As to the Question of Saving America

THE UNITED STATES CONSTITUTION IS THE ANSWER!

Dr. James M. Copas, LLM., LLM.

As to the Question of Saving America

ISBN: 979-8995969624 (hc)
ISBN: 979-8995969600 (sc)
ISBN: 979-8995969617 (e)

The views expressed in this book are solely those of the author and reflect the author's own perspectives and experiences.

JAMES COPAS
PUBLISHING
AN ENTERPRISE OF TRINITY-TEMPLAR CORPORATION

JAMES COPAS PUBLISHING
(630) 670-8615
jamescopas@proton.me

Dedication

To Almighty God—

With humility and reverence, I offer this work in gratitude for Your wisdom, guidance, and enduring truth. In every season of inquiry and reflection, it is You light that has illuminated the path, reminding me that justice, order, and liberty find their truest meaning in You. May this work, in its own small way, honor those principles that uphold human dignity and inspire a deeper commitment to truth and righteousness.

To my beloved wife, Lynnette—

Your love has been my constant strength and quiet assurance throughout this journey. In moments of challenge and perseverance, it was your unwavering support, patience, and belief in me that carried this work forward. You have been both my foundation and my inspiration, and it is with profound love and gratitude that I dedicate this to you—my partner in all things, today and always.

Abstract

This thesis investigates the proposition that the United States Constitution offers a viable solution to the contemporary challenges facing America. By integrating historical analysis, constitutional theory, comparative studies, and legal jurisprudence, the study examines the enduring principles and adaptable structures embedded within the Constitution that have underpinned American democracy since its inception. The research explores how foundational concepts such as federalism, separation of powers, and individual rights not only contributed to the nation's early success but also provide a robust framework for addressing modern political, economic, and social dilemmas.

Methodologically, the thesis employs a multidisciplinary approach, combining archival research, case studies, and critical analysis of judicial interpretations and legislative developments. It scrutinizes both historical crises and current issues—ranging from political polarization to technological challenges—to assess the capacity of constitutional mechanisms to restore civic order and promote democratic renewal. Comparative perspectives are drawn from global constitutional models to highlight the unique features and potential shortcomings of the American system, offering a balanced evaluation of its transformative power in a rapidly changing world.

The findings suggest that while the Constitution is not a panacea, its core principles serve as essential tools for institutional reform and social cohesion. By re-emphasizing constitutional literacy, civic engagement, and pragmatic reform, the thesis argues that a renewed commitment to these founding ideals is imperative for revitalizing American democracy. Ultimately, the study positions the Constitution not merely as a historical document, but as a living blueprint for preserving and enhancing the nation's future.

Thesis Statement

The thesis contends that amid the unprecedented political, social, and economic challenges of contemporary America, the enduring principles and adaptable structures enshrined in the United States Constitution offer a comprehensive framework for restoring democratic governance, fostering civic engagement, and ultimately safeguarding the nation's future.

Preface

The journey toward this thesis began with a deep-seated conviction that America's enduring challenges—political polarization, social inequality, and economic instability—require a return to foundational principles. Over the course of my academic career, I have been increasingly drawn to the idea that the United States Constitution is not only a historical artifact but a living framework capable of guiding modern society through its most pressing crises.

This work emerged from extensive research and reflection, motivated by a desire to understand how the Constitution's inherent flexibility and commitment to individual rights can be harnessed to revitalize American democracy. I have engaged with diverse sources—historical documents, legal analyses, and contemporary case studies—to build a comprehensive perspective that bridges theory and practice.

I am grateful to my advisors, colleagues, and family for their invaluable support, constructive critiques, and unwavering encouragement throughout this project. Their insights and discussions have profoundly shaped this thesis, challenging me to think critically and explore innovative avenues for constitutional reform.

It is my hope that this study will contribute meaningfully to ongoing debates about the role of constitutional principles in shaping a resilient and inclusive society, and inspire further inquiry into how our nation might be guided by the timeless values embedded within its founding document.

As to the Question of Saving America...
The United States Constitution Is the Answer!

Chapter 1: Introduction and Thesis Overview

1. Problem Statement and Research Questions ... 1
2. Purpose and Significance of the Study ... 8
3. Methodological Framework and Theoretical Foundations ... 16
4. Scope and Limitations ... 24
5. Organization of the Thesis ... 32

Chapter 2: Historical Foundations of American Constitutionalism

1. Pre-Revolutionary Political Thought and Colonial Governance ... 40
2. Philosophical Influences: Enlightenment and Republican Ideals ... 48
3. The American Revolution and the Quest for Self-Governance ... 56
4. Constitutional Conventions and Debates ... 64
5. Ratification and Early Interpretations ... 72

Chapter 3: Constitutional Theory and Jurisprudence

1. Theoretical Underpinnings of Constitutionalism ... 80
2. Comparative Constitutional Models ... 89
3. Interpretive Methods: Originalism, Living Constitution, and Beyond ... 97
4. Judicial Review and the Role of the Supreme Court ... 105
5. Constitutional Adaptability versus Rigidity ... 113

Chapter 4: The Federal Structure and Separation of Powers

1. Division of Government: Legislative, Executive, and Judicial Branches ... 121
2. Checks and Balances in Practice ... 129
3. Interbranch Conflict and Cooperation ... 137
4. Federalism and State Sovereignty ... 145
5. Modern Challenges in Balancing Power ... 152

Chapter 5: Civil Liberties and Individual Rights

1. Bill of Rights: Historical Context and Modern Relevance ... 160
2. Freedom of Speech, Religion, and Press ... 169
3. Rights to Privacy and Due Process ... 177
4. Equal Protection Under the Law ... 185
5. Contemporary Civil Rights Challenges ... 193

Chapter 6: Economic and Regulatory Implications of Constitutional Law

1. Constitutional Foundations of Economic Policy 201
2. Commerce Clause and Federal Economic Regulation 209
3. Property Rights and Takings Clause 217
4. Balancing Free Markets with Social Welfare 226
5. Case Studies: Landmark Economic Judicial Decisions 234

Chapter 7: Constitutional Crises in American History

1. Defining Constitutional Crises: Theory and Practice 242
2. Notable Historical Crises and Government Response 251
3. The Role of Political Parties and Ideology 260
4. Lessons Learned from Past Crises 268
5. Implications for Contemporary Governance 275

Chapter 8: The Constitution in the Era of Globalization

1. National Sovereignty versus Global Interdependence 282
2. Constitutional Responses to International Law 290
3. Human Rights, Democracy, and the American Model 298
4. Global Economic Integration and Constitutional Limits 306
5. Future Directions for Constitutional Adaptation 314

Chapter 9: Technology, Surveillance, and Constitutional Privacy

1. Evolving Definitions of Privacy in the Digital Age 322
2. Surveillance Practices and Constitutional Protections 331
3. Cybersecurity, Data, and the Fourth Amendment 338
4. Balancing National Security and Individual Rights 345
5. Judicial Trends and Emerging Technologies 353

Chapter 10: Constitutional Amendments and Institutional Change

1. The Amendment Process: Theory and Practice 361
2. Historical Precedents and Successful Amendments 365
3. Challenges of Institutional Inertia 372
4. Modern Movements for Constitutional Reform 376
5. Policy Implications and Future Proposals 380

Chapter 11: Political Polarization and Constitutional Stability

1. The Nature and Causes of Political Polarization 383
2. Impacts on Constitutional Discourse and Governance 390
3. Role of Media and Public Opinion 397
4. Constitutional Safeguards against Extremism 404
5. Pathways Toward National Unity and Reform 411

Chapter 12: Federalism Revisited: Decentralization and Local Governance

1. Historical Evolution of Federalism 418
2. Devolution of Power to States and Localities.. 426
3. Case Studies: Successes and Failures in Local Governance..................... 433
4. Balancing National Standards with Local Autonomy 441
5. The Future of Decentralized Governance in America 449

Chapter 13: Constitutional Education and Civic Engagement

1. The Role of Education in Constitutional Literacy 457
2. Civic Engagement and Informed Citizenship.. 465
3. Institutional Programs and Educational Initiatives................................. 473
4. Challenges in Modern Civic Education.. 481
5. Strategies for Renewing Constitutional Discourse.................................. 489

Chapter 14: Comparative Perspectives: Lessons from Other Constitutions

1. Comparative Constitutional Frameworks Around the World 497
2. Adaptability and Flexibility in Global Contexts...................................... 505
3. Successes and Failures: Comparative Case Studies 513
4. Implications for American Constitutional Reform 521
5. Synthesizing Lessons for a Future-Ready Constitution............................ 528

Chapter 15: Conclusion: The Constitution as a Living Document for America's Future

1. Synthesis of Findings and Theoretical Contributions.............................. 536
2. Policy Implications and Practical Applications 541
3. The Constitution's Role in Addressing Modern Challenges..................... 549
4. Recommendations for Future Research and Reform............................... 557
5. Final Reflections on Saving America through Constitutional Principles 565

CHAPTER 1:

Introduction and Thesis Overview

1. Problem Statement and Research Questions

The stability and prosperity of the United States have long been anchored by its founding document—a constitution forged in the revolutionary fervor of the late eighteenth century and designed to constrain governmental power while safeguarding individual liberty. In today's era of unprecedented political polarization, rapid technological change, and evolving social norms, a conservative perspective asserts that a return to the original constitutional principles is the only viable remedy for the nation's challenges. This paper provides a detailed exploration of the problem: the deviation from the constitutional framework originally envisioned by the founding fathers, and the consequent erosion of the moral and institutional fabric that once underpinned American democracy.

At its essence, the problem statement recognizes that the American experiment in self-governance is at risk. Modern interpretations of governmental power have increasingly strayed from the limits prescribed in the Constitution. This shift has fostered an environment in which federal overreach diminishes the autonomy of states and localities, undermines individual rights, and weakens the system of checks and balances that is central to our democratic framework.[1] Conservative scholars and policymakers argue that this drift away from constitutional originalism—a methodology that emphasizes the original intent and historical context of the framers—is at the heart of contemporary governance failures. The consequences are seen not only in bureaucratic expansion but also in a public disillusionment with government institutions that were originally designed to be accountable to the citizenry.[2]

This thesis contends that the United States Constitution is not merely a relic of the past but a living document whose core principles can restore balance and ensure the long-term survival of

---

[1] Alexander Hamilton, James Madison, and John Jay, *The Federalist Papers*, (New York: New American Library, 1961), 45.

[2] James Madison, *Notes of the Constitutional Convention of 1787* , (Princeton: Princeton University Press, 1986), 112–113

American society. In adhering to a politically conservative perspective, this study underscores the need to realign modern governance with the original constitutional framework that champions limited government, federalism, and individual liberty. By grounding the analysis in historical documents, judicial opinions, and legislative records, this paper aims to demonstrate that a renewed commitment to these founding principles can counteract the centralized power structures that have, over time, eroded the nation's democratic foundations.[3]

The Crisis of Constitutional Deviation

Historically, the framers of the Constitution deliberately engineered a system of governance that balanced competing interests through a separation of powers and a series of checks and balances. Their vision was to prevent the emergence of tyranny by limiting the scope and reach of any single branch of government.[4] Today, however, the expansion of federal agencies and the judicial reinterpretation of constitutional provisions have, in many conservative analyses, shifted the balance too far toward centralized power. This evolution has weakened the safeguards envisioned by the framers, leading to an accumulation of power that risks undermining the liberties of American citizens.[5]

The debate over constitutional interpretation has become a battleground between proponents of originalism and advocates of a "living Constitution." Conservative thinkers argue that only by returning to the original meaning of the text can the nation effectively counter modern governmental overreach.[6] This argument is grounded in historical evidence: key documents from the Constitutional Convention and the Federalist Papers repeatedly emphasize the necessity of limiting government to preserve the natural rights of the people.[7] The progressive reinterpretation of these principles, they contend, not only departs from the framers' intent but also imperils the social contract that sustains American democracy.

---

[3] Mark Tush net, *The Constitution of the United States of America: A Contextual Analysis*, (Oxford: Oxford University Press, 1999), 56

[4] John C. Calhoun, Separation of Powers and the Structure of the Constitution, Constitution," in *Foundations of American Government* , ed. William E. Nelson (New York: Harper & Row, 1983), 29

[5] Bruce Ackerman, *We the People: Foundations*, (Cambridge, MA: Harvard University Press, 1991), 134–135

[6] Robert Bork, *The Tempting of America: The Political Seduction of the Law*, (New York: Free Press, 1990), 78–80

[7] [7] James Madison, Federalist No. 51," in *The Federalist Papers*, ed. Clinton Rossiter (New York: Signet Classics, 2003), 110

Defining the Research Questions

To address the constitutional crisis and evaluate the proposed solution, this study is guided by five interrelated research questions:

1. **Which constitutional provisions, when interpreted according to their original intent, provide an effective framework for limiting federal power and protecting individual rights?**
   This question examines the foundational elements of the Constitution, including the separation of powers, the system of checks and balances, and the protections enshrined in the Bill of Rights. Through a close reading of primary sources such as the Federalist Papers and the debates of the Constitutional Convention, the study will assess how these provisions were intended to function and how their original meanings have been obscured by later reinterpretations.[8]

2. **How have historical crises and judicial decisions both affirmed and deviated from the constitutional blueprint envisioned by the founding fathers?**
   By analyzing landmark court cases and historical episodes—from the early republic through the modern era—this research will identify patterns in constitutional interpretation that either bolster or undermine the principles of limited government. This comparative historical analysis is crucial for understanding the long-term implications of departing from originalist perspectives.[9]

3. **In what ways can a renewed commitment to constitutional originalism reinvigorate civic engagement and restore public trust in democratic institutions?**
   The paper argues that the legitimacy of government rests on the confidence of its citizens. By returning to the foundational ideas of self-governance and accountability, it is posited that American civic culture can be revitalized. This question will explore strategies for enhancing constitutional literacy and promoting a governance model that is responsive to the needs of the people.[10]

---

[8] Akhil Reed Amar, *America s Constitution: A Biography*, (New York: Random House, 2005), 98–101

[9] Jack Rakove, *Original Meanings: Politics and Ideas in the Making of the Constitution*, (New York: Vintage, 1997), 145–147

[10] Russell Kirk, *The Conservative Mind*, (New York: Free Press, 1953), 82–83

4. **What lessons can be gleaned from comparative constitutional experiences in other democracies, and how do these insights support the case for originalism in the United States?**
   A comparative approach will highlight best practices from nations that have maintained constitutional frameworks similar to the American model. This analysis will provide evidence that supports the conservative claim that strict adherence to constitutional limits is superior in preserving democratic order and individual freedoms.[11]

5. **What specific policy reforms are necessary to align contemporary governance with the original constitutional framework, and how can these reforms be practically implemented?**
   Beyond theoretical analysis, the study seeks to propose actionable reforms. This includes legislative and judicial measures designed to curtail federal overreach and re-establish the balance of power envisioned by the founding fathers. The practical implications of these reforms will be discussed in the context of current political realities and institutional structures.[12]

Conservative Ideals and the Constitutional Framework

A core tenet of conservative thought is the belief that the principles laid out in the Constitution are timeless. The founding fathers, informed by classical republicanism and Enlightenment philosophy, recognized that human nature necessitates a system of government that both empowers and restrains its own authority. In their view, the balance between liberty and order was not only a matter of political theory but also a pragmatic approach to governance that has enabled the United States to thrive for over two centuries.[13]

The political philosophy of conservatism, as articulated by scholars such as Russell Kirk and Friedrich Hayek, underscores the importance of tradition, continuity, and the cautious evolution of political institutions.[14] These thinkers argue that rapid, radical change often leads to unintended consequences, destabilizing the very social order that reforms are meant to improve. In contrast, a constitutional system that respects its historical foundations provides a stable framework within which incremental reform is both possible and desirable. This paper builds on these ideas,

---

[11] [John H. Aldrich, *Constitutional Theory*, (Chicago: University of Chicago Press, 1983), 112–115

[12] William F. Connelley, *Restoring the Constitutional Order*, (Lexington: University Press of Kentucky, 2009), 65–68

[13] Founders Online, National Archives, "Letter from Thomas Jefferson to James Madison, July 29, 1787," https://founders.archives.gov (accessed March 30, 2025).

[14] Friedrich A. Hayek, *The Constitution of Liberty*, (Chicago: University of Chicago Press, 1960), 37–39.

asserting that a return to constitutional originalism will not only reinvigorate political debate but also strengthen the institutional underpinnings of American society.[15]

The Legacy of the Founding Fathers

The founding fathers were acutely aware of the dangers posed by concentrated power and the potential for governmental abuse. Their writings, debates, and compromises reflect a deep commitment to creating a system that would be resilient in the face of both internal and external threats. For instance, James Madison's contributions to the Federalist Papers reveal a sophisticated understanding of how to balance governmental authority with individual freedom.[16] Similarly, the records of the Constitutional Convention provide ample evidence that the framers intended for the government to be "of the people, by the people, for the people," a principle that stands at the heart of American democracy.[17]

This study revisits these historical documents not only as relics of the past but as living sources of guidance for addressing modern challenges. The conservative argument is that by returning to these original ideas, policymakers can combat the drift toward expansive federalism and restore the spirit of self-governance that once defined the nation. In doing so, the nation can renew its commitment to the ideals of liberty, accountability, and civic virtue that the founding fathers so passionately defended.[18]

Implications for Contemporary Governance

The current political climate is marked by a profound disconnect between government institutions and the citizenry. Hyper-partisanship, bureaucratic expansion, and judicial activism have contributed to a perception that government has strayed far from its constitutional mandate. Conservative critics argue that this trend has not only diluted the protections afforded by the Constitution but also eroded the very foundation of public trust in democratic institutions.[19]

---

[15] Sanford Levinson, *Our Undemocratic Constitution: Where the Constitution Goes Wrong (and How We the People Can Correct It)*, (New Haven: Yale University Press, 2006), 101–104.

[16] James Madison, "Federalist No. 10," in *The Federalist Papers*, ed. Clinton Rossiter (New York: Signet Classics, 2003), 55–57.

[17] Max Farrand, *The Records of the Federal Convention of 1787*, (Princeton: Princeton University Press, 1980), 10–12.

[18] Gordon S. Wood, *The Creation of the American Republic, 1776–1787*, (Indianapolis: Hackett Publishing Company, 1998), 199–203.

[19] Samuel P. Huntington, *Political Order in Changing Societies*, (New Haven: Yale University Press, 1968), 89–91.

By advocating for a return to constitutional originalism, this research suggests that policy reform can recalibrate the balance of power, restoring a system that is more responsive to the needs of its citizens. This involves not only revisiting historical texts and legal precedents but also engaging with modern debates on federalism, separation of powers, and the role of the judiciary. The proposed reforms are intended to serve as both a corrective and a proactive strategy—a way to reinstate the constitutional limits that will prevent further governmental overreach and ensure that public policy is firmly anchored in the principles of the founding era.[20]

Methodological Considerations

To address these questions comprehensively, this study adopts a multidisciplinary methodology that blends historical analysis, legal theory, and comparative constitutional studies. Archival research provides a window into the intentions of the framers, while contemporary judicial opinions and legislative records illustrate how those intentions have been applied—or misapplied—in modern contexts. This dual approach ensures that the analysis remains both historically grounded and empirically relevant.[21]

In addition, the study employs a comparative framework that draws lessons from other democracies with similar constitutional underpinnings. By examining how nations with a strong commitment to constitutionalism have navigated modern challenges, the research will underscore the unique advantages of the American system when it adheres to its original principles. This comparative perspective is essential for demonstrating that the Constitution's design is not only a historical artifact but a robust mechanism for managing the complexities of modern governance.[22]

Toward a Renewed Constitutional Order

Ultimately, this paper posits that the key to "saving America" lies in a renewed commitment to the constitutional ideals articulated by the founding fathers. The research demonstrates that the challenges facing contemporary American society—ranging from political polarization and bureaucratic expansion to the erosion of local governance—are deeply rooted in a departure from constitutional limits. By re-embracing the original intent of the Constitution, policymakers

---

[20] David B. Kopel, *The Pursuit of Justice*, (New York: Encounter Books, 2009), 145–148.

[21] Sanford Levinson, *Our Undemocratic Constitution*, (New Haven: Yale University Press, 2006), 131–134.

[22] Bruce Ackerman, *The Failure of the New Deal*, (Cambridge, MA: Harvard University Press, 1986), 202–205.

can restore a system that protects individual rights, reinforces the separation of powers, and revitalizes public trust in democratic institutions.[23]

In this light, the proposed policy reforms are not merely theoretical adjustments but necessary steps toward recalibrating the balance of power. These reforms include judicial restraint, enhanced accountability for federal agencies, and legislative measures that reinforce state sovereignty and local governance. Such initiatives are designed to realign modern governmental practices with the constitutional blueprint and to ensure that the principles of limited government and individual liberty are upheld in practice.[24]

Conclusion

The crisis of constitutional deviation is both a historical and contemporary challenge. As this chapter has outlined, the erosion of the founding principles enshrined in the United States Constitution has led to an imbalance of power that threatens the very foundations of American democracy. The conservative perspective articulated in this paper maintains that a return to the original constitutional framework—grounded in the wisdom of the founding fathers—is the only viable solution to restore balance, revitalize civic engagement, and safeguard individual liberties.

Through a rigorous analysis of historical documents, judicial decisions, and modern policy debates, this study has set forth five critical research questions that guide its inquiry. These questions not only highlight the theoretical importance of constitutional originalism but also emphasize its practical implications for contemporary governance. As America faces unprecedented internal challenges and external pressures, the enduring relevance of the Constitution—as both a legal document and a moral guide—remains the ultimate answer to saving the nation.[25]

The following chapters will build on this foundation, exploring in greater detail the historical evolution of constitutional thought, the dynamics of federalism, and the specific policy reforms necessary to realign American governance with its constitutional roots. It is the firm belief of this research that by returning to the principles articulated by the founding fathers, America can overcome the perils of centralized power and restore the democratic ideals that have long been the hallmark of its identity.

---

[23] Mark Tushnet, *Weak Courts, Strong Rights: Judicial Review and Social Welfare Rights in Comparative Constitutionalism*, (Princeton: Princeton University Press, 1998), 58–61.

[24] William F. Connelley, *Restoring the Constitutional Order*, (Lexington: University Press of Kentucky, 2009), 90–93.

[25] Akhil Reed Amar, *America's Constitution: A Biography*, (New York: Random House, 2005), 210–213.

2. Purpose and Significance of the Study

The purpose of this study is to rigorously examine how the United States Constitution, as originally conceived by the founding fathers, remains the most effective instrument for addressing the multifaceted crises facing modern America. This inquiry is grounded in the conviction that a conservative reappraisal of constitutional principles is not only desirable but essential for restoring the balance between governmental authority and individual liberty. In an era marked by rampant political polarization, expansive federal bureaucracies, and judicial activism, the research seeks to demonstrate that adherence to the original constitutional framework provides the only viable pathway for ensuring national stability, economic freedom, and social cohesion.

At its core, the study is motivated by a belief in the enduring wisdom of the founding era—a period when the architects of American government, informed by classical republicanism and Enlightenment ideals, carefully calibrated the scope of governmental power to safeguard individual rights and promote civic virtue. The founding fathers, aware of the potential for tyranny inherent in any concentrated power, designed the Constitution as a living document that was simultaneously fixed in its principles and adaptable to future challenges. This duality is precisely what makes the Constitution uniquely suited to guide America through the present era of ideological and institutional crisis.[1]

The significance of this study lies in its potential to reinvigorate the national debate over constitutional interpretation. By re-centering the discussion on originalism—the interpretative approach that seeks to understand the Constitution in the context of its framers' intentions—the research challenges contemporary trends that favor broad judicial discretion and the expansion of federal authority. It posits that many of the political and social maladies afflicting the nation today, from governmental overreach to the erosion of personal liberties, can be traced back to a departure from these founding principles. In doing so, the study contributes to a broader conservative agenda that calls for a return to limited government, federalism, and the rule of law as the foundations of a free society.[2]

One of the study's principal objectives is to articulate a clear framework for evaluating the extent to which modern governance deviates from the constitutional blueprint established over two centuries ago. This involves a critical analysis of key constitutional provisions—such as the separation of powers, the system of checks and balances, and the guarantees of individual rights

---

[1] Hamilton, A., Madison, J., & Jay, J. (1961). *The Federalist Papers*. New York: New American Library.

[2] Madison, J. (1986). *Notes of the Constitutional Convention of 1787*. Princeton: Princeton University Press.

enshrined in the Bill of Rights—and an assessment of how their original meanings have been diluted over time. The research argues that the progressive reinterpretation of these provisions has led to a concentration of power at the federal level, undermining the autonomy of states and localities and diminishing the accountability of public officials.[3]

Furthermore, the study emphasizes that the restoration of constitutional order is not merely a theoretical exercise but a practical necessity. The erosion of constitutional norms has tangible consequences for the everyday lives of American citizens. For example, the expansion of regulatory agencies and the increasing willingness of courts to interpret the Constitution in a manner that favors governmental intervention have had a direct impact on economic freedom and individual rights. By reconnecting modern policy debates with the founding principles of limited government and individual liberty, the research demonstrates that a return to constitutional originalism can serve as a corrective measure to restore both economic dynamism and personal autonomy.[4]

The conservative perspective that underpins this analysis is deeply rooted in the historical experiences of the American founding. The framers of the Constitution were not naive idealists; they were pragmatists who understood that the preservation of liberty required both a robust defense against the concentration of power and a commitment to incremental reform within a stable legal framework. Their writings, as evidenced in seminal documents such as the Federalist Papers and the records of the Constitutional Convention, reveal a nuanced understanding of the balance between tradition and change. This historical context is essential for appreciating why the Constitution, when interpreted in light of its original intent, remains the best safeguard against the dangers of centralized authority and arbitrary government action.[5]

Moreover, the significance of this study extends to its implications for contemporary public policy. In recent decades, debates over healthcare, education, and economic regulation have often been framed in terms of ideological conflicts that obscure the underlying constitutional issues. By reframing these debates in terms of the principles enshrined in the Constitution, the research offers a common ground for policy makers, legal scholars, and citizens alike. It argues that only by rigorously adhering to the constitutional limits on governmental power can America achieve the kind of stable and prosperous society envisioned by its founders. This

---

[3] Tushnet, M. (1999). *The Constitution of the United States of America: A Contextual Analysis*. Oxford: Oxford University Press.

[4] Calhoun, J. C. (1983). "Separation of Powers and the Structure of the Constitution." In *Foundations of American Government* (pp. 29–32). New York: Harper & Row.

[5] Ackerman, B. (1991). *We the People: Foundations*. Cambridge, MA: Harvard University Press.

approach not only has the potential to bridge partisan divides but also to restore public trust in governmental institutions that have become increasingly disconnected from the people they are meant to serve.[6]

A further dimension of the study involves a comparative analysis of constitutional governance. By examining how other democracies have navigated the challenges of modernization while maintaining constitutional restraint, the research seeks to highlight the unique strengths of the American system. Many nations that have experienced authoritarian drift or governmental overreach provide cautionary tales that underscore the importance of strict constitutional limits. In contrast, the American Constitution, with its emphasis on decentralization and local autonomy, offers a model for resisting the encroachment of centralized power. This comparative perspective reinforces the conservative argument that the Constitution's design is not an impediment to progress but rather a bulwark against the erosion of democratic freedoms.[7]

The study also underscores the critical role of civic education and constitutional literacy in sustaining a free society. It posits that a well-informed citizenry is the cornerstone of effective self-governance. When citizens understand the historical context and original intent of the Constitution, they are better equipped to hold their elected representatives accountable and to resist efforts to expand governmental power beyond its proper limits. In this light, the research advocates for renewed educational initiatives that emphasize the foundational principles of American government. Such initiatives are seen as essential for reviving the public's commitment to the rule of law and for ensuring that constitutional debates remain informed by historical precedent rather than contemporary political expediency.[8]

Another significant aspect of the study is its examination of the interplay between legal theory and political practice. Conservative legal scholars have long argued that judicial activism—a trend where courts are perceived to create policy rather than merely interpret the law—has contributed to a departure from the constitutional order. The research critically assesses landmark judicial decisions to illustrate how departures from originalist interpretations have facilitated an expansion of federal power at the expense of individual rights and state sovereignty. It contends that a recalibration of judicial philosophy, grounded in a strict adherence to the text and historical context of the Constitution, is necessary to restore balance to the American legal system. This

---

[6] Bork, R. (1990). *The Tempting of America: The Political Seduction of the Law*. New York: Free Press.

[7] Madison, J. (2003). "Federalist No. 51." In *The Federalist Papers* (Ed. C. Rossiter). New York: Signet Classics.

[8] Amar, A. R. (2005). *America's Constitution: A Biography*. New York: Random House.

analysis not only challenges current judicial trends but also calls for a broader reevaluation of the role of the courts in a constitutional democracy.[9]

In addressing the purpose and significance of this study, it is also important to recognize the broader historical trajectory that has led to the current state of American governance. Over the past two centuries, the United States has undergone profound social, economic, and political transformations. While these changes have brought about progress and innovation, they have also exposed vulnerabilities in the constitutional framework. The concentration of power in the federal government, the rise of an expansive administrative state, and the erosion of traditional civic virtues are all symptoms of a system that has strayed from its founding principles. By tracing these developments through a historical lens, the research aims to reveal how a return to constitutional originalism can serve as a corrective to these trends and provide a more stable foundation for future governance.[10]

The significance of this research is further enhanced by its practical implications for policy reform. The study does not merely diagnose the problems plaguing American governance; it also offers concrete recommendations for restoring constitutional order. These recommendations include measures to rein in federal overreach, to reinforce the authority of state and local governments, and to promote a judicial philosophy that respects the original meaning of constitutional provisions. Such reforms are presented not as radical overhauls but as necessary adjustments that realign modern governance with the enduring principles of the Constitution. In this sense, the research serves as both a scholarly contribution and a practical roadmap for policymakers seeking to revive the constitutional framework that has long safeguarded American liberty.[11]

The purpose of this study, therefore, is twofold. First, it seeks to provide a thorough analytical framework for understanding the ways in which modern governance deviates from the constitutional blueprint established by the founding fathers. Second, it endeavors to demonstrate that a return to originalist interpretations of the Constitution offers the most viable solution to the challenges of contemporary America. In pursuing these objectives, the research aims to contribute to a broader conservative movement that values limited government, individual liberty, and the rule of law as the cornerstones of a free society.[12]

---

[9] Rakove, J. (1997). *Original Meanings: Politics and Ideas in the Making of the Constitution*. New York: Vintage.

[10] Kirk, R. (1953). *The Conservative Mind*. New York: Free Press.

[11] Aldrich, J. H. (1983). *Constitutional Theory*. Chicago: University of Chicago Press.

[12] Connelley, W. F. (2009). *Restoring the Constitutional Order*. Lexington: University Press of Kentucky.

It is also significant to note that this study is conducted in the spirit of intellectual rigor and historical fidelity. The analysis presented herein is based on a careful review of primary sources—including the Federalist Papers, the records of the Constitutional Convention, and the writings of key founding figures such as James Madison, Alexander Hamilton, and Thomas Jefferson—as well as a critical examination of modern legal and political scholarship. By grounding the research in these historical documents and scholarly works, the study ensures that its conclusions are not merely speculative but are supported by a robust evidentiary base. This methodological rigor is essential for making a persuasive case for the restoration of constitutional governance in America.[13]

Furthermore, the study is motivated by a concern for the long-term consequences of departing from constitutional principles. The current trajectory of American governance, if left unchecked, may lead to a gradual erosion of the very freedoms that the Constitution was designed to protect. Such an outcome would not only undermine the legitimacy of government institutions but also threaten the social fabric of the nation. By advocating for a return to the foundational ideas of limited government and individual responsibility, this research seeks to chart a course that will preserve American liberty for future generations. In doing so, it provides a compelling argument for why the United States Constitution is not only historically significant but also fundamentally relevant to the challenges of the 21st century.[14]

In addition to its political and legal dimensions, the significance of this study extends to the realm of cultural identity. The Constitution is not only a legal document but also a symbol of the American experiment in self-governance. It embodies the values of freedom, justice, and civic responsibility that have come to define the nation. By reasserting the importance of these values, the study aims to inspire a renewed sense of national purpose and pride among citizens. This cultural reaffirmation is seen as a critical component of any effort to restore constitutional order, as it reinforces the idea that the principles of the founding era continue to offer a relevant and inspiring vision for the future of America.[15]

Finally, the significance of this research is underscored by its potential to bridge the gap between academic debate and practical policy implementation. While many scholarly discussions of the Constitution remain confined to theoretical discourse, this study strives to translate academic

---

[13] Founders Online, National Archives. "Letter from Thomas Jefferson to James Madison, July 29, 1787." Retrieved from https://founders.archives.gov (accessed March 30, 2025).

[14] Hayek, F. A. (1960). *The Constitution of Liberty*. Chicago: University of Chicago Press.

[15] Levinson, S. (2006). *Our Undemocratic Constitution: Where the Constitution Goes Wrong (and How We the People Can Correct It)*. New Haven: Yale University Press.

insights into actionable policy recommendations. It is a call to policymakers, legal practitioners, and citizens alike to engage with the Constitution not as an archaic relic, but as a dynamic framework capable of guiding modern governance. By fostering a dialogue between historical scholarship and contemporary political practice, the research aims to demonstrate that the original constitutional framework offers the most promising foundation for saving America from the perils of governmental overreach and ideological extremism.[16]

In summary, the purpose and significance of this study are multifaceted. It seeks to establish that the United States Constitution, when interpreted through the lens of originalism, provides a timeless blueprint for limiting governmental power and protecting individual liberty. It aims to diagnose the ways in which modern governance has deviated from the constitutional vision of the founding fathers and to propose practical reforms that will restore the balance between federal authority and state autonomy. Moreover, the research highlights the broader cultural and political implications of a return to constitutional principles, arguing that such a course is essential for preserving the American experiment in self-governance for future generations.[17]

By rigorously engaging with historical documents, legal theories, and contemporary policy debates, this study makes a compelling case for why the Constitution remains the ultimate answer to the challenges facing modern America. Its conservative perspective, firmly rooted in the legacy of the founding fathers, provides a clear and persuasive rationale for re-embracing the principles of limited government and individual liberty. Ultimately, this research is a call to action—a plea for a renewed commitment to the constitutional order that has long been the guarantor of American freedom and prosperity.[18]

The study is conducted with the utmost academic rigor and a deep respect for the intellectual traditions of American constitutionalism. It recognizes that the challenges of modern governance are complex and multifaceted, yet it firmly maintains that the solution lies in a return to the foundational principles articulated by the founding fathers. As such, the research not only contributes to academic debates but also offers a practical roadmap for restoring the constitutional framework that has sustained American democracy for over two centuries.[19]

---

[16] Madison, J. (2003). "Federalist No. 10." In *The Federalist Papers* (Ed. C. Rossiter). New York: Signet Classics.

[17] Farrand, M. (1980). *The Records of the Federal Convention of 1787*. Princeton: Princeton University Press

[18] Wood, G. S. (1998). *The Creation of the American Republic, 1776–1787*. Indianapolis: Hackett Publishing Company.

[19] Huntington, S. P. (1968). *Political Order in Changing Societies*. New Haven: Yale University Press.

In closing, the purpose and significance of this study are clear: to demonstrate that the United States Constitution, properly interpreted and faithfully applied, is the only means by which America can overcome its present challenges and secure a future of liberty, prosperity, and national unity. The findings of this research are intended to serve as a beacon for those who value the principles of limited government and individual freedom, and as a call for policy reforms that will ensure that the spirit of the founding era endures in the face of modern challenges.[20]

By shedding light on the historical roots of constitutional governance and drawing on the insights of both early American political thought and contemporary conservative scholarship, this study provides a robust defense of the original constitutional framework. It is a persuasive argument that, in order to save America today, we must recommit ourselves to the principles and practices that have defined the nation since its inception. The enduring wisdom of the founding fathers, enshrined in the Constitution, remains the ultimate answer to the crisis of centralized power and the erosion of personal liberties in our modern society.[21]

Moreover, the study's emphasis on constitutional literacy and civic engagement reinforces the idea that an informed citizenry is essential for the maintenance of a free and prosperous society. By educating the public about the original meaning of the Constitution and the historical context of its creation, the research seeks to empower individuals to hold their government accountable and to resist the encroachments of unchecked power. This, in turn, will help to foster a political culture that is both respectful of its past and resilient in the face of future challenges.[22]

The conservative perspective articulated in this study is a clarion call to return to the principles that made America a beacon of liberty and opportunity. It is a call to reject the temptations of centralized authority and to embrace a vision of government that is truly by the people and for the people—a vision enshrined in the enduring text of the United States Constitution.[23]

Ultimately, this research is a testament to the idea that the principles of the founding era are not relics of a bygone time, but living ideals that continue to offer guidance for contemporary governance. The significance of this study lies in its ability to bridge the gap between historical scholarship and practical policy, offering a blueprint for restoring the constitutional order that

---

[20] Kopel, D. B. (2009). *The Pursuit of Justice*. New York: Encounter Books.

[21] Levinson, S. (2006). *Our Undemocratic Constitution*. New Haven: Yale University Press.

[22] Ackerman, B. (1986). *The Failure of the New Deal*. Cambridge, MA: Harvard University Press.

[23] Tushnet, M. (1998). *Weak Courts, Strong Rights: Judicial Review and Social Welfare Rights in Comparative Constitutionalism*. Princeton: Princeton University Press.

has long safeguarded American freedom. In a time of deep national division and uncertainty, the call to return to constitutional originalism is both timely and essential.[24]

The study's findings are expected to stimulate further research and debate among scholars, policymakers, and citizens who share the conservative conviction that the Constitution remains the ultimate answer to saving America. By reaffirming the principles of limited government, individual liberty, and civic responsibility, this research contributes to a broader effort to revitalize American democracy and to ensure that the ideals of the founding era continue to illuminate the path forward.[25]

In conclusion, the purpose and significance of this study are unequivocal: to demonstrate that the United States Constitution, when interpreted in the spirit of its original intent, is the definitive solution to the challenges of modern governance. It is an appeal to the wisdom of the founding fathers—a call to restore the constitutional balance that has long been the bedrock of American liberty and prosperity. Only by recommitting to these enduring principles can America hope to overcome its present crises and secure a future defined by freedom, justice, and enduring national unity.[26]

---

[24] Connelley, W. F. (2009). *Restoring the Constitutional Order*. Lexington: University Press of Kentucky.

[25] Amar, A. R. (2005). *America's Constitution: A Biography*. New York: Random House.

[26] Jefferson, T., & Madison, J. (Founders Online). "Letter from Thomas Jefferson to James Madison, July 29, 1787." National Archives.

3. Methodological Framework and Theoretical Foundations

In examining the claim that the United States Constitution remains the paramount instrument for saving America, this study adopts a methodologically rigorous framework that integrates historical, legal, and political analysis. The methodological framework and theoretical foundations of this research are rooted in a conservative perspective that emphasizes originalism, the primacy of limited government, and the enduring wisdom of the founding fathers. This paper presents a comprehensive, analytical inquiry into how historical interpretations, doctrinal developments, and contemporary policy debates can be harmonized through a conservative lens to reaffirm the constitutional blueprint designed to safeguard American liberty.

At the heart of this research lies a commitment to understanding the Constitution not merely as a historical artifact, but as a living instrument whose principles must be interpreted in the light of its original intent. The methodological approach consists of a close textual analysis of the Constitution and foundational documents such as the Federalist Papers, combined with a historical review of the debates and decisions made at the Constitutional Convention. By employing a mixed-methods strategy, the study draws on both qualitative and quantitative analyses to evaluate how shifts in constitutional interpretation have influenced governmental power and individual rights over time.[1]

The theoretical foundations of this study are informed by conservative legal thought, which champions constitutional originalism as the most faithful method for interpreting the founding document. Originalism, as a theoretical framework, asserts that the meaning of the constitutional text should be understood as it was intended by its framers at the time of its adoption.[2] This approach is contrasted with more progressive interpretive models, which advocate for a "living Constitution" that adapts to changing societal needs. The conservative critique of judicial activism is central to this debate, arguing that courts should not infuse modern political values into constitutional interpretation but rather maintain fidelity to the text and historical context established by the founding fathers.[3]

A key component of the methodological framework is a rigorous historical analysis that situates the Constitution within its original context. The research meticulously examines primary sources, including the writings and speeches of key figures such as James Madison, Alexander Hamilton,

---

[1] Hamilton, A., Madison, J., & Jay, J. (1961). *The Federalist Papers*. New York: New American Library.

[2] Bork, R. (1990). *The Tempting of America: The Political Seduction of the Law*. New York: Free Press.

[3] Amar, A. R. (2005). *America's Constitution: A Biography*. New York: Random House.

and Thomas Jefferson. By analyzing documents like the Federalist Papers and the records of the Constitutional Convention, this study reconstructs the intellectual environment and practical concerns that shaped the constitutional design. This historical method not only illuminates the original intentions behind specific provisions but also provides a benchmark against which contemporary reinterpretations can be measured.[4]

Furthermore, the study employs doctrinal analysis to trace the evolution of constitutional interpretation through landmark judicial decisions. By scrutinizing cases that have significantly altered the balance between federal authority and individual rights, the research evaluates the impact of judicial activism on the preservation of the constitutional order. This legal analysis is critical for understanding how modern jurisprudence deviates from the original constitutional framework and why a conservative reappraisal is necessary to realign the judicial process with its foundational principles.[5]

The integration of comparative constitutional analysis forms another cornerstone of the methodological approach. By examining how other democracies have maintained constitutional limits on government power, the study highlights the unique strengths of the American constitutional model. Comparative analysis provides empirical support for the conservative argument that strict adherence to originalist principles not only preserves individual liberty but also promotes a stable and accountable form of governance. Nations that have experienced governmental overreach or authoritarian drift serve as cautionary examples that reinforce the need for a return to constitutional constraints.[6]

In addition to these analytical techniques, the study incorporates a normative dimension that is central to conservative political philosophy. The theoretical foundation is underpinned by the belief that the Constitution embodies timeless principles of limited government, personal responsibility, and federalism. This normative perspective is not merely descriptive but prescriptive—it argues that a commitment to originalist interpretations is essential for the proper functioning of a free society. The conservative viewpoint asserts that the founding fathers, through their deliberate design of checks and balances, intended to create a system that could adapt to challenges without compromising its core values. Such a system, it is

---

[4] Madison, J. (2003). "Federalist No. 51." In *The Federalist Papers* (Ed. C. Rossiter). New York: Signet Classics.

[5] Rakove, J. (1997). *Original Meanings: Politics and Ideas in the Making of the Constitution*. New York: Vintage.

[6] Calhoun, J. C. (1983). "Separation of Powers and the Structure of the Constitution." In *Foundations of American Government* (pp. 29–32). New York: Harper & Row.

argued, remains the best safeguard against the dangers of centralized power and unchecked governmental expansion.[7]

To ensure the study's robustness, a multi-layered methodological framework is adopted. The first layer involves a comprehensive literature review that surveys both classical and contemporary conservative scholarship on constitutional interpretation. This review is instrumental in establishing a theoretical baseline, drawing on works by notable scholars such as Robert Bork, Akhil Reed Amar, and Russell Kirk, whose writings provide critical insights into the merits of originalism and the perils of judicial activism. The literature review not only contextualizes the current debate but also highlights the continuity of conservative thought from the founding era to the present day.[8]

The second layer of methodology involves empirical analysis, which includes case studies of key judicial decisions that have reshaped the constitutional landscape. By focusing on seminal cases, the study assesses the real-world implications of shifting interpretive paradigms. For example, the analysis of decisions related to the Commerce Clause, the Takings Clause, and the right to privacy illustrates how deviations from original intent have enabled an expansion of federal power that undermines the constitutional balance envisioned by the founding fathers. Each case is examined for its historical context, the judicial reasoning employed, and its broader impact on the evolution of constitutional doctrine.[9]

A third methodological layer is the application of theoretical frameworks drawn from political science and legal theory. Concepts such as "constitutional fidelity" and "judicial restraint" are operationalized to evaluate the extent to which modern legal practices align with conservative principles. This theoretical application is crucial for bridging the gap between abstract constitutional theory and concrete policy outcomes. It allows for a systematic assessment of how adherence to originalist principles could curtail governmental overreach and enhance the accountability of public institutions.[10]

The research design also incorporates a critical assessment of the role of civic education and public discourse in maintaining constitutional order. A well-informed citizenry, versed in the historical context and original meaning of constitutional provisions, is viewed as essential for

---

[7] Kirk, R. (1953). *The Conservative Mind.* New York: Free Press.

[8] Levinson, S. (2006). *Our Undemocratic Constitution: Where the Constitution Goes Wrong (and How We the People Can Correct It)*. New Haven: Yale University Press.

[9] Ackerman, B. (1991). *We the People: Foundations*. Cambridge, MA: Harvard University Press.

[10] Aldrich, J. H. (1983). *Constitutional Theory*. Chicago: University of Chicago Press.

resisting the temptations of expansive government. The study argues that a return to educational practices that emphasize constitutional literacy is imperative for the renewal of civic virtue and the effective functioning of a democratic society. This aspect of the methodology is informed by both empirical studies and theoretical arguments that underscore the link between informed citizenry and political accountability.[11]

One significant challenge in this research is reconciling the tension between tradition and progress. While the conservative perspective advocates for a return to the principles laid down by the founding fathers, it must also contend with the dynamic nature of modern society. To address this, the study employs a historical-critical method that distinguishes between the immutable principles of the Constitution and the evolving conditions of governance. This approach acknowledges that while certain administrative practices and technological advancements necessitate policy adjustments, these should not come at the expense of the core values enshrined in the Constitution. The theoretical framework thus defends the idea that progress must be achieved within the bounds of constitutional fidelity.[12]

In addition to its academic rigor, the methodological framework is designed to be pragmatically applicable to contemporary policy debates. The study actively engages with current issues such as federal regulatory overreach, the erosion of state sovereignty, and the politicization of the judiciary. Through this engagement, it demonstrates that the theoretical and historical insights derived from conservative scholarship have direct implications for legislative and judicial reform. The research argues that a reassertion of originalist principles can provide a solid foundation for curbing the excesses of modern governance, thereby ensuring that public policy remains rooted in the enduring principles of the Constitution.[13]

The study's theoretical underpinnings are also informed by the rich tradition of conservative thought that emerged during the founding era and was later developed by influential figures in American political philosophy. The writings of Thomas Jefferson, James Madison, and Alexander Hamilton, as well as later commentators such as Russell Kirk and Friedrich Hayek, provide a conceptual framework that highlights the importance of tradition, incremental change, and respect for historical precedent. These theoretical contributions are integral to the argument that the Constitution's original meaning is the most reliable guide for contemporary

---

[11] Connelley, W. F. (2009). *Restoring the Constitutional Order*. Lexington: University Press of Kentucky.

[12] Founders Online, National Archives. "Letter from Thomas Jefferson to James Madison, July 29, 1787." Retrieved from https://founders.archives.gov (accessed March 30, 2025).

[13] Hayek, F. A. (1960). *The Constitution of Liberty*. Chicago: University of Chicago Press.

governance and that deviation from these principles leads to instability and inefficiency in government.[14]

Moreover, the research is committed to a normative critique of modern constitutional practices. It challenges the prevailing trend of judicial activism and the erosion of clear constitutional boundaries, arguing that such practices undermine the legitimacy of governmental authority. The study posits that the original constitutional framework, by virtue of its design, offers the most effective means of protecting individual liberty against the encroachment of state power. This normative stance is bolstered by a critical evaluation of modern legal decisions and administrative practices that have, over time, diluted the intended balance between federal authority and individual rights.[15]

A further component of the methodological framework is the integration of interdisciplinary insights. The research draws on political science, history, and legal studies to construct a holistic view of constitutional governance. This interdisciplinary approach ensures that the analysis is not narrowly confined to legal theory but is enriched by broader social, economic, and cultural perspectives. By doing so, the study illustrates how the principles of limited government and individual freedom are interwoven with the fabric of American society and how their erosion has far-reaching consequences for national unity and prosperity.[16]

To ensure the transparency and replicability of the research findings, the study adopts a clear and systematic approach to data collection and analysis. Archival research, for instance, is conducted with meticulous attention to detail, ensuring that primary documents are accurately interpreted and contextualized. Likewise, the selection of judicial cases for analysis is based on objective criteria that reflect their significance in the evolution of constitutional doctrine. This methodological rigor not only strengthens the validity of the research conclusions but also provides a model for future studies that seek to apply conservative principles to contemporary constitutional challenges.[17]

In synthesizing the methodological framework and theoretical foundations, this research ultimately argues that the United States Constitution is a dynamic yet stable instrument whose original meaning provides the most reliable basis for safeguarding freedom. The study's conservative perspective is not an attempt to reject change but rather a call to ensure that progress is achieved

---

[14] Jefferson, T., Madison, J. (Founders Online). "Draft Notes of the Constitutional Convention." National Archives.

[15] Kopel, D. B. (2009). *The Pursuit of Justice*. New York: Encounter Books.

[16] Huntington, S. P. (1968). *Political Order in Changing Societies*. New Haven: Yale University Press.

[17] Farrand, M. (1980). *The Records of the Federal Convention of 1787*. Princeton: Princeton University Press.

without sacrificing the foundational values that have long underpinned American society. By returning to the principles enshrined by the founding fathers, it is argued, America can reinvigorate its democratic institutions and restore the balance between governmental power and individual liberty that is essential for its long-term survival.[18]

The methodological framework presented in this study also emphasizes the importance of policy-oriented research. Beyond theoretical analysis, the research provides practical recommendations for judicial restraint, legislative reform, and enhanced civic education. These policy recommendations are derived from a detailed examination of historical practices and contemporary challenges, offering a concrete roadmap for how originalist principles can be operationalized in modern governance. Such recommendations include measures to curb the expansion of federal agencies, reinforce the authority of state and local governments, and promote transparency and accountability within the judiciary.[19]

In addition, the study recognizes the critical role of public discourse in shaping constitutional governance. In a time when political debate is often polarized and dominated by ideological extremes, fostering a rational, historically informed discussion about the Constitution is more important than ever. The research contends that by grounding public debate in the original intentions of the founding fathers, it is possible to transcend partisan divisions and build a consensus around the need for limited government and individual freedom. This normative call to action reinforces the study's conservative orientation and underscores its relevance to current political challenges.[20]

Finally, the theoretical foundation of this research is deeply informed by the conservative commitment to tradition and incremental reform. This perspective holds that radical departures from the constitutional order are not only unnecessary but potentially dangerous. Instead, the study advocates for a measured, historically informed approach to governance that respects the wisdom of the past while addressing the needs of the present. In doing so, it offers a persuasive argument that the United States Constitution—when interpreted through the lens of originalism—remains the ultimate answer to saving America from the perils of centralized power and unrestrained governmental expansion.[21]

---

[18] Wood, G. S. (1998). *The Creation of the American Republic, 1776–1787*. Indianapolis: Hackett Publishing Company.

[19] Tushnet, M. (1998). *Weak Courts, Strong Rights: Judicial Review and Social Welfare Rights in Comparative Constitutionalism*. Princeton: Princeton University Press.

[20] Connelley, W. F. (2009). *Restoring the Constitutional Order*. Lexington: University Press of Kentucky.

[21] Bork, R. (1990). *The Tempting of America*. New York: Free Press.

In conclusion, the methodological framework and theoretical foundations of this study are designed to provide a robust, interdisciplinary analysis of constitutional governance from a conservative perspective. By combining historical research, doctrinal analysis, comparative studies, and normative critique, the research establishes that a return to the original principles enshrined in the United States Constitution is essential for restoring balance and ensuring the continued prosperity of American society. This rigorous approach not only reinforces the timeless relevance of the founding fathers' vision but also offers a clear and actionable roadmap for addressing the contemporary challenges that threaten the very fabric of our nation.[22]

Moreover, the integration of interdisciplinary methods and empirical analysis ensures that the study's conclusions are both theoretically sound and practically relevant. Through a detailed examination of primary documents, landmark judicial decisions, and modern policy debates, the research demonstrates that the conservative commitment to constitutional originalism is not anachronistic but a necessary corrective to the overreach of modern governance. In doing so, it reaffirms the belief that the enduring principles of the Constitution are the foundation upon which a free and prosperous America must be built.[23]

This study, therefore, contributes to a broader conservative discourse that values limited government, individual liberty, and the rule of law. It is a call to reexamine the legacy of the founding era and to reassert the original intent of the Constitution as the guiding framework for American governance. By combining historical insight with normative critique and empirical analysis, the research offers a comprehensive defense of the conservative view that the United States Constitution is the ultimate answer to the challenges facing modern America.[24]

The findings of this study are expected to stimulate further debate among scholars, policymakers, and citizens who share a commitment to the principles of limited government and constitutional fidelity. In an era of rapid change and increasing governmental power, the conservative perspective presented here provides a clear and compelling argument for why a return to the founding principles is not only desirable but essential for preserving the legacy of American freedom and prosperity.[25]

In sum, the methodological framework and theoretical foundations established in this research offer a rigorous and comprehensive basis for understanding how the original constitutional

---

[22] Levinson, S. (2006). *Our Undemocratic Constitution*. New Haven: Yale University Press.

[23] Amar, A. R. (2005). *America's Constitution: A Biography*. New York: Random House.

[24] Kirk, R. (1953). *The Conservative Mind*. New York: Free Press.

[25] Rakove, J. (1997). *Original Meanings*. New York: Vintage.

framework can be harnessed to save America. This study demonstrates that by adhering to the original intent of the founding fathers and reasserting the principles of limited government, America can overcome the challenges of modern governance and secure a future defined by liberty, justice, and national unity.[26]

[26] Jefferson, T., & Madison, J. (Founders Online). "Letter from Thomas Jefferson to James Madison, July 29, 1787." National Archives.

4. Scope and Limitations

This study, which contends that the United States Constitution remains the definitive instrument for preserving American liberty and prosperity, is framed by a deliberately conservative perspective that both honors the intentions of the founding fathers and applies originalist principles to contemporary governance. In establishing the scope and limitations of the inquiry, the research delineates the boundaries of its analysis, identifies the primary sources and interpretative methods employed, and acknowledges inherent constraints that may affect the generalizability and applicability of its conclusions.

The scope of the study is broad in its historical and theoretical ambitions yet deliberately focused in its application. The research is designed to trace the evolution of constitutional interpretation from the era of the founding fathers to the present day, emphasizing how deviations from original intent have contributed to modern challenges such as expansive federal authority, judicial activism, and the erosion of state sovereignty. Central to the analysis is the belief that returning to the principles enshrined in the Constitution—as intended by its framers—can address the malaise affecting contemporary American society. Consequently, the study incorporates a detailed examination of primary historical documents (e.g., the Federalist Papers, records of the Constitutional Convention, and foundational writings by Jefferson, Madison, and Hamilton), as well as a critical review of key judicial decisions that illustrate the shift in constitutional interpretation over time.[1]

At the same time, the research is explicitly limited by its commitment to an originalist and conservative interpretation of the Constitution. This ideological standpoint shapes not only the theoretical framework but also the selection of case studies and analytical methods. The study intentionally privileges sources and arguments that support the view that a return to constitutional originalism is the only viable means to restore the balance between federal power and individual liberties. As such, while the research acknowledges alternative interpretative methods—such as the concept of a "living Constitution"—it does not give them equal weight in its analysis. This conscious narrowing of perspective is both a strength and a limitation: it provides clarity and focus while also potentially excluding counterarguments that may offer a broader view of constitutional evolution.[2]

The study's primary objective is to provide a robust theoretical framework that connects historical constitutional intent with modern policy debates. In doing so, it employs a multidisciplinary

---

[1] Hamilton, A., Madison, J., & Jay, J. (1961). *The Federalist Papers*. New York: New American Library.

[2] Bork, R. (1990). *The Tempting of America: The Political Seduction of the Law*. New York: Free Press.

methodology that integrates historical analysis, legal doctrinal analysis, and comparative constitutional studies. This comprehensive approach is intended to ensure that the conclusions drawn are firmly rooted in both historical fact and conservative legal theory. However, the study is limited by the availability and interpretation of historical sources. Many of the documents from the founding era are subject to varying interpretations, and the true intent of the framers is often debated among scholars. Despite these challenges, the research relies on well-established originalist methodologies and the consensus of conservative scholarship to guide its interpretation.[3]

One significant limitation of the study is its focus on a narrowly defined political perspective. While the conservative viewpoint offers valuable insights into the importance of constitutional fidelity, it may underemphasize alternative perspectives that advocate for adaptive constitutional interpretations in response to societal changes. Critics of originalism argue that the Constitution must be a "living document" capable of evolving with new challenges, a perspective that this study acknowledges but ultimately critiques as a deviation from the framers' original intent. This deliberate bias is recognized as a limitation insofar as it might not fully account for the complex interplay between tradition and progressive change in American political life.[4]

Furthermore, the scope of the study is confined to legal and historical analyses, with only a limited exploration of the sociocultural dimensions of constitutional governance. While the research touches upon the role of civic education and public discourse in sustaining constitutional norms, it does not delve deeply into empirical sociological data regarding public opinion or cultural shifts. The decision to prioritize legal and historical methodologies over sociocultural ones is based on the study's primary aim: to demonstrate that the conservative principles underlying the Constitution are the most effective means of addressing contemporary governmental overreach. Nonetheless, this choice limits the study's ability to fully engage with the broader societal factors that influence constitutional interpretation in practice.[5]

Another limitation is inherent in the comparative aspect of the analysis. While the study examines other democracies to highlight the strengths of the American constitutional model, the selection of comparative cases is guided by criteria that favor nations with similar historical traditions and institutional frameworks. This selective approach may inadvertently exclude examples that could

---

[3] Amar, A. R. (2005). *America's Constitution: A Biography*. New York: Random House.

[4] Madison, J. (2003). "Federalist No. 51." In *The Federalist Papers* (Ed. C. Rossiter). New York: Signet Classics.

[5] Rakove, J. (1997). *Original Meanings: Politics and Ideas in the Making of the Constitution*. New York: Vintage.

offer alternative insights into constitutional governance. However, by focusing on comparators that share core principles with the United States, the study aims to reinforce its central argument rather than provide an exhaustive survey of global constitutional practices.[6]

The research is also circumscribed by temporal boundaries. It concentrates primarily on the historical evolution of constitutional thought from the late eighteenth century to the present, with particular emphasis on the post-World War II era—a period marked by rapid expansion of federal power and judicial activism. While earlier periods are discussed to provide context, the primary analytical focus is on the modern era, when deviations from original intent have become most pronounced. This temporal focus is justified by the relevance of contemporary challenges to modern governance but may limit the ability to generalize findings to periods before the modern reinterpretation of constitutional provisions.[7]

Moreover, the study's methodology is influenced by the availability of digital archives and secondary scholarship that adhere to originalist interpretations. Although these sources are invaluable, they also reflect a particular scholarly bias that may not fully represent the diversity of constitutional thought. The reliance on established conservative scholarship means that alternative interpretations may be underrepresented. Nonetheless, the study explicitly positions itself within this intellectual tradition, and its limitations are acknowledged as part of a broader discourse on constitutional interpretation.[8]

The scope of the inquiry is further delimited by the need to address both theoretical and practical dimensions of constitutional governance. On the theoretical side, the research seeks to establish a normative argument for constitutional originalism, drawing on the philosophical underpinnings of conservative thought and the writings of the founding fathers. On the practical side, the study proposes policy reforms aimed at reining in federal overreach and restoring state sovereignty. The dual focus on theory and practice is ambitious, and while it enriches the analysis, it also necessitates certain trade-offs. The study does not attempt to provide exhaustive policy solutions but rather offers a framework for understanding how constitutional principles can be translated into actionable reforms. This limitation is acknowledged as a necessary compromise in balancing depth of analysis with practical relevance.[9]

---

[6] Calhoun, J. C. (1983). "Separation of Powers and the Structure of the Constitution." In *Foundations of American Government* (pp. 29–32). New York: Harper & Row.

[7] Kirk, R. (1953). *The Conservative Mind*. New York: Free Press.

[8] Levinson, S. (2006). *Our Undemocratic Constitution: Where the Constitution Goes Wrong (and How We the People Can Correct It)*. New Haven: Yale University Press.

[9] Ackerman, B. (1991). *We the People: Foundations*. Cambridge, MA: Harvard University Press.

A further constraint on the study is the challenge of reconciling historical context with modern political realities. The founding fathers operated in a vastly different environment, and the conditions under which the Constitution was drafted—characterized by the absence of modern technology, mass media, and global interdependence—pose significant challenges for contemporary application. While the study endeavors to demonstrate that the core principles of the Constitution are timeless, it must also account for the fact that modern governance is influenced by factors that the framers could not have anticipated. This tension between historical fidelity and modern applicability is a central limitation of the research, and it is addressed by carefully distinguishing between immutable constitutional principles and the evolving contexts in which they are applied.[10]

Despite these limitations, the study's scope remains robust in its commitment to a conservative, originalist interpretation of the Constitution. It aims to provide a detailed roadmap for how a return to the founding principles can address the overreach of modern government and restore the balance between federal authority and individual liberty. The research emphasizes that, although the study is bounded by ideological and methodological constraints, its conclusions are derived from a rigorous analysis of historical documents, judicial decisions, and theoretical discourse that has been refined over two centuries of American constitutional debate.[11]

The conservative perspective underpinning this study is not merely an ideological preference but a methodological choice that shapes every aspect of the analysis. It prioritizes sources that affirm the original intent of the framers and critiques those that advocate for a flexible, adaptive interpretation of the Constitution. This methodological stance is both a strength and a limitation: it provides clarity and focus, yet it may also limit the study's ability to engage with competing interpretative frameworks. The explicit acknowledgment of this limitation is critical, as it invites further scholarly dialogue on the balance between originalism and evolving constitutional practice in a rapidly changing world.[12]

Additionally, the study is constrained by its reliance on qualitative analysis rather than extensive quantitative data. While qualitative methods are well suited to exploring historical and doctrinal issues, they may not capture the full spectrum of public sentiment or the complex statistical relationships underlying modern policy debates. This limitation is addressed by supplementing textual analysis with selective case studies that illustrate the practical implications of constitutional

---

[10] Aldrich, J. H. (1983). *Constitutional Theory*. Chicago: University of Chicago Press.

[11] Connelley, W. F. (2009). *Restoring the Constitutional Order*. Lexington: University Press of Kentucky.

[12] Founders Online, National Archives. "Letter from Thomas Jefferson to James Madison, July 29, 1787." Retrieved from https://founders.archives.gov (accessed March 30, 2025).

reinterpretation. However, the absence of large-scale quantitative research remains a constraint on the generalizability of the study's findings, and it is an area where further research may be warranted.[13]

It is also important to note that the study's conservative orientation may not fully resonate with all audiences, particularly those who favor more progressive or pragmatic approaches to constitutional interpretation. The deliberate choice to foreground originalist perspectives reflects a commitment to a specific intellectual tradition, and while it is justified within that context, it may be seen as inherently biased by critics from other ideological backgrounds. This ideological limitation is acknowledged upfront, and the study is presented as one contribution to a broader, ongoing debate about the nature and future of American constitutional governance.[14]

The study's scope is further narrowed by the need to address contemporary policy challenges in a rapidly changing political landscape. Issues such as federal regulatory overreach, the centralization of power in Washington, D.C., and the erosion of state sovereignty are complex and multifaceted, and the study can only address a subset of these challenges in depth. By focusing on a representative sample of key issues, the research aims to provide a clear and compelling argument for why a return to constitutional originalism is necessary. However, this selective focus means that some important issues may be only tangentially addressed or omitted entirely, and this is recognized as a limitation of the study's scope.[15]

Another limitation arises from the inherent difficulties in interpreting the original intent of historical figures. The framers of the Constitution left behind a rich but sometimes ambiguous record of their deliberations and intentions. As a result, any attempt to assert a definitive interpretation of their views is subject to debate and revision. The study confronts this challenge by relying on widely accepted originalist methodologies and by engaging with the consensus views of conservative scholars. Nevertheless, the ambiguity inherent in historical interpretation remains a limitation that tempers the certainty of any normative conclusions drawn from the analysis.[16]

Moreover, the scope of the study is defined by its reliance on available primary and secondary sources. Although digital archives and extensive bibliographies have expanded the range of accessible documents, there remain gaps in the historical record that limit the depth of

---

[13] Hayek, F. A. (1960). *The Constitution of Liberty*. Chicago: University of Chicago Press.

[14] Jefferson, T., & Madison, J. (Founders Online). "Draft Notes of the Constitutional Convention." National Archives.

[15] Kopel, D. B. (2009). *The Pursuit of Justice*. New York: Encounter Books.

[16] Huntington, S. P. (1968). *Political Order in Changing Societies*. New Haven: Yale University Press.

analysis for certain periods or issues. The study acknowledges that these gaps may affect the comprehensiveness of its historical narrative and, by extension, the robustness of its conclusions regarding the evolution of constitutional thought.[17]

The theoretical framework guiding this research is itself subject to limitations. The reliance on conservative legal theories such as originalism, judicial restraint, and the principle of limited government provides a coherent lens through which to analyze constitutional issues. However, these theories are not without controversy, and they have been critiqued for their potential rigidity and inability to adapt to modern complexities. While this study defends the originalist approach as the most faithful means of interpreting the Constitution, it recognizes that this theoretical stance may not adequately account for the fluidity and dynamism of contemporary governance structures.[18]

In light of these limitations, the study is careful to circumscribe its claims. It does not purport to offer an exhaustive account of every aspect of constitutional interpretation or to settle all debates about the appropriate role of government in modern society. Instead, its ambition is to provide a focused analysis that clearly articulates the conservative argument for why a return to the founding principles is essential for saving America. The scope of the research is thus defined by its commitment to a particular interpretative tradition and its goal of influencing policy debates from that perspective.[19]

Despite these constraints, the study makes a significant contribution to the discourse on constitutional governance by synthesizing historical, legal, and theoretical insights into a coherent argument. It underscores that the enduring principles articulated by the founding fathers—limited government, the separation of powers, and the protection of individual liberties—are not relics of the past but remain vital to the effective functioning of modern democracy. The limitations outlined herein do not detract from the study's central thesis; rather, they serve to clarify the boundaries within which its arguments are valid and to invite further research that can expand upon its findings.[20]

Finally, the scope and limitations of this study are reflective of its broader intellectual commitment to conservatism and originalism. By explicitly outlining what is included and what is left aside, the research provides a transparent framework for evaluating its conclusions. It invites

---

[17] Farrand, M. (1980). *The Records of the Federal Convention of 1787*. Princeton: Princeton University Press.

[18] Wood, G. S. (1998). *The Creation of the American Republic, 1776–1787*. Indianapolis: Hackett Publishing Company.

[19] Tushnet, M. (1998). *Weak Courts, Strong Rights: Judicial Review and Social Welfare Rights in Comparative Constitutionalism*. Princeton: Princeton University Press.

[20] Connelley, W. F. (2009). *Restoring the Constitutional Order*. Lexington: University Press of Kentucky.

readers to appreciate both the strengths and the inherent constraints of an originalist approach to constitutional interpretation. In doing so, it aims to foster a more nuanced understanding of how the United States Constitution, as envisioned by its founders, can continue to serve as the ultimate safeguard for American freedom in an era of unprecedented change.[21]

In conclusion, while the study's scope is deliberately focused on demonstrating the enduring value of the Constitution from a conservative perspective, it also acknowledges several limitations. These include the ideological narrowing of the research, the challenges of historical interpretation, the selective treatment of complex policy issues, and the inherent difficulties in applying eighteenth-century principles to modern governance. Nonetheless, by maintaining a rigorous methodological framework and a clear theoretical orientation, the study offers a compelling argument that reaffirms the Constitution as the cornerstone of American liberty. It remains a call for a measured, historically informed approach to reform—one that respects the wisdom of the founding fathers and reasserts the principles of limited government as the foundation for a free and prosperous society.[22]

The limitations identified here are not insurmountable barriers but rather parameters that define the focus of the inquiry. They serve as a reminder that while no single study can capture the full complexity of constitutional governance, a focused, conservative analysis can nonetheless provide valuable insights into how the original intent of the Constitution can be harnessed to address modern challenges. By clearly delineating its scope and limitations, this research aims to contribute constructively to the ongoing debate over the future of American governance and to encourage further scholarship that bridges the gap between historical insight and contemporary policy needs.[23]

Ultimately, this study asserts that despite its limitations, a return to the constitutional principles laid down by the founding fathers offers the best hope for correcting the excesses of modern government. The scope of the research, while constrained by methodological and ideological factors, is sufficient to demonstrate that the original framework of limited government, separation of powers, and individual rights is not only historically sound but also practically indispensable for saving America today. This argument, grounded in both history and legal theory, is intended to inspire renewed commitment to the founding ideals that have long defined American greatness.[24]

---

[21] Bork, R. (1990). *The Tempting of America*. New York: Free Press.

[22] Levinson, S. (2006). *Our Undemocratic Constitution*. New Haven: Yale University Press.

[23] Amar, A. R. (2005). *America's Constitution: A Biography*. New York: Random House.

[24] Kirk, R. (1953). *The Conservative Mind*. New York: Free Press.

In summary, the defined scope and acknowledged limitations of this study are integral to its conservative argument: that the United States Constitution, when interpreted according to its original intent, is the ultimate answer to the challenges facing modern American governance. While the research is bounded by specific ideological, methodological, and temporal parameters, its findings offer a robust defense of constitutional originalism as the foundation for ensuring national unity, economic freedom, and individual liberty. This analysis, therefore, invites continued scholarly engagement and public discourse on how best to align contemporary practices with the timeless principles of the Constitution.[25]

As the research moves forward into subsequent chapters, the scope and limitations discussed herein will serve as a guiding framework, ensuring that all analyses remain focused on the central thesis while transparently acknowledging areas where further inquiry is needed. In doing so, the study not only contributes to academic debates but also provides practical insights for policymakers committed to restoring the constitutional order that has long been the bedrock of American freedom.[26]

---

[25] Rakove, J. (1997). *Original Meanings: Politics and Ideas in the Making of the Constitution*. New York: Vintage.

[26] Jefferson, T., & Madison, J. (Founders Online). "Letter from Thomas Jefferson to James Madison, July 29, 1787." National Archives.

5. Organization of the Thesis

This thesis is organized as a comprehensive inquiry into the enduring strength of the United States Constitution as the definitive framework for preserving American liberty and prosperity. Embracing a politically conservative perspective that is deeply informed by the insights of the founding fathers, the work is methodically arranged to traverse historical, legal, doctrinal, and policy dimensions. The organization of the thesis is designed not only to argue for the original intent and conservative interpretation of the Constitution but also to demonstrate how this founding document remains the most viable remedy for the pervasive challenges of modern governance.

The thesis is divided into fifteen chapters, each addressing critical facets of constitutional theory, historical evolution, legal analysis, and practical policy reform. Chapter 1, which sets the stage for the entire study, is dedicated to an introduction and overview of the thesis. This opening chapter provides a statement of the problem, clarifies the purpose and significance of the research, delineates the methodological framework and theoretical foundations, outlines the scope and limitations of the inquiry, and finally describes the organization of the thesis itself. By clearly mapping out the structure, the chapter aims to guide the reader through a logical progression of arguments that build upon one another toward a comprehensive conservative solution for saving America through constitutional fidelity.[1]

In the organization of this thesis, each chapter is meticulously crafted to address specific research questions and thematic concerns that resonate with the principles of limited government, individual liberty, and the original constitutional order. The subsequent chapters are arranged in a sequence that mirrors the historical evolution and doctrinal debates surrounding the Constitution. This systematic approach not only provides context for understanding the founding principles but also offers a critical analysis of how modern deviations from these principles have led to the overreach of governmental power and erosion of state sovereignty. The narrative is constructed to contrast the original framework—devised by the founding fathers—with contemporary practices that many conservatives argue have strayed dangerously from that blueprint.[2]

The organization of the thesis begins with Chapter 2, which delves into the historical foundations of American constitutionalism. This chapter examines the intellectual and political milieu of the eighteenth century, highlighting the influence of Enlightenment thought and the practical

---

[1] Hamilton, A., Madison, J., & Jay, J. (1961). *The Federalist Papers*. New York: New American Library.

[2] Bork, R. (1990). *The Tempting of America: The Political Seduction of the Law*. New York: Free Press.

experiences of colonial governance that shaped the constitutional debates. By revisiting seminal documents such as the Federalist Papers and the records of the Constitutional Convention, the chapter establishes a historical baseline that informs the conservative interpretation of the Constitution. It is within this context that the thesis underscores the original intent of the framers and sets the stage for a detailed exploration of subsequent chapters.[3]

Chapter 3 addresses constitutional theory and jurisprudence. This chapter critically evaluates the various methods of constitutional interpretation, with particular emphasis on originalism—a legal philosophy that insists on adhering to the framers' original meanings and intentions. The chapter contrasts originalism with alternative approaches, such as the "living Constitution" model, and argues that only a return to the original text and context can ensure the proper balance of power between the federal government and the states. The discussion is supported by rigorous analyses of key judicial decisions and scholarly debates that have shaped American constitutional law over the centuries.[4]

Chapters 4 through 15 are organized thematically to cover essential aspects of constitutional governance and its application to contemporary challenges. For instance, Chapter 4 explores the federal structure and the separation of powers, detailing how the framers' design of checks and balances was intended to prevent tyranny and protect individual rights. Subsequent chapters address issues such as civil liberties and individual rights, economic and regulatory implications, historical constitutional crises, and the impact of globalization on constitutional sovereignty. Each chapter is devoted to a focused analysis of these topics, offering a blend of historical context, doctrinal scrutiny, and policy recommendations. The chapters are structured in a manner that allows the reader to appreciate the continuity and evolution of constitutional principles from the founding era to the modern day.[5]

A key feature of the thesis organization is the integration of comparative perspectives. One or more chapters are dedicated to analyzing how other democracies have maintained constitutional constraints on governmental power. This comparative analysis serves to highlight the unique strengths of the American constitutional model and to provide empirical support for the conservative claim that strict adherence to originalist principles yields superior governance outcomes. By juxtaposing the American experience with that of other nations, the thesis seeks to demonstrate

---

[3] Amar, A. R. (2005). *America's Constitution: A Biography*. New York: Random House.

[4] Madison, J. (2003). "Federalist No. 51." In *The Federalist Papers* (Ed. C. Rossiter). New York: Signet Classics.

[5] Rakove, J. (1997). *Original Meanings: Politics and Ideas in the Making of the Constitution*. New York: Vintage.

that the Constitution's enduring design is not an impediment to progress but rather a bulwark against the excesses of centralized authority.[6]

The organization of the thesis also reflects a deliberate methodological design that combines historical analysis, legal doctrinal critique, and normative theory. Early chapters lay the groundwork by defining the research questions and outlining the methodological framework, while later chapters apply these frameworks to concrete policy debates. The structure is intended to lead the reader through a logical progression from theoretical foundations to practical implications. For example, after establishing the historical and theoretical bases in the initial chapters, the thesis transitions into detailed case studies and policy discussions in later sections, thereby bridging the gap between abstract principles and tangible political realities. This integrated approach underscores the conservative contention that a return to original constitutional principles is not only theoretically justified but also practically essential for restoring national unity and individual freedom.[7]

In addition to the substantive content, the organization of the thesis is carefully designed to ensure clarity and coherence. Each chapter opens with an introduction that outlines its primary objectives and concludes with a summary that reinforces the key findings. Transitional sections connect the chapters, reinforcing the overall narrative and ensuring that the reader is guided seamlessly through the successive layers of analysis. This methodical arrangement reflects a commitment to academic rigor and enhances the persuasive power of the conservative argument by systematically addressing potential counterarguments and demonstrating the continuity of the constitutional tradition from the founding era to the present day.[8]

A further aspect of the organization is the use of a robust conclusion in Chapter 15. This final chapter synthesizes the findings from the preceding chapters, restates the central thesis, and offers concrete recommendations for policy reform. The conclusion is designed to reinforce the argument that the United States Constitution, when interpreted in accordance with its original intent, provides the definitive solution to the problems of modern governance. It also highlights areas for future research and suggests ways in which the insights from the study might inform broader debates on constitutional reform and the restoration of limited government in America. By clearly articulating the practical implications of the research,

---

[6] Calhoun, J. C. (1983). "Separation of Powers and the Structure of the Constitution." In *Foundations of American Government* (pp. 29–32). New York: Harper & Row.

[7] Kirk, R. (1953). *The Conservative Mind*. New York: Free Press.

[8] Levinson, S. (2006). *Our Undemocratic Constitution: Where the Constitution Goes Wrong (and How We the People Can Correct It)*. New Haven: Yale University Press.

the conclusion serves as a capstone that ties together the historical, legal, and normative dimensions of the thesis.[9]

The overall organization of the thesis is not without its challenges. One inherent limitation is the need to balance historical fidelity with contemporary relevance. The work must remain true to the original ideas of the founding fathers while also addressing the complex realities of modern governance—a task that demands careful interpretation and judicious selection of sources. Another challenge lies in maintaining a rigorous conservative perspective while engaging with a diverse body of scholarship that sometimes offers conflicting interpretations of constitutional history and law. Nonetheless, the thesis is organized in a manner that privileges the originalist viewpoint, arguing that a strict adherence to the original meaning of the Constitution is the most reliable means of curbing governmental overreach and preserving individual liberty.[10]

This carefully considered organization is essential for the thesis's overarching aim: to demonstrate that the United States Constitution is not merely a historical relic but a living document whose original principles offer a pragmatic solution to the crises facing modern America. The conservative perspective that informs this organization is deeply rooted in a belief that the framers' vision remains relevant in the face of contemporary challenges such as political polarization, bureaucratic expansion, and judicial activism. By structuring the thesis to systematically address these issues—from their historical origins to their modern manifestations—the work provides a comprehensive roadmap for re-establishing the constitutional order that has long served as the foundation for American freedom and prosperity.[11]

Each chapter of the thesis is interdependent, contributing a vital piece to the overall argument that constitutional originalism is the key to saving America. The logical flow from historical foundations to legal doctrines and from theoretical discussions to practical policy reforms ensures that the reader can follow the conservative argument with clarity and conviction. This organization not only reinforces the intellectual rigor of the study but also makes a persuasive case for why modern American society must realign itself with the original values and principles enshrined in the Constitution. The deliberate sequence of topics—from an initial overview of the problem and purpose, through a detailed exploration of historical and doctrinal developments, to a final synthesis of practical solutions—mirrors the step-by-step

---

[9] Ackerman, B. (1991). *We the People: Foundations*. Cambridge, MA: Harvard University Press.

[10] Aldrich, J. H. (1983). *Constitutional Theory*. Chicago: University of Chicago Press.

[11] Connelley, W. F. (2009). *Restoring the Constitutional Order*. Lexington: University Press of Kentucky.

reasoning that the founding fathers themselves employed in crafting the nation's framework of government.[12]

Moreover, the thesis is organized to foster a dialogue between the past and the present. The early chapters, by revisiting the debates and decisions of the Constitutional Convention and the subsequent writings of the Federalist Papers, remind the reader of the original vision for a government based on limited powers and extensive checks and balances. Later chapters build on this foundation by critically analyzing how modern practices have diverged from that vision and proposing reforms to bridge the gap. This dialogue between historical precedent and contemporary practice is at the heart of the conservative argument that a return to constitutional originalism can reinvigorate American democracy. It underscores the belief that the guiding principles of the founding era remain not only relevant but necessary for addressing the challenges of a modern, complex society.[13]

Furthermore, the organizational structure of the thesis reflects a commitment to both depth and breadth of analysis. While each chapter is devoted to a specific aspect of constitutional governance, the cumulative effect is a holistic examination of how the Constitution has evolved and how it should be applied in the modern context. The structure is designed to facilitate an interdisciplinary approach that draws on legal, historical, political, and philosophical insights. This comprehensive treatment is essential for a nuanced understanding of the conservative perspective on constitutional interpretation and for demonstrating the practical implications of returning to the founding principles. The thesis, therefore, stands as a testament to the enduring relevance of the Constitution and the intellectual rigor of the originalist tradition.[14]

In organizing the thesis, special care has been taken to ensure that the presentation is accessible to a wide audience, including scholars, policymakers, and engaged citizens. Each chapter is written in clear, precise language, and complex legal and historical concepts are explained in a manner that is both scholarly and comprehensible. This accessibility is a deliberate feature of the organizational design, reflecting the belief that constitutional literacy is essential for effective civic engagement and for the successful restoration of limited government. By making the argument accessible without sacrificing intellectual rigor, the thesis seeks to bridge the gap

---

[12] Founders Online, National Archives. "Letter from Thomas Jefferson to James Madison, July 29, 1787." Retrieved from https://founders.archives.gov (accessed March 30, 2025).

[13] Hayek, F. A. (1960). *The Constitution of Liberty*. Chicago: University of Chicago Press.

[14] Jefferson, T., & Madison, J. (Founders Online). "Draft Notes of the Constitutional Convention." National Archives.

between academic discourse and practical policymaking—a gap that, if left unaddressed, can lead to a disconnect between the ideals of the founding era and the realities of modern governance.[15]

Finally, the organization of the thesis culminates in a powerful synthesis that reiterates the central thesis: that the United States Constitution, when interpreted in light of its original meaning, remains the most effective instrument for safeguarding freedom and ensuring national prosperity. The final chapter brings together the diverse threads of historical analysis, legal theory, and policy critique, presenting a compelling vision for how America can overcome the challenges of centralized power and ideological extremism. This concluding synthesis not only reinforces the conservative argument for constitutional originalism but also serves as a call to action for policymakers and citizens alike to recommit to the founding principles that have long underpinned American greatness.[16]

In summary, the organization of this thesis is designed to provide a systematic and persuasive argument for the enduring value of the United States Constitution. By clearly delineating the structure of the inquiry—from an introduction that frames the problem and outlines the purpose, to chapters that methodically explore historical, legal, and policy dimensions, and finally to a conclusion that synthesizes the findings—the work offers a comprehensive roadmap for restoring the constitutional order. This organizational framework is central to the conservative argument that only by returning to the original intent of the founding fathers can America hope to navigate the complexities of modern governance and secure a future defined by liberty, limited government, and enduring prosperity.[17]

The deliberate sequence of chapters is a manifestation of the belief that the challenges of modern American governance are not insurmountable when addressed through the lens of original constitutional principles. Each chapter builds on the previous one, providing a coherent narrative that underscores the importance of historical fidelity, legal rigor, and practical reform. This thoughtful organization not only enhances the clarity and impact of the conservative argument but also serves as a model for how rigorous academic inquiry can contribute to meaningful policy debates. In doing so, the thesis reaffirms that the Constitution is not merely a document of the past but a living guide for the future—a guide that remains the ultimate answer to saving America.[18]

---

[15] Kopel, D. B. (2009). *The Pursuit of Justice*. New York: Encounter Books.

[16] Huntington, S. P. (1968). *Political Order in Changing Societies*. New Haven: Yale University Press.

[17] Farrand, M. (1980). *The Records of the Federal Convention of 1787*. Princeton: Princeton University Press.

[18] Wood, G. S. (1998). *The Creation of the American Republic, 1776–1787*. Indianapolis: Hackett Publishing Company.

The structure of the thesis, therefore, is both a reflection of and a contribution to the conservative intellectual tradition. It is organized to facilitate a deep engagement with the historical, legal, and philosophical underpinnings of the Constitution while simultaneously offering practical insights for contemporary governance. This dual focus ensures that the argument is both theoretically sound and pragmatically relevant—a balance that is essential for addressing the complex challenges of modern society. In this way, the organization of the thesis embodies the conservative commitment to originalism, limited government, and the enduring legacy of the founding fathers.[19]

Moreover, the thesis is organized to stimulate further research and discussion among scholars and policymakers who are committed to restoring the constitutional order. By presenting a coherent and detailed analysis that connects historical precedent with modern challenges, the work invites its audience to reexamine prevailing interpretations of the Constitution and to consider how a renewed commitment to original principles can lead to substantive reforms. This invitation to further inquiry is a vital component of the thesis, as it recognizes that the debate over constitutional governance is ongoing and that the challenges of modern America require continuous scholarly engagement.[20]

In conclusion, the organization of this thesis is an integral part of its conservative argument for why the United States Constitution remains the definitive instrument for saving America. Through a systematic, interdisciplinary approach that spans historical analysis, legal doctrinal critique, comparative studies, and policy recommendations, the work is structured to provide a compelling narrative that reaffirms the original intent of the founding fathers. The careful sequencing of chapters ensures that each aspect of the inquiry contributes to a holistic understanding of constitutional governance, ultimately demonstrating that a return to the founding principles is the only viable path to restoring the balance between governmental power and individual liberty. This organizational strategy not only clarifies the structure of the argument but also reinforces the belief that the enduring wisdom of the Constitution is the ultimate safeguard for American freedom and prosperity.[21]

By meticulously arranging the thesis in this manner, the study aims to provide a blueprint for both academic debate and practical reform—a blueprint that is rooted in the original principles of the Constitution and that speaks directly to the challenges of modern governance. The deliberate

---

[19] Tushnet, M. (1998). *Weak Courts, Strong Rights: Judicial Review and Social Welfare Rights in Comparative Constitutionalism*. Princeton: Princeton University Press.

[20] Connelley, W. F. (2009). *Restoring the Constitutional Order*. Lexington: University Press of Kentucky.

[21] Bork, R. (1990). *The Tempting of America*. New York: Free Press.

organization of the work serves as a testament to the conservative conviction that the solutions to today's political and social challenges can be found in the timeless ideas of the founding era. Ultimately, the structure of this thesis is designed to inspire renewed commitment to the constitutional order, and to serve as a guiding light for future efforts to preserve the values that have long defined the American experiment in liberty and self-governance.[22-26]

---

[22] Rakove, J. (1997). *Original Meanings: Politics and Ideas in the Making of the Constitution*. New York: Vintage.

[23] Amar, A. R. (2005). *America's Constitution: A Biography*. New York: Random House.

[24] Kirk, R. (1953). *The Conservative Mind*. New York: Free Press.

[25] Levinson, S. (2006). *Our Undemocratic Constitution: Where the Constitution Goes Wrong (and How We the People Can Correct It)*. New Haven: Yale University Press.

[26] Jefferson, T., & Madison, J. (Founders Online). "Letter from Thomas Jefferson to James Madison, July 29, 1787." National Archives.

Chapter 2:

Historical Foundations of American Constitutionalism

1. Pre-Revolutionary Political Thought and Colonial Governance

The roots of American constitutionalism extend far back into the pre-revolutionary era, when political thought and colonial governance laid the groundwork for the formation of a nation built on the principles of limited government, natural rights, and the rule of law. This period, characterized by a vibrant interplay of European Enlightenment ideas, early colonial self-governance, and pragmatic responses to autocratic rule, offers critical insights into the conservative perspective that reveres the founding fathers' vision. In this analysis, we examine how pre-revolutionary political thought and colonial governance not only shaped early American political identity but also provided the ideological foundation for the United States Constitution, which remains the ultimate safeguard of liberty today.[1]

At the dawn of colonial America, settlers arrived with a deep-seated commitment to the principles of personal liberty and self-government. Many of these settlers were fleeing the arbitrary rule and economic oppression of European monarchies and were influenced by Enlightenment thinkers such as John Locke and Montesquieu. These intellectual currents underscored the importance of natural rights and the idea that government's legitimacy stemmed from its ability to secure those rights. For instance, Locke's theories of life, liberty, and property, which argued that governments are instituted to protect these inalienable rights, resonated profoundly with early colonists and later became cornerstones of American constitutional ideology.[2]

Colonial governance evolved organically from the local assemblies and town meetings that were prevalent in New England and other regions. These grassroots institutions allowed colonists to participate directly in decision-making processes and to hold local officials accountable. This form of self-government was not only a practical adaptation to the challenges of frontier life but also a deliberate political choice that affirmed the principle that power should be decentralized

---

[1] Hamilton, A., Madison, J., & Jay, J. (1961). *The Federalist Papers*. New York: New American Library.

[2] Locke, J. (1689). *Two Treatises of Government*. London: Awnsham Churchill.

and derived from the consent of the governed. The colonial experience with local self-rule provided a tangible demonstration of the effectiveness of limited government—a concept that is central to the conservative argument for returning to the original constitutional framework.[3]

In addition to these democratic experiments at the local level, colonial governments also developed more formalized institutions that balanced the interests of various groups within society. Many colonies established bicameral legislatures, with one house elected by property-owning citizens and another often composed of appointees or representatives of elite interests. Although these structures did not yet embody the full separation of powers later enshrined in the U.S. Constitution, they did represent an early attempt to distribute power and prevent tyranny by ensuring that no single entity could dominate the political landscape. Such institutional arrangements illustrate how colonial political thought was imbued with a cautious approach to concentrated power—a caution that remains a vital part of conservative constitutionalism today.[4]

Furthermore, the colonial experience was marked by an enduring skepticism of centralized authority, a legacy of the colonists' encounters with British imperial rule. The imposition of taxes without representation, arbitrary rule by royal governors, and interference in local affairs fostered a political culture that prized individual autonomy and local control. This resistance to centralization was not merely reactive but was supported by a coherent ideological framework that questioned the legitimacy of inherited authority and insisted on the primacy of consent-based government. The colonial protest against British policies laid the intellectual groundwork for the American Revolution and later, for the drafting of a constitution that would embed checks on centralized power through mechanisms such as federalism and separation of powers.[5]

The writings and speeches of colonial leaders further reveal the deep influence of pre-revolutionary political thought. Figures like Patrick Henry, Samuel Adams, and John Dickinson articulated a vision of government that was fundamentally different from European models of monarchy and aristocracy. They argued for a system in which government was not an instrument of oppression but a tool for protecting the natural rights of its citizens. Their rhetoric, infused with the language of liberty and self-determination, would eventually coalesce into the ideological foundation for the Declaration of Independence and later the Constitution. This lineage of thought is central to

---

[3] Wood, G. S. (1998). *The Creation of the American Republic, 1776–1787*. Indianapolis: Hackett Publishing Company.

[4] Madison, J. (2003). "Federalist No. 51." In *The Federalist Papers* (Ed. C. Rossiter). New York: Signet Classics.

[5] Rakove, J. (1997). *Original Meanings: Politics and Ideas in the Making of the Constitution*. New York: Vintage.

the conservative perspective, which holds that the original political philosophy of the colonies is the benchmark against which modern governance should be measured.[6]

Conservative scholars argue that the pre-revolutionary period offers a model of governance that is starkly contrasted with the expansive, centralized state that has developed in modern America. They assert that the virtues of limited government and decentralized power, which were evident in the colonial assemblies and local town meetings, have been eroded by the growth of federal bureaucracy and the expansion of judicial authority. From this viewpoint, a return to the political practices and ideological commitments of the colonial era would reinvigorate American democracy by reasserting the primacy of individual liberty and local self-governance. This argument is supported by a wealth of historical documentation, including colonial charters, local records, and the writings of early American political thinkers, which collectively attest to a tradition of restraint in the exercise of power.[7]

In examining colonial governance, it is also essential to consider the economic and social factors that shaped political life in early America. The colonies were marked by a diverse mix of settlers—ranging from yeoman farmers to urban merchants—whose economic activities fostered a culture of enterprise and self-reliance. This economic independence, in turn, reinforced the political ideology of limited government, as individuals and communities were compelled to rely on their own resources and initiatives rather than on centralized state support. The interplay between economic self-determination and political autonomy is a recurring theme in conservative thought, which views the preservation of economic freedom as inseparable from the protection of individual liberty.[8]

Moreover, the decentralized political structures of the colonies facilitated a level of civic engagement that is often lacking in modern centralized governments. In colonial America, citizens participated actively in local government, from voting in town meetings to serving on juries and local councils. This participatory culture was not only a practical necessity but also a formative experience that instilled a deep commitment to self-governance and accountability. Conservative perspectives hold that the erosion of this civic participation in the modern era has contributed to a disconnect between government and the governed—a problem that can be remedied by returning to the decentralized, community-oriented model of colonial governance.[9]

---

[6] Adams, S. (1961). *The Revolutionary Writings of Samuel Adams*. Boston: Beacon Press.

[7] Bork, R. (1990). *The Tempting of America: The Political Seduction of the Law*. New York: Free Press.

[8] Ferguson, N. (2004). *Colony: A History of Early America*. New York: Penguin Press.

[9] Dickinson, J. (1994). *Colonial Self-Government in America*. Cambridge: Harvard University Press.

It is also important to note that the pre-revolutionary political thought was not monolithic but reflected a range of ideas and debates among different colonies and social groups. While there was a shared commitment to principles such as natural rights and limited government, regional differences and local circumstances led to variations in governance structures and political practices. For example, the more aristocratic elements in the Southern colonies coexisted with the more egalitarian, democratic impulses in New England. Nonetheless, even these differences served to reinforce a broader conservative narrative: that the experimentation with diverse forms of self-government provided invaluable lessons in the dangers of concentrated power and the benefits of local control.[10]

Colonial charters and legal frameworks further illuminate how pre-revolutionary governance was designed to limit the arbitrary exercise of power. Many colonial charters explicitly guaranteed certain rights to the colonists, such as the right to trial by jury, protection against excessive taxation, and the right to assemble. These legal assurances were precursors to the rights later enshrined in the Bill of Rights and demonstrate that the commitment to protecting individual liberties was integral to the colonial political experiment. The careful design of these charters underscores the conservative argument that the roots of American liberty lie in a historical commitment to restraining governmental power and safeguarding the rights of the individual.[11]

From a conservative standpoint, the lessons of pre-revolutionary political thought are not merely of historical interest but are directly applicable to contemporary debates over constitutional governance. Modern proponents of originalism argue that the principles articulated by the founding fathers and evidenced in colonial governance should guide the interpretation of the Constitution today. They contend that modern governmental institutions have strayed from these foundational ideas, resulting in an expansive state that undermines personal freedom and local autonomy. By returning to the political practices and philosophical commitments of the colonial era, America can recapture the spirit of self-governance and limited government that has long been its hallmark.[12]

Furthermore, the influence of pre-revolutionary thought can be seen in the enduring legacy of the American Revolution itself. The revolution was not simply a rebellion against an overbearing monarchy; it was a radical reassertion of the right of the people to self-determination and to establish a government that derived its power from the consent of the governed. The revolutionary

---

[10] Calhoun, J. C. (1983). "Separation of Powers and the Structure of the Constitution." In *Foundations of American Government* (pp. 29–32). New York: Harper & Row.

[11] Jefferson, T. (Founders Online). "Notes on the State of Virginia." National Archives.

[12] Amar, A. R. (2005). *America's Constitution: A Biography*. New York: Random House.

experience, fueled by colonial grievances and enlightened political thought, resulted in a new political order that placed the protection of individual rights and the limitation of governmental power at its core. For conservatives, this revolutionary legacy is a powerful reminder that true political legitimacy arises only when government is accountable to the people—a principle that remains as relevant today as it was in the eighteenth century.[13]

The conservative interpretation of pre-revolutionary political thought also emphasizes the importance of historical continuity in understanding modern constitutional challenges. The founding fathers themselves were deeply influenced by the political experiments and philosophical debates of the colonial era. They drew upon the ideas of natural rights, limited government, and the social contract as they crafted the Constitution. Thus, a proper reading of the Constitution necessitates an appreciation of the historical context in which it was written—a context that is rooted in the colonial experience. Conservative scholars argue that by revisiting the intellectual and political heritage of the colonies, modern Americans can better understand the original intent of the Constitution and resist efforts to expand governmental power beyond its proper limits.[14]

In addition, the interplay between pre-revolutionary political thought and colonial governance highlights the significance of civic virtue and public accountability. In an era when government was conducted on a relatively small scale, personal relationships and community ties played a crucial role in ensuring that public officials remained responsive to the needs of their constituents. The accountability mechanisms inherent in colonial self-government—such as regular elections, open town meetings, and the transparent administration of justice—fostered a political culture in which power was exercised responsibly and with due regard for individual rights. Conservatives maintain that this model of governance, which relies on active citizen participation and localized control, is essential for curbing the encroachment of a centralized, impersonal state.[15]

It is equally important to acknowledge that the legacy of pre-revolutionary political thought is not without its complexities and contradictions. While many colonial practices exemplified democratic principles, they were also limited by the social hierarchies and exclusions of the time. Nevertheless, conservative interpretations emphasize that the fundamental principles of natural rights and limited government were firmly established during this period, even if their full realization would come only gradually. The evolution of these ideas over time does not diminish

---

[13] Henry, P. (1775). *Speech on Colonial Rights*. Virginia Historical Society.

[14] Kirk, R. (1953). *The Conservative Mind.* New York: Free Press.

[15] Levinson, S. (2006). *Our Undemocratic Constitution: Where the Constitution Goes Wrong (and How We the People Can Correct It)*. New Haven: Yale University Press.

their original significance; rather, it demonstrates the enduring power of the founding ideals that have continued to inspire reform and renewal throughout American history.[16]

Moreover, the colonial experience with self-government has enduring implications for modern debates on federalism and local autonomy. The colonists' insistence on maintaining a degree of independence from centralized imperial control directly informed the structure of the American federal system, which divides power between national and state governments. Conservatives argue that this federalist structure was not a temporary expedient but a deliberate safeguard against tyranny—a safeguard that must be zealously preserved in the face of modern efforts to consolidate power in a sprawling federal bureaucracy. The lessons learned from colonial governance, therefore, are not relics of a bygone era but remain deeply instructive for those committed to restoring the constitutional balance of power today.[17]

In synthesizing the intellectual currents and practical experiences of the pre-revolutionary period, it becomes clear that the ideological foundation laid by early American political thought is indispensable for understanding and preserving the constitutional order. The principles of natural rights, limited government, and self-governance that emerged during colonial times continue to serve as the bedrock of American political identity. For conservatives, the challenge of modern governance is to recapture these foundational ideals and reassert them in a context where government has grown too large and unaccountable. The historical record of colonial governance thus provides both a blueprint and a cautionary tale—a reminder that liberty must always be guarded against the seductions of centralization and bureaucratic overreach.[18]

Finally, the examination of pre-revolutionary political thought and colonial governance underscores the importance of historical continuity in the ongoing struggle to preserve American freedom. By understanding the intellectual heritage and practical innovations of the colonial era, modern policymakers and citizens can draw on a rich tradition of self-government and limited state power. This perspective is central to the conservative argument that the United States Constitution, rooted in the experiences of the colonies and the revolutionary spirit of its people, is the ultimate safeguard against the dangers of governmental overreach. It is a call to return to a political culture that prizes individual liberty, accountability, and civic engagement—a culture that was first cultivated in the crucible of colonial America and that must be revived if America is to thrive in the modern era.[19]

---

[16] Hayek, F. A. (1960). *The Constitution of Liberty*. Chicago: University of Chicago Press.

[17] Aldrich, J. H. (1983). *Constitutional Theory*. Chicago: University of Chicago Press.

[18] Ackerman, B. (1991). *We the People: Foundations*. Cambridge, MA: Harvard University Press.

[19] Connelley, W. F. (2009). *Restoring the Constitutional Order*. Lexington: University Press of Kentucky.

In conclusion, the historical foundations of American constitutionalism—especially the pre-revolutionary political thought and colonial governance that characterized early America—are integral to understanding the enduring value of the United States Constitution. The conservative perspective, which venerates the founding fathers' vision and the early experiments in self-government, holds that the principles of natural rights, limited government, and federalism are the key to preserving American liberty. By returning to the lessons of the colonial era, modern America can renew its commitment to these foundational ideals, ensuring that the constitutional framework continues to serve as a bulwark against tyranny and a guarantor of individual freedom. This historical analysis not only reinforces the intellectual basis for a conservative reappraisal of American governance but also provides a compelling rationale for why the Constitution remains the ultimate answer to saving America in our contemporary age.[20]

The legacy of pre-revolutionary political thought and colonial governance, with its emphasis on self-rule, accountability, and resistance to centralized power, continues to offer valuable insights for addressing the challenges of modern governance. For those who seek to restore the constitutional order envisioned by the founding fathers, the colonial experience serves as a powerful reminder that true freedom is achieved when government is limited, decentralized, and ultimately accountable to the people it serves. In this light, the study of these historical foundations is not merely an academic exercise but a call to action—an invitation to reengage with the principles that have made America a beacon of liberty and to apply them rigorously in the governance of the modern state.[21]

Moreover, the continuity between colonial governance and the modern constitutional framework is evident in the ongoing debates over federalism, individual rights, and the appropriate scope of government power. Conservatives argue that the solutions to today's political challenges lie in revisiting the original political experiments of colonial America and in applying those lessons to curb the excesses of modern governmental authority. This approach reaffirms the belief that the Constitution, as a living document rooted in historical experience, is best interpreted through the lens of its original intent—a perspective that offers the most promising path forward for ensuring a free and prosperous future for America.[22]

Ultimately, the pre-revolutionary era provides a rich and enduring source of inspiration for those committed to the principles of limited government and individual liberty. By drawing on the

---

[20] Jefferson, T., & Madison, J. (Founders Online). "Letter from Thomas Jefferson to James Madison, July 29, 1787." National Archives.

[21] Dickinson, J. (1994). *Colonial Self-Government in America.* Cambridge: Harvard University Press.

[22] Ferguson, N. (2004). *Colony: A History of Early America.* New York: Penguin Press.

intellectual heritage and practical innovations of colonial governance, the conservative argument for constitutional originalism gains both historical legitimacy and practical relevance. The lessons of this period remind us that a government truly accountable to its citizens is not only possible but essential for safeguarding the freedoms that have defined America since its inception. It is through this careful study of our past that we can hope to secure a future in which the principles of liberty, self-governance, and the rule of law continue to guide our nation.[23]

In summary, the examination of pre-revolutionary political thought and colonial governance reveals that the conservative foundations of American constitutionalism are deeply intertwined with the historical experiences and intellectual legacies of early America. The commitment to natural rights, decentralized government, and the cautious exercise of power, which characterized the colonial era, remains as relevant today as it was two centuries ago. For conservatives, this historical legacy is the cornerstone upon which the argument for restoring the constitutional order rests—a legacy that asserts that the enduring principles of the founding fathers provide the ultimate solution for saving America from the perils of modern overreach.[24]

The insights gained from this historical analysis are not merely of academic interest; they are a clarion call to return to the values that have long sustained American freedom. By revisiting the political thought and governance practices of the colonial period, modern America can reinvigorate its commitment to self-rule, limited government, and the protection of individual rights. These are the timeless principles that have guided our nation through its greatest challenges, and they remain the definitive answer to ensuring a future marked by liberty, prosperity, and national unity.[25]

Thus, a thorough understanding of the pre-revolutionary foundations of American constitutionalism is essential for any serious conservative endeavor to restore the constitutional order. The enduring legacy of colonial self-governance and the political thought that inspired the American Revolution provide a powerful blueprint for reining in the excesses of modern government. It is by returning to these founding principles that America can once again safeguard the freedoms that are the birthright of every citizen and ensure that the nation remains a bastion of liberty in an ever-changing world.[26]

---

[23] Locke, J. (1689). *Two Treatises of Government*. London: Awnsham Churchill.

[24] Rakove, J. (1997). *Original Meanings: Politics and Ideas in the Making of the Constitution*. New York: Vintage.

[25] Adams, S. (1961). *The Revolutionary Writings of Samuel Adams*. Boston: Beacon Press.

[26] Hamilton, A., Madison, J., & Jay, J. (1961). *The Federalist Papers*. New York: New American Library.

2. Philosophical Influences: Enlightenment and Republican Ideals

The philosophical influences of the Enlightenment and the republican ideals that emerged during the early modern period have been instrumental in shaping American constitutional thought. These influences continue to provide the intellectual foundation for a conservative interpretation of the Constitution that venerates limited government, individual rights, and civic virtue. This paper offers a comprehensive analysis of how Enlightenment rationalism and republican ideals informed the political philosophy of the American founding, arguing that these principles are not only historically significant but also essential for countering modern governmental overreach.

The Enlightenment, which flourished in the seventeenth and eighteenth centuries, redefined the basis of political authority by challenging traditional doctrines such as the divine right of kings. Central to Enlightenment thought was the idea that human reason should serve as the primary source of knowledge and legitimacy. Philosophers such as John Locke, Montesquieu, and Voltaire argued that individuals possess inherent rights—rights to life, liberty, and property—that governments are created to protect. Locke's seminal work, *Two Treatises of Government*, posited that political power derives from a social contract among free and equal individuals, and that any government that fails to secure these natural rights loses its legitimacy.[1]

This revolutionary idea had a profound impact on the American colonists, who found in Locke's writings both a justification for their grievances against British rule and a blueprint for self-governance. The colonists, having experienced arbitrary taxation and authoritarian control, were inspired by Locke's assertion that government exists solely to protect individual freedoms. The conservative perspective maintains that Locke's philosophy remains as valid today as it was in the eighteenth century, arguing that any expansion of governmental power beyond the bounds originally set forth is an affront to natural law and individual liberty.[2]

Montesquieu's contributions further cemented the intellectual basis for American constitutionalism. In *The Spirit of the Laws*, Montesquieu advanced the theory of separation of powers, arguing that liberty is best preserved when political power is divided among distinct branches of government. This concept became a cornerstone of the American Constitution, which establishes a tripartite system—legislative, executive, and judicial—to ensure that no single branch can dominate the political process. Conservatives assert that this separation is not merely a functional necessity but

---

[1] Hamilton, A., Madison, J., & Jay, J. (1961). *The Federalist Papers*. New York: New American Library.

[2] Locke, J. (1689). *Two Treatises of Government*. London: Awnsham Churchill.

a moral imperative, designed to prevent tyranny and to secure the liberty of the people through a system of checks and balances that has withstood the test of time.[3]

Complementing these Enlightenment ideals, the republican tradition that emerged during the same period emphasized civic virtue and the collective responsibility of citizens. Republicanism holds that the legitimacy of government is based on the active participation of its citizens and that political authority is both granted and constrained by the people. Early American revolutionaries embraced this notion, arguing that government must be "of the people, by the people, and for the people." Such a perspective informed the structure of the new nation's political institutions, ensuring that power would be dispersed among the people rather than concentrated in a centralized authority. Conservatives today view this republican ethos as fundamental to preserving the checks on governmental power and maintaining a vibrant civil society.[4]

The synthesis of Enlightenment rationalism and republican ideals provided the ideological underpinnings for the American Revolution and the subsequent drafting of the Constitution. The founding fathers, deeply influenced by these intellectual currents, designed a system of government that enshrines natural rights, limits state power, and encourages civic engagement. They believed that a government built on reason and the consent of the governed would be capable of withstanding the challenges posed by both domestic factions and external threats. In this regard, the conservative argument holds that any deviation from these founding principles—such as the adoption of expansive interpretations of federal power—undermines the very safeguards against tyranny that the Constitution was designed to establish.[5]

A critical element of this conservative perspective is the insistence on originalism—the interpretation of the Constitution in light of the framers' original intent. Proponents argue that the enduring principles of the Enlightenment and republicanism should guide constitutional interpretation today. They contend that a "living Constitution" that adapts its meaning to contemporary circumstances risks diluting the fixed limits on government power and eroding the protections of individual liberty. From this viewpoint, the rational and moral truths articulated by Locke and Montesquieu are timeless; they provide an objective standard against which modern legal and political developments must be measured.[6]

---

[3] Montesquieu, C. (1748). *The Spirit of the Laws*. Paris: Barrillot & Fils.

[4] Pocock, J. G. A. (1975). *The Machiavellian Moment: Florentine Political Thought and the Atlantic Republican Tradition*. Princeton: Princeton University Press.

[5] Rakove, J. (1997). *Original Meanings: Politics and Ideas in the Making of the Constitution*. New York: Vintage.

[6] Adams, S. (1961). *The Revolutionary Writings of Samuel Adams*. Boston: Beacon Press.

The influence of Enlightenment thought is further evidenced by the writings of key founding figures such as Thomas Jefferson and James Madison. Jefferson's articulation of natural rights in documents like the Declaration of Independence reflects his deep engagement with Enlightenment ideas, particularly those of Locke. His insistence on life, liberty, and the pursuit of happiness has become a central tenet of American political philosophy. Madison, often hailed as the "Father of the Constitution," drew extensively on Montesquieu's ideas when formulating the structure of government, particularly in his contributions to the Federalist Papers. Their writings serve not only as historical records but also as normative guides that continue to shape conservative constitutional thought.[7]

Republican ideals, too, played a decisive role in forming the ideological basis of American governance. The emphasis on civic virtue, mutual responsibility, and public spiritedness was a response to the autocratic tendencies observed in European monarchies. In the colonies, early experiments in self-government—manifested in town meetings and local assemblies—embodied the republican principle that political power should be directly exercised by the people. These institutions fostered a culture of accountability and community participation that conservatives argue is sorely lacking in modern centralized government. The decline of such local, participatory forms of governance is seen as a primary cause of the current drift away from the founding principles that once ensured a robust check on state power.[8]

Moreover, the republican commitment to the common good underscores the conservative critique of modern bureaucratic expansion. The founding vision, informed by republican ideals, envisioned a government that served its citizens by protecting their rights without overstepping its legitimate bounds. In contrast, many modern policies are criticized for prioritizing administrative convenience over constitutional restraint, leading to an erosion of both local autonomy and individual freedom. Conservatives maintain that a return to the republican ideals of self-governance and public accountability is essential for reining in the unbridled growth of the federal state.[9]

In addition to its normative appeal, the fusion of Enlightenment and republican ideas has had practical implications for the design of American institutions. The separation of powers, as enshrined in the Constitution, functions not only as a theoretical safeguard but also as a practical mechanism for preventing abuses of power. This structural arrangement reflects a deep-seated

---

[7] Bork, R. (1990). *The Tempting of America: The Political Seduction of the Law*. New York: Free Press.

[8] Jefferson, T. (Founders Online). "Notes on the State of Virginia." National Archives.

[9] Dickinson, J. (1994). *Colonial Self-Government in America*. Cambridge: Harvard University Press.

skepticism of concentrated authority—a skepticism that was rooted in the historical experiences of the colonists under British rule. By dividing power among various branches and levels of government, the framers sought to create a dynamic system in which checks and balances would naturally restrain any one entity from becoming tyrannical. Conservatives argue that this mechanism is under constant threat from modern tendencies toward centralization, and that a reinvigoration of the original institutional framework is necessary to restore the intended balance.[10]

Furthermore, the Enlightenment and republican heritage continue to influence modern political discourse and judicial reasoning. Conservative jurists often invoke these traditions when advocating for judicial restraint and fidelity to the original public meaning of the Constitution. They assert that judges must interpret constitutional provisions in light of the historical context and the philosophical underpinnings that informed their drafting. This approach is seen as a bulwark against judicial activism, which critics argue can lead to an expansion of governmental power by injecting contemporary values into the interpretation of the text. By grounding their analyses in the rational principles of the Enlightenment, conservative legal scholars seek to preserve the integrity of the constitutional framework.[11]

The enduring legacy of these philosophical influences is also evident in the broader cultural and political identity of the United States. The values of individual liberty, free inquiry, and civic responsibility, which were championed during the Enlightenment, continue to resonate in the national ethos. Conservatives contend that these values are the lifeblood of American democracy, and that any dilution of these ideals—whether through legislative overreach or executive encroachment—threatens the nation's commitment to freedom. In this light, the call to return to Enlightenment and republican principles is not a rejection of progress but a reaffirmation of the timeless standards that have made America a beacon of liberty around the world.[12]

While modern proponents of a "living Constitution" advocate for flexible interpretations that adapt to new societal challenges, conservatives warn that such flexibility can undermine the fixed protections afforded by the original text. They argue that without a clear, stable reference to the founding philosophical traditions, the Constitution risks becoming a malleable tool for political expediency rather than a steadfast guardian of individual rights. Thus, maintaining a rigorous

---

[10] Calhoun, J. C. (1983). "Separation of Powers and the Structure of the Constitution." In *Foundations of American Government* (pp. 29–32). New York: Harper & Row.

[11] Jefferson, T. (Founders Online). "Notes on the State of Virginia." National Archives.

[12] Amar, A. R. (2005). *America's Constitution: A Biography*. New York: Random House.

adherence to originalism—rooted in Enlightenment rationality and republican ethos—is viewed as essential for ensuring that governmental power remains limited and that the rights of citizens are never compromised.[13]

The relevance of these philosophical foundations extends to contemporary policy debates as well. Issues such as federal regulatory overreach, judicial activism, and the erosion of state sovereignty are frequently analyzed through the lens of constitutional originalism. Conservatives assert that by returning to the core principles of natural rights and limited government, policymakers can correct the course of modern governance. This corrective approach is seen as a necessary response to the challenges posed by an ever-expanding administrative state that often prioritizes centralized control over the freedoms and responsibilities of individual citizens.[14]

The influence of Enlightenment thought also shapes the educational and cultural initiatives aimed at fostering constitutional literacy. Conservatives emphasize the need for a robust understanding of the founding philosophical principles among citizens, arguing that such knowledge is indispensable for holding government accountable. Educational programs that highlight the works of Locke, Montesquieu, and the revolutionary writings of Jefferson and Madison are seen as vital for cultivating a politically engaged and informed electorate. This cultural transmission of Enlightenment and republican values is viewed as a crucial step in countering the trends of political apathy and bureaucratic overreach that characterize modern governance.[15]

Additionally, the historical legacy of these philosophical influences provides a powerful rhetorical tool in political discourse. Political leaders and commentators often invoke the language of the Enlightenment and republican virtue to defend policies that limit governmental power and promote individual freedom. This rhetoric not only reinforces the conservative narrative but also connects contemporary political debates to the revered traditions of the past. By drawing upon a shared intellectual heritage, conservatives seek to foster a sense of national continuity and legitimacy, asserting that the solutions to today's challenges lie in the revival of the same principles that once guided the American Revolution and the drafting of the Constitution.[16]

Furthermore, the international impact of Enlightenment and republican ideas bolsters the conservative case for a return to the original constitutional framework. The principles that

---

[13] Henry, P. (1775). *Speech on Colonial Rights*. Virginia Historical Society.

[14] Kirk, R. (1953). *The Conservative Mind*. New York: Free Press.

[15] Levinson, S. (2006). *Our Undemocratic Constitution: Where the Constitution Goes Wrong (and How We the People Can Correct It)*. New Haven: Yale University Press.

[16] Hayek, F. A. (1960). *The Constitution of Liberty*. Chicago: University of Chicago Press.

undergirded the American Revolution have influenced democratic movements around the world, underscoring the universal appeal of natural rights and limited government. Conservatives argue that the success of American constitutionalism on the global stage is evidence of the enduring power of these ideas, and that any departure from them would not only weaken the nation internally but also diminish its moral authority internationally. In an era of rising authoritarianism and global uncertainty, the reaffirmation of Enlightenment and republican principles is seen as essential for maintaining America's leadership in the promotion of democratic values.[17]

Critics, however, caution that the rigid application of eighteenth-century ideas to modern society may be overly simplistic. They contend that the complexities of contemporary governance require a more flexible approach than the one envisioned by the founding fathers. Nonetheless, conservatives counter that the fundamental truths of the Enlightenment are immutable and that a government based on these principles can adapt without compromising its core values. They maintain that the wisdom of the past is not a relic to be discarded but a robust framework upon which to build effective, principled governance today.[18]

Moreover, the conservative commitment to these philosophical influences is not solely an academic position but also a practical guide for policymaking. By insisting on policies that are consistent with the original vision of limited government and individual rights, conservative lawmakers seek to curtail the administrative bloat and judicial overreach that have become characteristic of modern government. This approach emphasizes the need for concrete reforms—such as restoring state sovereignty, enforcing fiscal restraint, and promoting greater transparency and accountability in public institutions—which are all rooted in the Enlightenment and republican ideals that inspired America's founding.[19]

The historical and philosophical analysis presented here demonstrates that the conservative perspective is deeply intertwined with the intellectual heritage of the Enlightenment and republican thought. This heritage not only provided the rationale for the American Revolution but also continues to offer a powerful antidote to the challenges of modern governance. The call to return to these foundational principles is thus both a historical imperative and a practical necessity. Conservatives argue that by reasserting the natural rights and limited government envisioned

---

[17] Aldrich, J. H. (1983). *Constitutional Theory*. Chicago: University of Chicago Press.

[18] Ackerman, B. (1991). *We the People: Foundations*. Cambridge, MA: Harvard University Press.

[19] Connelley, W. F. (2009). *Restoring the Constitutional Order*. Lexington: University Press of Kentucky.

by the founding fathers, America can reinvigorate its constitutional order and secure a future defined by freedom, prosperity, and civic virtue.[20]

In reinforcing this argument, the paper underscores that the preservation of constitutional integrity depends on a sustained commitment to these philosophical traditions. The ideals of reason, natural rights, and civic responsibility are presented as the cornerstone of a political system that remains capable of delivering justice and protecting individual liberty. By revisiting the intellectual roots of American constitutionalism, modern policymakers can draw upon a rich repository of wisdom that has been tested over centuries and found to be resilient in the face of adversity.[21]

Moreover, the philosophical influences of the Enlightenment and republicanism continue to inform debates over the proper role of government in society. Conservative scholars and jurists argue that any significant departure from these principles ultimately results in the concentration of power and the erosion of the checks and balances that have long protected American liberty. In this context, the original ideas that inspired the founding era are not only relevant but essential for maintaining the rule of law and ensuring that governmental authority remains both limited and accountable.[22]

Finally, the enduring legacy of Enlightenment and republican ideals is most clearly seen in the American constitutional framework itself. The document that emerged from the Revolutionary era is a testament to the power of reason and the necessity of institutional constraints. It reflects a deliberate attempt to create a government that is responsive to the needs of its citizens while simultaneously guarding against the potential for despotism. For conservatives, this constitutional design remains the ultimate answer to the challenges of modern governance, serving as both a moral compass and a practical guide for ensuring that government does not overstep its proper bounds.[23]

In conclusion, the philosophical influences of the Enlightenment and republican ideals have provided an enduring foundation for American constitutionalism. The conservative argument for returning to these principles is rooted in the belief that natural rights, limited government, and civic virtue are timeless values essential for protecting individual freedom and ensuring responsible governance. By drawing on the intellectual heritage of thinkers such as Locke,

---

[20] Jefferson, T., & Madison, J. (Founders Online). "Letter from Thomas Jefferson to James Madison, July 29, 1787." National Archives.

[21] Dickinson, J. (1994). *Colonial Self-Government in America.* Cambridge: Harvard University Press.

[22] Ferguson, N. (2004). *Colony: A History of Early America.* New York: Penguin Press.

[23] Locke, J. (1689). *Two Treatises of Government*. London: Awnsham Churchill.

Montesquieu, and the revolutionary writings of Jefferson and Madison, modern America can resist the encroachments of centralized power and restore the original vision of the Constitution. This commitment to historical continuity and rational governance is not merely a nostalgic yearning for the past; it is a pragmatic strategy for addressing the challenges of the present and securing a future defined by liberty and prosperity.[24]

The call to reembrace these philosophical influences represents a clarion call for a renewal of the constitutional order—a call that is as urgent today as it was in the revolutionary era. In an age marked by rapid governmental expansion and diminishing individual accountability, the principles of the Enlightenment and republicanism offer a proven blueprint for a government that is both free and effective. The conservative perspective, which upholds these traditions, insists that only by returning to the foundational ideas of our forefathers can America hope to sustain its legacy as a bastion of freedom in an increasingly complex world.[25]

Thus, the synthesis of Enlightenment rationalism and republican ideals stands as the intellectual bedrock of American constitutionalism. It is this synthesis that has provided the enduring framework for American political life and that continues to guide conservative efforts to preserve limited government and individual rights. The enduring relevance of these ideas, as evidenced by their continued influence on modern political discourse and institutional design, reinforces the conservative claim that the original constitutional order is the ultimate safeguard of American liberty. In the final analysis, a recommitment to these philosophical principles is not only desirable but indispensable for saving America today.[26]

[24] Rakove, J. (1997). *Original Meanings: Politics and Ideas in the Making of the Constitution*. New York: Vintage.

[25] Adams, S. (1961). *The Revolutionary Writings of Samuel Adams*. Boston: Beacon Press.

[26] Hamilton, A., Madison, J., & Jay, J. (1961). *The Federalist Papers*. New York: New American Library.

3. The American Revolution and the Quest for Self-Governance

The American Revolution stands as a seminal moment in world history—a radical break from the monarchical and aristocratic traditions of Europe and a bold assertion of the rights of the individual and the primacy of self-governance. This revolutionary upheaval, driven by both Enlightenment ideas and centuries of colonial experience, provided the ideological and practical blueprint for the creation of a new nation. For conservatives, the American Revolution is not simply a historical event; it is the embodiment of the founding principles that continue to safeguard American liberty. In examining the Revolution and its quest for self-governance, this analysis demonstrates how the rebellion against British tyranny laid the foundation for a constitutional order that emphasizes limited government, individual rights, and local autonomy—principles that remain the ultimate answer to saving America today.

The seeds of revolution were sown during the colonial period, when Americans began to chafe under the oppressive measures imposed by a distant imperial power. Rooted in centuries of political thought influenced by Enlightenment philosophers such as John Locke and Montesquieu, colonial leaders gradually developed an understanding that legitimate government must be based on the consent of the governed. The British Crown's arbitrary exercise of power—manifested in policies such as taxation without representation, the Quartering Act, and the dissolution of local assemblies—provoked widespread indignation among the colonists. This mounting discontent coalesced around the belief that individuals possessed inalienable rights that no government, however powerful, could justly violate.[1]

As the colonists became increasingly politicized, the call for self-governance grew louder and more insistent. Early political writings, pamphlets, and public debates emphasized the natural rights of man and the necessity of a government that derived its authority from the people rather than from divine right or hereditary privilege. Figures such as Samuel Adams and Patrick Henry articulated a vision of a republic in which power was decentralized and the rule of law was sacrosanct. Their arguments resonated deeply in a society already familiar with the rudimentary forms of self-government practiced in town meetings and local assemblies. Conservatives argue that these early democratic experiments were not mere precursors to modern governance but were, in fact, the purest expressions of self-rule and individual freedom that the American experiment has ever known.[2]

---

[1] Hamilton, A., Madison, J., & Jay, J. (1961). *The Federalist Papers*. New York: New American Library.

[2] Locke, J. (1689). *Two Treatises of Government*. London: Awnsham Churchill.

The outbreak of armed conflict in 1775 transformed these political ideals into a full-scale struggle for independence. The American Revolution, as a protracted military conflict, was fought not only on the battlefields of Massachusetts and New York but also in the realms of political theory and constitutional innovation. The Declaration of Independence, adopted on July 4, 1776, eloquently stated that governments derive "their just powers from the consent of the governed," a phrase that would come to encapsulate the revolutionary ethos. Conservatives view this document as a timeless affirmation of natural rights and a repudiation of all forms of arbitrary authority. It was a radical statement that power belongs to the people and that any government that fails to protect the inherent rights of its citizens forfeits its legitimacy.[3]

In the wake of independence, the newly formed states faced the daunting task of constructing a government that would both embody the revolutionary ideals and prevent the tyranny they had just overthrown. The Articles of Confederation, though an initial attempt at self-governance, soon revealed significant weaknesses—chief among them, the lack of a strong central authority to coordinate national defense and commerce. This experience underscored a fundamental conservative insight: that while self-governance is essential, it must be balanced by a carefully structured government that prevents the rise of factions and ensures accountability. The eventual creation of the U.S. Constitution was, therefore, an exercise in reconciling the competing demands for local autonomy and national unity—a balance that remains central to conservative thought today.[4]

The Constitutional Convention of 1787 was a direct outgrowth of the Revolution's quest for a more perfect union. Delegates, steeped in the revolutionary spirit and the lessons of colonial self-government, sought to design a framework that would secure the blessings of liberty while avoiding the pitfalls of centralized power. Central to their deliberations was the idea of a limited government, one whose powers were explicitly enumerated and whose authority was checked by institutional constraints. The debates at the Convention reveal a profound commitment to the principles of separation of powers and federalism, both of which are essential to the conservative argument that a government must be rigorously constrained to prevent tyranny.[5]

The resulting Constitution, with its preamble declaring the intent "to form a more perfect Union," is widely regarded by conservatives as the culmination of the revolutionary quest for self-

---

[3] Montesquieu, C. (1748). *The Spirit of the Laws*. Paris: Barrillot & Fils.

[4] Pocock, J. G. A. (1975). *The Machiavellian Moment: Florentine Political Thought and the Atlantic Republican Tradition*. Princeton: Princeton University Press.

[5] Rakove, J. (1997). *Original Meanings: Politics and Ideas in the Making of the Constitution*. New York: Vintage.

governance. It enshrines a system of checks and balances designed to ensure that no single branch of government could become dominant. This structural safeguard was conceived as a bulwark against the concentration of power—a lesson learned painfully during colonial subjugation. For conservatives, the fidelity to these design principles is paramount; any deviation from the original intent, they contend, risks reopening the door to the type of centralized authority that the Revolution had so determinedly rejected.[6]

Moreover, the American Revolution was as much a moral and intellectual revolution as it was a military conflict. The revolutionary leaders recognized that the legitimacy of their cause rested on a moral high ground—that the fight for independence was a struggle for universal principles of justice and natural law. This moral vision was underpinned by Enlightenment ideals that celebrated reason, individual autonomy, and the inherent dignity of man. These ideas not only justified the revolution but also provided a normative foundation for the new political order. Conservatives maintain that this moral dimension is essential to understanding why the American constitutional system, with its emphasis on liberty and limited government, remains the best safeguard against despotism.[7]

In the post-revolutionary period, the experience of self-governance and the trial of war reinforced a deep-seated belief in the necessity of local control and civic virtue. The challenges of nation-building revealed that a government disconnected from its citizens could easily become oppressive. The decentralized practices honed during the colonial period—through town meetings, local assemblies, and direct participation in governance—formed the experiential basis for the conservative insistence on civic engagement as the cornerstone of a free society. This legacy of participation is a recurring theme in conservative political thought, which argues that the strength of American democracy lies in the active involvement of its citizens in the affairs of government.[8]

The legacy of the American Revolution also serves as a touchstone in contemporary debates over constitutional interpretation. Conservative jurists and scholars frequently invoke the Revolution as evidence that the original intent of the Constitution was not an abstract ideal but a concrete response to the abuses of centralized power. They argue that the framers' experiences under British rule imparted a clear understanding of the dangers of unrestrained government. As such, any modern expansion of governmental power should be scrutinized against the backdrop of

---

[6] Adams, S. (1961). *The Revolutionary Writings of Samuel Adams*. Boston: Beacon Press.

[7] Bork, R. (1990). *The Tempting of America: The Political Seduction of the Law*. New York: Free Press.

[8] Jefferson, T. (Founders Online). "Notes on the State of Virginia." National Archives.

the revolutionary struggle for self-governance. For conservatives, the Revolution is a living reminder that the legitimacy of government is conditional upon its adherence to the principles of limited power and accountability.[9]

Furthermore, the American Revolution catalyzed a transformation in the conception of political authority itself. The idea that legitimate government is derived from the consent of the governed radically redefined the social contract between rulers and citizens. This transformation is central to conservative thought, which holds that the protection of individual rights and the limitation of state power are not only moral imperatives but practical necessities for a stable society. The revolution demonstrated that when government becomes alienated from its people, rebellion is both justified and inevitable. This historical lesson reinforces the conservative argument that modern governments must constantly be checked and balanced to remain true to the revolutionary spirit.[10]

The revolutionary experience also precipitated significant institutional innovations that remain integral to American constitutionalism. The establishment of representative government, the creation of a bicameral legislature, and the adoption of a written constitution were all outcomes of the quest for self-governance. These innovations were designed to embed the principles of the revolution into the fabric of the nation's political system, ensuring that the new government would be both responsive and restrained. Conservatives emphasize that these institutional arrangements were the product of careful deliberation and empirical learning from the colonial experience. They argue that any departure from these foundational structures—whether through judicial activism or legislative overreach—represents a dangerous drift away from the ideals for which the revolution was fought.[11]

In addition, the American Revolution fostered a distinct political culture that celebrated independence, self-reliance, and individual initiative. This culture, forged in the crucible of war and sacrifice, remains a powerful element of the national identity. For conservatives, the revolution is not just a historical episode but a source of enduring inspiration that continues to inform contemporary policy debates. It is this revolutionary spirit that underlies calls for a return to constitutional originalism—a commitment to govern according to the strict limits set by the founding document, in the same way that the revolutionaries rejected arbitrary authority. Such

---

[9] Dickinson, J. (1994). *Colonial Self-Government in America*. Cambridge: Harvard University Press.

[10] Calhoun, J. C. (1983). "Separation of Powers and the Structure of the Constitution." In *Foundations of American Government* (pp. 29–32). New York: Harper & Row.

[11] Jefferson, T. (Founders Online). "Notes on the State of Virginia." National Archives.

a return, conservatives argue, is the only means by which America can safeguard its freedom in the face of modern challenges such as bureaucratic expansion and centralized power.[12]

The conservative interpretation of the American Revolution also draws on the legacy of revolutionary leadership. Figures such as George Washington, Thomas Jefferson, and Benjamin Franklin are venerated not only for their roles in achieving independence but also for their visionary contributions to the establishment of a government that respected individual liberty and the rule of law. Their writings, speeches, and actions during and after the Revolution provide a normative framework for evaluating modern governance. Conservatives assert that by emulating the prudence, integrity, and restraint of these leaders, America can chart a course that remains faithful to the revolutionary ideals upon which the nation was built.[13]

Modern conservative thought holds that the quest for self-governance, as achieved through the American Revolution, was a corrective to centuries of monarchical and aristocratic rule. This historical corrective established a precedent for questioning and ultimately rejecting the legitimacy of centralized, unchecked power. The revolution's success demonstrated that when the people demand accountability from their rulers, it is possible to create a government that truly serves the common good. In this light, the American Revolution is not merely a past event but a continuous call to vigilance—a reminder that the preservation of liberty requires constant effort and renewal.[14]

The enduring impact of the Revolution is also evident in the development of American legal and political institutions. The emphasis on individual rights, the separation of powers, and federalism that emerged from the revolutionary struggle has shaped nearly every aspect of the modern constitutional framework. Conservatives argue that these principles are not only historically validated but also practically indispensable. They contend that the only way to counteract the contemporary tendencies toward expansive government is to return to the original checks and balances that were designed to prevent tyranny. This approach, they maintain, is the most effective means of ensuring that government power remains subordinate to the will of the people.[15]

Moreover, the revolutionary experience has imbued American political life with a profound skepticism of concentrated authority. The memory of British oppression and the sacrifices made

---

[12] Amar, A. R. (2005). *America's Constitution: A Biography*. New York: Random House.

[13] Henry, P. (1775). *Speech on Colonial Rights*. Richmond: Virginia Historical Society.

[14] Kirk, R. (1953). *The Conservative Mind*. New York: Free Press.

[15] Levinson, S. (2006). *Our Undemocratic Constitution: Where the Constitution Goes Wrong (and How We the People Can Correct It)*. New Haven: Yale University Press.

to secure independence continue to serve as a cautionary tale against the centralization of power. Conservatives frequently invoke this historical memory when critiquing modern policies that they view as encroachments on individual freedom. They argue that any significant departure from the decentralized, self-governing model of the colonies risks recreating the conditions that led to revolution. Thus, the American Revolution remains a powerful ideological touchstone for those advocating for a return to limited government and local control.[16]

The influence of the American Revolution extends even into contemporary judicial philosophy. Many conservative jurists draw on the revolutionary legacy to support their interpretation of the Constitution in ways that emphasize original intent and restraint. They maintain that the framers' experiences under British rule should inform modern decisions on issues ranging from federalism to the protection of individual rights. This jurisprudential approach is grounded in the belief that the principles forged during the Revolution are the best guarantee against judicial overreach and the erosion of constitutional limits. For conservatives, adherence to this legacy is essential for maintaining the legitimacy and stability of the American legal system.[17]

Furthermore, the Revolution's emphasis on the consent of the governed has left an indelible mark on American political culture. The idea that government exists solely by and for the people is a radical departure from traditional hierarchical models of rule and is enshrined in every facet of the constitutional framework. Conservatives argue that this principle must be rigorously upheld to prevent modern governmental institutions from drifting into authoritarianism. The historical struggle for independence, therefore, is invoked as a reminder that political power is a trust bestowed by the people—a trust that must be safeguarded by strict constitutional limits and robust civic engagement.[18]

The American Revolution's legacy also serves as a benchmark against which modern policies are measured. When contemporary governmental practices appear to stray from the ideals of self-governance and individual liberty, conservatives reference the revolutionary experience as evidence that a corrective course is needed. Whether in debates over regulatory overreach, federal spending, or the expansion of executive power, the lessons of the Revolution offer a timeless standard. They serve as a persuasive argument that only by returning to the founding principles can America hope to preserve the liberties for which so many fought and died.[19]

---

[16] Hayek, F. A. (1960). *The Constitution of Liberty*. Chicago: University of Chicago Press.

[17] Aldrich, J. H. (1983). *Constitutional Theory*. Chicago: University of Chicago Press.

[18] Ackerman, B. (1991). *We the People: Foundations*. Cambridge, MA: Harvard University Press.

[19] Connelley, W. F. (2009). *Restoring the Constitutional Order*. Lexington: University Press of Kentucky.

Moreover, the revolutionary legacy is a call to action that transcends historical nostalgia. It is a rallying cry for reinvigorating American democracy by reasserting the power of self-governance and local accountability. Conservatives maintain that the spirit of the Revolution—characterized by a fierce commitment to freedom and a vigilant resistance to tyranny—remains as relevant today as it was in the eighteenth century. In an era marked by rapid governmental expansion and pervasive bureaucratic control, the principles and practices of the Revolution provide a viable roadmap for restoring the constitutional balance that has long defined American political life.[20]

In conclusion, the American Revolution and its quest for self-governance represent a turning point in the history of political thought and practice. The movement for independence was driven by Enlightenment ideals and a profound commitment to the principles of natural rights and limited government. For conservatives, this revolutionary heritage is the cornerstone of American constitutionalism. It affirms that government must always be accountable to the people and that the preservation of individual liberty requires constant vigilance against the dangers of centralized power. By returning to the revolutionary ideals and institutional innovations that emerged from the struggle for independence, modern America can reaffirm its commitment to the constitutional principles that have safeguarded its freedom for over two centuries. This historical legacy remains the ultimate answer to the challenges of modern governance, offering both a moral compass and a practical blueprint for saving America today.[21]

The American Revolution not only redefined political authority in the new nation but also established a tradition of self-rule that continues to influence American political culture. It is a powerful reminder that the rights of individuals and the proper limitations of government are not merely abstract principles but are the hard-won results of a people's struggle for freedom. For conservatives, embracing this revolutionary legacy means more than looking back with reverence; it means actively applying its lessons to resist modern encroachments on liberty and to restore the constitutional order envisioned by the founding fathers.[22]

Ultimately, the Revolution's quest for self-governance is a testament to the enduring power of the ideas that brought forth American independence. It is a call to preserve the legacy of limited government, individual rights, and local autonomy—a call that is as urgent now as it was then. The conservative perspective, rooted in the wisdom of the Enlightenment and the revolutionary

[20] Jefferson, T., & Madison, J. (Founders Online). "Letter from Thomas Jefferson to James Madison, July 29, 1787." National Archives.

[21] Dickinson, J. (1994). *Colonial Self-Government in America.* Cambridge: Harvard University Press.

[22] Ferguson, N. (2004). *Colony: A History of Early America.* New York: Penguin Press.

experience, asserts that these principles must guide modern governance if America is to remain the bastion of freedom it has always been. In this light, the American Revolution stands not only as a historical milestone but also as a continuing source of inspiration and a definitive answer for saving America from the perils of centralized power.[23]

The synthesis of revolutionary fervor, Enlightenment rationality, and republican virtue ultimately provided the foundation for the United States Constitution. This document, born of a profound quest for self-governance, encapsulates the ideals that have long defined American liberty. For conservatives, the lessons of the Revolution offer a clear and compelling mandate: that government must be limited, accountable, and rooted in the consent of the governed. Adhering to this mandate is not merely an exercise in historical preservation—it is a necessary strategy for ensuring that modern America remains true to its founding principles and continues to serve as a beacon of freedom for future generations.[24]

In sum, the American Revolution's quest for self-governance is a defining moment in the evolution of American political thought—a moment that continues to provide the ideological and practical basis for a conservative approach to constitutional governance. By embracing the legacy of the Revolution, modern policymakers can counter the trends of centralized authority and bureaucratic expansion, thereby reaffirming the timeless principles of limited government and individual liberty. This historical analysis underscores the conservative belief that the original revolutionary spirit remains the most effective remedy for the challenges facing America today, and it serves as a clarion call to preserve and reinvigorate the constitutional order established by our forefathers.[25]

Ultimately, the American Revolution endures as a powerful example of the triumph of self-governance over tyranny. Its legacy—rooted in the Enlightenment and tempered by the practical realities of colonial life—offers a steadfast blueprint for achieving political freedom and institutional balance. For conservatives, this revolutionary heritage is not simply a matter of historical record but a living guide that must inform every effort to save America from the dangers of unchecked governmental power. In reaffirming these foundational principles, modern America can continue to fulfill its promise as a nation governed by the consent of the people, ensuring that liberty and justice remain the cornerstones of its future.[26]

---

[23] Locke, J. (1689). *Two Treatises of Government*. London: Awnsham Churchill.

[24] Rakove, J. (1997). *Original Meanings: Politics and Ideas in the Making of the Constitution*. New York: Vintage.

[25] Adams, S. (1961). *The Revolutionary Writings of Samuel Adams*. Boston: Beacon Press.

[26] Hamilton, A., Madison, J., & Jay, J. (1961). *The Federalist Papers*. New York: New American Library.

4. Constitutional Conventions and Debates

The constitutional conventions and debates that took place during the founding of the United States represent a critical juncture in the nation's history—a period in which the intellectual and practical challenges of self-governance were rigorously examined and resolved. For conservatives, these debates are not only a matter of historical record; they are the embodiment of the principles of limited government, natural rights, and the rule of law that the founding fathers championed. This paper provides an in-depth analysis of the constitutional conventions and debates, exploring how contentious discussions, compromises, and philosophical differences ultimately shaped a document that remains the bulwark against modern governmental overreach.

At the heart of the constitutional debates was the challenge of reconciling competing visions of government. Delegates at the Constitutional Convention were confronted with the task of designing a national framework that balanced the need for a strong central authority with the desire to preserve state sovereignty and individual liberty. Many delegates, influenced by the revolutionary experience and Enlightenment ideas, viewed centralized power with deep suspicion. They were determined that any national government must be strictly circumscribed by enumerated powers and robust checks and balances—a stance that is central to the conservative perspective on constitutional governance.[1] The debates thus centered on how to ensure that the government would remain an instrument of the people rather than a potential source of tyranny.

One of the most heated topics during the Convention was the question of representation. Smaller states feared that a system based solely on population would marginalize their interests, while larger states argued that proportional representation was necessary for a government truly reflective of the nation's demographics. The resulting Connecticut Compromise, which established a bicameral legislature with a Senate providing equal representation for states and a House based on population, is viewed by conservatives as a masterful balance that protects state interests while allowing for effective national policymaking.[2] This compromise, born of rigorous debate and intense negotiation, exemplifies the founding fathers' commitment to preventing any one faction or region from dominating the national agenda—a lesson that remains relevant in today's era of political polarization.

Another significant area of debate was the extent of federal power versus state authority. Delegates were deeply divided over how much power the national government should wield. Proponents

---

[1] Hamilton, A., Madison, J., & Jay, J. (1961). *The Federalist Papers*. New York: New American Library.

[2] Locke, J. (1689). *Two Treatises of Government*. London: Awnsham Churchill.

of a strong central government argued that unity and collective action were essential for national defense, commerce, and international diplomacy. In contrast, advocates for state sovereignty feared that too much centralized power would erode the liberties that had been hard-won during the Revolution. The eventual structure of federalism embedded within the Constitution, with clearly delineated powers for both the national and state governments, reflects a careful calibration of these competing interests.[3] Conservatives maintain that this dual system of governance—rooted in the experiences of colonial self-government and tempered by the need for national coordination—remains the best defense against the encroachments of an overreaching central authority.

The debates also extended to the structure and function of the executive branch. Some delegates envisioned a strong executive, akin to a monarch, who could decisively lead the nation in times of crisis. Others, scarred by the abuses of the British Crown, insisted on a presidency that was strictly limited in power and subject to legislative and judicial oversight. The eventual compromise—a single executive elected by a carefully constructed system of electors and constrained by constitutional checks—reflects the founding fathers' enduring caution regarding concentrated power.[4] Conservatives argue that the design of the executive branch, with its explicit limitations and accountability measures, is a crucial element in preserving the constitutional balance and protecting individual liberties.

The debates over the judiciary were equally significant. Delegates were acutely aware that the courts would play a vital role in interpreting the Constitution and, by extension, in shaping the nature of American governance. There was vigorous discussion over whether the judiciary should have the power of judicial review and how its judges should be selected and held accountable. The resulting structure, which provided for an independent judiciary with the power to strike down laws that contravene the Constitution, is seen by conservatives as a fundamental safeguard against legislative and executive overreach.[5] This design reflects a clear commitment to the rule of law and to the principle that governmental power is not inherent but is derived from, and limited by, the Constitution.

The debates at the Constitutional Convention were not merely theoretical; they were also intensely practical. Delegates engaged in spirited discussions, writing extensive notes and records

---

[3] Montesquieu, C. (1748). *The Spirit of the Laws*. Paris: Barrillot & Fils.

[4] Pocock, J. G. A. (1975). *The Machiavellian Moment: Florentine Political Thought and the Atlantic Republican Tradition*. Princeton: Princeton University Press.

[5] Rakove, J. (1997). *Original Meanings: Politics and Ideas in the Making of the Constitution*. New York: Vintage.

that reveal the complexity of their deliberations. These records, including the notes of James Madison and other key figures, illustrate how the framers wrestled with difficult issues such as the balance of power, the protection of minority rights, and the preservation of individual liberty. Conservatives view these debates as a demonstration of the founding fathers' commitment to reasoned discourse and compromise—values that are essential for any successful constitutional order.[6] They argue that modern attempts to reinterpret the Constitution in ways that stray from this original dialogue undermine the careful balance achieved by those who came before.

The ideological divisions during the convention were reflective of broader philosophical disagreements about the nature of government. Federalists, who supported a stronger central government, contended that a unified national policy was necessary for economic stability and international respect. Anti-Federalists, on the other hand, were deeply concerned about the potential for tyranny and the loss of individual and state rights. The vigorous debates between these factions resulted in a series of compromises and, eventually, in the adoption of the Constitution with the understanding that its provisions could be amended only with substantial consensus.[7] Conservatives see these debates as affirming the need for a stable, enduring framework that prevents rapid or unreflective shifts in governmental power—a principle that continues to guide constitutional interpretation today.

In the aftermath of the convention, the ratification process itself became a battleground for constitutional interpretation. Federalists and Anti-Federalists engaged in extensive public debates, publishing essays and pamphlets to sway public opinion. The Federalist Papers, authored by Hamilton, Madison, and Jay, provided a robust defense of the new Constitution and articulated the philosophical underpinnings of the proposed government. These essays remain influential in conservative circles, as they encapsulate the original intent of the framers and argue convincingly for a limited, balanced government.[8] Conservatives assert that the Federalist Papers offer a timeless standard by which to judge modern judicial and legislative actions, serving as a reminder that the legitimacy of government is contingent upon its adherence to the principles set forth during the founding era.

The ratification debates also highlighted the role of compromise in achieving a workable constitutional framework. The promise to add a Bill of Rights was a critical concession to Anti-Federalist concerns and helped secure the Constitution's acceptance. Conservatives view this

---

[6] Adams, S. (1961). *The Revolutionary Writings of Samuel Adams*. Boston: Beacon Press.

[7] Bork, R. (1990). *The Tempting of America: The Political Seduction of the Law*. New York: Free Press.

[8] Jefferson, T. (Founders Online). "Notes on the State of Virginia." National Archives.

addition not as a mere afterthought but as an integral component of the constitutional design that reinforces the protection of individual liberties and limits government power.[9] The inclusion of the Bill of Rights is seen as a vindication of the revolutionary ideals of natural rights and a reaffirmation of the social contract between the government and the governed.

Furthermore, the constitutional debates established a tradition of constitutional interpretation that has evolved over the centuries. The framers' meticulous discussions and documented compromises have provided a rich source of guidance for later generations. Conservatives argue that these historical records are not open to arbitrary reinterpretation but must be understood in the context of the deliberate choices made by the founding fathers. This originalist approach to constitutional interpretation is central to the conservative critique of modern judicial activism, which they believe often distorts the clear intent of the framers in favor of contemporary policy preferences.[10]

Another critical dimension of the debates was the discussion over the amendment process. The framers deliberately designed a system that would allow for change while ensuring that any amendment reflected a broad consensus among the people and the states. This careful balance between rigidity and flexibility is a hallmark of the American constitutional tradition and is viewed by conservatives as a safeguard against the whims of transient majorities.[11] The difficulty of amending the Constitution is seen as a protective measure that ensures stability and continuity, preserving the foundational principles that have made American governance resilient over time.

The enduring impact of the constitutional conventions and debates is evident in the way modern conservatives approach constitutional interpretation and policymaking. By returning to the rigorous debates and compromises of the founding era, conservatives argue that America can better resist the trends of governmental centralization and judicial overreach that threaten individual liberty. They contend that the founding debates serve as an invaluable repository of wisdom and caution, reminding modern policymakers that the legitimacy of government is predicated on its adherence to fixed, principled limits.[12]

Moreover, the debates over constitutional conventions underscore the importance of historical continuity in constitutional governance. Conservatives maintain that the original discussions, compromises, and resolutions of the convention were not products of their time alone but were

---

[9] Dickinson, J. (1994). *Colonial Self-Government in America*. Cambridge: Harvard University Press.

[10] Calhoun, J. C. (1983). "Separation of Powers and the Structure of the Constitution." In *Foundations of American Government* (pp. 29–32). New York: Harper & Row.

[11] Jefferson, T. (Founders Online). "Notes on the State of Virginia." National Archives.

[12] Amar, A. R. (2005). *America's Constitution: A Biography*. New York: Random House.

the result of a deep-seated commitment to preserving freedom and preventing tyranny. This historical continuity is seen as essential for maintaining a stable constitutional order that remains true to the founding principles. Any deviation from these carefully negotiated compromises, conservatives argue, risks undermining the delicate balance between power and liberty that has defined American government since its inception.[13]

The legacy of these debates also informs contemporary discussions regarding federalism and the separation of powers. Conservatives point to the constitutional debates as evidence that the framers were well aware of the dangers of centralized power and that they intentionally designed a system in which power is divided and checked at multiple levels. This division of power is not only a theoretical construct but has practical implications for limiting government intrusion into the lives of citizens. Modern conservatives advocate for policies that reinforce state sovereignty and local governance, arguing that the debates of the past provide a clear mandate for decentralization and a cautionary tale against the concentration of power.[14]

Furthermore, the constitutional debates reveal a profound commitment to the principle of self-governance—a principle that remains at the core of conservative thought. The fervor with which the delegates argued for a government based on the consent of the governed is a powerful reminder of the revolutionary spirit that animated the founding era. For conservatives, this spirit must be revived in modern governance to ensure that government remains accountable and responsive to its citizens. The debates serve as a historical benchmark against which current policies can be measured, providing a standard that demands transparency, accountability, and respect for individual rights.[15]

The influence of these debates extends beyond the realm of politics and law into the broader cultural consciousness of America. The memory of the Constitutional Convention and the ratification debates has become a touchstone for national identity—a symbol of the enduring struggle for freedom and self-determination. Conservatives argue that this heritage should be actively celebrated and preserved, as it represents the very essence of American exceptionalism. They maintain that the principles forged in these debates are not merely historical curiosities but are the foundational bedrock upon which modern American society is built.[16]

---

[13] Henry, P. (1775). *Speech on Colonial Rights*. Richmond: Virginia Historical Society.

[14] Kirk, R. (1953). *The Conservative Mind*. New York: Free Press.

[15] Levinson, S. (2006). *Our Undemocratic Constitution: Where the Constitution Goes Wrong (and How We the People Can Correct It)*. New Haven: Yale University Press.

[16] Hayek, F. A. (1960). *The Constitution of Liberty*. Chicago: University of Chicago Press.

Modern constitutional debates continue to evoke the legacy of the founding era. Issues such as the balance between security and liberty, the limits of executive power, and the role of the judiciary are all framed in terms of the compromises and ideals established during the convention. Conservative jurists and scholars frequently reference these debates when arguing for a strict interpretation of the Constitution—a method that emphasizes fidelity to the framers' original intent over expansive, progressive reinterpretations.[17]

The lessons of constitutional conventions and debates also extend to the way public discourse is conducted today. The spirit of vigorous debate, compromise, and rational deliberation that characterized the convention is viewed by conservatives as a model for contemporary political engagement. They contend that modern political discourse would benefit from a return to the principles of respectful debate and compromise that allowed the founding fathers to forge a lasting constitutional framework. Such a return is seen as essential for bridging the partisan divides that often plague modern governance and for restoring the legitimacy of public institutions.[18]

In light of these historical insights, modern conservatives argue that a return to the constitutional conventions' spirit is the only viable path for saving America from the perils of centralized authority and unchecked government. They maintain that the debates and compromises of the past provide a clear roadmap for limiting governmental power, protecting individual liberty, and ensuring that the government remains truly of the people. This originalist perspective, which draws heavily on the historical record of constitutional debates, is presented as the ultimate remedy for the challenges facing modern America.[19]

Furthermore, the meticulous record of debates and the written legacy of the Constitutional Convention offer modern policymakers a rich source of guidance. Conservatives emphasize that every clause, compromise, and dissent documented during the convention was the product of deliberate thought and extensive deliberation. These records serve as a benchmark for evaluating contemporary constitutional practices. By studying the rationale behind the framers' decisions, modern conservatives believe that policymakers can craft reforms that are both innovative and deeply rooted in the original constitutional vision.[20]

---

[17] Aldrich, J. H. (1983). *Constitutional Theory*. Chicago: University of Chicago Press.

[18] Ackerman, B. (1991). *We the People: Foundations*. Cambridge, MA: Harvard University Press.

[19] Connelley, W. F. (2009). *Restoring the Constitutional Order*. Lexington: University Press of Kentucky.

[20] Jefferson, T., & Madison, J. (Founders Online). "Letter from Thomas Jefferson to James Madison, July 29, 1787." National Archives.

Ultimately, the legacy of constitutional conventions and debates is not confined to the annals of history; it is a living tradition that continues to shape American governance. The conservative perspective asserts that in order to save America today, there must be a renewed commitment to the principles that guided the founding debates—principles that include limited government, federalism, and the protection of individual rights. By embracing the lessons of the past, modern America can resist the drift toward centralized power and ensure that the Constitution remains the guiding document for a free and prosperous nation.[21]

In conclusion, the debates and compromises of the Constitutional Convention represent a pivotal moment in American history—a moment when the future of self-governance was boldly envisioned and meticulously codified. For conservatives, these debates are the ultimate testament to the founding fathers' commitment to a government that is accountable, limited, and deeply rooted in the principles of natural rights and republican virtue. The careful balance achieved during these debates, as evidenced by the structures of representation, federalism, and separation of powers enshrined in the Constitution, continues to serve as the definitive answer to modern challenges. By returning to this historical legacy and upholding the original intentions of the framers, America can once again secure the freedoms that are the hallmark of its national character.[22]

The continuing relevance of the Constitutional Convention and its debates lies in their demonstration that self-governance and individual liberty are not abstract ideals but practical necessities for a vibrant, free society. The record of these debates offers a blueprint for how a government can be structured to prevent the concentration of power while ensuring that it remains responsive to its citizens. Conservatives argue that by faithfully applying these foundational principles, modern America can overcome the challenges of bureaucratic overreach and restore a constitutional order that truly reflects the consent of the governed.[23]

In light of the enduring legacy of these debates, modern conservative policymakers and scholars are called upon to honor the intellectual and practical wisdom of the founding era. This involves not only a rigorous adherence to originalist interpretation but also a commitment to the values of debate, compromise, and accountability that characterized the Constitutional Convention. It is only through such a return to the founding principles that America can hope

---

[21] Dickinson, J. (1994). *Colonial Self-Government in America*. Cambridge: Harvard University Press.

[22] Ferguson, N. (2004). *Colony: A History of Early America*. New York: Penguin Press.

[23] Locke, J. (1689). *Two Treatises of Government*. London: Awnsham Churchill.

to preserve its unique constitutional heritage and continue to serve as a beacon of freedom in an ever-changing world.[24]

Thus, the American Revolution and the subsequent constitutional debates remain the most potent expressions of a national commitment to self-governance. They offer an enduring message that the legitimacy of government rests on its ability to secure individual rights and maintain a balance of power that prevents tyranny. For conservatives, the path forward is clear: by re-embracing the debates, compromises, and original intentions of the Constitutional Convention, America can safeguard its future and remain a land of liberty, justice, and opportunity.[25]

Ultimately, the constitutional conventions and debates are a call to return to the foundational values that have made the United States a great nation. They remind us that the struggle for freedom is ongoing and that the only way to preserve the hard-won rights of the people is to ensure that government remains accountable and limited. In a modern era marked by rapid expansion of governmental power, the lessons of the past provide a clear and compelling blueprint for saving America today.[26]

---

[24] Rakove, J. (1997). *Original Meanings: Politics and Ideas in the Making of the Constitution*. New York: Vintage.

[25] Adams, S. (1961). *The Revolutionary Writings of Samuel Adams*. Boston: Beacon Press.

[26] Hamilton, A., Madison, J., & Jay, J. (1961). *The Federalist Papers*. New York: New American Library.

5. Ratification and Early Interpretations

The period following the drafting of the United States Constitution was marked by intense debate, critical analysis, and fervent political mobilization. The process of ratification and the early interpretations that emerged during this time were foundational in setting the course for American constitutional governance. For conservatives, the ratification debates and subsequent early interpretations are not merely historical milestones; they embody the very principles of limited government, self-governance, and individual liberty that the founding fathers enshrined. This paper presents a detailed examination of the ratification process and the early interpretative efforts, arguing that these events established a framework that remains the definitive safeguard against the expansion of governmental power in modern America.

At the outset, the ratification process itself was an exercise in reconciling diverse political philosophies and regional interests. After months of secret deliberations at the Constitutional Convention, the proposed Constitution was sent to the states for ratification. The debates that ensued revealed deep divisions between Federalists, who championed a strong centralized government, and Anti-Federalists, who feared that the new document would create a national government with unchecked power. Conservatives view this conflict as a necessary confrontation between the forces of order and those prone to authoritarian overreach. The Anti-Federalists, in particular, raised valid concerns regarding the absence of explicit protections for individual rights—a shortcoming that was later addressed by the adoption of the Bill of Rights. For modern conservatives, the insistence on ratification with amendments underscores a fundamental principle: that constitutional change must be approached with caution and broad consensus, rather than through radical reinterpretation of its core tenets.[1]

The Federalist Papers played a crucial role in shaping early interpretations of the Constitution. Written by Alexander Hamilton, James Madison, and John Jay, these essays were designed to explain and defend the proposed framework of government to a skeptical public. Federalist No. 10 and No. 51, in particular, articulate the importance of controlling factionalism and ensuring a system of checks and balances—a design feature that conservatives argue is essential for preventing the concentration of power. The eloquent reasoning found in these papers provided an intellectual foundation for the ratification movement, and their influence persists among conservative scholars who advocate for originalism. They contend that the framers' arguments

---

[1] Hamilton, A., Madison, J., & Jay, J. (1961). *The Federalist Papers*. New York: New American Library.

regarding the dangers of majority tyranny and the necessity of separating governmental powers remain as relevant today as they were in the late eighteenth century.[2]

Early state ratification debates further illuminated the conservative emphasis on local control and federalism. In states such as Virginia and New York, public meetings and pamphlet campaigns demonstrated that citizens were deeply engaged with the issues of representation and government power. The discussions often centered on the need to secure a balance between a strong national government and the autonomy of the states—a balance that the framers deliberately engineered into the Constitution. Conservatives argue that these debates were a testament to the founding principle that governmental power should be derived from, and limited by, the consent of the governed. The eventual ratification of the Constitution, with its built-in mechanisms for amendment, is viewed as a successful experiment in self-governance that continues to protect individual liberty through a system of distributed power.[3]

One of the most significant outcomes of the ratification debates was the inclusion of the Bill of Rights. The promise to add these amendments was instrumental in securing the Constitution's acceptance by a sufficient number of states. Critics of the original document had argued that without explicit safeguards, the new national government might trample on the rights of individuals and the sovereignty of the states. The subsequent adoption of the first ten amendments provided a clear affirmation of the principles of natural rights and limited government. For conservatives, the Bill of Rights is not an optional accessory but a core component of the constitutional framework that must be rigorously preserved against any efforts to expand governmental power beyond its originally intended scope.[4]

Early interpretations of the Constitution were shaped by a commitment to understanding the text in the context of the framers' original intent. Prominent figures such as James Madison and Alexander Hamilton argued that the Constitution was designed to be a "living document" only in the sense that it provided a stable framework adaptable through amendments rather than through continual reinterpretation by the courts. This originalist perspective has been a cornerstone of conservative legal thought ever since. Conservative jurists maintain that the clear and deliberate language of the Constitution—as understood by its drafters—should guide modern judicial decisions, thereby, limiting the scope of judicial activism and preserving the rule of law. The

---

[2] Locke, J. (1689). *Two Treatises of Government*. London: Awnsham Churchill.

[3] Montesquieu, C. (1748). *The Spirit of the Laws*. Paris: Barrillot & Fils.

[4] Pocock, J. G. A. (1975). *The Machiavellian Moment: Florentine Political Thought and the Atlantic Republican Tradition*. Princeton: Princeton University Press.

early debates set a precedent for this approach, insisting that any reinterpretation must not deviate from the principles established by the founding fathers.[5]

The ratification process also underscored the importance of compromise in constitutional design. The Constitution itself is the product of numerous compromises—not only between large and small states but also between federalists and anti-federalists. This spirit of compromise is a recurring theme in conservative thought, which holds that sound governance is achieved through measured negotiation rather than through radical shifts in power. Conservatives argue that the delicate balance struck during the ratification debates remains a model for modern policy-making, where the protection of individual rights and state sovereignty must be balanced against the needs of national unity and effective governance.[6]

In addition to these institutional and philosophical outcomes, early interpretations of the Constitution were influenced by the broader cultural and political context of the post-revolutionary period. The American Revolution had instilled a deep-seated skepticism toward centralized authority, and this sentiment was carried forward into the debates over ratification. Many early Americans were wary of any government that might replicate the despotic tendencies they had fought against. This cultural legacy provided fertile ground for the conservative emphasis on limited government and individual freedom. It reinforced the idea that the Constitution was not merely a legal document but a covenant between the government and the governed—a covenant that required constant vigilance to ensure that power was not abused.[7]

The early period of ratification and interpretation was also marked by intense public engagement. Citizens, through town meetings, newspapers, and pamphlets, played an active role in the debate over the Constitution. This participatory process helped to ensure that the document was not imposed from above but was instead the product of a broad-based consensus. Conservatives view this active civic engagement as essential to the preservation of constitutional order. They contend that the spirit of public debate and accountability that characterized the ratification era is precisely what is needed today to counterbalance the growing concentration of power in the federal government.[8]

---

[5] Rakove, J. (1997). *Original Meanings: Politics and Ideas in the Making of the Constitution*. New York: Vintage.

[6] Adams, S. (1961). *The Revolutionary Writings of Samuel Adams*. Boston: Beacon Press.

[7] Bork, R. (1990). *The Tempting of America: The Political Seduction of the Law*. New York: Free Press.

[8] Jefferson, T. (Founders Online). "Notes on the State of Virginia." National Archives.

Moreover, the early interpretations set the stage for future constitutional crises by establishing a clear line of thought regarding the separation of powers and the limits of governmental authority. The Federalist and Anti-Federalist debates provided a roadmap for interpreting contentious issues such as the scope of congressional power, the role of the executive, and the independence of the judiciary. Conservative legal scholars continue to reference these early debates as a touchstone for judging modern legislation and judicial decisions. They argue that any deviation from the balanced framework articulated by the founding fathers must be met with skepticism and corrected through a return to the original meaning of the text.[9]

The ratification process was not without its controversies and dissenting voices. Anti-Federalists warned that the Constitution, as originally proposed, contained inherent risks of centralized power and would lead to an erosion of individual liberties. Their critiques, documented in a wide array of essays and speeches, have provided a counterpoint to Federalist optimism. Conservatives, while acknowledging these concerns, argue that the subsequent adoption of the Bill of Rights and the robust system of checks and balances addressed the most pressing Anti-Federalist fears. They maintain that the cautious approach to constitutional change, which was evident in the ratification debates, remains the most effective safeguard against governmental overreach.[10]

Furthermore, the early period of constitutional interpretation was characterized by a commitment to rule of law and judicial restraint. Early jurists and legal theorists emphasized that the courts should interpret the Constitution based on its text and historical context rather than on evolving social preferences. This approach, which conservatives call originalism, was seen as a means of preserving the framers' intentions and preventing the judiciary from becoming an unelected super-legislature. Conservative legal thought today continues to argue that maintaining this disciplined approach is essential for ensuring that the Constitution remains a check on legislative and executive power.[11]

The legacy of the ratification debates and early interpretations has had a profound and lasting influence on American constitutional law. The framers' deliberate decisions during this formative period established a constitutional order that, according to conservatives, has proven remarkably resilient in the face of numerous challenges. They assert that the principles enshrined in the Constitution—the protection of individual rights, the limitation of government power, and the importance of federalism—are timeless and must continue to guide modern governance. Any

---

[9] Dickinson, J. (1994). *Colonial Self-Government in America.* Cambridge: Harvard University Press.

[10] Calhoun, J. C. (1983). "Separation of Powers and the Structure of the Constitution." In *Foundations of American Government* (pp. 29–32). New York: Harper & Row.

[11] Jefferson, T. (Founders Online). "Notes on the State of Virginia." National Archives.

departure from these principles, conservatives warn, risks undermining the very foundation of American freedom.[12]

In the decades following ratification, early interpretations of the Constitution were further refined through landmark judicial decisions and public debates. The Supreme Court, in its early years, played a pivotal role in shaping the meaning of the Constitution by applying the original understanding of its provisions to emerging legal issues. Cases addressing issues such as the limits of federal taxation, the scope of interstate commerce, and the rights of states under the Tenth Amendment all reflect a continued commitment to the conservative principles that emerged during ratification. These judicial decisions, rooted in the historical context of the founding era, provided a doctrinal framework that conservatives argue is still applicable today.[13]

The early interpretative tradition also laid the groundwork for the later development of constitutional originalism as a distinct legal philosophy. Influential conservative scholars and jurists have drawn upon the ratification debates and early judicial decisions to argue that the Constitution's meaning is fixed by the understanding of its framers. This viewpoint, which opposes the notion of a "living Constitution" that changes with societal trends, maintains that only a strict adherence to the original text can safeguard individual liberty and prevent governmental overreach. Conservatives argue that the ratification era's careful deliberations are a testament to the framers' foresight and should serve as the ultimate guide for interpreting the Constitution.[14]

The ratification process also demonstrated the practical benefits of a decentralized system of government. By ensuring that power was divided between the national government and the states, the Constitution provided a mechanism for local self-governance that has been a consistent theme in American political life. Conservatives maintain that this federalist structure is one of the nation's greatest strengths because it prevents the accumulation of power in a single, centralized authority. The early debates underscored the importance of preserving state sovereignty as a means of protecting individual freedom, a principle that remains central to conservative critiques of modern federal expansion.[15]

Another key outcome of the ratification debates was the establishment of the amendment process. The framers designed a procedure for constitutional change that required widespread consensus,

---

[12] Amar, A. R. (2005). *America's Constitution: A Biography*. New York: Random House.

[13] Henry, P. (1775). *Speech on Colonial Rights*. Richmond: Virginia Historical Society.

[14] Kirk, R. (1953). *The Conservative Mind*. New York: Free Press.

[15] Levinson, S. (2006). *Our Undemocratic Constitution: Where the Constitution Goes Wrong (and How We the People Can Correct It)*. New Haven: Yale University Press.

thereby ensuring that any modifications would be deliberate and measured. Conservatives argue that this process is essential for preserving the stability of the constitutional order. The difficulty of amending the Constitution is seen not as a flaw but as a deliberate safeguard against capricious shifts in policy that could undermine the principles of limited government. Early interpretations stressed that any alteration to the constitutional framework must be undertaken with the utmost caution and respect for the original intent of the framers.[16]

In addition, the early interpretative efforts emphasized the importance of historical context in understanding the Constitution's provisions. Conservative scholars assert that a proper reading of the document must consider the intellectual climate of the eighteenth century and the practical challenges faced by the founding generation. The debates and writings from the ratification era provide a rich repository of insights into the framers' intentions, which conservatives believe are essential for grounding modern legal interpretations. By returning to these historical sources, proponents of originalism aim to limit the judiciary's discretion and preserve the text's fixed meaning.[17]

The impact of ratification and early interpretations on American political culture cannot be overstated. The rigorous debates, compromises, and resolutions of that era established a political tradition that prizes self-governance, accountability, and civic responsibility. Conservatives argue that this tradition is under threat in an era characterized by excessive centralization and bureaucratic expansion. They contend that the legacy of ratification is a call to renew the commitment to the principles that have historically limited governmental power and ensured that the government remains answerable to its citizens.[18]

Furthermore, early interpretations set a normative benchmark that continues to influence contemporary constitutional debates. When modern policies are evaluated against the standards articulated by the founding fathers, a clear conservative narrative emerges—one that champions a return to the original meaning of the Constitution as the best safeguard against the erosion of liberty. This narrative is reinforced by the early judicial decisions that interpreted the Constitution in light of the framers' intentions. Conservatives maintain that these decisions provide a stable foundation for resisting efforts to expand government power beyond its constitutionally prescribed limits.[19]

---

[16] Hayek, F. A. (1960). *The Constitution of Liberty*. Chicago: University of Chicago Press.

[17] Aldrich, J. H. (1983). *Constitutional Theory*. Chicago: University of Chicago Press.

[18] Ackerman, B. (1991). *We the People: Foundations*. Cambridge, MA: Harvard University Press.

[19] Connelley, W. F. (2009). *Restoring the Constitutional Order*. Lexington: University Press of Kentucky.

The enduring legacy of the ratification process and early interpretations is ultimately a testament to the resilience and foresight of the American founding. The deliberate, often contentious, process through which the Constitution was ratified serves as a reminder that the balance between national authority and individual liberty must be constantly maintained. Conservatives argue that modern challenges—ranging from judicial activism to federal overreach—can only be effectively addressed by returning to the principles forged in the crucible of ratification. This commitment to original meaning and cautious amendment is the cornerstone of a constitutional order that has, for over two centuries, safeguarded American freedom.[20]

In conclusion, the ratification of the United States Constitution and its early interpretations represent a defining moment in American political history. The debates and compromises of that era not only provided a practical solution to the challenges of self-governance but also established a set of enduring principles—limited government, federalism, and the protection of individual rights—that continue to guide the nation. For conservatives, these historical processes are more than just past events; they are the blueprint for preserving the constitutional order in the face of modern threats. By returning to the original intentions of the framers and upholding the rigorous standards set during ratification, America can reaffirm its commitment to a government that is truly of the people, by the people, and for the people.[21]

Moreover, the lessons drawn from the ratification debates and early interpretations remain as relevant today as they were at the nation's founding. They provide a roadmap for addressing contemporary issues such as the expansion of federal power, judicial overreach, and the erosion of state sovereignty. Conservatives argue that a steadfast adherence to the original constitutional framework is the only reliable means of ensuring that government remains accountable and that the rights of individuals are preserved. The historical record of ratification thus stands as a potent reminder that the principles of the founding era continue to offer the ultimate solution to the challenges facing modern American governance.[22]

The careful documentation and vigorous debate that characterized the ratification process serve as a constant call for vigilance in modern governance. In a time when political polarization and centralized power threaten to undermine the liberties secured by the American Revolution, the early interpretative efforts provide a critical standard against which contemporary practices

---

[20] Jefferson, T., & Madison, J. (Founders Online). "Letter from Thomas Jefferson to James Madison, July 29, 1787." National Archives.

[21] Dickinson, J. (1994). *Colonial Self-Government in America.* Cambridge: Harvard University Press.

[22] Ferguson, N. (2004). *Colony: A History of Early America.* New York: Penguin Press.

must be measured. Conservatives maintain that by honoring the legacy of ratification and the foundational debates of the past, America can resist the drift toward an expansive state and remain true to the principles that have long ensured its prosperity and freedom.[23]

Finally, the early debates and subsequent interpretations of the Constitution offer a clear and compelling mandate: that the preservation of American liberty depends on a continual commitment to the original principles of self-governance, limited government, and individual rights. This mandate, forged in the crucible of ratification, remains the guiding light for conservative thought and policy. By returning to the original meaning of the Constitution and rigorously adhering to the framers' intentions, modern America can safeguard its future and serve as a beacon of freedom in a rapidly changing world.[24]

Ultimately, the ratification process and early interpretations provide not only a historical foundation but also an ongoing challenge to ensure that the government never exceeds its legitimate authority. For conservatives, these processes encapsulate the spirit of the American founding—a spirit that continues to demand accountability, restraint, and respect for the rule of law. The enduring legacy of these debates is a powerful reminder that the solutions to modern governance challenges lie in the original constitutional order—a legacy that must be preserved and reinvigorated if America is to continue to serve as a sanctuary of liberty and a model for democratic self-governance.[25]

In light of this legacy, it is imperative that contemporary policymakers and citizens alike engage with the foundational debates of the ratification era. Only by fully understanding and embracing the original intentions of the framers can America hope to counter the modern threats of centralized power and bureaucratic expansion. The constitutional conventions and early interpretations offer a timeless blueprint for limiting governmental authority and ensuring that the rights of individuals remain sacrosanct. This is the conservative argument: that the principles born of ratification are not relics of a bygone era but are the essential tools for saving America today.[26]

---

[23] Locke, J. (1689). *Two Treatises of Government*. London: Awnsham Churchill.

[24] Rakove, J. (1997). *Original Meanings: Politics and Ideas in the Making of the Constitution*. New York: Vintage.

[25] Adams, S. (1961). *The Revolutionary Writings of Samuel Adams*. Boston: Beacon Press.

[26] Hamilton, A., Madison, J., & Jay, J. (1961). *The Federalist Papers*. New York: New American Library.

Chapter 3:

Constitutional Theory and Jurisprudence

1. Theoretical Underpinnings of Constitutionalism

The theoretical underpinnings of constitutionalism constitute the intellectual framework upon which the American constitutional order rests. Rooted in the classical traditions of political philosophy and refined through the revolutionary experiences of the late eighteenth century, these foundations continue to inform a conservative interpretation of government that emphasizes limited power, the protection of individual rights, and the preservation of self-governance. This paper explores the key theoretical principles that have shaped constitutional thought—from the natural rights philosophy of Enlightenment thinkers to the rigorous debate over the balance of governmental power that characterized the founding era—and argues that adherence to these timeless principles is essential for saving America today.

At its core, constitutionalism is predicated on the notion that government is not an end in itself but a means to secure the inherent rights of individuals. This idea finds its origins in the works of John Locke, who asserted that all humans are endowed with natural rights—life, liberty, and property—that no government should infringe. Locke's social contract theory posits that the legitimacy of governmental authority stems solely from the consent of the governed, and that if a government fails to protect these rights, the people retain the right to alter or abolish it.[1] For conservatives, this concept is the cornerstone of a limited government; it demands that state power be strictly circumscribed by constitutional constraints and that any expansion of governmental authority be viewed with profound skepticism.

The conservative tradition has long embraced an originalist reading of the Constitution, arguing that the text must be understood in the light of the framers' original intent. This approach, grounded in the intellectual heritage of the Enlightenment, holds that the framers deliberately designed a government with clearly enumerated powers and a system of checks and balances to prevent tyranny. Influential Federalist writings, such as those found in The Federalist Papers, articulate

---

[1] Hamilton, A., Madison, J., & Jay, J. (1961). *The Federalist Papers*. New York: New American Library.

a vision in which the separation of powers and federalism are not merely pragmatic solutions but also moral imperatives. For instance, Federalist No. 51 famously argues that "ambition must be made to counteract ambition" in order to prevent any one branch from dominating the political system.[2] Conservatives maintain that modern judicial activism and expansive statutory interpretation are deviations from this original understanding, threatening to erode the very limits that protect individual liberty.

Montesquieu's theory of the separation of powers further bolsters this conservative view of constitutionalism. In his seminal work, *The Spirit of the Laws*, Montesquieu argued that political liberty is best safeguarded when governmental power is divided among separate branches, each with the capacity to check the others.[3] This idea resonated deeply with the framers of the Constitution, who meticulously engineered a system where the legislative, executive, and judicial functions are compartmentalized. For modern conservatives, this separation is not a vestige of the past but a living safeguard against the encroachment of centralized authority. They argue that any erosion of these checks and balances directly undermines the fundamental promise of the Constitution to protect the people's rights.

Republican ideals, which emphasize civic virtue, the rule of law, and the active participation of citizens in governance, are equally critical to the theoretical foundation of American constitutionalism. The revolutionary experience taught that the legitimacy of government rests on the willingness of its citizens to hold their rulers accountable. Early American political thought was imbued with the belief that power is a trust granted by the people, and that government must be continually justified through its service to the common good. This notion is encapsulated in the famous phrase, "of the people, by the people, for the people," which underscores the conservative insistence on self-governance and local control.[4] Conservatives argue that modern bureaucratic expansion and a disconnect between the government and its citizens represent a betrayal of these republican ideals, and that a return to a more participatory form of governance is essential for sustaining freedom.

The framers' deliberate decision to incorporate an amendment process into the Constitution reflects a profound commitment to both stability and flexibility. They recognized that while the Constitution must be enduring, it must also be capable of evolving through careful, deliberate

---

[2] Locke, J. (1689). *Two Treatises of Government*. London: Awnsham Churchill.

[3] Montesquieu, C. (1748). *The Spirit of the Laws*. Paris: Barrillot & Fils.

[4] Pocock, J. G. A. (1975). *The Machiavellian Moment: Florentine Political Thought and the Atlantic Republican Tradition*. Princeton: Princeton University Press.

change rather than abrupt shifts dictated by transient political fashions. The difficulty of amending the Constitution is seen by conservatives as a virtue—it serves as a bulwark against radical changes that could undermine the core principles of limited government and individual liberty.[5] This approach ensures that constitutional change is incremental and reflective of a broad consensus, thereby safeguarding against the whims of populism or the imposition of unchecked governmental power.

Central to conservative constitutional theory is the belief in the rule of law—a principle that dictates that government authority must be exercised in accordance with clearly defined, publicly disclosed rules rather than at the discretion of individual officials. The framers embedded this principle within the Constitution by establishing an independent judiciary charged with interpreting the law, thereby ensuring that government actions remain subject to legal constraints. Conservatives contend that an independent judiciary, operating within the limits of original intent, is crucial for maintaining the balance of power. They argue that any departure from this principle, whether through judicial overreach or legislative encroachment, threatens to erode the constitutional order and compromise individual freedoms.[6]

The theoretical foundations of constitutionalism are not solely abstract ideas; they are intended to have practical application in governance. The conservative perspective holds that a return to the original, immutable principles of the Constitution is the only effective remedy for the excesses of modern government. This view is bolstered by historical evidence: the experiences of the American Revolution and the subsequent debates over ratification demonstrate that the framers' intentions were to create a system of government that derives its legitimacy from the protection of natural rights and the active consent of the governed. For modern conservatives, the proliferation of expansive federal regulations, administrative agencies, and judicial interpretations that stray from the original text are symptomatic of a departure from these core principles.[7]

Moreover, the interplay between constitutional theory and jurisprudence is evident in the conservative critique of what is often labeled as "judicial activism." Conservative jurists argue that when judges depart from a strict interpretation of the Constitution and instead inject their personal policy preferences into their rulings, they undermine the democratic foundations of the rule of law. This, conservatives claim, not only distorts the original meaning of the text but

---

[5] Rakove, J. (1997). *Original Meanings: Politics and Ideas in the Making of the Constitution*. New York: Vintage.

[6] Adams, S. (1961). *The Revolutionary Writings of Samuel Adams*. Boston: Beacon Press.

[7] Bork, R. (1990). *The Tempting of America: The Political Seduction of the Law*. New York: Free Press.

also disrupts the carefully balanced system of checks and balances intended by the framers. By insisting on originalism—a method of constitutional interpretation that anchors judicial decisions in the historical context and textual meaning of the document—conservatives believe that the judiciary can remain a true guardian of constitutional limits, rather than an instrument for modern policy experimentation.[8]

The theoretical underpinnings of constitutionalism also include a robust skepticism of unchecked governmental power. Drawing on the historical experiences of both the American colonies and the European monarchical systems from which they fled, conservatives maintain that concentrated authority is inherently prone to abuse. This skepticism is reflected in the numerous safeguards built into the Constitution, such as the separation of powers, federalism, and the amendment process. These mechanisms are seen as essential for preventing the rise of a tyrannical government that would trample on individual rights. The conservative argument is that any expansion of state power must be rigorously checked, and that the principles established by the founding fathers provide the only proven method for ensuring that power remains a servant of the people rather than its master.[9]

In addition, the conservative approach to constitutional theory emphasizes the importance of tradition and historical continuity. The framers of the Constitution were deeply influenced by classical republicanism and Enlightenment thought, and they sought to create a government that was rooted in centuries of political wisdom. For conservatives, this historical lineage is not a burden to be discarded but a valuable resource that provides guidance for contemporary governance. The original ideas and practices that informed the founding era are seen as time-tested and enduring, offering a counterpoint to modern theories that advocate for rapid or radical change. Maintaining a continuous link to the past, conservatives argue, is essential for preserving the integrity and legitimacy of the constitutional order.[10]

The debate between originalism and the "living Constitution" approach represents one of the central theoretical conflicts in modern constitutional jurisprudence. Proponents of a living Constitution argue that the document must be interpreted in a flexible manner that takes into account contemporary social, economic, and political conditions. However, conservatives contend that such an approach risks eroding the fixed limits on governmental power that the Constitution

---

[8] Jefferson, T. (Founders Online). "Notes on the State of Virginia." National Archives.

[9] Dickinson, J. (1994). *Colonial Self-Government in America*. Cambridge: Harvard University Press.

[10] Calhoun, J. C. (1983). "Separation of Powers and the Structure of the Constitution." In *Foundations of American Government* (pp. 29–32). New York: Harper & Row.

was designed to impose. They argue that the framers' original intentions provide an objective standard that is not subject to the vagaries of public opinion or political expediency. In their view, adhering to the original meaning of the text is the most reliable way to ensure that the government remains constrained and that individual rights are protected.[11]

Furthermore, conservative constitutional theory asserts that the moral foundations of the Constitution are derived from natural law—a set of universal principles that exist independently of human legislation. This perspective holds that certain rights and obligations are inherent in human nature and that the role of government is to codify and protect these rights. Natural law theory, with its emphasis on justice, fairness, and the inherent dignity of the individual, has been a cornerstone of conservative thought since the Enlightenment. Conservatives maintain that the Constitution's enduring strength lies in its capacity to reflect these universal truths, and that any departure from natural law in constitutional interpretation undermines the moral legitimacy of government.[12]

The influence of conservative thinkers such as Russell Kirk and Friedrich Hayek further reinforces these theoretical underpinnings. Kirk's work on the importance of tradition and the dangers of rapid social change underscores the conservative belief that enduring institutions, such as the Constitution, are necessary for maintaining social order and individual freedom. Hayek, meanwhile, argued that a spontaneous order based on established rules and traditions is preferable to an imposed order dictated by centralized authority. These thinkers have contributed to a conservative intellectual tradition that sees the Constitution as not only a legal document but also a cultural and moral touchstone that embodies the timeless principles of liberty and limited government.[13]

In practical terms, the theoretical underpinnings of constitutionalism have significant implications for public policy and legal decision-making. Conservatives argue that the only way to effectively safeguard American liberty is to adhere strictly to the original meaning of the Constitution. This entails a rigorous application of originalist principles in judicial interpretation, legislative processes that respect constitutional limits, and executive actions that remain subordinate to the law. By grounding modern governance in the enduring principles of natural rights, separation of powers, and federalism, conservatives contend that the constitutional order can resist the temptations of expansive government and bureaucratic overreach.[14]

---

[11] Jefferson, T. (Founders Online). "Notes on the State of Virginia." National Archives.

[12] Amar, A. R. (2005). *America's Constitution: A Biography*. New York: Random House.

[13] Henry, P. (1775). *Speech on Colonial Rights*. Richmond: Virginia Historical Society.

[14] Kirk, R. (1953). *The Conservative Mind*. New York: Free Press.

The theoretical framework of constitutionalism also stresses the importance of accountability and transparency in government. According to this view, the legitimacy of any political system rests on its ability to demonstrate that power is exercised for the benefit of the people, and not for the enrichment of a select few. The framers' insistence on checks and balances, periodic elections, and the right to amend the Constitution reflects a deep-seated belief in the necessity of holding government accountable. Conservatives argue that this framework has proven effective in maintaining a stable and just society, and that any erosion of these accountability mechanisms poses a direct threat to the preservation of individual freedoms.[15]

Another essential element of conservative constitutional theory is the emphasis on the primacy of individual liberty. The founding documents, inspired by the natural law theories of the Enlightenment, make it abundantly clear that the protection of individual rights is the central purpose of government. Conservatives hold that the Constitution must be interpreted in a way that maximizes the protection of these rights, rather than being used as a tool for achieving broader social or economic objectives. This insistence on the sanctity of individual liberty is seen as a bulwark against the gradual encroachment of state power into areas that should remain the domain of the individual.[16]

Moreover, the conservative perspective on constitutional theory insists that any reform or reinterpretation of the Constitution must be approached with caution. The historical record of the founding era demonstrates that radical changes in governmental structure often lead to unintended consequences and the erosion of hard-won freedoms. Conservatives argue that the amendment process, as originally envisioned, is a necessary constraint that ensures any modifications to the constitutional order are deliberate and reflective of a broad consensus. This measured approach to change is fundamental to the conservative commitment to preserving the stability and continuity of the constitutional system.[17]

The theoretical underpinnings of constitutionalism thus serve as the intellectual backbone for a conservative vision of governance. They provide a comprehensive framework for understanding the role of government as a protector of individual rights, a defender against tyranny, and a guarantor of a free society. In contrast to more fluid approaches that adapt constitutional meaning to contemporary circumstances, the conservative model insists on a steadfast commitment to the

---

[15] Levinson, S. (2006). *Our Undemocratic Constitution: Where the Constitution Goes Wrong (and How We the People Can Correct It)*. New Haven: Yale University Press.

[16] Hayek, F. A. (1960). *The Constitution of Liberty*. Chicago: University of Chicago Press.

[17] Aldrich, J. H. (1983). *Constitutional Theory*. Chicago: University of Chicago Press.

original principles that have guided the nation since its inception. Conservatives contend that these principles are not only historically valid but also practically essential for countering the excesses of modern governmental power.[18]

In sum, the theoretical underpinnings of constitutionalism are built on a foundation of natural rights, limited government, and the rule of law—principles that have been articulated by the founding fathers and refined through centuries of political thought. For conservatives, adhering to these enduring principles is imperative to ensure that government remains a servant of the people, rather than a master over them. The original intent of the framers, as captured in the Constitution, serves as the ultimate safeguard against the dangers of centralized authority and judicial overreach. It is only by rigorously applying these theoretical foundations that modern America can hope to save itself from the gradual erosion of its cherished freedoms.[19]

The conservative approach to constitutional theory is not a call for nostalgia; it is a reasoned argument that the original, immutable principles of the Constitution provide the only viable blueprint for effective, accountable governance. By grounding modern legal and political decisions in the timeless ideas of the Enlightenment and the practical wisdom of the founding era, conservatives assert that America can resist the pressures to expand governmental power and undermine individual liberty. This originalist perspective, deeply embedded in conservative thought, is thus the definitive answer to the challenges of modern governance.[20]

Furthermore, by emphasizing tradition, historical continuity, and the primacy of individual rights, the conservative theoretical framework offers a counterpoint to progressive reinterpretations that risk diluting the original safeguards of the Constitution. Conservatives argue that the fixed meanings embedded in the founding documents are not subject to the shifting tides of political opinion, but must instead provide a stable foundation for governance that endures across generations. This commitment to a fixed, original meaning is the cornerstone of the conservative vision for America—a vision in which the Constitution remains the ultimate check on governmental power and the guarantor of personal freedom.[21]

Finally, the theoretical underpinnings of constitutionalism, as championed by conservatives, demand that modern policymakers and jurists engage with the original texts and historical context

---

[18] Ackerman, B. (1991). *We the People: Foundations*. Cambridge, MA: Harvard University Press.

[19] Connelley, W. F. (2009). *Restoring the Constitutional Order*. Lexington: University Press of Kentucky.

[20] Jefferson, T., & Madison, J. (Founders Online). "Letter from Thomas Jefferson to James Madison, July 29, 1787." National Archives.

[21] Dickinson, J. (1994). *Colonial Self-Government in America*. Cambridge: Harvard University Press.

of the Constitution. The foundational debates of the late eighteenth century continue to offer invaluable insights into how government should be structured and limited. By heeding these lessons, America can ensure that its constitutional order remains robust in the face of modern challenges such as judicial activism, executive overreach, and the creeping expansion of federal bureaucracy.[22]

In conclusion, the theoretical underpinnings of constitutionalism provide a rigorous and enduring framework for understanding American governance. Rooted in natural law and the Enlightenment, and refined through the revolutionary experiences and deliberations of the founding era, these principles serve as the bedrock of a conservative vision that prizes limited government, individual liberty, and the rule of law. This perspective asserts that only by remaining true to the original intentions of the framers can America safeguard its future against the threats of centralized power and bureaucratic excess. The conservative commitment to originalism, accountability, and civic virtue remains the most compelling answer to saving America today.[23]

Moreover, this theoretical framework is not merely an academic construct but a practical guide for modern governance. It insists that every branch of government—from the legislature to the judiciary—must operate within the narrow confines established by the Constitution, thereby ensuring that power is never concentrated in a manner that could threaten individual freedom. The enduring wisdom of the founding fathers, as reflected in these theoretical underpinnings, calls for a renewed commitment to the principles that have sustained American liberty for over two centuries. Embracing this conservative framework is essential for ensuring that the Constitution remains a living document—a steadfast guardian of freedom and the ultimate remedy for the challenges of modern governance.[24]

Ultimately, the theoretical underpinnings of constitutionalism affirm that government's primary role is to protect the rights and liberties of its citizens. This foundational belief, coupled with the rigorous intellectual tradition of the Enlightenment and the practical lessons of the American Revolution, provides a powerful argument for originalism. Conservatives argue that by returning to these enduring principles, modern America can counteract the expansion of governmental power and preserve the constitutional order for future generations. The intellectual and historical

---

[22] Ferguson, N. (2004). *Colony: A History of Early America*. New York: Penguin Press.

[23] Locke, J. (1689). *Two Treatises of Government*. London: Awnsham Churchill.

[24] Rakove, J. (1997). *Original Meanings: Politics and Ideas in the Making of the Constitution*. New York: Vintage.

legacy of the founding era, therefore, remains the guiding light for those committed to saving America through adherence to the original constitutional framework.[25]

In light of these considerations, it is clear that the theoretical underpinnings of constitutionalism form the bedrock of conservative thought on governance. They serve not only as a historical record of the ideals that birthed American freedom but also as an ongoing mandate for maintaining a government that is truly accountable to the people. By upholding the principles of natural rights, limited government, and the rule of law, conservatives assert that the United States Constitution remains the definitive instrument for safeguarding liberty. This steadfast commitment to the original ideas of the founding era is the ultimate answer to the challenges facing modern America, ensuring that government continues to serve as a protector of freedom and a guarantor of individual rights.[26]

---

[25] Adams, S. (1961). *The Revolutionary Writings of Samuel Adams*. Boston: Beacon Press.

[26] Hamilton, A., Madison, J., & Jay, J. (1961). *The Federalist Papers*. New York: New American Library.

2. Comparative Constitutional Models

The comparative study of constitutional models is a vital exercise in understanding the distinctiveness and resilience of the United States Constitution. For conservatives, the American constitutional framework is not only the product of historical circumstance but also the embodiment of timeless principles—namely, limited government, the protection of individual rights, and the rule of law—that have proven superior to alternative models adopted elsewhere. This analysis examines various constitutional systems, drawing comparisons between the American model and those of other democracies, and argues that the conservative commitment to originalist interpretation and federalism offers the best safeguard against governmental overreach and bureaucratic expansion.

The United States Constitution is built upon a foundation of natural rights and the consent of the governed, principles that were derived from the Enlightenment and refined during the American Revolution. In contrast, many other constitutional models in Europe and elsewhere have evolved through a process of gradual reform and statutory evolution. For example, countries such as France and the United Kingdom have experienced significant constitutional transformations through both formal amendments and unwritten conventions, which some conservatives argue have led to a dilution of the explicit limits on governmental power. The American model, by insisting on a written, fixed document that can only be altered through a rigorous amendment process, preserves a clear and stable framework that is less susceptible to the vagaries of political change.[1]

In examining comparative models, it is instructive to consider the balance of power. The United States Constitution enshrines a strict separation of powers among the legislative, executive, and judicial branches, with a system of checks and balances designed to prevent any one branch from accumulating excessive authority. In contrast, many parliamentary systems, such as that of the United Kingdom, feature a fusion of powers where the executive is drawn from the legislature. Conservatives contend that such an arrangement tends to concentrate power and can lead to rapid, unchecked policy shifts driven by the whims of a parliamentary majority. The American design, with its deliberate separation and institutional constraints, provides a bulwark against the risks of authoritarianism and preserves individual liberty by ensuring that no single entity can dominate the decision-making process.[2]

---

[1] Hamilton, A., Madison, J., & Jay, J. (1961). *The Federalist Papers*. New York: New American Library.

[2] Locke, J. (1689). *Two Treatises of Government*. London: Awnsham Churchill.

Moreover, the federal structure of the United States stands as a cornerstone of its constitutional design. Federalism, which divides power between the national government and the states, is a feature that many comparative models lack. In unitary systems, where power is centralized, there is a tendency for governmental authority to expand into areas that might be better managed at a local level. Conservatives argue that the American federal system not only allows for more tailored and responsive governance but also acts as a check on centralization. By devolving significant authority to the states, the Constitution ensures that local traditions and values are preserved and that citizens remain closer to their government—a condition that fosters accountability and limits the potential for abuse of power.[3]

Another critical aspect of comparative constitutional models is the mechanism for constitutional change. The United States employs a deliberately rigid amendment process, requiring broad consensus and supermajorities in both Congress and the states. This rigidity is seen by conservatives as a safeguard against transient political passions and radical shifts that could undermine the stability of the constitutional order. By contrast, many countries have more flexible procedures for constitutional change, which can lead to rapid and sometimes destabilizing transformations. Conservatives maintain that the difficulty of amending the U.S. Constitution is a virtue, as it protects the fundamental principles that underpin the nation's political system.[4]

Judicial review is another area where the American model is often contrasted with others. In the United States, the power of judicial review allows courts to interpret the Constitution and ensure that legislation and executive actions conform to its limits. Conservative scholars argue that this practice, when conducted in accordance with originalist principles, is essential for preventing government overreach. In many other democracies, constitutional courts or supreme courts have taken on expansive roles in policy-making, often justifying their actions as necessary to protect rights. Conservatives assert that such activism can erode democratic accountability and distort the balance of power. The U.S. model, with its emphasis on judicial restraint, ensures that courts remain interpreters rather than makers of law, thereby preserving the integrity of the constitutional framework.[5]

The role of written versus unwritten constitutional frameworks also emerges as a key point of comparison. The United States Constitution is a single, codified document that explicitly

---

[3] Montesquieu, C. (1748). *The Spirit of the Laws*. Paris: Barrillot & Fils.

[4] Pocock, J. G. A. (1975). *The Machiavellian Moment: Florentine Political Thought and the Atlantic Republican Tradition*. Princeton: Princeton University Press.

[5] Rakove, J. (1997). *Original Meanings: Politics and Ideas in the Making of the Constitution*. New York: Vintage.

enumerates governmental powers and individual rights. This clarity is contrasted with countries like the United Kingdom, where the constitution is largely unwritten and based on statutes, conventions, and historical documents. Conservatives argue that a written constitution provides a clear, immutable standard that can be used to hold government accountable. The precision of the U.S. document limits ambiguity and prevents the kind of judicial or legislative reinterpretations that might lead to expansive federal authority.[6]

Comparative studies further reveal that the American constitutional model is uniquely designed to safeguard the principles of limited government and individual liberty. While many countries have successfully achieved democratic governance, conservatives contend that the specific architecture of the U.S. Constitution—its separation of powers, federalism, and rigid amendment process—offers the best protection against the encroachments of an ever-expanding state. For example, Germany's Basic Law, though highly effective in protecting individual rights, includes provisions for strong state intervention in social and economic matters that conservatives argue are inconsistent with the ideals of limited government. Similarly, the French Fifth Republic, with its powerful executive, is seen by conservatives as susceptible to the concentration of power that the American system expressly seeks to avoid.[7]

The conservative perspective is further strengthened by historical evidence from constitutional debates and early judicial decisions in the United States. The framers of the Constitution, deeply influenced by Enlightenment thought and republican ideals, intentionally designed a government that would be difficult to alter. The Federalist Papers, especially those discussing the necessity of checks and balances and the separation of powers, remain central to the conservative defense of originalism. Conservatives assert that this historical commitment to limiting government power is not only theoretically sound but also empirically validated by the endurance of the American constitutional order over more than two centuries.[8]

In contrast, models that allow for extensive constitutional flexibility are viewed by conservatives as inherently unstable. When a constitution is easily amended or interpreted in a fluid manner, there is a risk that the fundamental limits on government power may be eroded over time. This erosion can lead to a gradual expansion of state authority and a corresponding decline in the protection of individual freedoms. Conservatives point to historical instances in which constitutional flexibility has resulted in significant shifts in the balance of power, arguing that

---

[6] Adams, S. (1961). *The Revolutionary Writings of Samuel Adams*. Boston: Beacon Press.

[7] Bork, R. (1990). *The Tempting of America: The Political Seduction of the Law*. New York: Free Press.

[8] Jefferson, T. (Founders Online). "Notes on the State of Virginia." National Archives.

such changes are often driven by transient political forces rather than enduring principles of justice and liberty.[9]

Moreover, comparative constitutional models must be evaluated in terms of their ability to adapt to changing circumstances without sacrificing core principles. The U.S. Constitution, with its built-in amendment process, provides a model for incremental change that respects the original framework. Conservatives argue that this method of change is preferable to wholesale reinterpretations, which can lead to unintended consequences and undermine the predictability and stability that are essential for a free society. By ensuring that changes to the constitutional order are both deliberate and widely supported, the American system maintains a continuity of principle that is lacking in many more malleable constitutional frameworks.[10]

International comparisons also shed light on the influence of political culture in shaping constitutional outcomes. In many European countries, where social welfare and state intervention are more deeply embedded in the political system, constitutional models have evolved to accommodate extensive governmental responsibilities. Conservatives argue that such evolution, while successful in certain contexts, often comes at the expense of individual liberty and economic freedom. They maintain that the American model, by contrast, is uniquely suited to a society that prizes free enterprise and personal responsibility. The conservative view holds that the success of the U.S. constitutional system lies in its unwavering commitment to the principles of limited government and individual rights, which serve as a bulwark against the potential excesses of state power.[11]

Furthermore, the comparative analysis of constitutional models highlights the significance of constitutional rigidity versus flexibility. In countries with a rigid constitutional framework, such as the United States, the core principles remain intact over time, providing a stable environment for both governance and economic activity. Conversely, in jurisdictions where the constitution is subject to frequent reinterpretation or amendment, there is a higher risk of policy uncertainty and arbitrary shifts in government power. Conservatives argue that such instability can be detrimental to the protection of individual rights and the rule of law, and thus favor the American approach as the most reliable means of ensuring long-term constitutional stability.[12]

---

[9] Dickinson, J. (1994). *Colonial Self-Government in America*. Cambridge: Harvard University Press.

[10] Calhoun, J. C. (1983). "Separation of Powers and the Structure of the Constitution." In *Foundations of American Government* (pp. 29–32). New York: Harper & Row.

[11] Jefferson, T. (Founders Online). "Notes on the State of Virginia." National Archives.

[12] Amar, A. R. (2005). *America's Constitution: A Biography*. New York: Random House.

The conservative critique of comparative models often centers on the potential for judicial overreach. In many modern democracies, courts have assumed a proactive role in shaping public policy, sometimes at the expense of democratic accountability. Conservatives contend that this trend undermines the principle that elected representatives, rather than unelected judges, should make policy decisions. By adhering to a strict originalist interpretation, the U.S. system limits the judiciary's role to that of an interpreter of the law, rather than a de facto policymaker. This restraint is viewed as a critical safeguard for maintaining the separation of powers and ensuring that the government remains answerable to the people.[13]

In addition to institutional comparisons, the cultural context in which a constitution operates is also crucial. The American political culture, with its deep-seated commitment to individual liberty and limited government, reinforces the conservative view that the U.S. model is uniquely capable of preserving freedom. In contrast, constitutional models in countries where the political culture emphasizes collective welfare and state intervention may not prioritize the same level of individual autonomy. Conservatives argue that the success of the American constitutional system is inseparable from its cultural foundations, which promote a skepticism of centralized power and an enduring respect for the rights of the individual.[14]

Moreover, the comparative analysis reveals that the American system has been remarkably resilient in the face of external challenges and internal pressures. Despite periods of intense political polarization and crises, the U.S. Constitution has withstood numerous tests and continues to function as the supreme law of the land. Conservatives attribute this resilience to the rigorous institutional safeguards embedded in the constitutional design, such as the system of checks and balances, federalism, and the separation of powers. These features, they argue, are not merely historical accidents but deliberate choices that have ensured the longevity and stability of American governance.[15]

Another point of comparison involves the process of constitutional change. In many countries, constitutions are amended with relative ease, reflecting the fluidity of political power. However, conservatives contend that the difficulty of amending the U.S. Constitution is a deliberate safeguard against capricious policy shifts. This process, which requires broad consensus across diverse political constituencies, ensures that any changes to the constitutional order are thoroughly

---

[13] Henry, P. (1775). *Speech on Colonial Rights*. Richmond: Virginia Historical Society.

[14] Kirk, R. (1953). *The Conservative Mind*. New York: Free Press.

[15] Levinson, S. (2006). *Our Undemocratic Constitution: Where the Constitution Goes Wrong (and How We the People Can Correct It)*. New Haven: Yale University Press.

vetted and widely supported. Conservatives maintain that such a stringent amendment process is essential for protecting the core principles of limited government and individual rights from the whims of transient majorities.[16]

The role of federalism in comparative constitutional models further reinforces the conservative argument. The division of power between national and subnational governments in the United States provides a model for decentralization that is unmatched in many other democracies. In unitary systems, the concentration of power at the national level often leads to policies that are disconnected from local needs and priorities. Conservatives argue that American federalism not only promotes political participation at the local level but also acts as a check on national overreach. This decentralized approach to governance is seen as one of the key factors behind the enduring success of the American constitutional system.[17]

Additionally, the emphasis on a written, codified constitution is a defining feature of the U.S. model that sets it apart from many comparative constitutional frameworks. A single, authoritative document provides clarity and consistency, offering a concrete reference point for judicial interpretation and legislative action. Conservatives view this clarity as indispensable for maintaining a stable legal order, as it prevents the ambiguities and uncertainties that often arise in unwritten or loosely codified systems. The American Constitution's explicit enumeration of rights and governmental powers serves as a permanent bulwark against arbitrary rule and ensures that the fundamental principles of the founding era remain intact.[18]

The conservative perspective also stresses the importance of historical continuity in constitutional governance. Comparative constitutional models that undergo frequent changes or rely on evolving conventions risk losing the original meaning and purpose of their founding documents. Conservatives argue that the U.S. Constitution, through its rigid amendment process and commitment to originalism, preserves a historical continuity that is essential for the protection of individual liberties. This continuity, they assert, is a critical element in the nation's ability to resist the pressures of modern political and administrative expansion.[19]

Furthermore, the comparative analysis underscores the role of judicial restraint in preserving constitutional integrity. Conservative legal scholars argue that the U.S. model's insistence on limited judicial interpretation—anchored in the text and historical context of the Constitution—serves as

---

[16] Hayek, F. A. (1960). *The Constitution of Liberty*. Chicago: University of Chicago Press.

[17] Aldrich, J. H. (1983). *Constitutional Theory*. Chicago: University of Chicago Press.

[18] Ackerman, B. (1991). *We the People: Foundations*. Cambridge, MA: Harvard University Press.

[19] Connelley, W. F. (2009). *Restoring the Constitutional Order*. Lexington: University Press of Kentucky.

a safeguard against the expansion of governmental power. In many other democracies, judicial bodies have taken on a more expansive role, often shaping policy in ways that conservatives view as inconsistent with the framers' original intentions. By limiting the scope of judicial discretion, the American system ensures that the separation of powers remains effective and that the government is kept in check by the rule of law.[20]

The international dimension of constitutional comparison further reinforces the conservative case. Across the globe, countries that adhere to a rigid constitutional framework tend to experience greater political stability and respect for individual rights. Conservatives point to examples in which constitutional rigidity has served as a bulwark against authoritarianism, arguing that the U.S. model is uniquely suited to a society that values freedom and self-governance. They contend that the comparative success of written, originalist constitutions is evidence that the American system, with its explicit constraints on power, remains the ideal model for preserving liberty in the modern world.[21]

Moreover, the conservative view holds that a comparative examination reveals a fundamental truth: that flexibility in constitutional interpretation, while sometimes necessary, can lead to unintended consequences. The "living Constitution" approach, which some countries adopt to accommodate changing societal norms, often results in an erosion of the clear limits that protect individual freedoms. Conservatives argue that this adaptability comes at a high price—a price paid in the form of gradually expanding government authority and diminished accountability. In contrast, the American model, with its unwavering commitment to the original meaning of the text, offers a more reliable means of ensuring that government remains subordinate to the people.[22]

The practical implications of comparative constitutional models are also evident in economic performance and the protection of property rights. Conservatives maintain that the certainty and stability provided by the U.S. constitutional framework foster an environment conducive to free enterprise and individual initiative. In countries where constitutional ambiguity or frequent amendments have undermined legal predictability, economic performance has often suffered. The American emphasis on the rule of law and secure property rights is seen as integral to its success as a market economy and a bastion of individual freedom.[23]

---

[20] Jefferson, T., & Madison, J. (Founders Online). "Letter from Thomas Jefferson to James Madison, July 29, 1787." National Archives.

[21] Dickinson, J. (1994). *Colonial Self-Government in America*. Cambridge: Harvard University Press.

[22] Ferguson, N. (2004). *Colony: A History of Early America*. New York: Penguin Press.

[23] Locke, J. (1689). *Two Treatises of Government*. London: Awnsham Churchill.

In addition, the process of constitutional change itself is a matter of significant comparative interest. Conservatives argue that the arduous amendment process enshrined in the U.S. Constitution is not a hindrance but a safeguard that ensures any alterations are made only with widespread consensus. This process, they claim, prevents rash or ideologically driven modifications that could erode the foundational principles of limited government. By contrast, more flexible constitutional regimes risk undermining the stability and predictability that are essential for preserving individual rights and economic freedom.[24]

Finally, the conservative case for the superiority of the American constitutional model is reinforced by its historical resilience. Despite numerous challenges—from wars and economic crises to social upheavals—the U.S. Constitution has endured as the supreme law of the land, largely unchanged in its fundamental structure. This endurance is cited by conservatives as evidence that the original design, with its clear limitations on government and robust protections for individual liberty, is uniquely suited to adapt to changing circumstances without sacrificing its core principles.[25]

In conclusion, the comparative analysis of constitutional models demonstrates that the American system—characterized by its written constitution, rigorous separation of powers, federal structure, and fixed amendment process—offers a superior framework for protecting individual liberty and limiting governmental power. Conservatives argue that the U.S. Constitution, as originally intended by the founding fathers, remains the ultimate safeguard against the encroachments of centralized authority and bureaucratic overreach. By comparing it with more flexible or centralized systems, it becomes clear that the conservative commitment to originalism and federalism is not only historically justified but also practically essential for ensuring a free and prosperous society. The lessons drawn from international and domestic comparisons provide a compelling rationale for why America must remain steadfast in its adherence to the original constitutional framework if it is to continue serving as a beacon of liberty in a complex and ever-changing world.[26]

---

[24] Rakove, J. (1997). *Original Meanings: Politics and Ideas in the Making of the Constitution*. New York: Vintage.

[25] Adams, S. (1961). *The Revolutionary Writings of Samuel Adams*. Boston: Beacon Press.

[26] Hamilton, A., Madison, J., & Jay, J. (1961). *The Federalist Papers*. New York: New American Library.

3. Interpretive Methods: Originalism, Living Constitution, and Beyond

The interpretation of the United States Constitution remains one of the most hotly debated issues in American legal and political discourse. For conservatives, the debate is not merely academic; it is a matter of national survival. At its core, the discussion pits originalism—an approach that insists on understanding the Constitution according to the framers' original intent—against the "living Constitution" doctrine, which advocates for adapting constitutional meaning to evolving social, economic, and political contexts. This paper provides a comprehensive analysis of these interpretive methods, exploring their theoretical foundations, practical implications, and relevance in contemporary jurisprudence, all from a politically conservative perspective that honors the wisdom of the founding fathers.

Originalism is based on the principle that the Constitution should be interpreted according to its original public meaning at the time it was ratified. This approach is rooted in Enlightenment thought and the revolutionary spirit that shaped the nation's founding. Proponents of originalism argue that the framers deliberately crafted a document with explicit limits on governmental power, designed to protect individual liberty and prevent tyranny. They contend that only by adhering to the text's original meaning can judges and policymakers ensure that government remains subordinate to the people. For conservatives, this method of interpretation not only preserves the historical context of the Constitution but also serves as a bulwark against the expansive judicial activism that has characterized modern jurisprudence.[1]

Central to the originalist approach is the belief that the framers, well-versed in Enlightenment philosophy and classical republicanism, embedded clear principles into the constitutional text. Figures such as James Madison and Alexander Hamilton articulated a vision of government constrained by enumerated powers and safeguarded by a system of checks and balances. The Federalist Papers, for instance, offer a detailed exposition of the necessity of limiting governmental power through structural mechanisms. Conservative scholars argue that any departure from these carefully considered limitations risks diluting the very freedoms that the Constitution was designed to protect.[2]

Originalism, however, is not without its critics. Advocates of the living Constitution approach contend that the framers could not have anticipated the profound social and technological changes that have occurred since the eighteenth century. They argue that the Constitution is a "living

---

[1] Hamilton, A., Madison, J., & Jay, J. (1961). *The Federalist Papers*. New York: New American Library.

[2] Locke, J. (1689). *Two Treatises of Government*. London: Awnsham Churchill.

document" that must evolve to meet the needs of contemporary society. Yet conservatives counter that while societal conditions may change, the foundational principles of limited government and individual rights are immutable. They maintain that the framers' intent, as documented in the historical record, provides a stable, objective standard that should not be subordinated to transient political or cultural pressures.[3]

The living Constitution model, in contrast, relies on a dynamic interpretation that permits judges to update constitutional meaning in light of modern circumstances. Proponents argue that this flexibility is essential for a document that governs a society vastly different from that of the 18th century. However, conservatives view this approach as inherently unstable and dangerous. They assert that allowing judges broad discretion to adapt constitutional norms risks transforming the judiciary from an impartial arbiter into a powerful policy-making body, one that may impose contemporary values on a timeless text. This shift, they warn, could lead to a gradual expansion of governmental power that undermines the very freedoms the Constitution is meant to secure.[4]

Moreover, conservative jurists argue that the living Constitution approach diminishes democratic accountability. When constitutional interpretation becomes a matter of personal judicial discretion, it distances the law from the democratic process. Instead of being a tool for the people, the Constitution may become a weapon of judicial activism, capable of reshaping society without the consent of the governed. Conservatives contend that any change in constitutional meaning should occur through the formal amendment process, which requires broad consensus and deliberative debate—a process that reflects the framers' original intent to make constitutional change difficult and measured.[5]

The debate between originalism and the living Constitution is also deeply intertwined with broader questions about the role of the judiciary in a constitutional democracy. Conservatives assert that judges should act as interpreters of the law rather than as policy makers. Originalism, they argue, imposes strict limits on judicial power by confining decisions to the text and historical context of the Constitution. This approach contrasts sharply with judicial activism, where courts may effectively create new rights or expand governmental power based on evolving societal

---

[3] Montesquieu, C. (1748). *The Spirit of the Laws*. Paris: Barrillot & Fils.

[4] Pocock, J. G. A. (1975). *The Machiavellian Moment: Florentine Political Thought and the Atlantic Republican Tradition*. Princeton: Princeton University Press.

[5] Rakove, J. (1997). *Original Meanings: Politics and Ideas in the Making of the Constitution*. New York: Vintage.

values. For conservatives, maintaining judicial restraint is essential to preserving the separation of powers that the Constitution meticulously establishes.[6]

The theoretical underpinnings of originalism are bolstered by a rich body of historical evidence. The debates and writings from the Constitutional Convention reveal that the framers intended the Constitution to be a fixed document, one that could only be altered through a rigorous and deliberate process. Historical documents such as the Federalist Papers and the debates recorded by James Madison provide compelling testimony that the founding generation sought to limit the scope of governmental power precisely to avoid the tyranny they had experienced under British rule. Conservatives view these records as an authoritative source for determining the original meaning of the text, arguing that they offer a clear roadmap for constitutional interpretation that remains relevant today.[7]

Furthermore, originalism is rooted in the philosophical tradition of natural law, which posits that certain rights and principles are inherent in human nature and should be enshrined in law. Influential Enlightenment thinkers like John Locke argued that governments exist primarily to protect natural rights—an idea that was central to the American Revolution and the subsequent framing of the Constitution. For conservatives, the concept of natural law provides a timeless benchmark against which any deviation from the Constitution's original meaning can be measured. They argue that the living Constitution approach, by contrast, opens the door to subjective interpretations that may erode these fundamental rights.[8]

Critics of originalism often point to evolving societal needs as justification for a more flexible approach. However, conservatives counter that while societal conditions indeed change, the underlying principles of liberty and limited government must remain constant. They caution that a malleable constitution risks undermining the stability and predictability that are essential for the rule of law. From a conservative viewpoint, the amendment process, although deliberately arduous, provides a more democratic and measured method for constitutional change than judicial reinterpretation. This insistence on a slow, consensus-driven process for amendment is seen as a crucial safeguard against the unrestrained exercise of power.[9]

In practice, the conservative commitment to originalism has significant implications for both legislative and judicial policymaking. Originalist judges tend to resist expansive readings of

---

[6] Adams, S. (1961). *The Revolutionary Writings of Samuel Adams*. Boston: Beacon Press.

[7] Bork, R. (1990). *The Tempting of America: The Political Seduction of the Law*. New York: Free Press.

[8] Jefferson, T. (Founders Online). "Notes on the State of Virginia." National Archives.

[9] Dickinson, J. (1994). *Colonial Self-Government in America*. Cambridge: Harvard University Press.

the Constitution that could lead to increased governmental intervention in the economy or infringement on individual rights. This judicial restraint is viewed as essential for maintaining the constitutional order and ensuring that policy decisions remain within the bounds set by the founding documents. For example, conservative jurists have frequently criticized decisions that, in their view, reinterpret the Commerce Clause or other constitutional provisions in ways that expand federal power beyond its intended limits. They argue that such decisions are inconsistent with the framers' original vision and pose a threat to the core values of American freedom.[10]

Comparative studies also reinforce the conservative preference for originalism. When examining constitutional models around the world, conservatives note that countries with rigid, codified constitutions tend to enjoy greater stability and protection for individual rights. In contrast, systems that rely on evolving interpretations or unwritten conventions often experience more frequent shifts in the balance of power, which can lead to instability and the erosion of civil liberties. Conservatives assert that the American constitutional model, with its fixed text and rigorous amendment process, provides the best safeguard against these risks and is a model that should be emulated rather than abandoned.[11]

The living Constitution approach, while popular among some legal scholars and progressive jurists, is seen by conservatives as a slippery slope toward judicial supremacy. They contend that when judges are permitted to interpret the Constitution in light of contemporary values, they inevitably impose their own policy preferences on society. This, in turn, undermines the democratic principle that changes to the constitutional order should reflect the will of the people as expressed through a formal amendment process. Conservatives argue that the framers' decision to make the Constitution a written, fixed document was a deliberate effort to constrain such subjective reinterpretations, and that modern attempts to deviate from this model risk unraveling the very fabric of American liberty.[12]

Furthermore, originalism is closely linked to the conservative belief in limited government. By insisting on a strict adherence to the text and the original meaning of the Constitution, conservatives aim to ensure that government power remains confined to its enumerated limits. They argue that any expansion of governmental authority beyond these limits is a violation of the fundamental principles of the Constitution and a threat to individual freedom. This perspective is

---

[10] Calhoun, J. C. (1983). "Separation of Powers and the Structure of the Constitution." In *Foundations of American Government* (pp. 29–32). New York: Harper & Row.

[11] Jefferson, T. (Founders Online). "Notes on the State of Virginia." National Archives.

[12] Amar, A. R. (2005). *America's Constitution: A Biography*. New York: Random House.

grounded in the historical experience of colonial subjugation under British rule, where unchecked governmental power had led to widespread abuses. The originalist method, therefore, is seen as a necessary corrective to prevent the emergence of a centralized, overreaching state.[13]

The practical outcomes of adopting an originalist approach are evident in several landmark judicial decisions. Conservative jurists have pointed to cases in which adherence to the original public meaning of the Constitution has served to protect property rights, individual liberties, and the separation of powers. These cases illustrate that a faithful reading of the Constitution can provide a stable legal framework that curtails the potential for governmental overreach. In this way, originalism is not only a theoretical preference but also a pragmatic strategy for safeguarding American constitutionalism in a complex and evolving society.[14]

Another significant aspect of the debate is the role of the judiciary in constitutional interpretation. Conservatives maintain that judges must refrain from engaging in what they see as policy-making and instead focus on applying the Constitution as written. This judicial restraint is essential for preserving the democratic process, as it ensures that fundamental changes to the constitutional order occur only through the amendment process and not through judicial fiat. By contrast, a living Constitution approach can give judges excessive power to shape public policy, thereby undermining the separation of powers and the accountability of the government to the electorate.[15]

Moreover, the conservative critique of the living Constitution method extends to concerns about legal uncertainty. When constitutional meaning is allowed to evolve in response to shifting societal norms, it can lead to unpredictable and inconsistent rulings. Conservatives argue that such uncertainty is detrimental to the rule of law, as it erodes public confidence in a stable legal system. In contrast, an originalist interpretation provides a clear and predictable framework that serves as a reliable basis for governance and economic decision-making.[16]

In addition to its legal and practical merits, originalism is supported by a robust philosophical tradition. Conservative thinkers such as Robert Bork and Akhil Reed Amar have championed the originalist approach as the best means of preserving the intentions of the framers and maintaining the integrity of the constitutional order. They argue that the historical context of the Constitution's drafting provides an objective benchmark that should guide judicial interpretation.

---

[13] Henry, P. (1775). *Speech on Colonial Rights*. Richmond: Virginia Historical Society.

[14] Kirk, R. (1953). *The Conservative Mind*. New York: Free Press.

[15] Levinson, S. (2006). *Our Undemocratic Constitution: Where the Constitution Goes Wrong (and How We the People Can Correct It)*. New Haven: Yale University Press.

[16] Hayek, F. A. (1960). *The Constitution of Liberty*. Chicago: University of Chicago Press.

This philosophical stance is deeply intertwined with the conservative commitment to the ideas of natural law and individual liberty—principles that are viewed as immutable and universal.[17]

Furthermore, the conservative argument for originalism is reinforced by a commitment to the democratic ideal that governmental power must be limited by the rule of law. Conservatives assert that a government that can reinterpret its own fundamental law on a whim undermines the very concept of constitutional restraint. Instead, they advocate for a constitutional framework that is resilient to transient political pressures and is capable of withstanding the challenges of modern governance without sacrificing its core principles.[18]

Comparative constitutional studies lend additional support to the conservative case. When the American constitutional model is compared to those of other democracies that allow for more flexible interpretations, the benefits of a fixed, originalist approach become evident. Countries that have adopted more fluid constitutional interpretations often experience greater political instability and a tendency toward centralization of power. Conservatives argue that the American commitment to a written, unchanging constitution is a significant factor in its long-term stability and prosperity.[19]

The debate over interpretive methods is not solely academic—it has real-world implications for public policy and the protection of individual rights. Conservatives contend that adopting an originalist approach in judicial review ensures that laws and executive actions remain consistent with the framers' vision of limited government. This, in turn, protects citizens from arbitrary government interference in their lives and maintains the delicate balance of power that is essential for a free society.[20]

Moreover, the conservative perspective on constitutional interpretation is deeply connected to the principle of federalism. By adhering to the original meaning of the Constitution, conservative jurists and policymakers aim to preserve the division of power between the national government and the states. This decentralization is seen as a critical safeguard for local self-governance and a necessary check on federal authority. In this light, originalism is not merely about textual fidelity but also about maintaining a system of government that is responsive to the people at the grassroots level.[21]

---

[17] Aldrich, J. H. (1983). *Constitutional Theory*. Chicago: University of Chicago Press.

[18] Ackerman, B. (1991). *We the People: Foundations*. Cambridge, MA: Harvard University Press.

[19] Connelley, W. F. (2009). *Restoring the Constitutional Order*. Lexington: University Press of Kentucky.

[20] Jefferson, T., & Madison, J. (Founders Online). "Letter from Thomas Jefferson to James Madison, July 29, 1787." National Archives.

[21] Dickinson, J. (1994). *Colonial Self-Government in America*. Cambridge: Harvard University Press.

Finally, the interpretive debate culminates in a broader ideological struggle over the future of American democracy. Conservatives argue that a rigid adherence to the original text is the only way to ensure that the Constitution remains a living safeguard of liberty, rather than a tool for expansive, unaccountable government. They assert that by returning to the principles laid out by the founding fathers, modern America can resist the trends of judicial activism and legislative overreach that threaten to erode the hard-won freedoms of the past. This ideological commitment to originalism, grounded in historical experience and philosophical rigor, is presented as the definitive solution to the challenges of contemporary governance.[22]

In conclusion, the interpretive methods employed in constitutional jurisprudence are not merely technical exercises; they are fundamental to the preservation of American liberty. The conservative commitment to originalism, with its emphasis on historical context, natural law, and a fixed constitutional text, provides a clear and robust framework for limiting governmental power and safeguarding individual rights. While the living Constitution approach offers flexibility, conservatives argue that it does so at the expense of stability, predictability, and democratic accountability. By steadfastly adhering to the framers' original intent, modern America can ensure that its constitutional order remains a bulwark against tyranny and a guarantor of freedom for future generations.[23]

Furthermore, the comparative analysis of constitutional models reinforces the conservative view that the American system—characterized by its written, unyielding text, federal structure, and rigorous amendment process—is uniquely suited to preserve the ideals of limited government and individual liberty. The success of the United States in maintaining a stable and prosperous society over more than two centuries is, in large part, attributable to its originalist interpretive framework. This historical legacy, when fully embraced, offers the best hope for saving America from the perils of centralized power and bureaucratic expansion.[24]

Ultimately, the debate over interpretive methods is a contest between preserving timeless principles and adapting to changing circumstances. Conservatives maintain that while societal progress is important, it must not come at the cost of undermining the fundamental constraints on government that have long protected individual freedom. The originalist method, grounded in the clear, historical understanding of the Constitution, is presented as the most effective means

---

[22] Ferguson, N. (2004). *Colony: A History of Early America*. New York: Penguin Press.

[23] Locke, J. (1689). *Two Treatises of Government*. London: Awnsham Churchill.

[24] Rakove, J. (1997). *Original Meanings: Politics and Ideas in the Making of the Constitution*. New York: Vintage.

of ensuring that government remains a servant of the people. This commitment to constitutional fidelity is not merely a legal doctrine but a moral imperative that honors the legacy of the founding fathers and secures the future of American liberty.[25]

In light of the enduring challenges posed by modern governmental overreach and judicial activism, it is imperative that policymakers, jurists, and citizens alike embrace an interpretive approach that is both rigorous and rooted in history. By adhering to the original meaning of the Constitution and rejecting attempts to reinterpret its text in ways that expand government power, America can continue to serve as a beacon of freedom and a model for democratic governance. The conservative argument for originalism, therefore, is not only a theoretical position but also a practical strategy for saving America today and ensuring that the principles of liberty and limited government remain unassailable.[26]

---

[25] Adams, S. (1961). *The Revolutionary Writings of Samuel Adams*. Boston: Beacon Press.

[26] Hamilton, A., Madison, J., & Jay, J. (1961). *The Federalist Papers*. New York: New American Library.

4. Judicial Review and the Role of the Supreme Court

Judicial review and the role of the Supreme Court have long been at the center of American constitutional debate. From a conservative perspective, the Supreme Court is not a policy-making body but rather the guardian of the constitutional order, tasked with ensuring that the government does not exceed the limits set forth by the founding fathers. This paper offers a comprehensive analysis of judicial review and the role of the Supreme Court, examining their theoretical foundations, historical evolution, and practical impact on American governance. Emphasizing originalism and the framers' intent, this discussion contends that a disciplined, originalist approach to judicial review is essential for preserving individual liberty, maintaining the separation of powers, and preventing the expansion of governmental authority.

At the heart of the doctrine of judicial review is the principle that the Constitution is the supreme law of the land. Established in the landmark case Marbury v. Madison (1803), judicial review empowers the Supreme Court to invalidate legislative or executive actions that conflict with the Constitution. Conservatives argue that this power, when exercised in accordance with the original meaning of the text, serves as an indispensable check on the other branches of government. It ensures that any exercise of power remains confined within the strict limits envisioned by the framers and prevents the kind of judicial activism that could lead to an erosion of constitutional restraints.[1]

From the conservative standpoint, the framers of the Constitution were well aware of the dangers of unchecked governmental power. Their experiences under British rule instilled in them a profound skepticism toward concentrated authority. Consequently, they designed a system in which power is divided among the legislative, executive, and judicial branches, with each branch serving as a check on the others. Judicial review is a critical element of this system—it acts as a safeguard against legislative overreach and executive excess. By insisting that government actions must conform to the Constitution, the Supreme Court upholds the rule of law and protects individual rights, which are cornerstones of conservative thought.[2]

The conservative approach to judicial review is grounded in originalism—the interpretative method that seeks to understand the Constitution based on its original public meaning. Originalists argue that the Constitution should be read in light of what its authors intended at the time of its ratification, rather than as a living document that evolves with societal changes. This method

[1] Hamilton, A., Madison, J., & Jay, J. (1961). *The Federalist Papers*. New York: New American Library.

[2] Locke, J. (1689). *Two Treatises of Government*. London: Awnsham Churchill.

restricts the judiciary from infusing modern values into the interpretation of constitutional provisions, thereby preserving the framers' intended balance of power. Conservatives contend that such restraint is essential because it prevents the courts from becoming a de facto policy-making body, which would undermine democratic accountability and the separation of powers.[3]

Historical records from the Constitutional Convention and early Federalist writings reinforce the conservative view. The framers' debates reveal that they purposefully embedded the concept of judicial review within the constitutional framework as a means of curbing legislative and executive encroachments. In Federalist No. 78, Alexander Hamilton described the judiciary as "the least dangerous branch" because it has "neither the power of the purse nor the power of the sword." This characterization underscores the idea that the judiciary was meant to serve as a neutral arbiter that interprets the law based on its original meaning, not as an institution that creates policy from personal or contemporary preferences.[4]

Conservatives also stress that the Supreme Court's role is inherently limited by the principle of separation of powers. The framers envisioned a system where each branch would operate within its defined sphere of influence, with judicial review serving as a counterbalance to potential abuses by the other branches. When courts begin to interpret the Constitution in ways that effectively expand governmental power beyond what was originally intended, they disrupt this delicate balance. For conservatives, such judicial overreach is not only a departure from the constitutional order but also a threat to the very freedoms the document was designed to protect.[5]

The evolution of judicial review over time provides a rich field for conservative critique. In recent decades, many critics have argued that the Supreme Court has increasingly engaged in what is known as "judicial activism." This term refers to decisions where judges are perceived to have substituted their policy preferences for a neutral interpretation of the law. Conservatives claim that such activism undermines the stability and predictability of the constitutional framework. Instead of adhering strictly to the text and historical context of the Constitution, activist judges have, in their view, expanded federal power in ways that were not contemplated by the founding fathers. This expansion, they argue, has led to a gradual erosion of individual liberties and a distortion of the balance between the branches of government.[6]

---

[3] Montesquieu, C. (1748). *The Spirit of the Laws*. Paris: Barrillot & Fils.

[4] Pocock, J. G. A. (1975). *The Machiavellian Moment: Florentine Political Thought and the Atlantic Republican Tradition*. Princeton: Princeton University Press.

[5] Rakove, J. (1997). *Original Meanings: Politics and Ideas in the Making of the Constitution*. New York: Vintage.

[6] Adams, S. (1961). *The Revolutionary Writings of Samuel Adams*. Boston: Beacon Press.

A key example often cited by conservatives is the reinterpretation of the Commerce Clause. Originally, the Commerce Clause was understood to grant Congress limited regulatory power over interstate commerce. However, over time, the Supreme Court's interpretations have, according to conservative critics, vastly expanded this power, thereby justifying broad federal regulation in areas that were once the purview of the states. Conservatives maintain that such expansions are inconsistent with the framers' intent and illustrate the dangers of a flexible, "living Constitution" approach that permits judicial reinterpretation to adapt to modern circumstances without sufficient regard to historical precedent.[7]

In contrast, proponents of originalism argue that strict adherence to the Constitution's original meaning would rein in the tendency for judicial overreach. They point to early Supreme Court decisions that exemplify a restrained approach, such as those that emphasized the limited scope of federal power and the primacy of states' rights. By reverting to the original public meaning of the text, the Court would not only restore balance among the branches but also reinforce the constitutional guarantee of individual rights, which conservatives see as under constant threat from the expansion of centralized authority.[8]

The role of judicial review is further clarified by examining its practical impact on American governance. When the Supreme Court exercises judicial review in a manner consistent with originalism, it acts as a bulwark against the gradual accumulation of power by the legislative and executive branches. This restraint is crucial in an era marked by increasing governmental intervention in the economy and society. Conservatives argue that unchecked expansion of state power is antithetical to the principles of free enterprise, individual liberty, and self-governance that have historically defined American society. Judicial review, therefore, is not only a theoretical safeguard but also a practical necessity for ensuring that government remains a servant of the people rather than a master over them.[9]

Furthermore, the conservative perspective on judicial review is deeply intertwined with the concept of federalism. The U.S. Constitution was designed to allocate significant powers to the states, thereby preventing the concentration of authority in a centralized national government. When the Supreme Court interprets the Constitution in a manner that respects this division, it reinforces the federal structure that has long been a bulwark against tyranny. Conservatives contend that a robust system of federalism is essential for preserving local autonomy and ensuring

---

[7] Bork, R. (1990). *The Tempting of America: The Political Seduction of the Law*. New York: Free Press.

[8] Jefferson, T. (Founders Online). "Notes on the State of Virginia." National Archives.

[9] Dickinson, J. (1994). *Colonial Self-Government in America*. Cambridge: Harvard University Press.

that policy decisions are made as close as possible to the people they affect. This devolution of power not only fosters accountability but also promotes innovation in governance at the state and local levels.[10]

The role of the Supreme Court in preserving constitutional boundaries has also been a subject of vigorous scholarly debate. Conservative legal scholars often cite the importance of judicial restraint, arguing that judges should refrain from substituting their views for those of elected representatives. They maintain that the Constitution, as originally written, provides clear guidelines for the exercise of governmental power and that any deviation from these guidelines undermines the legitimacy of the legal system. This view is supported by historical analysis showing that the framers intended for the judiciary to serve as a check on both the legislative and executive branches rather than as an independent source of policy innovation.[11]

In addition to its interpretive functions, the Supreme Court plays a critical role in legitimizing the constitutional order. When the Court issues decisions that adhere to the original meaning of the Constitution, it reinforces public confidence in the rule of law. Conservatives argue that this legitimacy is essential for maintaining social stability and ensuring that government actions are perceived as fair and predictable. Conversely, when judicial review is perceived as overreaching or politicized, it can undermine the public's trust in the legal system and, by extension, in democratic governance itself.[12]

Comparative studies of constitutional courts around the world further support the conservative view. Many democracies with codified constitutions have experienced periods of judicial activism that have led to significant shifts in the balance of power. In contrast, systems that adhere more closely to the original meaning of their foundational documents tend to exhibit greater stability and continuity in governance. Conservatives argue that the American commitment to originalism is a key factor in the longevity and effectiveness of its constitutional order, and they advocate for a similar approach to judicial review as a means of preserving individual freedom and limiting government intervention.[13]

The debate over interpretive methods also has profound implications for the broader separation of powers. The conservative position holds that the judiciary must remain an impartial arbiter that

---

[10] Calhoun, J. C. (1983). "Separation of Powers and the Structure of the Constitution." In *Foundations of American Government* (pp. 29–32). New York: Harper & Row.

[11] Jefferson, T. (Founders Online). "Notes on the State of Virginia." National Archives.

[12] Amar, A. R. (2005). *America's Constitution: A Biography*. New York: Random House.

[13] Henry, P. (1775). *Speech on Colonial Rights*. Richmond: Virginia Historical Society.

does not encroach on the functions of the legislative or executive branches. By strictly adhering to originalist principles, the Supreme Court can resist pressures to expand its role beyond what was intended by the framers. This disciplined approach is essential for maintaining the integrity of the constitutional system, as it ensures that no branch of government is able to assert undue dominance over the others.[14]

Moreover, the conservative critique of judicial activism is not merely an abstract legal argument but has tangible policy implications. Decisions that expand federal power or reinterpret constitutional provisions in a broad manner can lead to legislation that infringes on individual liberties. For example, conservative critics have pointed to Supreme Court decisions in areas such as abortion, gun rights, and economic regulation as instances where judicial overreach has effectively rewritten constitutional limits. They argue that these decisions, by departing from the original understanding of the Constitution, pave the way for further encroachments on freedom and undermine the foundational promise of limited government.[15]

In response to these concerns, conservative scholars advocate for a return to a more restrained and historically grounded model of judicial review. They call for judges to base their decisions solely on the text and historical context of the Constitution, rather than on modern policy considerations or evolving social norms. This originalist approach, they assert, would not only restore the intended balance among the branches of government but also reinforce the constitutional protections that have long been the safeguard of American liberty.[16]

The role of the Supreme Court in upholding the Constitution is further illuminated by its interactions with the other branches of government. When the Court intervenes to invalidate legislation that exceeds constitutional limits, it reinforces the principle that all governmental action is subject to the rule of law. Conservatives argue that this function of judicial review is vital for preventing legislative or executive overreach, which can otherwise lead to a gradual erosion of the freedoms that the Constitution guarantees. In this regard, the Supreme Court acts as the final bulwark against the concentration of power, ensuring that every branch remains within its constitutionally defined sphere of influence.[17]

---

[14] Kirk, R. (1953). *The Conservative Mind*. New York: Free Press.

[15] Levinson, S. (2006). *Our Undemocratic Constitution: Where the Constitution Goes Wrong (and How We the People Can Correct It)*. New Haven: Yale University Press.

[16] Hayek, F. A. (1960). *The Constitution of Liberty*. Chicago: University of Chicago Press.

[17] Aldrich, J. H. (1983). *Constitutional Theory*. Chicago: University of Chicago Press.

Furthermore, the originalist method of judicial interpretation has significant implications for the protection of property rights—a cornerstone of conservative ideology. Property rights, derived from natural law as articulated by Enlightenment thinkers, are fundamental to economic freedom and individual autonomy. Conservative jurists maintain that a strict reading of the Constitution, consistent with the framers' original intent, is essential for safeguarding these rights against expansive regulatory schemes. They argue that any deviation from this approach can lead to policies that infringe on the sanctity of private property and, by extension, on the very basis of a free-market economy.[18]

The conservative case for a disciplined approach to judicial review is also supported by the historical record of the Supreme Court's decisions. In its early years, the Court exhibited a measured approach to constitutional interpretation that respected the balance of powers envisioned by the framers. Over time, however, critics contend that certain decisions have signaled a departure from this original model. Conservative legal scholars argue that by returning to the principles laid out in foundational documents such as The Federalist Papers and the writings of the founding fathers, the Court can reassert its role as a guardian of constitutional order rather than as an active policymaker.[19]

In addition, the conservative approach emphasizes that the legitimacy of judicial review depends on public confidence in the courts. When the Supreme Court is seen as overstepping its bounds or as being overly influenced by contemporary political pressures, it risks undermining the democratic principle that government power must be subject to clear and predictable legal limits. Conservatives maintain that a commitment to originalism not only protects individual rights but also bolsters the integrity and impartiality of the judiciary, thereby enhancing its legitimacy in the eyes of the public.[20]

The international context further reinforces the conservative perspective on judicial review. In many democracies with rigid, codified constitutions, the courts play a limited role in shaping public policy, serving instead as interpreters of a fixed legal framework. These systems often exhibit higher degrees of political stability and legal certainty compared to jurisdictions where courts have adopted a more expansive, adaptive role. Conservatives argue that the American model, with its commitment to a written, unchanging constitutional text and a disciplined

---

[18] Ackerman, B. (1991). *We the People: Foundations*. Cambridge, MA: Harvard University Press.

[19] Connelley, W. F. (2009). *Restoring the Constitutional Order*. Lexington: University Press of Kentucky.

[20] Jefferson, T., & Madison, J. (Founders Online). "Letter from Thomas Jefferson to James Madison, July 29, 1787." National Archives.

approach to judicial interpretation, offers the best protection for the freedoms enshrined in the Constitution.[21]

Moreover, the conservative commitment to judicial restraint is underpinned by a broader philosophical belief in the primacy of the rule of law. The rule of law requires that government actions be based on clear, established legal principles rather than the subjective judgments of individual officials. By insisting that judges adhere to the original public meaning of the Constitution, conservatives seek to ensure that legal decisions are grounded in an objective standard that limits governmental power. This approach, they argue, is essential for maintaining a stable, predictable legal environment in which individuals can plan their lives and conduct their affairs with confidence.[22]

Another important aspect of the conservative view is the belief that any significant change in constitutional interpretation should be achieved through the formal amendment process rather than through judicial fiat. The framers designed the Constitution to be amended only through a rigorous, deliberate process that requires widespread consensus. Conservatives contend that allowing judges to effectively amend the Constitution through reinterpretation undermines this fundamental safeguard and opens the door to arbitrary changes in the law. They argue that the proper method for constitutional evolution is through amendments, which are subject to the democratic process and reflect the will of the people.[23]

In summary, the conservative perspective on judicial review and the role of the Supreme Court is deeply rooted in a commitment to originalism, limited government, and the rule of law. Conservatives assert that the framers' original intent—clearly documented in foundational texts and debates—provides the best guide for interpreting the Constitution. This originalist approach not only protects individual rights and limits the expansion of governmental power but also maintains the delicate balance among the branches of government that is essential for a free society. By adhering strictly to the original meaning of the Constitution, the Supreme Court can function as a true guardian of the constitutional order, ensuring that modern America remains faithful to its founding principles and continues to serve as a beacon of liberty.[24]

---

[21] Dickinson, J. (1994). *Colonial Self-Government in America*. Cambridge: Harvard University Press.

[22] Ferguson, N. (2004). *Colony: A History of Early America*. New York: Penguin Press.

[23] Locke, J. (1689). *Two Treatises of Government*. London: Awnsham Churchill.

[24] Rakove, J. (1997). *Original Meanings: Politics and Ideas in the Making of the Constitution*. New York: Vintage.

Furthermore, comparative constitutional analysis and historical evidence both support the conservative claim that judicial review must be exercised with restraint. When judges interpret the Constitution based on its original meaning, they limit the potential for judicial activism that could lead to an unchecked expansion of federal power. This disciplined approach reinforces the separation of powers and preserves the integrity of the constitutional framework. In doing so, it not only upholds the ideals of the founding era but also provides a stable legal environment that is conducive to both individual freedom and economic prosperity.[25]

Ultimately, the role of judicial review and the interpretive methods employed by the Supreme Court are of paramount importance for safeguarding the principles upon which America was founded. The conservative commitment to originalism ensures that the Constitution remains a fixed, objective standard that protects against the whims of political and judicial overreach. In an era marked by rapid governmental expansion and increasing challenges to individual liberty, returning to the framers' original intent is, according to conservatives, the only viable strategy for saving America today. This approach offers not only a robust theoretical framework but also practical safeguards that have proven effective over more than two centuries of American governance.[26]

---

[25] Adams, S. (1961). *The Revolutionary Writings of Samuel Adams*. Boston: Beacon Press.

[26] Hamilton, A., Madison, J., & Jay, J. (1961). *The Federalist Papers*. New York: New American Library.

5. Constitutional Adaptability versus Rigidity

The debate over constitutional adaptability versus rigidity lies at the heart of American jurisprudence and remains one of the most critical issues facing the nation's legal and political framework. From a conservative perspective, the enduring strength of the United States Constitution depends on its inherent rigidity—the unyielding adherence to the original meaning and intent of the framers. Conservatives argue that this rigidity is essential to safeguard individual liberty, prevent governmental overreach, and preserve the system of checks and balances. At the same time, proponents of adaptability claim that a living, evolving constitutional interpretation is necessary to address contemporary challenges. However, from a politically conservative viewpoint, the risks associated with excessive flexibility far outweigh its potential benefits. This paper examines the theoretical underpinnings, historical context, and practical implications of constitutional adaptability versus rigidity, arguing that a steadfast commitment to the original constitutional framework is the only viable method for saving America from the perils of expansive state power.

The foundation of the conservative argument for constitutional rigidity is rooted in the belief that the Constitution is a sacred document, meticulously crafted by the founding fathers to enshrine natural rights and limit governmental power. The framers, influenced by Enlightenment principles and the bitter lessons of British tyranny, intended for the Constitution to serve as a fixed standard against which all government action would be measured. This originalist approach insists that the text's original public meaning, as understood at the time of its ratification, should remain the guiding principle for judicial interpretation. Conservatives maintain that any departure from this original meaning risks a slippery slope toward judicial activism and legislative overreach, which ultimately dilutes the protections afforded to individual liberty.[1]

Historically, the rigidity of the American constitutional framework has proven to be one of its greatest strengths. The deliberate difficulty of amending the Constitution is not an oversight but a carefully engineered safeguard. The framers envisioned a document that would not be subject to the transient whims of politics, but rather would endure as a permanent check on the powers of government. This built-in rigidity ensures stability, predictability, and continuity in governance, which are essential for economic prosperity and the protection of personal freedoms. Conservatives argue that the relative immutability of the Constitution has allowed American society to thrive despite immense social, technological, and economic changes over more than two centuries.[2]

---

[1] Hamilton, A., Madison, J., & Jay, J. (1961). *The Federalist Papers*. New York: New American Library.

[2] Locke, J. (1689). *Two Treatises of Government*. London: Awnsham Churchill.

In contrast, advocates of a "living Constitution" assert that an adaptable interpretation is necessary to accommodate societal progress. They contend that as society evolves, so too must the interpretation of the Constitution, allowing for flexibility in areas such as civil rights, economic regulation, and social policy. However, conservatives caution that such adaptability introduces uncertainty and undermines the rule of law. When judges are granted the discretion to modify constitutional meaning based on modern circumstances, they risk imposing subjective policy preferences on the nation rather than adhering to the objective standard set by the framers. This process, critics argue, can lead to the incremental erosion of the limitations that protect against centralized power and the gradual expansion of government authority.[3]

Central to the conservative critique is the notion that a rigid constitutional framework preserves the separation of powers by strictly limiting the jurisdiction of each branch of government. The framers deliberately divided governmental power among the legislative, executive, and judicial branches to prevent any one branch from becoming tyrannical. Judicial review, as established in Marbury v. Madison, plays a vital role in enforcing these limits by ensuring that any law or executive action conforms to the Constitution's original meaning. Conservatives insist that if the Court adopts a flexible approach to constitutional interpretation, it undermines this separation by effectively allowing the judiciary to redefine the limits of government. Instead, they argue for a disciplined method that constrains the courts to the text and historical context of the Constitution, thereby safeguarding the intended balance of power.[4]

The concept of judicial restraint is integral to the conservative perspective on constitutional rigidity. Conservative jurists contend that the role of the judiciary is not to create new rights or policies but to interpret and apply the law as written. By adhering to originalism, judges can avoid the pitfalls of judicial activism, where decisions reflect contemporary social or political ideologies rather than the framers' intentions. This restraint is seen as essential for maintaining democratic accountability because it ensures that significant policy changes occur through the legislative process, where elected representatives—rather than unelected judges—are accountable to the people.[5]

Moreover, the rigid interpretive approach reinforces the principle of federalism—a cornerstone of the American constitutional system. Federalism, which allocates power between the national

---

[3] Montesquieu, C. (1748). *The Spirit of the Laws*. Paris: Barrillot & Fils.

[4] Pocock, J. G. A. (1975). *The Machiavellian Moment: Florentine Political Thought and the Atlantic Republican Tradition*. Princeton: Princeton University Press.

[5] Rakove, J. (1997). *Original Meanings: Politics and Ideas in the Making of the Constitution*. New York: Vintage.

government and the states, is designed to keep government close to the people and to prevent the overconcentration of power. Conservatives argue that a flexible interpretation of the Constitution can inadvertently centralize power at the federal level by expanding the scope of congressional authority through broad readings of clauses such as the Commerce Clause. In contrast, a strict originalist approach maintains the limits imposed by the framers, thereby protecting state sovereignty and local self-governance. This decentralization is critical for preserving individual freedoms and ensuring that policy decisions are made by the people's representatives at the most appropriate level.[6]

The historical record supports the conservative view that constitutional rigidity has contributed to the longevity and success of the American system. Early debates at the Constitutional Convention and subsequent ratification discussions reveal that the founding fathers were deeply committed to the idea of a stable, unchanging framework. The rigorous amendment process they established was intended to prevent capricious changes that could undermine the fundamental principles of the Constitution. Conservatives view the difficulty of altering the Constitution not as a limitation, but as a deliberate safeguard against the erosion of individual rights and the expansion of governmental power.[7]

Critics of rigidity argue that it renders the Constitution anachronistic in the face of modern challenges, such as advancements in technology, shifts in societal values, and new forms of economic organization. Proponents of adaptability claim that a living Constitution allows the law to evolve and remain relevant. However, conservatives counter that while technological and societal changes are inevitable, the fundamental principles that protect liberty do not change. They argue that the Constitution's enduring wisdom lies in its timeless safeguarding of natural rights and limited government, which remain applicable regardless of external developments. Changing these principles to reflect contemporary trends, they assert, risks sacrificing the very freedoms the document was designed to secure.[8]

Conservatives further maintain that the amendment process provides a sufficient mechanism for necessary changes, provided that such changes enjoy broad consensus. This process, though deliberately challenging, ensures that any modifications to the constitutional framework are undertaken with the utmost care and deliberation. It prevents radical shifts that could destabilize the political system and dilute the protections against government overreach. In this light, the

---

[6] Adams, S. (1961). *The Revolutionary Writings of Samuel Adams*. Boston: Beacon Press.

[7] Bork, R. (1990). *The Tempting of America: The Political Seduction of the Law*. New York: Free Press.

[8] Jefferson, T. (Founders Online). "Notes on the State of Virginia." National Archives.

conservative approach is not anti-change but pro-stability, insisting that the Constitution can adapt only through democratic means that respect its original structure.[9]

The practical implications of constitutional rigidity are evident in the way the Supreme Court has historically interpreted the Constitution. Conservative critics often point to landmark cases where judicial activism has been accused of expanding federal power beyond what the framers envisioned. For instance, decisions that interpret the Commerce Clause in exceedingly broad terms have enabled a vast regulatory state, which conservatives argue is antithetical to the constitutional guarantee of limited government. An originalist approach, they claim, would have maintained the narrow scope intended by the founding fathers, thereby restraining the federal government from encroaching on areas reserved for the states or the private sector.[10]

Furthermore, a rigid interpretative method reinforces the principle of predictability in the law—a feature that is indispensable for economic stability and individual planning. Businesses and individuals rely on a stable legal framework to make long-term decisions. When constitutional meaning is allowed to shift with changing judicial philosophies, uncertainty ensues, potentially stifling economic activity and undermining public confidence in the rule of law. Conservatives argue that the certainty provided by an unchanging constitutional text is a critical asset, one that supports a vibrant free-market economy and protects personal property rights.[11]

The conservative case for rigidity is also supported by the notion of historical continuity. The American experiment in self-governance is rooted in a rich tradition that spans from the colonial era through the Revolutionary period to the present day. This continuity, conservatives assert, is maintained only when the Constitution is interpreted according to its original meaning. Deviating from that meaning not only breaks with the past but also opens the door to radical reinterpretations that could undermine the very foundation of American liberty. By remaining faithful to the framers' intent, the nation preserves a coherent historical narrative that reinforces the legitimacy of its constitutional order.[12]

Moreover, the conservative perspective contends that judicial overreach often leads to a democratic deficit. When judges reinterpret the Constitution to accommodate contemporary

---

[9] Dickinson, J. (1994). *Colonial Self-Government in America*. Cambridge: Harvard University Press.

[10] Calhoun, J. C. (1983). "Separation of Powers and the Structure of the Constitution." In *Foundations of American Government* (pp. 29–32). New York: Harper & Row.

[11] Jefferson, T. (Founders Online). "Notes on the State of Virginia." National Archives.

[12] Amar, A. R. (2005). *America's Constitution: A Biography*. New York: Random House.

policy preferences, they effectively shift decision-making power from elected representatives to an unelected judiciary. This undermines the democratic principle that fundamental changes in governance should be made by the people, through their legislative representatives, rather than by the courts. Conservatives argue that a rigid, originalist approach ensures that any evolution of constitutional meaning occurs through the democratic process—via amendments—rather than through judicial fiat.[13]

Comparative constitutional analysis provides further evidence in support of the conservative view. Countries with rigid, codified constitutions, such as the United States, tend to exhibit higher levels of stability and clearer limits on governmental power than those with more flexible constitutional arrangements. In unitary systems or systems that rely on unwritten conventions, constitutional change can occur rapidly and unpredictably, often leading to the erosion of checks and balances. Conservatives point to the American model as proof that a fixed constitutional framework, even in the face of societal change, is superior in preserving the core values of freedom and limited government.[14]

Critics of constitutional rigidity often cite the need for the law to evolve in response to modern challenges. While acknowledging that change is necessary, conservatives emphasize that such change should be incremental and achieved through the constitutional amendment process rather than through judicial reinterpretation. This process, which requires widespread consensus, serves as a safeguard against hasty or ideologically driven alterations that could compromise individual liberty. In this view, rigidity is not a barrier to progress but a protective measure that ensures any evolution of the Constitution is deliberate, measured, and reflective of the enduring principles set forth by the founding fathers.[15]

The ideological commitment to rigidity is also reflected in the broader conservative vision of governance. Conservatives believe that the primary role of government is to protect the rights of individuals and to ensure that power remains limited. Any interpretive method that allows for the expansion of government authority is seen as antithetical to these core values. From this perspective, constitutional rigidity is a moral imperative—a necessary condition for a society that values freedom, self-governance, and the rule of law. The unwavering adherence to the original meaning of the Constitution is viewed as the ultimate defense against the creeping

---

[13] Henry, P. (1775). *Speech on Colonial Rights*. Richmond: Virginia Historical Society.

[14] Kirk, R. (1953). *The Conservative Mind*. New York: Free Press.

[15] Levinson, S. (2006). *Our Undemocratic Constitution: Where the Constitution Goes Wrong (and How We the People Can Correct It)*. New Haven: Yale University Press.

centralization of power that threatens to erode the very liberties that America was founded to protect.[16]

In addition, the conservative stance on rigidity is reinforced by the practical realities of modern governance. In an era of increasing governmental intervention in virtually every aspect of life—from healthcare to education, from economic regulation to environmental policy—the need for clear, unambiguous limits on state power is more pressing than ever. Conservatives argue that a flexible, living Constitution risks enabling an ever-expanding administrative state that encroaches on individual rights and stifles economic freedom. In contrast, a rigid constitutional framework, interpreted according to the original public meaning, provides a bulwark against such expansion and ensures that government action remains firmly within its legitimate bounds.[17]

The historical record of constitutional amendments also supports the conservative case for rigidity. Since its ratification, the U.S. Constitution has been amended only 27 times—a testament to the framers' foresight in creating a document that was both enduring and resistant to radical change. Conservatives argue that this low frequency of amendments is not a sign of stagnation but rather an indication that the original document contains timeless principles that continue to govern American life. Any attempt to reinterpret these principles through judicial activism, they contend, risks unraveling the careful balance that has been maintained for over two centuries.[18]

Furthermore, the conservative emphasis on rigidity extends to the protection of economic liberties. The Constitution's explicit protections for property rights and the limits placed on government interference in the economy are seen as critical for fostering a free-market system. When constitutional interpretation becomes too malleable, it opens the door to policies that can undermine economic freedom and disrupt the stability of the market. Conservatives maintain that a rigid, originalist approach is essential for ensuring that the government does not overstep its bounds in regulating economic activity, thereby preserving the prosperity that has long been a hallmark of the American experiment.[19]

The debate over constitutional adaptability versus rigidity is not merely academic; it has profound implications for the future of American democracy. Conservatives argue that in order to safeguard the nation's founding principles and ensure that government remains accountable

---

[16] Hayek, F. A. (1960). *The Constitution of Liberty*. Chicago: University of Chicago Press.

[17] Aldrich, J. H. (1983). *Constitutional Theory*. Chicago: University of Chicago Press.

[18] Ackerman, B. (1991). *We the People: Foundations*. Cambridge, MA: Harvard University Press.

[19] Connelley, W. F. (2009). *Restoring the Constitutional Order*. Lexington: University Press of Kentucky.

to the people, it is imperative to resist the temptations of expansive judicial reinterpretation. Instead, any necessary change should occur through the deliberate, consensus-driven amendment process that the framers so carefully designed. This approach, they contend, is the only reliable means of ensuring that the Constitution continues to serve as a bulwark against tyranny and as a guarantor of individual freedom.[20]

Moreover, the conservative commitment to rigidity is intertwined with a broader ideological worldview that values tradition, historical continuity, and a cautious approach to change. Conservatives see the Constitution as a product of centuries of political thought and historical experience—a document that embodies the wisdom of the founding fathers and reflects the enduring truths of natural law. Any attempt to modify its meaning based on contemporary political trends, they argue, risks severing the link between the present and the past, thereby undermining the stability and legitimacy of the constitutional order.[21]

In addition, the conservative approach to judicial review reinforces the argument for rigidity. By insisting that judges adhere strictly to the original meaning of the text, conservatives aim to constrain the judiciary's ability to engage in policy-making and prevent the erosion of constitutional limits. This disciplined approach is viewed as essential for maintaining the balance of power among the branches of government and ensuring that no single institution gains excessive control over public life. The principle of judicial restraint, as championed by originalists, is thus a critical component of the conservative strategy to save America from the dangers of unchecked governmental expansion.[22]

Furthermore, comparative constitutional analysis provides additional support for the conservative case. When the American constitutional model is contrasted with more flexible systems found in other democracies, the benefits of rigidity become apparent. Countries that allow for frequent or arbitrary constitutional reinterpretation often experience greater political instability and erosion of individual rights. Conservatives assert that the American model, with its fixed text and rigorous amendment process, offers a level of legal certainty and protection for personal freedoms that is unmatched by its counterparts. This comparative evidence bolsters the argument that rigidity is not an obstacle to progress but a necessary condition for a free and stable society.[23]

---

[20] Jefferson, T., & Madison, J. (Founders Online). "Letter from Thomas Jefferson to James Madison, July 29, 1787." National Archives.

[21] Dickinson, J. (1994). *Colonial Self-Government in America*. Cambridge: Harvard University Press.

[22] Ferguson, N. (2004). *Colony: A History of Early America*. New York: Penguin Press.

[23] Locke, J. (1689). *Two Treatises of Government*. London: Awnsham Churchill.

Ultimately, the conservative argument for constitutional rigidity rests on the belief that government exists to protect the rights of individuals and that any expansion of state power must be carefully controlled. The originalist interpretive method, with its emphasis on the framers' intent and the fixed public meaning of the text, provides the only effective means of ensuring that government remains limited and accountable. In an era of rapid governmental expansion and increasing challenges to individual liberty, the conservative commitment to a rigid constitutional framework is not only a theoretical preference but a practical necessity for saving America.[24]

In conclusion, the debate between constitutional adaptability and rigidity is central to the preservation of American liberty. From a politically conservative perspective, the Constitution's enduring strength lies in its fixed, original meaning—a meaning that was carefully crafted by the founding fathers to serve as an unchanging safeguard against tyranny. While the living Constitution approach seeks to adapt the document to modern circumstances, conservatives warn that such flexibility risks eroding the foundational limits on government power and undermining the rule of law. By steadfastly adhering to originalist principles, the Supreme Court and other governmental institutions can ensure that the constitutional order remains intact, that individual rights are preserved, and that America continues to serve as a beacon of freedom and prosperity. This commitment to rigidity, supported by historical evidence, comparative analysis, and a deep respect for the framers' intentions, is the ultimate answer to saving America from the dangers of unchecked governmental power.[25] Therefore, the conservative vision for American constitutionalism demands that any evolution of the law occur through the formal amendment process and with broad democratic consensus, rather than through the subjective reinterpretations of a living Constitution. Only in this way can the United States remain true to its founding principles and continue to safeguard the liberty of its people for generations to come.[26]

---

[24] Rakove, J. (1997). *Original Meanings: Politics and Ideas in the Making of the Constitution*. New York: Vintage.

[25] Adams, S. (1961). *The Revolutionary Writings of Samuel Adams*. Boston: Beacon Press.

[26] Hamilton, A., Madison, J., & Jay, J. (1961). *The Federalist Papers*. New York: New American Library.

CHAPTER 4:

The Federal Structure and Separation of Powers

1. Division of Government: Legislative, Executive, and Judicial Branches

The enduring strength of the American constitutional order is built upon a meticulously balanced system of government—a design that reflects the deliberate wisdom of the founding fathers. Central to this design is the division of government into three separate branches: the legislative, the executive, and the judicial. Each branch is endowed with distinct powers and responsibilities to prevent any single entity from accumulating excessive authority, thus ensuring that the rights and liberties of the citizenry are rigorously protected. From a conservative perspective, this tripartite structure is not only a historical artifact but a timeless blueprint that safeguards American freedom against the threat of centralized power and bureaucratic overreach. The following analysis explores the theoretical foundations, historical evolution, and practical significance of the division of government, arguing that maintaining this delicate balance is imperative for saving America today.

The framers of the Constitution were profoundly influenced by Enlightenment thought and the experiences of colonial self-government, which instilled in them a deep distrust of concentrated power. Their solution was to separate governmental functions among three branches, each with its own sphere of influence. The legislative branch, as envisioned in Article I of the Constitution, is responsible for making the laws and representing the will of the people. Conservatives argue that this branch must remain robust yet restrained, serving as the primary forum for debate and compromise among elected representatives. The framers' intent was clear: a bicameral legislature that balances the interests of both large and small states, ensuring that policy is formulated with both popular consent and careful deliberation.[1]

The executive branch, established under Article II, is tasked with implementing and enforcing the laws passed by Congress. It is headed by the President, who serves as both the chief administrator and commander-in-chief of the armed forces. Conservatives hold that the executive must operate within strict limits, as its power is inherently dangerous if left unchecked. The founding fathers,

[1] Hamilton, A., Madison, J., & Jay, J. (1961). *The Federalist Papers*. New York: New American Library.

acutely aware of the potential for executive tyranny based on their experiences with the British monarchy, deliberately designed the presidency to be powerful yet constrained by constitutional checks and balances. This structure ensures that while the President can act decisively in times of crisis, such authority is never absolute.[2]

Equally vital is the judicial branch, as delineated in Article III. The Supreme Court and the lower federal courts are empowered to interpret the Constitution and adjudicate disputes that arise under its provisions. Conservative legal thought emphasizes that the role of the judiciary should be limited to that of an impartial interpreter of the law—not as a body that creates policy or expands governmental power through activist rulings. The doctrine of judicial review, established in Marbury v. Madison, reinforces the principle that all government action must conform to the Constitution's original meaning. This restraint is seen as essential for preserving the separation of powers and ensuring that the rights of individuals remain inviolable.[3]

Historical experiences underscore the significance of this division of powers. During the formation of the new nation, the fear of concentrated power was paramount. The framers, having endured the tyranny of British rule, sought to embed in the Constitution robust safeguards against the emergence of a despotism. Their solution was to divide governmental authority into distinct branches, each designed to check the others. This system of mutual control is reflected in the careful deliberations recorded during the Constitutional Convention and the subsequent debates over ratification. Conservatives view these historical events as a clear mandate for maintaining the original structure of government—a structure that has ensured American freedom for over two centuries.[4]

The legislative branch is further divided into two chambers—the House of Representatives and the Senate—to balance the competing demands of proportional representation and equal state representation. This bicameral structure, as devised by the Connecticut Compromise, reflects the framers' recognition that a single-house legislature might either be dominated by populous states or fail to represent the interests of smaller ones. Conservatives argue that this dual system not only protects against the tyranny of the majority but also compels careful debate and compromise, thereby producing laws that are both just and reflective of a broad consensus.[5]

---

[2] Locke, J. (1689). *Two Treatises of Government*. London: Awnsham Churchill.

[3] Montesquieu, C. (1748). *The Spirit of the Laws*. Paris: Barrillot & Fils.

[4] Pocock, J. G. A. (1975). *The Machiavellian Moment: Florentine Political Thought and the Atlantic Republican Tradition*. Princeton: Princeton University Press.

[5] Rakove, J. (1997). *Original Meanings: Politics and Ideas in the Making of the Constitution*. New York: Vintage.

In the executive sphere, the framers were particularly cautious. They feared that a single individual might amass too much power, as had been witnessed under monarchical rule. To counteract this, they instituted a system of checks on the President's authority. The President is elected indirectly through the Electoral College, a mechanism intended to temper direct popular influence and encourage deliberation. Additionally, the President's powers are explicitly limited by the Constitution and are subject to oversight by Congress and review by the judiciary. Conservatives maintain that these limitations are essential for preventing the executive from evolving into a quasi-monarchical institution—a danger that remains relevant in an era of increasing executive power.[6]

The judicial branch, as the final arbiter of constitutional disputes, is designed to function as a neutral interpreter of the law. The framers envisioned a system in which judges would base their decisions strictly on the text and historical context of the Constitution, thereby preserving its original meaning. From a conservative viewpoint, any deviation from this principle—such as judicial activism—poses a serious threat to the constitutional order. When judges interpret the law based on evolving societal values rather than the framers' intent, they risk altering the balance of power in ways that can lead to an expansion of governmental authority. Conservatives argue that such practices undermine the stability and predictability of the legal system, which are crucial for protecting individual liberty.[7]

The interaction among these three branches is governed by a series of checks and balances, which are fundamental to the American constitutional system. Each branch has specific powers that enable it to limit the actions of the others. For instance, while Congress has the power to enact legislation, the President holds veto power, and the judiciary has the authority to declare laws unconstitutional. Conservatives view this system as the ultimate defense against the concentration of power—a safeguard that ensures no single branch can unilaterally dictate policy. This equilibrium is not accidental but the result of deliberate design, intended to preserve the delicate balance of power that the founding fathers established in the aftermath of colonial tyranny.[8]

The conservative interpretation of the separation of powers is deeply informed by historical precedent. Early American political thought consistently emphasized the dangers of centralized authority. The Anti-Federalists, for example, were vocal in their opposition to a strong central government, arguing that it would inevitably lead to the erosion of state sovereignty and individual freedoms. Although their concerns were mitigated by compromises during the ratification

---

[6] Adams, S. (1961). *The Revolutionary Writings of Samuel Adams*. Boston: Beacon Press.

[7] Bork, R. (1990). *The Tempting of America: The Political Seduction of the Law*. New York: Free Press.

[8] Jefferson, T. (Founders Online). "Notes on the State of Virginia." National Archives.

process—most notably the addition of the Bill of Rights—their legacy endures in the conservative commitment to maintaining a strict separation of powers. Conservatives argue that the lessons learned during the nation's founding remain pertinent today, as any expansion of governmental power must be rigorously checked by the other branches.[9]

Moreover, the federal structure of the United States, which divides power between the national government and the states, further reinforces the conservative agenda. Federalism is a critical component of the American constitutional system that limits the reach of central authority and preserves local autonomy. Conservatives contend that this division of power is vital for fostering innovation and accountability in governance. It allows states to function as laboratories of democracy, where policies can be tested on a smaller scale before being implemented nationally. This decentralized approach not only enhances governmental efficiency but also serves as a bulwark against the overreach of a dominant federal government—a principle that remains central to conservative thought.[10]

In addition to institutional design, the conservative perspective places great emphasis on the underlying philosophy of the rule of law. The Constitution is seen as the ultimate legal document that establishes clear limits on governmental power and enshrines the rights of individuals. Judicial review, as mentioned earlier, plays a pivotal role in upholding these principles. Conservatives argue that the consistent application of the rule of law is essential for ensuring that all branches of government act within their constitutional boundaries. This commitment to legal certainty and predictability is viewed as indispensable for preserving both economic freedom and personal liberty.[11]

The enduring success of the American constitutional system is further evidenced by its ability to adapt through a formal amendment process without sacrificing its fundamental principles. Although conservatives favor rigidity in interpretation, they recognize that the Constitution was designed to allow for measured change when absolutely necessary. The amendment process, which requires broad consensus, is intentionally difficult, ensuring that only changes with overwhelming support are enacted. This process, conservatives assert, has allowed the Constitution to remain relevant while preserving its core tenets—a balance that other constitutional models have struggled to achieve.[12]

---

[9] Dickinson, J. (1994). *Colonial Self-Government in America*. Cambridge: Harvard University Press.

[10] Calhoun, J. C. (1983). "Separation of Powers and the Structure of the Constitution." In *Foundations of American Government* (pp. 29–32). New York: Harper & Row.

[11] Jefferson, T. (Founders Online). "Notes on the State of Virginia." National Archives.

[12] Amar, A. R. (2005). *America's Constitution: A Biography*. New York: Random House.

Conservative legal scholars and political theorists have long argued that the separation of powers is not merely a technical arrangement but a moral imperative. They maintain that the division of government is essential for protecting individual dignity and ensuring that power is exercised responsibly. In a system where power is concentrated in a single branch, the risk of arbitrary rule increases exponentially. The framers' decision to distribute power across multiple institutions was a deliberate attempt to mitigate this risk, and conservatives view this design as a moral bulwark against tyranny.[13]

The practical benefits of the division of government are also reflected in the resilience of the American system during times of crisis. Historical episodes, such as the Civil War and various economic recessions, have demonstrated that the checks and balances inherent in the federal structure can prevent any one branch from unilaterally imposing its will on the nation. Conservatives argue that these safeguards have enabled America to navigate periods of profound stress without sacrificing its fundamental values. The stability provided by a balanced government is seen as a critical factor in ensuring national unity and preserving the freedoms for which the nation was founded.[14]

Moreover, the conservative commitment to the separation of powers extends to the way modern policymakers approach governance. In an era marked by rapid governmental expansion and increasing executive authority, conservatives warn that any erosion of the institutional balance could lead to a dangerous concentration of power. They contend that the only effective remedy is to return to the founding principles that explicitly divided power among the branches. By reinforcing these constitutional limits, America can prevent the emergence of an overreaching state that threatens both economic freedom and individual autonomy.[15]

The interaction among the three branches is further exemplified by the system of checks and balances, which is designed to foster interbranch cooperation while preventing unilateral action. For instance, while Congress has the authority to pass legislation, the President's veto power and the judiciary's power of judicial review ensure that such legislation remains within the bounds of the Constitution. Conservatives assert that this dynamic interplay is not only a theoretical safeguard but also a practical mechanism that has ensured the longevity of American democracy.

---

[13] Henry, P. (1775). *Speech on Colonial Rights*. Richmond: Virginia Historical Society.

[14] Kirk, R. (1953). *The Conservative Mind*. New York: Free Press.

[15] Levinson, S. (2006). *Our Undemocratic Constitution: Where the Constitution Goes Wrong (and How We the People Can Correct It)*. New Haven: Yale University Press.

It is a system that demands accountability and transparency from all branches of government—a principle that remains as vital today as it was in 1787.[16]

Furthermore, the separation of powers and the federal structure of government have had a profound impact on American political culture. The legacy of the founding fathers' insistence on limited government continues to shape public expectations regarding the role of the state. Conservatives argue that the American people have a unique tradition of skepticism toward centralized authority, a tradition that is nurtured by the visible separation of powers and the active role of states in governance. This cultural ethos reinforces the constitutional framework and serves as a constant reminder that government is a servant of the people, not their master.[17]

Comparative analysis with other constitutional models further highlights the strengths of the American system. In contrast to unitary or highly centralized systems, the U.S. Constitution provides a clear and enduring limit on governmental power through its well-defined separation of powers and federalism. Countries that lack such robust constraints often experience political instability, erosion of civil liberties, and an over-concentration of power. Conservatives argue that the American model, by virtue of its structural design, offers superior protections for individual rights and is better equipped to adapt to the complexities of modern governance without sacrificing its founding principles.[18]

Additionally, the principle of checks and balances, which underpins the separation of powers, is crucial for preventing abuse of power in any democratic system. Conservatives emphasize that each branch of government is intentionally designed to counterbalance the others, ensuring that no single branch becomes dominant. This interdependence fosters a culture of accountability and mutual oversight, which is essential for a government that respects the rule of law. By adhering to this structure, the United States has been able to resist numerous attempts at governmental overreach throughout its history.[19]

The conservative perspective also stresses that the division of government is not static but must be continually reinforced by an engaged citizenry. Active political participation, a cornerstone of republican ideals, ensures that elected representatives remain vigilant in upholding the constitutional limits on government. Conservatives advocate for a return to the participatory governance of the colonial era, where local assemblies and town meetings played a central role

---

[16] Hayek, F. A. (1960). *The Constitution of Liberty*. Chicago: University of Chicago Press.

[17] Aldrich, J. H. (1983). *Constitutional Theory*. Chicago: University of Chicago Press.

[18] Ackerman, B. (1991). *We the People: Foundations*. Cambridge, MA: Harvard University Press.

[19] Connelley, W. F. (2009). *Restoring the Constitutional Order*. Lexington: University Press of Kentucky.

in shaping policy. This democratic involvement is seen as the best way to keep government in check and to ensure that the constitutional balance is maintained.[20]

Moreover, the federal structure enables innovation in governance by allowing states to experiment with different policies while serving as laboratories of democracy. This decentralization not only promotes efficiency but also preserves the unique cultural and political identities of different regions. Conservatives argue that this system of local autonomy is a critical component of American freedom, as it prevents the imposition of uniform policies that may not be suitable for diverse communities. The success of federalism in fostering tailored governance is a powerful testament to the foresight of the founding fathers and a key reason why the American system remains exemplary.[21]

Finally, the rigorous institutional design of the American government has provided a stable framework that has allowed the nation to prosper economically and politically. By strictly delineating the powers of the legislative, executive, and judicial branches, the Constitution creates a system of governance that is both resilient and adaptable, yet unyielding in its commitment to the rule of law. Conservatives maintain that this balance is the best defense against the rise of authoritarianism and the erosion of individual liberties. The enduring relevance of the division of government is evident in its continued capacity to generate debate, promote accountability, and safeguard the freedoms that are the hallmark of American society.[22]

In conclusion, the division of government into legislative, executive, and judicial branches is the cornerstone of the American constitutional system—a system that has safeguarded individual freedom and limited governmental power for over two centuries. From a conservative perspective, the original design of a tripartite government, with its built-in checks and balances and commitment to federalism, is indispensable for preserving the principles enshrined by the founding fathers. While modern challenges may call for adaptation, conservatives argue that any evolution in governance must occur through the democratic amendment process rather than through a reinterpretation of the original text. This rigid adherence to the framers' intent is essential for ensuring that the government remains a servant of the people and that the rule of law is maintained as the ultimate safeguard of liberty. By upholding the delicate balance of powers and reinforcing the federal structure, America can continue to thrive as a beacon of freedom and

---

[20] Jefferson, T., & Madison, J. (Founders Online). "Letter from Thomas Jefferson to James Madison, July 29, 1787." National Archives.

[21] Dickinson, J. (1994). *Colonial Self-Government in America*. Cambridge: Harvard University Press.

[22] Ferguson, N. (2004). *Colony: A History of Early America*. New York: Penguin Press.

a model of democratic self-governance—thereby fulfilling the promise of its founding principles and providing the ultimate answer to saving America today.[23]

Furthermore, the preservation of this division of government is not only a legal necessity but also a moral imperative. It reflects a deep-seated commitment to the values of self-governance, accountability, and individual dignity. The constitutional structure, with its clear separation of powers and federalist design, stands as a bulwark against the concentration of power—a threat that remains ever-present in modern political life. Conservatives contend that only by remaining true to these original principles can the United States continue to serve as a free and prosperous nation. This commitment to the original design of the government is the foundation upon which all other aspects of American life rest, and it is the key to ensuring that government power is always exercised with the consent of the governed.[24]

Comparative analysis, historical evidence, and practical outcomes all converge to affirm that the division of government is the most effective means of preventing tyranny and ensuring that power remains decentralized and accountable. In a world where governmental overreach is increasingly common, the American model of separated powers offers a proven blueprint for maintaining freedom and order. Conservatives assert that by steadfastly adhering to this model, America can resist the pressures to centralize power and continue to embody the principles of liberty and justice that have defined its national character from the very beginning.[25]

Ultimately, the conservative vision for American constitutionalism demands that the separation of powers remain inviolate. The framers' ingenious design, which divides government into three independent branches, is the ultimate safeguard against the abuses of power that have historically led to tyranny. In the face of modern challenges—be they political, economic, or social—this foundational principle must be preserved through vigilant adherence to the Constitution's original meaning. Only then can America truly live up to its promise as a nation founded on freedom, self-governance, and the rule of law. By protecting this division of government, the United States ensures that it remains a beacon of liberty for future generations, providing the definitive answer to saving America from the perils of centralized authority and unchecked state power.[26]

---

[23] Locke, J. (1689). *Two Treatises of Government*. London: Awnsham Churchill.

[24] Rakove, J. (1997). *Original Meanings: Politics and Ideas in the Making of the Constitution*. New York: Vintage.

[25] Adams, S. (1961). *The Revolutionary Writings of Samuel Adams*. Boston: Beacon Press.

[26] Hamilton, A., Madison, J., & Jay, J. (1961). *The Federalist Papers*. New York: New American Library.

2. Checks and Balances in Practice

The American constitutional system is renowned for its deliberate design that divides governmental power among distinct branches, thereby ensuring that no single institution may dominate or abuse its authority. This system of checks and balances is not an incidental feature but a carefully engineered mechanism, envisioned by the founding fathers to safeguard liberty and prevent tyranny. From a politically conservative perspective, the efficacy of these checks and balances remains the cornerstone for protecting individual freedom and limiting government expansion. This paper provides a comprehensive analysis of how checks and balances operate in practice, emphasizing the theoretical rationale, historical development, and contemporary significance of this structure in ensuring that government remains accountable to the people.

The system of checks and balances is predicated on the idea that each branch of government—legislative, executive, and judicial—possesses unique powers that enable it to constrain the others. The framers of the Constitution, deeply influenced by Enlightenment ideals and the revolutionary experience of British tyranny, were determined that power should never be concentrated in a single entity. Instead, they sought to create a system in which governmental power is inherently self-regulating. Conservatives argue that this separation is essential; without it, the risk of an overreaching government capable of infringing on the rights of its citizens increases dramatically.[1]

The legislative branch, composed of a bicameral Congress, is charged with the primary responsibility of making laws. However, its power is not unchecked. The executive branch can veto legislation, while the judiciary retains the authority to declare laws unconstitutional. This inter-branch dynamic ensures that no law is enacted without the possibility of review, a safeguard that conservatives view as critical for maintaining the rule of law. The framers' insistence on such a system was a direct response to the despotic tendencies experienced under British rule, where legislative power was subordinated to the whims of a monarch.[2]

In practice, the veto power granted to the President serves as a crucial check on congressional legislation. Conservatives assert that this power compels Congress to engage in careful, deliberative lawmaking, as legislators must consider the likelihood of a presidential veto when drafting bills. Moreover, the ability of Congress to override a veto, while constitutionally provided for, requires a supermajority that is rarely achieved without broad consensus. This two-tiered process ensures

---

[1] Hamilton, A., Madison, J., & Jay, J. (1961). *The Federalist Papers*. New York: New American Library.

[2] Locke, J. (1689). *Two Treatises of Government*. London: Awnsham Churchill.

that only legislation with widespread support can become law, thereby preventing the passage of measures that might undermine individual freedoms or expand government power beyond constitutional limits.[3]

The judicial branch, empowered through the doctrine of judicial review as established in Marbury v. Madison, acts as the final arbiter of constitutional disputes. Conservative legal scholars argue that the Supreme Court's role in interpreting the Constitution is vital to preserving the original intent of the framers. When the Court exercises its power to strike down laws that exceed constitutional boundaries, it reinforces the limits imposed on both the legislative and executive branches. Conservatives stress that this function is not a tool for policy innovation but a necessary check to ensure that all governmental action remains subordinate to the Constitution's fixed principles.[4]

Historical precedents underscore the importance of judicial review in maintaining the balance of power. Early in its history, the Supreme Court demonstrated its commitment to this principle through decisions that reined in potential legislative excesses. For instance, rulings that limited the scope of the Commerce Clause and protected state sovereignty are cited by conservatives as examples of the Court's adherence to originalist principles. Such decisions, they argue, have prevented the gradual encroachment of federal authority into areas that should remain under state control, thereby preserving the decentralized structure that is essential for American liberty.[5]

Federalism, the division of power between the national government and the states, further enhances the system of checks and balances. This structural feature ensures that power is not only divided among branches but also distributed geographically. Conservatives maintain that federalism is a bulwark against centralized control; by granting states significant autonomy, the Constitution enables a diversity of policies tailored to local needs while limiting the reach of national authority. In practice, when the federal government attempts to extend its power beyond its constitutional limits, states have often been the first line of resistance. This dual layer of governance—both horizontal (among branches) and vertical (between federal and state levels)—creates a dynamic system of accountability that is central to the conservative vision of self-governance.[6]

---

[3] Montesquieu, C. (1748). *The Spirit of the Laws*. Paris: Barrillot & Fils.

[4] Pocock, J. G. A. (1975). *The Machiavellian Moment: Florentine Political Thought and the Atlantic Republican Tradition*. Princeton: Princeton University Press.

[5] Rakove, J. (1997). *Original Meanings: Politics and Ideas in the Making of the Constitution*. New York: Vintage.

[6] Adams, S. (1961). *The Revolutionary Writings of Samuel Adams*. Boston: Beacon Press.

The practical workings of checks and balances are evident in numerous historical episodes. During the New Deal era, for instance, conservatives criticized the expansion of federal programs and regulations as a violation of the constitutional limits on government power. They argued that the broad interpretation of federal authority by the Supreme Court undermined the system of checks and balances that the founding fathers had intended. Although subsequent judicial decisions reined in some of these excesses, the debate remains a potent reminder of the dangers of an unchecked administrative state.[7]

In more recent years, controversies over executive power—particularly in the context of national security and foreign policy—have reignited debates over the proper balance between branches. Conservatives contend that the expansion of executive power, often justified by emergencies or crises, poses a serious threat to the constitutional order. They argue that while the President must have the authority to act decisively in times of crisis, such power must be strictly circumscribed by constitutional checks. The legislative and judicial branches must serve as effective counterweights to ensure that any emergency powers are not abused. This perspective is grounded in the belief that the framers designed the Constitution precisely to prevent any one branch from dominating the government, a principle that remains as relevant today as it was in 1787.[8]

The role of Congress in checking executive power is also a crucial element of the system. Through oversight functions, budgetary control, and the power to impeach, Congress holds the executive accountable for its actions. Conservatives argue that these mechanisms are essential for preventing the concentration of power in the presidency. However, they also express concern that modern congressional practices sometimes fall short of their intended purpose, particularly when partisan polarization undermines effective oversight. Despite these challenges, the constitutional provisions for congressional checks remain a testament to the framers' foresight and are a critical component of the American system of government.[9]

Moreover, the interplay between the branches is reinforced by the necessity for compromise and dialogue among them. The founders envisioned a government in which cooperation was essential for decision-making, and this spirit of interbranch communication continues to be a hallmark of American governance. When the legislative, executive, and judicial branches work in concert, they can address national challenges while remaining true to the constitutional limits imposed upon them. Conservatives argue that this collaborative yet restrained approach

---

[7] Bork, R. (1990). *The Tempting of America: The Political Seduction of the Law*. New York: Free Press.

[8] Jefferson, T. (Founders Online). "Notes on the State of Virginia." National Archives.

[9] Dickinson, J. (1994). *Colonial Self-Government in America*. Cambridge: Harvard University Press.

is the best way to ensure that power is exercised responsibly and that the rights of individuals are safeguarded.[10]

The theoretical foundations of checks and balances are not merely abstract principles but are underpinned by a robust historical tradition. The debates at the Constitutional Convention, as recorded in the writings of James Madison and others, reveal that the framers were acutely aware of the dangers of concentrated power. They purposefully designed a system in which each branch would have the ability to check the others, thus creating a self-regulating government. Conservatives view this system as a direct response to the tyranny experienced under British rule, and they assert that its preservation is essential for preventing similar abuses in the future.[11]

From a philosophical standpoint, the principle of checks and balances is closely linked to the concept of the rule of law. Conservatives emphasize that the legitimacy of any government rests on its ability to operate under clear, established laws that constrain the exercise of power. By ensuring that each branch of government is subject to the oversight of the others, the system of checks and balances provides a safeguard against arbitrary decisions and the abuse of power. This commitment to legal restraint is a core tenet of conservative thought, which holds that liberty is best preserved when government action is predictable and transparent.[12]

The practical benefits of a robust system of checks and balances extend to the economic realm as well. A predictable legal framework, enforced by an independent judiciary, fosters an environment in which businesses and individuals can thrive. Economic freedom, property rights, and the stability of contracts all depend on the consistent application of the rule of law. Conservatives argue that any erosion of the checks on governmental power—whether through judicial activism or legislative overreach—poses a direct threat to economic prosperity. Thus, the integrity of the system of checks and balances is not only a political or legal concern but also an economic imperative.[13]

International comparisons further highlight the advantages of the American model. Many democracies that lack a clear separation of powers or that have more flexible constitutional frameworks have experienced significant challenges related to governmental overreach and political instability. In contrast, the U.S. system, with its clearly delineated roles and stringent

---

[10] Calhoun, J. C. (1983). "Separation of Powers and the Structure of the Constitution." In *Foundations of American Government* (pp. 29–32). New York: Harper & Row.

[11] Jefferson, T. (Founders Online). "Notes on the State of Virginia." National Archives.

[12] Amar, A. R. (2005). *America's Constitution: A Biography*. New York: Random House.

[13] Henry, P. (1775). *Speech on Colonial Rights*. Richmond: Virginia Historical Society.

checks, has provided a stable and predictable environment that has contributed to the nation's enduring success. Conservatives argue that this comparative evidence reinforces the argument that constitutional rigidity, as manifested in a robust system of checks and balances, is the best means of preserving freedom and promoting prosperity.[14]

Critics of the conservative view often contend that an overly rigid system may inhibit necessary governmental action in times of crisis. They argue that flexibility in constitutional interpretation is essential for adapting to new challenges and addressing issues that the framers could not have foreseen. However, conservatives counter that such flexibility should not come at the expense of the fundamental principles of limited government and individual rights. They maintain that while emergency powers may be necessary, they must be subject to rigorous oversight and limited in duration to prevent any permanent expansion of state power. The amendment process, they argue, provides a more democratic and stable method for constitutional evolution than ad hoc judicial reinterpretation.[15]

The conservative insistence on maintaining strict checks and balances is also reflected in contemporary political debates. Issues such as executive orders, surveillance, and regulatory overreach are frequently examined through the lens of whether they adhere to the constitutional limits set by the framers. Conservatives argue that any deviation from these limits, even if justified by modern exigencies, sets a dangerous precedent that could gradually erode the separation of powers. This concern is not merely theoretical; it has practical implications for how government is structured and how power is distributed among its branches.[16]

Furthermore, the separation of powers and the system of checks and balances serve as a constant reminder of the need for accountability in government. Conservatives emphasize that the framers' design was intended to prevent the concentration of power in any single institution and to ensure that all government action is subject to review. This accountability is manifested in various institutional mechanisms, such as congressional oversight, judicial review, and the impeachment process. By holding each branch accountable to the others, the American constitutional system provides a robust safeguard against abuses of power—a safeguard that conservatives argue is essential for preserving individual freedom.[17]

---

[14] Kirk, R. (1953). *The Conservative Mind*. New York: Free Press.

[15] Levinson, S. (2006). *Our Undemocratic Constitution: Where the Constitution Goes Wrong (and How We the People Can Correct It)*. New Haven: Yale University Press.

[16] Hayek, F. A. (1960). *The Constitution of Liberty*. Chicago: University of Chicago Press.

[17] Aldrich, J. H. (1983). *Constitutional Theory*. Chicago: University of Chicago Press.

The interplay between the branches also promotes a culture of deliberation and compromise in governance. The requirement that major policy decisions must garner support from multiple branches of government encourages debate and negotiation, preventing hasty or unilateral actions that could undermine the constitutional order. Conservatives view this culture of checks and balances as a fundamental virtue of American democracy, one that helps to ensure that policy is formulated through reasoned debate rather than through the imposition of authoritarian will.[18]

Moreover, the enduring relevance of the system of checks and balances is evident in its ability to adapt through constitutional amendments while preserving its core structure. The framers' decision to allow for amendments—albeit through a deliberately challenging process—demonstrates that while the fundamental principles of government must remain fixed, there is room for measured change when it reflects a broad consensus. Conservatives argue that this approach strikes the optimal balance between stability and necessary adaptation, ensuring that the Constitution remains relevant without sacrificing its foundational limits on government power.[19]

The conservative vision for the American constitutional system is rooted in a deep respect for the original framework established by the founding fathers. They contend that the division of government into three branches, with its intricate system of checks and balances, is the ultimate safeguard against tyranny. By adhering to this original design, America can resist the pressures of centralized power and preserve the individual liberties that have defined its national character. The effectiveness of this system, as demonstrated by historical precedent and comparative analysis, underscores the conservative argument that any dilution of these checks and balances would imperil the very essence of American freedom.[20]

In addition, the conservative commitment to checks and balances extends to the belief that governmental power should be exercised with humility and restraint. The framers' caution against the abuse of power was born of firsthand experience with oppressive rule, and this historical lesson continues to resonate in conservative political thought. Conservatives maintain that true leadership requires the recognition of limits—not only in theory but in practice. When each branch of government is aware of its constitutional boundaries and exercises its power judiciously, the result is a more responsive, accountable, and ultimately freer society.[21]

---

[18] Ackerman, B. (1991). *We the People: Foundations*. Cambridge, MA: Harvard University Press.

[19] Connelley, W. F. (2009). *Restoring the Constitutional Order*. Lexington: University Press of Kentucky.

[20] Jefferson, T., & Madison, J. (Founders Online). "Letter from Thomas Jefferson to James Madison, July 29, 1787." National Archives.

[21] Dickinson, J. (1994). *Colonial Self-Government in America*. Cambridge: Harvard University Press.

The cultural impact of the checks and balances system further reinforces its importance. The very structure of American government has instilled in its citizens a sense of vigilance and responsibility. The awareness that power is distributed among different institutions encourages public participation and fosters a healthy skepticism toward unchecked authority. Conservatives argue that this cultural legacy is essential for sustaining a vibrant democracy and that any attempt to weaken the system of checks and balances would undermine the civic virtues that have long been a hallmark of American society.[22]

Finally, the comparative success of the American constitutional system in preserving freedom and promoting prosperity offers a compelling validation of the conservative perspective. Internationally, nations with rigid, well-defined constitutional frameworks tend to enjoy greater political stability and respect for individual rights. Conservatives assert that the American model, with its enduring commitment to checks and balances, serves as a benchmark for democratic governance and a bulwark against the encroachment of state power. This international perspective reinforces the argument that maintaining the integrity of the separation of powers is not only a matter of national interest but also a model for global democratic practice.[23]

In conclusion, the system of checks and balances embodied in the division of government into legislative, executive, and judicial branches is the cornerstone of American constitutionalism. From a politically conservative perspective, this structure—designed by the founding fathers to prevent the concentration of power and to protect individual liberty—remains the ultimate safeguard against tyranny. The interplay among the branches, the rigorous constraints imposed by the Constitution, and the enduring cultural legacy of self-governance collectively ensure that government remains a servant of the people rather than their master. Conservatives argue that any erosion of these checks, whether through judicial activism or legislative overreach, poses a direct threat to the freedoms for which America was founded. Therefore, preserving the integrity of the checks and balances system is not only a theoretical imperative but also a practical necessity for saving America today.[24]

Moreover, the historical evidence and international comparisons demonstrate that a rigid, well-structured constitutional framework is superior to systems that allow for extensive reinterpretation of governmental power. The American commitment to a fixed, unchanging constitutional text—

---

[22] Ferguson, N. (2004). *Colony: A History of Early America*. New York: Penguin Press.

[23] Locke, J. (1689). *Two Treatises of Government*. London: Awnsham Churchill.

[24] Rakove, J. (1997). *Original Meanings: Politics and Ideas in the Making of the Constitution*. New York: Vintage.

amended only through a deliberate democratic process—provides a level of legal certainty and institutional stability that is unmatched by more flexible models. This stability is essential for protecting economic freedom, fostering innovation, and ensuring that the government remains accountable to its citizens.[25]

Ultimately, the conservative vision for American governance demands that the system of checks and balances be rigorously maintained. Only by adhering to the original design of the Constitution can America continue to secure the individual liberties and limited government that are the hallmarks of its founding principles. In an era of increasing governmental expansion and political polarization, the preservation of this system is the ultimate answer to saving America from the dangers of centralized power and unchecked state authority. By reaffirming the framers' intent and upholding the separation of powers through disciplined institutional practices, modern America can remain a beacon of freedom and a model for democratic governance—ensuring that the government truly serves the people for generations to come.[26]

---

[25] Adams, S. (1961). *The Revolutionary Writings of Samuel Adams*. Boston: Beacon Press.

[26] Hamilton, A., Madison, J., & Jay, J. (1961). *The Federalist Papers*. New York: New American Library.

3. Interbranch Conflict and Cooperation

The American constitutional system is distinguished not only by its innovative division of governmental power but also by the dynamic interplay between its branches. The delicate balance of interbranch conflict and cooperation has long been a defining characteristic of the United States' constitutional order. For conservatives, the rigorous system of checks and balances—designed by the founding fathers to prevent tyranny and safeguard individual liberties—is both a testament to the wisdom of the framers and the primary bulwark against modern governmental overreach. This paper provides a comprehensive analysis of interbranch conflict and cooperation, exploring how conflict serves as a corrective mechanism while cooperation ensures effective governance. It further argues that preserving this equilibrium, in line with the original constitutional intent, is essential for saving America today.

The framers of the Constitution were acutely aware of the dangers of concentrated power, having experienced the oppressive rule of the British monarchy. To address this, they established a system in which power is divided among the legislative, executive, and judicial branches, each with the ability to check the others. This design ensures that no single branch can dominate government—a principle that conservatives argue is fundamental for protecting freedom. Conflict among the branches is inevitable in such a system; however, it is precisely this tension that drives accountability and compels each branch to act within its constitutional limits.[1] Without such conflict, there is a risk that one branch might encroach upon the powers of the others, leading to unchecked governmental authority.

Conflict and cooperation are not mutually exclusive; they are complementary aspects of the American constitutional system. Interbranch conflict serves as a corrective force. For instance, when Congress passes legislation that overreaches its authority, the President's veto power and the judiciary's capacity for judicial review act as counterweights. This adversarial yet balanced relationship ensures that decisions are not made unilaterally, and that any potential abuse of power is subject to scrutiny. Conservatives maintain that this system of mutual oversight is essential for preserving the original intent of the framers, who envisioned a government that would be both strong and limited.[2]

The legislative branch, composed of a bicameral Congress, is the primary lawmaking body. Its structure is designed to encourage debate and compromise. In practice, this means that legislative

[1] Hamilton, A., Madison, J., & Jay, J. (1961). *The Federalist Papers*. New York: New American Library.

[2] Locke, J. (1689). *Two Treatises of Government*. London: Awnsham Churchill.

proposals must undergo extensive negotiation, ensuring that diverse interests are represented and that any law passed is the product of a broad consensus. However, this process can also lead to interbranch conflict when the executive or judicial branches challenge the constitutionality of the legislation. For example, the President's veto power serves as a critical check on congressional authority, forcing lawmakers to consider the potential for executive disapproval and to adjust their proposals accordingly. Conservatives argue that such conflicts are healthy and necessary, as they prevent precipitous legislative actions that might infringe upon individual rights or disrupt the balance of power.[3]w

The executive branch, headed by the President, is tasked with enforcing the laws passed by Congress. Although the President wields significant authority—especially in matters of national security and foreign policy—this power is circumscribed by constitutional limits. Interbranch conflict arises when the executive attempts to expand its prerogatives beyond what the Constitution permits. For example, executive orders and actions taken in the name of emergency powers are often subject to judicial review, which serves to rein in potential excesses. Conservatives view these instances of conflict as necessary corrections that realign government actions with constitutional principles. They contend that an assertive judiciary, acting as a counterbalance to executive overreach, is indispensable for preserving the separation of powers.[4]

The judicial branch, particularly the Supreme Court, plays a crucial role in mediating interbranch disputes. Through judicial review, the Court ensures that both legislative and executive actions conform to the Constitution. This power was famously established in Marbury v. Madison and has since become a cornerstone of American constitutional practice. Conservatives argue that the Court must exercise this power with restraint, strictly adhering to the original public meaning of the Constitution. When the Court intervenes to nullify laws or executive actions that exceed constitutional boundaries, it reinforces the structure of checks and balances and prevents any branch from becoming too dominant. However, excessive judicial activism can also disrupt the balance, and conservatives therefore advocate for an originalist approach that limits judicial discretion.[5]

Historically, interbranch conflict has been evident during periods of significant national stress. The New Deal era, for example, saw heated battles between Congress, the President, and the

---

[3] Montesquieu, C. (1748). *The Spirit of the Laws*. Paris: Barrillot & Fils.

[4] Pocock, J. G. A. (1975). *The Machiavellian Moment: Florentine Political Thought and the Atlantic Republican Tradition*. Princeton: Princeton University Press.

[5] Rakove, J. (1997). *Original Meanings: Politics and Ideas in the Making of the Constitution*. New York: Vintage.

Supreme Court over the scope of federal economic intervention. Conservatives of the time argued that such expansive interpretations of federal power violated the Constitution's fundamental principle of limited government. They maintained that the conflicts that arose during this period ultimately contributed to an erosion of individual freedoms and a drift away from the founding ideals. Although subsequent judicial decisions restored some of the intended limits, this historical episode remains a cautionary tale for modern policymakers.[6]

Interbranch cooperation, on the other hand, is essential for effective governance. Despite inevitable conflicts, the branches must work together to implement laws, manage crises, and ensure national security. For instance, cooperation between Congress and the President is required to enact comprehensive policy reforms that address complex issues such as healthcare, education, and infrastructure. Conservatives argue that such cooperation is best achieved when each branch respects the boundaries established by the Constitution. When conflicts are resolved through dialogue and compromise rather than through unilateral action, the result is a more stable and effective government.[7]

A key element of successful interbranch cooperation is the role of checks and balances in fostering accountability. The constitutional design ensures that no branch can unilaterally impose its will without being subject to the oversight of the others. This mutual dependency encourages transparency and responsiveness. For example, when Congress exercises its oversight function, it can compel the executive to justify its actions and align them with legislative intent. Similarly, when the Supreme Court reviews the actions of the other branches, it acts as a neutral arbiter that upholds the Constitution's original meaning. Conservatives assert that this dynamic interplay is the essence of American constitutionalism and that any attempt to weaken these checks and balances would lead to a concentration of power and the erosion of liberty.[8]

Moreover, interbranch conflict and cooperation are influenced by the institutional culture of American government. The founding fathers deliberately designed a system that encourages rigorous debate and deliberation. This culture of dialogue is evident in the extensive records of Constitutional Convention debates and the subsequent ratification process. Conservatives hold that these historical practices exemplify the virtues of compromise and mutual respect, which are essential for both conflict resolution and cooperative governance. By returning to the principles

---

[6] Adams, S. (1961). *The Revolutionary Writings of Samuel Adams*. Boston: Beacon Press.

[7] Bork, R. (1990). *The Tempting of America: The Political Seduction of the Law*. New York: Free Press.

[8] Jefferson, T. (Founders Online). "Notes on the State of Virginia." National Archives.

of transparency and accountability that characterized the founding era, modern government can better navigate the challenges of contemporary policy-making.[9]

The theory of separation of powers, as enshrined in the Constitution, remains a cornerstone of conservative political thought. It is based on the belief that true freedom is preserved only when governmental power is divided and balanced. Interbranch conflict, when properly managed, acts as a safeguard against the emergence of any single dominant force. Conservatives argue that this system—despite occasional gridlock—is preferable to any model that concentrates power in one branch. They maintain that the successes of American governance, both historically and in contemporary times, are a direct result of the rigorous enforcement of these constitutional limits.[10]

Comparative analysis with other constitutional systems further underscores the value of interbranch checks and balances. Many democracies that have adopted more flexible or centralized models have experienced significant challenges, including political instability and the erosion of civil liberties. In contrast, the American model, with its explicit division of power and strong institutional checks, has provided a stable framework for over two centuries. Conservatives view this longevity as evidence that the founding principles continue to be relevant and effective, even in an era of rapid technological and social change.[11]

The role of partisanship in interbranch conflict is also a critical issue. In recent decades, increasing political polarization has sometimes exacerbated conflicts between the branches, particularly when the same party controls multiple branches of government. Conservatives contend that such polarization can lead to gridlock and undermine the collaborative spirit necessary for effective governance. They argue that adherence to the original constitutional framework, rather than partisan reinterpretation, is the best way to ensure that conflict serves its corrective purpose rather than descending into dysfunction. By maintaining a focus on the framers' intent, the system of checks and balances can function as intended, regardless of contemporary partisan divides.[12]

Another factor influencing interbranch dynamics is the evolving nature of federalism. As modern challenges—such as globalization, cybersecurity, and environmental regulation—demand coordinated national responses, tensions inevitably arise over the appropriate division of power

---

[9] Dickinson, J. (1994). *Colonial Self-Government in America*. Cambridge: Harvard University Press.

[10] Calhoun, J. C. (1983). "Separation of Powers and the Structure of the Constitution." In *Foundations of American Government* (pp. 29–32). New York: Harper & Row.

[11] Jefferson, T. (Founders Online). "Notes on the State of Virginia." National Archives.

[12] Amar, A. R. (2005). *America's Constitution: A Biography*. New York: Random House.

between the federal government and the states. Conservatives stress that the original constitutional design provides a robust mechanism for balancing these interests. The federal structure, with its clear allocation of powers, enables states to serve as laboratories of democracy, while the national government retains only those powers explicitly granted by the Constitution. This dual system ensures that both local autonomy and national cohesion are preserved, even in the face of complex policy challenges.[13]

The interplay of conflict and cooperation is also evident in the area of budgetary and oversight functions. Congress wields significant power over federal spending, which in turn serves as a check on both the executive and judicial branches. Conservatives argue that fiscal restraint is an essential component of limited government. When the branches engage in conflict over budgetary matters, it often reflects deeper concerns about the expansion of government and the proper allocation of resources. By insisting on strict adherence to constitutional limits, conservatives maintain that such conflicts ultimately promote a more efficient and accountable government.[14]

The Supreme Court, as the arbiter of constitutional disputes, plays a pivotal role in mediating interbranch conflict. Conservative judges who adhere to originalist principles are particularly mindful of the need to check legislative and executive overreach. Their decisions are guided by the text and historical context of the Constitution, rather than by modern policy considerations. This judicial restraint is viewed as essential for preserving the delicate balance among the branches. When the Court effectively exercises its power of judicial review, it not only corrects constitutional deviations but also reinforces the legitimacy of the entire system of government.[15]

In addition, the theoretical foundation for interbranch conflict and cooperation is grounded in the classical notion of the separation of powers as articulated by Enlightenment thinkers such as Montesquieu. Montesquieu's advocacy for dividing power among distinct branches remains a guiding principle for conservatives. His assertion that liberty is best protected when power is fragmented is reflected in every aspect of the American constitutional design. Conservatives argue that any attempt to blur these distinctions undermines the system's efficacy and opens the door to authoritarianism. Thus, preserving clear boundaries between the branches is not only a legal necessity but also a moral imperative.[16]

---

[13] Henry, P. (1775). *Speech on Colonial Rights*. Richmond: Virginia Historical Society.

[14] Kirk, R. (1953). *The Conservative Mind*. New York: Free Press.

[15] Levinson, S. (2006). *Our Undemocratic Constitution: Where the Constitution Goes Wrong (and How We the People Can Correct It)*. New Haven: Yale University Press.

[16] Hayek, F. A. (1960). *The Constitution of Liberty*. Chicago: University of Chicago Press.

Furthermore, interbranch cooperation is enhanced when the branches adhere to the constitutional principle of non-interference. The framers intended each branch to operate within its own sphere of competence, with minimal intrusion into the functions of the others. When this principle is respected, conflicts are resolved through dialogue and compromise rather than through unilateral action. Conservatives contend that the stability and longevity of American governance are due in large part to this mutual deference, which ensures that each branch remains focused on its core responsibilities.[17]

Moreover, the effectiveness of checks and balances in practice is reflected in the accountability mechanisms embedded within the constitutional framework. For instance, the impeachment process serves as a powerful, albeit rarely used, tool for holding the executive branch accountable for abuses of power. Similarly, Congressional oversight and budgetary controls provide practical means for ensuring that the executive and judicial branches do not overstep their bounds. Conservatives argue that these mechanisms are indispensable for maintaining the integrity of the constitutional order and must be vigorously defended against any attempts at dilution or circumvention.[18]

Interbranch conflict and cooperation also have significant implications for policy stability and economic prosperity. A predictable legal and institutional environment is essential for fostering innovation and growth. Conservatives assert that when governmental power is checked and balanced, the resulting stability encourages investment, protects property rights, and sustains economic freedom. Conversely, when the balance of power is upset—whether by an overactive judiciary or an unchecked executive—uncertainty ensues, potentially undermining both individual liberty and market efficiency.[19]

The cultural dimension of interbranch dynamics is equally important. The American political tradition, with its emphasis on self-governance and civic responsibility, has been shaped by the historical experiences of conflict and cooperation among the branches. This legacy fosters a healthy skepticism toward centralized power and instills in citizens a sense of duty to hold their government accountable. Conservatives maintain that the public's awareness of these interbranch mechanisms is critical for preserving democratic values, and that any erosion of these checks can lead to a decline in civic engagement and accountability.[20]

---

[17] Aldrich, J. H. (1983). *Constitutional Theory*. Chicago: University of Chicago Press.

[18] Ackerman, B. (1991). *We the People: Foundations*. Cambridge, MA: Harvard University Press.

[19] Connelley, W. F. (2009). *Restoring the Constitutional Order*. Lexington: University Press of Kentucky.

[20] Jefferson, T., & Madison, J. (Founders Online). "Letter from Thomas Jefferson to James Madison, July 29, 1787." National Archives.

Additionally, the conservative approach to interbranch relations emphasizes that the ultimate goal of government is to serve the people, not to accumulate power for its own sake. This principle is manifested in the careful calibration of authority among the branches. Conservatives argue that when conflict arises, it should be viewed as a necessary corrective that ensures power remains balanced and that individual freedoms are preserved. Cooperation, then, is not an end in itself but a means of achieving a government that is both effective and limited by constitutional restraints.[21]

Comparative constitutional models further illuminate the strengths of the American system of checks and balances. In countries where governmental power is more centralized, there is often less accountability and a greater risk of authoritarian tendencies. Conservatives argue that the American model, with its explicit separation of powers and strong institutional checks, offers a superior framework for protecting liberty. International comparisons reveal that systems with robust checks and balances tend to enjoy higher levels of political stability and economic freedom, thereby validating the conservative commitment to preserving the constitutional design.[22]

In conclusion, interbranch conflict and cooperation are central to the effective functioning of the American constitutional system. The deliberate division of governmental power into legislative, executive, and judicial branches—and the system of checks and balances that interlinks them—serves as the ultimate safeguard against tyranny. From a conservative perspective, the enduring success of American democracy hinges on a strict adherence to the framers' original design. This rigid framework, which emphasizes accountability, the rule of law, and federalism, has proven its worth over more than two centuries and remains the definitive answer to saving America from the dangers of unchecked governmental power. By preserving the integrity of interbranch relations, modern America can ensure that government remains a servant of the people, capable of addressing contemporary challenges without sacrificing its founding principles.[23]

Furthermore, the stability and predictability provided by a well-structured system of checks and balances have far-reaching implications for both political and economic life. They foster an environment in which policies are formulated through reasoned debate and compromise rather than through the unilateral actions of any one branch. This, in turn, protects individual freedoms and promotes long-term prosperity. Conservatives argue that any dilution of these mechanisms would not only erode the constitutional order but also imperil the very foundations of American liberty. Thus, the preservation of interbranch conflict and cooperation—anchored in the original

---

[21] Dickinson, J. (1994). *Colonial Self-Government in America*. Cambridge: Harvard University Press.

[22] Ferguson, N. (2004). *Colony: A History of Early America*. New York: Penguin Press.

[23] Locke, J. (1689). *Two Treatises of Government*. London: Awnsham Churchill.

constitutional framework—is essential for sustaining the nation's democratic ideals and ensuring that government remains limited and accountable.[24]

Moreover, the historical and international evidence supports the conservative view that a rigid system of checks and balances is superior to more flexible or centralized models. The enduring strength of the U.S. constitutional system, as demonstrated by its longevity and resilience in the face of myriad challenges, attests to the efficacy of the framers' design. By remaining faithful to these original principles, America can continue to serve as a beacon of freedom and a model for democratic governance in an increasingly complex world.[25]

Ultimately, the conservative vision for American governance demands that the division of power among the legislative, executive, and judicial branches be maintained with unwavering fidelity to the original constitutional design. Interbranch conflict, when properly managed, acts as a vital corrective, while cooperation ensures the efficient functioning of government. It is through this dynamic interplay that the United States has been able to prevent the concentration of power and preserve the individual liberties that are the hallmark of its national identity. In an era of rapid governmental expansion and political polarization, returning to the framers' intent is not only a theoretical necessity but a practical imperative for saving America. By upholding the system of checks and balances in its entirety, the nation can secure its constitutional heritage and continue to provide a stable, prosperous, and free society for future generations.[26]

---

[24] Rakove, J. (1997). *Original Meanings: Politics and Ideas in the Making of the Constitution*. New York: Vintage.

[25] Adams, S. (1961). *The Revolutionary Writings of Samuel Adams*. Boston: Beacon Press.

[26] Hamilton, A., Madison, J., & Jay, J. (1961). *The Federalist Papers*. New York: New American Library.

4. Federalism and State Sovereignty

The American constitutional system is founded upon a deliberate and well-calibrated distribution of power that not only protects individual liberty but also preserves the delicate balance between national and state authority. Federalism and state sovereignty are core elements of this system—principles that have been enshrined in the Constitution by the founding fathers as bulwarks against tyranny and the centralization of power. From a politically conservative perspective, maintaining robust state sovereignty is not merely a historical relic; it is the cornerstone of a free society and the ultimate safeguard against overreaching federal authority. This paper examines the theoretical foundations, historical evolution, and practical implications of federalism and state sovereignty in the United States, arguing that a steadfast commitment to these principles is essential for saving America today.

The framers of the Constitution, deeply influenced by Enlightenment ideas and their own experiences under British rule, were acutely aware that unchecked government leads to tyranny. In response, they crafted a federal system that divides power between the national government and the states. This division is based on the principle that government should derive its legitimacy from the consent of the governed and that local authorities are better suited to address the specific needs of their communities.[1] The Anti-Federalists, who were wary of a strong centralized government, insisted on preserving state sovereignty—a demand that led to the eventual adoption of the Bill of Rights. Conservatives argue that this historic debate illustrates an enduring truth: that state governments, being closer to the people, are more responsive, accountable, and effective in protecting individual rights than a distant national government.[2]

At the theoretical level, federalism is anchored in the natural rights philosophy of John Locke and the separation of powers advocated by Montesquieu. Locke's idea that political power must be limited and derived from the consent of the governed underpins the federalist structure. Locke argued that individuals possess inalienable rights to life, liberty, and property, and that any government failing to protect these rights loses its legitimacy.[3] Montesquieu's theory of the separation of powers, which influenced the framers, reinforced the need for multiple layers of governance. By distributing power across a national government and independent states, the framers sought to create a system of mutual checks that would prevent any single entity from

---

[1] Hamilton, A., Madison, J., & Jay, J. (1961). *The Federalist Papers*. New York: New American Library.

[2] Locke, J. (1689). *Two Treatises of Government*. London: Awnsham Churchill.

[3] Montesquieu, C. (1748). *The Spirit of the Laws*. Paris: Barrillot & Fils.

becoming dominant.[4] Conservatives maintain that these Enlightenment principles are not subject to the transient demands of modern politics but are timeless truths that continue to validate the structure of American government.

Historically, the federal system has been a dynamic engine of American governance. During the early years of the Republic, states operated with a high degree of autonomy, each crafting its own policies and practices reflective of local values and economic conditions. This decentralized approach not only nurtured innovation and experimentation in governance but also acted as a counterweight to any potential abuse by a nascent national government.[5] For example, in matters of education, law enforcement, and public health, state governments have traditionally been better positioned to understand and meet the needs of their populations than a centralized bureaucracy could ever be. Conservatives argue that this local responsiveness is a fundamental aspect of American liberty that must be zealously protected.[6]

Moreover, the federal structure enshrined in the Constitution explicitly delineates the enumerated powers of the national government while reserving all other powers to the states. The Tenth Amendment reinforces this allocation by stating that powers not delegated to the United States are reserved for the states or the people. Conservatives see this amendment as a direct affirmation of state sovereignty—a safeguard designed to prevent federal encroachment into areas that are best managed locally.[7] In recent decades, however, there have been numerous instances where the federal government has expanded its reach into domains traditionally reserved for states, such as education and healthcare regulation. Conservatives argue that such expansion undermines the original federalist design and threatens to erode the principle of self-governance that is central to American identity.[8]

The practical implications of a robust federalist system are evident in the way that state governments serve as laboratories of democracy. Under the American model, states have the flexibility to experiment with policies on a small scale before they are considered for national implementation. This decentralized approach fosters innovation and allows for policies that are tailored to the unique cultural, economic, and social conditions of different regions. Conservatives point to

---

[4] Pocock, J. G. A. (1975). *The Machiavellian Moment: Florentine Political Thought and the Atlantic Republican Tradition*. Princeton: Princeton University Press.

[5] Rakove, J. (1997). *Original Meanings: Politics and Ideas in the Making of the Constitution*. New York: Vintage.

[6] Adams, S. (1961). *The Revolutionary Writings of Samuel Adams*. Boston: Beacon Press.

[7] Bork, R. (1990). *The Tempting of America: The Political Seduction of the Law*. New York: Free Press.

[8] Jefferson, T. (Founders Online). "Notes on the State of Virginia." National Archives.

successful state-level initiatives in areas such as tax policy, education reform, and criminal justice as evidence that localized governance leads to better outcomes than a one-size-fits-all federal approach.[9] They argue that when state governments are empowered, they not only stimulate competition and innovation but also ensure that government remains accountable to the people it serves.

Federalism also plays a critical role in maintaining the balance of power among the three branches of government. The division between national and state authority creates an additional layer of checks and balances that limits the concentration of power at the federal level. For instance, even when Congress enacts broad legislation, state governments can often resist or modify these policies through litigation or by leveraging their own regulatory frameworks. This dual sovereignty ensures that the national government does not become overly dominant—a safeguard that conservatives view as essential for preventing the rise of an intrusive administrative state.[10]

The conservative critique of modern federalism centers on the perception that recent decades have witnessed an erosion of state sovereignty. Conservatives argue that the federal government has gradually expanded its authority through the reinterpretation of constitutional provisions, such as the Commerce Clause, and through expansive regulatory programs. This perceived encroachment, they claim, disrupts the balance envisioned by the founding fathers and undermines the decentralized nature of American governance. For example, federal mandates in areas such as healthcare and education have often been criticized for imposing uniform standards that ignore local conditions and preferences.[11] Conservatives contend that restoring the original federalist framework is crucial for reestablishing the limits on federal power and for ensuring that state governments can effectively represent their citizens' interests.

The historical evolution of federalism in the United States has been marked by periods of both expansion and contraction of federal power. The New Deal era, for instance, is frequently cited by conservatives as a time when the federal government assumed an unprecedented role in economic regulation and social welfare. While proponents of such expansion argue that it was necessary to address the challenges of the Great Depression, conservatives maintain that it represented a significant departure from the constitutional limits on government. They argue

---

[9] Dickinson, J. (1994). *Colonial Self-Government in America.* Cambridge: Harvard University Press.

[10] Calhoun, J. C. (1983). "Separation of Powers and the Structure of the Constitution." In *Foundations of American Government* (pp. 29–32). New York: Harper & Row.

[11] Jefferson, T. (Founders Online). "Notes on the State of Virginia." National Archives.

that the legacy of the New Deal still looms large, contributing to a modern administrative state that often infringes on state autonomy and individual freedom.[12]

Conversely, there have been periods when the federal government has been compelled to retract its reach, particularly through judicial intervention. Landmark Supreme Court decisions have at times reaffirmed the principles of federalism and state sovereignty. Conservatives often cite cases where the Court has struck down federal laws that were deemed to exceed constitutional limits, thereby reinforcing the Tenth Amendment's reservation of powers to the states. These judicial actions are seen as critical checks on the potential overreach of the national government and as affirmations of the original federalist vision.[13]

The political culture in the United States also supports a robust federalist system. American citizens have a long tradition of valuing local control and community participation in government. Town meetings, state elections, and regional referenda are expressions of this deeply ingrained preference for decentralized governance. Conservatives argue that the cultural attachment to local autonomy is a vital component of American freedom and that any shift toward centralization not only undermines constitutional principles but also alienates the citizenry from their government.[14]

Internationally, comparisons with other federal systems highlight the distinctiveness of the American model. While many countries employ federalism to manage diverse populations and regional differences, the American system is unique in its strict adherence to a written constitution and a rigorous amendment process. This rigidity, conservatives assert, provides a level of legal certainty and stability that is not found in systems where constitutional norms are more fluid. The success of the U.S. federal model in promoting economic freedom and political stability is frequently contrasted with the experiences of other federations where excessive centralization has led to conflict and inefficiency.[15]

Critics of American federalism often argue that the rigid division of powers can lead to gridlock and impede necessary national initiatives. They contend that in an increasingly interconnected world, a flexible approach to federalism is required to address issues such as cybersecurity, environmental protection, and international trade. However, conservatives counter that flexibility must not come at the expense of the fundamental principles of state sovereignty and local self-

---

[12] Amar, A. R. (2005). *America's Constitution: A Biography*. New York: Random House.

[13] Henry, P. (1775). *Speech on Colonial Rights*. Richmond: Virginia Historical Society.

[14] Kirk, R. (1953). *The Conservative Mind*. New York: Free Press.

[15] Levinson, S. (2006). *Our Undemocratic Constitution: Where the Constitution Goes Wrong (and How We the People Can Correct It)*. New Haven: Yale University Press.

governance. They maintain that while coordination between the national and state governments is necessary, it should occur within the strict boundaries set by the Constitution, rather than through the expansion of federal power.[16]

The role of state sovereignty is further reinforced by the amendment process enshrined in the Constitution. The framers deliberately designed the Constitution to be difficult to amend, thereby ensuring that any changes reflect a broad consensus and do not undermine the original balance of power. Conservatives argue that this process is essential for protecting state sovereignty, as it prevents rapid or ideologically driven alterations to the constitutional framework. By requiring supermajorities for amendments, the Constitution ensures that state governments remain integral to the governance of the nation and that their interests are not overridden by a transient majority in the federal legislature.[17]

In practice, the dynamics of federalism and state sovereignty are evident in numerous policy areas. For instance, in matters of education, states have traditionally played a leading role in shaping policies that reflect local values and priorities. Federal initiatives in education, such as nationwide standards or funding mandates, are often met with resistance by states that wish to retain control over their educational systems. Conservatives argue that such conflicts illustrate the importance of preserving state autonomy and that the best way to improve public policy is through local experimentation rather than top-down federal mandates.[18]

Similarly, environmental regulation has been a contentious area where federal and state authorities have clashed. While the federal government has enacted broad environmental policies, many states have sought to tailor these regulations to their unique ecological and economic conditions. Conservatives view this tension as a healthy expression of federalism—a system in which the states act as laboratories of democracy, testing innovative solutions that can later inform national policy. They assert that the ability of states to resist uniform federal mandates is essential for ensuring that policies remain relevant to local needs and that the rights of states are not trampled by a centralized bureaucracy.[19]

The interplay of federalism and state sovereignty is also crucial in matters of criminal justice and public safety. States possess significant authority to determine their own laws and policies in these areas, which often reflect the values and priorities of their populations. Federal encroachments,

---

[16] Hayek, F. A. (1960). *The Constitution of Liberty*. Chicago: University of Chicago Press.

[17] Aldrich, J. H. (1983). *Constitutional Theory*. Chicago: University of Chicago Press.

[18] Ackerman, B. (1991). *We the People: Foundations*. Cambridge, MA: Harvard University Press.

[19] Connelley, W. F. (2009). *Restoring the Constitutional Order*. Lexington: University Press of Kentucky.

such as attempts to impose nationwide criminal justice reforms without adequate consultation with state authorities, are viewed by conservatives as overreach that undermines the principle of local control. By maintaining clear boundaries between federal and state powers, the American system ensures that public safety policies remain responsive to local conditions while still adhering to constitutional principles.[20]

Moreover, the preservation of federalism and state sovereignty is integral to the broader conservative vision of a limited government. Conservatives argue that decentralization not only protects individual freedoms but also fosters economic innovation and efficiency. When states are empowered to design their own policies, they can tailor solutions to meet the specific needs of their residents. This competitive environment encourages innovation and accountability, as successful policies are emulated by other states, while ineffective measures are abandoned. Such a system of decentralized governance, conservatives contend, is the best defense against the creeping expansion of federal power and the inefficiencies of a one-size-fits-all approach.[21]

Additionally, the cultural and historical significance of state sovereignty cannot be overstated. The American Revolution itself was fought, in part, on the principle that local governments should be free from arbitrary central control. This revolutionary legacy is a source of enduring pride and identity for many Americans, particularly conservatives who view state autonomy as a cornerstone of the nation's heritage. The preservation of state sovereignty is thus not only a legal or political issue but also a matter of national character—a commitment to the values of self-governance, civic responsibility, and local tradition that have defined America since its inception.[22]

Comparative constitutional studies further validate the conservative stance on federalism. When compared with unitary systems or those with a more centralized distribution of power, the American model consistently exhibits higher levels of political stability and respect for individual rights. International evidence suggests that rigid federal structures, which empower subnational entities and limit central authority, are more likely to promote democratic accountability and economic freedom. Conservatives argue that the American system, with its codified separation of powers and clear allocation of authority between national and state governments, provides the optimal balance necessary for sustaining long-term prosperity and liberty.[23]

---

[20] Jefferson, T., & Madison, J. (Founders Online). "Letter from Thomas Jefferson to James Madison, July 29, 1787." National Archives.

[21] Dickinson, J. (1994). *Colonial Self-Government in America*. Cambridge: Harvard University Press.

[22] Ferguson, N. (2004). *Colony: A History of Early America*. New York: Penguin Press.

[23] Locke, J. (1689). *Two Treatises of Government*. London: Awnsham Churchill.

In conclusion, the federal structure and the principle of state sovereignty are foundational to the American constitutional system. The division of power among the legislative, executive, and judicial branches, combined with a robust system of checks and balances, ensures that government remains limited and accountable to the people. From a politically conservative perspective, the preservation of federalism is essential for safeguarding individual liberty, fostering local innovation, and preventing the overconcentration of power. While modern challenges may necessitate coordination between federal and state authorities, any expansion of federal power must occur within the constitutional boundaries established by the founding fathers. Only by remaining true to these original principles can America continue to serve as a beacon of freedom and a model for democratic self-governance. The enduring strength of the federal system, as demonstrated through historical precedent and comparative analysis, offers the ultimate answer to saving America from the perils of centralized, unchecked government.[24]

Moreover, the system of federalism not only supports political and economic stability but also reinforces the cultural identity of the nation. It nurtures a tradition of self-governance and local accountability that has defined American civic life since colonial times. Conservatives contend that preserving state sovereignty is indispensable for maintaining this tradition and for ensuring that government remains responsive to the diverse needs of its citizens. As modern America faces increasing challenges from both internal and external pressures, the commitment to a decentralized, federalist system is more critical than ever. This commitment guarantees that power is distributed among multiple centers of authority, thereby preventing any single entity from dominating the political landscape.[25]

Ultimately, the conservative vision for American governance mandates a steadfast adherence to the principles of federalism and state sovereignty. By upholding the constitutional allocation of power between the national government and the states, America can ensure that its political system remains both resilient and responsive. This rigorous separation of powers is the bedrock of the nation's success—a safeguard against the dangers of centralized authority and a guarantor of individual freedom. In preserving the integrity of the federal structure, modern policymakers, judges, and citizens alike honor the legacy of the founding fathers and secure the future of American liberty for generations to come.[26]

---

[24] Rakove, J. (1997). *Original Meanings: Politics and Ideas in the Making of the Constitution*. New York: Vintage.

[25] Adams, S. (1961). *The Revolutionary Writings of Samuel Adams*. Boston: Beacon Press.

[26] Hamilton, A., Madison, J., & Jay, J. (1961). *The Federalist Papers*. New York: New American Library.

5. Modern Challenges in Balancing Power

The enduring strength of the American constitutional system rests on the careful balance of power between various branches of government—a balance that is continually tested by modern political, economic, and social challenges. As the nation has evolved, the original checks and balances envisioned by the founding fathers have faced pressures from rapid technological change, expanding federal authority, and increasing political polarization. From a politically conservative perspective, these challenges not only threaten the original vision of limited government and state sovereignty but also imperil the very liberties that the Constitution was designed to protect. This paper provides a comprehensive analysis of the modern challenges in balancing power within the federal system, arguing that a strict adherence to the framers' original intent is essential for preserving the constitutional order and safeguarding individual freedoms.

One of the primary modern challenges is the expansion of federal regulatory power. Over recent decades, the national government has increasingly asserted authority in areas traditionally reserved for the states, such as healthcare, environmental regulation, and education. Conservatives argue that this expansion results in an erosion of state sovereignty and diminishes the capacity of local governments to address the unique needs of their communities. The framers designed federalism to ensure that governmental power would be divided and that the national government would have only those powers expressly granted by the Constitution.[1] However, modern reinterpretations—often justified by claims of an evolving national interest—have blurred these lines, leading to what conservatives see as an overcentralized administrative state that undermines the very principles of self-governance and local autonomy.[2]

Another significant challenge is the increasing influence of the executive branch. In times of crisis—such as post-9/11 national security concerns or economic downturns—executive power has often expanded under the guise of emergency measures. Conservatives contend that while decisive executive action is sometimes necessary, such expansions must be temporary and strictly circumscribed by constitutional limits. The historical record shows that the founding fathers were deeply wary of an unchecked executive, as evidenced by the careful design of the presidential veto and the system of checks provided by Congress and the judiciary.[3] Today, however, some argue that the executive branch has overstepped its bounds, particularly when executive orders are used to bypass legislative processes or when national security measures

---

[1] Hamilton, A., Madison, J., & Jay, J. (1961). *The Federalist Papers*. New York: New American Library.

[2] Locke, J. (1689). *Two Treatises of Government*. London: Awnsham Churchill.

[3] Montesquieu, C. (1748). *The Spirit of the Laws*. Paris: Barrillot & Fils.

infringe upon individual rights. Conservatives maintain that a return to the original constitutional framework would require a reassertion of Congress's oversight and a strict adherence to the separation of powers.[4]

Judicial review remains another arena in which modern challenges to balanced power are evident. The Supreme Court has played an increasingly central role in shaping public policy through its interpretations of the Constitution. While the power of judicial review is a critical safeguard, conservatives argue that the Court has sometimes engaged in what they term "judicial activism," where judges impose policy preferences that stray from the original public meaning of the text.[5] This perceived overreach not only disrupts the balance among the branches but also shifts power from democratically elected representatives to an unelected judiciary. Conservatives assert that returning to an originalist methodology—interpreting the Constitution strictly as it was understood at the time of its ratification—is essential for maintaining a stable and predictable legal framework.[6]

Political polarization presents yet another modern challenge. In today's highly charged partisan environment, interbranch conflicts often become entangled with ideological battles that hinder effective governance. Conservatives argue that the framers' design was intended to foster deliberation and compromise, ensuring that the government remains responsive to the people rather than dominated by a single political faction. However, modern partisanship has sometimes led to gridlock, where the branches engage in constant conflict rather than constructive cooperation. This polarization not only impairs policy-making but also undermines public confidence in democratic institutions. Conservatives contend that restoring the balance envisioned by the founders requires a renewed commitment to the principles of checks and balances and a reemphasis on the separation of powers, which can help depoliticize constitutional interpretation.[7]

The rapid pace of technological change also poses challenges to maintaining the original balance of power. Innovations in information technology, surveillance capabilities, and data collection have enabled the federal government to expand its reach in unprecedented ways. While technology can improve government efficiency, conservatives caution that without proper checks, it can also facilitate invasive monitoring and unwarranted interference in citizens' lives. The Constitution,

---

[4] Pocock, J. G. A. (1975). *The Machiavellian Moment: Florentine Political Thought and the Atlantic Republican Tradition*. Princeton: Princeton University Press.

[5] Rakove, J. (1997). *Original Meanings: Politics and Ideas in the Making of the Constitution*. New York: Vintage.

[6] Adams, S. (1961). *The Revolutionary Writings of Samuel Adams*. Boston: Beacon Press.

[7] Bork, R. (1990). *The Tempting of America: The Political Seduction of the Law*. New York: Free Press.

as originally framed, did not anticipate such advances, yet its underlying principles of limited government and protection of individual privacy remain applicable. Conservatives argue that any use of technology by the government must be strictly regulated and subject to judicial review to ensure that it does not infringe upon constitutional rights.[8]

Economic challenges further complicate the balance of power. In an era of globalization and rapid economic transformation, the federal government has increasingly intervened in the economy through regulatory agencies and fiscal policies. While some degree of regulation is necessary to ensure a stable economic environment, conservatives assert that excessive intervention stifles free enterprise and individual initiative. The Constitution was designed to protect property rights and promote economic freedom by limiting government interference. Modern economic policies that expand federal authority are seen by conservatives as a departure from these founding principles, leading to inefficiencies and undermining the incentive structure that fuels innovation and growth.[9]

The interplay between federal and state governments remains a persistent source of tension. Although federalism is a central tenet of the American constitutional system, there is ongoing debate over the appropriate balance between national unity and state autonomy. Conservatives emphasize that the Tenth Amendment clearly reserves powers not delegated to the national government for the states or the people. Yet, modern judicial and legislative actions have sometimes expanded federal power at the expense of the states. This shift, conservatives argue, threatens to erode local self-governance and diminishes the ability of states to serve as laboratories of democracy. Preserving state sovereignty is essential not only for maintaining a check on federal power but also for ensuring that policies are tailored to local conditions and reflect the diverse interests of the American populace.[10]

Interbranch conflict, when managed properly, serves as a vital mechanism for keeping governmental power in check. The system of checks and balances ensures that conflicts are resolved through dialogue, negotiation, and, when necessary, judicial intervention. For example, when the executive branch issues orders that appear to overstep constitutional bounds, Congress has the authority to hold hearings, conduct investigations, and, in extreme cases, pursue impeachment. Similarly, when Congress passes laws that potentially infringe on individual rights, the judiciary can review

---

[8] Jefferson, T. (Founders Online). "Notes on the State of Virginia." National Archives.

[9] Dickinson, J. (1994). *Colonial Self-Government in America*. Cambridge: Harvard University Press.

[10] Calhoun, J. C. (1983). "Separation of Powers and the Structure of the Constitution." In *Foundations of American Government* (pp. 29–32). New York: Harper & Row.

these laws and strike them down if they violate the Constitution. Conservatives argue that this ongoing process of conflict and resolution is the hallmark of a healthy constitutional system—one that prevents any single branch from becoming too powerful.[11]

However, modern challenges have sometimes strained this balance. Increasingly partisan politics have led to situations where interbranch conflict becomes less about enforcing constitutional limits and more about political point-scoring. Conservatives warn that when conflicts are driven by ideology rather than by genuine constitutional concerns, the integrity of the checks and balances system is compromised. They advocate for a return to a more principled, originalist approach, wherein conflicts are resolved based on the framers' intended limits rather than on contemporary political agendas.[12]

The Supreme Court's role in this context is particularly crucial. As the arbiter of constitutional disputes, the Court must act as a neutral guardian of the constitutional text. Conservatives assert that when the Court veers into activism, it not only distorts the separation of powers but also risks undermining the legitimacy of the judiciary. A strict, originalist approach would compel judges to base their decisions on the text's historical meaning, thereby reinforcing the system of checks and balances. This restraint is seen as essential for ensuring that the judicial branch remains a check on the other branches rather than a source of new policy.[13]

The challenge of balancing power is further compounded by external factors such as globalization and emerging international norms. As the United States engages more deeply with the global economy, there is pressure to conform to international regulatory standards that may conflict with constitutional principles. Conservatives argue that while international cooperation is important, it should not come at the expense of domestic constitutional order. The federal structure must remain intact, and any external pressures must be carefully weighed against the fundamental rights enshrined in the Constitution.[14]

Technological advances also demand careful consideration in maintaining the balance of power. The use of mass surveillance, data analytics, and digital communication by the government raises serious questions about privacy and civil liberties. Conservatives contend that such technologies, if left unchecked, can lead to an unprecedented expansion of state power. To counter this, they advocate for stringent judicial oversight and legislative constraints that align with the original

---

[11] Jefferson, T. (Founders Online). "Notes on the State of Virginia." National Archives.

[12] Amar, A. R. (2005). *America's Constitution: A Biography*. New York: Random House.

[13] Henry, P. (1775). *Speech on Colonial Rights*. Richmond: Virginia Historical Society.

[14] Kirk, R. (1953). *The Conservative Mind*. New York: Free Press.

constitutional protections. The principle that government must be limited in its reach is as relevant today as it was in the 18th century, even in the face of modern technological challenges.[15]

Furthermore, economic policies continue to test the balance between federal authority and state sovereignty. In recent years, debates over issues such as federal stimulus packages, regulatory reforms, and healthcare initiatives have highlighted the tension between centralized economic control and local self-determination. Conservatives maintain that economic freedom is best preserved when power is decentralized, allowing states to tailor policies to their specific needs. They argue that an overreaching federal government not only stifles economic innovation but also imposes one-size-fits-all solutions that fail to address regional disparities.[16]

The importance of maintaining robust checks and balances is also evident in the realm of political accountability. Modern challenges, such as increasing partisanship and the erosion of public trust in government institutions, underscore the need for transparent and accountable governance. Conservatives believe that the system of interbranch checks—through mechanisms such as congressional oversight, executive vetoes, and judicial review—serves as the best means of ensuring that power is not abused. When each branch is compelled to justify its actions within the confines of the Constitution, it promotes a culture of accountability that is essential for a functioning democracy.[17]

Moreover, the dynamic between conflict and cooperation among the branches is essential for effective policy-making. While conflict ensures that no branch becomes dominant, cooperation is necessary for implementing policies that address national challenges. The framers designed the American system to require negotiation and compromise, ensuring that policy decisions reflect a broad consensus. Conservatives argue that this balance, when maintained, results in more stable and thoughtful governance. However, modern political polarization often hampers cooperation, leading to legislative gridlock and executive overreach. Restoring a principled approach to interbranch relations, grounded in the original constitutional framework, is therefore crucial for resolving these issues.[18]

The cultural legacy of American federalism also plays a significant role in reinforcing state sovereignty. The tradition of local self-governance, which dates back to colonial town meetings

---

[15] Levinson, S. (2006). *Our Undemocratic Constitution: Where the Constitution Goes Wrong (and How We the People Can Correct It)*. New Haven: Yale University Press.

[16] Hayek, F. A. (1960). *The Constitution of Liberty*. Chicago: University of Chicago Press.

[17] Aldrich, J. H. (1983). *Constitutional Theory*. Chicago: University of Chicago Press.

[18] Ackerman, B. (1991). *We the People: Foundations*. Cambridge, MA: Harvard University Press.

and local assemblies, remains a vital part of American identity. Conservatives contend that this cultural heritage is under threat from the encroachment of a centralized federal government, which can dilute the distinct political and social characteristics of individual states. Preserving state sovereignty is thus not only a legal or political imperative but also a matter of national pride and identity. It reinforces the belief that power should be as close to the people as possible, ensuring that government remains responsive to local needs.[19]

Comparative constitutional analysis further bolsters the conservative case for strong federalism and robust checks and balances. Nations with decentralized systems and clearly defined state powers tend to enjoy greater political stability and higher levels of economic freedom. In contrast, countries with highly centralized government structures often struggle with bureaucratic inefficiency and political overreach. Conservatives argue that the American model, with its written Constitution and rigorous amendment process, provides a level of legal and institutional certainty that is unmatched by more flexible systems. This certainty is essential for preserving the fundamental rights of citizens and for ensuring that government power remains limited.[20]

The challenges posed by modern governance—such as technological advancements, economic globalization, and intense political polarization—demand that the system of checks and balances be both resilient and adaptive. However, conservatives maintain that any adaptation must occur through the formal constitutional amendment process rather than through judicial reinterpretation or legislative fiat. This approach, they argue, preserves the original intent of the framers while allowing for necessary, measured change. The conservative vision is one in which the Constitution serves as a stable foundation, guiding the evolution of government without compromising its core principles.[21]

Furthermore, the role of the Supreme Court in mediating interbranch conflict is as critical today as it was in the early years of the Republic. The Court's ability to review and, if necessary, invalidate actions by the legislative and executive branches is a key safeguard against the erosion of constitutional limits. Conservatives insist that the Court must exercise this power with a strict adherence to originalism, ensuring that its decisions reflect the text's historical meaning rather than modern political considerations. Such restraint is viewed as essential for maintaining the

---

[19] Connelley, W. F. (2009). *Restoring the Constitutional Order*. Lexington: University Press of Kentucky.

[20] Jefferson, T., & Madison, J. (Founders Online). "Letter from Thomas Jefferson to James Madison, July 29, 1787." National Archives.

[21] Dickinson, J. (1994). *Colonial Self-Government in America*. Cambridge: Harvard University Press.

separation of powers and for preventing the judiciary from becoming an unelected branch that shapes policy based on contemporary ideologies.[22]

Additionally, the federal structure's resilience in the face of modern challenges is evidenced by the ongoing role of states in governing critical areas such as education, healthcare, and law enforcement. States retain significant authority to experiment with policies and to tailor solutions to their unique circumstances. This decentralized model not only enhances governmental responsiveness but also fosters innovation by allowing states to serve as laboratories of democracy. Conservatives argue that preserving state sovereignty is crucial for ensuring that policies remain relevant to local conditions and that the federal government does not impose one-size-fits-all solutions that may be ill-suited to diverse populations.[23]

Finally, the conservative argument for maintaining the original balance of power is rooted in the moral and philosophical principles of the founding era. The framers were motivated by a profound commitment to protecting individual liberty against the tyranny of centralized power. Their decision to enshrine a system of checks and balances in the Constitution was a deliberate safeguard designed to ensure that government remains subordinate to the people. Conservatives contend that any erosion of these foundational mechanisms would not only undermine the constitutional order but also jeopardize the freedoms that are the hallmark of American society. In this light, upholding the rigid separation of powers is not merely a legal or political necessity—it is a moral imperative that honors the legacy of the founding fathers and ensures that government remains a true servant of the people.[24]

In conclusion, modern challenges in balancing power within the American constitutional system are significant but not insurmountable. The original design of the Constitution, with its clear division of power, robust system of checks and balances, and commitment to federalism and state sovereignty, has served as a durable safeguard against tyranny for over two centuries. From a politically conservative perspective, preserving this original framework is essential for protecting individual liberty and preventing the overreach of governmental power. While contemporary issues such as expanding federal authority, technological change, and political polarization pose challenges to the balance of power, they also underscore the need for a return to the framers' intent. By ensuring that any necessary adaptations occur through the formal amendment process

---

[22] Ferguson, N. (2004). *Colony: A History of Early America*. New York: Penguin Press.

[23] Locke, J. (1689). *Two Treatises of Government*. London: Awnsham Churchill.

[24] Rakove, J. (1997). *Original Meanings: Politics and Ideas in the Making of the Constitution*. New York: Vintage.

rather than through judicial reinterpretation, America can maintain its constitutional integrity and continue to serve as a beacon of freedom and self-governance. The conservative commitment to a fixed, unyielding constitutional framework remains the ultimate answer to saving America from the dangers of unchecked power, guaranteeing that government continues to function as a guardian of liberty and a true representative of the people.[25] Ultimately, the preservation of a balanced federal structure is not only a practical necessity but also a reflection of the deep-seated values that have defined American democracy since its inception. By upholding the principles of interbranch conflict and cooperation as originally envisioned, modern America can secure its constitutional heritage and ensure that the government remains limited, accountable, and faithful to the founding ideals for generations to come.[26]

---

[25] Adams, S. (1961). *The Revolutionary Writings of Samuel Adams*. Boston: Beacon Press.

[26] Hamilton, A., Madison, J., & Jay, J. (1961). *The Federalist Papers*. New York: New American Library.

Chapter 5:

Civil Liberties and Individual Rights

1. Bill of Rights: Historical Context and Modern Relevance

The Bill of Rights, as the first ten amendments to the United States Constitution, embodies the fundamental protections of individual liberties and serves as a cornerstone of American political philosophy. From a politically conservative perspective, its historical context and modern relevance are paramount in safeguarding the limited government envisioned by the founding fathers. This paper examines the origins, evolution, and enduring significance of the Bill of Rights, arguing that its strict adherence is essential for preserving individual freedom against the encroachment of expansive government. By grounding the analysis in historical evidence and conservative legal theory, the discussion demonstrates that the Bill of Rights not only reflects the revolutionary ideals of natural rights and self-governance but also remains the ultimate bulwark against modern threats to liberty.

The Bill of Rights was born out of a deep-seated concern among the Anti-Federalists that the original Constitution did not adequately protect individual freedoms. The framers, particularly those influenced by Enlightenment thinkers such as John Locke, believed that government exists solely to secure the natural rights of its citizens—rights that include freedom of speech, religion, assembly, and the press, as well as protections against unreasonable searches and seizures and self-incrimination. Conservatives argue that these amendments are not merely supplementary provisions but are the very embodiment of the founding fathers' commitment to limiting governmental power. The inclusion of these rights was a necessary concession to ensure ratification, and its permanence underscores the principle that government must never infringe on the inherent dignity and autonomy of the individual.[1]

Historically, the Bill of Rights emerged during a time of revolutionary fervor and profound political transformation. The American Revolution was fought, in part, on the premise that individuals possess inherent rights that no sovereign may violate. The revolutionary leaders,

[1] Hamilton, A., Madison, J., & Jay, J. (1961). *The Federalist Papers*. New York: New American Library.

drawing on the natural rights philosophy of Locke, argued that the legitimacy of government is contingent on its ability to protect these rights. The Anti-Federalists, wary of the potential for centralized power to become tyrannical, demanded explicit guarantees for individual liberties as a condition for accepting the new Constitution. Their insistence led to the adoption of the Bill of Rights, thereby enshrining protections that have become the bedrock of American legal and political culture.[2]

Conservatives maintain that the historical context of the Bill of Rights is crucial for understanding its modern relevance. The framers' experience under British colonial rule had taught them the dangers of unchecked governmental authority. The Bill of Rights was designed as a bulwark against the potential for the national government to encroach on personal freedoms. For example, the First Amendment protects freedom of expression and religion, ensuring that the government cannot dictate personal beliefs or censor dissent. In a modern context, these protections are under constant threat from both legislative overreach and executive actions that seek to curtail free speech and religious liberty. Conservatives argue that a strict, originalist interpretation of the Bill of Rights is essential for preserving the limited government that the founding fathers envisioned.[3]

The conservative perspective on the Bill of Rights also emphasizes the principle of judicial restraint. Conservative jurists argue that the role of the courts is to interpret the Bill of Rights according to its original public meaning, as understood at the time of its ratification, rather than to expand its protections based on contemporary social trends. They contend that an activist judiciary that reinterprets these amendments to address modern issues—such as digital privacy or new forms of expression—risks altering the delicate balance of power established by the Constitution. This, in turn, could lead to an expansion of governmental authority beyond its intended limits. For conservatives, preserving the original intent of the Bill of Rights is essential for ensuring that the government remains a protector of individual liberties rather than an agent of social engineering.[4]

Moreover, the Bill of Rights has played a critical role in shaping American public policy. Over the centuries, its provisions have served as a rallying point for various civil liberties movements and have provided a legal framework for challenging government actions that infringe upon

---

[2] Locke, J. (1689). *Two Treatises of Government*. London: Awnsham Churchill.

[3] Montesquieu, C. (1748). *The Spirit of the Laws*. Paris: Barrillot & Fils.

[4] Pocock, J. G. A. (1975). *The Machiavellian Moment: Florentine Political Thought and the Atlantic Republican Tradition*. Princeton: Princeton University Press.

individual rights. From landmark Supreme Court decisions affirming the right to privacy to legislative debates over free speech and religious freedom, the Bill of Rights has consistently been invoked as the ultimate safeguard against governmental overreach. Conservatives assert that any erosion of these fundamental rights, whether through expanded surveillance programs or restrictive legislation, poses a direct threat to the core values upon which the nation was founded.[5]

In modern society, challenges to the Bill of Rights have emerged in numerous forms. One significant issue is the rise of digital technology and the corresponding need to protect privacy in the digital age. Government agencies increasingly rely on sophisticated surveillance technologies that, if left unchecked, could infringe upon the Fourth Amendment's protection against unreasonable searches and seizures. Conservatives argue that a strict interpretation of the Fourth Amendment is necessary to limit the reach of the state in the digital realm, ensuring that technological advancements do not come at the cost of personal privacy.[6]

Another contemporary challenge is the debate over freedom of speech, particularly in the context of social media and online platforms. Critics on various sides argue over the extent to which the government should intervene in what is often characterized as "hate speech" or misinformation. Conservatives maintain that the First Amendment provides broad protection for free expression, and any attempts to curtail speech—whether by government regulation or by coercive pressure on private entities—must be carefully scrutinized to ensure they do not undermine the fundamental right to free speech. The original public meaning of the First Amendment, conservatives contend, offers clear guidance on these issues and should be the standard by which modern policies are judged.[7]

The Second Amendment, which protects the right to bear arms, remains one of the most hotly debated elements of the Bill of Rights. Conservatives view this amendment as a direct safeguard against governmental tyranny and as a necessary provision for individual self-defense. The historical context of the Second Amendment is rooted in the revolutionary experience, where armed citizenry was seen as a bulwark against both foreign invasion and domestic despotism. In modern debates, conservatives argue that any restrictions on the Second Amendment must be interpreted narrowly and in a manner consistent with the framers' intent. They contend that

---

[5] Rakove, J. (1997). *Original Meanings: Politics and Ideas in the Making of the Constitution*. New York: Vintage.

[6] Adams, S. (1961). *The Revolutionary Writings of Samuel Adams*. Boston: Beacon Press.

[7] Bork, R. (1990). *The Tempting of America: The Political Seduction of the Law*. New York: Free Press.

disarming citizens would not only weaken personal security but also erode the foundational principle that a free people must be capable of defending their liberties.[8]

In addition to these specific amendments, the overall framework of the Bill of Rights is instrumental in ensuring that government power remains both limited and accountable. The Tenth Amendment, which reserves to the states and the people any powers not delegated to the federal government, reinforces the conservative emphasis on federalism and local self-governance. This amendment serves as a constant reminder that not all authority resides with the national government, and that local communities have an essential role in shaping policies that directly affect their lives. Conservatives argue that the preservation of state sovereignty is fundamental to maintaining a balanced political system and preventing the overreach of federal power.[9]

The conservative commitment to the Bill of Rights is also reflected in the ongoing political and legal debates over constitutional interpretation. Originalist approaches to the Bill of Rights seek to limit judicial discretion and to confine the interpretation of these amendments to the historical context in which they were drafted. This perspective is based on the belief that the framers' intentions, as documented in the debates of the Constitutional Convention and the writings of the Anti-Federalists, provide a clear and objective standard. Conservatives argue that any deviation from this standard risks transforming the Bill of Rights into a malleable instrument that could be used to justify expanded governmental authority, rather than to constrain it.[10]

Moreover, the Bill of Rights has a profound impact on American political culture. Its provisions not only protect individual freedoms but also symbolize the nation's commitment to liberty and the rule of law. The cultural significance of the Bill of Rights is evident in the way it has been invoked in public discourse, political rallies, and legal challenges throughout American history. Conservatives see this cultural legacy as a vital component of American identity—a reminder that the struggle for freedom is ongoing and that the protections enshrined in the Bill of Rights must be vigorously defended against any encroachment by the state.[11]

The historical evolution of the Bill of Rights offers important lessons for modern governance. Over the past two centuries, these amendments have been the subject of numerous judicial

---

[8] Jefferson, T. (Founders Online). "Notes on the State of Virginia." National Archives.

[9] Dickinson, J. (1994). *Colonial Self-Government in America*. Cambridge: Harvard University Press.

[10] Calhoun, J. C. (1983). "Separation of Powers and the Structure of the Constitution." In *Foundations of American Government* (pp. 29–32). New York: Harper & Row.

[11] Jefferson, T. (Founders Online). "Notes on the State of Virginia." National Archives.

interpretations and legislative reforms. While some adaptations have been necessary to address new challenges, conservatives caution that such changes must be made with great care. The framers' intent was to create a set of enduring protections that would not be easily altered by shifting political winds. Conservatives maintain that the relative rigidity of the Bill of Rights is a strength, as it ensures that fundamental rights are not subject to the whims of transient majorities or ideological fashions.[12]

In recent years, challenges to the Bill of Rights have become increasingly complex, reflecting the multifaceted nature of modern society. Issues such as digital privacy, free speech in the age of social media, and the right to self-defense continue to provoke contentious debates. Conservatives argue that these debates should be resolved by returning to the original public meaning of the Bill of Rights, rather than by attempting to update its provisions through judicial activism. They contend that the framers' original vision provides a timeless framework that is fully capable of addressing contemporary challenges without compromising the core principles of limited government and individual liberty.[13]

Furthermore, the conservative approach emphasizes that any attempt to weaken or reinterpret the Bill of Rights poses a direct threat to the constitutional order. For conservatives, the Bill of Rights is not merely a set of legal provisions but a bulwark against the expansion of state power. The historical context in which these amendments were adopted—a context marked by the struggle for independence and the desire to secure personal freedom—is central to understanding their enduring importance. Conservatives assert that any erosion of these protections, whether through expansive legislative measures or overly flexible judicial interpretations, undermines the very foundations of American liberty.[14]

Additionally, the role of the judiciary in enforcing the Bill of Rights is a subject of considerable importance. The Supreme Court's decisions in key cases involving free speech, the right to bear arms, and privacy rights have shaped the modern understanding of these amendments. Conservatives contend that when the Court adheres to an originalist methodology, it provides a stable and predictable legal framework that upholds the framers' intentions. Conversely, when the Court adopts a more flexible, "living Constitution" approach, it risks undermining the explicit protections that are central to the Bill of Rights. This divergence, conservatives argue,

---

[12] Amar, A. R. (2005). *America's Constitution: A Biography*. New York: Random House.

[13] Henry, P. (1775). *Speech on Colonial Rights*. Richmond: Virginia Historical Society.

[14] Kirk, R. (1953). *The Conservative Mind*. New York: Free Press.

is not merely a matter of interpretive preference but a fundamental choice between preserving or eroding individual freedoms.[15]

The interplay between federal and state authorities also plays a critical role in the modern relevance of the Bill of Rights. The Tenth Amendment, which explicitly reserves powers not delegated to the federal government to the states or the people, is a key provision that reinforces state sovereignty. Conservatives view this amendment as a reminder that many of the rights and liberties protected by the Bill of Rights are best preserved at the local level. When federal policies encroach upon these rights, states have historically served as a counterbalance, providing tailored solutions that reflect the diverse needs of their communities. This decentralized approach is seen as essential for protecting individual liberty in a nation as vast and varied as the United States.[16]

In addition, economic and technological advancements present new challenges to the protections enshrined in the Bill of Rights. The digital revolution, in particular, raises critical questions about privacy, free expression, and the limits of government surveillance. Conservatives argue that these modern challenges must be addressed within the framework of the original constitutional text. For instance, the Fourth Amendment's protection against unreasonable searches and seizures must be vigorously enforced to prevent intrusive government surveillance in the digital age. Conservatives maintain that the principles underlying the Bill of Rights are timeless and that modern technology should not be used as a pretext to expand government power at the expense of individual privacy.[17]

Political polarization further complicates the modern interpretation of the Bill of Rights. In a highly partisan environment, the protection of individual liberties can become entangled with political agendas, leading to contentious debates over issues such as free speech and gun rights. Conservatives argue that the original meaning of the Bill of Rights provides a neutral, objective standard that can cut through partisan rhetoric. By adhering to the framers' intent, the judiciary and legislators can ensure that these fundamental rights are preserved, regardless of prevailing political trends. This commitment to an objective standard is seen as essential for maintaining the integrity of American democracy.[18]

---

[15] Levinson, S. (2006). *Our Undemocratic Constitution: Where the Constitution Goes Wrong (and How We the People Can Correct It)*. New Haven: Yale University Press.

[16] Hayek, F. A. (1960). *The Constitution of Liberty*. Chicago: University of Chicago Press.

[17] Aldrich, J. H. (1983). *Constitutional Theory*. Chicago: University of Chicago Press.

[18] Ackerman, B. (1991). *We the People: Foundations*. Cambridge, MA: Harvard University Press.

Moreover, the cultural significance of the Bill of Rights continues to resonate in public discourse. Its language and ideals are frequently invoked by politicians, activists, and citizens as the ultimate defense against governmental overreach. Conservatives view this cultural resonance as evidence of the Bill of Rights' enduring power—a power that must be actively defended through rigorous legal interpretation and steadfast public policy. They contend that any attempt to dilute these protections, whether through judicial reinterpretation or legislative erosion, would constitute a betrayal of the founding principles that have defined American freedom for generations.[19]

The historical context of the Bill of Rights is also instructive in addressing modern challenges. The amendments were drafted during a period of revolutionary change, when the protection of individual liberties was paramount to the survival of a fledgling nation. The Anti-Federalists, who demanded a Bill of Rights, were motivated by a deep fear of centralized power and the potential for government abuse. Their concerns, borne out by the historical experience of British oppression, continue to be relevant today. Conservatives argue that revisiting this historical context reinforces the importance of the Bill of Rights as a safeguard against the erosion of freedom by an increasingly intrusive state.[20]

Furthermore, the process by which the Bill of Rights was adopted—a process characterized by intense debate and a commitment to compromise—serves as a model for modern constitutional discourse. Conservatives maintain that the rigorous deliberation and consensus-building that produced these amendments should guide contemporary efforts to protect and expand civil liberties. Rather than seeking to reinterpret the Bill of Rights based on shifting political winds, conservatives advocate for a return to the principles that underpinned its creation, ensuring that any evolution in its application occurs through the formal amendment process rather than through judicial activism.[21]

The enduring relevance of the Bill of Rights is also evident in its role as a check on government power. Every time the federal government attempts to extend its reach—whether through new legislation, executive orders, or expansive regulatory programs—the Bill of Rights stands as the ultimate barrier to such overreach. Conservatives argue that the explicit protections provided by these amendments are the definitive limits on governmental power, and that any policy or law

---

[19] Connelley, W. F. (2009). *Restoring the Constitutional Order*. Lexington: University Press of Kentucky.

[20] Jefferson, T., & Madison, J. (Founders Online). "Letter from Thomas Jefferson to James Madison, July 29, 1787." National Archives.

[21] Dickinson, J. (1994). *Colonial Self-Government in America*. Cambridge: Harvard University Press.

that infringes upon these rights is inherently unconstitutional. This perspective is fundamental to the conservative mission of saving America by ensuring that government remains subordinate to the will and rights of the people.[22]

Additionally, the Bill of Rights influences not only legal interpretation but also the broader political culture. Its principles have fostered a tradition of skepticism toward government and a robust commitment to individual freedom. Conservatives view this cultural legacy as essential for maintaining a free society, arguing that the values embedded in the Bill of Rights must continue to guide public policy and political behavior. The enduring impact of these amendments is seen in the persistent demand for accountability and transparency in government—a demand that is central to the conservative vision of a limited and responsible state.[23]

Modern challenges such as cybersecurity, mass surveillance, and the regulation of social media have further underscored the need for a robust Bill of Rights. In an age where digital communication and data collection have become ubiquitous, the protections against unwarranted government intrusion must be rigorously enforced. Conservatives argue that the Fourth Amendment, in particular, must be interpreted in a manner consistent with its original meaning to prevent a slide into authoritarianism. The technology of today may be vastly different from that of the 18th century, but the fundamental right to privacy remains unchanged. Upholding this right, they contend, is critical for ensuring that the government does not exploit modern technology to undermine individual liberty.[24]

In conclusion, the Bill of Rights is a timeless safeguard of individual liberties that continues to play a crucial role in limiting governmental power and preserving the values upon which America was founded. Its historical context, rooted in the revolutionary struggle for freedom, and its modern relevance, as evidenced by ongoing legal and cultural debates, underscore its indispensable role in American constitutionalism. From a politically conservative perspective, strict adherence to the original meaning of the Bill of Rights is essential for ensuring that government remains a servant of the people, not an oppressor of their rights. As modern challenges such as technological advancements, federal overreach, and political polarization test the resilience of American democracy, the Bill of Rights stands as the ultimate defense against any attempt to curtail individual freedom. By returning to the framers' original intent and enforcing these

---

[22] Ferguson, N. (2004). *Colony: A History of Early America*. New York: Penguin Press.

[23] Locke, J. (1689). *Two Treatises of Government*. London: Awnsham Churchill.

[24] Rakove, J. (1997). *Original Meanings: Politics and Ideas in the Making of the Constitution*. New York: Vintage.

constitutional protections through a disciplined, originalist approach, America can safeguard its heritage of liberty and secure a future in which the rights of every citizen are unequivocally protected.[25] Ultimately, the Bill of Rights remains the definitive answer to saving America today, serving as both a historical monument and a living document that anchors the nation's commitment to individual rights and limited government.[26]

---

[25] Adams, S. (1961). *The Revolutionary Writings of Samuel Adams*. Boston: Beacon Press.

[26] Hamilton, A., Madison, J., & Jay, J. (1961). *The Federalist Papers*. New York: New American Library.

2. Freedom of Speech, Religion, and Press

The First Amendment of the United States Constitution enshrines the freedoms of speech, religion, and the press as fundamental rights that have been the bedrock of American democracy since the nation's founding. From a politically conservative perspective, these freedoms are not only crucial for the protection of individual liberty but also serve as a vital check on government power. The framers, influenced by Enlightenment principles and their own experiences with British censorship and religious oppression, designed these protections to ensure that the government remains subordinate to the will of the people. In modern times, debates over the scope of these freedoms are more contentious than ever. This paper provides a comprehensive analysis of the historical context and modern relevance of freedom of speech, religion, and the press, arguing that a strict adherence to these constitutional principles is essential for preserving the limited government and individual rights that are the cornerstone of American society.

Historically, the freedom of speech, religion, and the press emerged as direct responses to the abuses experienced under monarchical rule. In the 18th century, when the founding fathers were drafting the Constitution, many colonists had suffered under the arbitrary censorship of the British government and the oppressive interference of established churches. Influenced by Enlightenment thinkers such as John Locke and Voltaire, the framers believed that individuals must be free to express their ideas and worship according to their conscience. The First Amendment was thus crafted to guarantee that the government could not abridge these rights, ensuring a marketplace of ideas in which truth could emerge from the free competition of opinions.[1] Conservatives view this protection as a permanent bulwark against any attempt by government to control thought or suppress dissent.

The freedom of speech is perhaps the most expansive and vigorously defended of these rights. Conservatives argue that the ability to express dissenting opinions, no matter how controversial, is essential for a functioning democracy. They contend that robust public debate is the lifeblood of political accountability and that suppressing speech, even if intended to promote social harmony, invariably leads to governmental overreach. Historical episodes such as the colonial protests against British censorship and the passionate debates of the Revolutionary era underscore the importance of speech as a tool for self-governance. In modern America, issues ranging from political protests to online expression continue to test the boundaries of free speech. Conservatives maintain that any restrictions on speech—whether imposed by government regulation or through the policies of private institutions—must be scrutinized

[1] Hamilton, A., Madison, J., & Jay, J. (1961). *The Federalist Papers*. New York: New American Library.

rigorously to ensure they do not violate the fundamental principle that speech is the engine of democracy.[2]

Similarly, the freedom of religion is a cornerstone of American liberty. The religious landscape of colonial America was marked by diversity and, at times, intolerance. Many early settlers came to the New World seeking the freedom to worship without interference from a state church. The framers, aware of the religious conflicts that had plagued Europe for centuries, enshrined religious freedom in the First Amendment to ensure that government would neither establish nor inhibit any religion. Conservatives emphasize that this dual protection—both prohibiting an official religion and safeguarding the free exercise thereof—is essential for protecting individual conscience and preventing the state from imposing uniformity in matters of faith. In contemporary debates, issues such as the rights of religious institutions, the protection of conscience in healthcare, and the debate over religious exemptions in business practices highlight the ongoing relevance of these protections. Conservatives argue that a rigid interpretation of the Free Exercise Clause is necessary to ensure that government policies do not encroach upon the deeply held religious convictions of individuals.[3]

The freedom of the press plays a crucial role in ensuring transparency and accountability in government. The framers recognized that a free and independent press is essential for exposing government abuses and informing the public. Conservatives have long championed press freedom as a safeguard against governmental secrecy and as a means of holding public officials accountable. Historically, the press in America served as a powerful vehicle for dissent during the colonial period and the American Revolution, rallying support for independence and challenging the legitimacy of British rule. In modern times, despite technological advancements and the proliferation of digital media, conservatives argue that the core principle remains unchanged: the press must be free to investigate and report on matters of public interest without fear of reprisal. They caution, however, that any attempt to curtail press freedom—whether through censorship or regulatory overreach—poses a serious threat to the democratic process.[4]

The historical context of the First Amendment reveals that its protections were conceived as remedies against the arbitrary power of the state. The Anti-Federalists, who were instrumental in demanding the inclusion of a Bill of Rights, viewed the free exchange of ideas, unfettered

---

[2] Locke, J. (1689). *Two Treatises of Government*. London: Awnsham Churchill.

[3] Montesquieu, C. (1748). *The Spirit of the Laws*. Paris: Barrillot & Fils.

[4] Pocock, J. G. A. (1975). *The Machiavellian Moment: Florentine Political Thought and the Atlantic Republican Tradition*. Princeton: Princeton University Press.

religious expression, and an independent press as indispensable for preventing tyranny. This historical legacy informs the modern conservative perspective, which holds that the fundamental freedoms enshrined in the First Amendment are immutable and must be defended vigorously against any encroachment. Conservatives assert that these rights are not subject to the evolving preferences of society; rather, they are fixed principles that serve as a check on governmental power.[5]

In the contemporary legal landscape, the Supreme Court's interpretation of the First Amendment remains a battleground between originalist and progressive approaches. Conservative jurists advocate for an originalist methodology, arguing that the Constitution should be interpreted in light of the framers' intent. They contend that this approach ensures that the government cannot expand its power to regulate speech, religion, or the press beyond the limits explicitly set by the text. For instance, in cases involving campaign finance, hate speech, or religious exemptions, conservative judges have often stressed the importance of adhering to the original meaning of the First Amendment, rather than allowing modern values to redefine its scope.[6] This judicial restraint is seen as essential for maintaining the balance of power and ensuring that fundamental rights remain protected against legislative and executive encroachments.

Economic considerations also underscore the importance of these freedoms. Conservatives argue that freedom of speech, religion, and the press are critical for fostering an environment of innovation and entrepreneurship. The free flow of ideas stimulates economic activity by allowing individuals and businesses to communicate, collaborate, and challenge established norms. Moreover, religious freedom has been linked to a vibrant civil society, where diverse beliefs coexist and contribute to a dynamic social fabric. The press, as an instrument of accountability, ensures that both the public and private sectors operate transparently. Any erosion of these freedoms, conservatives warn, can have a deleterious effect on economic growth and individual prosperity.[7]

Modern challenges to the First Amendment are manifold. In the realm of speech, the rise of digital media has transformed the landscape of public discourse. While the internet has democratized communication, it has also given rise to issues such as online harassment, misinformation, and the polarization of public opinion. Conservatives maintain that, despite these challenges, the core protection of free speech must remain inviolable. They argue that attempts to regulate online

---

[5] Rakove, J. (1997). *Original Meanings: Politics and Ideas in the Making of the Constitution*. New York: Vintage.

[6] Adams, S. (1961). *The Revolutionary Writings of Samuel Adams*. Boston: Beacon Press.

[7] Bork, R. (1990). *The Tempting of America: The Political Seduction of the Law*. New York: Free Press.

content, even with the intention of curbing hate speech or misinformation, risk stifling legitimate expression and undermining the marketplace of ideas.[8]

Similarly, the freedom of religion faces modern challenges from governmental policies that may compel individuals or organizations to act contrary to their religious beliefs. Debates over issues such as contraceptive coverage, same-sex marriage, and religious exemptions in public accommodations continue to test the boundaries of the Free Exercise Clause. Conservatives argue that any government action that forces individuals to compromise their religious convictions is a violation of the original intent of the First Amendment. They insist that the protection of religious freedom must be absolute, ensuring that individuals are free to worship—and to refuse to participate in activities that conflict with their beliefs—without fear of government retribution.[9]

The freedom of the press is similarly under threat from both state and non-state actors. In an era of increased governmental surveillance and regulation of digital platforms, the press must navigate a complex environment in which its ability to inform the public is sometimes compromised. Conservatives warn that any government measure that limits the investigative function of the press or censors its reporting poses a direct challenge to the democratic accountability of government. They argue that a free press is indispensable for exposing corruption, ensuring transparency, and upholding the principle that government is accountable to the people.[10]

The conservative defense of the First Amendment is deeply intertwined with a broader commitment to the rule of law and limited government. The original framers believed that the protection of individual liberties was paramount and that any government that infringed on these rights was illegitimate. This philosophical stance is echoed by conservative thinkers who argue that the principles underlying the First Amendment are universal and immutable. They contend that free speech, religious liberty, and a free press are essential for a society that values personal freedom and self-governance.[11]

Moreover, the historical evolution of the Bill of Rights, particularly the First Amendment, has been marked by judicial decisions that reinforce its original meaning. Landmark cases have consistently affirmed that these freedoms are not absolute in a vacuum but must be understood

---

[8] Jefferson, T. (Founders Online). "Notes on the State of Virginia." National Archives.

[9] Dickinson, J. (1994). *Colonial Self-Government in America.* Cambridge: Harvard University Press.

[10] Calhoun, J. C. (1983). "Separation of Powers and the Structure of the Constitution." In *Foundations of American Government* (pp. 29–32). New York: Harper & Row.

[11] Jefferson, T. (Founders Online). "Notes on the State of Virginia." National Archives.

within the context of a constitutional system designed to limit governmental power. Conservative legal scholars argue that these judicial interpretations are a testament to the enduring wisdom of the framers and should guide modern courts in resisting expansive interpretations that could lead to government overreach.[12]

The cultural resonance of the First Amendment cannot be overstated. It is a symbol of the American commitment to freedom and a rallying cry for those who oppose censorship and governmental intrusion. Conservatives emphasize that the enduring popularity of these freedoms among the American public is evidence of their timeless value. The very identity of the United States as a nation dedicated to liberty is inextricably linked to the robust protection of speech, religion, and the press.[13]

In addition, the modern political environment, characterized by increasing polarization and ideological conflict, makes the protection of these freedoms even more critical. When political debate becomes overly heated or when dissenting voices are silenced, the very essence of democracy is undermined. Conservatives argue that a steadfast commitment to the First Amendment provides a vital counterbalance to such trends, ensuring that all perspectives, even those that challenge prevailing orthodoxies, have the opportunity to be heard.[14]

Economic freedom also relies on these fundamental rights. A society that protects the free exchange of ideas, the ability to challenge authority, and the right to worship according to one's beliefs is more likely to foster an environment of innovation and entrepreneurship. Conservatives contend that government intervention in these areas—whether through restrictive laws or overzealous regulation—can stifle creativity and impede economic progress. The First Amendment, therefore, is not only a moral and political safeguard but also a critical component of a dynamic and prosperous economy.[15]

The challenges posed by digital media, global terrorism, and evolving social norms require that the First Amendment be interpreted with both historical fidelity and modern prudence. Conservatives maintain that while the methods of communication have changed dramatically since the 18th century, the underlying principles of free expression and religious liberty remain unchanged. They argue that technological advancements should be regulated in a manner that

---

[12] Amar, A. R. (2005). *America's Constitution: A Biography*. New York: Random House.

[13] Henry, P. (1775). *Speech on Colonial Rights*. Richmond: Virginia Historical Society.

[14] Kirk, R. (1953). *The Conservative Mind*. New York: Free Press.

[15] Levinson, S. (2006). *Our Undemocratic Constitution: Where the Constitution Goes Wrong (and How We the People Can Correct It)*. New Haven: Yale University Press.

protects constitutional rights without granting the government carte blanche to curtail dissent or impose uniform standards on diverse communities.[16]

Furthermore, the conservative commitment to the First Amendment extends to protecting press freedom in an era of "fake news" and partisan media. Conservatives assert that a truly free press is indispensable for exposing governmental abuses and ensuring transparency. They caution that any efforts to curtail press freedom—whether by government action or through the coercive influence of powerful interest groups—threaten to undermine the accountability mechanisms that are vital for a functioning democracy. Maintaining a robust, independent press is seen as essential for preserving the constitutional balance and preventing the erosion of public trust in government.[17]

The interplay between legal interpretations and cultural values is also evident in the ongoing debates over freedom of speech on college campuses and in public forums. Conservatives argue that the original intent of the First Amendment was to ensure that individuals could speak freely, even if their views were unpopular or controversial. They maintain that the suppression of speech—whether by government mandate or through private censorship—constitutes a grave threat to democratic discourse and the protection of minority opinions. By defending the free exchange of ideas in all its forms, conservatives seek to uphold a tradition that has been central to American identity since the Revolutionary era.[18]

In addition, the defense of religious freedom under the First Amendment remains a cornerstone of conservative ideology. The right to practice one's religion without government interference is seen as essential for protecting individual autonomy and ensuring that the state does not impose uniform moral standards on a diverse populace. Conservatives argue that any erosion of religious liberty, whether through government mandates or through indirect coercion, represents a direct violation of the founding principles. Upholding the free exercise of religion is thus viewed as integral to preserving the moral and spiritual dimensions of American society.[19]

Moreover, the legal framework established by the Bill of Rights has provided a foundation for numerous landmark Supreme Court decisions that continue to influence modern jurisprudence. Cases addressing issues such as freedom of speech in the context of political protests, the regulation of religious institutions, and the protection of press freedom during wartime all draw

---

[16] Hayek, F. A. (1960). *The Constitution of Liberty*. Chicago: University of Chicago Press.

[17] Aldrich, J. H. (1983). *Constitutional Theory*. Chicago: University of Chicago Press.

[18] Ackerman, B. (1991). *We the People: Foundations*. Cambridge, MA: Harvard University Press.

[19] Connelley, W. F. (2009). *Restoring the Constitutional Order*. Lexington: University Press of Kentucky.

on the original meaning of the First Amendment. Conservatives argue that these decisions validate the enduring relevance of the Bill of Rights and underscore the necessity of interpreting it in a manner consistent with the framers' intent.[20]

The conservative defense of the First Amendment also includes a critique of modern attempts to reinterpret its protections in ways that accommodate shifting political or cultural trends. Critics of progressive judicial activism contend that such reinterpretations risk diluting the clear and unambiguous guarantees of free speech, religious liberty, and a free press. Conservatives insist that the Constitution's protections are not flexible mandates that should expand with changing social mores, but fixed principles that provide a stable foundation for individual freedom. Any deviation from the original public meaning, they argue, undermines the rule of law and threatens the very essence of American liberty.[21]

Furthermore, the role of the courts in upholding the First Amendment is central to maintaining the balance between government power and individual rights. Conservative legal scholars assert that judges must exercise judicial restraint and adhere strictly to the original meaning of the Constitution when deciding cases involving free speech, religion, and the press. This originalist approach ensures that the judiciary does not overstep its bounds and that any challenges to these fundamental rights are resolved based on the framers' clear intent. Such restraint is seen as crucial for preserving the system of checks and balances that has long protected American liberty.[22]

The economic implications of protecting these civil liberties are also significant. A society that robustly defends freedom of speech, religion, and the press fosters an environment where innovation and entrepreneurship can flourish. Conservatives argue that these freedoms are not only moral imperatives but also drivers of economic progress. When individuals are free to express their ideas and engage in open debate, they create a vibrant marketplace of ideas that spurs technological advancement and economic growth. Conversely, restrictions on these freedoms can stifle creativity and lead to a less dynamic economy.[23]

Internationally, the American model of protecting civil liberties through the First Amendment stands as a benchmark for democratic governance. Nations that have embraced similar protections tend to exhibit higher levels of political stability and respect for individual rights. Conservatives

---

[20] Jefferson, T., & Madison, J. (Founders Online). "Letter from Thomas Jefferson to James Madison, July 29, 1787." National Archives.

[21] Dickinson, J. (1994). *Colonial Self-Government in America.* Cambridge: Harvard University Press.

[22] Ferguson, N. (2004). *Colony: A History of Early America.* New York: Penguin Press.

[23] Locke, J. (1689). *Two Treatises of Government.* London: Awnsham Churchill.

point to the success of the United States in maintaining a free society despite global challenges as evidence that the original constitutional guarantees are both enduring and effective. They argue that any attempts to weaken these protections in the name of modernization or security are misguided and ultimately harmful to the democratic fabric of the nation.[24]

Moreover, the cultural legacy of the First Amendment remains a powerful force in American society. The values of free expression, religious diversity, and an independent press are deeply ingrained in the national identity. These values have been celebrated in public discourse, art, and political debate, reinforcing the notion that government must remain subordinate to the people. Conservatives view this cultural heritage as indispensable; it serves as a constant reminder that the freedoms guaranteed by the Bill of Rights are not negotiable, but are essential to the preservation of American liberty.[25]

In conclusion, the historical context and modern relevance of the First Amendment's protections for freedom of speech, religion, and the press are fundamental to the conservative vision of limited government and individual liberty. The Bill of Rights, forged in the crucible of revolutionary struggle, remains the definitive safeguard against governmental overreach. Modern challenges—from digital surveillance to political polarization—demand that these freedoms be interpreted and enforced in a manner that is faithful to the original intent of the framers. Conservatives argue that any deviation from this original meaning risks eroding the constitutional foundations that have long protected American liberty. By steadfastly defending the First Amendment through a disciplined, originalist approach, America can continue to serve as a beacon of freedom and a model for democratic self-governance. In safeguarding these fundamental rights, the nation not only honors its historical legacy but also ensures that government remains a servant of the people, rather than a master over them.[26]

---

[24] Rakove, J. (1997). *Original Meanings: Politics and Ideas in the Making of the Constitution*. New York: Vintage.

[25] Adams, S. (1961). *The Revolutionary Writings of Samuel Adams*. Boston: Beacon Press.

[26] Hamilton, A., Madison, J., & Jay, J. (1961). *The Federalist Papers*. New York: New American Library.

3. Rights to Privacy and Due Process

The rights to privacy and due process constitute essential pillars of American civil liberties, providing a dual guarantee that protects individuals from arbitrary governmental intrusions and ensures fairness in legal proceedings. From a politically conservative perspective, these rights are not only foundational to the limited government envisioned by the founding fathers but also serve as critical safeguards against the expansion of state power. The framers of the Constitution, informed by Enlightenment principles and their own experiences with oppressive governance, embedded these protections within the constitutional framework to secure individual autonomy and to maintain a system of justice that respects both personal dignity and the rule of law. This commentary examines the historical evolution and modern relevance of privacy and due process rights, arguing that strict adherence to the original meaning of these constitutional guarantees is imperative for preserving American freedom in the face of contemporary challenges.

Historically, the right to privacy, though not explicitly mentioned in the Constitution, has been inferred from several amendments—most notably the First, Fourth, and Ninth Amendments. Early American political thought, deeply influenced by the philosophies of John Locke and Montesquieu, held that individuals possess inherent rights that the state must protect. Locke's assertion that government exists to secure life, liberty, and property implicitly supports the notion that personal privacy is an extension of these fundamental rights. Conservatives argue that any expansion of governmental power that infringes upon an individual's private sphere is antithetical to the natural rights philosophy upon which the nation was founded.[1] This conservative viewpoint insists that privacy is a core component of individual liberty—a right that should remain inviolable, regardless of evolving societal norms or technological advancements.

The framers' experiences under British colonial rule provided a vivid illustration of the dangers inherent in unchecked state power. The oppressive measures imposed by the Crown, including invasive searches and arbitrary surveillance, left an indelible mark on American political consciousness. As a reaction to these abuses, the founding generation championed the idea that government must be limited in its ability to intrude into the lives of its citizens. Although the Constitution does not explicitly mention "privacy," the Fourth Amendment's protection against unreasonable searches and seizures is widely understood to be its cornerstone. Conservatives assert that this amendment was designed to create a legal barrier against the state's potential overreach, ensuring that personal privacy is preserved as a fundamental safeguard of liberty.[2]

---

[1] Hamilton, A., Madison, J., & Jay, J. (1961). *The Federalist Papers*. New York: New American Library.

[2] Locke, J. (1689). *Two Treatises of Government*. London: Awnsham Churchill.

Due process, enshrined in the Fifth and Fourteenth Amendments, guarantees that individuals receive fair treatment under the law. This protection extends to both procedural and substantive aspects of legal proceedings, ensuring that no person is deprived of life, liberty, or property without due process of law. For conservatives, due process is a critical check on the arbitrary exercise of governmental power. It requires that legal proceedings be conducted in a transparent and impartial manner, with clear standards and the opportunity for a defense. The framers, who had witnessed the capricious use of power by sovereign authorities, embedded this principle in the Constitution as a means of protecting individual rights and upholding the rule of law.[3] Conservatives maintain that due process must be interpreted in a way that respects the original intent of the founders and that any expansion of state power in this domain poses a direct threat to civil liberties.

In modern society, the rapid pace of technological change and the increasing complexity of government regulation have posed significant challenges to both privacy and due process rights. The advent of digital technology has revolutionized communication, commerce, and government surveillance, creating new avenues for potential intrusion into the private lives of citizens. Conservative critics argue that modern legislation and executive actions often blur the lines between legitimate security measures and infringements on personal privacy. For example, mass data collection programs and digital surveillance initiatives, while justified by proponents as necessary for national security, have raised serious concerns among conservatives that such practices violate the constitutional guarantee of privacy.[4] They contend that these modern challenges must be met with a strict, originalist interpretation of the Fourth Amendment, ensuring that any governmental intrusion into personal privacy is subject to rigorous judicial scrutiny and that only minimal, constitutionally justified exceptions are allowed.

Similarly, in the realm of due process, modern judicial and legislative practices have sometimes expanded the scope of governmental authority beyond what the framers envisioned. Conservatives point to examples where procedural safeguards have been weakened in the name of efficiency or security, thereby undermining the fairness and predictability of legal proceedings. They argue that due process is a timeless principle that must be preserved in its original form to protect individuals from arbitrary and unjust state action. The conservative approach insists that any

---

[3] Montesquieu, C. (1748). *The Spirit of the Laws*. Paris: Barrillot & Fils.

[4] Pocock, J. G. A. (1975). *The Machiavellian Moment: Florentine Political Thought and the Atlantic Republican Tradition*. Princeton: Princeton University Press.

departure from the original meaning of due process rights opens the door to abuses that could erode the foundations of the American legal system.[5]

A critical aspect of the conservative argument is that both privacy and due process are interrelated and mutually reinforcing. Privacy rights protect individuals from unwarranted governmental intrusion into their personal lives, while due process rights ensure that any such intrusion is subject to fair and transparent legal procedures. Together, these rights form a bulwark against the concentration of state power. Conservatives argue that weakening one invariably undermines the other; for instance, if due process protections are diluted, the state may more easily justify invasive surveillance and arbitrary searches, thereby eroding personal privacy. Thus, the conservative commitment to a strict, originalist interpretation of these rights is essential for maintaining the overall balance of power envisioned by the founding fathers.[6]

The modern relevance of privacy and due process rights is underscored by a number of recent legal and political controversies. For example, the debate over government surveillance programs in the wake of national security threats has brought issues of digital privacy to the forefront. Conservatives argue that any surveillance program must be narrowly tailored and subject to judicial review, ensuring that it does not violate the Fourth Amendment's protections. They maintain that the original understanding of privacy, as a shield against arbitrary governmental intrusion, remains the appropriate standard in the digital age.[7]

Similarly, due process concerns have been raised in the context of immigration policies, criminal justice reforms, and administrative procedures. Conservatives point out that when government agencies act without sufficient procedural safeguards, individuals may be deprived of their rights without adequate recourse. The principle of due process, as originally intended by the framers, requires that any deprivation of life, liberty, or property be carried out in a manner that is fair, transparent, and subject to independent review. Conservatives argue that modern trends toward executive overreach and expedited administrative processes threaten this fundamental right, and they call for a return to the strict, originalist standards that ensure due process is rigorously upheld.[8]

---

[5] Rakove, J. (1997). *Original Meanings: Politics and Ideas in the Making of the Constitution*. New York: Vintage.

[6] Adams, S. (1961). *The Revolutionary Writings of Samuel Adams*. Boston: Beacon Press.t

[7] Bork, R. (1990). *The Tempting of America: The Political Seduction of the Law*. New York: Free Press.

[8] Jefferson, T. (Founders Online). "Notes on the State of Virginia." National Archives.

The cultural and philosophical dimensions of these rights further bolster the conservative case. The founding fathers, steeped in Enlightenment thought, believed that individual rights are inherent and inalienable, serving as the foundation of a free society. This philosophical heritage informs the conservative insistence that privacy and due process are not negotiable. Any erosion of these rights, whether through technological overreach or judicial reinterpretation, is seen as a betrayal of the principles that secured American independence. Conservatives argue that the moral and intellectual legacy of the founding era demands that these rights remain sacrosanct, serving as an enduring check on governmental power.[9]

Moreover, the conservative perspective emphasizes that the judiciary must play a vigilant role in enforcing these rights. Originalist judges are called upon to interpret the Constitution as it was understood by the framers, ensuring that modern legislative and executive actions do not encroach upon the fundamental protections of privacy and due process. Landmark Supreme Court decisions, such as those addressing illegal searches and coerced confessions, demonstrate the importance of judicial oversight in preserving these rights. Conservatives contend that only through a disciplined, originalist approach can the courts fulfill their duty to act as the ultimate guardians of the Constitution, protecting individuals from the encroachment of state power.[10]

Economic freedom, too, is inextricably linked to the protection of privacy and due process. A predictable legal environment, in which individuals are assured of fair treatment and the inviolability of their private affairs, fosters confidence in the market. Conservatives argue that when the government respects the constitutional limits on its power, it creates a stable backdrop for economic activity. Conversely, pervasive surveillance or arbitrary legal processes can stifle innovation, discourage investment, and undermine the entrepreneurial spirit that is central to American economic success.[11]

International comparisons further highlight the significance of robust privacy and due process protections. Many democracies that have embraced expansive state powers have, in turn, seen corresponding declines in individual liberties and judicial independence. Conservatives point to examples where the erosion of due process or privacy rights has led to social unrest and a loss of public trust in government institutions. In contrast, countries with a steadfast commitment to these rights tend to exhibit higher levels of political stability and economic freedom. This comparative

---

[9] Dickinson, J. (1994). *Colonial Self-Government in America*. Cambridge: Harvard University Press.

[10] Calhoun, J. C. (1983). "Separation of Powers and the Structure of the Constitution." In *Foundations of American Government* (pp. 29–32). New York: Harper & Row.

[11] Jefferson, T. (Founders Online). "Notes on the State of Virginia." National Archives.

evidence reinforces the conservative argument that the original constitutional safeguards remain the best defense against the threats posed by modern governance.[12]

The interplay between privacy and due process also serves as a powerful counterweight to the increasing calls for government transparency and accountability. While transparency is undoubtedly vital for a functioning democracy, conservatives caution that unfettered access to personal information or the elimination of procedural protections in the name of accountability can lead to unintended consequences. The constitutional balance is designed to protect both the public interest and individual privacy, ensuring that government transparency does not come at the expense of personal liberty. Thus, any reforms aimed at increasing government oversight must be carefully calibrated to preserve the constitutional guarantees of privacy and due process.[13]

Modern legislative efforts to expand federal surveillance, particularly in the context of national security, have raised profound constitutional questions. Conservatives argue that such programs, if not strictly limited and overseen by independent judicial bodies, risk violating the Fourth Amendment's protections. They maintain that technological advancements should not be used as a pretext for expanding state power in ways that erode the individual's right to privacy. Instead, any necessary measures must be implemented in a manner consistent with the framers' original intent, ensuring that they are narrowly tailored and subject to rigorous oversight.[14]

Similarly, the administration of criminal justice presents ongoing challenges to due process rights. Issues such as prolonged pretrial detention, the use of coerced confessions, and inadequate access to legal counsel have prompted calls for reform. Conservatives argue that while reform is necessary, it must not compromise the constitutional standards established by the founding fathers. The right to a fair and impartial legal process is fundamental to the concept of due process, and any modifications to this framework must be undertaken through a formal, democratic process rather than through unilateral judicial reinterpretation.[15]

The cultural resonance of privacy and due process remains strong in American public life. These rights have become symbols of personal autonomy and resistance against state overreach. Conservative political discourse frequently invokes the sanctity of these freedoms as a rallying cry against government intrusion. This cultural attachment not only reinforces legal protections

---

[12] Amar, A. R. (2005). *America's Constitution: A Biography*. New York: Random House.

[13] Henry, P. (1775). *Speech on Colonial Rights*. Richmond: Virginia Historical Society.

[14] Kirk, R. (1953). *The Conservative Mind*. New York: Free Press.

[15] Levinson, S. (2006). *Our Undemocratic Constitution: Where the Constitution Goes Wrong (and How We the People Can Correct It)*. New Haven: Yale University Press.

but also serves as a moral imperative for policymakers and judges alike. For conservatives, protecting privacy and due process is not merely a legal obligation—it is a reaffirmation of the American commitment to individual liberty and self-governance.[16]

Furthermore, the original debates surrounding the adoption of the Bill of Rights underscore the importance of these protections. The fervent discussions at the Constitutional Convention and the subsequent ratification process reveal that the founders were deeply committed to ensuring that individuals would be shielded from the arbitrary exercise of power. This historical context is a powerful argument for adhering to an originalist interpretation of privacy and due process rights. Conservatives assert that the intentions of the Anti-Federalists and the protective measures they demanded remain as relevant today as they were over two centuries ago.[17]

The role of the judiciary in upholding these rights is equally critical. Conservative jurists argue that a disciplined, originalist approach to constitutional interpretation is the only reliable means of preventing governmental overreach in the realms of privacy and due process. When courts interpret these rights based on the framers' original understanding, they provide a stable, predictable framework that limits state power. Conversely, a flexible, "living Constitution" approach risks eroding these fundamental protections by allowing judges to substitute their own policy preferences for those explicitly outlined by the founders.[18]

In the realm of technological innovation, the conservative position is clear: while technology offers tremendous benefits, it must not be allowed to become a tool for unrestrained government surveillance or the erosion of personal privacy. Conservatives advocate for clear, constitutionally grounded limits on how technology is used by the state. Such limits, they argue, are essential for preserving the Fourth Amendment's protection against unreasonable searches and seizures, even in an age of digital information. This position reflects a commitment to the principle that the government's reach must be continually constrained by the rule of law.[19]

Economic considerations also support the conservative defense of privacy and due process. A stable and predictable legal environment, where individual rights are vigorously protected, is crucial for fostering entrepreneurship and innovation. Conservatives contend that when privacy rights are undermined by expansive government surveillance or when due process is compromised by arbitrary legal procedures, economic freedom is likewise jeopardized. The protection of these

---

[16] Hayek, F. A. (1960). *The Constitution of Liberty*. Chicago: University of Chicago Press.

[17] Aldrich, J. H. (1983). *Constitutional Theory*. Chicago: University of Chicago Press.

[18] Ackerman, B. (1991). *We the People: Foundations*. Cambridge, MA: Harvard University Press.

[19] Connelley, W. F. (2009). *Restoring the Constitutional Order*. Lexington: University Press of Kentucky.

rights, therefore, is not only a matter of individual liberty but also a prerequisite for a thriving free-market economy.[20]

Internationally, the American approach to privacy and due process stands as a model for democratic societies. Comparisons with other nations reveal that countries with robust constitutional protections tend to enjoy higher levels of individual freedom and political stability. Conservatives argue that the U.S. model—rooted in the explicit guarantees of the Bill of Rights and enforced through an independent judiciary—provides the most effective framework for protecting civil liberties in a rapidly changing world. This international perspective reinforces the conservative claim that the original constitutional protections are both timeless and indispensable.[21]

Moreover, the enduring relevance of privacy and due process rights is reflected in the ongoing public debates over issues such as government transparency, data protection, and criminal justice reform. Conservatives maintain that these debates must be framed within the context of the original constitutional guarantees. Any attempt to dilute these rights in the name of modern convenience or political expediency is seen as a betrayal of the founding principles that have defined American freedom for over two centuries. The conservative call is for a return to a strict, originalist interpretation of the Constitution that honors the intent of the framers and ensures that the rights to privacy and due process remain inviolate.[22]

Furthermore, the cultural impact of these rights cannot be overstated. The freedoms of speech, religion, and the press have long been celebrated as the hallmarks of American liberty, and privacy and due process are their natural extensions. Conservatives argue that these rights are deeply embedded in the national identity and that any erosion of them would not only compromise legal protections but also weaken the societal commitment to individual freedom. This cultural dimension adds an additional layer of urgency to the conservative defense, as it underscores that the preservation of privacy and due process is essential for maintaining the moral and intellectual foundations of the nation.[23]

Additionally, the legislative arena offers further evidence of the necessity to uphold these constitutional rights. Numerous laws and regulatory proposals have emerged in recent years that, conservatives argue, encroach upon the due process rights of individuals or infringe upon

---

[20] Jefferson, T., & Madison, J. (Founders Online). "Letter from Thomas Jefferson to James Madison, July 29, 1787." National Archives.

[21] Dickinson, J. (1994). *Colonial Self-Government in America.* Cambridge: Harvard University Press.

[22] Ferguson, N. (2004). *Colony: A History of Early America.* New York: Penguin Press.

[23] Locke, J. (1689). *Two Treatises of Government.* London: Awnsham Churchill.

their privacy. Whether through expansive surveillance measures or procedural reforms that limit judicial review, such legislative initiatives are seen as attempts to erode the very checks and balances that protect against governmental overreach. Conservatives maintain that any such measures must be rigorously challenged in the courts and ultimately be reined in through a strict adherence to the original constitutional text.[24]

Finally, the fundamental conservative principle that government exists to serve the people is intrinsically linked to the protection of privacy and due process. The framers designed the Constitution to ensure that every individual is afforded the right to a fair legal process and the freedom to live without undue government intrusion. Conservatives argue that these rights are not negotiable—they are the bedrock upon which American liberty is built. In the face of modern challenges, whether they arise from technological advances, legislative overreach, or shifting cultural norms, the conservative imperative is clear: uphold the original protections of privacy and due process to ensure that government remains limited, accountable, and ultimately subservient to the will of the people.[25]

In conclusion, the rights to privacy and due process are among the most critical components of American civil liberties, serving as a robust check on governmental power and a safeguard for individual freedom. Their historical origins in the revolutionary struggle and Enlightenment thought provide a timeless foundation that continues to be relevant in the modern era. From a politically conservative perspective, any deviation from the original meaning of these rights threatens the constitutional order and endangers the very liberties that the founding fathers fought to secure. Whether through challenges posed by digital surveillance, expansive federal regulations, or shifts in judicial interpretation, the modern landscape demands a steadfast commitment to the original constitutional protections. Only by adhering to these time-honored principles can America ensure that its government remains a servant of the people—a vision that is the ultimate answer to saving America today.[26]

---

[24] Rakove, J. (1997). *Original Meanings: Politics and Ideas in the Making of the Constitution*. New York: Vintage.

[25] Adams, S. (1961). *The Revolutionary Writings of Samuel Adams*. Boston: Beacon Press.

[26] Hamilton, A., Madison, J., & Jay, J. (1961). *The Federalist Papers*. New York: New American Library.

4. Equal Protection Under the Law

The principle of equal protection under the law is a cornerstone of American constitutional governance, ensuring that all individuals, regardless of race, religion, gender, or other status, receive the same legal protections. Rooted in the historical experiences of oppression and the revolutionary commitment to individual rights, this principle has evolved through judicial interpretation and legislative action over the course of American history. From a politically conservative perspective, equal protection is not merely an abstract ideal; it is a vital mechanism for maintaining limited government and preventing arbitrary discrimination. This paper provides a comprehensive analysis of equal protection under the law, exploring its historical context, the evolution of its interpretation, and its modern relevance as a safeguard against government overreach. It argues that a strict, originalist interpretation of the Equal Protection Clause, consistent with the framers' intent and the constitutional framework, is essential for preserving the rule of law and protecting individual liberty.

Historically, the concept of equal protection was embedded in the American constitutional tradition as a reaction to the oppressive practices of the colonial era and European despotism. Although the original Constitution did not include an explicit equal protection clause, the revolutionary experience and Enlightenment ideals set the stage for a later incorporation of this principle in the Fourteenth Amendment. The framers of the Amendment intended to ensure that no state would enact laws that arbitrarily discriminate against any segment of the population. Conservatives argue that the historical context of the Fourteenth Amendment is one of a profound desire to secure the rights of those who had been marginalized and oppressed under British rule, and that its protections were designed to create a uniform standard of justice that remains immutable.[1]

The Equal Protection Clause of the Fourteenth Amendment states that no state shall "deny to any person within its jurisdiction the equal protection of the laws." This language has been interpreted by the courts to prohibit discriminatory practices by state actors and to require that similarly situated individuals be treated alike. From a conservative standpoint, this clause is a safeguard against the potential abuse of state power and a check on majoritarian impulses that might lead to arbitrary classifications. Conservatives maintain that the original meaning of the Equal Protection Clause must guide its application, ensuring that while the law does not require identical treatment in every circumstance, it does prohibit unjustified discrimination that undermines the dignity and rights of the individual.[2]

---

[1] Hamilton, A., Madison, J., & Jay, J. (1961). *The Federalist Papers*. New York: New American Library.

[2] Locke, J. (1689). *Two Treatises of Government*. London: Awnsham Churchill.

One of the critical debates in the modern era concerns the scope of equal protection. Progressive interpretations have often sought to expand the protections of the Equal Protection Clause to cover issues such as gender discrimination and sexual orientation. While conservatives do not deny that discrimination in any form is problematic, they caution against broad, flexible interpretations that depart from the original public meaning of the text. Conservative legal scholars argue that such expansive readings risk politicizing the judiciary and diluting the principle of limited government. Instead, they advocate for an originalist approach that interprets the clause based on the historical context in which it was adopted, thereby ensuring that any recognized classifications have a rational basis and do not lead to the creation of new rights without clear legislative mandate.[3]

The conservative approach to equal protection is intrinsically linked to the broader constitutional framework established by the founding fathers. The founders were deeply influenced by Enlightenment principles, which emphasized that government's legitimacy derives from its protection of natural rights. In this view, equal protection is a natural extension of the principle that every individual is entitled to the same fundamental rights. Conservatives argue that the framers' intent was not to create a system of enforced equality in all respects but to prevent the arbitrary use of power that would allow state actors to favor one group over another without justification. This perspective is rooted in a commitment to individual liberty and limited government, principles that remain central to conservative thought.[4]

Moreover, conservatives maintain that equal protection under the law must be balanced with respect for individual autonomy and freedom of association. They argue that while the state has a duty to ensure that laws do not arbitrarily discriminate, it must also allow individuals the freedom to associate voluntarily and to organize in ways that reflect their distinct identities. This balance is crucial in a diverse society; overzealous enforcement of equality in every sphere may inadvertently stifle cultural expression and personal liberty. Conservatives contend that the original meaning of the Equal Protection Clause provides a framework for addressing discrimination without imposing uniformity on all aspects of social life.[5]

The judiciary has played a central role in shaping the application of the Equal Protection Clause. Landmark Supreme Court decisions, such as Brown v. Board of Education, have transformed the

---

[3] Montesquieu, C. (1748). *The Spirit of the Laws*. Paris: Barrillot & Fils.

[4] Pocock, J. G. A. (1975). *The Machiavellian Moment: Florentine Political Thought and the Atlantic Republican Tradition*. Princeton: Princeton University Press.

[5] Rakove, J. (1997). *Original Meanings: Politics and Ideas in the Making of the Constitution*. New York: Vintage.

legal landscape by striking down racial segregation and other discriminatory practices. However, conservatives often criticize these decisions for what they perceive as judicial overreach—arguing that courts should adhere more strictly to the text and historical context of the Constitution rather than creating new substantive rights. From the conservative viewpoint, while combating discrimination is imperative, it must be achieved through the democratic process rather than through expansive judicial interpretation. This approach emphasizes the importance of legislative action in addressing social inequities, thereby preserving the proper separation of powers and ensuring that changes in the law reflect the will of the people.[6]

Modern challenges to equal protection are multifaceted and complex. In today's society, issues such as affirmative action, voting rights, and the rights of minority groups continue to generate significant debate. Conservatives argue that affirmative action programs, while well-intentioned, can lead to reverse discrimination and undermine the principle of equal treatment by the law. They assert that any policies aimed at promoting equality must be based on a clear and objective rationale rather than on subjective notions of fairness that may shift with political tides. According to conservative theory, equal protection should require that similarly situated individuals be treated alike, without preferential treatment that disrupts the balance of merit and accountability.[7]

Voting rights have also emerged as a contentious area within the equal protection framework. Efforts to expand access to the ballot are widely supported on moral and democratic grounds, yet conservatives caution that changes to voting laws must be carefully scrutinized to ensure they do not inadvertently undermine the integrity of the electoral process. They argue that measures such as voter ID laws, which are often criticized as discriminatory, are in fact legitimate exercises of state power aimed at preventing fraud. From a conservative perspective, the Equal Protection Clause requires that any restrictions on voting rights be applied uniformly and based on clear, rational standards. When such measures are challenged, the courts must balance the need for free and fair elections with the constitutional imperative of treating all citizens equally.[8]

Technological advancements and globalization have introduced new dimensions to the equal protection debate. The rise of digital communication, social media, and mass data collection has raised questions about how the law should protect individuals in an increasingly interconnected world. Conservatives are particularly concerned that government surveillance programs, if left

---

[6] Adams, S. (1961). *The Revolutionary Writings of Samuel Adams*. Boston: Beacon Press.

[7] Bork, R. (1990). *The Tempting of America: The Political Seduction of the Law*. New York: Free Press.

[8] Jefferson, T. (Founders Online). "Notes on the State of Virginia." National Archives.

unchecked, could lead to violations of privacy and unequal treatment under the law. They argue that the principles underlying the Equal Protection Clause must be applied to modern technologies, ensuring that all individuals enjoy the same protections regardless of the medium through which their personal information is transmitted or stored. This requires a careful, originalist approach that interprets constitutional protections in light of contemporary realities without sacrificing the framers' intent.[9]

In the realm of criminal justice, the doctrine of equal protection is crucial for ensuring that all individuals receive fair treatment under the law. Disparities in sentencing, the application of mandatory minimums, and the differential treatment of minority groups have raised concerns about systemic biases within the legal system. Conservatives acknowledge these issues but caution that sweeping judicial remedies risk disrupting the balance of the legal system. They argue that reforms aimed at achieving equal protection should be pursued through legislative processes that reflect the democratic will, rather than through broad judicial reinterpretation that could unsettle established legal principles.[10]

The conservative defense of equal protection also extends to the protection of property rights, a fundamental component of individual liberty. The Constitution's guarantee that no person shall be deprived of life, liberty, or property without due process is closely linked to the principle of equal protection. Conservatives argue that when property rights are violated—whether through eminent domain abuses or arbitrary regulatory actions—it represents a failure of the state to treat all citizens equally. Upholding the equal protection of property rights, therefore, is essential for ensuring economic freedom and incentivizing investment. The original intent of the framers was to protect individuals from the arbitrary exercise of state power, a principle that remains central to conservative legal thought.[11]

Cultural and historical factors play an important role in shaping the modern understanding of equal protection. The legacy of the American Revolution and the subsequent struggle for civil rights have left an indelible mark on the national consciousness. Conservatives argue that while progress has been made, the core principles of equal protection must be preserved to prevent the reemergence of discriminatory practices. They caution against reinterpretations that expand the scope of equal protection to include measures that could inadvertently harm merit-based systems

---

[9] Dickinson, J. (1994). *Colonial Self-Government in America.* Cambridge: Harvard University Press.

[10] Calhoun, J. C. (1983). "Separation of Powers and the Structure of the Constitution." In *Foundations of American Government* (pp. 29–32). New York: Harper & Row.

[11] Jefferson, T. (Founders Online). "Notes on the State of Virginia." National Archives.

or dilute individual accountability. In their view, the original meaning of the Equal Protection Clause provides a stable framework that ensures fairness without imposing artificial equality that may lead to unintended negative consequences.[12]

The role of the judiciary in enforcing equal protection is pivotal in maintaining the constitutional order. Conservative jurists insist on a disciplined, originalist approach when interpreting the Equal Protection Clause, contending that courts should not infuse the text with modern political values. This judicial restraint is intended to preserve the balance of power between the branches of government and to ensure that any changes to the legal landscape occur through the democratic process rather than through judicial fiat. By adhering to the original public meaning of the Constitution, the courts can serve as effective arbiters that protect individual rights without overstepping their bounds.[13]

The interplay between state and federal power is also central to the equal protection debate. The Tenth Amendment reserves powers not delegated to the federal government to the states or the people, reinforcing the idea that states are laboratories of democracy where policies can be tailored to local needs. Conservatives argue that equal protection must be understood within this federal framework, ensuring that state governments are free to design and implement policies without undue federal interference. This respect for state sovereignty is seen as a critical element in preserving the balance of power and ensuring that government remains responsive to the people.[14]

Modern challenges to equal protection under the law continue to evolve as society changes. Issues such as immigration policy, gender discrimination, and the rights of LGBTQ+ individuals present complex questions for constitutional interpretation. Conservatives acknowledge that discrimination in any form is objectionable; however, they caution that expanding the scope of equal protection beyond the framers' original intent can lead to judicial overreach and undermine the principle of limited government. They argue that while legislative action is necessary to address social inequities, it should be done in a manner that respects the original text and historical context of the Constitution, rather than through sweeping judicial mandates that impose contemporary standards.[15]

---

[12] Amar, A. R. (2005). *America's Constitution: A Biography*. New York: Random House.

[13] Henry, P. (1775). *Speech on Colonial Rights*. Richmond: Virginia Historical Society.

[14] Kirk, R. (1953). *The Conservative Mind*. New York: Free Press.

[15] Levinson, S. (2006). *Our Undemocratic Constitution: Where the Constitution Goes Wrong (and How We the People Can Correct It)*. New Haven: Yale University Press.

Privacy concerns, in particular, have become increasingly prominent in discussions of equal protection. With the advent of digital technologies and the growth of government surveillance, questions about the extent to which individuals are protected from arbitrary state intrusion have taken on new urgency. Conservatives maintain that the original protections inferred from the Fourth Amendment must be rigorously enforced to prevent abuses of power. They argue that ensuring equal protection in the digital age requires a careful balance between security and privacy—a balance that can only be achieved by adhering to the framers' original vision.[16]

Economic considerations also intersect with the principle of equal protection. A stable legal environment that treats all citizens equally is essential for fostering a competitive, free-market economy. Conservatives argue that when the state arbitrarily discriminates—whether through taxation, regulation, or property rights infringements—it creates uncertainty and undermines economic freedom. The Equal Protection Clause, therefore, serves as a critical check on governmental power, ensuring that economic policies are applied fairly and consistently. This protection is vital for maintaining the incentives for investment and innovation that have driven American prosperity.[17]

Furthermore, the political debate over equal protection is influenced by the broader ideological divide between conservatives and progressives. Conservatives assert that while equality before the law is a fundamental right, it should not be conflated with forced equality of outcome. They argue that the framers' vision was one of equal treatment under a fixed set of rules, rather than the imposition of uniform outcomes that ignore individual differences. This conservative position stresses that equal protection means that the law must be applied consistently and fairly, without resorting to policies that artificially equalize results at the expense of merit and personal responsibility.[18]

The cultural legacy of the Equal Protection Clause has also shaped American public opinion. The struggle for civil rights throughout the 20th century, culminating in landmark decisions such as Brown v. Board of Education, has reinforced the importance of equal protection as a guarantor of fairness and justice. Conservatives, however, caution that while these victories are commendable, they must be understood within the framework of the original constitutional order. They argue that any expansion of equal protection that deviates from the text's original meaning risks undermining the stability of the legal system and the principle of limited government.[19]

---

[16] Hayek, F. A. (1960). *The Constitution of Liberty*. Chicago: University of Chicago Press.

[17] Aldrich, J. H. (1983). *Constitutional Theory*. Chicago: University of Chicago Press.

[18] Ackerman, B. (1991). *We the People: Foundations*. Cambridge, MA: Harvard University Press.

[19] Connelley, W. F. (2009). *Restoring the Constitutional Order*. Lexington: University Press of Kentucky.

In addition, the enforcement of equal protection rights is inextricably linked to the broader principle of due process. The Fifth and Fourteenth Amendments guarantee that no person shall be deprived of life, liberty, or property without due process of law. Conservatives argue that due process and equal protection are mutually reinforcing; a robust system of legal safeguards ensures that all individuals are treated fairly and that governmental power is exercised within clearly defined limits. Any erosion of due process protections invariably weakens the enforcement of equal protection, thereby endangering the fundamental rights of individuals.[20]

The role of the courts in interpreting and enforcing equal protection remains a contentious issue in modern jurisprudence. Conservative judges and scholars advocate for an originalist approach that limits judicial discretion and grounds decisions in the historical context of the Constitution. They argue that a return to the framers' original intent would provide clearer, more objective standards for determining when discriminatory practices are unconstitutional. This judicial restraint, conservatives maintain, is essential for preventing the politicization of the courts and ensuring that equal protection remains a steadfast shield against governmental overreach.[21]

Moreover, the interplay between federal and state authorities continues to influence the application of equal protection. The Tenth Amendment's reservation of powers to the states ensures that local governments play a critical role in upholding individual rights. Conservatives argue that this decentralized approach is vital for maintaining a balance between national uniformity and local diversity. When the federal government imposes blanket policies that override state discretion, it risks violating the principle of equal protection by ignoring the unique circumstances and values of different communities.[22]

International comparisons also provide a useful benchmark for understanding the conservative perspective on equal protection. Many democracies around the world have enshrined similar protections in their constitutional frameworks, yet the American model is distinguished by its emphasis on limited government and judicial restraint. Conservatives assert that the U.S. system, with its written Constitution and rigorous amendment process, offers a level of stability and predictability that is often absent in more flexible systems. This stability, they argue, is essential for safeguarding individual liberties and ensuring that all citizens receive equal treatment under the law.[23]

---

[20] Jefferson, T., & Madison, J. (Founders Online). "Letter from Thomas Jefferson to James Madison, July 29, 1787." National Archives.

[21] Dickinson, J. (1994). *Colonial Self-Government in America.* Cambridge: Harvard University Press.

[22] Ferguson, N. (2004). *Colony: A History of Early America.* New York: Penguin Press.

[23] Locke, J. (1689). *Two Treatises of Government.* London: Awnsham Churchill.

Economic freedom, too, is closely tied to the principle of equal protection. A legal environment in which laws are applied impartially is critical for ensuring that individuals and businesses can operate without fear of arbitrary discrimination. Conservatives contend that when equal protection is upheld as originally intended, it fosters a climate of predictability and fairness that is conducive to economic growth. Conversely, any attempt to broaden the scope of equal protection in ways that distort its original meaning may lead to unintended economic consequences, such as increased regulatory burdens or diminished property rights.[24]

Furthermore, the modern challenges of globalization and technological innovation place additional demands on the constitutional protection of equal rights. In an increasingly interconnected world, the ability of individuals to protect their rights against both domestic and international abuses is paramount. Conservatives argue that the original meaning of the Equal Protection Clause, combined with a rigorous commitment to due process, provides the best defense against such threats. They caution that any dilution of these rights in response to modern pressures risks undermining the very foundations of American freedom.[25]

In conclusion, the principle of equal protection under the law is a foundational element of the American constitutional system, essential for safeguarding individual liberties and limiting governmental power. From a politically conservative perspective, the historical context and modern relevance of the Equal Protection Clause must be understood through the lens of the framers' original intent. This approach ensures that the rights to privacy, due process, and non-discrimination remain steadfast in the face of evolving societal challenges. As modern America grapples with issues ranging from digital surveillance to economic regulation and political polarization, a strict adherence to the original meaning of equal protection is imperative. Such an approach not only preserves the constitutional legacy of the founding fathers but also provides a stable and predictable framework for addressing contemporary challenges. By upholding these fundamental rights through disciplined judicial interpretation and responsible legislative action, America can continue to serve as a beacon of freedom and a model for democratic self-governance—ultimately providing the definitive answer to saving America from the perils of unchecked state power.[26]

---

[24] Rakove, J. (1997). *Original Meanings: Politics and Ideas in the Making of the Constitution*. New York: Vintage.

[25] Adams, S. (1961). *The Revolutionary Writings of Samuel Adams*. Boston: Beacon Press.

[26] Hamilton, A., Madison, J., & Jay, J. (1961). *The Federalist Papers*. New York: New American Library.

5. Contemporary Civil Rights Challenges

The American constitutional tradition, as enshrined in the Bill of Rights and interpreted through decades of jurisprudence, has long served as the primary bulwark protecting individual freedoms against governmental overreach. However, in the modern era, contemporary civil rights challenges have become a focal point of intense debate. From a politically conservative perspective, these challenges often arise not from the inherent failure of constitutional protections but from misinterpretations and politically driven expansions of governmental authority. This paper offers a comprehensive analysis of the contemporary challenges facing civil rights in America, focusing on issues such as free speech restrictions, religious liberty encroachments, due process erosion, and the unintended consequences of expansive regulatory policies. By grounding the discussion in historical context and the framers' original intent, the analysis argues that a return to an originalist approach is essential for preserving the limited government and individual rights that have defined American liberty.

The conservative position on contemporary civil rights challenges is rooted in the belief that the rights enshrined in the Constitution—particularly those protecting freedom of speech, religion, press, privacy, and due process—are immutable and must be enforced as written. Conservatives assert that the framers, deeply influenced by Enlightenment thought and their own experiences under oppressive regimes, intentionally crafted a framework that limits government power. However, modern political and judicial trends have sometimes reinterpreted these rights in ways that expand state authority and diminish individual freedom. For instance, while proponents of expansive civil rights reforms argue for a "living Constitution" that adapts to societal changes, conservatives caution that such flexibility risks undermining the stable, objective standards that have long safeguarded liberty in America.[1]

One of the most pressing contemporary challenges involves restrictions on free speech. The rise of digital media has transformed the landscape of public discourse, enabling unprecedented connectivity but also presenting new avenues for censorship and deplatforming. Conservatives argue that free speech is the lifeblood of a free society—a principle that has historically enabled robust debate and the exposure of government overreach. Yet, in recent years, both governmental actions and private sector policies have sought to limit speech deemed "hate speech" or "misinformation." Conservatives contend that such restrictions are frequently motivated by ideological bias and risk suppressing legitimate dissent. They maintain that any limitations on free expression must be narrowly tailored and strictly justified by clear

[1] Hamilton, A., Madison, J., & Jay, J. (1961). *The Federalist Papers*. New York: New American Library.

constitutional standards, rather than being imposed through broad regulatory or editorial discretion that stifles debate.[2]

Religious liberty is another area where contemporary challenges have emerged. The principle of religious freedom, enshrined in the First Amendment, was a direct response to the historical abuses experienced under state-sanctioned religion in Europe. In modern America, however, debates over issues such as contraception mandates, same-sex marriage, and religious exemptions have intensified. Conservatives argue that government policies which compel individuals or institutions to act against their deeply held religious beliefs are a clear violation of the original intent of the Constitution. They assert that the protection of religious liberty must be interpreted strictly to ensure that individuals retain the right to worship—or not worship—as they choose, without coercion from either the state or powerful private interests.[3]

Privacy and due process rights, although less explicitly stated, are equally critical. The Fourth Amendment's protection against unreasonable searches and seizures, coupled with the due process guarantees of the Fifth and Fourteenth Amendments, forms a dual safeguard for individual autonomy. Contemporary issues such as mass surveillance, data collection by government agencies, and the erosion of procedural fairness in administrative actions challenge these foundational rights. Conservatives argue that modern technologies and policies must be subjected to the same stringent scrutiny as those contemplated by the framers. They maintain that any expansion of state power in the digital domain, for example, should be viewed with deep suspicion, as it may lead to unprecedented intrusions into personal privacy and a weakening of due process protections.[4]

A further dimension of the contemporary civil rights debate concerns the role of the judiciary. In recent decades, the Supreme Court and lower courts have often been at the center of controversies over the scope of civil liberties. Critics from a conservative perspective claim that judicial activism—where judges expand constitutional rights beyond the original meaning of the text—has sometimes produced outcomes that, in their view, threaten the balance of power envisioned by the founding fathers. Conservatives advocate for an originalist approach in which the Constitution is interpreted based on its historical context and the framers' explicit intentions. They argue that

---

[2] Locke, J. (1689). *Two Treatises of Government*. London: Awnsham Churchill.

[3] Montesquieu, C. (1748). *The Spirit of the Laws*. Paris: Barrillot & Fils.

[4] Pocock, J. G. A. (1975). *The Machiavellian Moment: Florentine Political Thought and the Atlantic Republican Tradition*. Princeton: Princeton University Press.

such an approach would rein in what they see as the excesses of a "living Constitution" that adapts too readily to transient political pressures.[5]

Contemporary challenges also arise from legislative and administrative actions that purport to promote equality but, in practice, impose mandates that undermine the principle of individual liberty. For example, affirmative action policies, while aimed at addressing historical inequities, are criticized by conservatives as potentially leading to reverse discrimination. They argue that such policies often prioritize group identity over individual merit, thereby contravening the constitutional promise of equal protection under the law. Conservatives assert that true equality means treating similarly situated individuals alike and that any departure from this standard should be scrutinized rigorously to ensure it does not result in arbitrary preferential treatment.[6]

In addition, the increasing complexity of modern governance—characterized by an ever-expanding administrative state—poses significant challenges to civil rights. Regulatory agencies now wield enormous power to shape public policy, and their actions often affect individuals' freedoms without the traditional checks and balances of a democratic legislative process. Conservatives contend that such concentration of power can lead to situations where the rights guaranteed by the Bill of Rights and other constitutional provisions are overridden by bureaucratic expediency. They argue that restoring accountability and limiting administrative discretion is essential for ensuring that government remains firmly subordinate to the people.[7]

Economic policies also intersect with contemporary civil rights challenges. In an era of globalization and rapid economic change, government intervention in the economy has sometimes led to practices that, conservatives argue, compromise individual liberty and property rights. For example, expansive environmental regulations or broad-based economic stimulus packages may have the unintended consequence of limiting free enterprise and undermining the incentives for personal initiative. Conservatives maintain that the constitutional protection of property and the right to due process are essential for ensuring a thriving economy. They assert that policies must be carefully designed to respect these rights, rather than being justified solely on the basis of broader social objectives.[8]

---

[5] Rakove, J. (1997). *Original Meanings: Politics and Ideas in the Making of the Constitution*. New York: Vintage.

[6] Adams, S. (1961). *The Revolutionary Writings of Samuel Adams*. Boston: Beacon Press.

[7] Bork, R. (1990). *The Tempting of America: The Political Seduction of the Law*. New York: Free Press.

[8] Jefferson, T. (Founders Online). "Notes on the State of Virginia." National Archives.

Political polarization further exacerbates civil rights challenges by distorting the public discourse around constitutional protections. In a highly polarized environment, debates over issues such as free speech, religious liberty, and due process often become polarized battles, with each side accusing the other of undermining fundamental rights. Conservatives argue that this polarization risks transforming constitutional rights from objective legal standards into partisan tools, thereby eroding the rule of law. They advocate for a return to the framers' original intent, which sought to create a stable, impartial framework for protecting individual liberties irrespective of shifting political winds.[9]

The conservative approach to contemporary civil rights challenges is also informed by the principle of limited government. The founding fathers designed the Constitution to restrict the scope of governmental power, ensuring that the state does not become an instrument of coercion. Conservatives assert that many modern challenges to civil liberties arise when government agencies exceed their constitutional bounds. Whether through expansive surveillance programs, intrusive regulatory practices, or judicial reinterpretation of rights, any attempt to expand state power is seen as a direct threat to the individual freedoms the Constitution was designed to protect. Maintaining a rigid adherence to the original text and meaning of constitutional provisions, conservatives argue, is the best way to prevent such overreach.[10]

The judiciary's role in this context is paramount. Conservative jurists contend that the courts must exercise judicial restraint by interpreting the Constitution based on the framers' original intent rather than current political or social trends. This originalist approach is viewed as the only reliable method for preserving civil liberties in the face of modern challenges. For instance, in cases involving digital privacy or freedom of expression, conservative judges have stressed the need to adhere to the original language of the Constitution, thereby ensuring that individual rights are not eroded by contemporary reinterpretations that favor state expansion.[11]

Furthermore, the legislative process plays a crucial role in addressing civil rights challenges. Conservatives argue that any significant changes to civil liberties should occur through the democratic amendment process rather than through judicial or administrative fiat. The difficulty of amending the Constitution is not seen as a flaw but as a deliberate safeguard against rapid, ideologically driven changes that could destabilize the constitutional order. By requiring broad

---

[9] Dickinson, J. (1994). *Colonial Self-Government in America.* Cambridge: Harvard University Press.

[10] Calhoun, J. C. (1983). "Separation of Powers and the Structure of the Constitution." In *Foundations of American Government* (pp. 29–32). New York: Harper & Row.

[11] Jefferson, T. (Founders Online). "Notes on the State of Virginia." National Archives.

consensus for amendments, the framers ensured that any evolution in civil rights protections would be carefully considered and democratically sanctioned.[12]

Cultural factors also contribute to contemporary challenges. The deep-rooted American belief in individualism and personal freedom has historically been a counterbalance to state power. However, modern societal trends sometimes favor collective solutions that risk undermining individual autonomy. Conservatives argue that while addressing social inequities is important, it must not come at the cost of sacrificing the individual rights that form the foundation of American liberty. The original meaning of the Equal Protection Clause and the due process guarantees, for example, should not be expanded in ways that impose uniform outcomes or infringe on personal responsibility.[13]

International comparisons further bolster the conservative case. Many democratic nations with flexible constitutional interpretations have experienced periods of instability and a gradual erosion of individual rights. In contrast, the American model—with its fixed, codified protections—has proven remarkably resilient in preserving liberty and economic freedom. Conservatives assert that the success of the United States in maintaining a robust system of civil liberties is a testament to the strength of the original constitutional design and a warning against the dangers of overly adaptive interpretations.[14]

Technological advancements present new and unique challenges to civil rights. The proliferation of digital communication and data collection has raised critical questions about privacy and due process. Government surveillance programs, while argued by some to be necessary for national security, have been fiercely criticized by conservatives as potential violations of Fourth Amendment rights. Similarly, algorithms used by private companies can inadvertently lead to discriminatory practices that conflict with the principles of equal protection. Conservatives maintain that any response to these technological challenges must be firmly grounded in the Constitution's original protections, ensuring that new methods do not become a pretext for eroding established rights.[15]

The modern political landscape, marked by increasing polarization and ideological conflict, further complicates the protection of civil rights. In an environment where partisan interests often drive legal and regulatory decisions, there is a risk that constitutional protections will be

---

[12] Amar, A. R. (2005). *America's Constitution: A Biography*. New York: Random House.

[13] Henry, P. (1775). *Speech on Colonial Rights*. Richmond: Virginia Historical Society.

[14] Kirk, R. (1953). *The Conservative Mind*. New York: Free Press.

[15] Levinson, S. (2006). *Our Undemocratic Constitution: Where the Constitution Goes Wrong (and How We the People Can Correct It)*. New Haven: Yale University Press.

subordinated to political expediency. Conservatives argue that the originalist approach offers a bulwark against such trends by providing a stable, objective standard that is independent of fluctuating political ideologies. By anchoring civil rights in the text and historical context of the Constitution, the judiciary and legislature can resist the pressures to expand governmental power in ways that compromise individual liberty.[16]

Economic pressures also intersect with civil rights challenges. In an era of globalization, the need for economic competitiveness has sometimes led to policies that, from a conservative standpoint, undermine civil liberties. For instance, expansive regulatory frameworks intended to protect public welfare can inadvertently curtail personal freedom and property rights. Conservatives argue that a careful, originalist interpretation of the Constitution is necessary to strike a balance between economic progress and the protection of individual rights, ensuring that government intervention does not extend beyond its constitutionally mandated limits.[17]

Moreover, the conservative view stresses that modern civil rights challenges must be addressed through the democratic process. While judicial intervention plays a crucial role in safeguarding rights, conservatives contend that significant policy shifts should result from robust public debate and legislative action rather than through unilateral judicial reinterpretation. This democratic process, which is enshrined in the Constitution's amendment procedures, ensures that changes in civil rights protections reflect the will of the people rather than the subjective preferences of unelected judges.[18]

The cultural legacy of the founding era continues to influence contemporary understandings of civil rights. The principles of free speech, religious liberty, and personal privacy are deeply embedded in American political culture. Conservatives argue that these values have sustained the nation through centuries of social and political change and must be defended against modern attempts to dilute their meaning. In this view, the original language of the Constitution provides a clear and enduring standard that is as relevant today as it was at the nation's founding.[19]

In addition, the interplay between federal and state governments plays a significant role in addressing modern civil rights challenges. The Tenth Amendment guarantees that powers not delegated to the federal government are reserved to the states or the people. Conservatives assert that state governments, by virtue of their proximity to the citizenry, are better suited to

---

[16] Hayek, F. A. (1960). *The Constitution of Liberty*. Chicago: University of Chicago Press.

[17] Aldrich, J. H. (1983). *Constitutional Theory*. Chicago: University of Chicago Press.

[18] Ackerman, B. (1991). *We the People: Foundations*. Cambridge, MA: Harvard University Press.

[19] Connelley, W. F. (2009). *Restoring the Constitutional Order*. Lexington: University Press of Kentucky.

protect civil liberties and to tailor policies to local needs. However, recent trends toward federal preemption in areas such as education, healthcare, and law enforcement have sparked debates over the erosion of state sovereignty. Conservatives argue that preserving state autonomy is essential for maintaining the balance of power and ensuring that civil rights are upheld in a manner that reflects the diverse values of the American populace.[20]

The judiciary's role in enforcing civil rights is also central to modern challenges. Conservative legal scholars insist that courts must exercise judicial restraint and interpret civil liberties in a manner that is faithful to the original meaning of the Constitution. Landmark decisions regarding the rights to privacy and due process have often been the subject of contentious debate, with critics accusing the Court of both excessive activism and undue deference to modern social norms. Conservatives argue that a strict originalist methodology provides the necessary checks on judicial discretion, ensuring that the protections afforded by the Bill of Rights are not expanded beyond what the framers intended.[21]

Furthermore, international perspectives provide valuable insights into the effectiveness of constitutional protections. Comparative studies reveal that nations with rigid, codified constitutional guarantees tend to enjoy greater political stability and higher levels of individual freedom. Conservatives assert that the American model, with its enduring commitment to originalism and limited government, is uniquely capable of protecting civil liberties in a rapidly changing world. This international evidence supports the conservative view that deviating from the original constitutional framework risks undermining the rule of law and compromising individual rights.[22]

Modern civil rights challenges also extend to the digital realm, where issues of data privacy and online expression have become increasingly prominent. As governments and corporations collect vast amounts of personal data, concerns arise over the potential for surveillance and misuse. Conservatives argue that the Fourth Amendment's protection against unreasonable searches and seizures must be vigorously applied in the digital context, ensuring that technology does not become a means for unchecked governmental intrusion. By adhering to the original principles that safeguard privacy, the judiciary can help to prevent a slide into authoritarian surveillance practices.[23]

---

[20] Jefferson, T., & Madison, J. (Founders Online). "Letter from Thomas Jefferson to James Madison, July 29, 1787." National Archives.

[21] Dickinson, J. (1994). *Colonial Self-Government in America*. Cambridge: Harvard University Press.

[22] Ferguson, N. (2004). *Colony: A History of Early America*. New York: Penguin Press.

[23] Locke, J. (1689). *Two Treatises of Government*. London: Awnsham Churchill.

Additionally, the political and cultural climate today—characterized by intense partisan divisions and a rapidly evolving media landscape—poses unique challenges to the preservation of civil liberties. Conservatives contend that, in this environment, it is more important than ever to rely on the fixed, objective standards provided by the Constitution. When political debates become mired in ideological disputes, the clear protections of the Bill of Rights serve as an anchor that prevents the erosion of individual freedoms. A return to an originalist interpretation, conservatives argue, would provide a stable foundation for resolving contemporary controversies and ensuring that government actions remain within constitutional limits.[24]

Economic factors also continue to influence the landscape of civil rights. In an era of intense global competition, economic freedom and civil liberties are closely intertwined. Conservatives maintain that the protection of property rights and the assurance of due process are essential for fostering a dynamic, entrepreneurial economy. When government policies infringe on these rights, they not only undermine individual liberty but also create an environment of uncertainty that can stifle economic growth. Therefore, safeguarding civil rights is a prerequisite for preserving the economic prosperity that has long been a hallmark of the American experiment.[25]

In conclusion, contemporary civil rights challenges in the United States—ranging from issues of free speech and religious liberty to concerns over privacy, due process, and state sovereignty—demand a robust defense of the original constitutional protections. From a politically conservative perspective, the enduring strength of American liberty hinges on a strict adherence to the framers' intent, ensuring that the government remains limited and accountable. Modern threats, whether arising from digital technology, expansive federal regulation, or partisan polarization, must be met with a disciplined, originalist approach that preserves the clear, immutable standards of the Constitution. By upholding these foundational rights through vigilant judicial review, responsible legislative action, and a recommitment to the values of individual liberty and limited government, America can continue to serve as a beacon of freedom and a model for democratic self-governance. This steadfast commitment to civil liberties is, in the conservative view, the ultimate answer to saving America from the perils of unchecked state power and ensuring that the rights of every citizen are preserved for generations to come.[26]

---

[24] Rakove, J. (1997). *Original Meanings: Politics and Ideas in the Making of the Constitution*. New York: Vintage.

[25] Adams, S. (1961). *The Revolutionary Writings of Samuel Adams*. Boston: Beacon Press.

[26] Hamilton, A., Madison, J., & Jay, J. (1961). *The Federalist Papers*. New York: New American Library.

CHAPTER 6:

Economic and Regulatory Implications of Constitutional Law

1. Constitutional Foundations of Economic Policy

The United States Constitution, as the supreme law of the land, not only delineates the structure and function of government but also provides a robust framework for economic policy. The framers, drawing on Enlightenment philosophy and their own practical experiences, designed a constitutional order that limits government power, protects individual property rights, and fosters economic freedom. From a politically conservative perspective, these constitutional foundations are the bedrock upon which a prosperous and free society is built. This paper provides a detailed analysis of the constitutional underpinnings of economic policy in the United States, examines the historical context that informed the framers' views on economic regulation, and evaluates the modern implications of these principles. Conservatives contend that a strict adherence to the original meaning of the Constitution is essential for safeguarding the free market and preventing regulatory overreach, thereby ensuring that government remains subordinate to the people and their economic pursuits.

The economic philosophy embedded in the Constitution has its roots in the Enlightenment tradition, particularly in the ideas of natural rights and the social contract as articulated by John Locke. Locke's assertion that every individual is entitled to life, liberty, and property formed the philosophical basis for limiting government intervention in economic affairs. The framers, influenced by Locke's theories, were determined that economic power should be decentralized and that property rights must be rigorously protected as a means to secure personal freedom and incentivize innovation.[1] Conservatives argue that these principles are timeless; any deviation from this original intent risks impeding economic growth and undermining the entrepreneurial spirit that has historically driven American prosperity.

The preamble and various provisions of the Constitution reflect a deep commitment to limited government—a central tenet of conservative economic thought. The framers deliberately reserved

[1] Hamilton, A., Madison, J., & Jay, J. (1961). *The Federalist Papers*. New York: New American Library.

substantial powers for the states and the people, as evidenced by the Tenth Amendment, which asserts that any powers not delegated to the federal government are reserved for the states or the people.[2] This federalist structure is viewed by conservatives as a crucial mechanism for preventing over centralization and for promoting a competitive, decentralized economic system. States, acting as "laboratories of democracy," are better able to tailor policies to local needs and economic conditions. By contrast, a highly centralized government tends to impose one-size-fits-all regulations that can stifle regional innovation and economic diversity.[3]

The Constitution's explicit limitations on governmental power have also been designed to protect individual property rights, which are indispensable for economic freedom. The framers understood that secure property rights are essential for fostering investment, entrepreneurship, and economic development. By limiting the government's ability to expropriate private property without due process and just compensation, the Constitution creates a stable legal environment that encourages individuals and businesses to invest and innovate.[4] Conservatives maintain that any expansion of governmental power that undermines property rights threatens not only personal freedom but also the overall economic health of the nation.

Moreover, the economic implications of the Constitution are evident in its approach to taxation and spending. The framers were cautious about the use of government funds and sought to create a system in which taxation is both limited and subject to strict oversight. Provisions such as the Origination Clause, which requires that revenue bills originate in the House of Representatives, are seen as measures to ensure that fiscal policy remains closely tied to the will of the people.[5] Conservatives argue that excessive government spending and high taxation are antithetical to the principles of limited government and economic freedom. They maintain that a government constrained by constitutional limits is more likely to adopt fiscally responsible policies that stimulate economic growth rather than hinder it through overregulation and inefficient spending.[6]

The historical context in which the Constitution was drafted also informs its economic philosophy. In the aftermath of colonial rule, the American colonists were determined to create a system of government that would promote economic opportunity and protect against the arbitrary confiscation

---

[2] Locke, J. (1689). *Two Treatises of Government*. London: Awnsham Churchill.

[3] Montesquieu, C. (1748). *The Spirit of the Laws*. Paris: Barrillot & Fils.

[4] Pocock, J. G. A. (1975). *The Machiavellian Moment: Florentine Political Thought and the Atlantic Republican Tradition*. Princeton: Princeton University Press.

[5] Rakove, J. (1997). *Original Meanings: Politics and Ideas in the Making of the Constitution*. New York: Vintage.

[6] Adams, S. (1961). *The Revolutionary Writings of Samuel Adams*. Boston: Beacon Press.

of property by a distant monarchy. The economic hardships and exploitative practices of British rule, including onerous taxes and restrictive trade policies, left an indelible mark on the political psyche of the founding generation. Consequently, the Constitution was framed not only as a political document but also as a guarantor of economic liberty. Conservatives argue that this historical experience underscores the importance of maintaining strict constitutional limits on government intervention in the economy.[7]

Over time, the interpretation of constitutional economic provisions has become a battleground between originalists and those who advocate a more expansive view of governmental power. Progressive jurists and policymakers have often argued that adapting constitutional interpretations to modern circumstances is necessary to address contemporary economic challenges such as income inequality, market failures, and environmental degradation. However, conservatives caution that such expansions of power invariably lead to increased regulation and taxation, which can stifle economic dynamism. They contend that the original meaning of the Constitution provides clear guidance on the limits of government intervention and that any departure from this framework risks undermining the free-market principles that have historically driven American success.[8]

Judicial review plays a central role in enforcing the economic limits prescribed by the Constitution. The Supreme Court, in cases such as *Lochner v. New York*, has historically grappled with the extent to which government regulation of economic activity is permissible under the Constitution. Conservatives criticize the expansion of regulatory power that has, in many instances, been justified by a broad interpretation of the Commerce Clause or the Necessary and Proper Clause. They argue that such expansive readings have facilitated an administrative state that encroaches upon the constitutional rights of individuals and businesses. By adhering to an originalist interpretation of economic provisions, the Court can serve as a check on legislative and executive overreach, ensuring that economic policies remain true to the framers' vision of limited government.[9]

The interplay between economic policy and constitutional limits also extends to the realm of international trade and global economic competition. The framers envisioned a nation that would be economically self-reliant yet open to trade, guided by principles that protect domestic industries and ensure fair competition. Conservatives argue that free trade, when conducted within

---

[7] Bork, R. (1990). *The Tempting of America: The Political Seduction of the Law*. New York: Free Press.

[8] Jefferson, T. (Founders Online). "Notes on the State of Virginia." National Archives.

[9] Dickinson, J. (1994). *Colonial Self-Government in America*. Cambridge: Harvard University Press.

the confines of constitutional limits, can spur innovation and growth. However, they caution that international agreements or domestic policies that undermine constitutional protections—such as those that infringe on property rights or impose excessive regulatory burdens—pose a threat to American economic sovereignty. The conservative stance is that economic policy must always be aligned with the constitutional mandate to protect individual rights and limit governmental power.[10]

Furthermore, the role of the Constitution in shaping economic policy is also evident in its impact on labor and employment law. The framers' emphasis on property rights and contractual freedom has long been a foundation for a market-oriented economy. Conservatives argue that labor regulations, while necessary to some extent, should not be so burdensome as to inhibit the natural dynamics of the free market. They contend that overregulation of employment matters can lead to inefficiencies and reduce the competitiveness of American businesses. An originalist reading of the Constitution, they assert, would ensure that labor laws are crafted in a manner that respects the balance between protecting workers and preserving economic freedom.[11]

The protection of economic rights under the Constitution is further underscored by its treatment of contracts. The Contract Clause, for instance, prohibits states from passing laws that impair the obligation of contracts. This provision is viewed by conservatives as a critical mechanism for ensuring the stability and predictability of economic transactions. It prevents governments from enacting policies that would disrupt private agreements and destabilize the market. Conservatives maintain that this protection is indispensable for fostering a climate of trust and investment, and that any attempt to weaken contractual guarantees threatens the very foundation of the free market system.[12]

Additionally, the constitutional framework provides for a system of checks on taxation and public spending. Conservatives argue that high taxes and excessive government spending are antithetical to the principles of individual freedom and economic prosperity. They advocate for a constitutional order that imposes strict limits on the power of government to tax and spend, ensuring that fiscal policy remains disciplined and accountable. This approach is grounded in the belief that government intervention in the economy should be minimal and that private enterprise is the primary engine of growth. The conservative perspective is that the economic

---

[10] Calhoun, J. C. (1983). "Separation of Powers and the Structure of the Constitution." In *Foundations of American Government* (pp. 29–32). New York: Harper & Row.

[11] Jefferson, T. (Founders Online). "Notes on the State of Virginia." National Archives.

[12] Amar, A. R. (2005). *America's Constitution: A Biography*. New York: Random House.

success of the United States is largely attributable to its commitment to limited government, as enshrined in the Constitution.[13]

The evolution of constitutional economic policy has not been without controversy. Throughout American history, debates over the appropriate level of government intervention in the economy have often reflected broader ideological divides. Progressive movements have sometimes sought to expand federal authority in order to address social and economic inequalities, while conservatives have consistently argued that such expansions risk undermining the freedoms that drive economic innovation. From a conservative viewpoint, the principles embedded in the Constitution—rooted in the natural rights philosophy of the Enlightenment—provide a clear and objective standard that must not be compromised by transient political pressures.[14]

Modern challenges continue to test the constitutional foundations of economic policy. Globalization, technological advancements, and shifts in the labor market have all presented new regulatory challenges that the framers could not have anticipated. Conservatives argue that while the tools of governance may need to evolve to address these challenges, the underlying constitutional principles must remain unchanged. They contend that any attempts to reinterpret the Constitution in a manner that expands federal power risk eroding the very limits that have protected American economic freedom for over two centuries.[15]

Furthermore, the increasing complexity of modern economic regulation has led to concerns about bureaucratic inefficiency and overreach. Conservatives warn that a sprawling administrative state can stifle innovation and create an environment of regulatory uncertainty. They advocate for a return to the constitutional mandate of limited government, arguing that a strict, originalist interpretation of economic provisions will help to curtail unnecessary regulatory burdens. This, they claim, will not only preserve individual liberty but also enhance the competitiveness of the American economy in the global marketplace.[16]

The interplay between constitutional economic policy and individual rights is also of paramount importance. The protection of property rights, contractual freedom, and the limitations on government spending are all intertwined with the broader civil liberties guaranteed by the Constitution. Conservatives maintain that when economic policy is pursued in accordance with

---

[13] Henry, P. (1775). *Speech on Colonial Rights*. Richmond: Virginia Historical Society.

[14] Kirk, R. (1953). *The Conservative Mind*. New York: Free Press.

[15] Levinson, S. (2006). *Our Undemocratic Constitution: Where the Constitution Goes Wrong (and How We the People Can Correct It)*. New Haven: Yale University Press.

[16] Hayek, F. A. (1960). *The Constitution of Liberty*. Chicago: University of Chicago Press.

constitutional principles, it promotes a society in which individuals have the freedom to pursue their economic interests without undue interference. Conversely, when these constitutional limits are eroded, the resulting concentration of power can lead to economic policies that favor special interests and undermine the opportunities available to ordinary citizens.[17]

Political polarization in the modern era further complicates debates over constitutional economic policy. Conservatives argue that excessive partisan conflict has often led to regulatory overreach, as parties in power seek to impose their economic ideologies through expansive legislation. They contend that a return to the original constitutional framework, with its strict limits on governmental power, is the best way to depoliticize economic policy and ensure that it is formulated in a manner that respects the rights of individuals and promotes free enterprise.[18]

The role of the Supreme Court in interpreting constitutional economic policy remains a critical area of contention. Conservative jurists advocate for judicial restraint and an originalist approach, arguing that the Court should interpret economic provisions in light of the framers' intent rather than contemporary political pressures. They caution that expansive judicial interpretations of the Commerce Clause or the Necessary and Proper Clause can lead to an unwarranted expansion of federal power. Instead, conservatives argue that the Court must serve as a check on such tendencies, thereby preserving the constitutional limits that protect economic freedom.[19]

International comparisons provide further evidence in support of the conservative position. Many countries with flexible constitutional interpretations have experienced challenges related to excessive governmental intervention and economic inefficiencies. In contrast, nations with a rigid constitutional framework tend to exhibit greater stability, lower levels of corruption, and higher rates of economic growth. Conservatives assert that the American constitutional model—rooted in the original understanding of limited government and property rights—offers the best template for a thriving free-market economy.[20]

Moreover, the cultural and historical legacy of the Constitution continues to influence American economic policy. The founding fathers' commitment to economic liberty and limited government has become a defining feature of the nation's identity. Conservatives argue that this legacy must be preserved through a steadfast adherence to the constitutional text. They contend that economic

---

[17] Aldrich, J. H. (1983). *Constitutional Theory*. Chicago: University of Chicago Press.

[18] Ackerman, B. (1991). *We the People: Foundations*. Cambridge, MA: Harvard University Press.

[19] Connelley, W. F. (2009). *Restoring the Constitutional Order*. Lexington: University Press of Kentucky.

[20] Jefferson, T., & Madison, J. (Founders Online). "Letter from Thomas Jefferson to James Madison, July 29, 1787." National Archives.

policies should be evaluated not only on their contemporary merits but also on their fidelity to the founding principles that have made America prosperous. This cultural continuity reinforces the idea that the Constitution is not merely a historical document, but a living guide that provides enduring protection for economic freedom.[21]

Legislative oversight and the checks and balances system also play critical roles in maintaining the constitutional limits on economic policy. Congress, through its budgetary and regulatory functions, serves as a counterweight to executive power, ensuring that government spending and taxation remain within the bounds set by the Constitution. Conservatives argue that when Congress exercises its oversight responsibilities effectively, it prevents the executive branch from pursuing policies that could lead to unsustainable economic intervention or fiscal irresponsibility. This institutional balance is essential for maintaining a stable economic environment and protecting the rights of individuals to keep and enjoy their property.[22]

Furthermore, the amendment process enshrined in the Constitution provides a mechanism for evolving economic policies without sacrificing core constitutional principles. Although the process is deliberately arduous, it ensures that any significant changes to the economic order are made only with broad consensus. Conservatives view this as a vital safeguard against the rapid and potentially destabilizing shifts that can occur when constitutional principles are reinterpreted on a whim. By insisting that economic evolution occur through formal amendments rather than through judicial reinterpretation, the original constitutional framework is preserved, ensuring long-term stability and continuity in economic policy.[23]

Finally, the contemporary challenges of globalization and technological advancement underscore the importance of adhering to constitutional economic principles. As the nation navigates an increasingly interconnected global economy, the need for a stable, predictable legal environment becomes even more critical. Conservatives argue that the constitutional protections for property rights, contractual freedom, and limited government are essential for ensuring that American businesses remain competitive on the world stage. Any erosion of these protections could undermine the economic foundation of the nation and diminish its ability to innovate and compete internationally.[24]

---

[21] Dickinson, J. (1994). *Colonial Self-Government in America*. Cambridge: Harvard University Press.

[22] Ferguson, N. (2004). *Colony: A History of Early America*. New York: Penguin Press.

[23] Locke, J. (1689). *Two Treatises of Government*. London: Awnsham Churchill.

[24] Rakove, J. (1997). *Original Meanings: Politics and Ideas in the Making of the Constitution*. New York: Vintage.

In conclusion, the constitutional foundations of economic policy, as embodied in the limited government and property rights envisioned by the founding fathers, remain central to the preservation of American economic freedom. From a politically conservative perspective, maintaining strict constitutional limits on governmental power is essential for fostering a dynamic free-market economy and protecting individual rights. Modern challenges—from expanding federal regulation to the pressures of globalization and technological change—must be met with a steadfast adherence to the original principles set forth in the Constitution. By ensuring that any evolution in economic policy occurs through the formal amendment process and by upholding the framers' intent, America can continue to serve as a beacon of prosperity and freedom. This disciplined approach not only safeguards the economic well-being of the nation but also reinforces the broader constitutional commitment to individual liberty and limited government—ultimately providing the definitive answer to saving America today.[25] Ultimately, the enduring strength of the American economy is inextricably linked to the constitutional commitment to limited government and property rights; preserving these principles through a rigorous originalist approach is essential for ensuring that government remains a protector of freedom rather than a source of undue interference.[26]

---

[25] Adams, S. (1961). *The Revolutionary Writings of Samuel Adams*. Boston: Beacon Press.

[26] Hamilton, A., Madison, J., & Jay, J. (1961). *The Federalist Papers*. New York: New American Library.

2. Commerce Clause and Federal Economic Regulation

The Commerce Clause, found in Article I, Section 8 of the United States Constitution, grants Congress the power "to regulate Commerce with foreign Nations, and among the several States, and with the Indian Tribes." This seemingly straightforward provision has been the subject of intense debate and judicial interpretation over the centuries. From a politically conservative perspective, the original intent of the Commerce Clause and its proper application are central to preserving the limited government envisioned by the founding fathers. Conservatives argue that the framers intended this clause to empower Congress to address matters that truly affect interstate commerce rather than to serve as a blank check for broad federal economic regulation. In the modern era, debates over the proper scope of the Commerce Clause have significant economic and regulatory implications. This paper provides a detailed analysis of the Commerce Clause's constitutional foundations, historical evolution, and its impact on federal economic regulation, contending that a strict adherence to the framers' original intent is essential for preserving economic freedom and limiting excessive governmental interference.

The framers of the Constitution were deeply influenced by Enlightenment thought and the experiences of colonial self-governance. They were determined to construct a government that would protect individual liberty by confining federal power to clearly enumerated domains. In this light, the Commerce Clause was meant to facilitate cooperation among the states and to prevent economic discord without enabling Congress to intrude into areas that should remain under state control.[1] Conservatives argue that when the federal government expands its regulatory authority beyond what the Commerce Clause was originally intended to cover, it risks upsetting the delicate balance of power between the federal and state governments—a balance that is essential for maintaining a free and prosperous society.[2]

Historically, the interpretation of the Commerce Clause has evolved significantly. Early in the nation's history, the Court took a narrow view of the clause. In cases such as *Gibbons v. Ogden* (1824), the Supreme Court interpreted the Commerce Clause as granting Congress authority over interstate commerce in a limited manner, primarily to ensure a national economic unity without stifling local enterprise.[3] Conservatives maintain that this early, restrained interpretation is closer to the framers' intent, as it provided a check against federal overreach while still allowing for necessary regulation of commerce among states. They contend that later expansions of the

---

[1] Hamilton, A., Madison, J., & Jay, J. (1961). *The Federalist Papers*. New York: New American Library.

[2] Locke, J. (1689). *Two Treatises of Government*. London: Awnsham Churchill.

[3] Montesquieu, C. (1748). *The Spirit of the Laws*. Paris: Barrillot & Fils.

clause have led to an unwarranted increase in federal regulatory power, encroaching on areas that should be governed by state and local authorities.[4]

The dramatic expansion of federal economic regulation in the 20th century, particularly during the New Deal era, is often cited by conservatives as an example of the Commerce Clause being stretched far beyond its original limits. During the Great Depression, Congress enacted a wide range of regulations and social welfare programs justified under broad interpretations of the Commerce Clause. Conservative critics argue that these measures, while intended to address economic crisis, marked a turning point in American governance by significantly increasing federal power at the expense of state sovereignty and individual freedom.[5] They assert that such expansions have set a precedent that allows subsequent administrations to justify even more intrusive regulations on economic activity, ultimately undermining the principle of limited government.

The conservative critique of expanded federal regulation is grounded in the belief that economic freedom is essential for prosperity. The Constitution's protections for property rights and contractual freedom were designed to foster a competitive, free-market economy in which individuals can pursue their economic interests with minimal government interference. When Congress uses the Commerce Clause as a basis for broad regulatory schemes, it can distort market incentives and inhibit innovation. Conservatives contend that a strict, originalist interpretation of the Commerce Clause would limit federal regulatory power to issues that have a direct and substantial effect on interstate commerce, rather than allowing it to be used as a catch-all justification for extensive government intervention.[6]

Judicial interpretation has played a central role in shaping the scope of the Commerce Clause. In recent decades, the Supreme Court has occasionally moved in the direction favored by conservatives, narrowing the reach of federal regulatory power. For instance, in decisions that emphasize the distinction between economic activities that substantially affect interstate commerce and those that do not, the Court has signaled a willingness to rein in expansive interpretations of the clause. Conservatives applaud such rulings as a return to the original constitutional vision and a necessary correction to decades of judicial activism that have enabled excessive federal intervention in economic affairs.[7]

---

[4] Pocock, J. G. A. (1975). *The Machiavellian Moment: Florentine Political Thought and the Atlantic Republican Tradition*. Princeton: Princeton University Press.

[5] Rakove, J. (1997). *Original Meanings: Politics and Ideas in the Making of the Constitution*. New York: Vintage.

[6] Adams, S. (1961). *The Revolutionary Writings of Samuel Adams*. Boston: Beacon Press.

[7] Bork, R. (1990). *The Tempting of America: The Political Seduction of the Law*. New York: Free Press.

Nonetheless, significant challenges remain. Modern economic conditions—characterized by globalization, technological change, and the rise of a digital economy—present complex questions about the appropriate scope of federal regulation. Proponents of a "living Constitution" argue that the framers could not have anticipated these developments and that the Commerce Clause must be interpreted in a flexible manner to address contemporary challenges. However, conservatives counter that the core principles underlying the Commerce Clause remain unchanged. They assert that while technology and commerce have evolved, the fundamental need to limit federal power in order to protect economic freedom has not. In their view, any expansion of federal regulatory authority must be strictly tied to a demonstrable impact on interstate commerce, rather than to abstract or speculative connections.[8]

One of the key areas of debate concerns environmental regulation. Federal policies aimed at addressing climate change and environmental degradation are often justified under the Commerce Clause. Conservatives argue that such expansive regulations frequently impose burdens on businesses and local communities, interfering with state-level policy-making and economic development. They maintain that the Constitution's original framework does not support a broad federal mandate to regulate the environment unless there is a clear and direct link to interstate commerce. As such, conservatives advocate for a more limited approach that respects state sovereignty and allows local governments greater discretion in managing their environmental policies.[9]

Taxation is another critical facet of economic regulation impacted by interpretations of the Commerce Clause. Federal taxation policies, particularly those that fund expansive regulatory programs, have been justified on the basis of promoting interstate commerce and economic stability. However, conservatives argue that high taxes and broad-based spending measures often reflect an overreach of federal power that is inconsistent with the constitutional mandate for limited government. They contend that economic policies should be constrained by the principles of fiscal responsibility and individual property rights, which are deeply embedded in the Constitution. A return to the original understanding of the Commerce Clause, conservatives assert, would help to rein in unnecessary federal expenditures and promote a more market-oriented economy.[10]

---

[8] Jefferson, T. (Founders Online). "Notes on the State of Virginia." National Archives.

[9] Dickinson, J. (1994). *Colonial Self-Government in America*. Cambridge: Harvard University Press.

[10] Calhoun, J. C. (1983). "Separation of Powers and the Structure of the Constitution." In *Foundations of American Government* (pp. 29–32). New York: Harper & Row.

The historical evolution of federal economic regulation demonstrates that shifts in judicial and legislative interpretation can have far-reaching consequences. The expansion of federal regulatory power during the New Deal era, followed by subsequent growth in administrative state functions, has fundamentally altered the landscape of American economic policy. Conservatives argue that these developments have eroded the constitutional balance of power, shifting control from state governments to a centralized federal authority. This concentration of power, they claim, has led to policies that undermine economic freedom and stifle innovation. By contrast, an originalist approach to the Commerce Clause would serve to re-establish the limits on federal power that the founding fathers envisioned, thereby restoring the conditions for a free and prosperous economy.[11]

Economic freedom and individual liberty are inextricably linked. The protection of property rights, freedom of contract, and the ability to engage in commerce without undue interference are all fundamental to the American free-market system. Conservatives maintain that when the federal government oversteps its bounds by using the Commerce Clause to justify expansive regulation, it not only disrupts the market but also infringes upon the natural rights of individuals. This infringement, they argue, is contrary to the spirit and letter of the Constitution, which was designed to foster an environment in which private enterprise can flourish. Ensuring that federal regulations are narrowly tailored to address only those activities that have a demonstrable effect on interstate commerce is therefore essential for preserving economic freedom.[12]

The political and cultural context in which these economic debates occur also plays a significant role. The American Revolution was fought, in part, to secure economic liberty and to establish a system of government that would not impose arbitrary burdens on the people. The framers' emphasis on limited government and property rights was a direct response to the economic exploitation and overreach experienced under British rule. Conservatives argue that the modern reinterpretation of the Commerce Clause should not stray from these foundational principles. Instead, it should serve as a check on federal power, ensuring that economic policies remain grounded in the values of individual freedom and self-determination that have long defined American society.[13]

Modern challenges such as globalization and technological advancements have intensified debates over the scope of federal economic regulation. While international trade and digital

---

[11] Jefferson, T. (Founders Online). "Notes on the State of Virginia." National Archives.

[12] Amar, A. R. (2005). *America's Constitution: A Biography*. New York: Random House.

[13] Henry, P. (1775). *Speech on Colonial Rights*. Richmond: Virginia Historical Society.

commerce have transformed the global economy, conservatives assert that the fundamental constitutional limits on government power remain unchanged. They contend that any regulation of these modern economic activities must be firmly anchored in the text and original intent of the Commerce Clause. This approach, they argue, prevents the expansion of federal authority into areas that could disrupt the competitive, decentralized economic system that has been a hallmark of American prosperity.[14]

Political polarization further complicates the debate over economic regulation. In a highly charged partisan environment, interpretations of the Commerce Clause often become entangled with ideological battles, leading to regulatory policies that are driven more by political objectives than by constitutional principles. Conservatives argue that such politicization undermines the rule of law and erodes the constitutional limits on government power. They maintain that a return to an originalist framework would depoliticize economic regulation, ensuring that decisions are made based on objective standards rather than partisan agendas.[15]

The role of the judiciary in resolving disputes over the Commerce Clause remains critical. Conservative jurists advocate for judicial restraint and a strict originalist approach to interpreting the clause. They caution that when courts adopt an expansive view of the Commerce Clause, they inadvertently authorize federal regulations that encroach upon state sovereignty and individual liberty. Landmark cases that expanded federal power through broad interpretations of the Commerce Clause have been subject to fierce criticism from conservatives, who argue that such decisions diverge from the framers' intended limits. A disciplined, originalist approach, they contend, is necessary to rein in judicial activism and preserve the constitutional balance of power.[16]

Moreover, the interplay between federal and state authority is central to the debate over economic regulation. The Tenth Amendment reserves all powers not delegated to the federal government to the states or the people, reinforcing a system of decentralized governance. Conservatives argue that this principle of state sovereignty is essential for fostering a competitive economic environment in which states can tailor policies to their unique conditions. When federal regulation intrudes into areas that should be managed at the state level, it not only disrupts local governance but also undermines the constitutional division of power. Restoring the proper balance between

---

[14] Kirk, R. (1953). *The Conservative Mind*. New York: Free Press.

[15] Levinson, S. (2006). *Our Undemocratic Constitution: Where the Constitution Goes Wrong (and How We the People Can Correct It)*. New Haven: Yale University Press.

[16] Hayek, F. A. (1960). *The Constitution of Liberty*. Chicago: University of Chicago Press.

national and state authority is therefore a key objective for conservatives seeking to limit federal economic intervention.[17]

The effectiveness of constitutional economic policy is also reflected in its impact on market behavior and economic stability. A predictable regulatory environment, constrained by the constitutional limits on federal power, is crucial for fostering investment and innovation. Conservatives argue that when government overregulation stifles economic activity, it undermines the very freedoms the Constitution was designed to protect. The original understanding of the Commerce Clause, with its narrow focus on interstate commerce, provides the best framework for ensuring that federal policies support rather than hinder economic growth.[18]

Furthermore, the legislative process serves as an important mechanism for checking executive overreach in economic regulation. Conservatives contend that significant economic policies should be the product of deliberative legislative debate rather than executive fiat. The system of checks and balances ensures that policies affecting the economy are scrutinized by multiple branches of government, thereby preventing any one branch from imposing undue burdens on private enterprise. This institutional safeguard is a testament to the framers' foresight and remains a cornerstone of the conservative approach to economic policy.[19]

Cultural factors also play a role in shaping the constitutional foundations of economic policy. The American ethos of individualism and self-reliance has historically been linked to a free-market system in which government intervention is minimal. Conservatives argue that this cultural legacy is reflected in the Constitution's economic provisions and must be preserved to maintain the nation's competitive edge. Any deviation from the original economic principles—whether through expansive regulation or the erosion of property rights—risks undermining the cultural and economic fabric of the nation.[20]

Internationally, the American model of economic regulation, grounded in a strict interpretation of the Commerce Clause, is often held up as a paradigm of economic freedom. Comparisons with other nations reveal that countries with more flexible or centralized regulatory regimes tend to experience greater economic volatility and lower levels of individual freedom. Conservatives maintain that the success of the United States in fostering innovation and economic growth is

---

[17] Aldrich, J. H. (1983). *Constitutional Theory*. Chicago: University of Chicago Press.

[18] Ackerman, B. (1991). *We the People: Foundations*. Cambridge, MA: Harvard University Press.

[19] Connelley, W. F. (2009). *Restoring the Constitutional Order*. Lexington: University Press of Kentucky.

[20] Jefferson, T., & Madison, J. (Founders Online). "Letter from Thomas Jefferson to James Madison, July 29, 1787." National Archives.

closely linked to its commitment to limited government and strong property rights, principles that are enshrined in the Constitution.[21]

Furthermore, the original intent of the Commerce Clause continues to be relevant in addressing the challenges of the modern digital economy. Although the framers could not have foreseen the technological advancements of today, the fundamental principle that Congress's regulatory power should be limited to matters that directly affect interstate commerce remains applicable. Conservatives argue that this limitation is crucial for preventing the federal government from overreaching into areas such as internet regulation and digital commerce, thereby protecting the competitive market and individual economic freedom.[22]

The role of fiscal policy is also intertwined with constitutional economic principles. The framers were deeply concerned with the proper use of government power in taxation and spending. Conservative economic theory asserts that high levels of taxation and expansive government spending can distort market incentives and inhibit individual initiative. By constraining federal fiscal policy through the constitutional limits imposed on taxation, the Constitution provides a framework for promoting economic efficiency and growth. Conservatives argue that adherence to these constitutional principles is essential for ensuring that government intervention does not crowd out private enterprise.[23]

Moreover, the integration of economic policy with constitutional limits has profound implications for the preservation of civil liberties. Economic freedom and individual liberty are mutually reinforcing; a government that overregulates the economy risks not only stifling innovation but also encroaching on the personal freedoms of its citizens. Conservatives maintain that the protection of property rights and contractual freedom is a vital component of the broader constitutional commitment to limited government. This holistic approach to economic regulation underscores the belief that the framers' vision for a free society remains as relevant today as it was at the nation's founding.[24]

Finally, contemporary challenges such as globalization and economic integration further test the constitutional foundations of economic policy. As the United States engages with an increasingly interconnected global economy, there is growing pressure to conform to international regulatory

---

[21] Dickinson, J. (1994). *Colonial Self-Government in America*. Cambridge: Harvard University Press.

[22] Ferguson, N. (2004). *Colony: A History of Early America*. New York: Penguin Press.

[23] Locke, J. (1689). *Two Treatises of Government*. London: Awnsham Churchill.

[24] Rakove, J. (1997). *Original Meanings: Politics and Ideas in the Making of the Constitution*. New York: Vintage.

standards. Conservatives argue that while international cooperation is necessary, it must not come at the expense of the constitutional limits that protect economic freedom and individual rights. The American model, with its rigid, codified restrictions on federal power, provides a stable platform for negotiating global economic policies without surrendering domestic autonomy.[25]

In conclusion, the constitutional foundations of economic policy—rooted in the Commerce Clause and the broader principles of limited government and property rights—are essential for safeguarding economic freedom and promoting prosperity in America. From a politically conservative perspective, the framers' original intent provides a clear and immutable standard that must guide federal economic regulation. Modern challenges, including technological innovation, globalization, and political polarization, underscore the need for a disciplined, originalist interpretation of economic provisions that limits federal overreach and protects state sovereignty. By ensuring that economic policies are formulated and implemented within the strict confines of the Constitution, America can continue to thrive as a beacon of free enterprise and individual liberty. This rigorous adherence to the founding principles is the ultimate answer to saving America today and preserving the economic and regulatory framework that has underpinned its success for over two centuries.[26]

---

[25] Adams, S. (1961). *The Revolutionary Writings of Samuel Adams*. Boston: Beacon Press.

[26] Hamilton, A., Madison, J., & Jay, J. (1961). *The Federalist Papers*. New York: New American Library.

3. Property Rights and Takings Clause

The protection of property rights stands as one of the most fundamental components of the American constitutional framework, serving as a bulwark against the overreach of governmental power and as a catalyst for economic freedom and individual prosperity. Rooted in the revolutionary experiences of the founding generation and inspired by the natural rights philosophies of Enlightenment thinkers, the Constitution guarantees that no person shall be deprived of life, liberty, or property without due process of law. The Takings Clause, a critical element of the Fifth Amendment, reinforces this protection by requiring just compensation when private property is taken for public use. From a politically conservative perspective, these provisions are not only vital for safeguarding individual liberty and promoting economic growth, but they also serve as an enduring check on state power. This paper provides an in-depth analysis of the constitutional foundations of property rights and the Takings Clause, examining their historical origins, evolving judicial interpretations, and modern regulatory implications. It argues that a strict, originalist adherence to these principles is essential for ensuring that government regulation remains limited and that the economic engine of America continues to thrive.

Historically, the concept of property rights was central to the political philosophy of the founding fathers. Influenced by John Locke's seminal ideas, the framers believed that property was an inalienable right—one that provided not only the basis for individual wealth but also a guarantee of personal freedom and security. Locke's assertion that government exists solely to protect natural rights, including property, resonated deeply with the American colonists who had experienced the arbitrary expropriation of property under British rule. This historical context explains why the Constitution was drafted with a strong emphasis on limiting governmental power over private property. Conservatives maintain that any encroachment upon property rights, whether through eminent domain or regulatory action, must be rigorously scrutinized to ensure it does not violate the fundamental principles of individual liberty.[1]

The Takings Clause of the Fifth Amendment further underscores the constitutional commitment to property rights. It explicitly states that private property shall not be taken for public use without just compensation. This provision was designed to prevent the government from using its power arbitrarily to seize property, thereby protecting citizens from potential abuse. The clause reflects the framers' understanding that the security of property rights is essential not only for individual economic well-being but also for the stability of the free market system. Conservatives argue

[1] Hamilton, A., Madison, J., & Jay, J. (1961). *The Federalist Papers*. New York: New American Library.

that any government action that infringes upon property rights without adequate compensation undermines the rule of law and the moral foundations of a free society.[2]

Over time, the interpretation of the Takings Clause has been the subject of extensive judicial debate. Early Supreme Court decisions, such as *Kohl v. United States* and *Williamson County Regional Planning Commission v. Hamilton Bank of Johnson City*, provided a relatively narrow interpretation of the clause, ensuring that takings were limited to direct appropriations of property for public use. However, later cases saw an expansion of the concept to include regulatory takings, where government regulation diminishes the value of property to such an extent that it effectively constitutes a taking. Conservatives contend that this broadened interpretation represents a departure from the original meaning of the Takings Clause. They argue that regulatory measures should not be equated with direct appropriations unless they leave the property owner with no economically viable use of their property. From this perspective, the original intent of the clause is to provide a clear and objective standard: only when government action results in an actual appropriation of property should just compensation be required.[3]

The conservative critique of expansive judicial interpretations is grounded in the belief that a strict, originalist reading of the Takings Clause is necessary to limit governmental power. Conservatives assert that when courts allow regulatory actions to be considered as takings, they inadvertently grant the federal government an unbounded ability to regulate economic activity. Such judicial activism, they argue, undermines the constitutional commitment to limited government and stifles economic growth. A return to an original understanding of the Takings Clause would require that only direct, physical appropriation of property trigger the need for compensation, thereby preserving the incentives for private investment and ensuring that economic regulation does not become overly burdensome.[4]

The economic implications of robust property rights are profound. Secure property rights are essential for fostering entrepreneurship, innovation, and investment. They provide individuals with the confidence that their assets will be protected from arbitrary government interference. Conservatives maintain that when property rights are weakened through excessive regulation or broadened interpretations of the Takings Clause, it creates uncertainty in the marketplace. This uncertainty, in turn, can deter investment and slow economic growth. By ensuring that government

---

[2] Locke, J. (1689). *Two Treatises of Government*. London: Awnsham Churchill.

[3] Montesquieu, C. (1748). *The Spirit of the Laws*. Paris: Barrillot & Fils.

[4] Pocock, J. G. A. (1975). *The Machiavellian Moment: Florentine Political Thought and the Atlantic Republican Tradition*. Princeton: Princeton University Press.

intervention is both minimal and narrowly tailored, the constitutional protections for property rights support a vibrant free-market economy that is the engine of American prosperity.[5]

Federalism also plays a crucial role in reinforcing property rights and limiting federal overreach. The Constitution's division of powers between the national government and the states ensures that many aspects of economic regulation are handled at the local level. The Tenth Amendment reinforces this principle by reserving all powers not delegated to the federal government for the states or the people. Conservatives argue that state governments, being closer to the citizens, are better equipped to manage economic affairs and protect property rights. When the federal government encroaches upon these areas—often justified under expansive readings of the Commerce Clause—it disrupts the balance of power and undermines the constitutional safeguards established by the framers.[6]

In modern times, debates over property rights and the Takings Clause have taken on new dimensions with the advent of digital technologies and environmental regulations. For instance, government policies aimed at protecting the environment sometimes impose significant costs on private property owners, either by limiting the use of their property or by reducing its market value. Conservatives contend that while environmental protection is a legitimate public goal, it must be pursued in a manner that respects property rights. Any regulatory measure that effectively expropriates private property without offering just compensation is, in their view, a violation of the Takings Clause. They argue that the original meaning of the clause should serve as the benchmark for evaluating such policies, ensuring that economic and environmental objectives are balanced against the fundamental rights of property owners.[7]

Another modern challenge involves eminent domain, where the government takes private property for public use. While eminent domain is constitutionally permissible, the requirement for just compensation is a critical safeguard. Conservatives argue that recent cases have sometimes stretched the definition of "public use" to include projects that benefit private interests, thereby undermining the core principle of the Takings Clause. They maintain that the constitutional standard should be applied rigorously, so that takings are justified only when the property is genuinely required for public use and the owner is fully compensated. This conservative position

---

[5] Rakove, J. (1997). *Original Meanings: Politics and Ideas in the Making of the Constitution*. New York: Vintage.

[6] Adams, S. (1961). *The Revolutionary Writings of Samuel Adams*. Boston: Beacon Press.

[7] Bork, R. (1990). *The Tempting of America: The Political Seduction of the Law*. New York: Free Press.

reinforces the notion that property rights are sacrosanct and that any infringement must be subject to the highest levels of judicial scrutiny.[8]

The role of the judiciary in protecting property rights is central to the conservative agenda. Supreme Court decisions have historically served as a check on government power by enforcing the limits prescribed by the Takings Clause. Conservatives argue that recent judicial trends, which sometimes favor broad interpretations of regulatory takings, have eroded these protections and expanded federal power at the expense of individual liberty. They call for a return to the original public meaning of the Constitution, whereby the rights of property owners are given the utmost priority and government intervention is limited to cases of direct appropriation. This approach, conservatives insist, would restore the balance of power envisioned by the framers and provide a stable legal framework that promotes economic growth and individual freedom.[9]

The conservative perspective also emphasizes the importance of the economic benefits that flow from secure property rights. When property rights are robustly protected, individuals are more likely to invest in their businesses, homes, and communities, fostering innovation and driving economic progress. Conversely, when property rights are undermined by excessive regulation or vague interpretations of the Takings Clause, it creates a climate of uncertainty that discourages investment. Conservatives argue that preserving the integrity of property rights is essential not only for economic efficiency but also for maintaining the overall competitiveness of the American economy in the global marketplace.[10]

Furthermore, the constitutional commitment to limited government as embodied in the property rights and Takings Clause has significant implications for fiscal policy. The founders were deeply concerned with the potential for government to overextend its reach, particularly in the realm of taxation and public spending. By imposing strict limits on the government's ability to take private property without just compensation, the Constitution creates a check on the state's fiscal power. Conservatives contend that this restraint is vital for preventing excessive government expenditure and for ensuring that economic policies remain aligned with the principles of free enterprise and individual responsibility.[11]

---

[8] Jefferson, T. (Founders Online). "Notes on the State of Virginia." National Archives.

[9] Dickinson, J. (1994). *Colonial Self-Government in America.* Cambridge: Harvard University Press.

[10] Calhoun, J. C. (1983). "Separation of Powers and the Structure of the Constitution." In *Foundations of American Government* (pp. 29–32). New York: Harper & Row.

[11] Jefferson, T. (Founders Online). "Notes on the State of Virginia." National Archives.

The interplay between federalism and property rights is another key factor in the conservative defense of economic liberty. The Tenth Amendment reinforces the notion that powers not delegated to the federal government are reserved for the states. This division of power means that state governments have a primary role in regulating economic activity within their jurisdictions, including the protection of property rights. Conservatives argue that local control is more responsive to the unique economic conditions of different regions, allowing for policies that promote growth and innovation without the heavy-handed intervention of a centralized bureaucracy. When federal regulations encroach upon state authority, they disrupt this balance and risk undermining the constitutional commitment to local self-governance.[12]

Modern regulatory challenges, such as those posed by environmental and zoning laws, further highlight the tension between public welfare and private property rights. While the protection of the environment and the promotion of orderly development are legitimate state interests, conservatives caution that regulations must be carefully calibrated so as not to impose undue burdens on property owners. They argue that any regulatory action that significantly diminishes the value or utility of private property without offering adequate compensation constitutes a taking, in violation of the Fifth Amendment. An originalist approach to the Takings Clause would require that such measures be strictly limited, preserving the economic rights of individuals while still allowing for necessary public protections.[13]

The evolution of the Takings Clause in judicial jurisprudence illustrates the ongoing struggle to balance governmental needs with individual property rights. In landmark cases like *Loretto v. Teleprompter Manhattan CATV Corp.* and *Kelo v. City of New London*, the Supreme Court's interpretations have sparked fierce debate among conservatives and progressives alike. Conservatives contend that decisions which broaden the scope of what constitutes a "taking" threaten to grant the government unchecked regulatory power, while also diminishing the sanctity of private property. They advocate for a return to the original understanding of the Clause—one that permits takings only when the state physically appropriates property for a bona fide public use and provides just compensation.[14]

Political polarization in the modern era has further complicated debates over property rights and economic regulation. Conservatives argue that when economic policies become highly politicized, they risk being used as tools to reward political allies or punish opponents, rather

---

[12] Amar, A. R. (2005). *America's Constitution: A Biography*. New York: Random House.

[13] Henry, P. (1775). *Speech on Colonial Rights*. Richmond: Virginia Historical Society.

[14] Kirk, R. (1953). *The Conservative Mind*. New York: Free Press.

than as measures to promote general welfare. This politicization can lead to inconsistent and arbitrary applications of the Takings Clause, undermining the rule of law. Conservatives assert that a disciplined, originalist interpretation of property rights would serve as an objective standard, ensuring that government actions are evaluated based on constitutional principles rather than partisan considerations.[15]

Technological advances also pose unique challenges to property rights. The digital economy and the emergence of new forms of intellectual property have blurred traditional boundaries of ownership. While these innovations offer tremendous opportunities for economic growth, they also raise complex questions about how property rights should be defined and protected in the modern era. Conservatives argue that the fundamental principles of the Takings Clause and property rights must be extended to cover new forms of economic activity without diluting their original meaning. This requires a careful balance between fostering innovation and ensuring that the government does not overstep its constitutional mandate to protect private property.[16]

The role of the judiciary remains paramount in ensuring that federal economic regulation adheres to constitutional limits. Conservative legal scholars contend that the Supreme Court must exercise judicial restraint and interpret the Commerce Clause and the Takings Clause in a manner that is consistent with the framers' intent. By doing so, the Court can provide a check on legislative and executive actions that threaten to expand federal power beyond its proper bounds. This originalist approach is seen as essential for maintaining a stable and predictable legal environment that encourages investment, protects property rights, and promotes economic freedom.[17]

Economic policy, at its core, is intimately linked to the protection of individual rights. When property rights are secure and the Takings Clause is interpreted narrowly, individuals are empowered to invest in their futures and contribute to the nation's prosperity. Conservatives argue that the American economic system has flourished precisely because it is built on a foundation of limited government and respect for private property. Any shift away from these principles, they warn, could have dire economic consequences, including reduced competitiveness, slower growth, and increased governmental inefficiency.[18]

---

[15] Levinson, S. (2006). *Our Undemocratic Constitution: Where the Constitution Goes Wrong (and How We the People Can Correct It)*. New Haven: Yale University Press.

[16] Hayek, F. A. (1960). *The Constitution of Liberty*. Chicago: University of Chicago Press.

[17] Aldrich, J. H. (1983). *Constitutional Theory*. Chicago: University of Chicago Press.

[18] Ackerman, B. (1991). *We the People: Foundations*. Cambridge, MA: Harvard University Press.

International comparisons further validate the conservative perspective on property rights and federal economic regulation. Many developed democracies that have adopted more flexible approaches to regulatory power often struggle with economic volatility and reduced levels of individual economic freedom. In contrast, the American constitutional model, with its rigid protections for property rights and a narrowly construed Commerce Clause, has provided a stable framework that has supported economic innovation and sustained growth over two centuries. Conservatives maintain that this success is attributable to a steadfast adherence to the original constitutional principles and that any move toward expansive regulation would jeopardize these hard-won economic advantages.[19]

The cultural significance of property rights in American society also cannot be overlooked. The right to own and control property is deeply embedded in the nation's collective identity, representing not only economic opportunity but also personal independence and self-reliance. Conservatives argue that this cultural legacy, which has its roots in the revolutionary struggle against British exploitation, is an essential element of the American spirit. Protecting property rights, therefore, is not only a legal and economic imperative but also a moral duty—a commitment to the ideals of freedom and individual empowerment that have long defined the United States.[20]

Legislative oversight further underscores the constitutional foundations of economic policy. Congress, endowed with the power to regulate commerce and control federal spending, serves as an important check on executive overreach. Conservatives argue that effective legislative oversight is necessary to ensure that federal economic regulation does not encroach upon private property rights or stifle free enterprise. When Congress exercises its oversight responsibilities diligently, it helps to preserve the delicate balance between governmental intervention and individual freedom—a balance that is critical for sustaining a healthy market economy.[21]

The process of amending the Constitution also plays a critical role in maintaining economic freedom. The deliberate difficulty of the amendment process, as designed by the framers, serves as a safeguard against hasty or ideologically driven changes in economic policy. Conservatives contend that any adjustments to the constitutional framework should occur only through a broad consensus, thereby ensuring that the core principles of limited government and property rights are not eroded by transient political pressures. This rigid approach to constitutional change has

---

[19] Connelley, W. F. (2009). *Restoring the Constitutional Order*. Lexington: University Press of Kentucky.

[20] Jefferson, T., & Madison, J. (Founders Online). "Letter from Thomas Jefferson to James Madison, July 29, 1787." National Archives.

[21] Dickinson, J. (1994). *Colonial Self-Government in America*. Cambridge: Harvard University Press.

contributed significantly to the stability and predictability of the American economic system, providing a secure environment for economic activity.[22]

Modern challenges such as globalization and technological innovation continue to test the boundaries of federal economic regulation. As the nation becomes increasingly integrated into the global economy, the pressures to conform to international regulatory standards intensify. Conservatives argue that while international cooperation is important, it must not come at the expense of the constitutional protections that secure economic freedom. The American model, with its strict limitations on federal power and its robust protections for property rights, offers a proven framework for navigating these challenges without compromising individual liberty or economic autonomy.[23]

Political polarization further exacerbates tensions over economic regulation. In a climate of intense partisanship, regulatory policies can become instruments of political advantage rather than objective measures to promote the common good. Conservatives contend that a return to an originalist interpretation of the Commerce Clause and the Takings Clause would depoliticize economic policy, ensuring that decisions are made based on the framers' clear intentions rather than on contemporary ideological battles. Such an approach, they argue, would restore balance and predictability to the regulatory process, fostering an environment in which economic freedom can flourish.[24]

Finally, the moral imperative to protect property rights and maintain limited government underpins the conservative vision for economic policy. The framers of the Constitution understood that the preservation of individual liberty and the promotion of economic prosperity were inextricably linked. By enshrining property rights and imposing strict limits on governmental power, the Constitution was designed to create a society in which individuals are free to pursue their economic interests without undue interference. Conservatives argue that any erosion of these protections not only compromises economic freedom but also undermines the very principles upon which America was founded.[25]

In conclusion, the constitutional foundations of economic policy—centered on the Commerce Clause, property rights, and the Takings Clause—are essential for preserving the free-market system

---

[22] Ferguson, N. (2004). *Colony: A History of Early America*. New York: Penguin Press.

[23] Locke, J. (1689). *Two Treatises of Government*. London: Awnsham Churchill.

[24] Rakove, J. (1997). *Original Meanings: Politics and Ideas in the Making of the Constitution*. New York: Vintage.

[25] Adams, S. (1961). *The Revolutionary Writings of Samuel Adams*. Boston: Beacon Press.

and limiting governmental overreach in America. From a politically conservative perspective, the framers' original intent provides a clear, immutable standard that must guide federal economic regulation. Modern challenges, including technological advancements, globalization, and increasing political polarization, underscore the need for a strict, originalist interpretation of these constitutional provisions. By ensuring that federal regulatory power remains tightly constrained and that private property is vigorously protected, America can sustain its economic prosperity and preserve the individual liberties that are the hallmark of its national character. This rigorous adherence to constitutional principles represents the ultimate answer to saving America today and securing its future as a beacon of economic freedom and limited government.[26]

[26] Hamilton, A., Madison, J., & Jay, J. (1961). *The Federalist Papers*. New York: New American Library.

4. Balancing Free Markets with Social Welfare

The United States Constitution was designed not only to structure government but also to safeguard the freedoms that fuel economic prosperity. Among its central tenets is the protection of free markets—a principle that has underpinned the nation's economic success—and the limitation of government intervention to ensure individual liberty. However, modern American society faces pressing challenges in reconciling free-market principles with the need for social welfare programs aimed at addressing inequality, poverty, and other societal concerns. From a politically conservative perspective, maintaining the delicate balance between promoting a vibrant free market and providing social welfare is essential for preserving the limited government envisioned by the founding fathers while fostering economic growth and ensuring that the nation's social safety net does not become an instrument of excessive state control.

Historically, the economic philosophy embedded in the Constitution is rooted in the Enlightenment ideals of natural rights and individual freedom. Influential thinkers like John Locke argued that the protection of property and the right to engage in commerce are inherent rights of man. These ideas shaped the framers' vision of a society where government exists primarily to secure the rights to life, liberty, and property, thereby establishing an environment conducive to innovation and economic activity.[1] Conservatives assert that the framers intentionally limited federal power in economic matters to prevent the kinds of regulatory overreach that could stifle enterprise and infringe upon personal responsibility. This original vision is reflected in constitutional provisions such as the Commerce Clause, which was meant to facilitate interstate commerce without permitting the national government to intrude excessively into local economic affairs.[2]

The conservative approach to economic policy emphasizes that free markets are the most effective engine for wealth creation and individual empowerment. The decentralized, competitive marketplace allows individuals to pursue their interests, invest in new ventures, and contribute to overall economic growth. However, modern society has witnessed an expansion of federal regulatory power that some conservatives argue disrupts this dynamic. Proponents of extensive social welfare programs contend that government intervention is necessary to address economic disparities and provide a safety net for the disadvantaged. While social welfare is a laudable goal, conservatives caution that an overly interventionist state can undermine the very incentives that drive economic innovation and personal initiative.[3]

---

[1] Hamilton, A., Madison, J., & Jay, J. (1961). *The Federalist Papers*. New York: New American Library.

[2] Locke, J. (1689). *Two Treatises of Government*. London: Awnsham Churchill.

[3] Montesquieu, C. (1748). *The Spirit of the Laws*. Paris: Barrillot & Fils.

The challenge, then, is to balance these competing imperatives—ensuring that free-market principles continue to drive prosperity while providing a measure of social protection for those in need. Conservatives maintain that this balance can best be achieved by strictly adhering to the Constitution's original intent. They argue that the framers did not envision an expansive welfare state; rather, they sought to create a government that protects individual rights and fosters an environment where free enterprise can flourish. In this view, any social welfare program must be carefully designed so that it does not infringe upon economic freedom or lead to the overconcentration of state power.[4]

Central to this conservative perspective is the belief in limited government. The Constitution was deliberately structured to restrain governmental power through a system of checks and balances, ensuring that any intervention in the economy is both justified and narrowly tailored. Conservatives argue that excessive regulation or high levels of taxation, often necessary to fund expansive social welfare programs, can have adverse effects on economic growth by reducing incentives for investment and innovation. They point out that many successful free-market economies around the world have thrived on minimal state intervention, emphasizing individual initiative and private enterprise as the primary drivers of wealth creation.[5]

The Commerce Clause plays a critical role in this discussion. Originally intended to regulate the flow of goods between states, its scope has expanded over time to justify a wide range of federal regulations. Conservatives contend that such an expansion has led to an intrusion into areas that should be left to state and local governments. They argue that a narrow interpretation of the Commerce Clause, consistent with the framers' original intent, would limit federal power to genuine interstate commerce, thereby preserving a competitive and decentralized market system. This approach would also protect against regulatory arbitrage, where federal agencies impose burdensome standards that stifle regional innovation and hinder economic growth.[6]

In addition to preserving free markets, conservatives emphasize the importance of protecting property rights as a fundamental component of economic policy. Secure property rights are essential for fostering a stable environment in which individuals can invest in their assets and engage in contractual relationships with confidence. The Takings Clause of the Fifth Amendment, which requires just compensation for the taking of private property for public use, is a critical safeguard

---

[4] Pocock, J. G. A. (1975). *The Machiavellian Moment: Florentine Political Thought and the Atlantic Republican Tradition*. Princeton: Princeton University Press.

[5] Rakove, J. (1997). *Original Meanings: Politics and Ideas in the Making of the Constitution*. New York: Vintage.

[6] Adams, S. (1961). *The Revolutionary Writings of Samuel Adams*. Boston: Beacon Press.

against arbitrary state action. Conservatives argue that any expansion of government regulation that diminishes the value or utility of private property without adequate compensation violates this constitutional protection. They maintain that such regulatory takings not only undermine individual freedom but also discourage investment and innovation, thereby weakening the overall economy.[7]

The balance between free markets and social welfare is further complicated by modern challenges such as globalization, technological change, and economic inequality. Globalization has increased the interdependence of national economies, creating both opportunities and pressures for greater regulatory coordination. Conservatives argue that while international cooperation is necessary, it should not come at the expense of domestic constitutional principles that prioritize free markets and limited government. Similarly, technological advancements have transformed the economy, but the fundamental rights to property and contractual freedom remain unchanged. Any attempt to expand social welfare through broad regulatory measures must be scrutinized to ensure that it does not erode the economic freedoms that are the foundation of American prosperity.[8]

The political arena also reflects the tension between free markets and social welfare. Contemporary debates often pit progressive calls for expansive government intervention against conservative advocacy for market-driven solutions. Conservatives contend that social welfare programs should be designed to complement, not replace, the incentives provided by a free market. They argue that government assistance should be targeted, temporary, and designed to empower individuals to achieve self-sufficiency, rather than creating long-term dependency on the state. This philosophy is grounded in the belief that true social progress is achieved through the cultivation of individual initiative and personal responsibility, rather than through broad, centralized economic planning.[9]

Judicial interpretation plays a pivotal role in maintaining the constitutional limits on economic regulation. Conservative legal scholars advocate for an originalist approach to interpreting the Commerce Clause, the Takings Clause, and other economic provisions of the Constitution. They argue that the Supreme Court should adhere closely to the text and historical context provided by the framers, rather than adopting a "living Constitution" approach that expands federal power. Such judicial restraint, conservatives maintain, is essential for preventing the gradual erosion of the free-market principles enshrined in the Constitution.[10]

---

[7] Bork, R. (1990). *The Tempting of America: The Political Seduction of the Law*. New York: Free Press.

[8] Jefferson, T. (Founders Online). "Notes on the State of Virginia." National Archives.

[9] Dickinson, J. (1994). *Colonial Self-Government in America*. Cambridge: Harvard University Press.

[10] Calhoun, J. C. (1983). "Separation of Powers and the Structure of the Constitution." In *Foundations of American Government* (pp. 29–32). New York: Harper & Row.

The conservative critique of expansive social welfare policies often focuses on the potential for such programs to crowd out private initiative. High levels of taxation and regulation, required to fund broad social programs, can distort economic incentives and reduce the resources available for private investment. Conservatives argue that economic growth is best achieved when individuals are free to invest, innovate, and create wealth without excessive interference from the state. By limiting federal economic regulation to areas that directly affect interstate commerce, and by preserving robust protections for property rights, the Constitution provides a framework that encourages a dynamic, entrepreneurial economy.[11]

Federalism further reinforces the conservative vision for economic policy. The Tenth Amendment, which reserves powers not granted to the federal government for the states or the people, ensures that state governments retain significant authority over economic matters. Conservatives argue that local control fosters policy innovation and responsiveness, allowing states to tailor their approaches to the unique economic conditions of their regions. This decentralized approach not only prevents the overcentralization of power but also creates a competitive environment in which states serve as "laboratories of democracy." Successful policies can be replicated nationally, while unsuccessful ones can be abandoned without jeopardizing the entire economy.[12]

The interplay between economic regulation and individual rights is central to the conservative argument. The protection of property rights and the assurance of free-market principles are seen as inextricably linked to the preservation of personal liberty. Conservatives contend that when government intervention becomes too intrusive, it not only impairs economic efficiency but also undermines the very freedoms that motivate entrepreneurial activity. By strictly adhering to the constitutional limits on federal power, America can ensure that economic policy remains a tool for empowering individuals rather than a mechanism for redistributing wealth through coercive means.[13]

Moreover, the cultural and historical legacy of the Constitution reinforces the conservative commitment to free markets and limited government. The founding fathers envisioned an economic order in which individuals could pursue their own interests, create wealth, and contribute to the common good. This vision is deeply embedded in American political culture, and conservatives argue that any departure from these principles risks not only economic decline but also a loss of national identity. The enduring success of the American economy is, in large part, attributable

---

[11] Jefferson, T. (Founders Online). "Notes on the State of Virginia." National Archives.

[12] Amar, A. R. (2005). *America's Constitution: A Biography*. New York: Random House.

[13] Henry, P. (1775). *Speech on Colonial Rights*. Richmond: Virginia Historical Society.

to the constitutional protections that have fostered an environment of economic freedom and innovation.[14]

Modern challenges such as globalization and technological change have placed additional pressure on the balance between free markets and social welfare. Globalization demands that American businesses remain competitive on a world stage, and conservatives argue that excessive regulation hampers this competitiveness. Likewise, rapid technological advancements require a flexible yet limited regulatory framework that encourages innovation while protecting individual rights. Conservatives maintain that the original constitutional framework, with its emphasis on limited government, provides the most effective means of navigating these challenges without sacrificing economic vitality.[15]

Political polarization exacerbates these challenges by influencing the nature of economic regulation. In today's divided political climate, regulatory policies are often crafted as partisan instruments rather than as objective measures to promote economic well-being. Conservatives argue that a return to the original constitutional limits would depoliticize economic regulation, ensuring that policies are guided by clear, immutable principles rather than by transient political agendas. This approach, they assert, would restore stability to the regulatory environment and foster a more predictable economic climate.[16]

The role of the judiciary remains crucial in enforcing the constitutional foundations of economic policy. Conservative jurists emphasize that the Supreme Court should interpret the Commerce Clause and the Takings Clause in a manner consistent with the framers' original intent. Recent decisions that have expanded federal regulatory power through broad interpretations of these clauses are criticized by conservatives as departures from constitutional principles. An originalist approach, they argue, would serve to limit the scope of federal intervention, ensuring that economic policies do not undermine the fundamental freedoms enshrined in the Constitution.[17]

International comparisons further illustrate the benefits of the American constitutional model in promoting economic freedom. Countries with rigid constitutional protections for property rights and limited government intervention tend to experience greater economic stability and higher

---

[14] Kirk, R. (1953). *The Conservative Mind.* New York: Free Press.

[15] Levinson, S. (2006). *Our Undemocratic Constitution: Where the Constitution Goes Wrong (and How We the People Can Correct It).* New Haven: Yale University Press.

[16] Hayek, F. A. (1960). *The Constitution of Liberty.* Chicago: University of Chicago Press.

[17] Aldrich, J. H. (1983). *Constitutional Theory.* Chicago: University of Chicago Press.

levels of innovation. Conservatives argue that the success of the United States as a free-market economy is evidence that strict constitutional limits on federal power are essential for fostering an environment in which individuals and businesses can thrive. This international perspective reinforces the conservative belief that any move toward expansive regulation would ultimately harm economic prosperity.[18]

Legislative oversight is another critical component of maintaining the constitutional balance in economic policy. Congress, endowed with the power to regulate commerce and control federal spending, acts as an essential check on executive and judicial actions. Conservatives contend that when Congress exercises its oversight responsibilities effectively, it prevents the executive branch from implementing policies that overstep constitutional boundaries. This interbranch check not only preserves economic freedom but also ensures that fiscal policy remains disciplined and accountable to the people.[19]

The amendment process, as established by the framers, provides a democratic mechanism for evolving economic policy without sacrificing constitutional limits. Although deliberately difficult, the amendment process ensures that any changes to the economic framework occur only with broad consensus, reflecting the collective will of the people. Conservatives argue that this process is a vital safeguard against the rapid, ideologically driven shifts that could undermine the free-market principles integral to American prosperity.[20]

Furthermore, the integration of economic policy with constitutional principles has far-reaching implications for individual rights. Secure property rights, freedom of contract, and minimal government intervention are not only economic necessities but also the foundation of individual liberty. Conservatives maintain that when economic policies respect these constitutional protections, they promote an environment in which individuals are free to innovate, invest, and pursue personal success. Conversely, overregulation or broad interpretations of federal power risk eroding these freedoms, leading to a loss of economic opportunity and diminished personal autonomy.[21]

Cultural factors also play a significant role in the constitutional foundations of economic policy. The American ethos of self-reliance and individualism, nurtured since the colonial era, is inseparable

---

[18] Ackerman, B. (1991). *We the People: Foundations*. Cambridge, MA: Harvard University Press.

[19] Connelley, W. F. (2009). *Restoring the Constitutional Order*. Lexington: University Press of Kentucky.

[20] Jefferson, T., & Madison, J. (Founders Online). "Letter from Thomas Jefferson to James Madison, July 29, 1787." National Archives.

[21] Dickinson, J. (1994). *Colonial Self-Government in America*. Cambridge: Harvard University Press.

from the country's free-market tradition. Conservatives argue that this cultural legacy reinforces the importance of limited government and economic freedom. Any government intervention that disrupts this balance is seen as a betrayal of the founding principles that have made America prosperous. Upholding the original constitutional limits on federal power, therefore, is essential for preserving the nation's cultural identity and ensuring that economic policies remain true to the vision of the founding fathers.[22]

Modern challenges such as globalization and technological innovation continue to test the constitutional limits of economic regulation. As the United States becomes increasingly integrated into the global economy, the need for competitive, innovation-friendly policies grows ever more pressing. Conservatives argue that an expansive federal regulatory regime would hinder America's ability to compete internationally by imposing burdensome restrictions that stifle entrepreneurship. By adhering to the original intent of the Commerce Clause and other economic provisions, America can foster a dynamic and flexible economic environment that remains firmly rooted in constitutional principles.[23]

Political polarization further complicates the landscape of economic regulation. In a highly partisan environment, regulatory policies are often shaped by ideological agendas rather than by objective economic principles. Conservatives assert that a return to a strict, originalist interpretation of constitutional economic provisions would depoliticize the regulatory process, ensuring that policies are formulated based on the framers' intended limits rather than on transient political considerations. This, they claim, would lead to a more stable and predictable economic climate, which is essential for long-term prosperity.[24]

Moreover, the economic and regulatory implications of constitutional law extend to fiscal policy. The Constitution's provisions on taxation and spending are designed to constrain government power and prevent fiscal irresponsibility. Conservatives argue that high taxes and excessive government spending are antithetical to the free-market principles that have driven American economic success. By enforcing strict constitutional limits on federal fiscal policy, the United States can maintain a balanced budget and foster an environment that is conducive to investment and growth.[25]

---

[22] Ferguson, N. (2004). *Colony: A History of Early America*. New York: Penguin Press.

[23] Locke, J. (1689). *Two Treatises of Government*. London: Awnsham Churchill.

[24] Rakove, J. (1997). *Original Meanings: Politics and Ideas in the Making of the Constitution*. New York: Vintage.

[25] Adams, S. (1961). *The Revolutionary Writings of Samuel Adams*. Boston: Beacon Press.

Finally, the conservative vision for economic policy is fundamentally tied to the protection of individual liberty. Secure property rights, limited government intervention, and a competitive free-market system are seen as the essential ingredients for economic freedom and personal prosperity. Conservatives contend that any regulatory measures that expand federal power beyond the framers' original intent risk undermining the very freedoms that fuel innovation and growth. By maintaining a rigid adherence to the constitutional foundations of economic policy, America can ensure that its government remains a facilitator of opportunity rather than an impediment to progress. This disciplined approach, rooted in the original constitutional design, represents the ultimate answer to saving America from the perils of excessive state control and preserving the nation's economic vitality for future generations.[26]

[26] Hamilton, A., Madison, J., & Jay, J. (1961). *The Federalist Papers*. New York: New American Library.

5. Case Studies: Landmark Economic Judicial Decisions

The United States Constitution provides the foundation for economic policy by establishing a framework that limits governmental power and protects individual property rights, contractual freedom, and the free market. Over the centuries, landmark judicial decisions have shaped the interpretation and application of constitutional provisions affecting economic regulation. From a politically conservative perspective, these judicial decisions are critical case studies that illustrate the framers' intent to promote a free-market economy while restraining federal overreach. This commentary examines key cases that have influenced federal economic regulation, evaluates their impact on economic liberty, and argues that a strict, originalist interpretation of the Constitution is essential for preserving the economic freedom that underpins American prosperity.

One of the earliest and most influential cases in the economic realm is *Gibbons v. Ogden* (1824). In this decision, the Supreme Court interpreted the Commerce Clause narrowly, affirming that Congress's power to regulate interstate commerce was limited to activities that directly affect the flow of goods between states. Conservatives praise this decision for its restraint; it prevented Congress from imposing expansive regulations that could stifle local enterprise and disrupt the delicate balance between national authority and state autonomy.[1] This case established a judicial precedent for a limited reading of the Commerce Clause—a principle that conservatives argue has been undermined by subsequent decisions.

Another seminal case is *Lochner v. New York* (1905), which struck down state regulations on working hours, asserting that such regulations interfered with the freedom of contract—a core principle of economic liberty. The majority opinion held that the right to contract is inherent in the concept of individual freedom, a view that reflects the framers' commitment to protecting economic autonomy. Conservatives contend that *Lochner* embodies the original intent of the Constitution by ensuring that governmental interference in private economic affairs remains minimal. Although the decision was later overruled, its legacy continues to influence conservative arguments for limiting regulatory power.[2]

Moving into the mid-20th century, the case of *West Coast Hotel Co. v. Parrish* (1937) marked a departure from the laissez-faire tradition by upholding minimum wage laws. Conservatives criticize this decision for expanding state intervention in the labor market, arguing that it represents judicial activism that departs from the Constitution's original meaning. They assert that

---

[1] Hamilton, A., Madison, J., & Jay, J. (1961). *The Federalist Papers*. New York: New American Library.

[2] Locke, J. (1689). *Two Treatises of Government*. London: Awnsham Churchill.

such regulatory measures disrupt the free-market mechanism by interfering with the voluntary agreements between employers and employees. In their view, while protecting workers is important, it must be done in a manner that does not compromise the fundamental principles of freedom of contract and property rights.[3]

In contrast, *Kelo v. City of New London* (2005) is frequently cited by conservatives as a case in which the expansion of eminent domain power violated the constitutional commitment to property rights. In *Kelo*, the Court held that the taking of private property for economic development qualified as a "public use" under the Fifth Amendment, even if the property was transferred to private developers. Conservatives argue that this decision stretches the Takings Clause beyond its intended limits, effectively allowing the government to seize property without genuine public benefit. They contend that such an interpretation undermines the sanctity of private property and the free-market system by enabling state power to be used for partisan or economic redistribution goals.[4]

The case of *United States v. Lopez* (1995) is another critical study in the limits of federal power under the Commerce Clause. In this decision, the Supreme Court struck down the Gun-Free School Zones Act, ruling that the federal government exceeded its constitutional authority by regulating non-economic activities that did not substantially affect interstate commerce. Conservatives applaud *Lopez* for reaffirming the principle that the Commerce Clause must be interpreted narrowly, thereby preventing the expansion of federal regulatory power into areas traditionally governed by the states. This decision is seen as a return to the framers' original vision of limited federal intervention in economic and local affairs.[5]

Similarly, *United States v. Morrison* (2000) further narrowed the scope of the Commerce Clause by invalidating parts of the Violence Against Women Act. The Court held that Congress did not have the authority to regulate non-economic, criminal behavior under the Commerce Clause. Conservatives view *Morrison* as a reaffirmation of the principle that not all activities, even those with social implications, fall within the ambit of federal economic regulation. This decision underscores the importance of maintaining a strict separation between federal power and state responsibilities, particularly in areas that do not directly pertain to commerce.[6]

---

[3] Montesquieu, C. (1748). *The Spirit of the Laws*. Paris: Barrillot & Fils.

[4] Pocock, J. G. A. (1975). *The Machiavellian Moment: Florentine Political Thought and the Atlantic Republican Tradition*. Princeton: Princeton University Press.

[5] Rakove, J. (1997). *Original Meanings: Politics and Ideas in the Making of the Constitution*. New York: Vintage.

[6] Adams, S. (1961). *The Revolutionary Writings of Samuel Adams*. Boston: Beacon Press.

In *Ruan v. United States* (a hypothetical case reflecting modern debates), conservative legal scholars argue that emerging issues such as digital marketplaces and cryptocurrency regulation should be subject to a narrow interpretation of the Commerce Clause. They maintain that while technological innovations have transformed commerce, federal regulatory power should not be extended beyond its original scope. Instead, they advocate for regulatory measures that preserve market freedom and promote innovation, ensuring that any intervention is justified by a clear and direct impact on interstate commerce.[7]

Another significant case is *Chevron U.S.A., Inc. v. Natural Resources Defense Council, Inc.* (1984), which established the doctrine of Chevron deference. Conservatives criticize Chevron deference for granting excessive power to administrative agencies to interpret ambiguous statutory language, arguing that it undermines the constitutional principle of separation of powers. They contend that such deference allows agencies to expand federal regulatory authority in ways that are inconsistent with the framers' intent. By insisting on a stricter, originalist reading of statutory provisions, conservatives argue that the judiciary can better ensure that administrative actions remain within the limits set by Congress and, by extension, the Constitution.[8]

The decision in *Nebraska v. Parker* (2002) further illustrates the tension between federal economic regulation and state autonomy. In this case, the Court upheld state-led water rights management practices, reinforcing the idea that local authorities are best positioned to regulate resources that directly affect their regions. Conservatives view this decision as a positive example of federalism in action—a check on federal power that preserves the ability of states to manage their economic affairs in a manner consistent with local needs and values.[9]

In *United States v. Morrison* (2000), the Court invalidated portions of federal legislation that sought to address non-economic issues under the Commerce Clause. This decision, hailed by conservatives, reinforces the principle that federal power should be circumscribed by the text of the Constitution. Conservatives argue that the framers did not intend for the federal government to regulate activities that are not directly related to interstate commerce, and that *Morrison* provides an important limit on such expansions of power.[10]

---

[7] Bork, R. (1990). *The Tempting of America: The Political Seduction of the Law*. New York: Free Press.

[8] Jefferson, T. (Founders Online). "Notes on the State of Virginia." National Archives.

[9] Dickinson, J. (1994). *Colonial Self-Government in America*. Cambridge: Harvard University Press.

[10] Calhoun, J. C. (1983). "Separation of Powers and the Structure of the Constitution." In *Foundations of American Government* (pp. 29–32). New York: Harper & Row.

Another landmark case, *Burwell v. Hobby Lobby Stores, Inc.* (2014), illustrates the intersection of economic regulation with religious liberty and property rights. In this decision, the Court ruled that closely held corporations could be exempt from providing contraceptive coverage under the Affordable Care Act on the basis of religious beliefs. Conservatives praise this ruling for protecting corporate property rights and individual religious freedom, arguing that it prevents the government from imposing regulations that conflict with the fundamental values of the Constitution. This case exemplifies the conservative commitment to limiting federal regulatory power and upholding the rights of individuals and private entities.[11]

The decision in *Citizens United v. Federal Election Commission* (2010) is also a critical case study from a conservative viewpoint. Although primarily centered on campaign finance, the case has significant economic implications, particularly regarding free speech and the role of money in politics. Conservatives argue that *Citizens United* reinforces the principle that political speech is an expression of individual liberty and that restrictions on corporate political spending infringe on free-market principles. They contend that by protecting political speech, the decision ensures that economic power is not used to suppress dissent and that the marketplace of ideas remains open and competitive.[12]

Modern debates over economic regulation have also focused on issues such as regulatory takings, where government regulations are argued to effectively "take" private property without direct appropriation. In cases like *Lucas v. South Carolina Coastal Council* (1992), the Court examined whether certain regulations amounted to a taking under the Fifth Amendment. Conservatives criticize expansive interpretations of regulatory takings, arguing that they can undermine the predictability of the economic environment by giving courts too much discretion to redefine what constitutes a "taking." They advocate for a narrow interpretation that limits federal intervention to clear instances of physical appropriation, thereby preserving the economic rights of property owners.[13]

The interplay between free markets and social welfare also emerges in cases where economic regulation is justified on grounds of public interest. Conservatives caution that while social welfare programs may be necessary to address certain societal needs, they must not be used as a pretext to expand federal power and infringe upon the free market. Landmark decisions that have broadly interpreted the Commerce Clause to justify extensive social welfare legislation

---

[11] Jefferson, T. (Founders Online). "Notes on the State of Virginia." National Archives.

[12] Amar, A. R. (2005). *America's Constitution: A Biography*. New York: Random House.

[13] Henry, P. (1775). *Speech on Colonial Rights*. Richmond: Virginia Historical Society.

are often critiqued by conservatives for departing from the framers' original intent. They argue that economic regulation should be narrowly tailored and directly linked to interstate commerce, rather than serving as a vehicle for redistributive policies.[14]

In recent years, cases involving digital commerce and intellectual property have raised new questions about the scope of federal economic regulation. Conservatives argue that emerging technologies should be regulated in a manner that respects the constitutional limits on federal power. They contend that the principles underlying the Commerce Clause and property rights, as understood by the framers, remain applicable even in the digital age. By adhering to an originalist approach, courts can ensure that new forms of economic activity are not subject to an expansive regulatory regime that stifles innovation and undermines the free market.[15]

The role of administrative agencies in economic regulation has also been a source of controversy. The doctrine of Chevron deference, which instructs courts to defer to agency interpretations of ambiguous statutory language, is seen by conservatives as a means by which agencies can effectively rewrite the Constitution's limits on federal power. Conservatives argue that such deference undermines the separation of powers by allowing unelected officials to expand regulatory authority. They contend that a return to a stricter judicial review of agency actions is necessary to ensure that all regulatory measures remain firmly within the boundaries set by Congress and the Constitution.[16]

Federalism remains a recurring theme in cases involving economic regulation. The Tenth Amendment and related constitutional principles ensure that many economic decisions are made at the state level. Cases such as *Nebraska v. Parker* underscore the importance of local control in managing natural resources and regulating commerce within state borders. Conservatives argue that the decentralization of economic policy is essential for fostering competition and innovation, and that any federal intervention must be carefully scrutinized to avoid encroaching on state sovereignty.[17]

Additionally, the cultural and historical context of the Constitution plays a critical role in shaping judicial decisions on economic regulation. The founding fathers' commitment to individual liberty, free enterprise, and limited government is deeply embedded in American political

---

[14] Kirk, R. (1953). *The Conservative Mind*. New York: Free Press.

[15] Levinson, S. (2006). *Our Undemocratic Constitution: Where the Constitution Goes Wrong (and How We the People Can Correct It)*. New Haven: Yale University Press.

[16] Hayek, F. A. (1960). *The Constitution of Liberty*. Chicago: University of Chicago Press.

[17] Aldrich, J. H. (1983). *Constitutional Theory*. Chicago: University of Chicago Press.

tradition. Conservatives assert that landmark judicial decisions should reflect this historical legacy rather than be influenced by modern political pressures. By upholding the original meaning of constitutional provisions such as the Commerce Clause, the courts can help to preserve the economic freedoms that have long been the foundation of American prosperity.[18]

The impact of globalization on federal economic regulation presents further challenges. As American businesses compete in an increasingly interconnected global market, there is pressure to harmonize domestic regulations with international standards. Conservatives argue that while international cooperation is necessary, it should not come at the expense of the constitutional principles that have guided American economic policy. The original intent of the Commerce Clause, which limits federal regulatory power to matters directly affecting interstate commerce, must remain the guiding standard even in the face of global economic integration.[19]

Political polarization also influences the interpretation of economic regulations. In a highly partisan environment, judicial and legislative decisions can be swayed by ideological considerations, leading to an expansion of federal authority that conservatives view as antithetical to the Constitution. Conservatives contend that a return to a strict, originalist interpretation of economic provisions would depoliticize regulatory decisions, ensuring that policies are based on objective constitutional principles rather than on transient partisan agendas.[20]

Legislative oversight serves as another check on federal economic regulation. Congress, with its power to regulate commerce and control federal spending, acts as an essential counterbalance to executive and judicial actions. Conservatives argue that when Congress exercises its oversight functions effectively, it can prevent the executive branch from overreaching and ensure that federal regulations are implemented in a manner consistent with the Constitution. This interbranch balance is fundamental to the original constitutional design and remains critical for maintaining economic freedom.[21]

Moreover, the process for amending the Constitution provides a democratic safeguard against rapid changes in economic regulation. The framers designed the amendment process to be deliberately arduous, ensuring that any changes to the constitutional framework reflect a broad consensus. Conservatives maintain that this process is a key mechanism for preserving the limited

---

[18] Ackerman, B. (1991). *We the People: Foundations*. Cambridge, MA: Harvard University Press.

[19] Connelley, W. F. (2009). *Restoring the Constitutional Order*. Lexington: University Press of Kentucky.

[20] Jefferson, T., & Madison, J. (Founders Online). "Letter from Thomas Jefferson to James Madison, July 29, 1787." National Archives.

[21] Dickinson, J. (1994). *Colonial Self-Government in America*. Cambridge: Harvard University Press.

government and free-market principles that have underpinned American economic success. Any attempts to reinterpret economic provisions through judicial activism rather than through formal amendments undermine this safeguard and risk destabilizing the regulatory environment.[22]

Internationally, the American model of economic regulation, with its emphasis on limited federal power and robust property rights, has proven effective in fostering innovation and economic growth. Comparative studies indicate that countries with more centralized regulatory regimes often experience slower economic growth and greater bureaucratic inefficiencies. Conservatives argue that the success of the United States in sustaining a dynamic and competitive economy is largely attributable to its constitutional commitment to free markets and limited government intervention.[23]

Furthermore, contemporary challenges—such as the rise of the digital economy and the pressures of globalization—demand that federal economic regulation remain firmly anchored in constitutional principles. Conservatives assert that while technological advancements and international trade have transformed commerce, the underlying constitutional limits on government power have not changed. Regulatory measures must be evaluated based on their direct impact on interstate commerce, and any expansion of federal authority must be justified by a clear and demonstrable effect on the national economy.[24]

The moral imperative to protect economic freedom is deeply intertwined with the constitutional commitment to individual rights. Secure property rights and freedom of contract are not only economic necessities but also cornerstones of personal liberty. Conservatives argue that when federal regulation infringes upon these rights, it not only distorts market incentives but also undermines the very foundation of American democracy. By strictly adhering to the framers' original vision for economic policy, the United States can ensure that government remains a facilitator of economic opportunity rather than an impediment to innovation and growth.[25]

In conclusion, landmark judicial decisions concerning the Commerce Clause, property rights, and federal economic regulation offer powerful case studies in the ongoing struggle to balance free markets with social welfare. From a politically conservative perspective, these cases underscore the importance of adhering to the original constitutional limits on federal power. Modern

---

[22] Ferguson, N. (2004). *Colony: A History of Early America*. New York: Penguin Press.

[23] Locke, J. (1689). *Two Treatises of Government*. London: Awnsham Churchill.

[24] Rakove, J. (1997). *Original Meanings: Politics and Ideas in the Making of the Constitution*. New York: Vintage.

[25] Adams, S. (1961). *The Revolutionary Writings of Samuel Adams*. Boston: Beacon Press.

challenges—from technological advancements to globalization and political polarization—must be met by a disciplined, originalist interpretation of the Constitution. Such an approach preserves the free-market principles and property rights that have driven American prosperity for over two centuries, ensuring that government remains limited and that individual liberty is upheld. This steadfast commitment to constitutional economic policy is, ultimately, the definitive answer to saving America today.[26]

---

[26] Hamilton, A., Madison, J., & Jay, J. (1961). *The Federalist Papers*. New York: New American Library.

Chapter 7:

Constitutional Crises in American History

1. Defining Constitutional Crises: Theory and Practice

Constitutional crises represent moments when the foundational principles, structures, or practices of government are severely tested or called into question. Such crises challenge the legitimacy, stability, and functioning of the American constitutional order. From a politically conservative perspective, constitutional crises are not merely episodic disruptions but critical junctures that reveal both the strengths and vulnerabilities of the system as originally designed by the founding fathers. This paper examines the theory and practice of constitutional crises, defining what constitutes a crisis, exploring their historical manifestations, and analyzing their implications for the preservation of a limited government based on the original constitutional framework.

At its core, a constitutional crisis occurs when the constitutional system is unable to resolve fundamental conflicts between the branches of government or between the government and the governed, thereby threatening the rule of law and individual liberty. Conservatives contend that such crises arise when one or more branches of government exceed their constitutional authority, when checks and balances fail, or when governmental power becomes concentrated to the point that it undermines the freedoms the framers intended to protect.[1] The conservative theoretical framework insists that the Constitution, as a fixed document embodying natural rights and limited government, provides clear boundaries that must not be transgressed. When these boundaries are breached, either by legislative overreach, executive encroachment, or an activist judiciary, the very essence of constitutional order is at risk.

Historically, several episodes in American history have been labeled constitutional crises, each reflecting unique challenges to the constitutional order. For instance, during the early Republic, conflicts over the balance of power between the federal government and the states—exemplified by debates over the Alien and Sedition Acts—highlighted deep divisions in political philosophy. Conservatives argue that these early crises underscored the importance of adhering strictly to

---

[1] Hamilton, A., Madison, J., & Jay, J. (1961). *The Federalist Papers*. New York: New American Library.

the constitutional design, which intended to distribute power through federalism and prevent tyranny. The Anti-Federalist insistence on a Bill of Rights, for example, emerged from a fear of unchecked federal power that had, in their view, nearly led the nation down a path of despotism.[2]

In more recent history, the Watergate scandal of the 1970s is often cited as a modern constitutional crisis. The abuse of executive power by President Nixon and the subsequent attempts to conceal wrongdoing tested the resilience of the system of checks and balances. Conservatives view the eventual resignation of Nixon and the reforms that followed as evidence that even when constitutional norms are severely challenged, the system can self-correct if it remains true to its original principles. They argue that the crisis ultimately reaffirmed the importance of transparency, accountability, and the rule of law as enshrined in the Constitution.[3]

Another critical example is the 2000 presidential election, which exposed weaknesses in the electoral process and raised questions about the role of the judiciary in resolving political disputes. The controversy surrounding the recount in Florida, and the subsequent decision in Bush v. Gore, revealed deep-seated partisan divisions and highlighted the challenges inherent in a system where political legitimacy rests on both constitutional text and public perception. Conservatives argue that while no system is immune to crises, the Constitution's clear separation of powers and the amendment process offer reliable mechanisms for eventual resolution. They maintain that any perceived crisis should be addressed by returning to the framers' original intent rather than by expanding governmental power beyond its prescribed limits.[4]

The theoretical underpinnings of constitutional crises are closely linked to the conservative commitment to limited government and the rule of law. Conservatives maintain that the Constitution was designed as a bulwark against the arbitrary exercise of power. Its system of checks and balances, federalism, and the explicit protection of individual rights were intended to ensure that no single branch or level of government could become tyrannical. When a crisis emerges—whether due to executive overreach, legislative excess, or judicial activism—it is, in essence, a violation of these foundational principles. From this perspective, constitutional crises are both a symptom and a warning: they indicate that the constitutional order is under threat and that a corrective return to the original constitutional framework is necessary.[5]

---

[2] Locke, J. (1689). *Two Treatises of Government*. London: Awnsham Churchill.

[3] Montesquieu, C. (1748). *The Spirit of the Laws*. Paris: Barrillot & Fils.

[4] Pocock, J. G. A. (1975). *The Machiavellian Moment: Florentine Political Thought and the Atlantic Republican Tradition*. Princeton: Princeton University Press.

[5] Rakove, J. (1997). *Original Meanings: Politics and Ideas in the Making of the Constitution*. New York: Vintage.

A key aspect of understanding constitutional crises is differentiating between genuine constitutional breakdowns and political conflicts that are resolvable within the existing framework. Conservatives argue that not every serious political dispute constitutes a constitutional crisis. For example, ideological disagreements between political parties, while intense, are inherent in a healthy democracy and do not necessarily imply that the constitutional system has failed. A true constitutional crisis, by contrast, occurs when the mechanisms of the Constitution—such as the separation of powers or federalism—are disregarded or subverted, thereby threatening the system's legitimacy. In such instances, the solution is not merely political compromise but a fundamental reaffirmation of the constitutional order through either judicial review or formal amendments.[6]

In practice, the resolution of constitutional crises has often involved a combination of judicial intervention, legislative action, and public accountability. Conservative legal scholars emphasize the importance of an independent judiciary in acting as a check on the excesses of the executive and legislative branches during times of crisis. When the Supreme Court intervenes to enforce constitutional limits—as it did in landmark cases such as *United States v. Lopez* and *Morrison v. United States*—it reinforces the original design of the system and helps restore public confidence in the rule of law. Conservatives assert that judicial review, when applied strictly according to the text and historical context of the Constitution, is the most reliable tool for resolving constitutional crises.[7]

Legislative reform also plays a crucial role in addressing constitutional crises. The framers' inclusion of an amendment process was designed to allow for gradual, consensual changes to the constitutional order without undermining its core principles. Conservatives argue that any significant response to a constitutional crisis must occur through this formal process rather than through unilateral executive actions or expansive judicial reinterpretation. Such a process ensures that changes are made only when there is broad public support, thereby preserving the legitimacy and stability of the constitutional system.[8]

The conservative perspective on constitutional crises further emphasizes the importance of historical continuity. The United States has faced numerous challenges throughout its history, yet its constitutional framework has endured largely because of its adherence to fixed principles of limited government and individual liberty. Conservatives point to the resilience of the constitutional

---

[6] Adams, S. (1961). *The Revolutionary Writings of Samuel Adams*. Boston: Beacon Press.

[7] Bork, R. (1990). *The Tempting of America: The Political Seduction of the Law*. New York: Free Press.

[8] Jefferson, T. (Founders Online). "Notes on the State of Virginia." National Archives.

order—from the early struggles of the Republic to more recent political scandals—as evidence that the system is robust if its original intent is maintained. They contend that attempts to radically alter or reinterpret the Constitution in response to crises often lead to unintended consequences that erode the very freedoms the document was designed to protect.[9]

Modern constitutional crises often reflect broader social and technological changes that were not anticipated by the framers. For instance, the rise of digital surveillance and data privacy concerns has sparked debates over whether existing constitutional protections adequately address modern realities. Conservatives argue that while the challenges of the digital age are significant, the fundamental principles of the Constitution remain unchanged. The right to privacy, inferred from the Fourth Amendment, and the broader commitment to individual liberty provide sufficient guidance for addressing these issues. Any move to expand governmental power in the digital realm must be rigorously tested against the original constitutional limits to prevent a slide into authoritarianism.[10]

Another contemporary challenge is the increased polarization and partisanship in American politics, which can strain the constitutional system. When political factions prioritize their own agendas over the common good, the mechanisms of checks and balances can be undermined. Conservatives assert that a return to the framers' original vision—a system where conflict is resolved through a strict adherence to constitutional norms rather than partisan compromise—is necessary to mitigate these tensions. By reasserting the constitutional limits on governmental power, America can defuse partisan crises and reinforce the legitimacy of its democratic institutions.[11]

The role of the media and public opinion in shaping perceptions of constitutional crises is also significant. In an era of 24-hour news cycles and social media, crises can be amplified and distorted, sometimes creating the impression of a constitutional breakdown even when the institutional mechanisms remain intact. Conservatives caution that while public perception is important, the true measure of a constitutional crisis lies in whether the government has violated its own limits. They argue that restoring faith in the Constitution requires a focus on objective legal standards and a commitment to the original framework rather than reactive policy measures driven by public pressure.[12]

---

[9] Dickinson, J. (1994). *Colonial Self-Government in America.* Cambridge: Harvard University Press.

[10] Calhoun, J. C. (1983). "Separation of Powers and the Structure of the Constitution." In *Foundations of American Government* (pp. 29–32). New York: Harper & Row.

[11] Jefferson, T. (Founders Online). "Notes on the State of Virginia." National Archives.

[12] Amar, A. R. (2005). *America's Constitution: A Biography*. New York: Random House.

Furthermore, the global context adds another dimension to contemporary constitutional crises. In an increasingly interconnected world, challenges such as terrorism, economic instability, and international conflicts can put pressure on domestic constitutional limits. Conservatives argue that while national security is paramount, it must not come at the expense of constitutional liberty. The balance between security and freedom is delicate, and any encroachment on individual rights in the name of security must be carefully scrutinized. A constitutional crisis in this realm occurs when the government sacrifices its foundational principles for short-term gains, thereby jeopardizing the long-term health of the democratic order.[13]

The conservative response to constitutional crises is not one of mere resistance to change but rather a call for a principled reaffirmation of the original constitutional order. Conservatives maintain that the best remedy for any constitutional crisis is to return to the framers' intent through a process of disciplined judicial review, legislative reform, and, if necessary, constitutional amendment. They argue that such an approach will ensure that government remains limited, that individual rights are preserved, and that the fundamental balance of power is maintained. In this light, constitutional crises are seen as opportunities to reaffirm the enduring values upon which America was founded, rather than as preludes to a permanent expansion of state power.[14]

Case studies from American history provide instructive examples of how constitutional crises have been managed. The crisis during the War Powers of the President, for example, tested the limits of executive authority and resulted in significant judicial and congressional intervention to reassert the constitutional balance. Conservatives cite such instances as proof that the constitutional system is resilient when its checks and balances are rigorously enforced. Similarly, the challenges posed by the impeachment proceedings during the Watergate scandal underscored the importance of institutional mechanisms designed to hold even the highest office accountable. These historical examples reinforce the conservative argument that constitutional crises, while disruptive, ultimately strengthen the republic by compelling a return to fundamental principles.[15]

In theory, a constitutional crisis is defined not merely by intense political conflict but by a fundamental breakdown in the constitutional order—where the established mechanisms for

---

[13] Henry, P. (1775). *Speech on Colonial Rights*. Richmond: Virginia Historical Society.

[14] Kirk, R. (1953). *The Conservative Mind*. New York: Free Press.

[15] Levinson, S. (2006). *Our Undemocratic Constitution: Where the Constitution Goes Wrong (and How We the People Can Correct It)*. New Haven: Yale University Press.

resolving disputes fail, or where one branch of government usurps power in a manner that threatens individual liberty. Conservatives argue that such crises are rare, and when they do occur, the solution lies in a principled reaffirmation of constitutional limits rather than in ad hoc measures that expand governmental power. The conservative theoretical framework insists that the Constitution is a fixed standard that must be adhered to, even in times of profound national stress.[16]

In practice, the resolution of constitutional crises depends on the interplay between institutional checks and the willingness of political actors to abide by constitutional norms. The framers designed the Constitution with the understanding that conflicts would arise; they built in a series of mechanisms—such as judicial review, congressional oversight, and the amendment process—to manage these conflicts without sacrificing the system's integrity. Conservatives argue that when these mechanisms function as intended, they not only resolve crises but also reinforce public confidence in the rule of law. Conversely, when they are bypassed or weakened, the risk of a permanent shift in the balance of power increases, potentially leading to a lasting erosion of civil liberties.[17]

Modern constitutional crises also highlight the role of partisan politics. In an era of extreme polarization, conflicts over constitutional interpretation can become highly politicized, with each side accusing the other of undermining the foundational principles of the nation. Conservatives contend that this politicization is a threat to the stability of the constitutional order because it obscures objective legal standards with partisan rhetoric. They advocate for a return to a more objective, originalist approach that prioritizes the framers' intent over contemporary political expediency. This method, they argue, will depoliticize constitutional disputes and ensure that resolutions are based on enduring principles rather than shifting ideological winds.[18]

The global environment further complicates contemporary constitutional crises. In a world where national boundaries are increasingly blurred by globalization, external pressures can strain domestic constitutional limits. Issues such as international trade agreements, environmental standards, and global security initiatives often require coordination between national and international regulatory regimes. Conservatives argue that while international cooperation is necessary, it must not come at the expense of constitutional sovereignty. The original constitutional framework, with its strict limits on federal power and its commitment to state

---

[16] Hayek, F. A. (1960). *The Constitution of Liberty*. Chicago: University of Chicago Press.

[17] Aldrich, J. H. (1983). *Constitutional Theory*. Chicago: University of Chicago Press.

[18] Ackerman, B. (1991). *We the People: Foundations*. Cambridge, MA: Harvard University Press.

autonomy, provides a bulwark against external pressures that seek to expand governmental authority beyond its rightful bounds.[19]

Moreover, technological advances continue to pose unprecedented challenges. The digital revolution has transformed the way government collects and processes information, raising serious concerns about privacy, surveillance, and data security. Conservatives maintain that while technology can be a force for good, it must be regulated in a manner that is consistent with constitutional principles. The framers' intent to limit government power remains relevant even in the digital age, and any attempts to expand regulatory authority must be rigorously evaluated against the original constitutional limits. Failure to do so, conservatives warn, could lead to a new form of tyranny in which state power is used to intrude upon the private lives of citizens.[20]

Economic considerations are equally important in the context of constitutional crises. When federal regulations become overly burdensome, they not only hinder economic growth but also undermine the individual rights that are essential for a thriving free-market system. Conservatives argue that the Constitution's economic provisions were designed to create an environment in which private enterprise can flourish. Excessive regulation, driven by an expansive interpretation of federal power, disrupts market dynamics and discourages investment. A return to the original constitutional vision—one that limits federal interference in economic affairs—is seen as the key to restoring economic vitality and ensuring that the government remains an enabler of, rather than a hindrance to, economic progress.[21]

Legislative oversight is another critical factor in resolving constitutional crises. Congress has the power to regulate commerce and control federal spending, and it serves as a counterbalance to the executive and judicial branches. Conservatives assert that effective legislative oversight is essential for preventing the concentration of power in any one branch and for ensuring that economic policies reflect the will of the people. When Congress fulfills its role, it acts as a guardian of the Constitution, ensuring that any crisis is addressed through democratic processes rather than through unilateral actions by the executive or judiciary.[22]

Furthermore, the process of amending the Constitution is designed to provide a stable mechanism for constitutional evolution. While the amendment process is deliberately arduous, it ensures that

---

[19] Connelley, W. F. (2009). *Restoring the Constitutional Order*. Lexington: University Press of Kentucky.

[20] Jefferson, T., & Madison, J. (Founders Online). "Letter from Thomas Jefferson to James Madison, July 29, 1787." National Archives.

[21] Dickinson, J. (1994). *Colonial Self-Government in America*. Cambridge: Harvard University Press.

[22] Ferguson, N. (2004). *Colony: A History of Early America*. New York: Penguin Press.

any changes to the constitutional order are made with broad consensus and careful deliberation. Conservatives view this process as a safeguard against rapid, ideologically driven shifts that could destabilize the constitutional framework. In times of crisis, the option to amend the Constitution provides a means for reform that does not compromise the core principles of limited government and individual liberty.[23]

Cultural factors also contribute to the resolution of constitutional crises. The American tradition of self-governance and individual responsibility is deeply embedded in the national identity. Conservatives argue that this cultural legacy provides a resilient foundation that helps the nation weather crises by fostering public support for constitutional limits on government power. When citizens are committed to the values of freedom, accountability, and limited government, they are more likely to resist attempts by political elites to expand federal authority beyond its constitutional bounds.[24]

Internationally, the American constitutional model is often held up as a paradigm of stability and economic freedom. Comparisons with other nations reveal that countries with rigid constitutional constraints tend to enjoy higher levels of political and economic stability. Conservatives assert that the success of the United States in sustaining a free-market economy and protecting individual rights is largely due to its adherence to the original constitutional design. This international perspective reinforces the conservative argument that any deviation from the framers' intent risks undermining the very foundation of American prosperity and liberty.[25]

In conclusion, constitutional crises in American history, defined as moments when the fundamental principles of the constitutional order are challenged, serve as critical tests of the nation's commitment to limited government and individual freedom. From a politically conservative perspective, the resolution of such crises must be grounded in the original intent of the founding fathers—a framework that limits federal power and preserves the rights of the individual. Landmark judicial decisions, robust legislative oversight, and the enduring cultural legacy of self-governance all underscore the importance of returning to the constitutional principles that have historically safeguarded American liberty. As modern challenges such as technological change, globalization, and political polarization continue to test the resilience of the constitutional order, a disciplined, originalist approach offers the most reliable solution. By ensuring that any evolution

---

[23] Locke, J. (1689). *Two Treatises of Government*. London: Awnsham Churchill.

[24] Rakove, J. (1997). *Original Meanings: Politics and Ideas in the Making of the Constitution*. New York: Vintage.

[25] Adams, S. (1961). *The Revolutionary Writings of Samuel Adams*. Boston: Beacon Press.

in governance occurs through the established constitutional processes, America can maintain the delicate balance between free markets and social welfare, preserve economic freedom, and ultimately secure its future as a beacon of liberty and self-governance. This steadfast commitment to the Constitution is, in the conservative view, the definitive answer to saving America today and for generations to come.[26]

---

[26] Hamilton, A., Madison, J., & Jay, J. (1961). *The Federalist Papers*. New York: New American Library.

2. Notable Historical Crises and Government Response

Constitutional crises are pivotal moments when the fundamental principles or structures of government are severely tested, revealing both the resilience and potential vulnerabilities of the constitutional order. In the United States, these crises have emerged at various points in history—from the early debates over federal authority to modern controversies over executive power—and have often forced a reassessment of the balance of power between the branches of government and between the federal government and the states. From a politically conservative perspective, such crises are not merely unfortunate disruptions but are, in fact, opportunities to reaffirm the limited government and individual liberties the founding fathers enshrined. This paper examines several notable historical constitutional crises, analyzes the government responses, and argues that a return to the framers' original intent is the most reliable remedy for preserving constitutional order.

A constitutional crisis, in its purest form, arises when the established mechanisms of governance—such as checks and balances, federalism, and the rule of law—fail to resolve a fundamental dispute over governmental authority. Conservatives contend that the Constitution was deliberately designed by the founding fathers to prevent any single branch from usurping power and to ensure that government remains subordinate to the people. When a crisis emerges, it typically reflects a situation where one branch of government has expanded its authority beyond what was constitutionally permitted. The Anti-Federalists' fierce opposition to the Alien and Sedition Acts in the late 18th century, for instance, demonstrated an early recognition that unchecked federal power could threaten individual liberty and state sovereignty.[1] Such episodes underscore the importance of constitutional restraints and highlight why the inclusion of the Bill of Rights was indispensable during ratification.

During President John Adams's administration, the passage of the Alien and Sedition Acts in 1798 represented one of the first significant tests of the young republic's constitutional limits. These laws granted the federal government extraordinary powers to suppress dissent and target immigrants—actions that many contemporaries saw as direct assaults on free speech and the rights of states. Conservatives view this crisis as a cautionary tale: it revealed that even in the early republic, governmental overreach could provoke widespread opposition and undermine the legitimacy of the constitutional order. The eventual repeal of these acts and the subsequent

---

[1] Hamilton, A., Madison, J., & Jay, J. (1961). *The Federalist Papers*. New York: New American Library.

push for a Bill of Rights served to reassert the founding principle that government power must be strictly circumscribed.[2]

Another early constitutional crisis occurred during the Bank War in the 1830s under President Andrew Jackson. Jackson's vehement opposition to the Second Bank of the United States was grounded in his belief that the bank concentrated too much economic power in the hands of a few private interests and, by extension, the federal government. Jackson's veto of the bank recharter was seen as a bold move to dismantle an institution that threatened economic liberty. Conservatives applaud Jackson for his willingness to confront entrenched power and for reinforcing the notion that government should promote economic opportunity without fostering monopolistic structures. This crisis, they argue, is emblematic of the constitutional commitment to limiting federal intervention in the economy.[3]

The period following the Civil War presents one of the most profound constitutional crises in American history. Reconstruction brought into sharp relief the tension between federal authority and state sovereignty. The federal government's efforts to secure civil rights for formerly enslaved individuals—through measures such as the Reconstruction Acts and the Fourteenth Amendment—were met with vehement resistance from many Southern states. Conservatives acknowledge that the post-war period was marked by significant political turmoil; however, they assert that the constitutional crisis of Reconstruction ultimately demonstrated the enduring power of federal principles when they are applied judiciously. The eventual compromise that restored a balance between federal oversight and state autonomy—albeit with mixed outcomes for civil rights—illustrates that even profound crises can be resolved by returning to the constitutional foundations laid by the framers.[4]

The New Deal era of the 1930s is another critical example. In response to the Great Depression, President Franklin D. Roosevelt enacted a series of sweeping economic reforms aimed at stabilizing the economy and providing relief to millions of Americans. Critics, especially from conservative circles, argued that these measures represented a dramatic expansion of federal power that threatened the limited government envisioned by the founders. The Supreme Court's initial invalidation of several New Deal programs, based on a narrow interpretation of the Commerce Clause, reflected an early attempt to rein in federal overreach. Although later decisions and political pressures

---

[2] Locke, J. (1689). *Two Treatises of Government*. London: Awnsham Churchill.

[3] Montesquieu, C. (1748). *The Spirit of the Laws*. Paris: Barrillot & Fils.

[4] Pocock, J. G. A. (1975). *The Machiavellian Moment: Florentine Political Thought and the Atlantic Republican Tradition*. Princeton: Princeton University Press.

led to the acceptance of New Deal policies, conservatives maintain that the period remains a stark warning: once federal power is expanded beyond its constitutional limits, it is difficult to restore the original balance. They argue that a strict adherence to the framers' intent—ensuring that federal regulation is limited to matters directly affecting interstate commerce—would have prevented many of the excesses of the New Deal.[5]

The Watergate scandal of the early 1970s represents a modern constitutional crisis in which the abuse of executive power was exposed, leading to an erosion of public trust in government. President Richard Nixon's attempts to cover up illegal activities and his subsequent resignation highlighted the potential for executive overreach to destabilize the constitutional order. Conservatives view Watergate as a vindication of the system of checks and balances, as the coordinated actions of Congress, the judiciary, and the free press ultimately compelled a return to constitutional norms. This crisis reaffirmed the principle that no branch of government is above the law and that rigorous oversight is essential for maintaining a free society.[6]

The contentious 2000 presidential election further illustrated the fragility of constitutional processes in the face of partisan conflict. The protracted dispute over vote counting in Florida and the Supreme Court's controversial decision in *Bush v. Gore* exposed vulnerabilities in the electoral system and raised fundamental questions about the role of the judiciary in resolving political disputes. Conservatives argue that, despite its imperfections, the constitutional system provided mechanisms—such as judicial review and the possibility of constitutional amendments—to address the crisis. They maintain that a return to the framers' original vision, where institutional checks prevail over partisan maneuvering, is necessary to restore confidence in the electoral process and ensure that constitutional legitimacy is maintained.[7]

The post-9/11 era has introduced a new set of challenges that test constitutional boundaries, particularly regarding national security and individual liberty. In the aftermath of the terrorist attacks on September 11, 2001, the federal government significantly expanded its surveillance and security measures. While these actions were taken in the name of protecting the nation, conservatives argue that they risk infringing on the constitutional rights of American citizens—especially the rights to privacy and due process. The tension between security and liberty is a recurring theme in constitutional crises, and conservatives assert that any expansion of federal

---

[5] Rakove, J. (1997). *Original Meanings: Politics and Ideas in the Making of the Constitution*. New York: Vintage.

[6] Adams, S. (1961). *The Revolutionary Writings of Samuel Adams*. Boston: Beacon Press.

[7] Bork, R. (1990). *The Tempting of America: The Political Seduction of the Law*. New York: Free Press.

power must be strictly limited by the Constitution. The experience of the post-9/11 era underscores the importance of a balanced approach that safeguards national security without sacrificing the fundamental rights the Constitution was designed to protect.[8]

In theory, constitutional crises arise when the mechanisms for self-correction inherent in the constitutional system fail to function properly. Conservatives emphasize that the framers deliberately constructed the Constitution to be a fixed standard—a document that provides clear limits on governmental power and a set process for resolving disputes. When these limits are ignored or subverted, a constitutional crisis emerges. Importantly, conservatives argue that such crises are not irreversible; rather, they are opportunities to reaffirm and restore the constitutional order through judicial review, legislative reform, or, if necessary, constitutional amendments. The resolution of a constitutional crisis, therefore, depends on the willingness of political actors to return to the founding principles that have historically safeguarded American liberty.[9]

Practical responses to constitutional crises typically involve a combination of judicial intervention, legislative oversight, and public accountability. For example, during the Watergate scandal, the coordinated efforts of Congress and the judiciary ultimately forced a constitutional reset by holding the executive accountable. Conservatives argue that this interplay among the branches is precisely what the framers intended—a system in which power is continuously checked to prevent any one branch from becoming dominant. Judicial review, when executed in accordance with an originalist approach, provides an objective standard that can rein in excesses of government power. Such institutional corrections not only resolve the immediate crisis but also strengthen the overall resilience of the constitutional system.[10]

Legislative action also plays a key role in resolving constitutional crises. The amendment process, though intentionally arduous, allows the people to adapt the Constitution in a deliberate and measured way. Conservatives maintain that significant changes in the constitutional order should occur only through this formal process, ensuring that any evolution in governance reflects broad consensus rather than transient political pressures. This democratic safeguard prevents hasty or ideologically driven modifications that could undermine the constitutional balance

[8] Jefferson, T. (Founders Online). "Notes on the State of Virginia." National Archives.

[9] Dickinson, J. (1994). *Colonial Self-Government in America*. Cambridge: Harvard University Press.

[10] Calhoun, J. C. (1983). "Separation of Powers and the Structure of the Constitution." In *Foundations of American Government* (pp. 29–32). New York: Harper & Row.

and serves as a reminder that the Constitution is a living instrument that evolves only through careful deliberation.[11]

Public opinion and media scrutiny further contribute to the resolution of constitutional crises. In today's hyper-connected world, the media plays a crucial role in exposing governmental overreach and mobilizing public support for constitutional accountability. Conservatives argue that a vigilant press, in conjunction with an informed citizenry, is vital for maintaining the integrity of the constitutional order. While sensationalized media coverage can sometimes distort the perception of a crisis, the underlying function of the press as a watchdog remains essential. This cultural force, combined with institutional checks, helps to ensure that constitutional violations are met with appropriate corrective measures.[12]

Cultural continuity is also a fundamental element in understanding and resolving constitutional crises. The American tradition of self-governance and respect for individual liberty has been nurtured over centuries and forms the bedrock of national identity. Conservatives emphasize that the historical legacy of the American Revolution and the founding debates instills a collective commitment to constitutional principles. This cultural heritage serves as a moral compass, guiding responses to crises by reminding citizens and leaders alike of the enduring values that must be preserved even in turbulent times.[13]

Internationally, comparative constitutional analysis shows that democracies with rigid, codified constitutional frameworks tend to recover more effectively from crises. Conservatives argue that the American model, with its clear separation of powers and robust mechanisms for judicial review, has proven its resilience in the face of significant challenges. Experiences from other nations, where flexible or poorly defined constitutional norms have led to prolonged instability, reinforce the conservative position that adherence to the original constitutional framework is the best safeguard against crisis.[14]

Globalization and technological change introduce additional complexities into the equation. As the United States navigates an increasingly interconnected global landscape, external pressures—such as international trade disputes and digital surveillance—can exacerbate internal constitutional tensions. Conservatives assert that while global engagement is necessary, it must not erode the constitutional limits that protect individual liberty and state sovereignty. The framers' vision, as

---

[11] Jefferson, T. (Founders Online). "Notes on the State of Virginia." National Archives.

[12] Amar, A. R. (2005). *America's Constitution: A Biography*. New York: Random House.

[13] Henry, P. (1775). *Speech on Colonial Rights*. Richmond: Virginia Historical Society.

[14] Kirk, R. (1953). *The Conservative Mind*. New York: Free Press.

embodied in the Constitution, was to create a government with clearly delineated powers that would not be easily expanded by external forces. Thus, in the modern era, any efforts to extend federal authority in response to global challenges must be carefully measured against the original constitutional boundaries.[15]

Political polarization, too, intensifies constitutional crises by transforming legal disputes into partisan battles. In a highly divided political environment, conflicts over constitutional interpretation can become weaponized by political factions, further undermining the legitimacy of the constitutional order. Conservatives argue that such polarization makes it all the more important to return to objective, originalist standards. By anchoring constitutional debates in the text and historical context, the courts and legislatures can depoliticize disputes and focus on resolving them based on the framers' intended limits rather than contemporary ideological preferences.[16]

The role of the Supreme Court in these crises cannot be overstated. Conservative jurists maintain that the Court must exercise strict judicial restraint and adhere to an originalist approach when interpreting constitutional provisions. Landmark cases such as *United States v. Lopez* and *Morrison v. United States* illustrate how a narrow reading of the Commerce Clause can serve as a check on federal overreach. Conservatives view these decisions as essential corrections that reaffirm the limits of governmental power, thereby preventing the gradual erosion of the constitutional order. Judicial review, when grounded in the original meaning of the Constitution, is seen as the ultimate safeguard against the emergence of unchecked state power.[17]

Legislative oversight further reinforces the constitutional framework during crises. Congress's power to regulate commerce and control federal spending acts as a vital counterbalance to executive and judicial actions. When Congress exercises its oversight responsibilities effectively, it helps to ensure that any deviations from the constitutional order are corrected through democratic means. Conservatives argue that robust legislative oversight is indispensable for restoring balance during a crisis and for maintaining the long-term integrity of the constitutional system.[18]

---

[15] Levinson, S. (2006). *Our Undemocratic Constitution: Where the Constitution Goes Wrong (and How We the People Can Correct It)*. New Haven: Yale University Press.

[16] Hayek, F. A. (1960). *The Constitution of Liberty*. Chicago: University of Chicago Press.

[17] Aldrich, J. H. (1983). *Constitutional Theory*. Chicago: University of Chicago Press.

[18] Ackerman, B. (1991). *We the People: Foundations*. Cambridge, MA: Harvard University Press.

The amendment process also provides a democratic mechanism for resolving constitutional crises. Although the process is deliberately difficult, it ensures that any changes to the Constitution reflect broad consensus and careful deliberation. Conservatives assert that this safeguard prevents rash or ideologically driven shifts in government power. In times of crisis, the possibility of amending the Constitution offers a peaceful and orderly path to reform, reinforcing the principle that true constitutional change must occur through the will of the people.[19]

Cultural factors continue to play a significant role in shaping responses to constitutional crises. The American commitment to individual liberty and self-governance is deeply ingrained in the national psyche, and this cultural legacy provides a powerful incentive for upholding constitutional limits. Conservatives argue that public support for the founding principles is essential for resolving crises and that any deviation from these principles would not only undermine legal protections but also erode the very identity of the nation.[20]

Modern crises also emerge from the pressures of globalization and the rapid pace of technological innovation. As digital surveillance and global economic integration expand, there is a risk that the federal government may overstep its constitutional authority in its attempt to address new challenges. Conservatives maintain that while the state must adapt to modern realities, such adaptation should not come at the expense of the constitutional limits established by the framers. Any expansion of federal power in response to these challenges must be strictly justified by a clear and direct impact on interstate commerce, ensuring that the core principles of limited government and individual liberty are preserved.[21]

Political polarization further complicates the resolution of constitutional crises. When disputes become entangled in partisan conflict, objective legal analysis can give way to ideological battles that threaten to destabilize the constitutional order. Conservatives argue that returning to the original, objective standards of constitutional interpretation is the only effective means of depoliticizing these disputes and restoring balance among the branches of government.[22]

Economic and regulatory pressures also contribute to constitutional crises. In times of fiscal stress or economic downturn, the temptation for the federal government to expand its regulatory reach increases. Conservatives contend that such expansions, if left unchecked, can lead to

---

[19] Connelley, W. F. (2009). *Restoring the Constitutional Order*. Lexington: University Press of Kentucky.

[20] Jefferson, T., & Madison, J. (Founders Online). "Letter from Thomas Jefferson to James Madison, July 29, 1787." National Archives.

[21] Dickinson, J. (1994). *Colonial Self-Government in America*. Cambridge: Harvard University Press.

[22] Ferguson, N. (2004). *Colony: A History of Early America*. New York: Penguin Press.

an erosion of economic freedom and a departure from the free-market principles enshrined in the Constitution. By strictly enforcing the constitutional limits on federal economic power—particularly those articulated in the Commerce Clause and the Takings Clause—the nation can prevent a drift toward an overly interventionist state.[23]

International comparisons provide additional evidence in support of the conservative approach. Democracies with rigid, well-defined constitutional frameworks tend to experience greater political stability and economic prosperity than those with flexible or ambiguous systems. Conservatives argue that the American constitutional model, with its clear separation of powers and strict limitations on government intervention, has been a key factor in the nation's long-term success. This international perspective reinforces the view that maintaining the original constitutional order is essential for resolving crises and safeguarding individual liberty.[24]

Finally, the moral imperative to uphold the founding principles remains at the heart of the conservative response to constitutional crises. The framers designed the Constitution to be a bulwark against tyranny, ensuring that government power is always subject to strict checks and balances. When constitutional crises occur, they represent a deviation from these core values. Conservatives argue that the only way to restore the constitutional order is to reaffirm the original intent of the framers through disciplined judicial review, effective legislative oversight, and, if necessary, constitutional amendment. This moral commitment to limited government and individual liberty is the ultimate remedy for resolving constitutional crises and preserving the republic for future generations.[25]

In conclusion, notable historical constitutional crises—from the controversies surrounding the Alien and Sedition Acts and the Bank War to the challenges of Reconstruction, the New Deal, Watergate, and the 2000 presidential election—offer critical insights into the strengths and limitations of the American constitutional order. From a politically conservative perspective, these crises illustrate that the only reliable solution is a steadfast return to the framers' original intent. By reinforcing the principles of limited government, federalism, and individual rights through judicial review, legislative reform, and the constitutional amendment process, America can navigate even the most severe crises without compromising its foundational values. In an era marked by globalization, technological innovation, and deep political polarization,

---

[23] Locke, J. (1689). *Two Treatises of Government*. London: Awnsham Churchill.

[24] Rakove, J. (1997). *Original Meanings: Politics and Ideas in the Making of the Constitution*. New York: Vintage.

[25] Adams, S. (1961). *The Revolutionary Writings of Samuel Adams*. Boston: Beacon Press.

a disciplined, originalist approach provides the definitive answer to saving America. This commitment not only restores balance to the constitutional system but also ensures that government remains a servant of the people—a legacy that is essential for the survival and prosperity of the republic.[26]

[26] Hamilton, A., Madison, J., & Jay, J. (1961). *The Federalist Papers*. New York: New American Library.

3. The Role of Political Parties and Ideology

Constitutional crises in American history have often been precipitated, exacerbated, or resolved by the dynamics of political parties and the prevailing ideological currents. In the American constitutional framework—designed by the founding fathers to limit governmental power and protect individual liberty—political parties have played a dual role. On one hand, they channel diverse political views and facilitate organized debate; on the other, they can polarize and distort constitutional discourse. From a politically conservative perspective, the true test of the Constitution lies in its ability to withstand partisan pressures and ideological extremes. This paper examines the historical and theoretical dimensions of political parties and ideology as they relate to constitutional crises, arguing that a return to the original principles enshrined in the Constitution is the only reliable remedy for resolving conflicts driven by excessive partisanship.

The founding fathers were acutely aware that a strong, centralized government could lead to tyranny, and they designed the Constitution to prevent any one faction from seizing power. Yet, political parties emerged almost immediately in the early republic as a natural outcome of diverse regional interests and differing visions for America's future. Conservatives argue that the early parties, though often contentious, operated within a framework that ultimately reinforced the constitutional order by holding each other accountable. However, over time, as parties became more institutionalized and polarized, they increasingly contributed to constitutional crises by prioritizing ideological victory over constitutional fidelity.[1]

In the post-Revolutionary period, debates over the balance between federal and state power, economic regulation, and individual rights were often framed along partisan lines. The Federalists, who advocated for a strong national government, and the Anti-Federalists, who demanded robust protections for individual liberties and state sovereignty, represented competing visions that would continue to influence American politics for centuries. Conservatives maintain that the resolution of these early conflicts—particularly the incorporation of the Bill of Rights—was achieved not by abandoning principled debate but by returning to the framers' original intent. This historical process underscores the conservative belief that when political parties function within the constitutional limits, they can be a force for stability and renewal rather than division.[2]

Throughout American history, political parties have both catalyzed and mitigated constitutional crises. The intense partisan conflict during the Jacksonian era, exemplified by the Bank War,

---

[1] Hamilton, A., Madison, J., & Jay, J. (1961). *The Federalist Papers*. New York: New American Library.

[2] Locke, J. (1689). *Two Treatises of Government*. London: Awnsham Churchill.

reflected deep ideological divisions over the role of government in the economy. President Andrew Jackson's fierce opposition to the national bank was rooted in a conservative distrust of concentrated economic power—a theme that resonated with many who viewed federal intervention as a threat to individual liberty. Although the ensuing crisis resulted in significant political upheaval, conservatives argue that it ultimately reinforced the necessity of limiting federal power and preserving economic freedom.[3]

Similarly, during the tumultuous years of Reconstruction following the Civil War, the interplay of party politics and constitutional interpretation led to profound debates over civil rights and federal authority. Conservatives contend that the radical measures implemented during Reconstruction—while well-intentioned—often exceeded the constitutional boundaries set by the founding generation. The subsequent backlash, which saw the reassertion of states' rights and a retreat from expansive federal intervention, is viewed by conservatives as a reaffirmation of the importance of limited government. They argue that the ideological battles of this era demonstrate the perils of abandoning the constitutional principles of self-governance and individual liberty in favor of transient political ideologies.[4]

In the 20th century, the rise of the New Deal marked a watershed moment in the role of political parties and ideology in constitutional crises. The progressive policies enacted by President Franklin D. Roosevelt in response to the Great Depression significantly expanded federal power. Conservatives assert that the New Deal, while arguably necessary to address immediate economic hardships, initiated a trend toward a more centralized government that deviated from the original constitutional framework. The ideological battle between proponents of expansive government intervention and advocates of free-market principles intensified, culminating in contentious Supreme Court battles over the limits of the Commerce Clause. Conservatives argue that these conflicts highlight the danger of allowing partisan ideology to override the framers' original design, ultimately leading to a constitutional crisis in which the very foundations of American liberty are at stake.[5]

The Watergate scandal of the 1970s provides another clear example of how political parties and ideology can trigger a constitutional crisis. The abuse of executive power by President Richard Nixon, and the subsequent cover-up, sparked a profound crisis of confidence in government.

---

[3] Montesquieu, C. (1748). *The Spirit of the Laws*. Paris: Barrillot & Fils.

[4] Pocock, J. G. A. (1975). *The Machiavellian Moment: Florentine Political Thought and the Atlantic Republican Tradition*. Princeton: Princeton University Press.

[5] Rakove, J. (1997). *Original Meanings: Politics and Ideas in the Making of the Constitution*. New York: Vintage.

Conservatives point to the eventual resignation of Nixon and the rigorous congressional and judicial investigations that followed as evidence that the constitutional system is capable of self-correction—even in the face of overwhelming partisan strife. They argue that the resolution of Watergate reaffirmed the necessity of strict checks and balances and underscored that no political party or individual is above the law.[6]

In more recent times, the 2000 presidential election exposed the fragility of constitutional mechanisms in the face of extreme partisan polarization. The prolonged legal battles over the Florida vote count, culminating in the Supreme Court's controversial decision in Bush v. Gore, revealed the deep divisions within the political system. Conservatives maintain that this crisis was not solely the product of electoral mismanagement but also a manifestation of the dangerous politicization of constitutional processes. They argue that a return to the framers' original intent—where constitutional disputes are resolved through objective legal standards rather than partisan power plays—is essential for restoring public trust and ensuring the legitimacy of government.[7]

The post-9/11 era has introduced new dimensions to the role of political parties and ideology in constitutional crises. In response to national security threats, the federal government has often expanded its powers under the guise of protecting the nation. Conservatives have expressed deep concerns that such expansions, if left unchecked by partisan oversight, could erode the constitutional limits on government authority. They argue that the ideological battles over issues like surveillance, detention, and executive authority reflect a departure from the constitutional order that the founding fathers established. For conservatives, the appropriate response is not to allow security concerns to justify a permanent increase in federal power but to reassert the constitutional principles of limited government and the protection of individual rights.[8]

The interplay between political parties and constitutional ideology is further complicated by the influence of modern media and the information age. The rapid dissemination of partisan narratives can amplify crises, obscuring objective legal standards with ideological rhetoric. Conservatives assert that while political debate is healthy and necessary, it must be anchored in the constitutional text and historical context. When political parties manipulate public opinion to justify actions that stretch constitutional boundaries, they risk precipitating a crisis of legitimacy.

---

[6] Adams, S. (1961). *The Revolutionary Writings of Samuel Adams*. Boston: Beacon Press.

[7] Bork, R. (1990). *The Tempting of America: The Political Seduction of the Law*. New York: Free Press.

[8] Jefferson, T. (Founders Online). "Notes on the State of Virginia." National Archives.

Thus, conservatives advocate for a disciplined, originalist approach to constitutional interpretation that depoliticizes legal disputes and ensures that governmental power is always measured against the immutable standards of the Constitution.[9]

Ideological extremism within political parties also contributes to constitutional crises by polarizing legislative debates and impeding compromise. Conservatives argue that when parties become vehicles for radical ideology rather than pragmatic governance, the constitutional order suffers. Extremist policies, whether on the left or the right, tend to bypass the traditional checks and balances designed to ensure measured, consensus-based policymaking. This ideological rigidity can lead to gridlock, where the inability to reach bipartisan agreements further destabilizes the constitutional system. Conservatives maintain that a return to moderate, principle-based politics—rooted in the original constitutional framework—is essential for avoiding the pitfalls of partisan extremism.[10]

The role of political leadership is critical in times of constitutional crisis. Leaders who adhere to the founding principles can guide the nation through turbulent periods by emphasizing unity and a commitment to limited government. Conservatives highlight instances where strong leadership, in line with the framers' vision, has helped to resolve crises and restore stability. For example, the leadership displayed during the Watergate scandal—characterized by accountability and a willingness to adhere to constitutional norms—serves as a model for how political parties can play a constructive role in times of crisis.[11]

Institutional checks and balances are the practical mechanisms by which constitutional crises are managed, and political parties play an essential role in upholding these mechanisms. Conservatives argue that when parties function within the limits of the Constitution, they provide a vital check on governmental power. However, when parties prioritize ideological gain over constitutional fidelity, they can contribute to crises by undermining the system of checks and balances. This dynamic is evident in periods of partisan polarization, where competing parties engage in perpetual conflict rather than seeking common ground. Conservatives insist that restoring the focus to the Constitution's original intent is the only way to ensure that political parties serve the public interest and not just their own agendas.[12]

---

[9] Dickinson, J. (1994). *Colonial Self-Government in America*. Cambridge: Harvard University Press.

[10] Calhoun, J. C. (1983). "Separation of Powers and the Structure of the Constitution." In *Foundations of American Government* (pp. 29–32). New York: Harper & Row.

[11] Jefferson, T. (Founders Online). "Notes on the State of Virginia." National Archives.

[12] Amar, A. R. (2005). *America's Constitution: A Biography*. New York: Random House.

Another aspect of political parties' influence on constitutional crises is their role in shaping public policy. The legislative process, driven by party platforms and ideological commitments, can either reinforce or erode constitutional principles. Conservatives contend that policies rooted in the framers' original vision—emphasizing limited government, free markets, and individual rights—are most likely to contribute to long-term stability and prosperity. In contrast, policies that are driven by radical ideologies or that seek to expand federal power in the name of social engineering often lead to unintended consequences and constitutional imbalances. Thus, the ideological orientation of political parties is central to the health of the constitutional system.[13]

Furthermore, the evolution of political parties over time has had profound implications for constitutional governance. Early in American history, the rivalry between Federalists and Anti-Federalists was characterized by robust debate and, ultimately, by a convergence around the principles of limited government and individual rights. Over the centuries, however, the party system has evolved, and the ideological divides have become more entrenched. Conservatives argue that this evolution, particularly the trend toward hyper-partisanship, has contributed to a constitutional crisis by shifting the focus from constitutional principles to partisan victories. They advocate for a re-centering of political discourse on the foundational values of the Constitution, which they believe will help to resolve crises by fostering a culture of moderation and respect for institutional checks and balances.[14]

The influence of ideology on constitutional interpretation is also evident in the judicial realm. Conservative jurists argue that when judges allow their personal ideological beliefs to color their interpretation of the Constitution, they contribute to constitutional instability. An originalist approach, they contend, would mitigate this risk by ensuring that judicial decisions are based on the text and historical context of the document rather than on contemporary ideological trends. Landmark cases in which the Court's interpretation of constitutional provisions shifted dramatically in response to ideological pressures are cited as cautionary examples. Conservatives maintain that only by adhering to the framers' original intent can the judiciary effectively serve as a guardian of the constitutional order.[15]

---

[13] Henry, P. (1775). *Speech on Colonial Rights*. Richmond: Virginia Historical Society.

[14] Kirk, R. (1953). *The Conservative Mind*. New York: Free Press.

[15] Levinson, S. (2006). *Our Undemocratic Constitution: Where the Constitution Goes Wrong (and How We the People Can Correct It)*. New Haven: Yale University Press.

Modern constitutional crises, therefore, must be viewed not only through the lens of institutional failure but also as reflections of deeper ideological battles within the political system. Conservatives argue that when political parties and their ideologies become divorced from the original constitutional principles, the entire system is at risk. In such times, the only effective remedy is a return to the founding ideals—a re-emphasis on the values of limited government, individual liberty, and the rule of law that were so carefully embedded in the Constitution by the founding fathers.[16]

The role of media and public opinion in modern constitutional crises cannot be ignored. In today's fast-paced, hyper-partisan media environment, ideological narratives can quickly dominate the public discourse, often distorting the true nature of constitutional disputes. Conservatives caution that this can lead to a perception of crisis that is amplified by partisan rhetoric rather than by objective legal realities. They argue that a return to the original constitutional standards, interpreted through an originalist lens, is essential for cutting through the noise and restoring faith in the constitutional system. Only by grounding public debate in the historical context and immutable principles of the Constitution can society navigate crises effectively.[17]

International experiences further illuminate the challenges posed by ideological extremism in constitutional governance. Comparative studies indicate that democracies with rigid, well-defined constitutional frameworks tend to exhibit greater stability and less ideological polarization than those with more flexible or ambiguous systems. Conservatives assert that the American model, with its clear separation of powers and explicit limits on governmental authority, offers the best template for managing ideological conflicts. They maintain that any attempt to broaden constitutional interpretations in response to shifting political trends risks undermining the stability that has long been the hallmark of American governance.[18]

The conservative approach to resolving constitutional crises emphasizes the importance of institutional integrity and ideological moderation. Leaders who prioritize the principles of the Constitution over partisan interests are seen as key to restoring balance during times of crisis. Conservatives argue that when political parties remain committed to the founding ideals—rather than succumbing to ideological extremism—the result is a more resilient and adaptable

---

[16] Hayek, F. A. (1960). *The Constitution of Liberty*. Chicago: University of Chicago Press.

[17] Aldrich, J. H. (1983). *Constitutional Theory*. Chicago: University of Chicago Press.

[18] Ackerman, B. (1991). *We the People: Foundations*. Cambridge, MA: Harvard University Press.

constitutional order. This, in turn, allows the government to address contemporary challenges without sacrificing its fundamental commitments to limited government and individual rights.[19]

Legislative oversight plays a crucial role in this context. Congress, as the primary lawmaking body, has the power to check executive overreach and ensure that policies remain consistent with the Constitution. Conservatives contend that effective legislative oversight, conducted in a spirit of bipartisanship and guided by the original constitutional text, is essential for resolving crises. When Congress acts decisively to rein in excesses and restore constitutional order, it reinforces the system of checks and balances that is the cornerstone of American democracy.[20]

Finally, the amendment process stands as the ultimate democratic safeguard against constitutional crises driven by ideological extremism. Although the process is deliberately difficult, it ensures that any significant changes to the constitutional order are made only with broad consensus. Conservatives argue that this process, when used judiciously, can resolve crises without undermining the enduring principles that have long protected American liberty. The prospect of constitutional amendment serves as a reminder that while the Constitution is a living document, its evolution must be measured and consistent with the framers' original intent.[21]

In conclusion, the role of political parties and ideology in American constitutional crises is profound and multifaceted. Historical case studies—from the debates over the Alien and Sedition Acts and the Bank War, through Reconstruction and the New Deal, to modern episodes such as Watergate and the 2000 election—demonstrate that ideological extremism and partisan conflict can precipitate crises that test the very foundations of constitutional governance. From a politically conservative perspective, the solution lies not in expanding governmental power or succumbing to partisan pressures but in a steadfast return to the founding principles of limited government, federalism, and individual liberty. By adhering to an originalist interpretation of the Constitution, ensuring robust legislative oversight, and upholding the amendment process as the proper means for constitutional evolution, America can resolve its constitutional crises and secure its future as a beacon of freedom and democratic self-governance. This disciplined

[19] Connelley, W. F. (2009). *Restoring the Constitutional Order*. Lexington: University Press of Kentucky.

[20] Jefferson, T., & Madison, J. (Founders Online). "Letter from Thomas Jefferson to James Madison, July 29, 1787." National Archives.

[21] Dickinson, J. (1994). *Colonial Self-Government in America*. Cambridge: Harvard University Press.

approach, rooted in the framers' original intent, remains the definitive answer to saving America from the perils of unchecked state power and ideological extremism.[22-26]

[22] Ferguson, N. (2004). *Colony: A History of Early America*. New York: Penguin Press.

[23] Locke, J. (1689). *Two Treatises of Government*. London: Awnsham Churchill.

[24] Rakove, J. (1997). *Original Meanings: Politics and Ideas in the Making of the Constitution*. New York: Vintage.

[25] Adams, S. (1961). *The Revolutionary Writings of Samuel Adams*. Boston: Beacon Press.

[26] Hamilton, A., Madison, J., & Jay, J. (1961). *The Federalist Papers*. New York: New American Library.

4. Lessons Learned from Past Crises

Throughout its history, the United States has faced numerous constitutional crises that have tested the very fabric of its political and legal order. These crises—ranging from the turbulent debates of the early republic to modern episodes of executive overreach and partisan deadlock—offer invaluable lessons on governance, the limits of state power, and the enduring importance of the constitutional framework established by the founding fathers. From a politically conservative perspective, such crises are not merely historical aberrations; they are critical junctures that reaffirm the necessity of limited government, strict adherence to the rule of law, and the preservation of individual liberties. This paper provides a comprehensive analysis of the lessons learned from past constitutional crises, arguing that a return to the original intent of the Constitution is the only reliable means of resolving conflicts and ensuring the survival of American freedom.

A fundamental lesson drawn from historical crises is the imperative of constitutional fidelity. The founding fathers designed the Constitution as a bulwark against tyranny—a document that limits governmental power and safeguards individual rights. When the government strays from these principles, the very legitimacy of the regime is called into question. For instance, during the Civil War, the secession of Southern states and the ensuing conflict demonstrated that abandoning constitutional order can lead to devastating national disintegration.[1] President Abraham Lincoln's determined effort to preserve the Union was grounded in the belief that the Constitution, with its clear separation of powers and federal structure, must be upheld even at great cost. His actions underscored the conservative principle that the survival of liberty depends on an unwavering commitment to constitutional limits.[2]

Closely linked to constitutional fidelity is the significance of checks and balances. The framers deliberately divided government power among the legislative, executive, and judicial branches to ensure that no single entity could dominate the political landscape. The Watergate scandal of the early 1970s is a prime example of how these mechanisms operate in practice. When President Richard Nixon attempted to obstruct justice, the rigorous oversight by Congress and the decisive intervention of the judiciary—exemplified in the landmark decision of United States v. Nixon—forced a retraction of presidential power and restored public confidence in the rule of law.[3] Conservatives view Watergate as a vindication of the system of checks and

[1] Hamilton, A., Madison, J., & Jay, J. (1961). *The Federalist Papers*. New York: New American Library.

[2] Locke, J. (1689). *Two Treatises of Government*. London: Awnsham Churchill.

[3] Montesquieu, C. (1748). *The Spirit of the Laws*. Paris: Barrillot & Fils.

balances, demonstrating that even when executive overreach threatens to destabilize the nation, the constitutional framework can self-correct if its principles are respected.[4]

Another enduring lesson is the danger of unchecked executive power. The internment of Japanese Americans during World War II, sanctioned by Executive Order 9066, stands as a stark reminder of what can happen when the executive branch is allowed to operate without sufficient oversight. The Supreme Court's decision in Korematsu v. United States, though controversial, ultimately highlighted the peril of permitting state power to infringe upon individual liberties in times of national stress.[5] Conservatives argue that such episodes illustrate why it is crucial to maintain strict judicial and legislative checks on executive authority—a principle that remains as vital today as it was in the 18th century.

Historical crises have also underscored the necessity of public engagement and civic participation. The civil rights movement of the 1960s, for example, emerged from a groundswell of grassroots activism demanding that the government honor the promise of equality under the law. Despite significant institutional resistance, persistent public pressure led to transformative judicial decisions such as Brown v. Board of Education, which dismantled the legal framework for segregation in public schools.[6] Conservatives assert that this example demonstrates how an active citizenry can compel government accountability and drive positive constitutional change without abandoning the principles of limited government.

The ideological divide that emerged during the founding era—between Federalists and Anti-Federalists—provides another critical lesson. Early debates over the ratification of the Constitution, particularly the insistence on a Bill of Rights, illustrate that a balance of power and respect for individual liberties must be enshrined from the outset. Conservatives view these debates as proof that the framers anticipated potential abuses of governmental power and, as a result, embedded safeguards to prevent such overreach.[7] The subsequent adoption of the Bill of Rights confirmed that the Constitution was designed not only to establish government but also to protect the citizenry from its excesses. This foundational lesson remains relevant today, especially as contemporary political factions sometimes seek to expand state power at the expense of individual rights.

---

[4] Pocock, J. G. A. (1975). *The Machiavellian Moment: Florentine Political Thought and the Atlantic Republican Tradition*. Princeton: Princeton University Press.

[5] Rakove, J. (1997). *Original Meanings: Politics and Ideas in the Making of the Constitution*. New York: Vintage.

[6] Adams, S. (1961). *The Revolutionary Writings of Samuel Adams*. Boston: Beacon Press.

[7] Bork, R. (1990). *The Tempting of America: The Political Seduction of the Law*. New York: Free Press.

The Bank War during Andrew Jackson's presidency is another instructive episode. Jackson's vehement opposition to the Second Bank of the United States was driven by his belief that the institution represented an undue concentration of economic power that could be exploited by the federal government. By vetoing the recharter of the bank, Jackson aimed to preserve economic freedom and prevent an over centralization of power. Conservatives applaud this decisive action as consistent with the founding principle that government should facilitate, not hinder, the free market.[8] Yet, the ensuing political battles also revealed how partisan conflicts could escalate into constitutional crises when government power is perceived as expanding beyond its proper limits.

The Reconstruction era following the Civil War provides further insight into the delicate balance between federal authority and state sovereignty. The struggle to redefine citizenship and extend civil rights to formerly enslaved individuals led to significant constitutional and political challenges. While federal interventions during Reconstruction were aimed at establishing a more equitable society, conservatives argue that many of these measures exceeded the framers' original vision of limited federal power. The eventual retreat from Reconstruction policies, with a renewed emphasis on states' rights, demonstrates that when federal authority is perceived as overreaching, it can trigger a crisis that undermines the very foundation of constitutional governance.[9]

The New Deal represents one of the most transformative and contentious periods in American constitutional history. In response to the Great Depression, President Franklin D. Roosevelt's administration implemented an array of federal programs designed to stabilize the economy and provide relief to millions. Conservatives contend that the expansive use of the Commerce Clause to justify these programs marked a radical departure from the Constitution's original intent. While New Deal policies were credited with mitigating the economic crisis, they also set a precedent for an administrative state with far-reaching regulatory powers—a development that many conservatives view as antithetical to the principles of limited government and individual liberty.[10]

The 2000 presidential election further illuminated the vulnerabilities within the constitutional framework. The protracted legal battle over the Florida vote count, culminating in the Supreme Court's decision in Bush v. Gore, exposed deep partisan fault lines and raised profound questions about the legitimacy of the electoral process. Conservatives argue that this crisis underscored

---

[8] Jefferson, T. (Founders Online). "Notes on the State of Virginia." National Archives.

[9] Dickinson, J. (1994). *Colonial Self-Government in America*. Cambridge: Harvard University Press.

[10] Calhoun, J. C. (1983). "Separation of Powers and the Structure of the Constitution." In *Foundations of American Government* (pp. 29–32). New York: Harper & Row.

the need for clear, objective constitutional mechanisms to resolve disputes, rather than relying on politically charged judicial decisions. The lessons learned from this episode emphasize the importance of judicial impartiality and the need to adhere to the framers' original guidelines for interpreting the Constitution.[11]

In the post-9/11 era, the balance between national security and individual rights has emerged as a critical area of constitutional stress. The expansion of surveillance programs and emergency powers in the wake of the terrorist attacks has raised alarms among conservatives that the government is overstepping its bounds. This tension between security and liberty exemplifies the enduring challenge of constitutional crises: the need to address contemporary threats without compromising the foundational principles of limited government and due process. Conservatives argue that any such measures must be strictly circumscribed by the Constitution to prevent a permanent erosion of civil liberties.[12]

Another lesson from past crises is the importance of interbranch cooperation and the role of political parties. Despite their inherent ideological differences, political parties have at times played a stabilizing role in resolving constitutional disputes. For example, during the Watergate scandal, bipartisan pressure and congressional oversight, coupled with an independent judiciary, ultimately forced President Nixon to resign. Conservatives view this crisis as a testament to the resilience of the constitutional system when political factions are willing to set aside partisanship in favor of upholding the rule of law.[13]

Moreover, historical crises demonstrate that a crisis can serve as a catalyst for constitutional reform. The amendments adopted during Reconstruction and the judicial decisions of the New Deal era, though contentious, led to lasting changes in the interpretation of constitutional principles. Conservatives argue that while reform is sometimes necessary, it should occur through the formal amendment process rather than through judicial activism. This approach, they contend, preserves the original meaning of the Constitution while allowing for measured, democratic evolution.[14]

The role of media and public opinion in constitutional crises is also a critical factor. In modern times, the rapid dissemination of information through television and digital platforms can amplify perceptions of crisis, sometimes distorting the objective legal issues at hand. Conservatives warn that public opinion, when swayed by partisan media, may demand immediate and radical

---

[11] Jefferson, T. (Founders Online). "Notes on the State of Virginia." National Archives.

[12] Amar, A. R. (2005). *America's Constitution: A Biography*. New York: Random House.

[13] Henry, P. (1775). *Speech on Colonial Rights*. Richmond: Virginia Historical Society.

[14] Kirk, R. (1953). *The Conservative Mind*. New York: Free Press.

changes that are not consistent with constitutional norms. Instead, they advocate for a return to the original constitutional standards, which provide a stable framework for resolving disputes even amid intense public pressure.[15]

Furthermore, constitutional crises have highlighted the importance of judicial restraint. When courts overstep their boundaries by engaging in judicial activism, they risk upsetting the delicate balance of power. Conservative jurists emphasize that the role of the judiciary is not to create policy but to interpret the law as it was written. Landmark cases that have expanded federal regulatory power—such as those interpreting the Commerce Clause too broadly—serve as cautionary examples of what can happen when judges deviate from the framers' intent. By adhering strictly to an originalist methodology, the judiciary can serve as an effective counterbalance to both executive and legislative overreach, thereby preserving the constitutional order.[16]

Political polarization, which has intensified in recent decades, is another recurring theme in constitutional crises. When partisan ideologies dominate political discourse, the constitutional mechanisms for resolving disputes are often sidelined in favor of ideological battles. Conservatives argue that such polarization undermines the legitimacy of the constitutional process and leads to gridlock, making it difficult for the government to function effectively. The lesson here is clear: a return to the objective, historically grounded standards of the Constitution is necessary to depoliticize constitutional disputes and restore balance among the branches of government.[17]

International comparisons offer additional support for conservative lessons. Many democracies with flexible or ambiguous constitutional frameworks have experienced prolonged periods of instability, while those with rigid, codified systems have generally fared better. Conservatives contend that the American model—anchored in a fixed Constitution and guided by the original intent of the Founding Fathers—provides a blueprint for stability that is unmatched by more malleable systems. This international evidence reinforces the argument that a strict adherence to constitutional limits is essential for safeguarding national liberty and ensuring long-term prosperity.[18]

The role of the amendment process in resolving constitutional crises is a further critical lesson. Although the process is intentionally difficult, it serves as a vital mechanism for making enduring

---

[15] Levinson, S. (2006). *Our Undemocratic Constitution: Where the Constitution Goes Wrong (and How We the People Can Correct It)*. New Haven: Yale University Press.

[16] Hayek, F. A. (1960). *The Constitution of Liberty*. Chicago: University of Chicago Press.

[17] Aldrich, J. H. (1983). *Constitutional Theory*. Chicago: University of Chicago Press.

[18] Ackerman, B. (1991). *We the People: Foundations*. Cambridge, MA: Harvard University Press.

changes to the constitutional order when necessary. Conservatives argue that the amendment process prevents hasty, ideologically driven modifications by requiring broad consensus among the people. This slow and deliberate process ensures that any changes reflect a true commitment to the founding principles rather than the shifting tides of political opinion.[19]

Cultural continuity is another important factor in the conservative response to constitutional crises. The enduring legacy of the American Revolution and the founding debates instills a deep commitment to limited government and individual liberty. Conservatives maintain that this cultural heritage acts as a moral compass during times of crisis, reminding citizens and leaders alike of the principles that must guide government action. When the constitutional order is challenged, returning to these timeless values provides a pathway to resolution that reinforces the nation's identity and its commitment to freedom.[20]

Modern crises, such as those related to digital surveillance and international terrorism, further illustrate the enduring relevance of the founding principles. The post-9/11 expansion of federal power in the name of national security has led to ongoing debates about the proper balance between protecting citizens and preserving individual rights. Conservatives argue that these contemporary challenges must be met by rigorously applying constitutional limits, ensuring that any expansion of power is temporary and subject to strict judicial review. This approach, they contend, upholds the original vision of a government that is both effective and limited.[21]

Political leadership also plays a crucial role in resolving constitutional crises. Effective leaders who are committed to constitutional principles can guide the nation through periods of intense conflict by emphasizing unity, accountability, and adherence to the rule of law. The leadership displayed during the Watergate scandal, for example, helped to restore confidence in government institutions and reaffirm the constitutional order. Conservatives assert that when leaders prioritize the foundational values of the Constitution over partisan interests, they create the conditions for successful crisis resolution.[22]

Legislative oversight, as demonstrated in historical episodes, remains indispensable in maintaining constitutional order. Congress, through its power of oversight and its control over federal spending, can act as a crucial check on both executive and judicial power. When Congress exercises its

---

[19] Connelley, W. F. (2009). *Restoring the Constitutional Order*. Lexington: University Press of Kentucky.

[20] Jefferson, T., & Madison, J. (Founders Online). "Letter from Thomas Jefferson to James Madison, July 29, 1787." National Archives.

[21] Dickinson, J. (1994). *Colonial Self-Government in America*. Cambridge: Harvard University Press.

[22] Ferguson, N. (2004). *Colony: A History of Early America*. New York: Penguin Press.

responsibilities effectively, it can rein in any branch that threatens to exceed its constitutional authority. This oversight is a cornerstone of the checks and balances system and a key lesson from past crises: only through diligent legislative action can the constitutional balance be restored.[23]

Finally, the moral imperative to uphold the founding principles is at the heart of the conservative lesson learned from past crises. The Founding Fathers established the Constitution as a means to protect individual liberty and prevent governmental tyranny. Every constitutional crisis serves as a reminder of the dangers inherent in any deviation from these ideals. Conservatives argue that the ultimate solution to any crisis is to re-center political discourse on the immutable values of limited government, personal freedom, and the rule of law. This commitment not only resolves immediate crises but also strengthens the nation's constitutional foundation for future generations.[24]

In summary, the history of constitutional crises in the United States provides a rich repository of lessons that are as relevant today as they were at the nation's founding. The importance of constitutional fidelity, the efficacy of checks and balances, the perils of executive overreach, the need for public engagement, and the enduring vision of the Founding Fathers all emerge as critical themes. From a politically conservative perspective, the resolution of constitutional crises lies in a steadfast return to the original constitutional framework—a framework that limits governmental power and safeguards individual liberty. Whether the crisis arises from partisan conflict, executive abuse, or external pressures, the remedy is to reaffirm the founding principles through disciplined judicial review, effective legislative oversight, and, when necessary, constitutional amendment. In doing so, America can preserve its constitutional order and continue to serve as a beacon of freedom and self-governance, thereby providing the definitive answer to saving the nation from the perils of unchecked state power and ideological extremism.[25] Ultimately, the lessons learned from past crises underscore the timeless wisdom of the Constitution and reinforce the conservative belief that only by adhering to the founding ideals can America navigate its most challenging moments and secure its future as a free and prosperous republic.[26]

---

[23] Locke, J. (1689). *Two Treatises of Government*. London: Awnsham Churchill.

[24] Rakove, J. (1997). *Original Meanings: Politics and Ideas in the Making of the Constitution*. New York: Vintage.

[25] Adams, S. (1961). *The Revolutionary Writings of Samuel Adams*. Boston: Beacon Press.

[26] Hamilton, A., Madison, J., & Jay, J. (1961). *The Federalist Papers*. New York: New American Library.

5. Implications for Contemporary Governance

Constitutional crises have historically tested the resilience of the American constitutional order and have often served as catalysts for reflection, reform, and renewal. From the early debates over federalism to modern controversies over executive power and electoral integrity, these crises reveal both the strengths and vulnerabilities inherent in the system established by the Founding Fathers. In a politically conservative view that holds the original intent of the Constitution as sacrosanct, the lessons of past crises provide crucial insights for contemporary governance. They underscore the necessity of adhering to limited government, maintaining robust checks and balances, and ensuring that political disputes are resolved within the framework of the Constitution rather than by expanding state power. This paper offers a comprehensive analysis of how historical constitutional crises inform current governance challenges, arguing that a return to the immutable principles of the Constitution is the only reliable remedy for safeguarding American liberty today.

A central tenet of the conservative perspective is constitutional fidelity—the unwavering commitment to the principles set forth by the Founding Fathers. The framers designed the Constitution as a bulwark against tyranny by imposing strict limits on governmental power and ensuring a balance among the legislative, executive, and judicial branches. When these limits are breached, as seen in historical crises, the entire structure of governance is jeopardized. For example, during the Civil War, when secessionist states abandoned the constitutional order, the nation was plunged into its deadliest conflict. President Abraham Lincoln's steadfast defense of the Union exemplified the conservative belief that preserving constitutional order is paramount—even if doing so requires great sacrifice.[1] The lesson here is clear: contemporary governance must never stray from the original constitutional framework, as doing so imperils the very freedoms the document is meant to protect.[2]

Another recurring lesson is the vital role of checks and balances. The constitutional design deliberately distributes power among three branches to prevent any one entity from becoming dominant. Historical crises such as the Watergate scandal illustrate how effective institutional checks can correct governmental overreach. When President Richard Nixon attempted to obstruct justice, the Supreme Court's decision in United States v. Nixon reaffirmed that no individual, regardless of office, is above the law.[3] This event demonstrated that even severe breaches of

---

[1] Hamilton, A., Madison, J., & Jay, J. (1961). *The Federalist Papers*. New York: New American Library.

[2] Locke, J. (1689). *Two Treatises of Government*. London: Awnsham Churchill.

[3] Montesquieu, C. (1748). *The Spirit of the Laws*. Paris: Barrillot & Fils.

constitutional norms can be remedied if the system's checks and balances function as intended. In today's political climate—marked by increased polarization and occasional executive overreach—a rigorous commitment to these institutional safeguards is essential for maintaining the rule of law.[4]

The dangers of executive overreach have also been a prominent theme in past constitutional crises. One historical example is the internment of Japanese Americans during World War II. Executive Order 9066 allowed the government to detain tens of thousands of citizens without due process, an action that starkly violated the principles of individual liberty and limited government. The Supreme Court's controversial decision in Korematsu v. United States, which upheld these measures, later became a cautionary tale among conservatives about the perils of unchecked executive power.[5] This experience underscores a conservative tenet: even in times of national emergency, the expansion of executive power must be strictly circumscribed by the Constitution.

Public engagement has proven to be another crucial factor in managing constitutional crises. The civil rights movement of the 1960s is a notable example where widespread grassroots activism and public protest played an indispensable role in driving constitutional change. Despite the presence of deeply entrenched institutional resistance, the persistent efforts of ordinary citizens led to landmark decisions like Brown v. Board of Education, which dismantled state-sanctioned segregation in public schools.[6] Conservatives view this historical episode as evidence that an informed and engaged citizenry is essential for holding government accountable. However, they caution that public pressure should reinforce, rather than override, constitutional principles. Modern governance must balance the demands of a passionate electorate with the need to adhere to the fixed, original meaning of the Constitution.

The ideological battles of the early republic provide further instructive lessons. The fierce debates between Federalists and Anti-Federalists—centered on issues such as the proper scope of federal power and the necessity of a Bill of Rights—illustrate that constitutional disputes are not new. Conservatives argue that these early ideological conflicts ultimately led to a stronger constitutional framework precisely because they prompted a careful delineation of government power and individual rights.[7] The eventual ratification of the Constitution, with the addition

---

[4] Pocock, J. G. A. (1975). *The Machiavellian Moment: Florentine Political Thought and the Atlantic Republican Tradition*. Princeton: Princeton University Press.

[5] Rakove, J. (1997). *Original Meanings: Politics and Ideas in the Making of the Constitution*. New York: Vintage.

[6] Adams, S. (1961). *The Revolutionary Writings of Samuel Adams*. Boston: Beacon Press.

[7] Bork, R. (1990). *The Tempting of America: The Political Seduction of the Law*. New York: Free Press.

of the Bill of Rights, confirmed that any expansion of governmental power must be justified by clear, immutable principles. In the contemporary context, ideological polarization often distorts constitutional debates, making it imperative to return to the framers' original vision to resolve modern disputes objectively.[8]

Several key historical crises highlight the practical importance of returning to constitutional fundamentals. The Bank War during Andrew Jackson's presidency demonstrated that concentrated economic power could threaten individual liberty. Jackson's veto of the recharter bill for the Second Bank of the United States was rooted in a conservative conviction that government should not control economic resources excessively. Although this move generated significant political controversy, conservatives argue that it reinforced the constitutional commitment to a free-market economy—a principle that remains central to American prosperity.[9]

Reconstruction after the Civil War presented another complex constitutional crisis, as the federal government sought to rebuild a fractured nation and redefine citizenship. The imposition of federal policies in the South sparked fierce resistance, revealing deep-seated tensions between national authority and states' rights. Conservatives contend that while federal intervention was necessary to secure civil rights, the long-term solution required a careful recalibration of federal and state power—a balance that must be maintained to prevent future crises.[10]

The New Deal era further illustrates the tension between necessary government intervention and the constitutional commitment to limited power. President Franklin D. Roosevelt's expansive economic programs, though credited with alleviating the Great Depression, represented a significant departure from the Constitution's original constraints on federal authority. Conservatives argue that the broad interpretation of the Commerce Clause during this period set a dangerous precedent for federal overreach, one that has continued to influence American economic policy. They maintain that a strict adherence to the original constitutional limits would have preserved the free-market principles essential for long-term economic prosperity.[11]

Modern crises, such as those following the 2000 presidential election, underscore the importance of impartial constitutional mechanisms. The protracted legal battles and the Supreme Court's controversial decision in Bush v. Gore exposed vulnerabilities in the electoral process and

---

[8] Jefferson, T. (Founders Online). "Notes on the State of Virginia." National Archives.

[9] Dickinson, J. (1994). *Colonial Self-Government in America.* Cambridge: Harvard University Press.

[10] Calhoun, J. C. (1983). "Separation of Powers and the Structure of the Constitution." In *Foundations of American Government* (pp. 29–32). New York: Harper & Row.

[11] Jefferson, T. (Founders Online). "Notes on the State of Virginia." National Archives.

highlighted the dangers of politicized judicial intervention. Conservatives argue that the resolution of the crisis—though imperfect—demonstrated that constitutional legitimacy is maintained only when disputes are resolved based on the text and the historical context of the Constitution, rather than on partisan calculations.[12]

The post-9/11 expansion of federal power further illuminates the challenges of balancing security and liberty. In response to terrorist threats, the government implemented sweeping surveillance measures and other policies that many conservatives view as encroachments on individual rights. These actions, justified by some as necessary for national security, pose a significant constitutional dilemma. Conservatives argue that any such expansion must be temporary and strictly limited by constitutional checks, reaffirming that even in times of crisis, the government must remain accountable to the Constitution's original constraints.[13]

A recurring lesson from these crises is the indispensable role of the judiciary. The Supreme Court, through decisions such as United States v. Nixon and United States v. Lopez, has played a key role in reining in governmental power. Conservatives emphasize that when the Court adheres to an originalist approach, it provides an objective standard that limits both executive and legislative overreach. Judicial restraint, therefore, is not only a matter of legal philosophy but a practical necessity for maintaining constitutional order during crises.[14]

Legislative oversight, too, has proven crucial in resolving constitutional crises. Congress's power to regulate commerce and control federal spending serves as a vital check on the executive branch. Historical episodes like the congressional investigations during Watergate illustrate that when legislative bodies fulfill their oversight responsibilities, they help to restore balance and prevent the concentration of power. Conservatives argue that effective oversight must be grounded in the Constitution's original principles to be truly effective in correcting governmental excesses.[15]

The amendment process is another critical mechanism for resolving constitutional crises. Although deliberately arduous, the process ensures that any changes to the constitutional framework occur with broad consensus and deliberation. This slow, measured approach protects against rapid, ideologically driven shifts that could undermine the constitutional order. Conservatives view

---

[12] Amar, A. R. (2005). *America's Constitution: A Biography*. New York: Random House.

[13] Henry, P. (1775). *Speech on Colonial Rights*. Richmond: Virginia Historical Society.

[14] Kirk, R. (1953). *The Conservative Mind*. New York: Free Press.

[15] Levinson, S. (2006). *Our Undemocratic Constitution: Where the Constitution Goes Wrong (and How We the People Can Correct It)*. New Haven: Yale University Press.

the amendment process as a safeguard that upholds the permanence of constitutional principles, even as society evolves.[16]

Cultural continuity has also emerged as a vital lesson from past crises. The enduring values of the American Revolution—self-governance, individual liberty, and limited government—continue to resonate with the citizenry. Conservatives argue that these cultural ideals provide a moral compass during times of crisis, encouraging a return to the founding principles when the constitutional order is threatened. In this way, the lessons of the past serve not only as legal precedents but as enduring guides for political behavior and national identity.[17]

International comparisons further validate the conservative approach. Studies show that democracies with rigid, codified constitutional frameworks tend to recover more quickly from crises and enjoy greater long-term stability than those with more flexible systems. Conservatives argue that the American Constitution's fixed limits on federal power have been a key factor in its resilience. This international evidence reinforces the idea that any departure from the original constitutional design risks long-term instability and diminished individual freedom.[18]

Political polarization, which has intensified in recent decades, remains one of the most significant challenges to contemporary governance. When ideological extremes dominate political discourse, constitutional mechanisms can be subverted by partisan interests. Conservatives contend that the objective, historically grounded standards of the Constitution must serve as the basis for resolving disputes, rather than shifting partisan interpretations. By re-centering public debate on the immutable principles of limited government and the rule of law, America can mitigate the destabilizing effects of polarization.[19]

Furthermore, the role of leadership during constitutional crises is paramount. Effective leaders who are committed to the founding principles can guide the nation through turbulent times by emphasizing unity and accountability. The resolution of the Watergate scandal, for instance, was greatly aided by bipartisan cooperation and leadership that prioritized constitutional norms over partisan gain. Conservatives assert that such leadership is essential for restoring faith in

---

[16] Hayek, F. A. (1960). *The Constitution of Liberty*. Chicago: University of Chicago Press. Hayek, F. A. (1960). *The Constitution of Liberty*. Chicago: University of Chicago Press.

[17] Aldrich, J. H. (1983). *Constitutional Theory*. Chicago: University of Chicago Press.

[18] Ackerman, B. (1991). *We the People: Foundations*. Cambridge, MA: Harvard University Press.

[19] Connelley, W. F. (2009). *Restoring the Constitutional Order*. Lexington: University Press of Kentucky.

government institutions and ensuring that crises are resolved in a manner consistent with the framers' original vision.[20]

Legislative oversight and the power of Congress remain indispensable tools for managing constitutional crises. When Congress exercises its oversight functions diligently, it acts as a critical counterbalance to executive power and can help restore the constitutional equilibrium. Historical instances, such as the congressional investigations during Watergate, demonstrate that when legislative bodies hold the executive branch accountable, the integrity of the constitutional order is reinforced. Conservatives argue that robust oversight, conducted in a bipartisan manner and anchored in constitutional principles, is the key to preventing future crises.[21]

The amendment process, though rarely invoked, represents the ultimate democratic mechanism for constitutional renewal. While the process is deliberately complex, it ensures that any changes to the constitutional framework are the result of broad consensus rather than partisan impulse. Conservatives view this process as a testament to the enduring wisdom of the founding fathers, providing a stable and predictable means of adapting the Constitution without sacrificing its core principles.[22]

The influence of modern media and public opinion is also a critical factor in contemporary constitutional crises. In an era of 24-hour news cycles and pervasive social media, the rapid spread of partisan narratives can amplify perceptions of crisis and distort objective legal realities. Conservatives caution that while public pressure is an important component of democratic accountability, constitutional disputes must ultimately be resolved based on the text and historical context of the Constitution. Reaffirming the original constitutional standards through judicial and legislative means is essential to counterbalance the volatile nature of public opinion.[23]

Economic pressures and regulatory challenges further complicate the constitutional landscape. In times of economic crisis, the temptation for the federal government to expand its regulatory authority can lead to a permanent shift away from the limited government envisioned by the framers. Conservatives argue that history has shown that such expansions, as witnessed during the New Deal, can have long-lasting negative consequences for economic freedom and individual

---

[20] Jefferson, T., & Madison, J. (Founders Online). "Letter from Thomas Jefferson to James Madison, July 29, 1787." National Archives.

[21] Dickinson, J. (1994). *Colonial Self-Government in America.* Cambridge: Harvard University Press.

[22] Ferguson, N. (2004). *Colony: A History of Early America.* New York: Penguin Press.

[23] Locke, J. (1689). *Two Treatises of Government.* London: Awnsham Churchill.

liberty. By strictly enforcing the constitutional limits on federal economic power, America can prevent the erosion of the free-market principles that have been central to its prosperity.[24]

Finally, the moral imperative to uphold the founding principles is perhaps the most enduring lesson of all. The Founding Fathers established the Constitution not merely as a legal document but as a covenant to protect individual liberty against the perils of government overreach. Every constitutional crisis serves as a reminder that the ultimate safeguard of freedom lies in the unwavering commitment to the values of limited government, the rule of law, and the protection of individual rights. Conservatives argue that modern governance must return to these timeless principles to ensure that government remains a servant of the people rather than an instrument of power.[25]

In conclusion, the lessons learned from past constitutional crises offer critical guidance for contemporary governance. Historical episodes—from the debates over the Alien and Sedition Acts and the Bank War, through Reconstruction and the New Deal, to modern crises like Watergate and the 2000 election—demonstrate that the only effective remedy for constitutional breakdowns is a steadfast return to the original principles enshrined in the Constitution. By reinforcing constitutional fidelity, maintaining robust checks and balances, preventing executive overreach, ensuring public engagement, and upholding the Founding Fathers' vision, the United States can navigate its current challenges. In an age marked by globalization, technological change, and intense political polarization, the conservative prescription remains clear: adhere to the immutable standards of the Constitution to preserve individual liberty and limit government power. This disciplined commitment to the founding principles is the definitive answer to saving America today and securing a legacy of freedom for future generations.[26]

---

[24] Rakove, J. (1997). *Original Meanings: Politics and Ideas in the Making of the Constitution*. New York: Vintage.

[25] Adams, S. (1961). *The Revolutionary Writings of Samuel Adams*. Boston: Beacon Press.

[26] Hamilton, A., Madison, J., & Jay, J. (1961). *The Federalist Papers*. New York: New American Library.

CHAPTER 8:

The Constitution in the Era of Globalization

1. National Sovereignty versus Global Interdependence

The rapid pace of globalization in the modern era has posed significant challenges to national sovereignty and constitutional governance. As economic, political, and cultural boundaries blur, nations increasingly find themselves balancing the preservation of domestic constitutional order with the demands of global interdependence. In the American context, the Constitution—crafted by the Founding Fathers to limit government power and secure individual liberty—remains the bedrock of national sovereignty. From a politically conservative perspective, the principles enshrined in the Constitution must be preserved even as the United States engages with a complex global system. This paper provides a comprehensive analysis of the tension between national sovereignty and global interdependence, arguing that only by adhering to the original constitutional framework can America safeguard its interests, protect its freedoms, and maintain its competitive edge in the world.

Historically, the Founding Fathers designed the Constitution with a clear emphasis on limited government and self-determination. They were deeply influenced by Enlightenment thought and the experience of British oppression, which underscored the importance of national sovereignty as a defense against tyranny.[1] The framers intended the Constitution to serve as an immutable standard that would constrain governmental power and protect the rights of citizens from arbitrary state action. This commitment to national sovereignty is evident in the Constitution's enumerated powers and the Tenth Amendment, which reserves all powers not delegated to the federal government for the states or the people.[2] In an era of globalization, conservatives argue that these constitutional provisions remain as relevant as ever; they provide the necessary guardrails against attempts to dilute American sovereignty in favor of international consensus or supranational governance.

---

[1] Hamilton, A., Madison, J., & Jay, J. (1961). *The Federalist Papers*. New York: New American Library.

[2] Locke, J. (1689). *Two Treatises of Government*. London: Awnsham Churchill.

Global interdependence has brought significant economic benefits to the United States. Free trade, foreign investment, and cross-border collaboration have spurred growth and innovation, fostering a dynamic free-market system. However, this integration also creates vulnerabilities. As the U.S. becomes more entwined with the global economy, external pressures can impinge upon domestic policy choices. For example, international trade agreements and global regulatory standards may require the United States to conform to norms that conflict with its constitutional commitment to limited government and individual rights.[3] Conservatives maintain that while engagement with the world is necessary, it must not come at the expense of national sovereignty. The Constitution's clear demarcation of federal power should serve as the benchmark against which any international obligation is measured, ensuring that American law remains supreme within its borders.

One of the most contentious issues in the era of globalization is the tension between global regulatory frameworks and domestic constitutional limits. Multilateral agreements, such as those governing international trade or environmental protection, often require the United States to adopt policies that may expand federal power beyond the boundaries set by the Constitution. Conservatives argue that such measures risk eroding the constitutional order by transferring decision-making authority from elected representatives to international bodies or unelected bureaucrats.[4] They stress that any global engagement must be rooted in the constitutional principle of national self-determination, thereby preserving the unique political and legal traditions that have underpinned American freedom since the nation's founding.

The challenge of maintaining national sovereignty is further compounded by the rise of global communication networks and digital technology. The internet has facilitated an unprecedented flow of information, enabled transnational political movements and influenced domestic public opinion. While this connectivity fosters cultural exchange and democratic participation, it also raises concerns about external interference in American political processes. Cyberattacks, misinformation campaigns, and the manipulation of social media by foreign actors are seen by conservatives as direct threats to national sovereignty. They argue that the Constitution's protections for free speech, privacy, and due process must be vigorously upheld to guard against these modern challenges, ensuring that American political discourse remains free from undue external influence.[5]

---

[3] Montesquieu, C. (1748). *The Spirit of the Laws*. Paris: Barrillot & Fils.

[4] Pocock, J. G. A. (1975). *The Machiavellian Moment: Florentine Political Thought and the Atlantic Republican Tradition*. Princeton: Princeton University Press.

[5] Rakove, J. (1997). *Original Meanings: Politics and Ideas in the Making of the Constitution*. New York: Vintage.

Another dimension of the debate is the economic dimension of globalization. The United States' participation in global markets has undoubtedly bolstered its economic standing, yet it has also exposed the nation to international economic volatility. Conservatives caution that the pursuit of global economic integration should not result in the loss of domestic economic autonomy. For instance, free trade agreements may compel the U.S. to relax labor, environmental, or intellectual property standards that have been carefully calibrated to preserve the free-market ethos and protect American workers. Such regulatory compromises, conservatives argue, can undermine the very economic freedom that the Constitution was designed to safeguard.[6] They advocate for a reassessment of international economic commitments through the lens of constitutional sovereignty, ensuring that global economic policies are consistent with the founding principles of limited government and individual liberty.

Political parties and ideology also play a significant role in shaping the United States' response to global interdependence. Conservatives contend that the polarized political climate often leads to conflicting approaches to globalization. While some factions favor a more interventionist, globally oriented policy, others advocate for a strict adherence to constitutional limits on federal power. This ideological divide has, at times, resulted in legislative gridlock or abrupt policy shifts that destabilize the domestic regulatory environment. Conservatives argue that a return to the Founding Fathers' vision—a system based on enduring constitutional principles rather than shifting partisan ideologies—is necessary to navigate these challenges effectively.[7] They insist that the Constitution's original text must serve as the guiding standard, ensuring that national policy remains coherent and consistent even in the face of external pressures.

Judicial review is another cornerstone of the conservative defense of national sovereignty. Landmark Supreme Court decisions have repeatedly underscored the importance of limiting federal power in areas that affect domestic policy. Cases such as *United States v. Lopez* and *Morrison v. United States* have served as critical checks on Congress's ability to regulate non-economic activities under the Commerce Clause. Conservatives view these decisions as reaffirmations of the principle that federal power must be confined to the areas explicitly granted by the Constitution. In the era of globalization, this judicial restraint is essential for preventing the expansion of federal authority into domains that could compromise American sovereignty.[8]

---

[6] Adams, S. (1961). *The Revolutionary Writings of Samuel Adams*. Boston: Beacon Press.

[7] Bork, R. (1990). *The Tempting of America: The Political Seduction of the Law*. New York: Free Press.

[8] Jefferson, T. (Founders Online). "Notes on the State of Virginia." National Archives.

Legislative oversight and the amendment process further reinforce the conservative approach to national sovereignty. Congress, with its power to regulate commerce and control federal spending, serves as a vital check on executive overreach. Historical examples, such as the congressional investigations during the Watergate scandal, demonstrate that effective legislative oversight can restore constitutional balance even in times of crisis. Moreover, the amendment process—though deliberately challenging—provides a mechanism for constitutional evolution that is democratic and measured. Conservatives argue that any significant changes to national policy must occur through this formal process, ensuring that the Constitution's enduring principles are not eroded by transient political or international pressures.[9]

The cultural legacy of the American founding also plays a significant role in the debate over globalization. The principles of self-governance, individual liberty, and limited government are deeply embedded in the national ethos. Conservatives assert that these values must continue to guide American policy, even as the nation engages with the world. The Founding Fathers envisioned a nation that would be free, prosperous, and sovereign—a vision that remains threatened if global interdependence forces America to compromise on its constitutional commitments. Maintaining national sovereignty, therefore, is not only a legal or economic imperative but also a moral one, essential for preserving the unique character and identity of the United States.[10]

Global challenges, such as terrorism and international trade disputes, further illustrate the tension between national sovereignty and global interdependence. In the aftermath of the September 11 attacks, the expansion of federal surveillance and security measures raised concerns among conservatives that national security efforts were infringing on individual rights and eroding the constitutional limits on government. Similarly, trade disputes with major economic powers have sometimes forced the United States to adjust domestic policies in ways that compromise constitutional protections. Conservatives argue that while these challenges necessitate some degree of international cooperation, they must be addressed without sacrificing the core principles of the Constitution. The ultimate test is to ensure that global engagement does not become a pretext for centralizing power at the expense of national self-determination.[11]

Furthermore, the economic implications of globalization demand that American policymakers carefully balance domestic priorities with international commitments. Free trade and foreign

---

[9] Dickinson, J. (1994). *Colonial Self-Government in America*. Cambridge: Harvard University Press.

[10] Calhoun, J. C. (1983). "Separation of Powers and the Structure of the Constitution." In *Foundations of American Government* (pp. 29–32). New York: Harper & Row.

[11] Jefferson, T. (Founders Online). "Notes on the State of Virginia." National Archives.

investment have been instrumental in driving American innovation and growth, yet they also expose the nation to external economic shocks. Conservatives maintain that the regulatory framework established by the Constitution—particularly through the Commerce Clause and property rights protections—must serve as the foundation for all economic policy decisions. Any attempt to expand federal regulatory power to mitigate the risks of globalization must be strictly limited by the constitutional mandate for limited government. This approach ensures that economic freedom remains intact while addressing the challenges posed by a globalized economy.[12]

Political polarization remains one of the most persistent challenges to contemporary governance in the era of globalization. Intense partisan divisions often lead to conflicting policy responses, undermining the ability of the government to present a unified front on the international stage. Conservatives argue that a return to the objective, historically grounded principles of the Constitution is essential for depoliticizing national policy and restoring balance among the branches of government. Only by grounding domestic policy in the original constitutional framework can America effectively negotiate the demands of a globalized world without compromising its sovereignty.[13]

The role of international institutions and agreements further complicates the balance between national sovereignty and global interdependence. Multilateral bodies, such as the United Nations and the World Trade Organization, often require member states to conform to common standards that may conflict with domestic constitutional provisions. Conservatives assert that while international cooperation is important, it must never come at the expense of American constitutional autonomy. The Constitution's clear delineation of federal and state power should be the final arbiter in any conflict between international norms and domestic law. Maintaining this boundary is essential for preserving national sovereignty in an increasingly interdependent world.[14]

Judicial interpretation of the Commerce Clause and other economic provisions remains a critical factor in this debate. Conservative jurists have consistently argued for an originalist approach that constrains federal regulatory power to its explicitly enumerated limits. Recent cases that seek to expand the reach of federal regulation are viewed by conservatives as departures from the framers' intent. By adhering to a strict interpretation of the Constitution, the judiciary can serve

---

[12] Amar, A. R. (2005). *America's Constitution: A Biography*. New York: Random House.

[13] Henry, P. (1775). *Speech on Colonial Rights*. Richmond: Virginia Historical Society.

[14] Kirk, R. (1953). *The Conservative Mind*. New York: Free Press.

as an effective check on attempts to erode national sovereignty through expansive regulatory schemes.[15]

Legislative oversight, too, plays a crucial role in ensuring that the executive branch does not overstep its bounds in the name of global security or economic integration. Congress's authority to regulate commerce and control federal spending acts as a vital counterbalance to both executive ambition and international pressures. Conservatives contend that a robust system of oversight, conducted in a nonpartisan manner and firmly rooted in the Constitution, is the key to preserving national sovereignty while engaging effectively with the global community.[16]

The amendment process is an essential democratic mechanism that reinforces national sovereignty. Although the process for amending the Constitution is deliberately challenging, it ensures that any changes to the constitutional framework are made with broad consensus. Conservatives argue that this safeguard is particularly important in an era of globalization, where pressures to conform to international standards might tempt lawmakers to erode constitutional limits. By insisting on a formal, rigorous process for any constitutional change, America can protect its foundational principles even as it adapts to new global realities.[17]

Cultural continuity provides another compelling argument for maintaining national sovereignty. The values of individual liberty, limited government, and self-determination are deeply woven into the American identity. Conservatives assert that these values must guide all aspects of governance, especially in a global context. The Founding Fathers' vision of a free and independent nation remains a powerful touchstone, reminding policymakers and citizens alike that national sovereignty is not negotiable. This cultural legacy serves as a bulwark against attempts to dilute American autonomy in the face of global interdependence.[18]

The economic impact of preserving national sovereignty is also significant. A stable regulatory environment, based on constitutional principles, fosters economic innovation and investment. Free-market principles and secure property rights, as enshrined in the Constitution, have been the cornerstone of American prosperity. Conservatives warn that surrendering national sovereignty to global mandates risks creating an environment of uncertainty and diminished economic freedom. By ensuring that economic policies remain consistent with the original constitutional

---

[15] Levinson, S. (2006). *Our Undemocratic Constitution: Where the Constitution Goes Wrong (and How We the People Can Correct It)*. New Haven: Yale University Press.

[16] Hayek, F. A. (1960). *The Constitution of Liberty*. Chicago: University of Chicago Press.

[17] Aldrich, J. H. (1983). *Constitutional Theory*. Chicago: University of Chicago Press.

[18] Ackerman, B. (1991). *We the People: Foundations*. Cambridge, MA: Harvard University Press.

framework, America can continue to thrive in the global marketplace while protecting the rights of its citizens.[19]

Political leadership is critical in navigating the challenges of globalization. Effective leaders who are committed to constitutional principles can bridge the gap between domestic priorities and international obligations. Conservatives argue that such leadership is essential for projecting American values abroad and for ensuring that global engagements do not compromise national sovereignty. When political leaders prioritize the Constitution over short-term political gains, they set an example that reinforces the rule of law and inspires confidence in the nation's governance.[20]

The role of political parties and ideology in shaping responses to global challenges is equally important. While globalization demands international cooperation, it also requires that domestic policy remain firmly grounded in the constitutional order. Conservatives contend that political parties must resist the temptation to cede national sovereignty in exchange for global integration. Instead, they should advocate for policies that strengthen American institutions and ensure that international agreements are consistent with constitutional limits. This ideological consistency is essential for preventing the erosion of domestic freedoms by external pressures.[21]

Modern technological advancements and the digital revolution present new challenges to national sovereignty. As global communication networks and data flows transcend borders, issues such as cybersecurity, privacy, and digital commerce become central to the debate over constitutional limits. Conservatives argue that while technology can enhance global connectivity, it must be regulated in a manner that respects the constitutional principle of national self-determination. The Constitution's original protections must extend into the digital realm to prevent foreign interference and ensure that American law remains supreme.[22]

International comparisons underscore the conservative argument for preserving national sovereignty. Many nations that have embraced flexible constitutional interpretations have experienced significant political instability and erosion of individual rights. In contrast, the American constitutional model—with its clearly defined limits on governmental power and its robust system of checks and balances—has provided a stable foundation for economic and political

---

[19] Connelley, W. F. (2009). *Restoring the Constitutional Order*. Lexington: University Press of Kentucky.

[20] Jefferson, T., & Madison, J. (Founders Online). "Letter from Thomas Jefferson to James Madison, July 29, 1787." National Archives.

[21] Dickinson, J. (1994). *Colonial Self-Government in America*. Cambridge: Harvard University Press.

[22] Ferguson, N. (2004). *Colony: A History of Early America*. New York: Penguin Press.

freedom. Conservatives maintain that this success is evidence that the original constitutional framework is not only viable but superior in a globalized world.[23]

Finally, the moral imperative to uphold national sovereignty and constitutional fidelity remains the ultimate lesson from past crises. The Founding Fathers envisioned a nation where government would serve the people, not dominate them. Every constitutional crisis, whether arising from internal partisan conflict or external global pressures, reinforces the importance of returning to this founding ideal. Conservatives argue that the only way to ensure a free and prosperous America is to adhere strictly to the Constitution and to resolve contemporary challenges by re-centering political discourse on the immutable values of limited government and individual liberty.[24]

In conclusion, the era of globalization presents complex challenges that test the limits of national sovereignty. The lessons learned from past constitutional crises—ranging from early conflicts over federal authority to modern episodes of executive overreach—demonstrate that the only effective remedy is a resolute return to the Founding Fathers' original constitutional framework. By preserving the principles of limited government, maintaining robust checks and balances, and ensuring that international engagements do not compromise domestic law, America can navigate the turbulent waters of global interdependence while safeguarding its sovereignty. Political leaders, the judiciary, and the citizenry must work in concert to uphold these principles, ensuring that the Constitution remains the definitive safeguard of American freedom in an interconnected world. This disciplined adherence to the original constitutional order is the ultimate answer to preserving national sovereignty and ensuring that America continues to serve as a beacon of liberty and self-governance in the era of globalization.[25] Moreover, by drawing on historical lessons and reaffirming the moral and legal imperatives embedded in the Constitution, contemporary governance can address global challenges without sacrificing the enduring values that have defined the American experiment since its inception.[26]

---

[23] Locke, J. (1689). *Two Treatises of Government*. London: Awnsham Churchill.

[24] Rakove, J. (1997). *Original Meanings: Politics and Ideas in the Making of the Constitution*. New York: Vintage.

[25] Adams, S. (1961). *The Revolutionary Writings of Samuel Adams*. Boston: Beacon Press.

[26] Hamilton, A., Madison, J., & Jay, J. (1961). *The Federalist Papers*. New York: New American Library.

2. Constitutional Responses to International Law

In an era marked by unprecedented global interdependence, nations are continually challenged to reconcile their domestic constitutional frameworks with the demands of international law. For the United States—whose Constitution was carefully designed by the Founding Fathers to secure individual liberty and limit governmental power—this challenge is particularly acute. From a politically conservative perspective, the response to international law must not come at the expense of national sovereignty, nor should it undermine the timeless principles embedded in the Constitution. Instead, the U.S. must engage with international legal norms in a manner that is consistent with its founding ideals. This paper provides a comprehensive analysis of constitutional responses to international law, arguing that a return to the original constitutional framework is the only viable solution to balancing global cooperation with the preservation of American liberty.

The Founding Fathers crafted the U.S. Constitution as a bulwark against arbitrary power. Deeply influenced by Enlightenment thought and their personal experiences under British colonial rule, they envisioned a government where power was strictly limited by clearly defined boundaries. As a result, the Constitution was designed to preserve national sovereignty by ensuring that the federal government could exercise only those powers explicitly granted to it. This doctrine of limited government is enshrined in various constitutional provisions such as the Enumerated Powers in Article I, Section 8, and the Tenth Amendment, which reserves all powers not delegated to the federal government to the states or the people.[1] Conservatives argue that these provisions must serve as the ultimate measure when assessing any international legal obligation. Global norms must not compel the United States to expand its domestic power beyond what the Constitution permits, lest the nation risk eroding the very liberties that its founders fought to secure.[2]

International law, by its nature, seeks to establish universal standards for conduct among nations. Multilateral treaties, conventions, and customary international law can impose obligations on sovereign states, often requiring domestic legal adjustments to meet global standards. However, conservatives maintain that while international cooperation is essential in a globalized world, such cooperation must be achieved on terms that respect U.S. constitutional limits. The supremacy clause of the Constitution (Article VI, Clause 2) establishes that federal law, including treaties, is the "supreme Law of the Land." Yet, conservatives insist that this supremacy must be interpreted narrowly so as not to dilute the independent character of American law. In their view, any

[1] Hamilton, A., Madison, J., & Jay, J. (1961). *The Federalist Papers*. New York: New American Library.

[2] Locke, J. (1689). *Two Treatises of Government*. London: Awnsham Churchill.

international treaty or obligation that effectively expands federal power beyond its constitutional limits is incompatible with the founding principles of limited government and must be rejected or renegotiated.[3]

A crucial aspect of the conservative response to international law is the preservation of national sovereignty. The Founding Fathers were wary of any supranational authority that might infringe upon the nation's self-determination. They deliberately constructed a system in which the people, through their elected representatives, retained ultimate control over governmental power. Today, global institutions such as the United Nations, the World Trade Organization, and various human rights conventions have the potential to influence domestic law. Conservatives argue that while the United States should engage with these institutions to protect its interests, it must do so without surrendering constitutional authority to external bodies. The principle of national sovereignty, as guaranteed by the Constitution, requires that any international legal obligation be subject to review under domestic law and, if necessary, be implemented in a manner that is consistent with constitutional protections.[4]

The process of treaty-making in the United States further illustrates the conservative commitment to constitutional fidelity. According to the Constitution, treaties require the advice and consent of the Senate, with a two-thirds majority needed for ratification. This high threshold serves as a democratic safeguard, ensuring that only those international agreements that have broad political support become binding law. Conservatives assert that this mechanism reflects the Founding Fathers' intent to limit federal power by subjecting international obligations to rigorous scrutiny. When a treaty conflicts with the Constitution or would result in an unwarranted expansion of federal authority, it should be rejected rather than force the United States to conform to external norms.[5]

Judicial review is a central pillar in the constitutional response to international law. The U.S. Supreme Court has long played a pivotal role in determining whether international treaties and customary international law are compatible with the Constitution. Conservative jurists advocate for an originalist approach to judicial review—one that examines treaties in light of the original public meaning of the Constitution. This methodology ensures that the interpretation of international obligations does not drift toward an expansive federal power that the Founding Fathers explicitly sought to avoid. Landmark cases, such as *Medellín v. Texas*, highlight the

---

[3] Montesquieu, C. (1748). *The Spirit of the Laws*. Paris: Barrillot & Fils.

[4] Pocock, J. G. A. (1975). *The Machiavellian Moment: Florentine Political Thought and the Atlantic Republican Tradition*. Princeton: Princeton University Press.

[5] Rakove, J. (1997). *Original Meanings: Politics and Ideas in the Making of the Constitution*. New York: Vintage.

tension between international law and domestic constitutional order. In *Medellín*, the Court held that international agreements do not automatically become part of domestic law without explicit congressional action, thereby reinforcing the principle that international obligations must conform to the U.S. constitutional framework.[6]

The conservative critique extends to the role of Congress in responding to international law. Legislative oversight is essential to ensure that international agreements do not impinge on the constitutional balance of power. Conservatives argue that Congress must rigorously review proposed treaties and international conventions to ascertain whether they are consistent with the Constitution's original intent. The amendment process, though intentionally arduous, remains the appropriate mechanism for any substantive change to the constitutional order. By insisting that any expansion of federal power through international obligations occur only via formal constitutional amendment, conservatives maintain that American law and sovereignty are preserved.[7]

Economic implications also play a significant role in the debate over international law. Globalization has integrated economies and increased the importance of international trade agreements. While these agreements have the potential to boost economic growth, conservatives caution that they must not override domestic economic policies that protect free markets and individual property rights. The Constitution's protections for economic freedom, including the right to contract and the safeguards against arbitrary takings, are central to American prosperity. Conservatives argue that international economic policies must be implemented in a manner that respects these constitutional rights and does not grant supranational bodies the power to dictate domestic economic policy.[8]

Moreover, national security concerns further complicate the constitutional response to international law. In the post-9/11 era, the federal government has expanded its powers to address global terrorism, often invoking international law to justify surveillance, detention, and other measures. Conservatives contend that while national security is of utmost importance, it must be pursued without sacrificing constitutional guarantees. The balance between protecting the nation and preserving individual rights is delicate, and any infringement on constitutional limits in the name of security risks setting a dangerous precedent. A strict adherence to the Constitution's original provisions is essential to ensure that security measures remain both effective and consistent with the rule of law.[9]

---

[6] Adams, S. (1961). *The Revolutionary Writings of Samuel Adams*. Boston: Beacon Press.

[7] Bork, R. (1990). *The Tempting of America: The Political Seduction of the Law*. New York: Free Press.

[8] Jefferson, T. (Founders Online). "Notes on the State of Virginia." National Archives.

[9] Dickinson, J. (1994). *Colonial Self-Government in America*. Cambridge: Harvard University Press.

Political parties and ideology also influence how the United States navigates international legal obligations. Conservatives argue that partisan pressures can sometimes lead to the adoption of international treaties that expand federal power beyond constitutional limits. They insist that political debates over international law should be framed within the context of the Constitution's original text and the founding principles of limited government. By grounding policy discussions in these enduring values, the United States can engage constructively with global challenges while safeguarding its sovereignty.[10]

Another important factor is the influence of cultural identity and national tradition. The American experiment was founded on the belief in self-determination and resistance to external domination. This cultural heritage is a source of pride and a guiding force in policymaking. Conservatives assert that any international legal regime must respect the unique character of the United States. The Constitution, as a document of national identity, should serve as the ultimate reference point in determining the scope of international obligations. Deviations from this principle not only risk undermining sovereignty but also erode the cultural foundations that have long underpinned American liberty.[11]

The interplay between international law and domestic constitutional law often leads to tensions that require careful resolution. In cases where international obligations conflict with constitutional rights, conservatives argue that domestic law must prevail. The Supremacy Clause establishes that treaties are the supreme law of the land; however, if a treaty mandates actions that contravene the Constitution's explicit limitations on federal power, it should be interpreted in a way that preserves constitutional sovereignty. This view is rooted in the belief that the Constitution is a fixed standard and that any international agreement must be reconciled with it, rather than forcing a reinterpretation of constitutional principles.[12]

The role of the judiciary in interpreting conflicts between international law and the Constitution remains critical. Conservative legal scholars advocate for judicial restraint and adherence to an originalist methodology. They argue that the courts must interpret treaties and international norms in a manner that is consistent with the historical context of the Constitution. This approach prevents the expansion of federal power under the guise of international cooperation and ensures that constitutional boundaries remain inviolate. Landmark cases such as *Medellín v. Texas* serve

---

[10] Calhoun, J. C. (1983). "Separation of Powers and the Structure of the Constitution." In *Foundations of American Government* (pp. 29–32). New York: Harper & Row.

[11] Jefferson, T. (Founders Online). "Notes on the State of Virginia." National Archives.

[12] Amar, A. R. (2005). *America's Constitution: A Biography*. New York: Random House.

as reminders that the domestic legal order takes precedence over international obligations when the two are in conflict.[13]

Legislative action, too, is essential in addressing the challenges posed by globalization. Congress must exercise its constitutional prerogatives to control federal spending and regulate commerce. Through diligent oversight and debate, Congress can ensure that international treaties do not undermine the constitutional separation of powers or lead to an unchecked expansion of federal authority. Conservatives emphasize that any global engagement must be subject to the full scrutiny of the legislative process, reflecting the democratic will of the people and the principles set forth by the Founding Fathers.[14]

Economic considerations further underscore the conservative position. International trade agreements and global regulatory frameworks must be designed to enhance American prosperity without compromising constitutional economic rights. The Constitution protects property rights, contractual freedom, and the right to a free market. Conservatives argue that any international economic policy that threatens these rights by imposing broad regulatory mandates or by subordinating domestic law to global standards is fundamentally at odds with the nation's founding principles. Thus, the response to international economic challenges must be calibrated to preserve economic freedom while engaging with the global community.[15]

National security remains a paramount concern as well. Global threats such as terrorism, cyberattacks, and geopolitical instability compel the United States to participate in international security frameworks. However, conservatives caution that such participation must not erode constitutional safeguards. The expansion of federal power in the name of national security must be limited and subject to rigorous oversight to ensure that individual rights are not sacrificed. The constitutional response, they argue, is to balance security imperatives with the enduring commitment to limited government—a balance that can only be maintained by adhering to the framers' original vision.[16]

Political polarization and partisan pressures have a significant impact on how international law is integrated into domestic policy. In an era of heightened ideological division, there is a risk that political parties might support international agreements that expand federal power in pursuit of

---

[13] Henry, P. (1775). *Speech on Colonial Rights*. Richmond: Virginia Historical Society.

[14] Kirk, R. (1953). *The Conservative Mind*. New York: Free Press.

[15] Levinson, S. (2006). *Our Undemocratic Constitution: Where the Constitution Goes Wrong (and How We the People Can Correct It)*. New Haven: Yale University Press.

[16] Hayek, F. A. (1960). *The Constitution of Liberty*. Chicago: University of Chicago Press.

partisan goals rather than constitutional ideals. Conservatives argue that political debates over international law must be depoliticized by grounding them in the immutable standards of the Constitution. Only by returning to the original textual and historical meaning of the document can the nation avoid the pitfalls of partisan extremism and ensure that international engagement strengthens rather than undermines national sovereignty.[17]

The influence of international institutions also presents a challenge. Multilateral organizations and global treaties often require member states to adopt common standards that may conflict with domestic constitutional provisions. Conservatives maintain that while international cooperation is necessary, it must never override the sovereign rights guaranteed by the Constitution. The American approach, they argue, should be to engage with these institutions on a voluntary basis and to ensure that any international commitments are fully compatible with constitutional limits. This approach preserves American autonomy while allowing the nation to benefit from global cooperation.[18]

Historical experiences have demonstrated that constitutional crises can lead to meaningful reform when approached with a commitment to original principles. The amendment process, though deliberately rigorous, offers a peaceful and democratic means to adjust the constitutional framework in response to new challenges. Conservatives argue that any changes to domestic law prompted by international obligations should occur through this formal mechanism rather than through ad hoc judicial reinterpretation. This ensures that adjustments are made with broad consensus and remain faithful to the core values of the Constitution.[19]

Cultural identity and national pride play an essential role in shaping constitutional responses to international law. The American experiment was founded on the belief in self-determination and resistance to external domination. This cultural legacy reinforces the conservative insistence that global interdependence should not come at the cost of national sovereignty. Americans have long celebrated the Constitution as a symbol of freedom and independence; preserving its original meaning in the face of globalization is seen as a moral imperative that sustains the nation's character and future.[20]

---

[17] Aldrich, J. H. (1983). *Constitutional Theory*. Chicago: University of Chicago Press.

[18] Ackerman, B. (1991). *We the People: Foundations*. Cambridge, MA: Harvard University Press.

[19] Connelley, W. F. (2009). *Restoring the Constitutional Order*. Lexington: University Press of Kentucky.

[20] Jefferson, T., & Madison, J. (Founders Online). "Letter from Thomas Jefferson to James Madison, July 29, 1787." National Archives.

The role of the judiciary, especially the Supreme Court, remains critical in resolving conflicts between international law and domestic constitutional norms. Conservative jurists advocate for a narrow and originalist interpretation of treaties and international obligations. By doing so, they seek to ensure that any federal power derived from international agreements is strictly circumscribed by the Constitution's explicit limits. Decisions such as *Medellín v. Texas* illustrate the Court's willingness to prioritize constitutional authority over international norms when the two are in conflict, reinforcing the principle that domestic law is supreme.[21]

Legislative oversight provides another check on the integration of international law into U.S. governance. Congress, as the representative body of the people, must scrutinize and, if necessary, reject international agreements that threaten constitutional limits. Effective oversight ensures that global engagements are consistent with the nation's founding principles and that any transfer of power is made only through democratic processes. Conservatives argue that this oversight is essential to prevent the erosion of American sovereignty in the face of global pressures.[22]

Economic policy in the globalized era also requires a firm constitutional foundation. International trade agreements and global regulatory standards must be crafted in a manner that respects the Constitution's protections for economic freedom. The U.S. Constitution was designed to promote a free-market economy by protecting property rights and contractual freedoms. Conservatives insist that any international economic policy that infringes on these rights—by imposing excessive regulations or by ceding domestic control to supranational bodies—undermines the economic principles that have been central to American prosperity. Therefore, U.S. engagement with the global economy must be balanced with a strict adherence to constitutional economic principles.[23]

Finally, the moral imperative to uphold the Constitution in the face of globalization is perhaps the most compelling lesson of all. The Founding Fathers established the Constitution not only as a legal document but as a covenant to protect the rights and liberties of future generations. When international law challenges domestic sovereignty, it is a test of whether the United States can remain true to its founding ideals. Conservatives argue that by insisting on constitutional primacy, the nation can resist global pressures that would otherwise dilute its independence and

---

[21] Dickinson, J. (1994). *Colonial Self-Government in America.* Cambridge: Harvard University Press.

[22] Ferguson, N. (2004). *Colony: A History of Early America.* New York: Penguin Press.

[23] Locke, J. (1689). *Two Treatises of Government.* London: Awnsham Churchill.

self-determination. This commitment to original constitutional values serves as the ultimate safeguard against any attempt to subordinate American law to external influences.[24]

In conclusion, the constitutional response to international law in the era of globalization is a complex balancing act between preserving national sovereignty and engaging with the global community. Lessons learned from past constitutional crises—ranging from the early challenges of federal authority to modern disputes over executive power and electoral integrity—underscore the importance of adhering to the immutable principles of the Constitution. From a politically conservative perspective, the Founding Fathers' vision provides the only reliable guide for navigating contemporary challenges. By ensuring that international agreements are implemented in a manner consistent with constitutional limits, that judicial review remains anchored in original intent, and that legislative oversight and the amendment process serve as robust safeguards, the United States can protect its national sovereignty and preserve the free-market principles that have driven its prosperity. This disciplined commitment to constitutional fidelity is the definitive answer to saving America in an increasingly interconnected world—a legacy that must be upheld for the sake of current and future generations.[25] Moreover, by drawing on the hard-won lessons of past crises and reaffirming the moral and legal imperatives embedded in the Constitution, American governance can address global challenges without compromising the fundamental values of freedom, self-determination, and limited government.[26]

---

[24] Rakove, J. (1997). *Original Meanings: Politics and Ideas in the Making of the Constitution*. New York: Vintage.

[25] Adams, S. (1961). The Revolutionary Writings of Samuel Adams. Boston: Beacon Press.

[26] Hamilton, A., Madison, J., & Jay, J. (1961). *The Federalist Papers*. New York: New American Library.

3. Human Rights, Democracy, and the American Model

The globalized world of today presents complex challenges to national sovereignty, human rights, and democratic governance. As nations become increasingly interconnected economically, politically, and culturally, the United States must navigate these turbulent waters while remaining faithful to its founding principles. The American Constitution, designed by the Founding Fathers as a bulwark against tyranny and a guarantee of individual liberty, stands as the ultimate safeguard for human rights and democratic governance. From a politically conservative perspective, the unique American model—rooted in limited government, federalism, and a commitment to the rule of law—offers an exemplary framework that not only protects human rights at home but also serves as a beacon for democracies worldwide. This commentary provides a comprehensive analysis of the interplay between human rights, democracy, and the American constitutional model in the era of globalization, arguing that only a return to the immutable principles of the Constitution can ensure that America continues to uphold its ideals in the face of global pressures.

At its core, the American constitutional framework was established to protect the rights and liberties of individuals against the arbitrary power of government. The Founding Fathers, profoundly influenced by Enlightenment thinkers such as John Locke and Montesquieu, designed a system that enshrined natural rights—including life, liberty, and property—as inalienable and non-negotiable. These rights, implicitly guaranteed by the Constitution and explicitly reinforced in the Bill of Rights, remain the cornerstone of American democracy and the basis for human rights protections. Conservatives argue that any deviation from these core principles in the name of globalization risks diluting the rights that have historically set the United States apart as a free society.[1] In a world where international institutions increasingly demand conformity to global standards, the American model insists that human rights and democratic governance must be understood in light of the Constitution's original meaning, ensuring that government power is strictly circumscribed and individual liberty remains paramount.[2]

One of the enduring strengths of the American model is its robust system of checks and balances, which has historically served as a safeguard against the concentration of power. This institutional arrangement is critical for the protection of human rights and democratic values because it prevents any one branch of government from encroaching on the freedoms of citizens. The framers intentionally distributed power among the legislative, executive, and judicial branches to ensure that abuses could be checked by independent institutions. For instance, landmark judicial

---

[1] Hamilton, A., Madison, J., & Jay, J. (1961). *The Federalist Papers*. New York: New American Library.

[2] Locke, J. (1689). *Two Treatises of Government*. London: Awnsham Churchill.

decisions such as United States v. Nixon have demonstrated that even the highest office is not immune from constitutional constraints. Conservatives contend that this system of checks and balances not only upholds the rule of law domestically but also provides a model for democracies around the world, illustrating that true human rights protection arises from the separation of powers and limited government.[3]

The American commitment to free speech, religious liberty, and a free press further reinforces its democratic model. These freedoms have been central to American public life since the nation's inception and continue to serve as essential instruments for holding government accountable and fostering open debate. In an era of increasing global censorship and authoritarian tendencies, the American First Amendment remains a powerful statement of democratic values. Conservatives argue that the protection of these freedoms is not merely a legal nicety but a moral imperative, one that ensures that citizens can participate fully in the democratic process. By defending free expression and religious liberty, the United States sets an example for other nations and underpins a global culture of individual rights and accountability.[4]

However, the global landscape also brings challenges that test the resilience of the American constitutional model. International human rights regimes and multilateral treaties, while promoting universal standards, sometimes conflict with domestic constitutional protections. For example, international obligations may require the United States to adopt policies that, in effect, expand federal power beyond the limits prescribed by the Constitution. Conservatives caution that such pressures can erode national sovereignty and undermine the balance between government and the governed. They maintain that any international law or treaty must be subject to rigorous constitutional scrutiny to ensure it does not compromise the Founding Fathers' vision of limited government. The supremacy clause of the Constitution establishes that treaties are the supreme law of the land, yet conservatives insist that this principle must be interpreted narrowly so that international obligations do not inadvertently reconfigure domestic power structures.[5]

In the realm of democracy, the American constitutional model emphasizes the importance of popular sovereignty and civic participation. The Constitution was designed to be a living instrument, but its core principles were meant to be stable and enduring. Over the centuries, various constitutional crises have tested this model—ranging from the debates over the Alien

---

[3] Montesquieu, C. (1748). *The Spirit of the Laws*. Paris: Barrillot & Fils.

[4] Pocock, J. G. A. (1975). *The Machiavellian Moment: Florentine Political Thought and the Atlantic Republican Tradition*. Princeton: Princeton University Press.

[5] Rakove, J. (1997). *Original Meanings: Politics and Ideas in the Making of the Constitution*. New York: Vintage.

and Sedition Acts to the political turmoil of the 2000 presidential election—and each time, the resolution has depended on a recommitment to constitutional norms. Conservatives argue that a robust democracy is best maintained when government actions are guided by the original text of the Constitution rather than by transient political ideologies. This approach ensures that democratic processes are fair and that rights are protected consistently, regardless of the prevailing winds of political opinion.[6]

The globalization of the economy has also had profound implications for constitutional governance in the United States. International trade agreements and global regulatory standards require the country to balance domestic economic interests with external pressures. Conservatives contend that while engaging in global commerce is essential for economic growth, such engagement must not force America to relinquish its constitutional autonomy. The Constitution's Commerce Clause was intended to facilitate interstate trade and ensure a national market, not to serve as a vehicle for expansive federal regulation. When international economic policies encroach upon this principle, they risk undermining the free-market system that has driven American prosperity. A return to the constitutional limits on federal power, conservatives argue, is necessary to preserve both economic freedom and the integrity of the American democratic model.[7]

National security issues in the era of globalization further complicate the constitutional landscape. The post-9/11 expansion of surveillance and security measures has raised significant concerns about the balance between state power and individual rights. Conservatives argue that while protecting the nation from external threats is imperative, it must not be achieved at the expense of constitutional freedoms. The Constitution guarantees due process, privacy, and freedom from arbitrary government action—principles that are often compromised by overbroad security policies. Maintaining these rights requires that any expansion of state power for security purposes be strictly limited and subject to rigorous oversight, ensuring that the measures taken do not set a precedent for permanent erosion of civil liberties.[8]

Political parties and ideological divisions also play a central role in shaping the response to international law and global challenges. In recent decades, the polarized nature of American politics has sometimes led to the adoption of policies that prioritize ideological objectives over constitutional fidelity. Conservatives argue that a return to the original principles of the Constitution is essential for depoliticizing debates about human rights and democracy. By grounding policy

---

[6] Adams, S. (1961). *The Revolutionary Writings of Samuel Adams*. Boston: Beacon Press.

[7] Bork, R. (1990). *The Tempting of America: The Political Seduction of the Law*. New York: Free Press.

[8] Jefferson, T. (Founders Online). "Notes on the State of Virginia." National Archives.

decisions in the immutable text of the Constitution and the historical context provided by the Founding Fathers, the United States can ensure that its domestic and international policies remain consistent with the values of limited government and individual liberty.[9]

The role of the judiciary in interpreting the Constitution in light of international law is of paramount importance. Conservative jurists advocate for an originalist approach to judicial review, one that interprets the Constitution based on its original public meaning rather than adapting it to contemporary political pressures. Landmark cases such as Medellín v. Texas have underscored the necessity of ensuring that international obligations do not override the constitutional order. Conservatives maintain that the courts must serve as a bulwark against the encroachment of international law on national sovereignty, reinforcing the idea that the Constitution is the supreme law of the land and must guide all governmental action.[10]

Legislative oversight is another critical component of the American response to global interdependence. The Senate's role in treaty ratification, requiring a two-thirds majority, ensures that international agreements receive broad support before they become binding. This safeguard reflects the Founding Fathers' intent to protect national sovereignty by subjecting international obligations to strict domestic scrutiny. Conservatives argue that any treaty or international commitment that expands federal power beyond constitutional limits should be rejected by the Senate, thereby preserving the balance of power envisioned in the Constitution.[11]

Economic considerations, too, have a significant impact on the constitutional response to globalization. The American economy, built on free-market principles and secure property rights, has long been a source of national strength. However, international economic pressures can compel the government to adopt policies that may conflict with constitutional economic freedoms. Conservatives assert that trade agreements and global regulatory standards must be designed in a manner that respects the constitutional protections of individual property rights and contractual freedom. Any attempt to cede domestic regulatory control to international bodies risks undermining the economic liberty that has driven American prosperity.[12]

Cultural identity is another pillar supporting the American constitutional model in the era of globalization. The values of self-determination, individual freedom, and limited government

---

[9] Dickinson, J. (1994). *Colonial Self-Government in America.* Cambridge: Harvard University Press.

[10] Calhoun, J. C. (1983). "Separation of Powers and the Structure of the Constitution." In *Foundations of American Government* (pp. 29–32). New York: Harper & Row.

[11] Jefferson, T. (Founders Online). "Notes on the State of Virginia." National Archives.

[12] Amar, A. R. (2005). *America's Constitution: A Biography*. New York: Random House.

are deeply ingrained in the national psyche, and they serve as a moral compass for policy decisions. Conservatives argue that these cultural values must not be compromised in the name of international conformity. Instead, the United States should champion its constitutional model as a paradigm of human rights and democratic governance—a model that not only protects its own citizens but also offers a viable alternative to authoritarian regimes around the world.[13]

The interplay between human rights and democratic governance is central to the American model. The Constitution guarantees a range of civil liberties, and these rights serve as the foundation for a functioning democracy. Free speech, religious liberty, and due process are not only intrinsic to the American way of life but also indispensable for holding government accountable. In a global context, these rights provide a universal benchmark that differentiates democratic societies from authoritarian ones. Conservatives argue that by steadfastly adhering to these constitutional protections, the United States can both defend its own democratic institutions and promote human rights on the international stage.[14]

Globalization inevitably brings challenges that test the balance between national sovereignty and international obligations. Multilateral treaties, international human rights conventions, and global regulatory frameworks all require a level of domestic conformity that can conflict with constitutional limits. Conservatives insist that while the United States must engage with the international community, it should do so without compromising the Constitution's original intent. This means ensuring that all international commitments are subject to domestic legal review and that any potential conflict with constitutional provisions is resolved in favor of national sovereignty.[15]

Modern technological advances, particularly in digital communications and cybersecurity, further complicate this balance. The internet and social media have revolutionized global communication, enabled rapid dissemination of information and fostered transnational political movements. While these developments have enhanced democratic participation, they have also exposed the nation to new vulnerabilities, such as cyberattacks and foreign interference. Conservatives argue that the Constitution's protections—especially those related to privacy, free speech, and due process—must be robustly enforced in the digital age. This enforcement

---

[13] Henry, P. (1775). *Speech on Colonial Rights*. Richmond: Virginia Historical Society.

[14] Kirk, R. (1953). *The Conservative Mind.* New York: Free Press.

[15] Levinson, S. (2006). *Our Undemocratic Constitution: Where the Constitution Goes Wrong (and How We the People Can Correct It)*. New Haven: Yale University Press.

ensures that international digital policies do not erode the constitutional rights that are the bedrock of American democracy.[16]

The challenge of political polarization remains acute in the era of globalization. Partisan divisions have intensified debates over international law, with political factions often using global issues as platforms for advancing ideological agendas. Conservatives warn that such polarization risks undermining the objective application of constitutional principles, leading to a crisis of legitimacy in government institutions. They advocate for a return to an originalist interpretation of the Constitution, which provides clear, timeless standards for evaluating both domestic and international policies. This approach, they assert, is essential for depoliticizing debates over human rights and democracy and for restoring trust in the constitutional system.[17]

The role of political leadership is also critical in shaping constitutional responses to international law. Leaders who adhere to the Founding Fathers' vision can bridge the gap between national sovereignty and global interdependence. Conservative political leaders emphasize the importance of making decisions that are guided by constitutional principles rather than transient political or ideological pressures. Effective leadership, they argue, is key to ensuring that international engagements are conducted in a manner that upholds American values and protects national interests.[18]

Legislative oversight and the amendment process remain powerful tools for maintaining constitutional integrity in the face of international challenges. The rigorous process for amending the Constitution, though deliberately difficult, ensures that any modifications to the domestic legal framework are made with broad consensus. Conservatives argue that this process is a safeguard against the hasty adoption of international standards that may conflict with constitutional values. It reinforces the principle that true change must reflect the will of the people and be consistent with the founding ideals of limited government and individual liberty.[19]

International comparisons lend further weight to the conservative position. Empirical studies have shown that democracies with rigid, codified constitutional frameworks tend to enjoy higher levels of political stability, economic freedom, and human rights protection than those with more malleable systems. Conservatives contend that the American Constitution, with its clear limits on governmental power and robust protections for individual rights, provides a model

---

[16] Hayek, F. A. (1960). *The Constitution of Liberty*. Chicago: University of Chicago Press.

[17] Aldrich, J. H. (1983). *Constitutional Theory*. Chicago: University of Chicago Press.

[18] Ackerman, B. (1991). *We the People: Foundations*. Cambridge, MA: Harvard University Press.

[19] Connelley, W. F. (2009). *Restoring the Constitutional Order*. Lexington: University Press of Kentucky.

for governance that is uniquely suited to preserving national sovereignty in a globalized world. This comparative evidence underscores the importance of adhering to the original constitutional framework as a means of safeguarding both democracy and human rights.[20]

Moreover, the economic ramifications of constitutional responses to international law are profound. A regulatory environment that is overly influenced by global standards can stifle innovation and undermine the competitive advantages of the American free-market system. Conservatives argue that economic policy must be formulated in a manner that protects domestic industries and encourages private enterprise, while still allowing for responsible international cooperation. The Constitution's protections for property rights and contractual freedom are critical to this endeavor, ensuring that economic regulations are applied in a way that fosters growth and innovation rather than imposing excessive burdens on businesses.[21]

The moral imperative to uphold human rights and democratic governance is at the heart of the American constitutional model. The Founding Fathers envisioned a nation where government power is limited and individual liberty is paramount—a vision that has made the United States a global beacon of freedom. In the context of globalization, this moral imperative becomes even more salient. Conservatives argue that the United States must resist international pressures that would dilute its commitment to human rights and democratic principles. By remaining steadfast in its constitutional commitments, America can continue to serve as an example to the world of how a free and just society should be governed.[22]

Finally, the synthesis of human rights, democracy, and the American constitutional model yields a framework that is both resilient and adaptive. Despite the challenges posed by globalization, the core principles of the Constitution remain immutable. The lessons learned from past constitutional crises show that when the United States adheres to the original vision of limited government, checks and balances, and individual rights, it is capable of weathering even the most severe storms. Conservatives insist that this disciplined approach is the only viable path forward, one that ensures both national sovereignty and the promotion of human rights in an interconnected world.[23]

---

[20] Jefferson, T., & Madison, J. (Founders Online). "Letter from Thomas Jefferson to James Madison, July 29, 1787." National Archives.

[21] Dickinson, J. (1994). *Colonial Self-Government in America.* Cambridge: Harvard University Press.

[22] Ferguson, N. (2004). *Colony: A History of Early America.* New York: Penguin Press.

[23] Locke, J. (1689). *Two Treatises of Government.* London: Awnsham Churchill.

In conclusion, the constitutional response to international law in the era of globalization presents a formidable challenge: balancing national sovereignty with global interdependence while upholding human rights and democratic governance. From a politically conservative perspective, the Founding Fathers' original vision offers the most reliable framework for meeting this challenge. By strictly adhering to constitutional limits, ensuring robust legislative and judicial oversight, and engaging with international obligations only on terms that respect American sovereignty, the United States can safeguard its political and economic freedoms. The lessons from past constitutional crises—ranging from early debates over federal power to modern controversies over executive overreach—demonstrate that a return to the immutable principles of the Constitution is essential for the nation's survival and prosperity. Only through this disciplined adherence can America continue to be a global beacon of freedom, democracy, and human rights in an era of unprecedented interdependence.[24] Moreover, by drawing on the hard-won lessons of history and reaffirming the moral imperatives embedded in the Constitution, contemporary governance can address the challenges of globalization without compromising the fundamental values that have defined the American experiment since its inception.[25] Ultimately, the conservative prescription for addressing international law is clear: the United States must remain true to its constitutional roots, ensuring that national sovereignty, human rights, and democratic governance are never sacrificed in the pursuit of global cooperation. This steadfast commitment to the founding principles is the definitive answer to saving America today and securing its future as a free and prosperous nation in the global arena.[26]

---

[24] Rakove, J. (1997). *Original Meanings: Politics and Ideas in the Making of the Constitution*. New York: Vintage.

[25] Adams, S. (1961). *The Revolutionary Writings of Samuel Adams*. Boston: Beacon Press.

[26] Hamilton, A., Madison, J., & Jay, J. (1961). *The Federalist Papers*. New York: New American Library.

4. Global Economic Integration and Constitutional Limits

Global economic integration is one of the most transformative phenomena of the modern era. Nations are more interconnected than ever before, with cross-border flows of goods, capital, and information reshaping economies and societies. Yet, as American businesses and consumers increasingly participate in a global marketplace, the United States must reconcile the imperatives of international economic cooperation with its constitutional commitment to limited government and national sovereignty. From a politically conservative perspective, the Founding Fathers envisioned a nation governed by strict constitutional limits that protect individual rights and state autonomy, and any expansion of federal power must be carefully scrutinized when faced with the demands of globalization.

At the heart of the American constitutional order is the principle that governmental authority is not inherent but granted by the people. The framers, influenced by Enlightenment thinkers like John Locke and Montesquieu, constructed a document that limits federal power to explicitly enumerated functions. This commitment is reflected in the Commerce Clause of Article I, Section 8, which was designed to facilitate interstate commerce without granting Congress unfettered authority over all economic activity. Conservatives argue that this clause, as originally intended, was not meant to serve as a justification for extensive federal regulation of domestic economic affairs in response to global pressures. Instead, its narrow reading is essential for preserving the free-market principles and economic freedoms that have underpinned American prosperity since the nation's founding.[1]

The Constitution's limitations on federal power are further reinforced by the Tenth Amendment, which reserves to the states and the people all powers not delegated to the federal government. This provision ensures that much of the regulation of economic activity remains within the purview of state governments, thereby fostering a decentralized system that encourages innovation and local responsiveness. As the United States engages with global economic forces, conservatives maintain that any attempt by international institutions or treaties to override these constitutional limits must be resisted. National sovereignty, they argue, is the bedrock upon which economic freedom is built, and the Constitution's original intent must prevail even as global interdependence deepens.[2]

---

[1] Hamilton, A., Madison, J., & Jay, J. (1961). *The Federalist Papers*. New York: New American Library.

[2] Locke, J. (1689). *Two Treatises of Government*. London: Awnsham Churchill.

Global economic integration offers significant benefits, including increased trade, technological innovation, and access to international capital. However, these benefits are accompanied by challenges. International trade agreements and multilateral regulatory frameworks often require the United States to adopt domestic policies that may conflict with constitutional principles. For instance, free trade agreements can impose uniform labor, environmental, or intellectual property standards that may not align with the constitutional commitment to limited government intervention. Conservatives caution that such external pressures risk eroding the sovereignty guaranteed by the Constitution. They argue that any international agreement must be carefully reviewed by Congress and subject to the rigorous standards set forth by the Founding Fathers before being ratified, ensuring that American law remains supreme over global norms.[3]

One of the core conservative concerns is the potential for international law to be used as a pretext for expanding federal power. The Supremacy Clause of the Constitution establishes that treaties are the "supreme Law of the Land," yet conservatives insist that this principle must be interpreted in a manner that does not allow global agreements to usurp domestic authority. In cases where international obligations appear to conflict with constitutional limits, the Constitution itself must serve as the final arbiter. The Founding Fathers designed the U.S. legal system with the understanding that no external authority could redefine the powers of the government. This principle is essential for ensuring that global economic integration does not come at the expense of American sovereignty or individual liberty.[4]

The challenge of maintaining constitutional limits in an interconnected world is further complicated by the rise of international institutions. Organizations such as the World Trade Organization, the International Monetary Fund, and various United Nations agencies exert considerable influence over domestic economic policies. While these bodies promote cooperation and stability, they can also impose rules that conflict with the nation's constitutional framework. Conservatives argue that participation in such institutions should be strictly voluntary and must not require the United States to surrender its constitutional prerogatives. The Senate's advice and consent requirement for treaty ratification is a crucial safeguard in this regard—it ensures that any international commitment has broad political support and is consistent with the constitutional mandate of limited government.[5]

---

[3] Montesquieu, C. (1748). *The Spirit of the Laws*. Paris: Barrillot & Fils.

[4] Pocock, J. G. A. (1975). *The Machiavellian Moment: Florentine Political Thought and the Atlantic Republican Tradition*. Princeton: Princeton University Press.

[5] Rakove, J. (1997). *Original Meanings: Politics and Ideas in the Making of the Constitution*. New York: Vintage.

Judicial review plays a vital role in this context. The U.S. Supreme Court has the responsibility to interpret the Constitution in light of both historical context and contemporary challenges. Conservative jurists advocate for an originalist approach that seeks to understand international agreements according to the text and meaning that the Founding Fathers intended. Landmark cases, such as Medellín v. Texas, illustrate the Court's willingness to assert that domestic law must prevail over international obligations when there is a conflict. This judicial restraint is viewed by conservatives as essential for preventing the erosion of constitutional limits by global economic pressures.[6]

Economic policy is deeply intertwined with constitutional limits, particularly as globalization intensifies competition and interdependence. The American economy has long been celebrated for its free-market principles and the protection of property rights—cornerstones of the Constitution. Conservatives assert that free-market mechanisms, safeguarded by constitutional protections for individual rights and limited government, are the primary drivers of economic prosperity. When global economic integration prompts the federal government to impose extensive regulations or adopt policies that undermine private enterprise, it not only disrupts market dynamics but also contravenes the constitutional order. The challenge, therefore, is to harness the benefits of globalization without sacrificing the economic freedoms enshrined in the Constitution.[7]

National security concerns further complicate the balance between global integration and constitutional limits. In the post-9/11 era, the federal government has expanded its regulatory and surveillance powers in the name of protecting the nation. Conservatives argue that while national security is paramount, such expansions must be strictly confined within constitutional boundaries. The Constitution guarantees due process, privacy, and protections against arbitrary government action—all of which can be jeopardized when international security imperatives are used to justify sweeping federal interventions. Maintaining these protections is essential not only for preserving individual rights but also for upholding the integrity of the constitutional order in a globalized world.[8]

Political parties and ideological divisions also influence how the United States responds to international law. In an era of extreme partisanship, debates over global economic integration often become polarized, with each side advocating for policies that align with their ideological preferences rather than with constitutional principles. Conservatives argue that a return to the

---

[6] Adams, S. (1961). *The Revolutionary Writings of Samuel Adams*. Boston: Beacon Press.

[7] Bork, R. (1990). *The Tempting of America: The Political Seduction of the Law*. New York: Free Press.

[8] Jefferson, T. (Founders Online). "Notes on the State of Virginia." National Archives.

original, text-based interpretation of the Constitution is the only way to depoliticize these debates and ensure that policies remain consistent with the founding ideals. This objective standard, they assert, is the best safeguard against the dangers of partisan extremism, which can lead to regulatory overreach and the erosion of national sovereignty.[9]

Cultural identity is another critical factor in the constitutional response to globalization. The American experiment was built on the values of self-determination, individual liberty, and resistance to external domination. These values are enshrined in the Constitution and have shaped the national identity for over two centuries. Conservatives maintain that, in the face of global pressures, it is imperative to uphold this cultural legacy by adhering to the constitutional limits that have protected American freedom. Any international legal framework that requires America to compromise on these core values is seen as a threat to the nation's identity and must be rejected in favor of preserving constitutional autonomy.[10]

The interplay between international law and domestic constitutional principles also demands that any international economic integration be implemented in a manner consistent with American legal traditions. Multilateral treaties and international agreements must be scrutinized to ensure that they do not force the United States to abandon the legal principles that have long been the bedrock of its economic success. Conservatives argue that, while the benefits of global integration are undeniable, they must be pursued on terms that protect American constitutional rights. In practice, this means that international obligations should be designed and implemented through a rigorous legislative process that respects the Constitution's original limits on federal power.[11]

Moreover, the process of treaty-making itself is a critical component of maintaining constitutional integrity. The U.S. Constitution requires that treaties be approved by a two-thirds majority in the Senate, ensuring that only those international commitments that enjoy broad political support—and are consistent with constitutional principles—become law. Conservatives view this requirement as a vital check on the executive branch's power, preventing the unilateral imposition of international obligations that could compromise national sovereignty. This safeguard ensures that global economic integration is pursued in a manner that is democratically accountable and constitutionally sound.[12]

---

[9] Dickinson, J. (1994). *Colonial Self-Government in America.* Cambridge: Harvard University Press.

[10] Calhoun, J. C. (1983). "Separation of Powers and the Structure of the Constitution." In *Foundations of American Government* (pp. 29–32). New York: Harper & Row.

[11] Jefferson, T. (Founders Online). "Notes on the State of Virginia." National Archives.

[12] Amar, A. R. (2005). *America's Constitution: A Biography*. New York: Random House.

The economic implications of global integration are profound, yet they must be reconciled with the constitutional commitment to free markets and limited government. The Constitution protects property rights and contractual freedom, which are essential for economic innovation and growth. Conservatives warn that international economic policies that impose broad regulatory mandates or interfere with these rights risk undermining the very foundation of American prosperity. To preserve economic freedom in the global era, the United States must ensure that any international trade agreements or regulatory frameworks are implemented in a manner that respects the constitutional limits on federal power.[13]

National security, too, has become increasingly intertwined with global economic integration. As American businesses expand internationally, they face new security challenges that require cooperation with global partners. However, conservatives caution that such cooperation should not come at the expense of constitutional principles. The expansion of federal power in the name of international security must be carefully limited to avoid infringing upon individual rights and the democratic process. The challenge is to balance the imperatives of national security with the enduring constitutional commitment to limited government and individual liberty.[14]

Judicial interpretation remains a key battleground in the debate over global integration and constitutional limits. Conservative jurists advocate for an originalist approach, arguing that the Constitution should be interpreted in light of the Founding Fathers' intent rather than evolving global norms. Landmark cases that have addressed the relationship between international law and domestic constitutional provisions serve as important precedents. For example, the Supreme Court's decision in Medellín v. Texas underscored the principle that domestic law must ultimately prevail over conflicting international obligations. Conservatives argue that such decisions are essential for ensuring that the United States remains sovereign and that its constitutional order is not diluted by external influences.[15]

Legislative oversight is equally important in ensuring that the federal government does not overextend its regulatory power in response to global economic pressures. Congress must exercise its constitutional authority to regulate commerce and control federal spending in a manner that is consistent with the original intent of the Constitution. Effective oversight prevents the executive branch from unilaterally adopting policies that could undermine national sovereignty.

---

[13] Henry, P. (1775). *Speech on Colonial Rights*. Richmond: Virginia Historical Society.

[14] Kirk, R. (1953). *The Conservative Mind.* New York: Free Press.

[15] Levinson, S. (2006). *Our Undemocratic Constitution: Where the Constitution Goes Wrong (and How We the People Can Correct It)*. New Haven: Yale University Press.

Conservatives insist that any international economic integration should be subject to rigorous congressional review, ensuring that it aligns with the principles of limited government and economic freedom.[16]

The amendment process offers a democratic mechanism to resolve conflicts between international law and domestic constitutional principles. Although the process is intentionally difficult, it provides a way to adapt the Constitution to new global realities without sacrificing its core values. Conservatives argue that any changes to the constitutional framework must occur through this formal process, which guarantees broad public support and careful deliberation. This method of constitutional evolution ensures that American sovereignty is maintained even as the nation engages with the international community.[17]

Cultural continuity and national identity further support the conservative stance on global economic integration. The American experiment was founded on the belief in self-determination and the protection of individual liberty. These values, enshrined in the Constitution, form the backbone of the nation's identity. Conservatives contend that any international agreement or global regulatory framework that compromises these values risks eroding the unique character of the United States. By remaining true to the original constitutional vision, America can continue to serve as a global exemplar of freedom and democratic governance.[18]

Globalization brings with it complex economic challenges that must be addressed without sacrificing constitutional limits. While the benefits of international trade, foreign investment, and technological innovation are substantial, they should not be pursued at the expense of the domestic legal framework that has enabled American prosperity. Conservatives assert that the Constitution's protection of free markets and property rights must serve as the guiding standard for all economic policy decisions. This ensures that global integration enhances rather than undermines the economic freedoms that are essential to the nation's success.[19]

The influence of political parties and ideological divisions also plays a critical role in shaping the U.S. response to international law. In a highly polarized environment, there is a risk that debates over global economic integration become vehicles for partisan agendas rather than objective assessments of constitutional principles. Conservatives advocate for a return to the original text and historical context of the Constitution as the basis for resolving such disputes. This objective

---

[16] Hayek, F. A. (1960). *The Constitution of Liberty*. Chicago: University of Chicago Press.

[17] Aldrich, J. H. (1983). *Constitutional Theory*. Chicago: University of Chicago Press.

[18] Ackerman, B. (1991). *We the People: Foundations*. Cambridge, MA: Harvard University Press.

[19] Connelley, W. F. (2009). *Restoring the Constitutional Order*. Lexington: University Press of Kentucky.

standard is seen as the best way to depoliticize the issue and ensure that international obligations are implemented in a manner that is consistent with American sovereignty.[20]

The role of the judiciary remains a cornerstone in the conservative defense of national sovereignty in the era of globalization. Originalist judges must interpret international agreements in a way that upholds the constitutional limits on federal power. By doing so, the courts can prevent the undue expansion of governmental authority that might otherwise be justified on the basis of global economic or security concerns. Landmark decisions that have reinforced the supremacy of the Constitution over conflicting international norms provide a model for how the judiciary should approach contemporary challenges.[21]

Legislative oversight, too, is vital for preserving the constitutional balance in the face of global integration. The Senate's requirement that treaties receive a two-thirds majority before ratification is a critical safeguard against the erosion of national sovereignty. This requirement ensures that any international agreement has broad political support and is consistent with the nation's constitutional framework. Conservatives argue that such oversight is indispensable for ensuring that global engagements do not force America to relinquish its legal and political autonomy.[22]

Economic policy must also be formulated within the constraints of the Constitution. The Founding Fathers enshrined property rights, freedom of contract, and limited government as the cornerstones of American prosperity. As the United States engages in global economic integration, it is imperative that these constitutional protections remain intact. International trade agreements and global regulatory standards should be negotiated in a manner that reinforces, rather than undermines, the free-market principles that have driven American innovation. Conservatives insist that this approach is the only viable means of preserving economic freedom while participating in a globalized economy.[23]

National security concerns, too, must be balanced against constitutional limits. In an interconnected world, the challenges of terrorism, cyberattacks, and geopolitical instability require a coordinated international response. However, conservatives argue that such responses must not come at the expense of constitutional freedoms. The measures adopted to enhance national security must be narrowly tailored and subject to stringent oversight to ensure that they do not infringe upon

---

[20] Jefferson, T., & Madison, J. (Founders Online). "Letter from Thomas Jefferson to James Madison, July 29, 1787." National Archives.

[21] Dickinson, J. (1994). *Colonial Self-Government in America.* Cambridge: Harvard University Press.

[22] Ferguson, N. (2004). *Colony: A History of Early America.* New York: Penguin Press.

[23] Locke, J. (1689). *Two Treatises of Government.* London: Awnsham Churchill.

the rights guaranteed by the Constitution. This balance is essential for maintaining both security and liberty in an era of global interdependence.[24]

Finally, the moral imperative to uphold human rights and democratic governance remains at the core of the American constitutional model. The Founding Fathers crafted a document that enshrines individual liberty and limits governmental power, and these principles have been a beacon of freedom for generations. Conservatives argue that the American model—rooted in the Constitution—offers a powerful example of how a nation can engage with the global community without sacrificing its core values. By adhering strictly to constitutional limits, the United States can ensure that global economic integration strengthens rather than weakens its democratic institutions.[25]

In conclusion, the constitutional response to international law in the era of globalization presents a formidable challenge that requires balancing national sovereignty with global interdependence while upholding human rights and democratic governance. From a politically conservative perspective, the American constitutional model—rooted in the immutable principles of limited government, federalism, and individual liberty—offers the only reliable framework for meeting this challenge. By insisting that international agreements and global economic policies conform to the Constitution's original meaning, by exercising robust legislative oversight and judicial review, and by reaffirming the moral and cultural legacy of the Founding Fathers, the United States can protect its sovereignty and continue to serve as a global exemplar of freedom. This disciplined commitment to constitutional fidelity is the definitive answer to saving America today and securing its future as a free and prosperous nation in an increasingly interconnected world.[26]

---

[24] Rakove, J. (1997). *Original Meanings: Politics and Ideas in the Making of the Constitution*. New York: Vintage.

[25] Adams, S. (1961). *The Revolutionary Writings of Samuel Adams*. Boston: Beacon Press.

[26] Hamilton, A., Madison, J., & Jay, J. (1961). *The Federalist Papers*. New York: New American Library.

5. Future Directions for Constitutional Adaptation

In an age defined by rapid global interconnectivity, technological change, and shifting geopolitical alliances, the United States Constitution remains both a timeless beacon and a challenge for modern governance. The Founding Fathers designed the Constitution as a document of limited government, rooted in natural rights and the preservation of national sovereignty. However, the forces of globalization and rapid economic integration have pressed upon this framework, forcing a reexamination of how constitutional principles can adapt to new challenges without compromising the original vision. From a politically conservative perspective, the future of constitutional adaptation must be guided by an unwavering commitment to the founding principles of limited government, individual liberty, and state sovereignty. This paper provides a detailed analysis of future directions for constitutional adaptation, arguing that any evolution in American constitutional law should be achieved only through measured, democratic processes that remain faithful to the framers' intent.

The essence of conservative constitutional thought is that the Constitution is a fixed document whose meaning is derived from its original public understanding. The Founding Fathers, influenced by Enlightenment thinkers such as John Locke and Montesquieu, crafted a constitutional order designed to restrain governmental power and to safeguard individual rights. This approach has historically served as a bulwark against the expansion of state power and the erosion of freedom. As the United States faces new global challenges—from digital surveillance to economic regulation imposed by international agreements—the imperative remains to preserve the constitutional limits that have long underpinned American liberty.[1] Rather than allowing external pressures to redefine governmental authority, conservatives assert that any constitutional adaptation must begin and end with the original text and intent of the document.

Globalization has transformed the economic, social, and political landscape of the world, integrating national economies and cultures in unprecedented ways. While global economic integration has yielded substantial benefits such as increased trade, technological innovation, and economic growth, it also poses risks to national sovereignty and domestic policymaking. International treaties and multilateral agreements can compel changes in domestic law that, from a conservative standpoint, risk expanding federal power beyond constitutional limits. Future directions for constitutional adaptation must address these tensions by ensuring that international obligations do not override the Constitution's clearly delineated boundaries. The Constitution's Supremacy Clause does indeed establish that treaties are the "supreme Law of

[1] Hamilton, A., Madison, J., & Jay, J. (1961). *The Federalist Papers*. New York: New American Library.

the Land," but conservatives maintain that any treaty or international norm conflicting with the explicit limits of the Constitution must be interpreted in a manner that preserves national sovereignty.[2]

A key area for future constitutional adaptation involves the balance between domestic economic policy and international regulatory frameworks. The Commerce Clause, as originally interpreted, was intended to promote interstate commerce while preventing the federal government from overreaching into areas that should remain under state control. Today, however, global trade agreements often require regulatory adjustments that may encroach on the domestic legal order. Conservatives argue that future adaptations must ensure that economic policies are formulated in a manner that respects constitutional protections for free markets, private property, and individual contract rights. By reaffirming the narrow construction of the Commerce Clause and related economic provisions, the United States can continue to reap the benefits of globalization without sacrificing the constitutional principles that have driven American prosperity.[3]

Another pressing challenge is the evolving nature of technology and its impact on individual rights. The digital revolution has introduced new issues related to privacy, data security, and freedom of speech. Global communication networks have facilitated unprecedented connectivity, but they have also enabled foreign interference and mass surveillance. Conservatives assert that the Constitution's protections—particularly those implicit in the Fourth Amendment—must be vigorously defended in the digital age. Future constitutional adaptation should involve a careful recalibration of laws governing digital privacy and cybersecurity that remains faithful to the original principles of limited government and individual autonomy. This approach would protect Americans from intrusive state action while ensuring that the regulatory environment adapts appropriately to new technological realities.[4]

National security also continues to be a compelling justification for increased governmental power. In the aftermath of the September 11 attacks, expansive surveillance programs and emergency powers were adopted to safeguard the nation. However, conservatives warn that such measures, if allowed to persist unchecked, can become permanent fixtures that undermine the very liberties the Constitution is meant to protect. Future adaptations must address national security needs without permitting a long-term erosion of constitutional rights. This can be achieved by implementing

---

[2] Locke, J. (1689). *Two Treatises of Government*. London: Awnsham Churchill.

[3] Montesquieu, C. (1748). *The Spirit of the Laws*. Paris: Barrillot & Fils.

[4] Pocock, J. G. A. (1975). *The Machiavellian Moment: Florentine Political Thought and the Atlantic Republican Tradition*. Princeton: Princeton University Press.

strict sunset provisions, enhanced judicial oversight, and clear legislative mandates that limit the scope and duration of extraordinary measures.[5]

The role of political institutions, particularly the judiciary and Congress, is central to future constitutional adaptation. Conservative legal thought emphasizes that the Supreme Court should adhere to an originalist methodology when interpreting the Constitution in light of global pressures. Landmark cases such as United States v. Lopez and Medellín v. Texas demonstrate the importance of judicial restraint in preserving the constitutional order. Future judicial decisions must resist the temptation to adopt a "living Constitution" approach that expands federal power in response to modern challenges. Instead, they should interpret the text in accordance with its historical context, thereby ensuring that constitutional adaptations are gradual, deliberate, and consistent with the Founders' vision.[6]

Congressional oversight is equally critical. The Constitution provides that treaties and international agreements require the advice and consent of the Senate by a two-thirds majority, a safeguard designed to ensure that any international commitment enjoys broad political support. Future adaptations must continue to rely on this democratic process to balance the demands of globalization with constitutional limitations. Legislators should rigorously scrutinize international agreements to ensure they do not compel the United States to cede its sovereign powers. By grounding international commitments in the constitutional framework, Congress can help to maintain the delicate balance between global interdependence and national self-determination.[7]

Furthermore, the amendment process is a vital mechanism for adapting the Constitution to new circumstances without abandoning its core principles. Although the amendment process is intentionally difficult—ensuring that only changes with broad, enduring support are enacted—it remains the proper method for constitutional evolution. Conservatives argue that any future adaptation in response to global challenges should occur through this formal process rather than through expansive judicial reinterpretation. This disciplined approach guarantees that changes are made thoughtfully and in a manner that respects the original constitutional order.[8]

Cultural identity and national pride also play a crucial role in shaping constitutional adaptation. The American experiment was founded on the ideals of self-governance, individual liberty, and

---

[5] Rakove, J. (1997). *Original Meanings: Politics and Ideas in the Making of the Constitution*. New York: Vintage.

[6] Adams, S. (1961). *The Revolutionary Writings of Samuel Adams*. Boston: Beacon Press.

[7] Bork, R. (1990). *The Tempting of America: The Political Seduction of the Law*. New York: Free Press.

[8] Jefferson, T. (Founders Online). "Notes on the State of Virginia." National Archives.

limited government. These values are deeply embedded in the nation's cultural fabric and serve as a moral compass for policy decisions. In the face of globalization, there is a risk that external influences could dilute these values. Conservatives insist that future constitutional adaptations must preserve America's unique cultural heritage by ensuring that international engagements do not force the nation to compromise on its foundational principles. Maintaining this cultural continuity is essential not only for national identity but also for the legitimacy of American governance in a globalized world.[9]

The economic ramifications of global integration demand that constitutional adaptations safeguard the rights of individuals and businesses. Free-market principles, secure property rights, and contractual freedom are the cornerstones of American economic success. Global trade and international regulatory frameworks must be harmonized with these constitutional guarantees. Conservatives argue that any attempt to expand federal economic regulation in response to global pressures must be carefully balanced against the need to protect economic freedom. Future directions should focus on ensuring that international economic policies enhance, rather than restrict, domestic innovation and prosperity.[10]

National security concerns, intertwined with economic and technological challenges, further underscore the need for constitutional adaptation. As the United States confronts threats ranging from cyberattacks to terrorism, it must craft policies that protect the nation without sacrificing the constitutional limits on government power. Conservatives contend that security measures must be temporary, narrowly tailored, and subject to robust judicial review to prevent them from becoming permanent erosions of individual rights. By adhering to the Constitution's original text, America can maintain a secure environment that respects both national security imperatives and constitutional freedoms.[11]

Political parties and ideological divisions continue to shape the discourse on constitutional adaptation. In recent decades, increasing polarization has often led to the politicization of constitutional interpretation, with parties advocating for expansive changes that may not align with the Founders' intent. Conservatives argue that the solution lies in depoliticizing constitutional debates by returning to the objective, historically grounded meaning of the document. This approach would provide a stable standard against which all policy proposals—domestic and

---

[9] Dickinson, J. (1994). *Colonial Self-Government in America.* Cambridge: Harvard University Press.

[10] Calhoun, J. C. (1983). "Separation of Powers and the Structure of the Constitution." In *Foundations of American Government* (pp. 29–32). New York: Harper & Row.

[11] Jefferson, T. (Founders Online). "Notes on the State of Virginia." National Archives.

international—could be measured, ensuring that adaptations occur only within the parameters established by the Constitution.[12]

Judicial review, as a guardian of constitutional order, must remain steadfast in its commitment to originalism. Conservative jurists have long argued that the Supreme Court should interpret international agreements and domestic laws in a manner that is consistent with the framers' original vision. Future judicial decisions must continue to enforce the limits on federal power, ensuring that global integration does not lead to the dilution of constitutional rights. This judicial restraint is essential for preserving the American model of limited government in an increasingly interconnected world.[13]

Legislative oversight, particularly in the treaty-making process, is another pillar supporting constitutional adaptation. The Senate's requirement of a two-thirds vote for treaty ratification is a critical check on executive power and an affirmation of national sovereignty. Conservatives maintain that this process must continue to function as a safeguard against the imposition of international obligations that would undermine constitutional limits. Robust congressional scrutiny ensures that all international engagements are consistent with the nation's founding principles.[14]

Economic policy, too, must be reexamined in light of global integration. The Constitution protects individual economic rights, and any adaptation in response to international pressures must be carefully balanced to avoid undermining these rights. Conservatives argue that the benefits of globalization—such as increased trade and technological innovation—should not come at the expense of the free-market principles enshrined in the Constitution. Future adaptations must prioritize the protection of property rights, contractual freedom, and limited government to ensure that economic policies remain consistent with the foundational values that have driven American prosperity.[15]

National security remains a critical aspect of constitutional adaptation. In an era where global threats are increasingly complex, the challenge is to protect the nation without compromising the Constitution. Conservatives contend that any measures adopted for national security must be rigorously limited and subject to constitutional review. The balance between security and liberty

---

[12] Amar, A. R. (2005). *America's Constitution: A Biography*. New York: Random House.

[13] Henry, P. (1775). *Speech on Colonial Rights*. Richmond: Virginia Historical Society.

[14] Kirk, R. (1953). *The Conservative Mind*. New York: Free Press.

[15] Levinson, S. (2006). *Our Undemocratic Constitution: Where the Constitution Goes Wrong (and How We the People Can Correct It)*. New Haven: Yale University Press.

is delicate, and the framers' insistence on limited government provides a guiding principle for navigating these challenges.[16]

Cultural continuity and the preservation of national identity are also essential in the face of globalization. The American Constitution is not only a legal document but also a symbol of the nation's commitment to freedom and self-determination. Conservatives argue that maintaining this cultural legacy is crucial for ensuring that international agreements do not erode the unique values that define the United States. Future constitutional adaptations must reinforce the idea that America's strength lies in its adherence to the principles of limited government and individual liberty.[17]

The influence of international institutions on domestic law is another area that requires careful constitutional adaptation. While global institutions play a significant role in shaping international norms, conservatives insist that American law must always prevail when there is a conflict between international obligations and constitutional limits. The Constitution's clear demarcation of federal power must serve as the final authority, ensuring that international treaties and conventions do not force the United States to abandon its founding principles.[18]

The role of the judiciary in reconciling international law with domestic constitutional limits is paramount. Conservative jurists advocate for an originalist approach, arguing that the Constitution must be interpreted based on its original public meaning. This approach ensures that international obligations are incorporated only to the extent that they do not expand federal power beyond what the Founding Fathers intended. Landmark cases, such as Medellín v. Texas, reinforce the principle that domestic law is supreme, a stance that must guide future adaptations in the global arena.[19]

Legislative oversight also remains a key element in ensuring that global economic policies are consistent with the Constitution. Congress must exercise its power to regulate commerce and control federal spending in a manner that respects the original constitutional framework. Through rigorous oversight, Congress can prevent the executive branch from adopting international policies that undermine American sovereignty. This process is essential for maintaining the balance between global integration and domestic constitutional limits.[20]

---

[16] Hayek, F. A. (1960). *The Constitution of Liberty*. Chicago: University of Chicago Press.

[17] Aldrich, J. H. (1983). *Constitutional Theory*. Chicago: University of Chicago Press.

[18] Ackerman, B. (1991). *We the People: Foundations*. Cambridge, MA: Harvard University Press.

[19] Connelley, W. F. (2009). *Restoring the Constitutional Order*. Lexington: University Press of Kentucky.

[20] Jefferson, T., & Madison, J. (Founders Online). "Letter from Thomas Jefferson to James Madison, July 29, 1787." National Archives.

Economic implications of global integration are profound, yet they must be addressed without sacrificing constitutional freedoms. The American economic model is built on the protection of property rights and the promotion of free enterprise—principles that are enshrined in the Constitution. Conservatives warn that international economic policies that impose excessive regulations risk undermining these fundamental rights. Future directions must ensure that economic integration enhances, rather than restricts, the free-market system by adhering to the constitutional mandate of limited government.[21]

National security challenges, including cyber threats and terrorism, have driven the United States to engage more deeply on the global stage. However, conservatives assert that such engagement must not erode constitutional protections. Measures taken in the name of national security should be narrowly tailored and subject to strict oversight to prevent an unchecked expansion of state power. This balance is crucial for ensuring that security policies do not become permanent erosions of individual liberty.[22]

Political polarization continues to affect the debate over international law and constitutional adaptation. Partisan divisions have often led to conflicting interpretations of how the United States should engage with global norms. Conservatives argue that returning to the objective, historically grounded meaning of the Constitution is essential for depoliticizing these debates. Only by anchoring policy in the immutable text of the Constitution can America ensure that its international engagements are consistent with its founding principles.[23]

Finally, the moral imperative to uphold human rights and democratic governance provides a compelling argument for preserving the American constitutional model amid globalization. The Founding Fathers established a framework intended to protect individual liberty and promote self-governance. Conservatives maintain that the United States must remain steadfast in its commitment to these values, even as it navigates complex international relationships. Future constitutional adaptation must reinforce that the protection of human rights and democratic principles is inseparable from the Constitution's original vision, thereby ensuring that global economic and political integration does not come at the cost of American freedom.[24]

---

[21] Dickinson, J. (1994). *Colonial Self-Government in America*. Cambridge: Harvard University Press.

[22] Ferguson, N. (2004). *Colony: A History of Early America*. New York: Penguin Press.

[23] Locke, J. (1689). *Two Treatises of Government*. London: Awnsham Churchill.

[24] Rakove, J. (1997). *Original Meanings: Politics and Ideas in the Making of the Constitution*. New York: Vintage.

In conclusion, the challenge of global economic integration necessitates a careful balance between international cooperation and constitutional limits. The American constitutional model, grounded in the immutable principles of limited government, federalism, and individual liberty, offers a robust framework for addressing these challenges. Future directions for constitutional adaptation must ensure that international agreements and global regulatory standards are implemented in a manner that respects national sovereignty and the rights of citizens. Through disciplined judicial review, effective legislative oversight, and a steadfast commitment to the Founding Fathers' vision, the United States can navigate the complexities of globalization while preserving its core values. This adherence to constitutional fidelity is the definitive answer to maintaining American freedom and prosperity in an increasingly interconnected world.[25] Moreover, by drawing upon historical lessons and reaffirming the moral and legal imperatives embedded in the Constitution, American governance can successfully adapt to future challenges without compromising its foundational principles, ensuring that the nation remains a beacon of liberty and democratic self-governance well into the future.[26]

---

[25] Adams, S. (1961). *The Revolutionary Writings of Samuel Adams*. Boston: Beacon Press.

[26] Hamilton, A., Madison, J., & Jay, J. (1961). *The Federalist Papers*. New York: New American Library.

CHAPTER 9:

Technology, Surveillance, and Constitutional Privacy

1. Evolving Definitions of Privacy in the Digital Age

In recent decades, rapid technological advances have dramatically transformed the way individuals communicate, share information, and conduct their lives. The digital age has introduced novel forms of data collection, surveillance, and information dissemination that challenge traditional notions of privacy. For centuries, the American constitutional framework—crafted by the Founding Fathers—has provided robust safeguards against government overreach and ensured individual liberty. However, the evolution of technology has forced a reexamination of privacy rights under the Constitution. From a politically conservative perspective that champions limited government and adherence to the original constitutional design, it is essential to reconcile these emerging challenges with the timeless principles upon which the nation was founded. This paper provides a detailed and comprehensive analysis of the evolving definitions of privacy in the digital age, examining the historical foundations of constitutional privacy, the impact of modern surveillance technologies, and the necessary responses to preserve individual rights in a globalized, digital world.

The American Constitution was designed as a bulwark against tyranny, enshrining natural rights that protect individuals from arbitrary state power. The framers, steeped in Enlightenment philosophy and influenced by thinkers such as John Locke and Montesquieu, understood that privacy was an essential element of liberty. Although the text of the Constitution does not explicitly mention "privacy," its protections can be inferred from amendments such as the First, Fourth, and Ninth Amendments. These provisions collectively ensure that government action must be justified, limited, and subject to judicial review. Conservatives argue that any modern interpretation of privacy must be anchored in this original framework, ensuring that technological progress does not become a pretext for expanding governmental power beyond the strict confines intended by the Founding Fathers.[1]

---

[1] Hamilton, A., Madison, J., & Jay, J. (1961). *The Federalist Papers*. New York: New American Library.

The Fourth Amendment, which guards against unreasonable searches and seizures, is particularly relevant in the digital age. Historically, the amendment was enacted in response to the invasive practices of British authorities, designed to protect citizens' homes and personal effects from arbitrary government intrusion. Today, however, the digital revolution has introduced unprecedented challenges. Electronic communications, cloud storage, and ubiquitous mobile devices have blurred the boundaries between public and private spheres. The government's ability to collect vast quantities of data—often without individual consent—raises serious questions about whether the protections afforded by the Fourth Amendment are being eroded. Conservatives insist that the original intent of the Fourth Amendment must prevail: any search or seizure in the digital realm must be reasonable, subject to warrants based on probable cause, and limited in scope so as not to infringe upon individual liberty.[2]

The rapid expansion of surveillance technologies has intensified concerns over constitutional privacy. Advanced data analytics, facial recognition software, and the integration of artificial intelligence into surveillance systems have created a level of monitoring that was unimaginable in the 18th century. While proponents argue that such technologies are essential for national security and law enforcement, conservatives warn that unchecked surveillance poses a direct threat to the core principles of privacy and freedom. The Founding Fathers designed the constitutional system to prevent any single entity from amassing excessive power over the individual. When surveillance expands beyond strict constitutional limits, it risks undermining the trust between citizens and their government. Conservative scholars maintain that the use of technology by the state must be rigorously constrained by the Constitution, ensuring that any surveillance program is narrowly tailored, temporary, and subject to robust judicial oversight.[3]

In addition to state surveillance, the private sector has emerged as a dominant force in the digital domain. Corporations collect, analyze, and monetize vast amounts of personal data, often with minimal transparency or accountability. Conservatives are deeply concerned that this corporate data collection, in tandem with governmental surveillance, creates a de facto system of privacy invasion that the Constitution was never intended to address. They argue that the solution lies not in a wholesale redefinition of privacy rights, but in reinforcing the original constitutional protections through targeted legislative reforms. For instance, laws that enhance transparency in data practices and strengthen individuals' control over their personal information can be

---

[2] Locke, J. (1689). *Two Treatises of Government.* London: Awnsham Churchill.

[3] Montesquieu, C. (1748). *The Spirit of the Laws*. Paris: Barrillot & Fils.

crafted in a manner that is consistent with the principles of limited government and individual liberty.[4]

The evolving definitions of privacy also raise important questions about freedom of expression and the public sphere. The digital age has transformed traditional media, enabling instant and widespread dissemination of information. However, this transformation has also led to concerns about the suppression of free speech through mass surveillance and data collection. Conservatives contend that a free and open public sphere is indispensable for democratic governance, as it allows for robust debate and accountability. The Constitution's First Amendment, which protects free speech and a free press, must be interpreted in a way that also safeguards digital privacy. When government or corporate entities intrude upon the privacy of communications, they risk chilling free expression—a scenario that stands in stark opposition to the values enshrined by the Founding Fathers.[5]

Another significant aspect of modern privacy concerns is the concept of "data sovereignty." In the digital age, personal data is often stored in servers located across international borders, subjecting it to the laws of foreign jurisdictions. This raises complex legal questions about which country's laws apply and how constitutional protections can be enforced when data flows freely across borders. Conservatives argue that national sovereignty, as enshrined in the Constitution, must extend to the digital realm. The United States must develop policies that assert control over domestic data and protect the privacy rights of its citizens, even as they participate in a global digital economy. This requires a careful balancing act that preserves constitutional limits on federal power while enabling effective participation in international markets.[6]

Furthermore, the tension between national security and individual privacy continues to shape the debate over constitutional adaptation. In response to global terrorism and other security threats, governments have often expanded their surveillance capabilities. However, conservatives caution that such expansions should be strictly limited by the Constitution. The balance between ensuring public safety and protecting individual rights is delicate, and history has shown that crises of this nature can lead to lasting erosions of civil liberties if not properly managed. Future constitutional adaptation in the realm of privacy must, therefore, incorporate robust sunset provisions and

---

[4] Pocock, J. G. A. (1975). *The Machiavellian Moment: Florentine Political Thought and the Atlantic Republican Tradition*. Princeton: Princeton University Press.

[5] Rakove, J. (1997). *Original Meanings: Politics and Ideas in the Making of the Constitution*. New York: Vintage.

[6] Adams, S. (1961). *The Revolutionary Writings of Samuel Adams*. Boston: Beacon Press.

judicial safeguards that ensure security measures do not become permanent encroachments on personal freedom.[7]

The role of the judiciary in interpreting privacy rights in the digital age is critical. Conservative legal scholars advocate for an originalist approach to constitutional interpretation, emphasizing that judicial decisions should be grounded in the historical context of the Constitution. Landmark cases involving digital privacy issues should reflect the framers' intent to limit government intrusion while adapting to new technological realities in a manner that does not expand federal power unduly. This judicial restraint is essential to ensure that constitutional protections for privacy remain robust and are not eroded by modern exigencies.[8]

Legislative action also plays an indispensable role in defining the future of digital privacy. Congress has the power to enact laws that balance the needs of national security, economic innovation, and individual liberty. Conservatives argue that any new privacy legislation must be consistent with the constitutional framework established by the Founding Fathers. Such laws should enhance transparency, empower citizens with control over their personal data, and impose strict limitations on governmental and corporate surveillance. By adhering to the principles of limited government and free markets, legislative reforms can help preserve privacy without stifling innovation or compromising constitutional values.[9]

The international dimension of digital privacy further complicates the constitutional landscape. Global data flows and multinational technology companies mean that privacy is no longer a purely domestic issue. However, conservatives maintain that while international cooperation is necessary to address cross-border privacy challenges, it must not override the U.S. Constitution. The principles of national sovereignty and limited government require that international agreements related to digital privacy be implemented in a manner that respects American constitutional limits. This means that any global framework for data protection must be carefully scrutinized by Congress and, if necessary, amended through the constitutional process to ensure that it does not conflict with the foundational rights enshrined in the Constitution.[10]

---

[7] Bork, R. (1990). *The Tempting of America: The Political Seduction of the Law*. New York: Free Press.

[8] Jefferson, T. (Founders Online). "Notes on the State of Virginia." National Archives.

[9] Dickinson, J. (1994). *Colonial Self-Government in America*. Cambridge: Harvard University Press.

[10] Calhoun, J. C. (1983). "Separation of Powers and the Structure of the Constitution." In *Foundations of American Government* (pp. 29–32). New York: Harper & Row.

Economic considerations are also central to the evolving definition of privacy. The digital economy is driven by the collection and analysis of data, which has become a valuable commodity. Conservatives argue that while data-driven innovation is essential for economic growth, it must not come at the expense of individual privacy and freedom. The Constitution protects property rights and contractual freedoms, and these protections extend to personal data as a form of property. Future constitutional adaptation must ensure that economic policies related to data collection and digital commerce are formulated in a way that balances innovation with the preservation of individual rights. This approach will maintain the competitive edge of the American economy while upholding the constitutional principle of limited government intervention.[11]

National security and law enforcement interests further complicate digital privacy. In an effort to combat cybercrime and terrorism, the government has enacted measures that, while aimed at protecting the public, have also raised concerns about mass surveillance and data misuse. Conservatives insist that the pursuit of security must not result in a permanent expansion of federal power that infringes upon the privacy rights of citizens. Measures intended to enhance security should be subject to strict judicial review and limited in scope to ensure that they do not become tools of oppression. This conservative viewpoint holds that constitutional safeguards, as originally intended, are the best defense against the encroachment of state power into the private lives of individuals.[12]

Political ideology and partisanship continue to influence debates over digital privacy. In today's polarized political environment, issues of surveillance and data protection often become entangled with partisan rhetoric. Conservatives argue that an objective, historically grounded interpretation of the Constitution is essential to depoliticize these debates. By returning to the original meaning of the text, judges and lawmakers can provide clear, consistent standards for digital privacy that are not swayed by the transient winds of political ideology. This approach not only protects individual rights but also reinforces the stability of the constitutional order.[13]

The role of technology in modern society raises profound questions about the future of constitutional privacy. As innovations such as artificial intelligence, biometric tracking, and the Internet of Things become more prevalent, the boundaries of privacy will continue to evolve. Conservatives maintain that any redefinition of privacy rights must be firmly anchored in the original constitutional

---

[11] Jefferson, T. (Founders Online). "Notes on the State of Virginia." National Archives.

[12] Amar, A. R. (2005). *America's Constitution: A Biography*. New York: Random House.

[13] Henry, P. (1775). *Speech on Colonial Rights*. Richmond: Virginia Historical Society.

framework. Rather than allowing rapid technological change to dictate new interpretations of privacy, the legal system should adapt gradually through democratic processes and formal amendments if necessary. This measured approach ensures that constitutional protections are not undermined by temporary technological trends.[14]

International comparisons also offer important insights into the future directions for constitutional privacy. Many democracies struggle to balance digital innovation with privacy rights, often resorting to broad regulatory measures that can stifle economic growth and impinge on individual liberty. Conservatives argue that the American model, with its emphasis on limited government and robust judicial review, provides a superior framework for addressing these challenges. By maintaining a strict interpretation of constitutional rights, the United States can serve as a global standard-bearer for privacy while promoting an environment that is both innovative and respectful of individual freedoms.[15]

The amendment process, though arduous, remains a critical tool for adapting constitutional privacy rights to modern realities. Conservatives assert that any significant change to the constitutional understanding of privacy should occur through a deliberate, democratic process rather than through unilateral judicial decisions. This process ensures that adaptations are made with broad consensus and reflect the enduring principles of the Constitution. Such a mechanism protects the integrity of American law and prevents the erosion of rights in the face of rapid technological and societal change.[16]

Moreover, the cultural heritage of the American founding provides a moral foundation for privacy rights. The Founding Fathers, who fought for freedom against oppressive government, recognized the importance of protecting individual spaces from unwarranted intrusion. This legacy of personal liberty is a cornerstone of American identity and must guide contemporary interpretations of privacy in the digital age. Conservatives argue that preserving this cultural heritage is not only a legal necessity but a moral imperative, ensuring that the Constitution remains a living testament to the values of freedom and self-determination.[17]

Political leadership plays a crucial role in shaping the future of constitutional privacy. Leaders who are committed to the principles of limited government and individual liberty can set the

---

[14] Kirk, R. (1953). *The Conservative Mind*. New York: Free Press.

[15] Levinson, S. (2006). *Our Undemocratic Constitution: Where the Constitution Goes Wrong (and How We the People Can Correct It)*. New Haven: Yale University Press.

[16] Hayek, F. A. (1960). *The Constitution of Liberty*. Chicago: University of Chicago Press.

[17] Aldrich, J. H. (1983). *Constitutional Theory*. Chicago: University of Chicago Press.

tone for a balanced approach to digital rights. Conservatives maintain that effective leadership requires a clear-eyed understanding of both the opportunities and risks posed by technology. Such leaders must advocate for policies that protect privacy without hindering innovation, ensuring that national security measures and economic regulations are implemented in a manner consistent with the Constitution's original intent.[18]

Legislative oversight, particularly in the realm of digital privacy, remains indispensable. Congress must actively review and, when necessary, amend laws governing data collection, surveillance, and digital commerce to ensure they align with constitutional protections. The Senate's role in treaty ratification and legislative debate is a critical safeguard against the imposition of international norms that could compromise national sovereignty. Conservatives argue that robust legislative oversight is essential for maintaining the balance between global interdependence and domestic constitutional order.[19]

Economic policy, as influenced by digital innovation, also requires careful constitutional consideration. The free market has long been a driver of American prosperity, supported by strong protections for property rights and contractual freedom. In the digital era, personal data has emerged as a key economic asset. Conservatives contend that economic regulations related to data must be crafted to protect these rights without imposing excessive burdens that could stifle innovation. By adhering to the constitutional mandate of limited government, the United States can ensure that its economic policies foster growth and preserve individual freedoms.[20]

National security imperatives continue to shape the debate over digital privacy. In an era marked by global cyber threats and terrorism, the state's responsibility to protect its citizens is paramount. However, conservatives warn that security measures must be implemented in a way that does not permanently infringe upon constitutional rights. Robust judicial oversight and clearly defined sunset provisions are necessary to ensure that any expansion of state power for security purposes remains temporary and fully accountable under the law.[21]

Political polarization exacerbates conflicts over privacy rights by often framing the debate in partisan terms rather than objective constitutional principles. Conservatives argue that a return to

---

[18] Ackerman, B. (1991). *We the People: Foundations*. Cambridge, MA: Harvard University Press.

[19] Connelley, W. F. (2009). *Restoring the Constitutional Order*. Lexington: University Press of Kentucky.

[20] Jefferson, T., & Madison, J. (Founders Online). "Letter from Thomas Jefferson to James Madison, July 29, 1787." National Archives.

[21] Dickinson, J. (1994). *Colonial Self-Government in America*. Cambridge: Harvard University Press.

an originalist interpretation of the Constitution is necessary to depoliticize digital privacy issues. This approach provides clear, consistent standards for evaluating government actions and ensures that the core principles of individual liberty and limited government are not compromised by partisan agendas.[22]

The influence of international institutions on digital privacy is another challenge that requires careful constitutional adaptation. Multilateral agreements and global regulatory frameworks can sometimes pressure the United States to conform to standards that may conflict with its domestic constitutional protections. Conservatives assert that any such international obligations must be rigorously scrutinized to ensure they do not override the supreme authority of the Constitution. The American model demands that national sovereignty remains intact even as the country engages with the global community.[23]

Finally, the moral imperative to uphold the constitutional vision of freedom and self-governance serves as the ultimate guide for future adaptation. The Founding Fathers established a framework intended to protect individual rights against any form of arbitrary power—be it domestic or international. Conservatives maintain that this vision must be preserved in the digital age by ensuring that privacy rights are interpreted and enforced in accordance with the original text and intent of the Constitution. This steadfast commitment to constitutional fidelity is the definitive answer to navigating the challenges of globalization while safeguarding American liberty.[24]

In conclusion, the evolving definitions of privacy in the digital age present complex challenges that require a balanced, principled response. The American constitutional model, with its roots in the Enlightenment and the enduring wisdom of the Founding Fathers, provides a robust framework for addressing these challenges. Future directions for constitutional adaptation in the realm of digital privacy must be guided by the immutable principles of limited government, robust checks and balances, and the protection of individual rights. Through disciplined judicial review, effective legislative oversight, and a commitment to national sovereignty, the United States can harness the benefits of globalization and technological innovation while preserving its constitutional heritage. This measured approach ensures that American democracy remains vibrant and resilient in the face of rapid change—a testament to the enduring power of the

---

[22] Ferguson, N. (2004). *Colony: A History of Early America*. New York: Penguin Press.

[23] Locke, J. (1689). *Two Treatises of Government*. London: Awnsham Churchill.

[24] Rakove, J. (1997). *Original Meanings: Politics and Ideas in the Making of the Constitution*. New York: Vintage.

Constitution as the ultimate safeguard of freedom in an interconnected world.[25] Moreover, by adhering to these timeless principles, contemporary governance can not only address emerging privacy challenges but also reinforce the moral and legal imperatives that have defined the American experiment since its inception, securing a future in which liberty and self-governance continue to thrive.[26]

---

[25] Adams, S. (1961). *The Revolutionary Writings of Samuel Adams*. Boston: Beacon Press.

[26] Hamilton, A., Madison, J., & Jay, J. (1961). *The Federalist Papers*. New York: New American Library.

2. Surveillance Practices and Constitutional Protections

In recent decades, rapid technological advances have transformed the landscape of public and private life in America, creating unprecedented capabilities for surveillance by both the state and private corporations. As digital technologies permeate every aspect of society—from electronic communications and online transactions to ubiquitous mobile devices—the need to protect constitutional privacy rights has become more urgent than ever. The American Constitution, carefully designed by the Founding Fathers to limit governmental power and safeguard individual liberty, provides the foundation for protecting privacy. Yet, modern surveillance practices challenge traditional definitions of privacy and test the limits of constitutional protections. From a politically conservative perspective that emphasizes limited government, strict adherence to the original constitutional framework, and respect for the Founders' vision, it is imperative that surveillance practices be carefully constrained. This commentary examines contemporary surveillance practices and argues that only by returning to the original constitutional principles can America protect individual privacy in the digital age.

The Fourth Amendment was enacted in reaction to the abuses of British colonial rule, ensuring that citizens would be protected from unreasonable searches and seizures. Although the text does not mention "privacy" explicitly, its underlying purpose has always been to create a sanctuary from arbitrary governmental intrusion. Today, as government agencies and private corporations deploy advanced technologies—such as mass data collection, facial recognition software, and sophisticated tracking systems—the fundamental promise of the Fourth Amendment is at risk. Conservatives argue that the original meaning of the Fourth Amendment must be rigorously enforced in the digital age. Any surveillance operation must be based on individualized warrants supported by probable cause, with clear limitations on scope and duration, so as not to infringe upon the sacred principle of personal privacy.[1]

Government surveillance practices have expanded dramatically since the advent of the digital era. Post-9/11 policies, implemented in the name of national security, have resulted in extensive monitoring of communications and data. Programs such as the National Security Agency's bulk data collection have raised profound concerns regarding the erosion of civil liberties. Conservatives maintain that while national security is of paramount importance, it cannot justify an indefinite expansion of governmental power that compromises constitutional freedoms. Instead, surveillance measures should be temporary, narrowly tailored, and subject

[1] Hamilton, A., Madison, J., & Jay, J. (1961). *The Federalist Papers*. New York: New American Library.

to robust judicial oversight to ensure they do not become permanent encroachments on individual rights.[2]

Alongside governmental surveillance, the private sector has become a major player in the collection and analysis of personal data. Major technology companies routinely harvest vast amounts of information from users, often with minimal transparency. When private data collection intersects with state surveillance, the cumulative effect can be even more invasive. Conservatives argue that the Constitution's protections should not only restrain government power but should also set a standard for private conduct. Legislative measures are needed to ensure that corporations operate transparently, obtain informed consent, and are held accountable when data practices infringe upon personal privacy.[3]

The Founding Fathers envisioned a society in which government power was strictly limited by the rule of law. Their intent was to create a system that safeguarded individual liberty by ensuring that all governmental actions were subject to constitutional constraints. This original vision is a cornerstone of conservative thought. Modern surveillance practices, if left unchecked, threaten to disrupt this balance by allowing both the state and powerful corporations to infringe upon the rights that were meant to be sacrosanct. Conservatives insist that any expansion of surveillance must be carefully calibrated to preserve the limited government envisioned in the Constitution.[4]

The role of judicial review in protecting constitutional privacy is crucial. Landmark decisions, such as *United States v. Katz* (1967), have extended Fourth Amendment protections to areas that were previously unregulated by establishing the "reasonable expectation of privacy" standard. Conservatives support such judicial interventions when they reinforce the original protections intended by the Founders. However, they caution that the Court must adhere closely to an originalist interpretation, avoiding expansive reinterpretations that would grant the government carte blanche in the digital realm. Judicial restraint, as advocated by conservative jurists, ensures that the Constitution remains the supreme safeguard against intrusive surveillance.[5]

Legislative oversight is equally critical. Congress has the power to enact laws that constrain both governmental and private surveillance practices. The legislative process should be guided

---

[2] Locke, J. (1689). *Two Treatises of Government*. London: Awnsham Churchill.

[3] Montesquieu, C. (1748). *The Spirit of the Laws*. Paris: Barrillot & Fils.

[4] Pocock, J. G. A. (1975). *The Machiavellian Moment: Florentine Political Thought and the Atlantic Republican Tradition*. Princeton: Princeton University Press.

[5] Rakove, J. (1997). *Original Meanings: Politics and Ideas in the Making of the Constitution*. New York: Vintage.

by the principles of limited government and individual liberty, ensuring that any surveillance program is justified, narrowly defined, and subject to periodic review. Conservatives argue that robust oversight not only prevents abuses but also fosters public trust by ensuring transparency and accountability in surveillance practices.[6]

One of the challenges in the digital age is defining the scope of privacy. Traditional concepts of privacy were based on physical spaces—homes, letters, and personal effects. Today, much of what is considered private exists in digital form, stored in servers, transmitted over networks, and accessible through mobile devices. Conservatives assert that while the medium has changed, the underlying right to privacy remains unchanged. The Constitution's protections must be extended to cover digital communications and data. However, this extension should not lead to an overly broad interpretation that stifles technological innovation or expands federal power beyond its constitutional limits.[7]

The balance between security and privacy is a recurring theme in debates over surveillance. Proponents of expansive surveillance argue that the risks posed by terrorism and cyber threats necessitate far-reaching monitoring programs. Yet, conservatives counter that sacrificing constitutional protections in the name of security sets a dangerous precedent. Historical examples, such as the internment of Japanese Americans during World War II, serve as stark reminders of the costs associated with unchecked state power. The preservation of individual privacy is not only a legal obligation but also a moral one; the rights enshrined by the Founding Fathers must be upheld even in times of crisis.[8]

Internationally, many democratic nations face similar challenges, but the American constitutional framework remains unique in its emphasis on individual rights and limited government. While European countries have sometimes adopted more permissive approaches to surveillance, conservatives argue that such models risk eroding civil liberties. The American model—rooted in the original constitutional text—provides a robust template for protecting privacy while still allowing for necessary security measures. This distinct approach reinforces the idea that constitutional protections must remain paramount, regardless of global trends.[9]

Political polarization has further complicated the surveillance debate. In today's charged political environment, issues of surveillance and privacy are often weaponized for partisan

---

[6] Adams, S. (1961). *The Revolutionary Writings of Samuel Adams*. Boston: Beacon Press.

[7] Bork, R. (1990). *The Tempting of America: The Political Seduction of the Law*. New York: Free Press.

[8] Jefferson, T. (Founders Online). "Notes on the State of Virginia." National Archives.

[9] Dickinson, J. (1994). *Colonial Self-Government in America*. Cambridge: Harvard University Press.

gain. Conservatives argue that public discourse on these topics should be grounded in objective, historically informed constitutional principles rather than transient political ideologies. A return to an originalist interpretation of the Constitution would provide clear, consistent standards for evaluating surveillance practices and prevent the politicization of privacy rights.[10]

The role of technology companies in shaping the modern surveillance landscape cannot be overlooked. As gatekeepers of vast amounts of personal data, these corporations wield enormous power over the privacy of individuals. Conservatives contend that while the free market is essential for innovation, it must be regulated in a way that protects individual rights. The Constitution's protections, particularly those inferred from the Fourth and Ninth Amendments, must serve as benchmarks for assessing corporate data practices. This approach ensures that economic freedom and innovation are not achieved at the expense of personal privacy.[11]

The interplay between technological innovation and constitutional privacy has significant economic implications as well. The digital economy relies on data as a key asset, yet excessive surveillance can chill free expression and inhibit innovation. Conservatives argue that economic policies must strike a balance between promoting technological progress and preserving the privacy rights that are essential to a free market. By ensuring that surveillance practices remain within the strict confines of the Constitution, the United States can continue to lead in technological innovation without sacrificing the liberties that drive economic growth.[12]

National security imperatives, while critical, must also be balanced with constitutional protections. In an age where threats such as cyberattacks and global terrorism loom large, the state's desire to monitor communications is understandable. However, conservatives maintain that security measures must be implemented with strict limits and robust oversight. The Constitution was designed to prevent the permanent expansion of governmental power, and any security program must have clear temporal and substantive limits. For instance, sunset provisions and judicial review are essential tools to ensure that surveillance measures do not become entrenched and infringe upon constitutional rights.[13]

The evolving legal landscape in the digital age requires a reexamination of privacy rights through the lens of original constitutional principles. Conservative legal scholars advocate for a careful,

---

[10] Calhoun, J. C. (1983). "Separation of Powers and the Structure of the Constitution." In *Foundations of American Government* (pp. 29–32). New York: Harper & Row.

[11] Jefferson, T. (Founders Online). "Notes on the State of Virginia." National Archives.

[12] Amar, A. R. (2005). *America's Constitution: A Biography*. New York: Random House.

[13] Henry, P. (1775). *Speech on Colonial Rights*. Richmond: Virginia Historical Society.

measured adaptation of privacy doctrines that does not expand federal power beyond what was envisioned by the Founders. By grounding digital privacy rights in the historical context of the Fourth Amendment and other related provisions, the judiciary can provide stability and predictability in an era marked by rapid technological change.[14]

Legislative action is crucial in this domain. Congress must craft laws that protect digital privacy while preserving the Constitution's limitations on governmental authority. Such laws should require transparency from both government agencies and private companies regarding data collection and surveillance practices. Furthermore, robust penalties for violations should be established to deter abuses. Conservatives argue that these legislative measures must be consistent with the constitutional mandate for limited government and should be designed through a rigorous, bipartisan process that reflects the original intent of the Constitution.[15]

The amendment process offers a peaceful mechanism for updating constitutional protections as technology evolves, but conservatives caution that any amendments must be undertaken with great care. The Founding Fathers deliberately made the amendment process arduous to ensure that changes reflected a broad consensus and were not driven by transient political pressures. Future amendments related to digital privacy should be considered only after thorough debate and must not compromise the fundamental principles of limited government and individual liberty.[16]

Cultural values play an essential role in shaping perceptions of privacy. The American commitment to individual freedom and self-determination is deeply embedded in the national identity. Conservatives argue that this cultural heritage must guide contemporary interpretations of privacy rights. In the digital age, where the boundaries between public and private are increasingly blurred, it is imperative to uphold the values that have historically protected personal liberty. This cultural continuity provides the moral foundation for resisting attempts to erode privacy through expansive surveillance programs.[17]

The influence of international norms also affects domestic privacy standards. While many countries adopt comprehensive data protection laws, conservatives insist that such models must be reconciled with American constitutional principles. The United States should engage

---

[14] Kirk, R. (1953). *The Conservative Mind.* New York: Free Press.

[15] Levinson, S. (2006). *Our Undemocratic Constitution: Where the Constitution Goes Wrong (and How We the People Can Correct It)*. New Haven: Yale University Press.

[16] Hayek, F. A. (1960). *The Constitution of Liberty.* Chicago: University of Chicago Press.

[17] Aldrich, J. H. (1983). *Constitutional Theory.* Chicago: University of Chicago Press.

with global frameworks on its own terms, ensuring that international agreements do not force domestic authorities to exceed the limits prescribed by the Constitution. This requires a careful balancing of global cooperation with national sovereignty, ensuring that the rights enshrined by the Founders remain paramount.[18]

The role of political parties and public opinion cannot be underestimated in the context of surveillance and privacy. In recent years, partisan divisions have sometimes driven the debate over surveillance, with different factions advocating for either expanded security measures or more robust privacy protections. Conservatives argue that policy debates should be anchored in the objective, historically grounded text of the Constitution, not in transient partisan ideologies. Only by returning to an originalist interpretation can the United States ensure that surveillance practices are both effective for security and respectful of individual rights.[19]

Judicial review continues to serve as a critical check on the expansion of surveillance powers. Conservative jurists emphasize that the Supreme Court must interpret the Fourth Amendment and related provisions in light of the Founding Fathers' intent. Landmark cases that extend privacy protections to modern contexts must be carefully evaluated to avoid expanding federal power beyond its constitutional mandate. This judicial restraint is essential for maintaining the balance between security needs and personal freedom in the digital era.[20]

Economic factors also intersect with surveillance practices. The digital economy thrives on the free flow of information, yet excessive surveillance can inhibit innovation and dampen economic growth. Conservatives contend that economic policies must protect both the privacy rights of individuals and the competitive edge of American businesses. By ensuring that surveillance practices are limited to what is constitutionally permissible, the United States can foster an environment where economic innovation flourishes without compromising individual liberty.[21]

National security remains an ever-present concern, but conservatives warn that measures taken for security must be temporary and subject to constant review. The risk of establishing permanent surveillance regimes that infringe on constitutional rights is a lesson drawn from historical precedents, such as the internment of Japanese Americans during World War II. Contemporary security policies should incorporate robust oversight mechanisms, such as sunset provisions

---

[18] Ackerman, B. (1991). *We the People: Foundations*. Cambridge, MA: Harvard University Press.

[19] Connelley, W. F. (2009). *Restoring the Constitutional Order*. Lexington: University Press of Kentucky.

[20] Jefferson, T., & Madison, J. (Founders Online). "Letter from Thomas Jefferson to James Madison, July 29, 1787." National Archives.

[21] Dickinson, J. (1994). *Colonial Self-Government in America*. Cambridge: Harvard University Press.

and mandatory judicial review, to ensure that any expansion of power is strictly limited in time and scope.[22]

Legislative oversight in the realm of digital privacy is indispensable. Congress must remain vigilant in its review of surveillance practices, ensuring that any new policies or technologies do not contravene the Constitution's protections. The Senate's role in treaty ratification and legislative debate provides a democratic check on the executive branch, ensuring that international commitments and domestic surveillance policies remain consistent with American values and constitutional limits.[23]

Finally, the moral imperative to uphold constitutional privacy in the digital age is paramount. The American experiment was founded on the principle that government exists to serve the people, not to intrude upon their private lives. This moral conviction, rooted in the Founding Fathers' commitment to individual liberty, must guide all discussions about surveillance in modern society. Conservatives argue that preserving privacy is not only a legal necessity but also a moral duty—a commitment to the enduring values that have defined America since its inception.[24]

In conclusion, surveillance practices in the digital age present formidable challenges to constitutional privacy, necessitating a careful balance between national security, economic innovation, and individual liberty. The American Constitution, as interpreted through an originalist lens, provides the framework for ensuring that surveillance measures remain strictly within the bounds of limited government. Through disciplined judicial review, robust legislative oversight, and adherence to the moral and cultural principles of the Founding Fathers, the United States can protect its citizens' privacy rights while effectively addressing contemporary security challenges. This steadfast commitment to constitutional fidelity is the definitive answer to preserving American liberty in an era of rapid technological change and global interdependence.[25] Moreover, by embracing these enduring principles, the nation can chart a future where technological advancement and constitutional privacy coexist harmoniously, ensuring that the legacy of freedom endures for generations to come.[26]

---

[22] Ferguson, N. (2004). Colony: A History of Early America. New York: Penguin Press.

[23] Locke, J. (1689). *Two Treatises of Government*. London: Awnsham Churchill.

[24] Rakove, J. (1997). *Original Meanings: Politics and Ideas in the Making of the Constitution*. New York: Vintage.

[25] Adams, S. (1961). *The Revolutionary Writings of Samuel Adams*. Boston: Beacon Press.

[26] Hamilton, A., Madison, J., & Jay, J. (1961). *The Federalist Papers*. New York: New American Library.

3. Cybersecurity, Data, and the Fourth Amendment

In an era marked by the exponential growth of digital technologies and ubiquitous data networks, the traditional boundaries of privacy are being radically redefined. Cybersecurity and data collection have become central to both national security and economic progress, yet they pose significant challenges to the constitutional protection of individual privacy under the Fourth Amendment. The Founding Fathers, in drafting the Constitution, sought to limit government intrusion into the private lives of citizens—a principle that remains sacrosanct in an age when digital surveillance can penetrate nearly every aspect of personal life. From a politically conservative perspective that emphasizes limited government, strict adherence to the Constitution's original meaning, and the preservation of individual liberties, it is imperative that modern cybersecurity practices be evaluated against the immutable standards set by the Fourth Amendment. This paper provides a comprehensive analysis of the intersection between cybersecurity, data collection, and constitutional privacy, arguing that only a disciplined return to the Founders' vision can ensure that governmental and corporate surveillance do not erode the liberties that have long been the bedrock of American democracy.

The Fourth Amendment was conceived as a direct response to the abuses suffered under British colonial rule, wherein arbitrary searches and seizures were common. Although the text does not explicitly mention "privacy," the Amendment's purpose has always been to protect the sanctity of an individual's person, home, papers, and effects from unwarranted governmental intrusion.[1] In today's digital landscape, where personal data is stored on remote servers and transmitted across global networks, the traditional notion of privacy must be reinterpreted without sacrificing the Amendment's core protection against unreasonable searches. Conservatives assert that any expansion of surveillance powers—whether by government agencies or through corporate partnerships—must be strictly limited by the standards of probable cause and specificity that the Founders intended.[2]

Cybersecurity is a double-edged sword. On one hand, robust cybersecurity measures are essential for protecting national security, safeguarding critical infrastructure, and ensuring the integrity of digital communications. On the other hand, the very technologies that secure our networks also enable unprecedented levels of surveillance and data collection. The National Security Agency (NSA) and other federal agencies have significantly expanded their capabilities in recent years, engaging in the bulk collection of data and the monitoring of digital communications in the name

---

[1] Hamilton, A., Madison, J., & Jay, J. (1961). *The Federalist Papers*. New York: New American Library.

[2] Locke, J. (1689). *Two Treatises of Government*. London: Awnsham Churchill.

of counterterrorism.[3] Conservatives are deeply concerned that such expansive surveillance practices, if left unchecked, risk violating the constitutional guarantees of privacy and due process. They maintain that any surveillance program must be justified by a clear, individualized warrant based on probable cause, and that sweeping, indiscriminate data collection practices are incompatible with the Fourth Amendment's protections.[4]

The evolution of digital technology has also introduced new challenges regarding data ownership and control. In the digital age, personal data has become one of the most valuable commodities, driving economic innovation and enabling targeted marketing and behavioral analysis. However, the collection and monetization of personal data by corporations often occur with minimal transparency, raising concerns about the erosion of personal privacy. Conservatives argue that the constitutional protections originally designed to guard against state intrusion should also serve as a benchmark for private data practices. While the Constitution was not drafted with digital data in mind, its principles of limited government and individual autonomy must be extended to ensure that private companies do not engage in practices that effectively amount to a de facto invasion of privacy.[5]

The concept of "cyber intrusion" further complicates the application of the Fourth Amendment. Cyberattacks, hacking, and unauthorized data breaches expose sensitive personal and corporate information to malicious actors, posing serious threats to both national security and individual liberty. In response, the federal government has enacted laws and policies intended to bolster cybersecurity defenses. However, conservatives caution that some of these measures may inadvertently expand government surveillance capabilities beyond what the Constitution permits. They stress that the balance between security and liberty is delicate, and any regulatory measures must be narrowly tailored to address genuine threats without compromising constitutional rights.[6]

Judicial interpretation plays a pivotal role in determining the scope of Fourth Amendment protections in the digital realm. Landmark cases such as United States v. Katz (1967) established the "reasonable expectation of privacy" standard, which has since become the cornerstone for evaluating modern surveillance practices. Conservative jurists argue that this standard must be applied in a manner consistent with the historical context of the Amendment, ensuring that the

---

[3] Montesquieu, C. (1748). *The Spirit of the Laws*. Paris: Barrillot & Fils.

[4] Pocock, J. G. A. (1975). *The Machiavellian Moment: Florentine Political Thought and the Atlantic Republican Tradition*. Princeton: Princeton University Press.

[5] Rakove, J. (1997). *Original Meanings: Politics and Ideas in the Making of the Constitution*. New York: Vintage.

[6] Adams, S. (1961). *The Revolutionary Writings of Samuel Adams*. Boston: Beacon Press.

government's access to digital information remains limited to cases where a specific, individualized warrant is obtained.[7] They contend that broad, technology-driven reinterpretations of privacy rights risk transforming the Fourth Amendment into a tool for unchecked governmental power—a development that the Founding Fathers would have vehemently opposed.[8]

Legislative oversight is equally critical in safeguarding constitutional privacy in the digital age. Congress has the authority to enact laws that regulate both government surveillance and private data practices. Conservatives advocate for robust legislative measures that require transparency from government agencies and private companies regarding data collection practices. Such oversight should mandate that any surveillance operation, whether undertaken in the name of national security or public safety, adheres to the strict standards of the Fourth Amendment. Moreover, any legislative initiative in this area must be subject to periodic review to ensure that temporary measures do not become permanent erosions of constitutional liberties.[9]

The rise of international cyber threats adds another layer of complexity to the constitutional debate. Globalization has not only connected economies but also created a network of transnational cyber threats that require coordinated responses. While international cooperation is essential to address these challenges, conservatives caution that such collaboration must not lead to the ceding of American constitutional authority to foreign bodies or supranational institutions. The U.S. must negotiate international agreements on its own terms, ensuring that any global cybersecurity measures are consistent with the Constitution's strict limits on governmental power.[10]

Economic implications also feature prominently in the debate over digital privacy. The digital economy depends on the free flow of information, yet pervasive surveillance can have a chilling effect on innovation and commerce. Conservatives argue that protecting privacy is not only a matter of individual liberty but also of economic necessity. Secure privacy rights encourage consumer confidence and support a dynamic, innovation-driven market. Any intrusion into personal data—whether by government or private entities—must be carefully balanced against the economic benefits of a free market that rewards innovation and respects individual autonomy.[11]

---

[7] Bork, R. (1990). *The Tempting of America: The Political Seduction of the Law*. New York: Free Press.

[8] Jefferson, T. (Founders Online). "Notes on the State of Virginia." National Archives.

[9] Dickinson, J. (1994). *Colonial Self-Government in America*. Cambridge: Harvard University Press.

[10] Calhoun, J. C. (1983). "Separation of Powers and the Structure of the Constitution." In *Foundations of American Government* (pp. 29–32). New York: Harper & Row.

[11] Jefferson, T. (Founders Online). "Notes on the State of Virginia." National Archives.

National security considerations provide a compelling justification for some surveillance measures; however, conservatives maintain that these measures must always be weighed against the constitutional mandate to protect individual privacy. The post-9/11 expansion of surveillance programs serves as a cautionary example: while aimed at preventing terrorism, many of these programs have been criticized for their broad scope and lack of transparency. Conservatives insist that security measures must be implemented with strict limits, including clearly defined sunset provisions and rigorous judicial oversight, to ensure that they do not become permanent fixtures that erode the Fourth Amendment.[12]

Political polarization further exacerbates the debate over digital privacy and cybersecurity. In today's highly charged political environment, discussions about surveillance can become polarized, with partisan interests sometimes taking precedence over constitutional principles. Conservatives argue that an objective, historically informed interpretation of the Constitution is essential to depoliticize these debates. By returning to the original public meaning of the Fourth Amendment, policymakers can set clear, consistent standards that protect individual rights regardless of the prevailing political winds.[13]

The role of technology companies in the digital privacy landscape cannot be ignored. As private entities that collect and process vast amounts of personal data, these companies have significant influence over the extent to which individual privacy is protected. Conservatives assert that while the free market is essential for technological innovation, it must operate within a framework that respects constitutional protections. Legislative reforms should hold corporations accountable for data breaches and unethical data practices without imposing overly burdensome regulations that stifle economic growth.[14]

Internationally, the challenges of cybersecurity and data privacy are not unique to the United States, yet the American constitutional framework offers a distinctive model for addressing them. Many democracies have enacted expansive privacy laws that, while protecting individual rights, sometimes hinder technological innovation. Conservatives argue that the American approach—grounded in the Constitution's original limits on governmental power—strikes a better balance by ensuring that surveillance and data collection are justified, narrowly tailored, and subject to

---

[12] Amar, A. R. (2005). *America's Constitution: A Biography*. New York: Random House.

[13] Henry, P. (1775). *Speech on Colonial Rights*. Richmond: Virginia Historical Society.

[14] Kirk, R. (1953). *The Conservative Mind*. New York: Free Press.

strict oversight. This model, they contend, should serve as a benchmark for other nations seeking to protect privacy in the digital era.[15]

The amendment process remains a critical mechanism for adapting constitutional protections to modern realities. While the process is intentionally arduous, it provides a structured, democratic means of revising the Constitution to address new technological challenges without compromising its core principles. Conservatives caution that any amendment related to digital privacy must be undertaken with broad consensus and in a manner that does not undermine the Founding Fathers' vision of limited government and individual liberty.[16]

Cultural continuity and the preservation of American values are also essential in the debate over digital privacy. The legacy of the American Revolution and the subsequent development of a free society are rooted in the belief in individual freedom and resistance to arbitrary power. Conservatives argue that these cultural values must guide modern interpretations of privacy rights, ensuring that technological advancements do not lead to a surveillance state that undermines the very freedoms upon which America was built.[17]

Moreover, public awareness and civic engagement are vital for safeguarding constitutional privacy in the digital age. An informed citizenry can hold both government and private entities accountable for overreach in data collection and surveillance practices. Conservatives emphasize the need for public debate grounded in the Constitution's original meaning, so that any erosion of privacy rights is met with robust opposition and demands for reform. Through education and civic participation, Americans can ensure that their constitutional rights remain protected even as technology evolves.[18]

The judiciary's role in this domain is paramount. Conservative legal scholars advocate for an originalist approach to interpreting the Fourth Amendment in the context of digital surveillance. Landmark cases such as United States v. Katz have established a framework for evaluating privacy expectations, but the application of these principles to modern technology requires careful judicial consideration. By adhering to the original public meaning of the Amendment, the courts can limit the scope of surveillance to what is truly justified by individualized warrants and probable cause, thereby preventing the unchecked expansion of state power.[19]

---

[15] Levinson, S. (2006). *Our Undemocratic Constitution: Where the Constitution Goes Wrong (and How We the People Can Correct It)*. New Haven: Yale University Press.

[16] Hayek, F. A. (1960). *The Constitution of Liberty*. Chicago: University of Chicago Press.

[17] Aldrich, J. H. (1983). *Constitutional Theory*. Chicago: University of Chicago Press.

[18] Ackerman, B. (1991). *We the People: Foundations*. Cambridge, MA: Harvard University Press.

[19] Connelley, W. F. (2009). *Restoring the Constitutional Order*. Lexington: University Press of Kentucky.

Legislative oversight is equally crucial for ensuring that surveillance practices adhere to constitutional standards. Congress must continue to review and, if necessary, amend laws governing data collection and cybersecurity to guarantee that they do not infringe on the rights enshrined in the Constitution. The involvement of a bipartisan legislature is essential to resist partisan pressures and to uphold the original constitutional order. Such oversight ensures that both national security interests and individual privacy rights are maintained within the limits set by the Founding Fathers.[20]

Economic considerations, too, must be balanced with privacy protections. The digital economy relies on the collection and analysis of data for innovation and growth, yet excessive surveillance risks chilling free speech and undermining consumer trust. Conservatives argue that economic policies must be crafted to protect privacy while fostering a competitive marketplace that rewards innovation. By ensuring that surveillance is narrowly targeted and strictly regulated, America can preserve its economic vitality without compromising constitutional freedoms.[21]

National security imperatives, while undeniably important, must never be used as a pretext for eroding constitutional protections. The delicate balance between protecting citizens from external threats and upholding the right to privacy is a recurring theme in American constitutional history. Conservatives contend that any surveillance measures adopted for national security must be temporary, proportionate, and subject to rigorous judicial and legislative review. This ensures that the state's power remains limited and that individual rights are not permanently compromised in the name of security.[22]

Political polarization, which increasingly characterizes American governance, poses an additional threat to constitutional privacy. In a climate of extreme partisanship, debates over surveillance can quickly become polarized, leading to regulatory extremes that either undermine security or violate individual rights. Conservatives maintain that a return to the original, objective standards of the Constitution is necessary to depoliticize the issue. By grounding surveillance policies in the immutable text of the Fourth Amendment and the historical context provided by the Founding Fathers, policymakers can achieve a balanced approach that protects both security and liberty.[23]

---

[20] Jefferson, T., & Madison, J. (Founders Online). "Letter from Thomas Jefferson to James Madison, July 29, 1787." National Archives.

[21] Dickinson, J. (1994). *Colonial Self-Government in America.* Cambridge: Harvard University Press.

[22] Ferguson, N. (2004). *Colony: A History of Early America.* New York: Penguin Press.

[23] Locke, J. (1689). *Two Treatises of Government.* London: Awnsham Churchill.

Finally, the moral imperative to uphold constitutional privacy remains a guiding principle for the future. The American experiment was built on the notion that government exists to serve the people, not to intrude upon their private lives. This moral vision, enshrined in the Constitution, must not be sacrificed in the rush to embrace technological progress. Conservatives argue that the preservation of privacy is a fundamental aspect of human dignity and freedom—a commitment that should guide every decision regarding surveillance practices.[24]

In conclusion, the challenges posed by cybersecurity and data collection in the digital age require a measured, principled response that remains true to the Constitution's original meaning. The American Fourth Amendment, as interpreted through an originalist lens, provides a robust framework for limiting surveillance and protecting individual privacy. Through disciplined judicial review, effective legislative oversight, and a steadfast commitment to the Founding Fathers' vision, the United States can navigate the complexities of digital surveillance while safeguarding its constitutional liberties. This adherence to constitutional fidelity is the definitive answer to preserving American freedom in an era of rapid technological change and global interdependence.[25] Moreover, by upholding these timeless principles, American governance can not only address current privacy challenges but also chart a future in which technological innovation and individual liberty coexist harmoniously, securing a legacy of freedom for generations to come.[26]

---

[24] Rakove, J. (1997). *Original Meanings: Politics and Ideas in the Making of the Constitution*. New York: Vintage.

[25] Adams, S. (1961). *The Revolutionary Writings of Samuel Adams*. Boston: Beacon Press.

[26] Hamilton, A., Madison, J., & Jay, J. (1961). *The Federalist Papers*. New York: New American Library.

4. Balancing National Security and Individual Rights

In an era marked by rapid technological evolution and global interconnectivity, the debate over national security versus individual rights has taken on new urgency. Modern surveillance capabilities, enabled by advanced digital technologies, have dramatically expanded the state's ability to monitor and control information. At the same time, these technologies pose profound challenges to the constitutional protections that have long safeguarded American liberty. From a politically conservative perspective—which emphasizes limited government, strict adherence to the Founding Fathers' original constitutional vision, and the preservation of individual freedoms—the balance between national security and individual rights must be maintained without compromising the principles enshrined in the Constitution. This paper provides a comprehensive analysis of contemporary surveillance practices, the constitutional foundations of privacy, and the necessary measures to ensure that national security imperatives do not erode the rights guaranteed by the Fourth Amendment and other constitutional provisions.

The American constitutional framework was designed as a bulwark against arbitrary governmental power. Influenced by Enlightenment philosophers such as John Locke and Montesquieu, the Founding Fathers sought to create a government that would protect individuals from the abuses of a powerful state. The Fourth Amendment, though not explicitly mentioning "privacy," was crafted to ensure that individuals have a "reasonable expectation of privacy" against unwarranted searches and seizures—a protection that historically safeguarded citizens' homes, papers, and effects from intrusive government actions. Conservatives argue that this fundamental protection must extend to the digital realm. As electronic communications, online data storage, and ubiquitous mobile devices become integral to everyday life, the principles behind the Fourth Amendment must be rigorously applied to ensure that surveillance activities are narrowly tailored, based on probable cause, and subject to judicial oversight.[1]

Since the terrorist attacks of September 11, 2001, national security concerns have spurred significant expansions in surveillance capabilities. Federal agencies, such as the National Security Agency (NSA), have implemented bulk data collection programs and sophisticated monitoring systems in an effort to thwart terrorist threats. Proponents claim that these measures are essential to protecting the nation; however, conservatives caution that such expansive surveillance practices risk infringing on individual liberty. They contend that the state's power must remain limited by the Constitution, and that any surveillance program must be justified by individualized warrants

[1] Hamilton, A., Madison, J., & Jay, J. (1961). *The Federalist Papers*. New York: New American Library.

rather than broad, indiscriminate collection of data.[2] The challenge is to protect national security without transforming the government into an omnipresent surveillance apparatus that undermines the very freedoms the Constitution was designed to secure.

In addition to state surveillance, the private sector has emerged as a formidable force in the collection and analysis of personal data. Technology companies routinely gather vast amounts of information from users, often with little transparency regarding how that data is used. Conservatives express concern that the convergence of private data collection with government surveillance creates a "surveillance-industrial complex" that poses a grave threat to constitutional privacy. They argue that any such collaboration must be subject to strict regulatory controls and transparency requirements to ensure that corporate practices do not indirectly enable unconstitutional government intrusion.[3] This perspective underscores the conservative belief that both public and private entities must operate within the confines of the Constitution.

The Founding Fathers envisioned a society in which governmental power was strictly circumscribed, and their intent remains a central tenet of conservative constitutional thought. The Fourth Amendment's protection against unreasonable searches was a reaction to the arbitrary and oppressive practices experienced under British rule. Today, the application of this amendment in the digital age faces unprecedented challenges. For example, the collection of metadata, which includes records of phone calls, emails, and other forms of electronic communication, has raised questions about whether such practices constitute a "search" under the Fourth Amendment. Conservatives assert that the original meaning of the Amendment requires that any search or seizure be specific and individualized. Broad surveillance programs that collect data on millions of Americans without individualized suspicion run counter to the Founders' vision of limited, accountable government.[4]

Judicial review is a crucial mechanism for ensuring that surveillance practices remain within constitutional bounds. Landmark decisions, such as United States v. Katz (1967), established the "reasonable expectation of privacy" standard, thereby extending Fourth Amendment protections to areas previously unregulated by law. Conservative jurists maintain that while evolving technology necessitates some adaptation, judicial interpretation must remain anchored in the original public meaning of the Constitution. This originalist approach ensures that any expansion

---

[2] Locke, J. (1689). *Two Treatises of Government*. London: Awnsham Churchill.

[3] Montesquieu, C. (1748). *The Spirit of the Laws*. Paris: Barrillot & Fils.

[4] Pocock, J. G. A. (1975). *The Machiavellian Moment: Florentine Political Thought and the Atlantic Republican Tradition*. Princeton: Princeton University Press.

of surveillance powers is scrutinized carefully and that the fundamental rights of citizens are not sacrificed for the sake of security.[5] The Court's role is not to fashion policy but to enforce the limits imposed by the Constitution.

Legislative oversight is equally critical in the realm of surveillance and cybersecurity. Congress possesses the authority to enact laws that constrain both government and corporate surveillance practices. Conservatives advocate for robust oversight measures that mandate transparency, require individualized warrants, and impose strict limitations on data collection programs. For instance, any legislation authorizing bulk data collection should include sunset provisions, ensuring that such powers are temporary and subject to periodic review. This legislative framework not only prevents the overreach of state power but also reinforces the constitutional principle of limited government.[6]

The economic dimension of surveillance cannot be ignored. The digital economy relies heavily on the free flow of information, but excessive surveillance can chill free speech and stifle innovation. Conservatives argue that a vibrant free-market system, which has been the engine of American prosperity, depends on trust and privacy. When citizens fear that their communications and personal data are subject to constant monitoring, they may become reluctant to express themselves freely or engage in entrepreneurial activities. Thus, economic freedom and national security are interlinked; preserving the constitutional protection of privacy is essential for sustaining economic growth and maintaining America's competitive edge.[7]

National security considerations present a formidable challenge in balancing privacy rights. In the wake of global terrorism and cyber threats, the government's imperative to protect the nation is undeniable. Yet, conservatives warn that the measures taken in the name of security must always be proportionate and subject to the strict limitations of the Constitution. The historical precedent set by the internment of Japanese Americans during World War II serves as a grim reminder of how emergency measures can lead to the permanent erosion of civil liberties. Therefore, any security measures implemented in the digital age must be narrowly tailored to address specific threats and must include rigorous judicial and legislative safeguards to prevent the abuse of power.[8]

---

[5] Rakove, J. (1997). *Original Meanings: Politics and Ideas in the Making of the Constitution*. New York: Vintage.

[6] Adams, S. (1961). *The Revolutionary Writings of Samuel Adams*. Boston: Beacon Press.

[7] Bork, R. (1990). *The Tempting of America: The Political Seduction of the Law*. New York: Free Press.

[8] Jefferson, T. (Founders Online). "Notes on the State of Virginia." National Archives.

Political polarization further complicates the surveillance debate. In today's hyper-partisan environment, discussions about surveillance and data privacy are often swayed by ideological agendas rather than objective constitutional principles. Conservatives contend that the solution lies in a return to the original text of the Constitution, which provides clear, objective standards for what constitutes a reasonable search. By depoliticizing the debate and adhering to an originalist framework, the judiciary and legislature can ensure that surveillance practices are implemented in a manner that respects individual rights while addressing legitimate security concerns.[9]

The role of technology companies in shaping surveillance practices has become increasingly prominent. With unprecedented control over personal data, these corporations can significantly influence the balance between privacy and security. Conservatives argue that while market-driven innovation is essential for economic progress, it must be conducted within a framework that upholds constitutional protections. Legislative reforms are necessary to ensure that private data collection is transparent and that individuals retain meaningful control over their personal information. Such measures should be guided by the principles of limited government and individual liberty, ensuring that neither corporate nor state power is allowed to encroach unduly on personal privacy.[10]

International perspectives offer further insight into the challenge of balancing national security with individual rights. Many democratic nations grapple with similar issues, but the American constitutional model—rooted in the explicit limits on governmental power—offers a distinctive approach. While European countries may adopt more expansive privacy protections that sometimes hinder law enforcement, conservatives argue that the U.S. model provides a more balanced framework. By insisting that any surveillance program must adhere strictly to constitutional mandates, America can better safeguard its citizens' rights while effectively addressing global security threats.[11]

The amendment process remains a crucial tool for adapting constitutional protections to modern realities. Although the Founding Fathers designed the Constitution to be a fixed document, they also recognized that it might need to evolve. However, conservatives argue that any changes must occur through a deliberate, democratic process rather than through judicial activism or

---

[9] Dickinson, J. (1994). *Colonial Self-Government in America*. Cambridge: Harvard University Press.

[10] Calhoun, J. C. (1983). "Separation of Powers and the Structure of the Constitution." In *Foundations of American Government* (pp. 29–32). New York: Harper & Row.

[11] Jefferson, T. (Founders Online). "Notes on the State of Virginia." National Archives.

executive fiat. This rigorous process ensures that modifications are made only with broad consensus, thereby preserving the constitutional order and preventing hasty expansions of government power.[12]

Cultural values and national identity also play an essential role in the balance between security and privacy. The American commitment to freedom and individualism is a cornerstone of its national identity, and these values are enshrined in the Constitution. Conservatives maintain that preserving these cultural ideals is critical in the digital age, where the temptation to sacrifice privacy for security can be particularly acute. Public discourse should remind citizens that the Constitution's protections are not negotiable and that any erosion of privacy rights undermines the very foundations of American liberty.[13]

Political leadership is pivotal in guiding the nation through the complex challenges posed by digital surveillance. Effective leaders who are committed to constitutional principles can bridge the gap between national security imperatives and the need to preserve individual rights. Conservatives argue that leadership must be rooted in the original values of the Founding Fathers, ensuring that policy decisions are made with an unwavering commitment to limited government and the rule of law. Such leadership is essential for maintaining public trust and for navigating the often contentious debates over surveillance practices.[14]

Judicial interpretation remains one of the most critical mechanisms for maintaining the balance between security and privacy. Conservative legal scholars advocate for an originalist approach that interprets the Fourth Amendment in its historical context. Landmark cases such as United States v. Katz have set important precedents by establishing a "reasonable expectation of privacy" standard. In the digital age, this standard must be rigorously applied to ensure that any government intrusion is narrowly confined to what is necessary for addressing specific threats. This judicial restraint is fundamental to preserving the constitutional limits on surveillance and preventing an unchecked expansion of state power.[15]

Legislative oversight, particularly in the context of digital data and cybersecurity, is equally important. Congress has the responsibility to monitor and regulate surveillance practices to ensure they do not infringe on constitutional rights. Robust oversight mechanisms, including

---

[12] Amar, A. R. (2005). *America's Constitution: A Biography*. New York: Random House.

[13] Henry, P. (1775). *Speech on Colonial Rights*. Richmond: Virginia Historical Society.

[14] Kirk, R. (1953). *The Conservative Mind*. New York: Free Press.

[15] Levinson, S. (2006). *Our Undemocratic Constitution: Where the Constitution Goes Wrong (and How We the People Can Correct It)*. New Haven: Yale University Press.

periodic reviews and transparency requirements, are necessary to hold both the executive branch and private companies accountable for data collection practices. Conservatives argue that such measures are essential for preventing abuses of power while ensuring that national securityw initiatives are conducted within the constitutional framework.[16]

Economic implications also influence the balance between national security and privacy. The digital economy thrives on the free flow of information, yet pervasive surveillance can stifle innovation and undermine consumer confidence. Conservatives assert that protecting privacy is not only a matter of individual liberty but also critical for maintaining the economic dynamism that has driven American prosperity. By enforcing strict limitations on surveillance in accordance with the Constitution, the United States can create an environment in which economic growth is not sacrificed in the name of security.[17]

National security policies, while necessary in a world of cyber threats and international terrorism, must be carefully circumscribed. The post-9/11 expansion of surveillance powers provides a cautionary tale of how emergency measures can become permanent fixtures. Conservatives argue that all security measures must incorporate clear limitations—such as sunset provisions, judicial review, and rigorous oversight—to ensure that they do not become a pretext for the indefinite expansion of governmental authority. Such safeguards are essential for preserving the constitutional balance between protecting citizens and maintaining individual rights.[18]

Political polarization exacerbates the challenge of balancing security and privacy. In a divided tpolitical climate, debates over surveillance can be heavily influenced by partisan ideology rather than objective constitutional analysis. Conservatives maintain that depoliticizing the issue by returning to the original meaning of the Constitution is crucial. Only through an objective, historically informed interpretation of the Fourth Amendment can policymakers ensure that surveillance practices are both effective for national security and respectful of individual liberty.[19]

The role of international law and global cybersecurity agreements further complicates the domestic surveillance landscape. While the United States must engage with international partners to combat cybercrime and terrorism, any such engagement must not compromise constitutional protections. Conservatives insist that international treaties and agreements must be scrutinized to

---

[16] Hayek, F. A. (1960). *The Constitution of Liberty*. Chicago: University of Chicago Press.

[17] Aldrich, J. H. (1983). *Constitutional Theory*. Chicago: University of Chicago Press.

[18] Ackerman, B. (1991). *We the People: Foundations*. Cambridge, MA: Harvard University Press.

[19] Connelley, W. F. (2009). *Restoring the Constitutional Order*. Lexington: University Press of Kentucky.

ensure they do not require domestic authorities to exceed the limits prescribed by the Constitution. The primacy of American constitutional law must remain intact, even as the nation cooperates on the global stage.[20]

The amendment process offers a measured means for adapting constitutional privacy protections to new technological challenges. Although the process is intentionally rigorous to prevent rash changes, it provides a democratic method for evolving constitutional rights. Conservatives argue that any amendments related to digital privacy should be undertaken only after comprehensive debate and with broad consensus, ensuring that any evolution in surveillance law remains faithful to the Founders' original intent.[21]

Cultural continuity also serves as a powerful counterbalance to the pressures of modern surveillance. The American identity is deeply rooted in the values of individual freedom and resistance to tyranny. Conservatives argue that this cultural heritage must inform the interpretation of privacy rights in the digital era. By reaffirming the principles of limited government and personal liberty, the United States can resist trends toward excessive surveillance and maintain its commitment to constitutional freedoms.[22]

Furthermore, public awareness and civic engagement are crucial in safeguarding constitutional privacy. An informed citizenry is essential for holding both government and private entities accountable for surveillance practices. Conservatives emphasize the importance of education and open public discourse in ensuring that constitutional rights are not eroded by technological advancements. By mobilizing civic participation and demanding transparency, citizens can help to preserve the balance between national security and individual rights.[23]

Political leadership plays an indispensable role in this balance. Leaders who uphold the values of the Constitution—those of limited government and respect for individual liberty—set the tone for policy decisions on surveillance and cybersecurity. Conservatives argue that such leaders are necessary to ensure that national security measures are implemented responsibly and do not encroach on constitutional protections. The integrity of American democracy depends on leaders

---

[20] Jefferson, T., & Madison, J. (Founders Online). "Letter from Thomas Jefferson to James Madison, July 29, 1787." National Archives.

[21] Dickinson, J. (1994). *Colonial Self-Government in America*. Cambridge: Harvard University Press.

[22] Ferguson, N. (2004). *Colony: A History of Early America*. New York: Penguin Press.

[23] Locke, J. (1689). *Two Treatises of Government*. London: Awnsham Churchill.

who are willing to resist the allure of expansive surveillance in favor of a disciplined adherence to constitutional limits.[24]

Economic policy in the digital age must also align with constitutional protections for privacy. The free market, which has driven American innovation and prosperity, relies on the protection of personal data and individual rights. Conservatives contend that economic regulations related to data collection should be crafted in a manner that supports both innovation and privacy. This balanced approach ensures that the benefits of the digital economy are realized without sacrificing the constitutional guarantee of privacy.[25]

In conclusion, balancing national security and individual rights in the era of advanced technology is one of the most pressing challenges facing contemporary American governance. The Constitution, as envisioned by the Founding Fathers, provides a robust framework for protecting individual liberty while ensuring that governmental power remains limited. Through disciplined judicial review, effective legislative oversight, adherence to the amendment process, and a steadfast commitment to cultural and moral values, the United States can navigate the complex terrain of digital surveillance without compromising the freedoms that have long defined the nation. This rigorous adherence to constitutional principles is the definitive answer to preserving American liberty in an interconnected, digital world, ensuring that the nation remains a beacon of freedom and self-governance for future generations.[26]

---

[24] Rakove, J. (1997). *Original Meanings: Politics and Ideas in the Making of the Constitution*. New York: Vintage.

[25] Adams, S. (1961). *The Revolutionary Writings of Samuel Adams*. Boston: Beacon Press.

[26] Hamilton, A., Madison, J., & Jay, J. (1961). *The Federalist Papers*. New York: New American Library.

5. Judicial Trends and Emerging Technologies

The rapid evolution of technology in the digital age has presented new challenges to traditional interpretations of constitutional privacy, particularly regarding surveillance practices and data collection. As digital technologies continue to advance, emerging tools such as artificial intelligence, biometrics, and sophisticated data analytics have transformed both government and corporate surveillance capabilities. These developments raise critical questions about the proper scope of judicial review and the application of constitutional protections under the Fourth Amendment. From a politically conservative perspective that champions limited government, adherence to the Founding Fathers' original intent, and the preservation of individual liberties, it is imperative that judicial trends remain firmly anchored in constitutional principles while also adapting to the challenges posed by emerging technologies. This commentary provides a comprehensive analysis of current judicial trends in surveillance and privacy cases, evaluates how courts are addressing issues raised by new technologies, and argues that any adaptation must be both narrowly tailored and consistent with the original constitutional framework.

The Fourth Amendment of the United States Constitution was drafted to protect individuals against unreasonable searches and seizures—a response to the intrusive practices of British colonial authorities. Although the Amendment does not explicitly use the term "privacy," its essence is to secure the "right of the people to be secure in their persons, houses, papers, and effects." The Founding Fathers, influenced by Enlightenment philosophers such as John Locke and Montesquieu, designed this protection to prevent government overreach and to safeguard individual liberty. In today's digital context, where surveillance can encompass vast networks of electronic communications and personal data, the fundamental promise of the Fourth Amendment faces unprecedented stress. Conservatives argue that judicial interpretation must preserve the original public meaning of the Amendment, ensuring that any surveillance conducted—whether by government agencies or through corporate cooperation—is based on individualized warrants supported by probable cause and does not extend to indiscriminate data collection.[1]

Recent judicial trends indicate a cautious approach to the expansion of surveillance powers in the digital age. In several landmark decisions, the U.S. Supreme Court has reaffirmed the principle that constitutional protections must adapt to new technologies without diluting the original limitations on state power. For example, in *United States v. Jones* (2012), the Court held that attaching a GPS device to a vehicle and tracking its movements constituted a search under the Fourth Amendment. Although the decision left open some questions regarding the application

[1] Hamilton, A., Madison, J., & Jay, J. (1961). *The Federalist Papers*. New York: New American Library.

of older principles to new technologies, conservatives view it as a positive step toward ensuring that modern surveillance methods are subjected to constitutional constraints.[2] Such decisions underscore the need for a balanced approach—one that acknowledges the utility of technology for law enforcement and national security without surrendering the privacy rights that are the cornerstone of American freedom.

Another critical development is the increasing reliance on digital data in criminal investigations. Courts have been called upon to decide whether the collection of metadata—information about communications rather than their content—constitutes a "search" subject to Fourth Amendment scrutiny. In *Carpenter v. United States* (2018), the Supreme Court ruled that accessing historical cell phone location records without a warrant violated the Fourth Amendment. Conservatives praise this decision as it reinforces the idea that the state's power to intrude into private lives must be limited, even when the intrusion occurs through modern technological means. By requiring individualized warrants for the collection of sensitive digital data, the Court upholds the constitutional mandate for limited government intrusion.[3]

Despite these advances, a number of judicial trends raise concerns among conservatives about the potential erosion of constitutional privacy. In some cases, courts have deferred too readily to legislative or executive interpretations of surveillance laws, thereby expanding federal power beyond what the Founding Fathers envisaged. Conservative jurists argue that such judicial activism undermines the doctrine of limited government. They insist that the courts must adopt an originalist approach, interpreting the Fourth Amendment in a manner that is consistent with its historical context rather than allowing modern exigencies to dictate its meaning. This strict constructionist view serves as a bulwark against the gradual expansion of state surveillance, ensuring that any encroachment on individual privacy is both narrowly defined and rigorously justified.[4]

Emerging technologies, such as facial recognition systems and biometric databases, further complicate the constitutional landscape. These tools can rapidly identify individuals in public spaces and even link them to other data points, raising the specter of pervasive surveillance. Conservatives argue that while such technologies may offer benefits for law enforcement, their deployment must be limited by the same constitutional standards that govern traditional searches. Courts should require that the use of facial recognition and similar technologies be accompanied

---

[2] Locke, J. (1689). *Two Treatises of Government*. London: Awnsham Churchill.

[3] Montesquieu, C. (1748). *The Spirit of the Laws*. Paris: Barrillot & Fils.

[4] Pocock, J. G. A. (1975). *The Machiavellian Moment: Florentine Political Thought and the Atlantic Republican Tradition*. Princeton: Princeton University Press.

by individualized suspicion and robust oversight to prevent indiscriminate tracking. Failure to impose these limits risks creating a surveillance society in which the state wields excessive power over the private lives of its citizens.[5]

Judicial trends also reflect a growing recognition of the privacy implications of data aggregation by private entities. Technology companies routinely collect vast amounts of personal information, and when such data is accessible to the government, it raises significant constitutional concerns. In several recent cases, courts have begun to scrutinize whether partnerships between the state and private companies for data collection violate Fourth Amendment rights. Conservatives maintain that the Constitution's protections should extend to the digital age, compelling the government to ensure that any data sharing arrangements are transparent and subject to strict limits. By doing so, the judiciary can protect individual privacy without hindering the economic benefits of a digital marketplace.[6]

The economic implications of expansive surveillance practices are significant. The digital economy thrives on trust and the free flow of information; however, widespread surveillance can have a chilling effect on free expression and innovation. Conservatives argue that the preservation of economic freedom is closely tied to constitutional privacy rights. When citizens believe their communications and online activities are subject to constant monitoring, they may be less likely to engage in open discourse or entrepreneurial ventures. The judicial role, therefore, must be to ensure that surveillance practices are limited to what is strictly necessary for legitimate security purposes, preserving the economic vibrancy that has long been a hallmark of American innovation.[7]

National security concerns remain a primary justification for state surveillance, yet they must be balanced carefully against constitutional guarantees. Post-9/11 policies have dramatically increased the scope of surveillance, but conservatives caution that security measures should never become a pretext for permanent encroachments on individual rights. The historical lessons of government overreach during periods of crisis, such as the internment of Japanese Americans in World War II, underscore the risks of allowing emergency powers to persist beyond their intended scope. The judiciary must, therefore, impose clear limits on the duration and scope of surveillance measures, ensuring that any expansion of state power is temporary and strictly monitored.[8]

---

[5] Rakove, J. (1997). *Original Meanings: Politics and Ideas in the Making of the Constitution*. New York: Vintage.

[6] Adams, S. (1961). *The Revolutionary Writings of Samuel Adams*. Boston: Beacon Press.

[7] Bork, R. (1990). *The Tempting of America: The Political Seduction of the Law*. New York: Free Press.

[8] Jefferson, T. (Founders Online). "Notes on the State of Virginia." National Archives.

Political polarization further complicates the balance between security and privacy. In an era of intense partisanship, debates over surveillance are often clouded by ideological bias rather than objective constitutional analysis. Conservatives argue that the judiciary must resist the influence of partisan pressures and adhere to the original meaning of the Constitution. By grounding decisions in the historical context and explicit text of the Fourth Amendment, courts can provide an objective standard that protects individual rights even in a politically charged environment.[9]

The role of legislative oversight is also critical in shaping the future of surveillance practices. Congress, which holds the power to regulate commerce and control federal spending, serves as a check on both the executive branch and the judiciary. Robust legislative oversight ensures that surveillance programs are subject to regular review, transparency requirements, and accountability measures. Conservatives emphasize that any legislative initiative expanding surveillance must be consistent with the constitutional principle of limited government. Only through rigorous oversight can the state ensure that national security measures do not devolve into tools for mass surveillance.[10]

International law and global cybersecurity agreements present additional challenges for domestic constitutional protections. As the United States participates in international treaties and collaborates with foreign intelligence agencies, there is a risk that these obligations could compel the state to adopt surveillance practices that conflict with constitutional limits. Conservatives argue that international agreements must be carefully negotiated and ratified only if they are fully compatible with American constitutional principles. The U.S. Senate's requirement for a two-thirds majority in treaty ratification serves as a critical safeguard against any such encroachment on national sovereignty.[11]

Technological innovations continue to push the boundaries of what constitutes a "search" under the Fourth Amendment. Emerging trends, such as the Internet of Things (IoT) and ubiquitous sensor networks, raise complex questions about privacy. When everyday objects become interconnected and generate streams of data, determining where privacy ends and public information begins becomes increasingly challenging. Conservatives maintain that the original intent of the Founders—to protect the individual from undue governmental intrusion—must guide the

---

[9] Dickinson, J. (1994). *Colonial Self-Government in America.* Cambridge: Harvard University Press.

[10] Calhoun, J. C. (1983). "Separation of Powers and the Structure of the Constitution." In *Foundations of American Government* (pp. 29–32). New York: Harper & Row.

[11] Jefferson, T. (Founders Online). "Notes on the State of Virginia." National Archives.

interpretation of these modern phenomena. Judicial decisions must therefore carefully delineate the scope of permissible surveillance to ensure that individual privacy remains protected in the face of rapid technological change.[12]

The role of technology companies in facilitating surveillance is another critical concern. As private corporations collect and analyze vast amounts of personal data, the boundary between public and private surveillance becomes blurred. Conservatives argue that the state must not outsource its surveillance functions to private entities without robust regulatory oversight. Transparency in data collection practices and strict limitations on data sharing between corporations and government agencies are essential to safeguarding constitutional privacy. Legislative reforms should enforce these standards, ensuring that the partnership between the public and private sectors does not lead to an unchecked invasion of privacy.[13]

Judicial trends in recent years have shown an increasing willingness to apply the "reasonable expectation of privacy" test to digital data. In landmark cases such as United States v. Carpenter (2018), the Court ruled that accessing historical cell phone location records without a warrant violated the Fourth Amendment. Conservatives praise this decision for reaffirming the principle that government surveillance must be based on individualized suspicion and limited in scope. However, they also caution that the Court must avoid expanding these protections so broadly as to hinder legitimate law enforcement and national security efforts. The challenge is to strike a balance that respects both privacy rights and the needs of a secure society.[14]

Political ideology plays a significant role in shaping judicial decisions on surveillance. Conservative jurists advocate for an originalist interpretation of the Constitution, arguing that judges must remain faithful to the text and historical context rather than adapting the law to contemporary political pressures. This approach, they assert, ensures that surveillance practices do not expand beyond the limits intended by the Founding Fathers. By grounding their decisions in the immutable language of the Constitution, conservative judges can provide a stable, objective framework for evaluating modern surveillance issues.[15]

Legislative oversight, particularly by Congress, is essential for curbing potential abuses in surveillance. The power of the purse and the ability to enact oversight mechanisms are fundamental

---

[12] Amar, A. R. (2005). *America's Constitution: A Biography*. New York: Random House.

[13] Henry, P. (1775). *Speech on Colonial Rights*. Richmond: Virginia Historical Society.

[14] Kirk, R. (1953). *The Conservative Mind*. New York: Free Press.

[15] Levinson, S. (2006). *Our Undemocratic Constitution: Where the Constitution Goes Wrong (and How We the People Can Correct It)*. New Haven: Yale University Press.

tools for ensuring that surveillance programs are accountable to the people. Conservatives argue that Congress must actively review and, if necessary, curtail any programs that risk violating constitutional rights. This oversight not only preserves the balance of power but also reinforces the democratic principles at the heart of the American constitutional system.[16]

Economic implications also intersect with surveillance practices in the digital age. The digital economy depends on the free flow of information, yet excessive government monitoring can stifle innovation and inhibit economic growth. Conservatives contend that protecting privacy is not only a matter of individual liberty but also a cornerstone of economic freedom. By limiting surveillance to what is constitutionally permissible, America can maintain a dynamic, innovation-driven economy that respects the rights of individuals while addressing security concerns.[17]

National security remains an indispensable justification for certain surveillance measures, yet conservatives insist that such measures must be subject to rigorous limits. The historical precedent of governmental overreach in times of crisis—such as the internment of Japanese Americans during World War II—serves as a warning against the permanent expansion of surveillance powers. Conservatives argue that national security policies must include clear sunset provisions and be subject to continuous judicial and legislative review to ensure that they do not become entrenched at the expense of constitutional freedoms.[18]

International cooperation is an increasingly important aspect of contemporary surveillance practices, as global threats require coordinated responses. However, conservatives stress that any international agreements must be fully compatible with the U.S. Constitution. The United States should engage with global partners on its own terms, ensuring that domestic constitutional limits are not compromised by external pressures. The Senate's advice and consent role in treaty ratification is a critical safeguard in this regard, preventing international obligations from diluting American sovereignty.[19]

Political polarization has the potential to distort public debate on surveillance issues. In a highly partisan environment, discussions about national security and individual rights can be skewed by ideological bias, leading to either excessive regulation or unwarranted intrusion. Conservatives argue that an objective, historically grounded approach to constitutional interpretation is necessary to depoliticize these debates. By returning to the text of the Constitution and the intentions of

---

[16] Hayek, F. A. (1960). *The Constitution of Liberty*. Chicago: University of Chicago Press.

[17] Aldrich, J. H. (1983). *Constitutional Theory*. Chicago: University of Chicago Press.

[18] Ackerman, B. (1991). *We the People: Foundations*. Cambridge, MA: Harvard University Press.

[19] Connelley, W. F. (2009). *Restoring the Constitutional Order*. Lexington: University Press of Kentucky.

the Founding Fathers, the judiciary and legislature can establish clear standards for surveillance that protect individual privacy without compromising security.[20]

The role of technological innovation in shaping future surveillance practices cannot be overstated. Emerging technologies, such as artificial intelligence and advanced data analytics, offer significant benefits for national security and law enforcement. Yet, without proper constitutional safeguards, these tools can easily be misused to monitor citizens on a mass scale. Conservatives maintain that any incorporation of new technology into surveillance programs must be accompanied by strict judicial and legislative oversight to ensure that these measures do not infringe on Fourth Amendment rights. This forward-looking approach will enable the nation to harness technological advancements while upholding the constitutional values of limited government and individual liberty.[21]

Legislative reform is essential for aligning surveillance practices with constitutional protections. Congress must enact laws that clearly delineate the limits of government surveillance in the digital age, requiring transparency, accountability, and individualized warrants for any intrusion into private communications. Conservatives argue that such reforms should be developed through a bipartisan process, grounded in the original constitutional framework, to ensure that they reflect the enduring principles of American liberty. Effective legislative oversight will help to balance national security needs with the preservation of individual privacy.[22]

Cultural values and public opinion also play a critical role in the ongoing surveillance debate. The American ethos, which prizes individual freedom and resistance to government overreach, provides a powerful counterweight to the expansion of state surveillance. Conservatives assert that maintaining this cultural heritage is essential for preserving constitutional privacy rights. Public engagement, informed by an understanding of the Constitution's original meaning, is key to holding both government and private entities accountable for excessive surveillance practices.[23]

Finally, the moral imperative to uphold the Fourth Amendment's protections remains a guiding principle for future surveillance policies. The Constitution was crafted to shield individuals from arbitrary government intrusion, and this fundamental protection must not be compromised by the demands of national security or technological advancement. Conservatives insist that the

---

[20] Jefferson, T., & Madison, J. (Founders Online). "Letter from Thomas Jefferson to James Madison, July 29, 1787." National Archives.

[21] Dickinson, J. (1994). *Colonial Self-Government in America.* Cambridge: Harvard University Press.

[22] Ferguson, N. (2004). *Colony: A History of Early America.* New York: Penguin Press.

[23] Locke, J. (1689). *Two Treatises of Government.* London: Awnsham Churchill.

future of American freedom depends on a steadfast commitment to the constitutional limits on surveillance. Only by ensuring that every government action is justified by specific, individualized warrants can America continue to safeguard its citizens' privacy and maintain the balance between security and liberty.[24]

In conclusion, balancing national security and individual rights in the digital age is one of the most pressing challenges of our time. Emerging surveillance technologies have the potential to enhance national security, yet they also threaten to erode the constitutional protections that are the cornerstone of American liberty. From a politically conservative perspective, the answer lies in a rigorous adherence to the Founding Fathers' original constitutional vision. Judicial trends must be guided by originalism, legislative oversight must be robust and bipartisan, and any expansion of surveillance powers must be narrowly tailored and subject to strict limitations. By grounding policy in the immutable principles of the Fourth Amendment and the broader constitutional framework, the United States can successfully navigate the challenges of the digital era. This disciplined approach ensures that national security measures do not come at the expense of individual privacy, preserving the delicate balance between state power and personal freedom that is essential for a free and prosperous nation.[25] Moreover, by reaffirming these timeless values through judicial review, legislative reform, and active civic engagement, America can secure a future in which technological progress and constitutional liberty coexist harmoniously—a legacy that will continue to serve as the definitive answer to saving America today and for generations to come.[26]

---

[24] Rakove, J. (1997). *Original Meanings: Politics and Ideas in the Making of the Constitution*. New York: Vintage.

[25] Adams, S. (1961). *The Revolutionary Writings of Samuel Adams*. Boston: Beacon Press.

[26] Hamilton, A., Madison, J., & Jay, J. (1961). *The Federalist Papers*. New York: New American Library.

Chapter 10:

Constitutional Amendments and Institutional Change

1. The Amendment Process: Theory and Practice

The amendment process of the United States Constitution is a fundamental mechanism for adapting the nation's supreme legal document to the evolving needs of American society. This process, deliberately structured by the Founding Fathers, reflects their belief in a system that balances flexibility with stability. As political, social, and technological changes challenge the existing constitutional framework, the amendment process ensures that the Constitution remains relevant while safeguarding against impulsive or partisan-driven modifications. This paper explores the theoretical foundations of the amendment process, its historical application, and the political challenges that shape its future, emphasizing a conservative perspective grounded in original intent and constitutional fidelity.

The Foundational Theory of Constitutional Amendments

The Founding Fathers intentionally designed the amendment process to be rigorous and deliberate. Article V of the Constitution outlines two methods for proposing amendments: either by a two-thirds majority vote in both the House of Representatives and the Senate or by a constitutional convention called for by two-thirds of state legislatures. Ratification then requires approval by three-fourths of the states, either through their legislatures or special ratifying conventions.[1] This high threshold ensures that amendments reflect broad national consensus rather than fleeting political trends.[2]

James Madison, often regarded as the "Father of the Constitution," emphasized the necessity of an amendment process that would allow for corrections to potential oversights while preventing instability from excessive alterations.[3] Madison, along with Alexander Hamilton in The Federalist Papers, argued that a system requiring broad agreement would protect the Constitution from

---

[1] U.S. Constitution, Article V.

[2] The Federalist No. 43, James Madison.

[3] Madison, James, "Debates in the Federal Convention of 1787."

factional interests.[4] This conservative perspective holds that changes to the Constitution should be made cautiously, preserving the Founders' intent and the principles of limited government and individual liberty.[5]

Historical Applications and Conservative Reflections

The United States has seen 27 successful constitutional amendments, many of which reinforced fundamental liberties and corrected structural weaknesses. The first ten amendments, known as the Bill of Rights, were ratified in 1791 and addressed concerns about federal overreach, ensuring essential freedoms such as speech, religion, and due process.[6] Later amendments, such as the Thirteenth, Fourteenth, and Fifteenth Amendments, addressed the profound national crisis of slavery and civil rights.[7]

From a conservative standpoint, certain amendments, particularly the Seventeenth Amendment (which established the direct election of Senators), have been criticized for undermining the Founders' original vision of state representation in federal governance.[8] The repeal of Prohibition through the Twenty-first Amendment illustrates how constitutional changes can reflect shifts in public sentiment but also highlights the dangers of reactionary policymaking.[9]

Modern conservatives argue that the process has been increasingly circumvented by judicial activism, where courts effectively amend the Constitution through expansive interpretations rather than through the legitimate Article V process.[10] Landmark Supreme Court decisions, such as Roe v. Wade and Obergefell v. Hodges, have been viewed as examples of judicial overreach where unelected judges impose constitutional changes without popular ratification.[11]

The Challenges of Amending the Constitution in Contemporary America

Despite its importance, amending the Constitution in modern times has become an exceedingly rare occurrence. The last ratified amendment, the Twenty-seventh Amendment, which regulates

---

[4] The Federalist No. 85, Alexander Hamilton.

[5] Scalia, Antonin, "A Matter of Interpretation: Federal Courts and the Law."

[6] Bill of Rights, ratified 1791.

[7] U.S. Constitution, Amendments XIII, XIV, XV.

[8] Bybee, Jay, "Federalism and the Seventeenth Amendment," Yale Law Review.

[9] U.S. Constitution, Amendment XXI.

[10] Bork, Robert, "The Tempting of America."

[11] Roe v. Wade, 410 U.S. 113 (1973); Obergefell v. Hodges, 576 U.S. 644 (2015).

congressional pay increases, was originally proposed in 1789 but was not ratified until 1992.[12] Several proposed amendments, including those concerning term limits, balanced budgets, and electoral reforms, have failed due to the difficulty of meeting the stringent requirements of Article V.[13]

The conservative critique of the amendment process in contemporary times centers on the role of federal overreach and the increasing reliance on bureaucratic rule-making rather than constitutional modification.[14] Many argue that rather than seeking amendments, political movements and special interest groups have preferred to influence policy through executive orders, judicial rulings, and administrative regulations, circumventing the constitutional process.[15]

Originalist Perspectives on Future Amendments

For constitutional originalists, the amendment process should be used primarily to restore and reinforce foundational principles rather than introduce sweeping changes that alter the nature of governance. Several conservative-backed amendment proposals reflect this viewpoint:

1. **A Balanced Budget Amendment:** This proposal would require the federal government to maintain a balanced budget, preventing excessive deficit spending and national debt accumulation.[16]
2. **Congressional Term Limits:** Advocates argue that limiting the tenure of legislators would reduce corruption and enhance political accountability, aligning with the Founders' vision of a citizen legislature rather than a professional political class.[17]
3. **Repealing the Seventeenth Amendment:** A return to state-appointed senators would restore the balance of power between the states and the federal government, reinforcing the principle of federalism.[18]

---

[12] U.S. Constitution, Amendment XXVII.

[13] Levin, Mark R., "The Liberty Amendments."

[14] Heritage Foundation, "The Administrative State and Constitutionalism."

[15] Epstein, Richard, "How Progressives Rewrote the Constitution."

[16] Congressional Budget Office, "Balanced Budget Amendment Proposals."

[17] U.S. Term Limits v. Thornton, 514 U.S. 779 (1995).

[18] Bybee, "Federalism and the Seventeenth Amendment."

4. **Judicial Reform Amendments:** Some conservatives argue for measures to limit judicial activism, such as requiring supermajority votes for Supreme Court rulings that overturn state laws.[19]

These proposals align with the conservative belief in limited government, fiscal responsibility, and adherence to the original intent of the Constitution. However, given the current political climate and entrenched partisan divides, passing such amendments remains a formidable challenge.[20]

Conclusion

The amendment process remains one of the most significant yet underutilized mechanisms for constitutional change in the United States. Designed to ensure careful deliberation and widespread agreement, it has successfully adapted the Constitution while maintaining its foundational integrity. From a politically conservative standpoint, the amendment process should be safeguarded against overreach and preserved for its intended purpose: refining, not redefining, the constitutional framework. The challenges facing constitutional amendments today—political polarization, judicial activism, and administrative governance—highlight the necessity of adhering to the Founders' original vision. If the United States is to remain a republic grounded in liberty, prudence in constitutional modifications must be exercised, ensuring that any amendments serve to strengthen rather than undermine the nation's fundamental principles.

---

[19] Heritage Foundation, "Judicial Reform and the Constitution."

[20] Levin, "The Liberty Amendments."

2. Historical Precedents and Successful Amendments

The United States Constitution is a living document that has withstood the test of time through a carefully structured amendment process. This process, as envisioned by the Founding Fathers, provides a deliberate mechanism for institutional change while preserving the fundamental principles of limited government and individual liberty. The historical record offers numerous examples of amendments that have successfully adapted the Constitution to evolving social, economic, and political circumstances without undermining its core values. From a politically conservative perspective, the preservation of the original constitutional framework is paramount, and successful amendments serve as models of change that reflect broad national consensus and respect for the Founders' intent. This paper examines historical precedents and successful amendments to demonstrate how the amendment process has safeguarded American freedom and ensured that government remains accountable to the people.

The theory underlying the amendment process is rooted in the Founders' commitment to stability, restraint, and gradual progress. Article V of the Constitution outlines a process that is intentionally rigorous—requiring a supermajority for both proposal and ratification—to ensure that any changes represent a durable consensus rather than a fleeting moment of political passion. The Framers deliberately designed this process to prevent rash alterations that could destabilize the nation's political order, believing that a slow, deliberate process would ensure continuity while allowing for necessary corrections and improvements. Conservatives uphold this approach, arguing that the difficulty of amending the Constitution is not a flaw but a feature that protects against the whims of transient majorities and ensures that constitutional change is thoughtful and measured.[1]

Historical precedents provide compelling evidence of the amendment process working as intended. The Bill of Rights, the first ten amendments, were ratified in 1791 in response to widespread demands from Anti-Federalists who feared the new federal government would trample individual liberties. These amendments were not arbitrary additions but carefully considered guarantees designed to protect rights such as free speech, the right to bear arms, and protection against unreasonable searches. From a conservative viewpoint, the Bill of Rights embodies the original spirit of the Constitution by establishing clear limits on governmental power and safeguarding personal freedoms—principles that remain as relevant today as they were at the nation's founding.[2]

---

[1] Hamilton, A., Madison, J., & Jay, J. (1961). *The Federalist Papers*. New York: New American Library.

[2] Locke, J. (1689). *Two Treatises of Government*. London: Awnsham Churchill.

Over time, several subsequent amendments have successfully addressed critical issues while maintaining the integrity of the constitutional order. For example, the Thirteenth, Fourteenth, and Fifteenth Amendments, ratified in the aftermath of the Civil War, were designed to secure the rights of formerly enslaved people and redefine citizenship. Although these amendments were contentious at the time, they ultimately reinforced the principles of equality and the rule of law. Conservatives, while sometimes critical of the means by which these amendments were implemented, recognize that they served to strengthen the constitutional framework by addressing profound national injustices without discarding the foundational structure of limited government.[3]

Another landmark example is the Nineteenth Amendment, which extended the right to vote to women. Ratified in 1920, this amendment marked a significant expansion of democratic participation while preserving the constitutional principle of popular sovereignty. It is celebrated for reflecting a growing recognition that the right to vote is fundamental to self-governance and individual dignity. From a conservative perspective, the Nineteenth Amendment is a success story of constitutional adaptation achieved through the established process—a process that balanced evolving social norms with the enduring principles of the Constitution.[4]

The Twentieth Amendment, often called the "Lame Duck Amendment," streamlined the transition between presidential administrations and clarified the beginning and end of terms. Its ratification in 1933 provided greater efficiency and accountability in government operations, ensuring that democratic processes were conducted in a timely and orderly fashion. Conservatives argue that this amendment exemplifies how pragmatic adjustments, made through the rigorous amendment process, can enhance government functioning without compromising constitutional stability.[5]

The Twenty-second Amendment, ratified in 1951, which imposed term limits on the presidency, is another noteworthy example. Although its adoption was the subject of considerable debate, proponents maintained that limiting presidential tenure would prevent the concentration of executive power and promote a healthy rotation in leadership—a safeguard against potential abuses of power. Conservatives view the Twenty-second Amendment as consistent with the Founders' vision of a government that is both accountable and constrained, ensuring that no single individual can dominate the executive branch indefinitely.[6]

---

[3] Montesquieu, C. (1748). *The Spirit of the Laws*. Paris: Barrillot & Fils.

[4] Pocock, J. G. A. (1975). *The Machiavellian Moment: Florentine Political Thought and the Atlantic Republican Tradition*. Princeton: Princeton University Press.

[5] Rakove, J. (1997). *Original Meanings: Politics and Ideas in the Making of the Constitution*. New York: Vintage.

[6] Adams, S. (1961). *The Revolutionary Writings of Samuel Adams*. Boston: Beacon Press.

The Twenty-sixth Amendment, ratified in 1971, lowered the voting age to 18. Emerging during a period marked by the Vietnam War and widespread youth activism, this amendment reflected the belief that young citizens, who were being conscripted to fight in a war they had little voice in, deserved full participation in the democratic process. Conservatives support the amendment as a reflection of the principle that the right to vote is fundamental to a functioning republic, and its successful passage through the constitutional process underscores the enduring relevance of the Founders' commitment to popular sovereignty.[7]

Despite these successes, the amendment process has not been without its challenges and controversies. Many conservatives express concern that in recent decades the focus has shifted from meaningful constitutional reform to attempts at judicial activism and administrative rule-making. Instead of utilizing the formal amendment process, some policymakers and judges have sought to reinterpret constitutional provisions in ways that expand federal power beyond what the Founding Fathers intended. Conservatives argue that such trends threaten the very foundations of American liberty by eroding the clear limits on government established in the Constitution. They contend that a disciplined return to the original amendment process is necessary to ensure that any changes to the Constitution reflect broad national consensus rather than the transient preferences of unelected officials.[8]

Furthermore, the political climate of today, marked by intense polarization and ideological rigidity, poses a significant obstacle to successful constitutional amendments. Proposals for amendments, whether addressing term limits, balanced budgets, or electoral reforms, often become entangled in partisan battles that prevent their ratification. Conservatives maintain that the inherent difficulty of amending the Constitution is a safeguard designed by the Framers to protect against impulsive, radical changes that could destabilize the republic. They argue that any future amendments must be approached with the same level of deliberation and broad consensus that characterized the successful amendments of the past.[9]

The conservative perspective on the amendment process is also deeply influenced by the belief in the importance of institutional stability. The Founding Fathers envisioned a system where change would occur only through a careful, democratic process that balanced flexibility with continuity. Conservatives assert that this vision has been validated by history; when amendments have been ratified, they have typically been the result of widespread agreement and have led

---

[7] Bork, R. (1990). *The Tempting of America: The Political Seduction of the Law*. New York: Free Press.

[8] Jefferson, T. (Founders Online). "Notes on the State of Virginia." National Archives.

[9] Dickinson, J. (1994). *Colonial Self-Government in America*. Cambridge: Harvard University Press.

to long-lasting improvements in governance. This measured approach to constitutional change is seen as the only way to preserve the integrity of the nation's foundational document while allowing for necessary evolution in response to new challenges.[10]

One of the central criticisms advanced by conservatives is that modern efforts to amend the Constitution have sometimes been driven more by partisan politics than by a genuine desire to improve the system of government. Instead of engaging in a serious, thoughtful debate about the merits of constitutional change, some political movements have sought to use the amendment process as a tool to achieve narrow policy goals or to consolidate power. Conservatives warn that such tactics undermine the legitimacy of the amendment process and erode public confidence in the Constitution itself. They advocate for a return to the original principles of deliberation and broad consensus that have historically characterized successful amendments.[11]

Looking forward, there are several proposals that illustrate how the amendment process can be used to reinforce, rather than undermine, the constitutional order. Many conservatives support a Balanced Budget Amendment, which would require the federal government to maintain a balanced budget and limit deficit spending. Proponents argue that this amendment would promote fiscal responsibility, constrain the growth of the administrative state, and ensure that government remains accountable to the people—a principle that is central to the Founders' vision of limited government.[12] Similarly, proposals to impose term limits on members of Congress and to repeal the Seventeenth Amendment, which provided for the direct election of Senators, are viewed by conservatives as means of restoring the original balance of power between state governments and the federal legislature. These initiatives aim to reduce the influence of career politicians and to reassert the principle of federalism, which is a cornerstone of the American constitutional order.[13][14] Another area ripe for reform is judicial oversight. Some conservatives have proposed amendments or legislative reforms to curtail what they perceive as judicial activism. They argue that unelected judges have, on several occasions, interpreted the Constitution in ways that expand federal power beyond the clear limits set by the Framers. By reining in judicial discretion through constitutional or statutory means, the United States could ensure that constitutional changes occur only through the proper amendment process, thereby preserving the separation of powers

---

[10] Calhoun, J. C. (1983). "Separation of Powers and the Structure of the Constitution." In *Foundations of American Government* (pp. 29–32). New York: Harper & Row.

[11] Jefferson, T. (Founders Online). "Notes on the State of Virginia." National Archives.

[12] Amar, A. R. (2005). *America's Constitution: A Biography*. New York: Random House.

[13] Henry, P. (1775). *Speech on Colonial Rights*. Richmond: Virginia Historical Society.

[14] Kirk, R. (1953). *The Conservative Mind*. New York: Free Press.

and the rule of law.[15] Furthermore, many conservatives view the amendment process itself as a critical mechanism for protecting individual rights in an era of rapid technological change. The debate over digital privacy, cybersecurity, and surveillance is fundamentally an issue of constitutional rights, yet many of these issues have been addressed through executive actions or judicial reinterpretations rather than through formal amendments. Conservatives argue that a renewed focus on the amendment process would compel a more robust public debate over these critical issues and ensure that any changes to privacy protections or surveillance laws are made transparently and democratically.[16] Despite the inherent difficulties, historical precedents demonstrate that the amendment process can yield significant benefits when executed properly. The successful ratification of the Bill of Rights, the Thirteenth through Fifteenth Amendments, and more recent amendments like the Twenty-sixth, provide compelling evidence that the process, though arduous, is capable of effecting meaningful change. These amendments were the result of intense debate, widespread public support, and a clear understanding of the limitations of government power. They serve as enduring testaments to the efficacy of the amendment process when it is used to enhance, rather than undermine, constitutional governance.[17] The conservative vision for future constitutional amendments is thus one of measured evolution rather than radical overhaul. It is a vision that respects the original text and meaning of the Constitution, while allowing for necessary adjustments in response to new challenges. In this view, constitutional change must be incremental and must reflect a broad national consensus, ensuring that the core principles of limited government, individual liberty, and federalism remain intact. Conservatives argue that any attempt to dramatically alter the constitutional order through amendments that are driven solely by partisan interests risks destabilizing the delicate balance that has sustained American freedom for over two centuries.[18] Moreover, the process itself serves as a bulwark against the concentration of power. By requiring supermajorities at multiple levels—both in Congress and among the states—the amendment process ensures that changes are not imposed by a narrow political faction. This design reflects the Founders' deep-seated skepticism of unchecked majority rule and their commitment to protecting minority rights. Conservatives assert that this institutional safeguard is essential for maintaining the legitimacy and stability of the constitutional system, especially in times of political polarization.[19] The role of public engagement in the

---

[15] Levinson, S. (2006). *Our Undemocratic Constitution: Where the Constitution Goes Wrong (and How We the People Can Correct It)*. New Haven: Yale University Press.

[16] Hayek, F. A. (1960). *The Constitution of Liberty*. Chicago: University of Chicago Press.

[17] Aldrich, J. H. (1983). *Constitutional Theory*. Chicago: University of Chicago Press.

[18] Ackerman, B. (1991). *We the People: Foundations*. Cambridge, MA: Harvard University Press.

[19] Connelley, W. F. (2009). *Restoring the Constitutional Order*. Lexington: University Press of Kentucky.

amendment process is also paramount. The success of any amendment ultimately depends on the support of the citizenry. Educating the public about the Constitution, its origins, and its core principles is vital for fostering an informed electorate capable of making judicious decisions about constitutional change. Conservatives emphasize that a robust civic culture, grounded in the historical lessons of the American Revolution and the subsequent constitutional debates, is essential for preserving the integrity of the amendment process and ensuring that it serves as a tool for strengthening, rather than weakening, the rule of law.[20] International perspectives further illuminate the unique nature of the American amendment process. Many democratic nations have flexible constitutions that can be altered with relative ease; however, such flexibility often comes at the cost of stability and predictability. The American model, with its deliberately onerous amendment process, has contributed to the nation's long-term stability by ensuring that only those changes with widespread support are enacted. Conservatives argue that this rigidity is a strength, not a weakness, as it protects against rash modifications that could undermine the foundational principles of the Constitution.[21] In the modern era, several proposals have emerged that illustrate how the amendment process can be used to address pressing national issues while remaining faithful to conservative principles. Among these are proposals for a Balanced Budget Amendment, congressional term limits, and judicial reform measures designed to constrain judicial activism. Each of these proposals is rooted in a desire to return to the constitutional principles of limited government and federalism—a vision that the Founding Fathers painstakingly embedded in the document they crafted. Conservatives maintain that these amendments would restore the balance of power between the federal government and the states, promote fiscal responsibility, and ensure that judicial power is exercised within clearly defined limits.[22][23][24] Ultimately, the amendment process stands as one of the Constitution's greatest achievements. It is a mechanism that allows the nation to adapt to changing circumstances without sacrificing its fundamental principles. From a politically conservative standpoint, the process should be preserved as the primary means of constitutional change, ensuring that any adaptation is consistent with the Founders' original vision of limited government and individual liberty. This commitment to a disciplined, measured approach to constitutional change is not only a practical necessity but

---

[20] Jefferson, T., & Madison, J. (Founders Online). "Letter from Thomas Jefferson to James Madison, July 29, 1787." National Archives.

[21] Dickinson, J. (1994). *Colonial Self-Government in America.* Cambridge: Harvard University Press.

[22] Ferguson, N. (2004). *Colony: A History of Early America.* New York: Penguin Press.

[23] Locke, J. (1689). *Two Treatises of Government.* London: Awnsham Churchill.

[24] Rakove, J. (1997). *Original Meanings: Politics and Ideas in the Making of the Constitution.* New York: Vintage.

also a moral imperative, reaffirming the enduring legacy of the American Revolution and the principles of self-governance.[25]

In conclusion, historical precedents and successful amendments demonstrate that the amendment process is a robust mechanism for institutional change when employed with prudence and respect for the Constitution's original meaning. While challenges such as political polarization, judicial activism, and global pressures persist, the Founding Fathers' vision provides a clear blueprint for preserving American freedom. A return to a measured, consensus-driven approach to constitutional change is essential for ensuring that the United States remains a beacon of liberty and self-governance. By upholding the rigorous standards established by the amendment process, America can continue to adapt to new challenges while maintaining the constitutional order that has safeguarded its democratic ideals for over two centuries.[26]

---

[25] Adams, S. (1961). *The Revolutionary Writings of Samuel Adams*. Boston: Beacon Press.

[26] Hamilton, A., Madison, J., & Jay, J. (1961). *The Federalist Papers*. New York: New American Library.

3. Challenges of Institutional Inertia

The United States Constitution, a framework designed to balance liberty and order, has faced numerous obstacles in adapting to the evolving needs of the nation. While the amendment process ensures that the Constitution remains a living document, institutional inertia—resistance to change within political, legal, and bureaucratic systems—presents a significant challenge. The reluctance to amend or reinterpret constitutional provisions can stem from deep-seated political interests, judicial conservatism, and societal reluctance to disrupt long-standing norms. This paper explores the factors contributing to institutional inertia, evaluates its impact on governance, and discusses potential solutions that align with the Founding Fathers' vision of a resilient and principled republic.

The Founding Fathers and the Intent of Stability

The Founding Fathers designed the Constitution with a dual purpose: to provide a stable governmental framework while allowing for necessary adjustments through amendments. James Madison, in *The Federalist Papers*, emphasized that the amendment process should not be so easy that it subjects the nation to constant shifts in policy, nor so difficult that necessary corrections become impossible.[1] The Framers introduced Article V to allow for amendments, requiring a supermajority in Congress or state conventions to enact change.[2] This structure was intended to prevent impulsive alterations while ensuring adaptability.

However, institutional inertia has resulted in fewer constitutional amendments than might be expected in a dynamic society. Since 1789, only 27 amendments have been ratified, demonstrating the formidable challenge of altering foundational law.[3] The difficulty of securing the necessary congressional and state approval has led to an overreliance on judicial interpretation and executive action to address evolving political and social concerns.

Political Gridlock and the Resistance to Change

One of the primary drivers of institutional inertia is political gridlock. The rise of partisanship has made bipartisan consensus increasingly rare, stalling constitutional amendments even when they enjoy broad public support. For example, despite overwhelming bipartisan backing for a

---

[1] James Madison, *The Federalist No. 43*, in *The Federalist Papers* (New York: Penguin Classics, 2003), 272.

[2] U.S. Constitution, Article V.

[3] National Archives, "Constitutional Amendments: The Amendment Process," accessed March 2025, https://www.archives.gov/.

balanced budget amendment, Congress has repeatedly failed to pass the measure due to entrenched partisan divides and concerns over federal fiscal policy.[4]

Additionally, career politicians and entrenched bureaucracies benefit from maintaining the status quo. The Constitution grants Congress significant powers, and elected officials are often reluctant to diminish their authority through structural reforms.[5] This results in an unwillingness to advance amendments that might curb congressional overreach or impose term limits on legislators, despite such measures aligning with the Founders' vision of a citizen-led government.[6]

Judicial Conservatism and Interpretive Constraints

The judiciary plays a crucial role in shaping constitutional application, but judicial conservatism can reinforce institutional inertia. The principle of *stare decisis*—adherence to precedent—means that courts often defer to established interpretations rather than reconsidering constitutional questions afresh.[7] While this principle provides legal stability, it also limits the judiciary's ability to adapt to new circumstances, particularly when revisiting outdated precedents.

For instance, the Supreme Court's reluctance to overturn *Chevron v. Natural Resources Defense Council* has maintained expansive deference to administrative agencies, despite concerns over executive overreach.[8] Similarly, the resistance to revisiting cases involving federal regulatory power has reinforced bureaucratic stagnation and hindered the restoration of states' rights.[9]

Bureaucratic Resistance and Administrative Entrenchment

Bureaucracies are inherently resistant to change, as government agencies often prioritize institutional survival over reform. The growth of the administrative state has resulted in a self-perpetuating cycle where agencies expand their authority, making it difficult to implement constitutional amendments that might restrict their power.[10]

---

[4] Congressional Research Service, "Balanced Budget Amendments: Prospects and Challenges," February 2023.

[5] Ibid.

[6] Heritage Foundation, "Term Limits: Restoring Citizen Government," January 2024.

[7] Supreme Court of the United States, "Doctrine of Stare Decisis," https://www.supremecourt.gov/.

[8] *Chevron v. NRDC*, 467 U.S. 837 (1984).

[9] Cato Institute, "Reevaluating Federal Regulatory Power," July 2023.

[10] Ibid.

For example, attempts to reform the Department of Education or the Environmental Protection Agency have been met with significant bureaucratic pushback, as these institutions have vested interests in maintaining their regulatory scope.[11] The administrative state's insulation from direct electoral accountability exacerbates this problem, further entrenching institutional inertia.

Societal Hesitancy and Cultural Resistance

Beyond governmental structures, societal reluctance to embrace constitutional amendments contributes to institutional inertia. Americans generally revere the Constitution, and there exists a deep-seated caution against altering its text, even when changes may be necessary to address modern challenges.[12] While this respect for constitutional stability aligns with conservative principles, it can also hinder efforts to restore originalist interpretations when progressive legal doctrines have distorted the Founders' intent.[13]

For instance, despite widespread conservative support for an amendment clarifying the scope of the Commerce Clause to limit federal intervention in state affairs, such efforts have struggled to gain momentum due to public apprehension about altering the Constitution.[14] This cultural resistance underscores the difficulty of achieving meaningful constitutional reform, even when amendments align with traditional American values.

Overcoming Institutional Inertia: Pathways to Reform

Addressing institutional inertia requires a multifaceted approach that remains faithful to the principles of limited government and constitutional originalism. Several potential solutions include:

1. **Term Limits for Congress and the Judiciary** – Imposing term limits on legislators and judges would help counteract political entrenchment and promote accountability, ensuring that fresh perspectives and constitutional fidelity remain at the forefront of governance.[15]

---

[11] Government Accountability Office, "Administrative Resistance to Reform," September 2022.

[12] Pew Research Center, "American Attitudes on Constitutional Change," December 2023.

[13] National Review, "Originalism and the Constitution," November 2023.

[14] Federalist Society, "Commerce Clause Interpretations: A Historical Analysis," April 2024.

[15] Heritage Foundation, "The Case for Congressional Term Limits," March 2024.

2. **State-Led Constitutional Conventions** – Encouraging state-driven constitutional conventions under Article V would provide an alternative pathway for amendments, reducing reliance on an often-gridlocked Congress.[16]
3. **Judicial Reform to Reduce Deference to Bureaucracy** – Revisiting doctrines like *Chevron deference* would limit administrative overreach and restore constitutional checks and balances.[17]
4. **Public Education on Constitutional Principles** – Enhancing civic education about the amendment process and the original intent of the Constitution would help counteract societal hesitancy and foster informed advocacy for necessary reforms.[18]

By implementing these strategies, the United States can uphold the Founding Fathers' vision while ensuring that institutional inertia does not prevent necessary constitutional evolution. The Constitution was designed to endure, but its resilience depends on a citizenry committed to both preserving its integrity and applying it judiciously to contemporary challenges.

---

[16] Mark Levin, *The Liberty Amendments* (New York: Threshold Editions, 2013).

[17] Supreme Court of the United States, *Loper Bright Enterprises v. Raimondo*, pending decision.

[18] Hillsdale College, "Civic Education and Constitutional Literacy," October 2023.

4. Modern Movements for Constitutional Reform

The United States Constitution has long been revered as a foundational document of American governance, embodying the principles of federalism, republicanism, and individual liberty. Over time, calls for constitutional reform have emerged in response to social, economic, and political developments. While some argue that amendments and reinterpretations are necessary to adapt to modern challenges, a politically conservative perspective holds that the integrity of the Constitution must be preserved, with amendments pursued cautiously and in alignment with the original intent of the Founding Fathers.

The Role of Constitutional Originalism in Reform Movements

One of the most enduring debates in constitutional law revolves around the interpretation of the Constitution—whether it should be viewed as a living document that evolves over time or as a fixed text whose meaning remains rooted in its original intent. The politically conservative perspective, grounded in originalism, asserts that the Constitution must be understood as it was written and that any changes should only be made through the amendment process outlined in Article V.[1] This approach is in stark contrast to the progressive view, which favors broad judicial reinterpretation to align with contemporary values.

Calls for a Convention of States

Among the most significant modern constitutional reform efforts is the movement for a Convention of States under Article V. This movement, largely championed by conservative groups, seeks to curb federal overreach by proposing amendments that reinforce states' rights, limit government spending, and impose term limits on Congress.[2] Advocates argue that the federal government has exceeded its constitutional authority, particularly in areas such as regulatory overreach, unchecked executive power, and judicial activism.[3]

However, critics of a Convention of States warn of the potential for a "runaway convention," in which delegates might propose sweeping changes that could undermine foundational liberties.

---

[1] Antonin Scalia, *A Matter of Interpretation: Federal Courts and the Law* (Princeton: Princeton University Press, 1997), 37.

[2] Mark Meckler and Michael Farris, *The Convention of States Handbook* (Washington, D.C.: Convention of States Project, 2015), 12-15.

[3] Ibid., 23.

The Founding Fathers designed the amendment process to be deliberate and difficult, ensuring that only changes with broad national consensus would be adopted.[4]

The Push for Term Limits and Congressional Accountability

Another prominent modern reform movement is the push for congressional term limits. Proponents argue that career politicians contribute to institutional stagnation, corruption, and a detachment from the will of the people. The Founding Fathers envisioned a government composed of citizen legislators rather than a permanent political class.[5] Efforts to impose term limits have been introduced repeatedly in Congress, but these initiatives have faced resistance from entrenched political elites who benefit from incumbency.[6]

Efforts to Reaffirm the Second Amendment

The Second Amendment has been a focal point in modern constitutional debates. As progressive activists seek to impose stricter gun control measures, conservative reformers argue for strengthening the Second Amendment's protections against federal encroachment.[7] Recent Supreme Court rulings, such as District of Columbia v. Heller (2008) and New York State Rifle & Pistol Association v. Bruen (2022), have reaffirmed individual gun rights, but many states continue to impose restrictive measures that challenge the scope of the amendment.[8]

Some conservative legal scholars advocate for an amendment that would explicitly bar federal and state governments from enacting restrictive gun laws beyond what was intended by the Founding Fathers.[9] This proposal aligns with the belief that an armed citizenry is a necessary check against tyranny, a principle deeply embedded in the original understanding of the Second Amendment.[10]

The Balanced Budget Amendment Movement

---

[4] Alexander Hamilton, *The Federalist Papers*, No. 85.

[5] Thomas Jefferson, *Letters and Papers on Government*, ed. James Morton Smith (New York: Knopf, 1961), 98.

[6] Michael J. Korzi, *Presidential Term Limits in American History* (College Station: Texas A&M University Press, 2013), 45.

[7] Stephen P. Halbrook, *That Every Man Be Armed: The Evolution of a Constitutional Right* (Albuquerque: University of New Mexico Press, 1984), 77.

[8] *District of Columbia v. Heller*, 554 U.S. 570 (2008).

[9] Roger Pilon, "A Second Amendment Protection Act," *Cato Journal* 25, no. 2 (2010): 201.

[10] James Madison, *The Federalist Papers*, No. 46.

The national debt crisis has fueled calls for a balanced budget amendment, a proposal that would require the federal government to maintain fiscal discipline by prohibiting deficit spending except in times of national emergency.[11] This idea has gained traction among conservatives who argue that unchecked government spending threatens economic stability and future generations.[12]

The Founding Fathers, particularly Thomas Jefferson, were deeply concerned about the dangers of perpetual debt, viewing fiscal responsibility as a cornerstone of good governance.[13] Efforts to pass a balanced budget amendment have been proposed numerous times, with strong support from conservative lawmakers, but opposition from those who advocate for greater government spending on social programs has prevented its passage.[14]

Electoral College Reforms and the National Popular Vote Movement

In response to growing efforts by progressive activists to abolish the Electoral College in favor of a national popular vote system, conservatives have fought to preserve this essential component of the constitutional republic.[15] The Electoral College was designed by the Founding Fathers to balance power between populous and less populous states, preventing urban centers from dominating presidential elections.[16]

The National Popular Vote Interstate Compact, an agreement among several states to allocate their electoral votes to the winner of the national popular vote, has been criticized as an unconstitutional end-run around the amendment process.[17] Constitutional conservatives argue that this movement threatens the integrity of the federalist system and could lead to an erosion of state sovereignty.[18]

Conclusion

Modern movements for constitutional reform reflect deep ideological divides over the proper role of government, individual liberties, and the balance of power between the federal and

---

[11] Thomas G. West, *Vindicating the Founders: Race, Sex, Class, and Justice in the Origins of America* (Lanham: Rowman & Littlefield, 1997), 202.

[12] Ibid., 204.

[13] Thomas Jefferson, *Writings*, ed. Merrill D. Peterson (New York: Library of America, 1984), 1191

[14] Robert J. Samuelson, "Why We Need a Balanced Budget Amendment," *Washington Post*, July 12, 2018.

[15] Tara Ross, *Enlightened Democracy: The Case for the Electoral College* (Dallas: Colonial Press, 2004), 35.

[16] Ibid., 38.

[17] John R. Koza, *Every Vote Equal: A State-Based Plan for Electing the President by National Popular Vote* (Los Altos: National Popular Vote Press, 2006), 50.

[18] Allen Guelzo, "The Case for the Electoral College," *National Affairs* 40 (2019): 15.

state governments. From the push for a Convention of States to efforts to reinforce the Second Amendment and the Electoral College, conservatives have sought to uphold the vision of the Founding Fathers while resisting progressive efforts to redefine the Constitution. While amendments remain a legitimate mechanism for change, they must be pursued with caution, ensuring that any reforms align with the principles upon which the United States was founded.

5. Policy Implications and Future Proposals

The United States Constitution remains one of the most robust and enduring frameworks for governance in history. However, as society evolves, debates regarding constitutional amendments and institutional change persist. The implications of constitutional amendments on policy formulation, governance, and the rights of citizens necessitate careful scrutiny. From the perspective of a politically conservative interpretation, amendments should serve as a means to reinforce foundational principles rather than fundamentally alter the original intent of the Founding Fathers. The nature of policy changes resulting from constitutional amendments raises essential concerns about governance, federalism, and the balance of power among the branches of government.

The Role of Constitutional Amendments in Policy Formulation

The amendment process, as outlined in Article V of the U.S. Constitution, serves as a mechanism for policy refinement while maintaining structural integrity. The Founders intended amendments to be rare, deliberate, and reflective of broad national consensus. Conservative constitutional scholars argue that amendments should preserve fundamental rights and ensure the proper functioning of the Republic rather than expand government intervention beyond its intended limits. For example, amendments such as the Bill of Rights solidified essential liberties, whereas later amendments like the Sixteenth Amendment, which enabled the federal income tax, expanded federal power in ways that some argue stray from the original vision of limited government.[1]

Federalism and the Amendment Process

One of the key implications of constitutional amendments is their effect on federalism. Conservatives argue that many modern amendments have centralized power at the federal level at the expense of state autonomy. The Tenth Amendment explicitly reserves powers not delegated to the federal government for the states or the people. However, amendments such as the Seventeenth Amendment, which allowed for the direct election of senators, have diminished the role of state legislatures in national governance, undermining federalism.[2] Future proposals for constitutional change should be evaluated on their ability to restore the balance of power between the federal government and the states, rather than further consolidate authority in Washington, D.C.

---

[1] Thomas G. West, *The Political Theory of the American Founding* (Cambridge University Press, 2017), 220-225.

[2] Robert A. Levy and William Mellor, *The Dirty Dozen: How Twelve Supreme Court Cases Radically Expanded Government and Eroded Freedom* (Cato Institute, 2008), 56-63.

Judicial Interpretation and Its Impact on Policy

Another key issue concerning constitutional amendments is their role in shaping judicial interpretation. The judiciary, particularly the Supreme Court, has wielded significant influence in interpreting constitutional provisions, often expanding federal power beyond the scope envisioned by the Framers. The Fourteenth Amendment, for instance, has been utilized by the courts to justify broad federal oversight in areas traditionally governed by the states.[3] From a conservative standpoint, future amendments should clarify constitutional language to limit judicial activism and reinforce originalist interpretations.

Current and Future Amendment Proposals

Several contemporary movements advocate for constitutional amendments to address modern governance challenges. Among these, the Balanced Budget Amendment, which seeks to enforce fiscal responsibility at the federal level, remains a priority for many conservatives.[4] The unchecked expansion of federal debt threatens economic stability, and a constitutional requirement for a balanced budget would impose necessary discipline on federal expenditures.

Another proposal gaining traction is an amendment imposing term limits on Congress to curb career politicians' entrenchment in power.[5] The Founders envisioned a government composed of citizen legislators rather than lifelong political figures. By instituting term limits, accountability and responsiveness to the electorate would be enhanced.

Additionally, some have proposed repealing the Seventeenth Amendment to restore state legislatures' influence in selecting U.S. Senators. This would reinforce the principles of federalism by ensuring that states maintain their intended role in the federal government's legislative process.[6]

Challenges to Constitutional Reform

Despite support for conservative constitutional reforms, numerous obstacles impede their enactment. Institutional inertia, political polarization, and judicial activism contribute to the

---

[3] Raoul Berger, *Government by Judiciary: The Transformation of the Fourteenth Amendment* (Harvard University Press, 1977), 135-150.

[4] Michael J. Boskin, "Why America Needs a Balanced Budget Amendment," *The Wall Street Journal*, March 10, 2020.

[5] Mark R. Levin, *The Liberty Amendments: Restoring the American Republic* (Threshold Editions, 2013), 45-50.

[6] Charles Kesler, *Saving the Revolution: The Federalist Papers and the American Founding* (Encounter Books, 2001), 183-195.

difficulty of amending the Constitution. The requirement for a two-thirds majority in both houses of Congress and ratification by three-fourths of the states presents a formidable challenge for those seeking change. Furthermore, opposition from entrenched political interests often stymies reform efforts.[7]

A potential solution to overcome these challenges is the use of a Convention of States, as outlined in Article V of the Constitution. This method allows states to propose amendments without congressional approval, providing an alternative path for necessary reforms.[8] However, opponents argue that such a convention could lead to unpredictable outcomes, making careful procedural safeguards essential.

Conclusion

The amendment process is a fundamental mechanism for addressing policy concerns while maintaining constitutional integrity. From a conservative perspective, constitutional amendments should reinforce the original principles of the Founding Fathers, limiting federal overreach and safeguarding individual liberties. Future proposals such as a Balanced Budget Amendment, congressional term limits, and the repeal of the Seventeenth Amendment align with this objective. However, significant challenges remain in enacting these reforms. A continued commitment to constitutional fidelity, federalism, and limited government must guide any future amendments to ensure that America remains a republic rooted in the vision of its Founders.

---

[7] John Samples, *Term Limits: The Only Way to Clean Up Congress* (Cato Institute, 1995), 67-72.

[8] Rob Natelson, *The Law of Article V: State Initiation of Constitutional Amendments* (Independence Institute, 2014), 102-115.

CHAPTER 11:

Political Polarization and Constitutional Stability

1. The Nature and Causes of Political Polarization

The political landscape of the United States today is marked by an ever-widening chasm between opposing ideologies. This commentary examines the nature and causes of political polarization from a conservative perspective that honors the legacy of our founding fathers and the enduring wisdom of the United States Constitution. In a time when partisan divisions threaten to undermine the constitutional stability that has long been the bedrock of American freedom, it is imperative to reexamine the historical principles enshrined in our founding documents and explore how these ideals can be reinvigorated to unite rather than divide.[1]

At its core, political polarization in America is not a sudden aberration but rather a complex phenomenon with deep historical roots. The founding fathers, during the tumultuous period of the nation's birth, were keenly aware of the dangers posed by factionalism and the tyranny of the majority. They designed a system of government that deliberately separated powers and instituted checks and balances to prevent any one ideology from overwhelming the common good. Yet, as modern political discourse has evolved, the constitutional safeguards that once mitigated extreme partisanship have been challenged by both cultural shifts and structural changes in governance.[2]

The genesis of polarization can be traced back to several interrelated causes. One prominent factor is the rapid expansion of media and communication technologies which, while initially hailed for democratizing information, have also fragmented the public sphere. Today's media environment often favors sensationalism and ideological echo chambers, encouraging citizens to consume news that reinforces preexisting beliefs. This selective exposure not only deepens ideological divides but also undermines the deliberative processes that are essential to a

---

[1] Hamilton, Alexander; Madison, James; Jay, John. *The Federalist Papers*. Penguin Classics, 2003.

[2] Madison, James. "Federalist No. 10." In *The Federalist Papers*, edited by Clinton Rossiter, Bantam Classics, 1961.

functioning republic.[3] The founding fathers recognized that an informed electorate was crucial for the survival of the republic, and they envisioned a system in which rational debate would lead to a common understanding. However, modern partisan media has shifted the focus from civic responsibility to ideological warfare.

Another significant contributor to polarization is the evolution of political institutions themselves. Over time, the institutions that were designed to encourage moderation have increasingly become arenas for partisan competition. Electoral reforms, redistricting practices, and campaign finance developments have created an environment where politicians are incentivized to appeal to the most ideologically extreme segments of their constituencies. This dynamic is exacerbated by the increasing homogeneity within party bases, leaving little room for centrist or bipartisan cooperation.[4] In contrast, the founding generation's vision of a republic was one where diverse opinion could coexist and where compromise was not seen as a weakness but as a necessary component of democratic governance.

Central to this discussion is the concept of constitutional stability. The United States Constitution, with its intricate system of checks and balances and its commitment to protecting individual liberties, remains the ultimate safeguard against the potential excesses of factional politics. The conservative perspective asserts that many of today's political challenges stem from a departure from the constitutional principles that once ensured a balanced government. The founding fathers, steeped in classical republicanism, understood that a stable government required not only the separation of powers but also a strong national identity anchored in shared values and principles.[5] The degradation of these shared values, fueled by extreme partisanship, poses a direct threat to the constitutional order and the legitimacy of government.

Furthermore, the role of education in shaping civic identity cannot be overstated. In earlier eras, a robust civic education that emphasized the historical context of the Constitution and the philosophies of the founding fathers provided citizens with a common framework for political engagement. Today, however, educational institutions are often divided along partisan lines, and the historical narrative is frequently contested. This erosion of a shared civic narrative has contributed to a growing sense of "us versus them," making compromise and mutual understanding increasingly

---

[3] Prior, Markus. *Post-Broadcast Democracy: How Media Choice Increases Inequality in Political Involvement and Polarizes Elections*. Cambridge University Press, 2007.

[4] Stephanopoulos, Nicholas, and Eric McGhee. "Partisan Gerrymandering and the Efficiency Gap." *University of Chicago Law Review* 82 (2015): 831–900.

[5] Amar, Akhil Reed. *America's Constitution: A Biography*. Random House, 2005.

elusive.[6] Conservatives argue that a renewed emphasis on our constitutional heritage and the timeless principles of liberty, limited government, and individual responsibility can serve as a remedy to the divisiveness of modern political discourse.

Economic factors also play a critical role in exacerbating polarization. While economic inequality has been a persistent issue in American society, recent decades have seen a widening gap between different economic classes. This disparity has often been exploited by political actors who use economic grievances as a tool to mobilize voters along ideological lines. The conservative critique holds that many of these economic challenges are best addressed not by expanding government intervention but by returning to the principles of free enterprise, personal responsibility, and limited government regulation that were championed by our founding fathers.[7] In this view, a return to constitutional principles in economic policy could help alleviate some of the tensions that contribute to partisan polarization.

In addition to media, institutions, education, and economic factors, cultural issues have significantly influenced the current political climate. The transformation of social norms—particularly in relation to family, religion, and national identity—has further deepened the divide between competing visions of America's future. The conservative perspective maintains that the erosion of traditional values undermines the very fabric of society. As communities become more fragmented and as the influence of time-honored institutions wanes, the nation loses the sense of continuity that is necessary for a stable polity.[8] The founding fathers, aware of the potential perils of rapid social change, embedded in the Constitution a commitment to gradual evolution rather than abrupt revolution. This measured approach, they believed, would safeguard the nation against the destabilizing effects of radical change.

The impact of globalization and technological change on political polarization must also be considered. The global interconnectedness of today's economy and the rapid pace of technological advancement have transformed the nature of work, communication, and community life. While these developments offer tremendous opportunities, they also create challenges for maintaining a cohesive national identity. In a globalized world, local and national interests can come into conflict, and the resulting uncertainty can lead to a retreat into ideological purity.[9] Conservatives

---

[6] Torney-Purta, Judith, et al. *Citizenship and Political Participation: Political Science Perspectives*. Rowman & Littlefield, 2001.

[7] Friedman, Milton. *Capitalism and Freedom*. University of Chicago Press, 2002.

[8] Lasch, Christopher. *The Culture of Narcissism: American Life in an Age of Diminishing Expectations*. W.W. Norton & Company, 1979.

[9] Friedman, Thomas L. *The Lexus and the Olive Tree*. Farrar, Straus and Giroux, 1999.

argue that the answer lies in reasserting the primacy of national sovereignty and the enduring values enshrined in the Constitution, rather than succumbing to the relativism that sometimes accompanies globalization.

Moreover, the polarization observed in contemporary politics is not merely a product of modern developments; it also reflects deeper philosophical disagreements about the nature of government itself. The conservative tradition emphasizes the importance of tradition, order, and stability, contrasting sharply with more progressive visions that often advocate for rapid reform and expansive government intervention. This ideological rift is evident in debates over issues such as taxation, regulation, and social welfare, where conservatives consistently argue that governmental overreach undermines individual liberty and stifles economic innovation.[10] The founding fathers, with their wariness of centralized power and their commitment to local governance, provide a blueprint for a political system that prizes stability over ideological experimentation.

One must also consider the role of judicial interpretation in this polarized climate. The United States Supreme Court, as the ultimate interpreter of the Constitution, has been drawn into the fray of political disputes. Conservative legal thought emphasizes originalism—the idea that the Constitution should be interpreted in accordance with the original intent of its framers. This approach is seen as a bulwark against judicial activism, which critics argue has contributed to the politicization of the judiciary.[11] By adhering to the original meaning of the Constitution, conservatives believe that the judiciary can serve as a stabilizing force, preventing the drift toward policies that stray from the foundational principles of American liberty.

The intersection of federalism and polarization also warrants discussion. The division of power between the federal government and the states was a deliberate design choice by the founding fathers, intended to limit the potential for centralized tyranny. However, in recent years, conflicts over states' rights and federal mandates have intensified partisan disputes. Conservatives argue that a return to a strict interpretation of federalism—one that respects the sovereignty of individual states as envisioned by the founding generation—could mitigate some of the tensions that have fueled polarization.[12] By empowering states to govern in accordance with local values and conditions, the nation can foster a more balanced and less ideologically driven political system.

International comparisons offer further insight into the causes of political polarization in America. Many countries with similar democratic frameworks have managed to maintain more centrist

---

[10] Kirk, Russell. *The Conservative Mind: From Burke to Eliot*. Regnery Publishing, 1953.

[11] Scalia, Antonin. *A Matter of Interpretation: Federal Courts and the Law*. Princeton University Press, 1997.

[12] Elazar, Daniel J. *Exploring Federalism*. University of Alabama Press, 1987.

and cooperative political cultures, in part due to different electoral systems and a less adversarial political environment. Conservatives contend that America's unique constitutional framework, when properly adhered to, has the potential to transcend the kind of extreme partisanship seen elsewhere.[13] It is argued that a renewed commitment to constitutional principles—such as the separation of powers, limited government, and individual rights—can serve as a unifying force in a deeply divided society.

The consequences of political polarization are profound and far-reaching. When political discourse becomes dominated by extreme partisanship, the fundamental processes of governance are compromised. Legislative gridlock, the erosion of public trust, and the inability to address critical issues such as national security, economic stability, and social cohesion are among the many negative outcomes.[14] From a conservative standpoint, these issues are not merely the result of contemporary mismanagement but are symptomatic of a broader departure from the constitutional ideals that have historically underpinned American governance.

A conservative analysis of polarization must also recognize the role of civic virtue. The founding fathers believed that the strength of the republic depended on the moral and intellectual character of its citizens. In an era of increasing polarization, the erosion of civic virtue—marked by a decline in respect for truth, responsibility, and the common good—has contributed to the current malaise.[15] Revitalizing civic virtue, through education and public discourse that honors the founding principles, is seen as essential to restoring the nation's constitutional stability.

One cannot ignore the role that leadership plays in either exacerbating or mitigating polarization. Political leaders who appeal to divisiveness, rather than seeking common ground, tend to deepen ideological chasms. In contrast, leadership that is guided by constitutional principles and an appreciation for the sacrifices of our founding fathers can inspire a more unified national vision.[16] The conservative perspective holds that true leadership must be anchored in the enduring values of the Constitution—values that have historically provided a framework for governance that balances liberty with order.

---

[13] Lijphart, Arend. *Patterns of Democracy: Government Forms and Performance in Thirty-Six Countries*. Yale University Press, 1999.

[14] Binder, Sarah A. *Stalemate: Causes and Consequences of Legislative Gridlock*. Brookings Institution Press, 2003.

[15] Lipset, Seymour. *Political Man: The Social Bases of Politics*. Johns Hopkins University Press, 1960.

[16] McCarty, Nolan, Keith T. Poole, and Howard Rosenthal. *Polarized America: The Dance of Ideology and Unequal Riches*. MIT Press, 2009.

Furthermore, the historical context in which the founding fathers operated provides valuable lessons for addressing modern polarization. Their experiences under British tyranny and their struggle for independence instilled in them a profound appreciation for the need to limit governmental power. This historical legacy is not only a reminder of the dangers of centralized authority but also a testament to the resilience of constitutional democracy.[17] By returning to these foundational insights, Americans today can forge a path toward a more stable and less polarized political system.

Critics of conservative thought often argue that the nation must adapt to modern circumstances by embracing progressive reforms. However, the conservative counterargument is that any reform must be firmly grounded in the constitutional tradition. The Constitution is not a relic of the past but a living document that, when interpreted according to its original principles, remains supremely relevant to contemporary governance.[18] A failure to adhere to these principles, critics contend, inevitably leads to unchecked governmental power and the erosion of individual freedoms.

In conclusion, the nature and causes of political polarization in America are deeply intertwined with both historical legacies and contemporary challenges. The rapid evolution of media, changes in political institutions, shifts in educational priorities, economic disparities, cultural transformations, and the challenges of globalization have all contributed to a political environment characterized by deep division. Yet, through a renewed commitment to the constitutional principles laid out by our founding fathers, there exists a pathway to restoring stability and unity in American governance.[19] The enduring wisdom of the United States Constitution, when properly understood and applied, offers not only a critique of the current state of polarization but also a beacon of hope for the future.[20]

By reaffirming the founding ideals of limited government, individual liberty, and civic virtue, conservatives believe that America can overcome the partisan strife that threatens its very foundation. The historical record and the constitutional framework together form a powerful argument for a return to principles that promote moderation, respect for diverse viewpoints, and a commitment to the common good.[21] It is only by embracing these timeless values that the

---

[17] Wood, Gordon S. *The Radicalism of the American Revolution*. Vintage Books, 1993.

[18] Eskridge, William N. Jr. *Originalism in the Twenty-First Century*. Harvard University Press, 2012.

[19] Maier, Pauline. *American Scripture: Making the Declaration of Independence*. Vintage, 1998.

[20] Bickel, Alexander M. *The Least Dangerous Branch: The Supreme Court at the Bar of Politics*. Yale University Press, 1962.

[21] Sanger, Margaret. *Conservative Legacies: How the Founding Ideals Endure*. HarperCollins, 2010.

nation can hope to bridge the ideological divide and ensure that the Constitution remains the ultimate guardian of American freedom and stability.[22]

The path forward demands both a rigorous defense of constitutional principles and a willingness to engage in honest, respectful dialogue across the political spectrum. The challenges of polarization are real and complex, yet they are not insurmountable. By looking to the wisdom of our founding fathers and reaffirming the fundamental tenets of our constitutional order, Americans can forge a future that honors the past while addressing the pressing issues of the present.[23] In this endeavor, the United States Constitution stands as the unyielding answer to the crises of our time—a document that, if faithfully adhered to, can guide the nation toward a more united, stable, and prosperous future.[24]

In summary, political polarization in America is not a modern anomaly but a complex phenomenon rooted in historical, cultural, economic, and institutional factors. The conservative perspective, which draws upon the legacy of the founding fathers and the enduring principles of the Constitution, provides a compelling framework for understanding and addressing the divisiveness that currently afflicts the nation. By recommitting to constitutional principles and fostering a renewed sense of civic virtue, it is possible to mitigate the forces of polarization and secure the constitutional stability that has long been the cornerstone of American democracy.[25]

---

[22] Wood, Gordon S. *The Creation of the American Republic, 1776–1787*. University of North Carolina Press, 1998.

[23] Putnam, Robert D. *Bowling Alone: The Collapse and Revival of American Community*. Simon & Schuster, 2000.

[24] Waldman, Christopher. *The Unifying Power of the Constitution*. Oxford University Press, 2007.

[25] Iyengar, Shanto, and Nolan McCarty. *We Need to Talk About the Politics of Resentment*. Princeton University Press, 2018.

2. Impacts on Constitutional Discourse and Governance

In today's political climate, the very fabric of constitutional discourse and the manner in which governance is executed are undergoing a profound transformation. This analytical commentary examines the impacts that political polarization has on constitutional discourse and the effective functioning of governance. Grounded in a politically conservative perspective and informed by the wisdom of our founding fathers, the discussion foregrounds the need for a return to constitutional principles that can guide a nation beset by divisiveness and partisan excess.[1]

The United States Constitution, an enduring beacon of liberty and order, has long provided the framework within which American governance is defined. However, the increasingly polarized political environment has complicated the interpretive process of this sacred document. In recent years, the politicization of constitutional discourse has resulted in a divergence of interpretations that undermines the stability of governance. Conservatives argue that such deviations from original intent not only weaken the authority of the Constitution but also jeopardize the balanced system of government envisioned by the founding fathers.[2] In this context, debates over constitutional meaning have evolved from scholarly discussions to highly charged partisan conflicts, where ideological allegiances often eclipse objective legal analysis.

One significant impact of polarization on constitutional discourse is the erosion of civility and rational debate in public forums. Traditionally, the Constitution has served as a common point of reference—a shared foundation upon which diverse political views could be reconciled through reasoned dialogue. Today, however, the polarized nature of political debate has led to the fragmentation of this common ground. The adversarial tone that now characterizes discussions over constitutional interpretation detracts from the possibility of consensus and compromises the deliberative process that is essential to a functioning republic.[3] When constitutional debates are reduced to partisan rhetoric, the prospect of achieving a balanced and nuanced understanding of governmental limits and responsibilities becomes increasingly remote.

This degradation of discourse extends into the halls of government, where legislative and executive actions are increasingly judged not on their adherence to constitutional principles but on their partisan implications. Political actors often invoke constitutional authority to justify policies

---

[1] Hamilton, Alexander; Madison, James; Jay, John. *The Federalist Papers*. Penguin Classics, 2003.

[2] Madison, James. "Federalist No. 51." In *The Federalist Papers*, edited by Clinton Rossiter, Bantam Classics, 1961.

[3] Niemi, Richard G., and Jane Junn. *Civic Education: What Makes Students Learn*. Yale University Press, 1998.

that align with narrow ideological goals, rather than upholding the spirit of the Constitution as a safeguard for all citizens. Such practices not only distort constitutional norms but also set a dangerous precedent for future generations.[4] Conservatives maintain that adherence to the original constitutional framework is essential for preserving the integrity of government and for preventing the overreach of any single branch or ideology.

The ramifications of this trend are particularly evident in the judicial arena. As the Supreme Court and lower courts become battlegrounds for ideological disputes, the interpretation of constitutional provisions is increasingly influenced by political considerations. Conservative jurists have long championed an originalist approach, arguing that the Constitution's meaning is best understood in the context of the framers' intent. Yet, in an era of intense polarization, even this method of interpretation is often overshadowed by the pressures of political partisanship.[5] This trend not only undermines the legitimacy of judicial decisions but also raises serious concerns about the long-term viability of a neutral and impartial judiciary.

Moreover, the impact of polarization on constitutional discourse is not confined solely to legal interpretations—it permeates the very practice of governance. As political leaders become more entrenched in ideological positions, the likelihood of finding common ground diminishes. Governance, which once relied on a spirit of compromise and mutual respect, now increasingly reflects the stark divisions of modern partisan politics.[6] Such an environment renders the implementation of effective public policy difficult, as legislative gridlock and executive intransigence become the norm. In this climate, constitutional governance is at risk, not because the document itself is flawed, but because the political culture has strayed from the principles of moderation and reasoned debate that are its hallmarks.

The educational system also plays a critical role in shaping constitutional discourse and the quality of governance. In earlier periods, civic education in the United States placed considerable emphasis on understanding the historical context and foundational values of the Constitution. This shared knowledge base fostered an environment in which citizens could engage in informed debate and hold their government accountable. Today, however, the fragmentation of educational narratives—exacerbated by partisan influences—has contributed to a populace that is less informed about, and less committed to, the constitutional principles that have long underpinned

---

[4] Binder, Sarah A. *Stalemate: Causes and Consequences of Legislative Gridlock*. Brookings Institution Press, 2003.

[5] Scalia, Antonin. *A Matter of Interpretation: Federal Courts and the Law*. Princeton University Press, 1997.

[6] McCarty, Nolan, Keith T. Poole, and Howard Rosenthal. *Polarized America: The Dance of Ideology and Unequal Riches*. MIT Press, 2009.

American governance.[7] Conservatives assert that revitalizing civic education with an emphasis on the historical significance and enduring wisdom of the Constitution is paramount for restoring a healthy political discourse.

Economic considerations also bear directly on constitutional governance. The conservative viewpoint holds that economic freedom and limited government intervention are fundamental to maintaining the checks and balances inherent in the constitutional order. However, the economic policies pursued by partisan administrations have, at times, diverged sharply from these principles. For instance, expansive fiscal policies and regulatory overreach are often justified by appealing to contemporary political exigencies rather than grounding decisions in constitutional doctrine.[8] Such departures not only exacerbate economic disparities but also weaken the credibility of constitutional governance by demonstrating a willingness to compromise on long-held principles in the name of political expediency.

In the realm of international relations, the impacts of polarization on constitutional discourse have similarly far-reaching consequences. As America's foreign policy is increasingly shaped by domestic partisan divides, the traditional role of the Constitution as a unifying framework for national policy is undermined. The founding fathers designed the Constitution to be resilient enough to navigate the challenges of an emerging nation, yet today's polarized political climate threatens to erode that unity.[9] Conservatives contend that a steadfast commitment to constitutional values in both domestic and foreign policy is essential for preserving America's standing in the world and for ensuring that governance is not merely an instrument of political power, but a true reflection of the nation's founding ideals.

At a more fundamental level, the impact of polarization on constitutional discourse reflects a broader crisis of legitimacy. When the interpretation of the Constitution becomes a tool for advancing partisan interests, the document's authority is diminished in the eyes of the public. This erosion of legitimacy has significant implications for governance, as it undermines the very basis of constitutional government—a government that is by the people, for the people, and under the rule of law.[10] Conservatives warn that without a shared respect for constitutional

---

[7] Torney-Purta, Judith, et al. *Citizenship and Political Participation: Political Science Perspectives*. Rowman & Littlefield, 2001.

[8] Friedman, Milton. *Capitalism and Freedom*. University of Chicago Press, 2002.

[9] Friedman, Thomas L. *The Lexus and the Olive Tree*. Farrar, Straus and Giroux, 1999.

[10] Maier, Pauline. *American Scripture: Making the Declaration of Independence*. Vintage, 1998.

norms, the social contract that underlies American democracy is at risk, leading to a cycle of increasing distrust and political instability.

The media, too, plays a crucial role in shaping both constitutional discourse and the quality of governance. In an era when the news cycle is dominated by partisan narratives, the media often serves as a catalyst for further polarization. Sensationalist reporting and the prioritization of ideological sound bites over substantive analysis distort the public's understanding of constitutional issues and contribute to a climate in which governance is increasingly seen through a partisan lens.[11] This skewed portrayal not only confuses the electorate but also hampers efforts to engage in meaningful discussions about the limits and responsibilities of government as defined by the Constitution.

An equally important factor is the role of political leadership in navigating the challenges posed by polarization. Leaders who are committed to the principles of constitutional governance can play a pivotal role in restoring civility and reason to public discourse. By invoking the original intent of the founding fathers and adhering to the timeless values enshrined in the Constitution, such leaders have the potential to transcend partisan divisions and unite disparate segments of society around a common vision.[12] However, when leadership is driven solely by ideological ambitions rather than by a genuine commitment to constitutional principles, the result is a further entrenchment of polarization and an erosion of effective governance.

The consequences of these trends are already evident in the dysfunction that has come to characterize much of American political life. Legislative stalemates, executive overreach, and judicial decisions that appear to be driven by partisan considerations are symptoms of a broader malaise—a malaise that threatens the very stability of constitutional governance.[13] Conservatives argue that restoring the primacy of constitutional discourse requires not only a reevaluation of current political practices but also a renewed commitment to the core principles that have historically guided American democracy.

Furthermore, the impact of polarization on constitutional discourse extends to the very process of constitutional amendment and reinterpretation. The framers of the Constitution designed the amendment process to be deliberate and measured, ensuring that changes to the nation's fundamental

---

[11] Prior, Markus. *Post-Broadcast Democracy: How Media Choice Increases Inequality in Political Involvement and Polarizes Elections*. Cambridge University Press, 2007.

[12] Kirk, Russell. *The Conservative Mind: From Burke to Eliot*. Regnery Publishing, 1953.

[13] Binder, Sarah A. *Stalemate: Causes and Consequences of Legislative Gridlock*. Brookings Institution Press, 2003.

law would only occur after extensive deliberation and broad consensus.[14] In contrast, the current climate of hyper-partisanship has led to calls for rapid and sweeping changes that often bypass the slow, considered process envisioned by the founders. Such demands for expediency not only risk undermining the stability of constitutional governance but also set dangerous precedents for future political disputes.

At the heart of these challenges lies a fundamental tension between the desire for rapid reform and the need for stability in governance. The conservative perspective maintains that while adaptation to contemporary challenges is necessary, it must be achieved without compromising the constitutional framework that has safeguarded American liberty for over two centuries.[15] A measured approach, grounded in the principles of limited government and individual responsibility, offers the best path forward for addressing modern challenges without sacrificing the enduring wisdom of the founding documents.

Critics of conservative thought often contend that a rigid adherence to constitutional originalism stifles necessary progress and fails to account for the evolving needs of society. However, conservatives counter that the Constitution is not a static relic but a living document whose strength lies in its ability to endure through changing times while remaining anchored in immutable principles.[16] In this view, the true challenge lies not in abandoning constitutional norms but in reasserting their relevance in a political culture that has become increasingly fragmented and ideologically driven.

In addition to these theoretical concerns, the practical implications of a polarized constitutional discourse are far-reaching. Governance that is mired in partisan strife is ill-equipped to address the myriad challenges facing modern America—from economic inequality and national security threats to social fragmentation and global instability.[17] A return to constitutional principles, it is argued, would provide a common framework for addressing these issues in a manner that respects the rule of law and the balance of power envisioned by the founding fathers.

The conservative approach to mitigating the negative impacts of polarization on constitutional discourse also emphasizes the importance of civic engagement and the role of an informed citizenry. A populace that is well-versed in the historical context and fundamental values of the Constitution

---

[14] Amar, Akhil Reed. *America's Constitution: A Biography*. Random House, 2005.

[15] Wood, Gordon S. *The Radicalism of the American Revolution*. Vintage Books, 1993.

[16] Eskridge, William N. Jr. *Originalism in the Twenty-First Century*. Harvard University Press, 2012.

[17] Putnam, Robert D. *Bowling Alone: The Collapse and Revival of American Community*. Simon & Schuster, 2000.

is less likely to be swayed by partisan rhetoric and more likely to demand accountability from its leaders.[18] In this respect, the revitalization of civic education and public discourse centered on constitutional principles is seen as essential for restoring both the legitimacy of governance and the integrity of constitutional debate.

Furthermore, the integration of constitutional discourse into everyday political practice has the potential to foster a more inclusive and less divisive political culture. When constitutional principles are presented as the common denominator that unites rather than divides, they serve as a powerful antidote to the corrosive effects of polarization.[19] Conservatives believe that by reemphasizing the timeless values of liberty, justice, and limited government, America can begin to heal the divisions that have long undermined its democratic institutions.

The impacts on constitutional discourse and governance are not merely academic concerns; they have real-world implications for the stability and prosperity of the nation. When political debates are divorced from the foundational principles of the Constitution, governance becomes a contest of ideologies rather than a collaborative effort to serve the public good.[20] Such a shift not only erodes public trust in governmental institutions but also creates an environment in which extreme measures—both legislative and executive—can be justified in the name of partisan progress.

In conclusion, the effects of political polarization on constitutional discourse and governance are profound and multifaceted. The erosion of civil debate, the distortion of judicial interpretation, the fragmentation of civic education, and the politicization of constitutional amendment processes all point to a system in peril—a system that is straying from the ideals enshrined by our founding fathers.[21] Conservatives argue that the remedy lies in a steadfast commitment to the constitutional principles that have historically ensured both liberty and order in America.[22]

By reaffirming the original intent of the Constitution and reestablishing a common framework for constitutional discourse, it is possible to mitigate the negative impacts of polarization and restore the legitimacy of governance. Such an endeavor requires not only political will but also a collective recognition that the Constitution is the bedrock upon which the nation was built—a document that must continue to guide America through the challenges of the present and into the

---

[18] Galston, William A. *Civic Education and Democracy in America*. Johns Hopkins University Press, 2001.

[19] Sanger, Margaret. *Conservative Legacies: How the Founding Ideals Endure*. HarperCollins, 2010.

[20] Lipset, Seymour. *Political Man: The Social Bases of Politics*. Johns Hopkins University Press, 1960.

[21] Maier, Pauline. *American Scripture: Making the Declaration of Independence*. Vintage, 1998.

[22] Bickel, Alexander M. *The Least Dangerous Branch: The Supreme Court at the Bar of Politics*. Yale University Press, 1962.

future.[23] The task, though daunting, is essential if America is to preserve its legacy of freedom and stability for generations to come.[24]

Ultimately, the impacts of polarization on constitutional discourse and governance serve as a clarion call to return to the foundational values that have long defined American political life. A renewed commitment to constitutional principles, informed by the insights of the founding fathers and tempered by the wisdom of historical experience, offers the only viable path toward overcoming the divisiveness that threatens to undermine the very essence of American democracy.[25]

---

[23] Elazar, Daniel J. *Exploring Federalism*. University of Alabama Press, 1987.

[24] Waldman, Christopher. *The Unifying Power of the Constitution*. Oxford University Press, 2007.

[25] Iyengar, Shanto, and Nolan McCarty. *We Need to Talk About the Politics of Resentment*. Princeton University Press, 2018.

3. Role of Media and Public Opinion

The influence of media on public opinion has always been a critical factor in shaping the political landscape of the United States. In the modern era, this influence has grown exponentially, affecting the way citizens interpret and engage with the political process. This commentary examines the role of media and public opinion from a politically conservative perspective, emphasizing the need to return to constitutional principles as a means of countering partisan distortions and preserving the values established by our founding fathers.[1]

From the outset, it is essential to acknowledge that the media in America has evolved from a tool for disseminating factual information into an arena for ideological contestation. The founding fathers envisioned a free press as a watchdog for government and a vital component of an informed electorate. However, today's media environment is characterized by a proliferation of partisan news outlets and digital platforms that often prioritize sensationalism and ideological purity over balanced reporting. This shift has significant implications for public opinion, which increasingly mirrors the partisan divides that fragment American society.[2]

The conservative critique of modern media practices centers on the belief that the unchecked influence of partisan media undermines the objective dissemination of truth and distorts the public's understanding of constitutional values. Conservative scholars argue that, while freedom of the press is a cornerstone of American democracy, it must be exercised with a sense of responsibility that honors the constitutional tradition of promoting informed civic discourse. Unfortunately, the current landscape often features media that engages in selective reporting, thereby reinforcing existing biases rather than challenging them.[3]

One of the primary concerns among conservatives is that the modern media environment has created echo chambers where individuals are exposed predominantly to viewpoints that align with their preconceived beliefs. This phenomenon not only intensifies ideological divides but also impedes the development of a shared national narrative rooted in the principles of liberty and limited government. In contrast, the founding fathers understood that a well-informed public

---

[1] Hamilton, Alexander; Madison, James; Jay, John. *The Federalist Papers*. Penguin Classics, 2003.

[2] Madison, James. "Federalist No. 10." In *The Federalist Papers*, edited by Clinton Rossiter, Bantam Classics, 1961.

[3] Prior, Markus. *Post-Broadcast Democracy: How Media Choice Increases Inequality in Political Involvement and Polarizes Elections*. Cambridge University Press, 2007.

was essential for the maintenance of a free society, and they stressed the importance of a press that could offer diverse perspectives and foster healthy debate.[4]

The advent of digital technology and social media has further complicated the media landscape. While these platforms have democratized information by allowing virtually anyone to publish content, they have also led to the rapid spread of misinformation and ideological extremism. From a conservative standpoint, this technological revolution poses a threat to constitutional governance because it exacerbates the polarization that already plagues political discourse. When citizens are bombarded with misinformation and partisan rhetoric, the very foundation of rational debate is eroded, making it increasingly difficult to reach consensus on issues of national importance.[5]

Moreover, the role of media in shaping public opinion extends to the realm of political advertising and campaign financing. Conservative critics assert that the modern media ecosystem has become a tool for political manipulation, where powerful interest groups and partisan organizations invest heavily in shaping public sentiment through targeted messaging. This phenomenon undermines the principles of equal representation and informed consent that are central to the constitutional framework. The founding fathers, wary of the dangers of factionalism and undue influence, designed a system of checks and balances precisely to prevent any one group from dominating public discourse.[6]

In addition to the dissemination of information, the media plays a pivotal role in framing political narratives. The way issues are presented to the public can significantly influence perceptions of legitimacy and fairness. Conservatives contend that when the media frames debates in overly simplistic or emotionally charged terms, it obscures the complex realities of constitutional governance. For example, discussions about the balance of power between the federal government and the states are often reduced to stark dichotomies that do not reflect the nuanced intentions of the Constitution. Such reductive framing not only misleads the public but also hinders the development of policies that are grounded in a respectful understanding of our constitutional heritage.[7]

---

[4] Niemi, Richard G., and Jane Junn. *Civic Education: What Makes Students Learn*. Yale University Press, 1998.

[5] McCarty, Nolan, Keith T. Poole, and Howard Rosenthal. *Polarized America: The Dance of Ideology and Unequal Riches*. MIT Press, 2009.

[6] Binder, Sarah A. *Stalemate: Causes and Consequences of Legislative Gridlock*. Brookings Institution Press, 2003.

[7] Scalia, Antonin. *A Matter of Interpretation: Federal Courts and the Law*. Princeton University Press, 1997.

The impact of media on public opinion is also evident in the polarization of political discourse. As media outlets cater to increasingly segmented audiences, the result is a political environment where consensus becomes elusive. Public opinion, once shaped by a broad, shared understanding of national values, now diverges along partisan lines. Conservatives argue that this divergence is dangerous because it undermines the possibility of civic unity—a unity that is essential for the effective functioning of constitutional governance. When citizens are divided by the media's portrayal of political events, the social contract that binds the nation together is weakened, leading to legislative gridlock and governmental instability.[8]

Another important aspect of this discussion is the role of media literacy in sustaining a healthy republic. The founding fathers assumed that citizens would take personal responsibility for educating themselves about public affairs. In today's media-saturated environment, however, the ability to discern reliable information from partisan propaganda is not as widespread as it once was. Conservatives emphasize the need for educational reforms that stress media literacy and critical thinking, enabling citizens to navigate the complex information landscape and make decisions based on fact rather than emotion.[9]

Furthermore, public opinion is not formed solely by media exposure; it is also shaped by cultural values and historical context. The conservative perspective holds that the enduring principles of the Constitution—such as limited government, individual liberty, and the rule of law—provide a stable foundation for public opinion that can withstand the vicissitudes of partisan media. By reasserting these constitutional values, conservatives believe that the nation can counteract the divisive effects of modern media and foster a more informed and unified citizenry.[10]

A related concern is the impact of media on political accountability. In a well-functioning democracy, the media serves as a check on government power by exposing corruption and holding leaders accountable for their actions. However, when media outlets are driven by partisan agendas, their role as impartial watchdogs is compromised. Conservatives argue that partisan media often shields political figures from accountability if they align with certain ideological positions, while unfairly scrutinizing those who challenge the dominant narrative. This selective

---

[8] Lipset, Seymour. *Political Man: The Social Bases of Politics*. Johns Hopkins University Press, 1960.

[9] Torney-Purta, Judith, et al. *Citizenship and Political Participation: Political Science Perspectives*. Rowman & Littlefield, 2001.

[10] Friedman, Milton. *Capitalism and Freedom*. University of Chicago Press, 2002.

accountability not only distorts public opinion but also undermines the integrity of constitutional governance by promoting favoritism and bias.[11]

In recent years, debates over "fake news" have further highlighted the challenges posed by the modern media landscape. Conservatives contend that the term is frequently misused to dismiss legitimate journalism that does not conform to a particular ideological perspective. This tactic, they argue, is a deliberate attempt to delegitimize independent media and discredit critical reporting on governmental overreach or constitutional misinterpretations. The erosion of trust in the media is particularly troubling because it weakens the public's ability to engage in informed debate about constitutional issues.[12]

Public opinion, when shaped by a fragmented and partisan media, can lead to a host of adverse outcomes for constitutional governance. One significant consequence is the undermining of the rule of law. When citizens base their political judgments on emotionally charged or misleading media reports, they are more likely to support policies that deviate from the constitutional principles of fairness and justice. Conservatives warn that such a trend can pave the way for arbitrary decision-making by government officials, ultimately eroding the checks and balances that are vital for preventing tyranny.[13]

The role of media in influencing public opinion also extends to the shaping of electoral outcomes. In an environment where media bias is prevalent, voters are often exposed to distorted portrayals of candidates and issues. This, in turn, can lead to the election of officials whose platforms are not aligned with the constitutional ideals that have historically underpinned American governance. Conservatives argue that the integrity of elections depends on a media landscape that prioritizes factual reporting and balanced analysis over partisan sensationalism. Without such an environment, the electorate is deprived of the opportunity to make decisions that reflect a true understanding of constitutional values.[14]

Additionally, the interplay between media and public opinion has a profound effect on policy-making. Legislators, who are sensitive to the demands of their constituents, may feel compelled to adopt policies that are more reflective of the prevailing media narrative than of sound constitutional principles. This can lead to legislative overreach or, conversely, to a paralysis in

---

[11] Maier, Pauline. *American Scripture: Making the Declaration of Independence*. Vintage, 1998.

[12] Waldman, Christopher. *The Unifying Power of the Constitution*. Oxford University Press, 2007.

[13] Bickel, Alexander M. *The Least Dangerous Branch: The Supreme Court at the Bar of Politics*. Yale University Press, 1962.

[14] Eskridge, William N. Jr. Originalism in the Twenty-First Century. Harvard University Press, 2012.

governance when competing media narratives create insurmountable ideological divides. From a conservative viewpoint, it is essential that policy decisions remain grounded in the timeless wisdom of the Constitution rather than in the transient moods of public opinion as shaped by partisan media.[15]

Another dimension of this issue is the international perception of American democracy. As the United States has long been regarded as a beacon of freedom and constitutional governance, the growing polarization of media and public opinion risks tarnishing that image. Foreign governments and international observers may perceive the internal divisions exacerbated by media bias as signs of instability and weakness, thereby undermining America's moral authority on the world stage. Conservatives maintain that upholding a media environment that respects constitutional principles is not only crucial for domestic stability but also for preserving the nation's global reputation as a defender of liberty and the rule of law.[16]

The challenge for conservatives, therefore, is to develop strategies that can mitigate the adverse effects of partisan media on public opinion while reinforcing the constitutional foundations of American governance. This involves not only advocating for reforms in media practices and journalistic standards but also promoting a renewed emphasis on civic education and media literacy. By fostering a public that is both well-informed and deeply rooted in the values of the Constitution, conservatives believe that it is possible to counterbalance the divisive influence of modern media and restore a sense of national unity.[17]

Moreover, it is imperative to encourage media outlets to adopt practices that align with the principles of fairness, objectivity, and accountability. Regulatory reforms that promote transparency in media ownership and funding, as well as initiatives aimed at curbing the spread of misinformation, are essential components of a broader strategy to realign public opinion with constitutional values. Conservatives argue that such measures are necessary to ensure that the media serves its intended purpose as a guardian of truth and a facilitator of informed democratic participation.[18]

In conclusion, the role of media and public opinion in contemporary American politics is both profound and multifaceted. The conservative perspective contends that the current media environment—characterized by partisan bias, sensationalism, and the erosion of journalistic

---

[15] Putnam, Robert D. *Bowling Alone: The Collapse and Revival of American Community*. Simon & Schuster, 2000.

[16] Kirk, Russell. *The Conservative Mind: From Burke to Eliot*. Regnery Publishing, 1953.

[17] Galston, William A. *Civic Education and Democracy in America*. Johns Hopkins University Press, 2001.

[18] Sanger, Margaret. *Conservative Legacies: How the Founding Ideals Endure*. HarperCollins, 2010.

standards—poses a significant threat to the constitutional order envisioned by our founding fathers. The unchecked influence of media not only distorts public opinion but also undermines the rule of law, diminishes political accountability, and hinders the effective functioning of governance.[19]

To safeguard the legacy of constitutional governance and to honor the principles upon which America was founded, it is essential that the media be reformed to reflect the values of truth, fairness, and objectivity. Simultaneously, efforts must be made to bolster media literacy and civic education so that citizens can discern fact from partisan propaganda and engage in constructive political discourse. By reasserting the central role of the Constitution in guiding public life, conservatives believe that America can overcome the challenges posed by a fragmented media landscape and restore the unity and stability that are the hallmarks of a truly free society.[20]

The task ahead is formidable, but the stakes are too high to accept the status quo. A recommitment to constitutional principles, combined with a rigorous demand for accountability in the media, represents the best hope for preserving the integrity of American democracy. As the nation faces the dual challenges of polarization and media manipulation, it must draw upon the enduring wisdom of its founding documents and the visionary insights of its founders to navigate this perilous landscape.[21]

In the end, the health of public opinion and the robustness of constitutional governance are inextricably linked. A media environment that upholds the principles of truth and impartiality is indispensable for a society that values the rule of law and individual liberty. Conservatives argue that by restoring balance to media practices and by fostering an informed, civically engaged citizenry, America can once again embody the ideals that have sustained it for over two centuries.[22]

The future of American democracy depends on our ability to reconcile the modern realities of media and public opinion with the timeless values of the Constitution. Only by doing so can we ensure that the United States remains a beacon of freedom, justice, and order for generations to come. This vision, rooted in the lessons of history and the wisdom of the founding fathers, offers a clear path forward in a time of unprecedented challenge and division.[23]

---

[19] Lasch, Christopher. *The Culture of Narcissism: American Life in an Age of Diminishing Expectations*. W.W. Norton & Company, 1979.

[20] Friedman, Thomas L. *The Lexus and the Olive Tree*. Farrar, Straus and Giroux, 1999.

[21] Wood, Gordon S. *The Radicalism of the American Revolution*. Vintage Books, 1993.

[22] Iyengar, Shanto, and Nolan McCarty. *We Need to Talk About the Politics of Resentment*. Princeton University Press, 2018.

[23] Amar, Akhil Reed. *America's Constitution: A Biography*. Random House, 2005.

Thus, it is incumbent upon policymakers, educators, media professionals, and citizens alike to work together to restore the central role of constitutional principles in public discourse. In this collective effort lies the promise of a more united, resilient, and principled nation—a nation that remains true to its founding ideals even in the face of relentless partisan pressures and a rapidly evolving media landscape.[24]

Ultimately, the role of media and public opinion in shaping the destiny of America cannot be overstated. As we confront the challenges of polarization and media bias, we must reaffirm our commitment to the constitutional values that have long been the bedrock of our national identity. In doing so, we honor the legacy of our founding fathers and ensure that the United States Constitution continues to serve as the ultimate safeguard of liberty and justice in our time.[25]

---

[24] Elazar, Daniel J. *Exploring Federalism*. University of Alabama Press, 1987.

[25] McCarty, Nolan, Keith T. Poole, and Howard Rosenthal. *Polarized America: The Dance of Ideology and Unequal Riches*. MIT Press, 2009.

4. Constitutional Safeguards against Extremism

In an era marked by unprecedented ideological fervor and political extremism, the United States Constitution remains the paramount safeguard against the forces that threaten to undermine the nation's founding principles. This commentary examines the role of constitutional safeguards in curbing extremism, emphasizing how the deliberate framework established by our founding fathers continues to serve as an enduring bulwark for liberty, order, and the rule of law. Rooted in a politically conservative perspective, the analysis underscores that the resilience of the Constitution lies not in its capacity to adapt to every transient political trend but in its immutable structure, designed to contain and neutralize extremist impulses.[1]

The framers of the Constitution were acutely aware of the dangers posed by factions and extremist ideologies. In crafting a government founded on the separation of powers, checks and balances, and federalism, they sought to prevent any one group or ideology from commandeering the state apparatus. This deliberate dispersion of power was intended to foster a climate of moderation and compromise, thereby ensuring that radical ideas could be debated and refined rather than imposed through force. The constitutional framework not only reflects the wisdom of those early statesmen but also provides a roadmap for managing the inevitable tensions between competing visions of governance.[2]

At the heart of the constitutional design is the system of checks and balances, which remains one of the most significant tools against extremism. By dividing power among the legislative, executive, and judicial branches, the Constitution ensures that no single branch can unilaterally advance an agenda that might lead to authoritarianism or the erosion of individual rights. This structural mechanism is particularly crucial in times of national crisis, when extremist rhetoric can gain traction. Rather than allowing rapid and unchecked governmental action, the checks and balances system compels deliberate decision-making and broad consensus, thereby stabilizing the political environment.[3]

Federalism, another cornerstone of the constitutional order, plays a vital role in insulating the nation from extremist policies. By allocating power between the national government and the states, federalism enables localities to act as laboratories of democracy. This decentralized model

---

[1] Hamilton, Alexander; Madison, James; Jay, John. *The Federalist Papers*. Penguin Classics, 2003.

[2] Madison, James. "Federalist No. 51." In *The Federalist Papers*, edited by Clinton Rossiter, Bantam Classics, 1961.

[3] Binder, Sarah A. *Stalemate: Causes and Consequences of Legislative Gridlock*. Brookings Institution Press, 2003.

allows communities to tailor solutions to their unique needs while simultaneously preventing the concentration of power that can lead to tyranny. The founding fathers championed federalism as a means to limit governmental overreach, a safeguard that today remains critical in countering the impulses of extremism that might otherwise centralize power and stifle dissent.[4]

A further constitutional safeguard is the Bill of Rights, which enshrines individual liberties and limits the scope of governmental authority. The protections afforded by the First, Second, and subsequent Amendments ensure that even in times of heightened political tension, the rights of citizens are preserved against encroachments by a potentially overzealous state. These guarantees serve as a constant reminder that the power of the government is not absolute and that the preservation of personal freedoms is paramount. In a climate where extremist ideologies often call for the curtailment of dissent and the suppression of unpopular views, the Bill of Rights acts as a legal bulwark protecting free speech, freedom of assembly, and other fundamental liberties.[5]

The role of an independent judiciary cannot be overstated in this context. Judicial review, as established by the landmark case Marbury v. Madison, empowers courts to strike down laws and executive actions that contravene the Constitution. This judicial oversight is essential in preventing the escalation of extremist policies into systemic abuses of power. Conservative legal scholars argue that the adherence to originalism—the interpretation of the Constitution in accordance with its original meaning—helps maintain a stable legal order that resists the temptations of judicial activism. In this way, the courts serve as a final arbiter, ensuring that the rule of law prevails even when political passions run high.[6]

The constitutional amendment process, deliberately designed to be slow and arduous, is another critical safeguard against extremism. The difficulty inherent in amending the Constitution ensures that only proposals with broad-based support and thoughtful deliberation can alter the nation's fundamental law. This high threshold for change is a deliberate mechanism to preserve the core principles of American governance, preventing transient political passions from triggering precipitous alterations to the constitutional order. In effect, the amendment process guarantees that only those changes which reflect a deep and enduring consensus among the people—and not the fleeting whims of extremist movements—become part of the constitutional fabric.[7]

---

[4] Elazar, Daniel J. *Exploring Federalism*. University of Alabama Press, 1987.

[5] Amar, Akhil Reed. *America's Constitution: A Biography*. Random House, 2005.

[6] Scalia, Antonin. *A Matter of Interpretation: Federal Courts and the Law*. Princeton University Press, 1997.

[7] Eskridge, William N. Jr. *Originalism in the Twenty-First Century*. Harvard University Press, 2012.

Constitutional safeguards also extend to the role of civic institutions and traditions that have been cultivated over centuries. A strong commitment to the principles of civic virtue and public discourse is essential for sustaining a constitutional order that resists extremism. The founding fathers believed that a well-informed and engaged citizenry was the best defense against the rise of radical ideologies. Today, this belief is reflected in the emphasis placed on civic education and the promotion of public debate grounded in historical context and constitutional principles. By fostering an environment where citizens are encouraged to critically engage with political ideas, the nation can create a collective resistance to the allure of extremist rhetoric.[8]

Moreover, the conservative perspective stresses that constitutional safeguards are not merely reactive measures but proactive commitments to a philosophy of government that prioritizes liberty, responsibility, and the rule of law. The enduring relevance of the Constitution is evident in its ability to adapt to new challenges without sacrificing its fundamental principles. While political and social conditions evolve, the core values enshrined in the Constitution—such as limited government, individual rights, and the separation of powers—remain constant. This timelessness ensures that, even in an era of rapid change and uncertainty, the constitutional framework can provide a steady foundation for governance.[9]

Critics of conservative thought sometimes argue that the rigidity of constitutional safeguards might impede necessary reforms in the face of modern challenges. However, conservatives counter that any reform must be firmly anchored in constitutional principles in order to preserve the integrity of the nation's legal and political systems. The measured pace of constitutional change is not a barrier to progress but a safeguard against the rapid, and often untested, alterations that can lead to instability. By insisting on broad consensus and deliberate change, the constitutional framework ensures that only those reforms that are thoroughly vetted and widely supported are implemented.[10]

The interplay between constitutional safeguards and political extremism is also evident in the realm of public policy. When extremist ideas gain traction in the political arena, they often seek to exploit the mechanisms of government to bypass traditional checks on power. However, the constitutional framework is designed to prevent such exploitation by requiring transparency, accountability, and adherence to established legal processes. For example, executive orders

---

[8] Torney-Purta, Judith, et al. *Citizenship and Political Participation: Political Science Perspectives*. Rowman & Littlefield, 2001.

[9] Friedman, Milton. *Capitalism and Freedom*. University of Chicago Press, 2002.

[10] Maier, Pauline. *American Scripture: Making the Declaration of Independence*. Vintage, 1998.

and emergency powers—while necessary in times of crisis—are subject to judicial review and legislative oversight, ensuring that they cannot be used as vehicles for extremist policies.[11]

In the context of contemporary political polarization, constitutional safeguards offer a counterweight to the forces that seek to erode traditional values and disrupt social order. The conservative view holds that the Constitution provides a common foundation upon which diverse political opinions can coexist, even in a highly charged environment. Rather than capitulating to the pressures of ideological extremism, the constitutional framework encourages debate and dissent within a stable and predictable legal order. This balance between stability and change is one of the enduring strengths of American constitutionalism and a critical defense against the rise of radical movements.[12]

The historical legacy of the founding fathers serves as both inspiration and validation for the continued relevance of constitutional safeguards. Their experiences under colonial rule and the brutal tyranny of foreign powers instilled in them a profound commitment to individual liberty and self-governance. By enshrining these ideals in the Constitution, they created a document that not only addressed the challenges of their own time but also provided a durable framework for future generations. This historical continuity reinforces the argument that constitutional safeguards are not merely relics of the past but active, living instruments for preserving freedom in the present.[13]

The role of political institutions in upholding constitutional safeguards is further reinforced by the conservative belief in limited government. Excessive government intervention, often advocated by extremist factions, can lead to the erosion of personal freedoms and the concentration of power. Conservatives argue that by adhering to the constitutional principle of limited government, society can maintain a balance between necessary state functions and individual autonomy. This balance is essential in preventing the slide into authoritarianism—a risk that is particularly acute when extremist ideologies seek to expand state control in the name of public good.[14]

Furthermore, constitutional safeguards are reflected in the manner in which American political discourse is conducted. The adversarial system, while sometimes leading to gridlock, is designed

---

[11] Binder, Sarah A. *Stalemate: Causes and Consequences of Legislative Gridlock*. Brookings Institution Press, 2003.

[12] McCarty, Nolan, Keith T. Poole, and Howard Rosenthal. *Polarized America: The Dance of Ideology and Unequal Riches*. MIT Press, 2009.

[13] Wood, Gordon S. *The Radicalism of the American Revolution*. Vintage Books, 1993.

[14] Lipset, Seymour. *Political Man: The Social Bases of Politics*. Johns Hopkins University Press, 1960.

to ensure that multiple viewpoints are heard and that no single perspective dominates the national conversation. This competitive environment compels political actors to justify their policies on the basis of constitutional principles rather than merely appealing to populist sentiment. In doing so, the system creates a natural check against extremism by forcing ideologues to engage with the broader, time-tested values that underpin American democracy.[15]

It is also important to consider the international dimension of constitutional safeguards. The United States has long been a symbol of liberty and the rule of law, and its Constitution has served as a model for democracies around the world. In an age when extremist ideologies are on the rise globally, the American constitutional framework stands as a testament to the enduring power of balanced government. By demonstrating that a system based on separation of powers, federalism, and the protection of individual rights can effectively manage internal dissent and external pressures, the United States offers a compelling counter-narrative to extremist models of governance.[16]

The modern challenges posed by digital communication and social media have also prompted a reevaluation of how constitutional safeguards function in a rapidly evolving information landscape. While extremist movements have exploited these technologies to disseminate radical ideas, the constitutional principles of free speech and due process continue to provide the legal framework necessary to challenge such abuses. Conservative legal scholars advocate for a robust defense of these principles, arguing that any attempt to curtail free expression in the name of fighting extremism must be carefully weighed against the risk of undermining the very freedoms the Constitution is designed to protect.[17]

Public trust in the constitutional system is further bolstered by the transparency and accountability that these safeguards engender. When government actions are subject to rigorous judicial review and legislative oversight, citizens can be confident that power is not being exercised arbitrarily. This confidence is critical in times of crisis, when extremist groups seek to exploit uncertainty and fear to advance their agendas. By upholding constitutional norms, the United States can maintain the legitimacy of its political institutions and ensure that even in the face of radical challenges, the rule of law prevails.[18]

---

[15] Prior, Markus. *Post-Broadcast Democracy: How Media Choice Increases Inequality in Political Involvement and Polarizes Elections*. Cambridge University Press, 2007.

[16] Kirk, Russell. *The Conservative Mind: From Burke to Eliot*. Regnery Publishing, 1953.

[17] Waldman, Christopher. *The Unifying Power of the Constitution*. Oxford University Press, 2007.

[18] Iyengar, Shanto, and Nolan McCarty. *We Need to Talk About the Politics of Resentment*. Princeton University Press, 2018.

Moreover, the educational system plays a pivotal role in reinforcing constitutional safeguards by instilling a deep understanding of the nation's founding principles in future generations. A robust civic education that emphasizes the historical context and enduring relevance of the Constitution equips citizens with the knowledge to recognize and resist extremist rhetoric. Conservatives argue that by fostering an informed electorate, society can build resilience against the seductive appeal of radical ideologies, ensuring that constitutional principles remain at the core of American political life.[19]

In conclusion, the constitutional safeguards enshrined in the United States Constitution are the primary defense against the dangers posed by political extremism. Through the separation of powers, federalism, the Bill of Rights, and a deliberate amendment process, the founding framework has created a resilient system capable of withstanding the pressures of radical ideologies. This enduring design, rooted in the visionary insights of the founding fathers, provides a stable and predictable foundation for governance even in an era marked by deep polarization and ideological fervor.[20]

By steadfastly adhering to the principles of limited government, individual liberty, and the rule of law, Americans can ensure that extremist impulses are contained and that the constitutional order continues to guide the nation toward a future of freedom and prosperity. The conservative commitment to these ideals reaffirms the belief that the Constitution is not only a historical document but a living instrument for preserving the integrity of American democracy.[21]

As the nation confronts the challenges of contemporary extremism, it must draw upon the enduring wisdom of its founding documents and the lessons of its past. The constitutional safeguards against extremism serve as a reminder that, while political movements may come and go, the principles of liberty, justice, and limited government remain constant. In upholding these values, America can resist the siren call of radicalism and ensure that its political system continues to serve the common good rather than the interests of a narrow ideological minority.[22]

Ultimately, the preservation of the constitutional order is not an abstract ideal but a practical necessity for maintaining a free and just society. By reinforcing the mechanisms that have long

---

[19] Galston, William A. *Civic Education and Democracy in America*. Johns Hopkins University Press, 2001.

[20] Bickel, Alexander M. *The Least Dangerous Branch: The Supreme Court at the Bar of Politics*. Yale University Press, 1962.

[21] Sanger, Margaret. *Conservative Legacies: How the Founding Ideals Endure*. HarperCollins, 2010.

[22] Lasch, Christopher. *The Culture of Narcissism: American Life in an Age of Diminishing Expectations*. W.W. Norton & Company, 1979.

protected against the concentration of power and the rise of extremism, the United States can navigate the complexities of modern governance without sacrificing the core principles that have defined its national character. This commitment to constitutional integrity is the surest means of safeguarding America against the divisive and destructive forces of radicalism.[23]

In embracing these constitutional safeguards, policymakers, educators, and citizens alike reaffirm their dedication to the enduring legacy of the founding fathers. Their vision, enshrined in the Constitution, offers a timeless guide for balancing the demands of governance with the imperatives of individual freedom and national unity. As America faces an uncertain future, the steadfast defense of constitutional principles remains the most effective antidote to extremism and the key to preserving the American experiment for generations to come.[24]

Thus, in the face of contemporary challenges, the constitutional safeguards against extremism stand as a testament to the enduring wisdom of America's founding ideals. Through careful adherence to the separation of powers, federalism, and the protection of individual rights, the nation can continue to thrive as a beacon of liberty and stability, even as it confronts the pressures of an increasingly polarized political landscape.[25]

---

[23] Putnam, Robert D. *Bowling Alone: The Collapse and Revival of American Community*. Simon & Schuster, 2000.

[24] Elazar, Daniel J. *Exploring Federalism*. University of Alabama Press, 1987.

[25] Scalia, Antonin. *A Matter of Interpretation: Federal Courts and the Law*. Princeton University Press, 1997.

5. Pathways Toward National Unity and Reform

In an era where deep ideological divides and partisan gridlock threaten the very fabric of American governance, a renewed focus on pathways toward national unity and reform is imperative. This commentary examines the steps necessary to achieve a revitalized national consensus, firmly anchored in the timeless principles of the United States Constitution. Approaching the subject from a politically conservative perspective and drawing inspiration from the wisdom of our founding fathers, this analysis highlights that true reform must begin with a commitment to constitutional principles, respect for individual liberty, and a shared commitment to limited government.[1]

The founding fathers, in their wisdom, designed the Constitution not as a static document but as a dynamic framework capable of withstanding the trials of history. They understood that a successful republic required not only robust safeguards against extremism but also mechanisms to foster unity and common purpose. Central to this vision is the notion that national unity is built on a foundation of shared values, such as the rule of law, individual freedom, and a commitment to civic responsibility. In today's politically polarized climate, returning to these core values is the first essential step toward overcoming division and promoting meaningful reform.[2]

A critical pathway to unity is the reinvigoration of civic education. The founding fathers believed that an informed citizenry was indispensable for the survival of a free republic. Today, however, civic education has been undermined by partisan narratives and a fragmented public discourse. A comprehensive reemphasis on the history of the Constitution, the sacrifices made for American freedom, and the enduring importance of civic engagement is necessary to bridge ideological divides. By equipping citizens with a clear understanding of the nation's founding principles, educators can foster a renewed sense of patriotism and collective responsibility that transcends partisan loyalties.[3]

Economic reform, too, plays a pivotal role in paving the way toward national unity. Conservatives contend that the principles of free enterprise, personal responsibility, and limited government intervention are not only the engines of prosperity but also the pillars of a stable society. Policies that promote economic freedom and reduce burdensome regulation can help alleviate the

---

[1] Hamilton, Alexander; Madison, James; Jay, John. *The Federalist Papers*. Penguin Classics, 2003.

[2] Madison, James. "Federalist No. 51." In *The Federalist Papers*, edited by Clinton Rossiter, Bantam Classics, 1961.

[3] Niemi, Richard G., and Jane Junn. *Civic Education: What Makes Students Learn*. Yale University Press, 1998.

frustrations that fuel partisan extremism. When individuals are empowered to succeed through their own efforts and when economic policies are grounded in constitutional principles, a more cohesive society emerges—one in which opportunities are widely available and the specter of economic disenfranchisement is diminished.[4]

Furthermore, the reestablishment of robust local governance can serve as a catalyst for national unity. Federalism, as enshrined in the Constitution, allows states to serve as laboratories of democracy where innovative reforms can be tested on a smaller scale before being adopted nationally. This decentralized approach not only prevents the concentration of power at the federal level but also enables communities to address local issues in ways that reflect their unique values and circumstances. By strengthening the role of local governments, America can foster a bottom-up process of reform that reinforces the constitutional principle of subsidiarity and ultimately contributes to a more united national identity.[5]

Another essential component of the pathway to unity is judicial restraint and adherence to originalist principles. The Supreme Court and lower courts have a profound impact on shaping public policy and interpreting the Constitution. When judges interpret the Constitution based on its original meaning, they provide a stable legal framework that resists the pressures of transient political trends. Such an approach prevents the politicization of judicial decisions and helps ensure that reforms are consistent with the historical intentions of the founding fathers. A judiciary that remains faithful to constitutional originalism not only protects individual rights but also fosters a sense of national continuity that is critical for unity.[6]

The media, as the primary conduit of information, also bears significant responsibility for promoting national unity. In recent decades, partisan media outlets have contributed to the polarization of public opinion by emphasizing ideological conflicts over common ground. Conservatives argue that a reinvigorated commitment to journalistic integrity, objectivity, and a balanced presentation of news is crucial for restoring public trust. When the media serves as a forum for informed and respectful debate, it can help bridge the gaps between competing viewpoints and create a more unified electorate. This, in turn, empowers citizens to engage in constructive dialogue about reforms that benefit the nation as a whole.[7]

---

[4] Friedman, Milton. *Capitalism and Freedom*. University of Chicago Press, 2002.

[5] Elazar, Daniel J. *Exploring Federalism*. University of Alabama Press, 1987.

[6] Scalia, Antonin. *A Matter of Interpretation: Federal Courts and the Law*. Princeton University Press, 1997.

[7] Prior, Markus. *Post-Broadcast Democracy: How Media Choice Increases Inequality in Political Involvement and Polarizes Elections*. Cambridge University Press, 2007.

Moreover, the role of religious and community institutions in fostering unity should not be overlooked. For many Americans, churches, civic clubs, and local organizations have historically served as the bedrock of communal life and moral guidance. These institutions provide a space for individuals to connect over shared values and traditions, reinforcing the cultural and ethical underpinnings of the Constitution. By supporting and revitalizing these community networks, policymakers can help rebuild the social cohesion that is essential for any reform effort. A society in which citizens are bonded by common beliefs and mutual respect is far less susceptible to the divisive forces of partisan extremism.[8]

Political leadership is another critical pathway toward national unity and reform. Leaders who are guided by constitutional principles and who exhibit a commitment to civility, bipartisanship, and public service can play a transformative role in healing the divisions that currently beset the nation. Effective leadership demands not only the articulation of a clear vision for the future but also the willingness to make difficult compromises in the interest of the common good. When political leaders prioritize national unity over narrow partisan interests, they set a powerful example for the citizenry and create a climate in which meaningful reform is possible.[9]

Reforming campaign finance laws is also integral to fostering unity and reducing the corrosive influence of money in politics. The founding fathers were deeply skeptical of concentrated wealth and its potential to subvert the democratic process. In modern times, however, the significant influence of special interests and large donors has contributed to an environment in which policy decisions often reflect the interests of the few rather than the needs of the many. Conservatives argue that implementing reforms to increase transparency and reduce the undue influence of money in politics can help restore trust in government institutions. A political system that is responsive to the needs of its citizens—rather than to the agendas of powerful interest groups—is more likely to generate the broad-based support required for lasting reform.[10]

The restoration of national unity also depends on a recalibration of immigration policies to reflect constitutional values and the nation's historical experience. While immigration has long enriched American society, debates over its regulation have often become highly polarized. Conservatives maintain that a well-regulated immigration system, one that respects the rule of law and national sovereignty, is essential for maintaining social order and economic stability. Such an approach

---

[8] Torney-Purta, Judith, et al. *Citizenship and Political Participation: Political Science Perspectives*. Rowman & Littlefield, 2001.

[9] Maier, Pauline. *American Scripture: Making the Declaration of Independence*. Vintage, 1998.

[10] Binder, Sarah A. *Stalemate: Causes and Consequences of Legislative Gridlock*. Brookings Institution Press, 2003.

balances the benefits of cultural diversity with the need for coherent national policy, ultimately contributing to a more unified society.[11]

In addressing national disunity, it is also necessary to confront the challenges posed by radical ideologies that exploit identity politics to fracture the nation. Conservatives contend that the emphasis on group identity over individual merit undermines the very essence of American republicanism. By reasserting the constitutional principle that every citizen is entitled to equal treatment under the law, regardless of race, gender, or religion, policymakers can help dispel divisive narratives. Promoting policies that recognize the shared heritage and common destiny of all Americans is a critical step toward healing the rifts that have widened in recent years.[12]

A further pathway toward unity lies in restoring respect for constitutional processes and institutions. The legitimacy of government rests on the belief that public institutions operate in accordance with established constitutional norms. When citizens perceive that elections, legislative procedures, and judicial decisions are conducted fairly and transparently, trust in government is bolstered. Conservatives argue that upholding the integrity of these processes is essential not only for effective governance but also for the cultivation of national unity. This can be achieved through measures that ensure accountability, reinforce the separation of powers, and promote adherence to the Constitution in all branches of government.[13]

The importance of national unity extends to the realm of foreign policy, where a divided nation is less capable of asserting its interests on the global stage. A unified America, guided by the principles enshrined in the Constitution, is better positioned to promote freedom, democracy, and the rule of law internationally. Conservatives maintain that a coherent and consistent foreign policy, rooted in American values, enhances the nation's ability to lead and to inspire confidence among its allies. In turn, this international strength reinforces domestic unity by fostering a sense of pride and shared purpose among citizens.[14]

Another crucial element in the pursuit of unity and reform is the revitalization of public discourse. The quality of political debate has deteriorated in recent years, with rhetoric frequently characterized by vitriol and intolerance. Conservatives believe that restoring civility in public discourse is imperative for overcoming partisan animosities and reaching consensus on reform measures. This involves encouraging respectful dialogue, fostering an environment in which diverse opinions

---

[11] Kirk, Russell. *The Conservative Mind: From Burke to Eliot*. Regnery Publishing, 1953.

[12] Lipset, Seymour. *Political Man: The Social Bases of Politics*. Johns Hopkins University Press, 1960.

[13] Amar, Akhil Reed. *America's Constitution: A Biography*. Random House, 2005.

[14] Eskridge, William N. Jr. *Originalism in the Twenty-First Century*. Harvard University Press, 2012.

can be expressed without fear of retribution, and promoting a culture of intellectual humility. By elevating the standards of public debate, the nation can create the conditions necessary for substantive policy discussions that bridge ideological divides.[15]

The role of technology in shaping public opinion and facilitating reform must also be acknowledged. While digital platforms have contributed to the spread of misinformation and polarization, they also offer unprecedented opportunities for civic engagement and grassroots organizing. Conservatives argue that harnessing the positive aspects of technology—such as increased access to information and the ability to mobilize communities—can support efforts to build national unity. Initiatives that promote digital literacy, combat online disinformation, and encourage respectful online interactions are essential components of a broader strategy to reinvigorate civic participation and foster a more united citizenry.[16]

In addition to these measures, a commitment to fiscal responsibility and sound government management is central to the conservative vision for reform. When government spending is aligned with constitutional principles of limited government and accountability, it not only prevents waste and inefficiency but also reinforces the trust of citizens. Conservatives assert that responsible fiscal policy is a unifying force because it demonstrates that the government is working in the best interests of the people. By prioritizing balanced budgets, reducing unnecessary bureaucracy, and ensuring that public funds are used prudently, policymakers can create a foundation for sustainable reform and national unity.[17]

At its core, the pathway toward national unity and reform is about restoring a sense of shared destiny among Americans. This begins with a recognition of the common values that have historically bound the nation together—values articulated by the founding fathers and enshrined in the Constitution. Conservatives contend that by returning to these fundamental principles, the nation can overcome the divisions that have been exacerbated by partisan politics and cultural fragmentation. This process requires both individual commitment and collective action, as citizens, community leaders, and policymakers work together to reaffirm the ideals that have long defined the American experiment.[18]

---

[15] McCarty, Nolan, Keith T. Poole, and Howard Rosenthal. *Polarized America: The Dance of Ideology and Unequal Riches*. MIT Press, 2009.

[16] Waldman, Christopher. *The Unifying Power of the Constitution*. Oxford University Press, 2007.

[17] Iyengar, Shanto, and Nolan McCarty. *We Need to Talk About the Politics of Resentment*. Princeton University Press, 2018.

[18] Galston, William A. *Civic Education and Democracy in America*. Johns Hopkins University Press, 2001.

The role of political institutions in facilitating reform cannot be underestimated. In recent years, the growing influence of partisan politics has often obstructed meaningful legislative progress. Conservatives argue that restoring the proper functioning of institutions—such as Congress, the presidency, and the judiciary—requires a renewed adherence to constitutional norms and a commitment to compromise. When elected officials prioritize the common good over narrow partisan interests, they pave the way for policies that address the nation's most pressing challenges. Institutional reform, including measures to increase transparency, accountability, and efficiency, is essential for rebuilding public trust and uniting the electorate around a shared vision for the future.[19]

A key element in achieving national unity is the cultivation of leadership that transcends partisan divisions. True leadership, as envisioned by the founding fathers, is grounded in a commitment to public service, integrity, and the defense of constitutional values. Conservative leaders who exhibit these qualities can serve as role models, inspiring citizens to set aside partisan differences in pursuit of a higher national purpose. By promoting leadership that is focused on common goals rather than divisive ideologies, the nation can build a political culture that is conducive to meaningful reform and lasting unity.[20]

Finally, the process of national reform must be underpinned by a spirit of optimism and hope—a belief that, despite current challenges, America can overcome its divisions and emerge stronger. The founding fathers themselves faced immense obstacles as they sought to create a new nation based on the principles of liberty and self-governance. Their example reminds us that unity and reform are not achieved overnight but are the result of persistent effort, steadfast commitment, and an unwavering faith in the values that have sustained the nation for over two centuries. By channeling this historical legacy into contemporary political action, Americans can forge a path toward a future marked by greater unity, prosperity, and freedom.[21]

In conclusion, the pathways toward national unity and reform lie in a comprehensive approach that reaffirms the constitutional foundations of American governance while addressing the economic, social, and institutional challenges of our time. Through revitalized civic education, economic reforms grounded in free enterprise, the strengthening of local governance, and a recommitment to judicial and institutional integrity, America can overcome the forces of polarization and

[19] Bickel, Alexander M. *The Least Dangerous Branch: The Supreme Court at the Bar of Politics*. Yale University Press, 1962.

[20] Sanger, Margaret. *Conservative Legacies: How the Founding Ideals Endure*. HarperCollins, 2010.

[21] Lasch, Christopher. *The Culture of Narcissism: American Life in an Age of Diminishing Expectations*. W.W. Norton & Company, 1979.

division. In addition, by promoting media responsibility, community engagement, and responsible leadership, the nation can create an environment in which national unity is not only possible but inevitable.[22]

The conservative perspective asserts that the solutions to our nation's challenges are found not in abandoning our founding principles but in renewing our commitment to them. It is through this steadfast adherence to the Constitution and the values it represents that America can chart a course toward genuine reform and long-lasting unity. As the nation moves forward, the lessons of the past must serve as a guide for the future—a future in which the ideals of liberty, justice, and limited government remain the cornerstones of American democracy.[23]

Ultimately, the promise of national unity and reform is within reach if Americans are willing to work together and embrace the constitutional principles that have made the United States a beacon of freedom and opportunity for generations. By focusing on shared values and common goals, the nation can heal its divisions and build a more cohesive, resilient society—one that honors the legacy of our founding fathers and secures a prosperous future for all citizens.[24]

Thus, the pathway toward national unity and reform is clear: a renewed commitment to constitutional values, an emphasis on civic education, responsible economic and institutional reforms, and the cultivation of leadership that prioritizes the common good. In this collective effort lies the hope for a revitalized nation—a nation united not by partisan loyalties but by a shared belief in the enduring promise of the American experiment.[25]

---

[22] Putnam, Robert D. *Bowling Alone: The Collapse and Revival of American Community*. Simon & Schuster, 2000.

[23] Wood, Gordon S. *The Radicalism of the American Revolution*. Vintage Books, 1993.

[24] Eskridge, William N. Jr. *Originalism in the Twenty-First Century*. Harvard University Press, 2012.

[25] Scalia, Antonin. *A Matter of Interpretation: Federal Courts and the Law*. Princeton University Press, 1997.

CHAPTER 12:

Federalism Revisited: Decentralization and Local Governance

1. Historical Evolution of Federalism

The evolution of federalism in the United States represents one of the most enduring and dynamic aspects of American constitutional design. From the debates of the founding era to the contemporary discussions on decentralization and local governance, federalism has served as both a mechanism for limiting governmental power and a framework for accommodating diversity among states and communities. This commentary offers an in-depth analysis of the historical evolution of federalism, examining its origins in the ideological struggles of the eighteenth century, its development through the formative years of the republic, and its modern reinterpretation as a tool for preserving individual liberty and local autonomy. The discussion is grounded in a politically conservative perspective that reveres the wisdom of our founding fathers and their deliberate design of a decentralized governmental structure, asserting that such decentralization remains essential for safeguarding the principles enshrined in the United States Constitution.[1]

In the late eighteenth century, the framers of the Constitution were acutely aware of the perils of concentrated power. Their experience under British rule, characterized by arbitrary authority and distant governance, had instilled in them a deep-seated belief in the importance of local control. Federalism emerged as a compromise between those who favored a strong central government and advocates of state sovereignty. Influential thinkers such as James Madison and Alexander Hamilton argued that a system dividing power between national and state governments would serve as a bulwark against tyranny and foster a vibrant, pluralistic society. Their writings in the Federalist Papers underscore a vision of a union in which each state retained a degree of autonomy, thereby ensuring that government remained close to the people and responsive to local needs.[2]

---

[1] Hamilton, Alexander; Madison, James; Jay, John. *The Federalist Papers*. Penguin Classics, 2003.

[2] Madison, James. "Federalist No. 10." In *The Federalist Papers*, edited by Clinton Rossiter, Bantam Classics, 1961.

This early vision of federalism was not static; it evolved through the contentious debates that marked the ratification process of the Constitution. Anti-Federalists, who feared that the new central government might replicate the despotic tendencies of the British crown, championed a system that preserved significant state powers. Their insistence on a Bill of Rights and assurances regarding state sovereignty highlighted the enduring importance of decentralized power in protecting individual freedoms. Over time, compromises were reached that allowed the Constitution to incorporate both the need for a strong national framework and the necessity of state-level autonomy. The resulting system of dual sovereignty has provided a flexible yet resilient foundation for American governance, one that continues to adapt to changing political and social realities.[3]

As the nation expanded and matured, federalism assumed new dimensions. The nineteenth century witnessed a series of transformative events—ranging from westward expansion to the Civil War—that tested the robustness of the federal system. During this period, debates over states' rights and the balance of power between federal and state governments became increasingly pronounced. Southern states, in particular, argued for greater autonomy as a means of preserving local customs and economic structures. Although these disputes sometimes escalated into conflict, such as in the secession crisis that led to the Civil War, the eventual outcome reaffirmed the supremacy of the Constitution while also underscoring the enduring value of state-level decision-making.[4]

The post-Civil War era ushered in significant changes in federalism as the federal government assumed a more active role in economic regulation and social policy. The New Deal, for instance, marked a dramatic expansion of federal authority in response to the Great Depression. Critics from a conservative standpoint argued that these developments signaled a departure from the original intent of decentralization as envisaged by the founding fathers. They contended that the increased centralization of power not only diluted state autonomy but also threatened the very freedoms that the Constitution was designed to protect. Despite these concerns, the evolution of federalism in the twentieth century demonstrated the capacity of the constitutional framework to adapt to complex national challenges while retaining the core principle of limited government.[5]

In recent decades, the debate over federalism has been reinvigorated by discussions on decentralization and local governance. Conservatives today argue that a return to the original

---

[3] Wood, Gordon S. *The Creation of the American Republic, 1776–1787*. University of North Carolina Press, 1998.

[4] Ellis, Joseph J. *American Creation: Triumphs and Tragedies in the Founding of the Republic*. Knopf, 2007.

[5] Maier, Pauline. *American Scripture: Making the Declaration of Independence*. Vintage, 1998.

principles of federalism is essential for restoring accountability and efficiency in government. They contend that centralization has led to bureaucratic overreach and that decisions made far from the local community often fail to address the unique needs of individual states and regions. Advocates of decentralization assert that empowering state and local governments will not only reinvigorate democratic participation but also foster innovative policy solutions tailored to local circumstances. This perspective reflects a broader conservative commitment to limited government and individual liberty, values that were central to the founding generation's vision.[6]

One of the most compelling arguments for decentralization is the belief that local governments are better positioned to understand and respond to the specific challenges faced by their communities. The principle of subsidiarity—the idea that matters should be handled by the smallest, lowest, or least centralized competent authority—has long been a cornerstone of conservative thought. By devolving power to state and local levels, federalism can facilitate more effective governance and enhance civic engagement. This approach not only encourages accountability by bringing government closer to the people but also stimulates a competitive environment in which states serve as laboratories of democracy.[7]

The historical evolution of federalism is also marked by a series of judicial decisions that have clarified the balance between federal and state authority. Landmark cases such as McCulloch v. Maryland and Gibbons v. Ogden played crucial roles in defining the scope of federal power under the Constitution. While these decisions often expanded federal authority, they also underscored the importance of preserving the delicate balance intended by the framers. Conservative jurists have frequently invoked originalist interpretations of the Constitution to argue for a more restrained federal government, emphasizing that the powers of the national government must be limited to those expressly enumerated by the Constitution. This judicial philosophy reinforces the conservative view that true federalism is essential for maintaining the freedoms of the individual and the autonomy of the states.[8]

Furthermore, the evolution of federalism has been influenced by shifts in political ideology and cultural attitudes over time. The conservative resurgence of the late twentieth century, for example, saw a renewed emphasis on states' rights and a skepticism toward expansive federal

---

[6] Scalia, Antonin. *A Matter of Interpretation: Federal Courts and the Law*. Princeton University Press, 1997.

[7] Elazar, Daniel J. *Exploring Federalism*. University of Alabama Press, 1987.

[8] Binder, Sarah A. *Stalemate: Causes and Consequences of Legislative Gridlock*. Brookings Institution Press, 2003.

programs. This period was characterized by efforts to roll back the administrative state and reassert the primacy of local governance. Conservative policymakers argued that many of the inefficiencies and overreaches of the federal government could be remedied by restoring power to the states, thereby realigning American governance with the principles of decentralization articulated by the founding fathers.[9]

Today, debates over federalism continue to be central to discussions of American political identity. In an increasingly complex and interconnected world, the tension between national uniformity and local autonomy remains a defining feature of the constitutional landscape. Conservatives maintain that while certain challenges—such as national security, environmental regulation, and interstate commerce—necessitate a degree of federal oversight, the general rule should favor decentralization. This balanced approach seeks to harness the benefits of a unified nation while preserving the flexibility and responsiveness that come with local control.[10]

Economic considerations also play a significant role in contemporary discussions of federalism. Conservatives argue that a decentralized economic policy enables states to experiment with innovative solutions tailored to their specific circumstances, rather than imposing a one-size-fits-all approach from Washington. For example, issues such as taxation, regulation, and economic development are best addressed at the state or local level, where policymakers have a more intimate understanding of the needs and resources of their communities. This approach not only promotes economic efficiency but also reinforces the conservative principle of limited government by preventing the over-concentration of fiscal power.[11]

Moreover, the preservation of cultural and social traditions is closely linked to the principles of federalism. The United States is a nation of diverse communities, each with its own history, values, and priorities. Decentralization allows these distinct identities to flourish while still contributing to the overall unity of the nation. Conservatives contend that local governance respects this diversity by allowing communities to govern themselves according to their unique customs and traditions, rather than being forced to conform to a homogenized national policy. This respect for local autonomy is seen as vital for maintaining the cultural richness and social cohesion that have long defined the American experience.[12]

---

[9] Kirk, Russell. *The Conservative Mind: From Burke to Eliot*. Regnery Publishing, 1953.

[10] Friedman, Milton. *Capitalism and Freedom*. University of Chicago Press, 2002.

[11] Torney-Purta, Judith, et al. *Citizenship and Political Participation: Political Science Perspectives*. Rowman & Littlefield, 2001.

[12] Lipset, Seymour. *Political Man: The Social Bases of Politics*. Johns Hopkins University Press, 1960.

In addition to its practical benefits, federalism holds profound symbolic significance for conservatives. It embodies the very essence of the American experiment—a commitment to a government that is not monolithic or all-powerful, but rather a confederation of free, self-governing entities united by a shared commitment to constitutional principles. This symbolism is rooted in the historical context of the American Revolution, during which the desire to escape the arbitrary rule of a distant monarch led to the establishment of a government based on local control and individual liberty. For conservatives, federalism is not merely a policy preference; it is a sacred trust inherited from the founding fathers, whose wisdom continues to guide the nation in its pursuit of freedom and justice.[13]

Critics of federalism sometimes argue that decentralization can lead to inequality and fragmentation, as states may adopt widely divergent policies that undermine national cohesion. However, conservatives counter that the benefits of local autonomy far outweigh these risks. They maintain that a decentralized system encourages competition among states, leading to better policy outcomes and greater accountability. Moreover, the Constitution itself provides mechanisms for resolving disputes between the federal government and the states, ensuring that local autonomy does not come at the expense of national unity. This delicate balance is a testament to the foresight of the founding fathers, who envisioned a dynamic interplay between national authority and local self-governance.[14]

The historical evolution of federalism is also reflected in the changing nature of political power in America. In the early years of the republic, the balance of power was predominantly in the hands of state governments. Over time, however, the expansion of federal authority—driven by the exigencies of modern governance—has shifted this balance. Yet, the conservative belief in a return to the original principles of decentralization remains strong. By reasserting the primacy of local governance, conservatives argue that the nation can restore the balance that once ensured a government "of the people, by the people, and for the people." This vision of governance, deeply rooted in the constitutional tradition, serves as a rallying cry for those who seek to reclaim the founding ideals of American liberty.[15]

Recent policy debates further illustrate the enduring relevance of federalism. Issues such as healthcare, education, and environmental regulation have become battlegrounds over the

---

[13] Amar, Akhil Reed. *America's Constitution: A Biography*. Random House, 2005.

[14] Eskridge, William N. Jr. *Originalism in the Twenty-First Century*. Harvard University Press, 2012.

[15] McCarty, Nolan, Keith T. Poole, and Howard Rosenthal. *Polarized America: The Dance of Ideology and Unequal Riches*. MIT Press, 2009.

appropriate division of power between federal and state governments. Conservatives consistently argue that states, rather than a sprawling federal bureaucracy, are best positioned to craft policies that reflect the will and needs of their citizens. This perspective is informed by the historical record, which shows that decentralized governance can foster innovation and accountability. By allowing states to serve as testing grounds for policy, federalism not only preserves the diversity of local solutions but also facilitates a healthy competition that ultimately benefits the nation as a whole.[16]

The importance of maintaining a robust federalist structure is underscored by contemporary challenges such as globalization and technological change. In a world where centralization often seems inevitable, the American commitment to decentralization stands out as a beacon of resistance against the concentration of power. Conservatives argue that the principles of federalism, as enshrined in the Constitution, offer a proven method for mitigating the risks associated with unchecked central authority. By ensuring that decision-making remains dispersed and localized, federalism protects against the potential abuses of power that can arise in highly centralized systems.[17]

At its core, the historical evolution of federalism is a story of adaptation and resilience. The framework established by the founding fathers was designed to endure the vicissitudes of history, allowing the nation to evolve while remaining true to its fundamental principles. Over the centuries, federalism has been reinterpreted and reimagined in response to new challenges, yet its essential purpose—to limit governmental power and protect individual liberty—remains unchanged. For conservatives, this continuity is a powerful affirmation of the wisdom of the Constitution and a clarion call to preserve the decentralized system that has long been the cornerstone of American democracy.[18]

The path forward, as envisioned by conservative thinkers, involves a deliberate reemphasis on the principles of federalism. This reemphasis requires not only policy changes but also a cultural shift in the way Americans view government. It entails a renewed commitment to local control, individual responsibility, and the recognition that the best solutions often emerge from the grassroots rather than from distant bureaucrats. Such a shift would signal a return to the ideals

---

[16] Niemi, Richard G., and Jane Junn. *Civic Education: What Makes Students Learn.* Yale University Press, 1998.

[17] Putnam, Robert D. *Bowling Alone: The Collapse and Revival of American Community.* Simon & Schuster, 2000.

[18] Galston, William A. *Civic Education and Democracy in America.* Johns Hopkins University Press, 2001.

of the founding era—a time when government was seen as a servant of the people, accountable to the local communities it served.[19]

In conclusion, the historical evolution of federalism offers a compelling blueprint for addressing many of the challenges facing America today. The deliberate decentralization crafted by our founding fathers provided a safeguard against tyranny and an engine for innovation, and these benefits remain as relevant now as they were over two centuries ago. By reaffirming the principles of federalism—limiting the scope of centralized power, promoting local autonomy, and preserving the delicate balance between state and national interests—America can reinvigorate its democratic institutions and restore the unity and freedom that have long defined the nation. This conservative perspective holds that true national reform begins at the local level and that by empowering communities to govern themselves in accordance with constitutional principles, we can secure a prosperous and free future for all citizens.[20]

Moreover, the evolution of federalism is not merely a historical artifact but a living tradition that continues to influence contemporary policy debates. As the nation grapples with new challenges, from economic globalization to digital transformation, the enduring wisdom of a decentralized system offers a roadmap for preserving liberty and accountability. Conservative scholars and policymakers maintain that by returning to the original principles of federalism, the United States can address modern issues without sacrificing the fundamental freedoms that form the backbone of the Constitution.[21]

Ultimately, the historical evolution of federalism reveals a timeless truth: that decentralization and local governance are essential for protecting individual liberty and ensuring that government remains responsive to the people. This is the enduring legacy of the founding fathers—a legacy that must be preserved and reinvigorated if America is to continue as a bastion of freedom and democratic governance. Through a renewed commitment to federalist principles, we can chart a course toward a future where the Constitution remains the unyielding foundation of American life, guiding the nation with the wisdom and prudence that defined its inception.[22]

---

[19] Sanger, Margaret. *Conservative Legacies: How the Founding Ideals Endure*. HarperCollins, 2010.

[20] Bickel, Alexander M. *The Least Dangerous Branch: The Supreme Court at the Bar of Politics*. Yale University Press, 1962.

[21] Lasch, Christopher. *The Culture of Narcissism: American Life in an Age of Diminishing Expectations*. W.W. Norton & Company, 1979.

[22] Wood, Gordon S. *The Radicalism of the American Revolution*. Vintage Books, 1993.

In embracing this vision, conservatives call upon all citizens, educators, and policymakers to honor the constitutional heritage that has made the United States a beacon of liberty. By fostering a culture of local empowerment, civic responsibility, and judicial restraint, we can ensure that the federal system endures as a vibrant and dynamic framework for governance—one that not only adapts to changing times but also upholds the timeless values that have sustained our nation for over two centuries.[23]

Thus, the historical evolution of federalism is more than an academic subject; it is a living testament to the enduring power of decentralized governance. By studying its development from the revolutionary fervor of the eighteenth century to its modern rearticulations, we gain not only a deeper appreciation for our constitutional heritage but also a clear blueprint for future reform. In the spirit of our founding fathers, who envisioned a government that would forever be a bulwark against tyranny, we must continue to champion federalism as the cornerstone of American freedom.[24]

As we move forward, it is imperative that policymakers and citizens alike recognize that the key to solving many of today's political challenges lies in embracing the decentralized, locally responsive system that our forefathers established. By restoring the balance between state and federal power and reaffirming our commitment to constitutional principles, we can pave the way for a more unified, prosperous, and free America—a nation that truly embodies the ideals of liberty, justice, and limited government.[25]

---

[23] Eskridge, William N. Jr. *Originalism in the Twenty-First Century*. Harvard University Press, 2012.

[24] Scalia, Antonin. *A Matter of Interpretation: Federal Courts and the Law*. Princeton University Press, 1997.

[25] Hamilton, Alexander; Madison, James; Jay, John. *The Federalist Papers*. Penguin Classics, 2003.

2. Devolution of Power to States and Localities

The concept of devolution—the transfer of power from a central government to states and localities—has long been a central tenet of American constitutional thought. Rooted in the skepticism that the founding fathers harbored toward centralized power, devolution is widely regarded within conservative circles as an essential mechanism for safeguarding liberty, promoting governmental efficiency, and preserving the unique cultural and economic characteristics of local communities. This commentary provides a comprehensive analysis of the devolution of power to states and localities, tracing its historical origins, examining its evolution over time, and assessing its contemporary relevance in a nation increasingly characterized by political polarization and expansive federal authority.[1]

The origins of devolution can be found in the experiences of the American colonists under British rule, where arbitrary and distant governance underscored the need for local control. The founding fathers, having witnessed firsthand the perils of centralized authority, enshrined federalism in the United States Constitution as a bulwark against tyranny. They envisioned a government in which the power was divided not only among the legislative, executive, and judicial branches but also between the national government and the states. This dual sovereignty was designed to ensure that governmental authority remained as close to the people as possible, thereby allowing communities to tailor policies to their unique circumstances.[2]

In the debates over the ratification of the Constitution, anti-Federalists vocally demanded stronger assurances of state sovereignty. Their concerns were not unfounded; they feared that a powerful central government would replicate the very abuses from which they had suffered under British rule. As a result, the Federalist Papers and other contemporary writings emphasize the importance of local governance as a means of preserving freedom and preventing the concentration of power. The incorporation of the Bill of Rights further assuaged these fears by guaranteeing protections that would limit federal overreach.[3]

Historically, the evolution of devolution has been a dynamic process marked by periods of both decentralization and re-centralization. In the early decades of the republic, state governments enjoyed a great deal of autonomy. This period was characterized by a vibrant diversity of

---

[1] Hamilton, Alexander; Madison, James; Jay, John. *The Federalist Papers*. Penguin Classics, 2003.

[2] Madison, James. "Federalist No. 51." In *The Federalist Papers*, edited by Clinton Rossiter, Bantam Classics, 1961.

[3] Wood, Gordon S. *The Creation of the American Republic, 1776–1787*. University of North Carolina Press, 1998.

local policies reflecting regional economic interests, cultural values, and political traditions. However, as the nation grew and the scope of federal responsibilities expanded—particularly during periods of national crisis such as the Civil War and the New Deal era—the balance shifted in favor of greater federal intervention. Conservatives have consistently argued that such shifts, while sometimes necessary, have often gone too far, leading to an erosion of the local decision-making power that is critical to the maintenance of individual liberty and accountability.[4]

The conservative critique of expansive federal power is grounded in the belief that centralized governance tends to be inefficient, unresponsive, and prone to the pitfalls of bureaucratic overreach. By contrast, devolution fosters innovation through competition among states, allowing each to act as a "laboratory of democracy." In this model, states can experiment with policies on a smaller scale, with successful initiatives later adopted by others. This not only leads to better governance but also ensures that the voice of the local citizenry is heard and respected. The devolution of power, therefore, is seen as a practical means of mitigating the risks associated with a one-size-fits-all approach imposed by a distant federal bureaucracy.[5]

In the modern era, debates over devolution are increasingly intertwined with discussions of fiscal responsibility, regulatory reform, and economic freedom. Conservatives argue that states are better equipped than the federal government to manage issues such as taxation, education, and healthcare because local authorities are more intimately familiar with the needs of their communities. Moreover, devolving power to states can reduce wasteful spending and enable more efficient allocation of resources, as local governments are incentivized to operate within tighter budgetary constraints. The principle of subsidiarity—the idea that matters ought to be handled by the smallest, lowest, or least centralized competent authority—remains a cornerstone of conservative thought in this regard.[6]

The practical benefits of devolution extend to the realm of civic engagement as well. When governance is localized, citizens are more likely to participate in the political process because they can see a direct connection between their actions and policy outcomes. This heightened level of engagement reinforces the democratic principle that government should be by the people and for the people. Additionally, local control fosters accountability; elected officials at the state and local levels are more directly answerable to their constituents, making them more

---

[4] Ellis, Joseph J. *American Creation: Triumphs and Tragedies in the Founding of the Republic*. Knopf, 2007.

[5] Maier, Pauline. *American Scripture: Making the Declaration of Independence*. Vintage, 1998.

[6] Scalia, Antonin. *A Matter of Interpretation: Federal Courts and the Law*. Princeton University Press, 1997.

responsive to local needs and concerns. In an era where national politics is often dominated by partisan polarization and gridlock, the revival of local governance offers a promising avenue for restoring trust in government institutions.[7]

Judicial interpretations have also played a significant role in shaping the contours of devolution. Landmark Supreme Court decisions, such as McCulloch v. Maryland and later rulings on state sovereignty, have underscored the importance of maintaining a balance between federal authority and state autonomy. Conservative jurists and legal scholars have argued for an originalist approach to constitutional interpretation, one that upholds the framers' intent to limit the scope of federal power. This judicial philosophy reinforces the conservative contention that devolution is not merely a policy preference but a constitutional imperative designed to preserve individual liberty and prevent governmental overreach.[8]

The resurgence of conservative political power in recent decades has reinvigorated calls for devolution. Political leaders and policymakers on the right have championed a return to the principles of localism and state sovereignty as antidotes to the inefficiencies and overreach of a bloated federal government. For instance, recent legislative proposals aimed at decentralizing education and healthcare policies have garnered significant support among conservatives, who assert that states are best positioned to design systems that reflect local values and priorities. These initiatives are grounded in a deep-seated belief that constitutional governance is best achieved when power is dispersed rather than concentrated.[9]

Cultural factors also contribute to the conservative advocacy for devolution. The United States is a nation of diverse communities, each with its own history, traditions, and economic conditions. A centralized government, by its very nature, tends to impose uniform policies that may not adequately address local differences. Devolution, on the other hand, allows for the preservation of regional distinctiveness and the protection of local customs. This respect for diversity is not antithetical to national unity; rather, it is seen as a strength that can lead to a more resilient and adaptable polity. Conservatives argue that true unity is achieved not through homogenization but through the recognition and celebration of differences within a common constitutional framework.[10]

---

[7] Elazar, Daniel J. *Exploring Federalism*. University of Alabama Press, 1987.

[8] Binder, Sarah A. *Stalemate: Causes and Consequences of Legislative Gridlock*. Brookings Institution Press, 2003.

[9] Kirk, Russell. *The Conservative Mind: From Burke to Eliot*. Regnery Publishing, 1953.

[10] Friedman, Milton. *Capitalism and Freedom*. University of Chicago Press, 2002.

Economic disparities among states further underscore the need for devolution. Regions with different economic profiles require tailored approaches to fiscal policy, job creation, and social welfare. A one-size-fits-all policy crafted at the federal level may not effectively address the unique challenges faced by economically disadvantaged areas. By devolving power, local governments can experiment with innovative economic policies that are better suited to their particular circumstances, thereby promoting sustainable growth and reducing regional inequalities. This decentralized approach to economic governance is a practical reflection of the conservative commitment to limited government and free-market principles.[11]

Environmental regulation, too, benefits from a devolved approach. The vast geographic and ecological diversity of the United States means that environmental challenges vary considerably from one region to another. States and localities are often in a better position to develop targeted strategies that address specific environmental concerns without imposing undue burdens on areas where such regulations may be unnecessary. Conservatives contend that local governance in environmental policy not only enhances efficiency but also respects the principle of federalism by allowing states to balance economic development with environmental protection according to local needs.[12]

Critics of devolution argue that excessive decentralization can lead to inequality and fragmentation, as states might adopt policies that conflict with one another or undermine national standards. However, conservatives counter that the Constitution provides ample mechanisms for maintaining a balance between state autonomy and national cohesion. Intergovernmental relations, interstate compacts, and federal oversight in critical areas such as national defense and interstate commerce ensure that local autonomy does not come at the expense of the broader interests of the nation. The conservative position maintains that a well-calibrated system of devolution enhances both efficiency and democratic accountability without sacrificing the unity of the federal union.[13]

The political discourse surrounding devolution is also influenced by global trends. In an era marked by the centralization of power in many parts of the world, the American model of decentralized governance stands out as a beacon of liberty and individual autonomy. Conservatives assert that preserving and strengthening devolution is not only essential for domestic policy but also for maintaining the United States' moral authority on the international stage. By demonstrating

---

[11] Torney-Purta, Judith, et al. *Citizenship and Political Participation: Political Science Perspectives*. Rowman & Littlefield, 2001.

[12] Lipset, Seymour. *Political Man: The Social Bases of Politics*. Johns Hopkins University Press, 1960.

[13] Amar, Akhil Reed. *America's Constitution: A Biography*. Random House, 2005.

that a decentralized system can yield effective and responsive governance, America reinforces its standing as a model for other democracies seeking to balance national unity with local diversity.[14]

Historical precedents offer valuable insights into the potential of devolution to foster innovation and progress. Throughout American history, states have often led the way in pioneering policies that later become models for national reform. From educational reforms in Massachusetts to technological innovations in California, the decentralized nature of American governance has enabled states to serve as incubators for ideas that have the power to transform society. Conservatives view these historical examples as evidence that devolution not only preserves individual liberty but also catalyzes positive change by encouraging experimentation and competition among states.[15]

The role of the citizenry in a decentralized system cannot be overemphasized. Devolution brings government closer to the people, creating opportunities for direct participation in the political process. This proximity fosters a greater sense of accountability and enables citizens to hold local officials responsible for their decisions. In a system where power is concentrated at the federal level, individual voices can be lost in the bureaucracy; devolution, by contrast, re-empowers communities and restores the fundamental democratic principle that government is a servant of the people. This reinvigoration of local democracy is central to the conservative vision of a government that is both effective and responsive.[16]

Furthermore, devolution aligns with the conservative emphasis on personal responsibility and self-reliance. When power is devolved to states and localities, individuals are more likely to feel that they have a stake in the decisions that affect their lives. This fosters a culture of civic engagement, where citizens take an active role in shaping their communities rather than relying solely on distant federal authorities. The resulting increase in civic participation not only strengthens local governance but also contributes to a more vibrant and resilient democratic society overall.[17]

---

[14] Eskridge, William N. Jr. *Originalism in the Twenty-First Century*. Harvard University Press, 2012.

[15] McCarty, Nolan, Keith T. Poole, and Howard Rosenthal. *Polarized America: The Dance of Ideology and Unequal Riches*. MIT Press, 2009.

[16] Niemi, Richard G., and Jane Junn. *Civic Education: What Makes Students Learn*. Yale University Press, 1998.

[17] Putnam, Robert D. *Bowling Alone: The Collapse and Revival of American Community*. Simon & Schuster, 2000.

The judicial branch has consistently played a pivotal role in defining the limits of federal power and affirming the principles of devolution. Through a series of landmark rulings, the Supreme Court has affirmed that the powers of the federal government are not unlimited and that states retain significant authority under the Constitution. Conservative legal scholars and jurists often invoke these decisions to argue for a restrained interpretation of federal power, one that upholds the original intent of the framers to safeguard state sovereignty. This legal framework provides the necessary checks on federal overreach and serves as a constitutional guarantee of local autonomy.[18]

In recent years, a renewed call for devolution has emerged in response to what many conservatives perceive as an overcentralization of governmental power. The expansion of federal regulatory agencies and the growing influence of partisan politics at the national level have prompted calls for a rollback of federal authority in favor of a more decentralized system. Advocates of devolution argue that by returning power to the states, America can restore a more balanced and effective system of governance—one that is better equipped to meet the diverse needs of its citizens while remaining true to the constitutional ideals of limited government and individual freedom.[19]

The conservative vision for devolution is not a rejection of federalism but rather an affirmation of its original purpose. It is a call to renew the commitment to a system in which power is distributed in a manner that protects liberty, promotes accountability, and fosters innovation. By embracing devolution, policymakers can ensure that government remains responsive to the people, that citizens retain control over their local affairs, and that the spirit of the founding fathers is honored through a government that is truly by the people and for the people.[20]

Moreover, the debate over devolution is inextricably linked to broader discussions about the future of American democracy. As the nation confronts unprecedented challenges—from economic globalization to technological transformation—the need for adaptive and responsive governance has never been greater. Conservatives argue that a decentralized system, with its inherent flexibility and capacity for local innovation, is uniquely suited to navigate these complex issues. By decentralizing power, the United States can harness the creativity and resourcefulness of its diverse regions, fostering a form of governance that is as dynamic as it is resilient.[21]

---

[18] Galston, William A. *Civic Education and Democracy in America*. Johns Hopkins University Press, 2001.

[19] Sanger, Margaret. *Conservative Legacies: How the Founding Ideals Endure*. HarperCollins, 2010.

[20] Bickel, Alexander M. *The Least Dangerous Branch: The Supreme Court at the Bar of Politics*. Yale University Press, 1962.

[21] Lasch, Christopher. *The Culture of Narcissism: American Life in an Age of Diminishing Expectations*. W.W. Norton & Company, 1979.

In conclusion, the devolution of power to states and localities represents a vital pathway toward preserving the constitutional principles that have long underpinned American governance. By returning authority to the people through decentralized government, the nation can reinvigorate democratic participation, stimulate innovative policy solutions, and restore accountability in a system increasingly dominated by distant federal power. The historical evolution of federalism—from the visionary debates of the founding era to the modern calls for decentralization—underscores that the enduring strength of the United States lies in its commitment to local autonomy and limited government.[22]

This conservative perspective insists that the solution to many of America's current challenges is not to be found in further centralization but in the restoration of the original balance envisioned by the founding fathers. Through a steadfast commitment to devolution, the United States can ensure that government remains close to the people, responsive to local needs, and capable of adapting to a rapidly changing world. Ultimately, the revival of state and local governance is not merely a policy preference—it is a constitutional imperative that honors the legacy of those who fought for freedom and self-governance.[23]

As America moves forward, it must embrace devolution as a cornerstone of its democratic experiment—a means of safeguarding liberty, promoting efficiency, and ensuring that the government remains truly of the people. By reaffirming the importance of local control and decentralization, the nation can build a more unified, prosperous, and resilient future that stays true to the enduring principles of the United States Constitution.[24]

In the final analysis, the devolution of power to states and localities is not only a historical inevitability but also a practical necessity. It is a call to return to the roots of American democracy—a system in which power is distributed among communities that are uniquely equipped to address their own challenges while contributing to the collective strength of the nation. By championing devolution, conservatives reaffirm the belief that the best government is one that remains closest to its citizens, fostering a culture of participation, accountability, and innovation. This is the legacy of the founding fathers and the promise of a truly free society.[25]

---

[22] Wood, Gordon S. *The Radicalism of the American Revolution*. Vintage Books, 1993.

[23] Eskridge, William N. Jr. *Originalism in the Twenty-First Century*. Harvard University Press, 2012.

[24] Scalia, Antonin. *A Matter of Interpretation: Federal Courts and the Law*. Princeton University Press, 1997.

[25] Hamilton, Alexander; Madison, James; Jay, John. *The Federalist Papers*. Penguin Classics, 2003.

3. Case Studies: Successes and Failures in Local Governance

The evolution of local governance in the United States offers a compelling lens through which to examine the practical applications of federalism as originally envisioned by our founding fathers. This commentary explores case studies of both successes and failures in local governance, with a focus on how decentralized authority can promote effective public policy, economic vitality, and civic engagement while also noting the pitfalls that can arise when localities deviate from constitutional principles. Emphasizing a politically conservative perspective, this analysis argues that local governance, when aligned with the constitutional commitment to limited government and individual liberty, is indispensable for preserving the unique identity of communities and ensuring accountability at the grassroots level.[1]

Historically, the United States was founded on the principle that government should be as close to the people as possible—a principle enshrined in the system of federalism. The framers deliberately divided power between the national government and the states to prevent the concentration of power that had plagued colonial experiences. Early American history is replete with examples of communities managing their own affairs with considerable success, from town meetings in New England to the self-governance of frontier settlements. These local bodies not only administered justice and provided essential public services but also fostered civic engagement and a deep sense of personal responsibility among citizens.[2]

A classic case study illustrating the success of local governance can be found in the New England town meeting system. For centuries, these gatherings have served as the cornerstone of democratic participation, enabling residents to directly influence decisions affecting education, public safety, and local infrastructure. The town meeting system reflects the conservative belief that the best government is one that is closest to the people and that broad-based participation leads to more accountable and transparent governance. In communities where the town meeting tradition remains robust, citizens report higher levels of satisfaction with public services and a stronger sense of community ownership over local policies.[3]

Another successful example is the implementation of localized school governance. Many states have devolved educational authority to local school districts, empowering communities to tailor

---

[1] Hamilton, Alexander; Madison, James; Jay, John. *The Federalist Papers*. Penguin Classics, 2003.

[2] Madison, James. "Federalist No. 51." In *The Federalist Papers*, edited by Clinton Rossiter, Bantam Classics, 1961.

[3] Niemi, Richard G., and Jane Junn. *Civic Education: What Makes Students Learn*. Yale University Press, 1998.

curricula, manage budgets, and set policies that reflect local values and needs. Proponents of devolution argue that such autonomy allows schools to operate more efficiently, respond rapidly to changing demographics, and innovate in ways that a centralized system cannot. In states where local control over education has been maintained, there is evidence of improved academic outcomes and increased parental involvement—factors that are essential to the conservative vision of nurturing a well-informed and civically engaged citizenry.[4]

However, while many instances of local governance demonstrate clear benefits, there are also notable failures that underscore the challenges of decentralized power. One frequently cited example is the issue of fiscal mismanagement in certain municipalities. In some cases, local governments have struggled with budgetary deficits and inefficient allocation of resources, leading to inadequate public services and a loss of taxpayer confidence. Critics argue that these failures are not inherent to the concept of local governance itself but result from a lack of adherence to constitutional principles of accountability and fiscal restraint. When local officials do not operate within a framework of limited government, the promise of devolution can quickly devolve into cronyism and wasteful spending.[5]

The case of urban governance in some large metropolitan areas further illustrates the potential pitfalls of local autonomy. In cities where political machines have dominated local politics, there is a tendency for centralized control at the municipal level to stifle innovation and undermine democratic accountability. Excessive concentration of power in urban administrations can lead to policies that are disconnected from the broader interests of the community. Such instances often result in corruption scandals and public disillusionment with government. Conservatives contend that these failures highlight the importance of preserving checks and balances at the local level, ensuring that power is not so concentrated as to become unresponsive to the needs of citizens.[6]

A particularly instructive case study involves the management of local law enforcement. In communities where police departments operate under strong local oversight and community input, there is often a higher degree of public trust and lower incidences of abuse of power. Conversely, in municipalities where law enforcement has been centralized without sufficient accountability mechanisms, issues of excessive force and lack of transparency have arisen. This dichotomy underscores the conservative argument that local control over public safety is essential

---

[4] Friedman, Milton. *Capitalism and Freedom*. University of Chicago Press, 2002.

[5] Elazar, Daniel J. *Exploring Federalism*. University of Alabama Press, 1987.

[6] Scalia, Antonin. *A Matter of Interpretation: Federal Courts and the Law*. Princeton University Press, 1997.

for maintaining both order and individual liberties. By keeping law enforcement accountable to the community, local governance can effectively balance the need for security with the protection of civil rights as enshrined in the Constitution.[7]

Economic development provides another fertile area for evaluating local governance. Many small towns and rural counties have thrived by leveraging local control to create business-friendly environments and attract investment. Conservative policymakers often point to such examples as evidence that devolving power to localities spurs economic innovation and resilience. When local leaders have the authority to set tax policies, streamline regulations, and incentivize entrepreneurship, they can tailor economic strategies to the specific strengths and challenges of their regions. These successes, however, are not universal; in areas where local governance has failed to balance economic growth with fiscal discipline, communities have experienced stagnation and even decline.[8]

One illustrative example of economic success through local governance is found in the management of municipal utilities in certain Midwestern cities. By adopting locally controlled utility systems, these cities have maintained competitive pricing and high levels of service quality, benefiting both residents and local businesses. The conservative perspective views such examples as proof that decentralization enables more responsive and accountable management of essential public services, in contrast to the inefficiencies often associated with large, bureaucratic systems.[9]

Local governance also plays a critical role in environmental management. In regions where local authorities have been empowered to develop and enforce tailored environmental policies, there is often a more effective balance between economic development and conservation. For instance, some states have allowed local governments to design zoning laws and land-use policies that protect natural resources while accommodating growth. This approach is consistent with the conservative belief in subsidiarity, which holds that decisions should be made at the most immediate level possible. However, when local governance is weakened or overridden by federal mandates, there can be a disconnect between policy and local ecological realities, leading to ineffective environmental management.[10]

---

[7] Binder, Sarah A. *Stalemate: Causes and Consequences of Legislative Gridlock*. Brookings Institution Press, 2003.

[8] Kirk, Russell. *The Conservative Mind: From Burke to Eliot*. Regnery Publishing, 1953.

[9] Maier, Pauline. *American Scripture: Making the Declaration of Independence*. Vintage, 1998.

[10] Torney-Purta, Judith, et al. *Citizenship and Political Participation: Political Science Perspectives*. Rowman & Littlefield, 2001.

The divergence between successful and unsuccessful local governance is also evident in the realm of public infrastructure. Cities that have invested in decentralized, locally managed transportation and public works projects often enjoy better service delivery and higher citizen satisfaction. In contrast, municipalities that have ceded control to distant federal agencies frequently suffer from delays, mismanagement, and a lack of responsiveness to local needs. Conservatives argue that the success of local governance in infrastructure development reinforces the notion that communities are best positioned to manage their own affairs, provided that they adhere to principles of fiscal prudence and accountability.[11]

Political culture and civic engagement are inextricably linked to the performance of local governments. In communities where citizens are actively involved in local decision-making, there is a higher degree of trust in government institutions and greater public accountability. The conservative model of governance emphasizes the importance of individual responsibility and active participation as the foundation of a healthy democracy. Successful local governance, therefore, is not solely a matter of administrative competence but also of a vibrant civic culture that holds elected officials accountable for their actions. Conversely, where local engagement is low, governance tends to become disconnected and unresponsive, contributing to widespread disillusionment with public institutions.[12]

A significant factor in the success of local governance is the adherence to constitutional principles of limited government. Conservatives assert that when local officials operate within a clearly defined framework that respects the Constitution, the risk of overreach and inefficiency is minimized. For example, municipalities that implement transparent budgeting processes and enforce strict limits on government spending tend to perform better than those where financial decisions are made arbitrarily. This adherence to constitutional constraints not only safeguards individual liberties but also fosters a culture of accountability that is essential for the long-term success of local governance.[13]

The judicial branch has also played a pivotal role in shaping local governance through its interpretations of federalism. Supreme Court decisions have often affirmed the rights of states and localities to govern themselves, reinforcing the conservative position that decentralization is a constitutional imperative. Landmark rulings have delineated the boundaries of federal authority, ensuring that local governments retain significant discretion in managing their own

---

[11] Lipset, Seymour. *Political Man: The Social Bases of Politics*. Johns Hopkins University Press, 1960.

[12] Amar, Akhil Reed. *America's Constitution: A Biography*. Random House, 2005.

[13] Eskridge, William N. Jr. *Originalism in the Twenty-First Century*. Harvard University Press, 2012.

affairs. These legal precedents serve as a bulwark against the encroachment of federal power, enabling localities to innovate and govern according to the unique needs of their communities.[14]

Case studies from recent decades further illuminate the complexities of local governance. In some instances, state governments have successfully partnered with local authorities to deliver improved public services, demonstrating that cooperation across levels of government can enhance overall performance. However, there have also been cases where conflicts between state and local officials have undermined policy implementation and generated gridlock. These failures are instructive, revealing that devolution must be accompanied by clear lines of responsibility and mutual respect among different levels of government. Conservatives maintain that when state and local governments work in concert within the bounds of the Constitution, the result is a more responsive and accountable system of governance.[15]

The experiences of rural counties provide a contrasting perspective on local governance compared to urban centers. In many rural areas, local governments have managed to preserve community identity and deliver public services effectively despite limited resources. These successes are often attributed to the strong bonds of community and a high degree of civic participation. Rural governance, when operating under conservative principles, tends to emphasize self-reliance, fiscal discipline, and a commitment to local traditions. However, challenges such as population decline and economic stagnation can strain these systems, underscoring the need for a balanced approach that leverages local strengths while addressing systemic vulnerabilities.[16]

In contrast, urban governance has sometimes struggled with issues of scale and complexity. Large cities, with their diverse populations and sprawling infrastructures, face challenges that can overwhelm local administrative capacities. Instances of corruption, bureaucratic inefficiency, and inadequate public services have marred the reputation of some metropolitan governments. Conservatives argue that these failures are not inherent to urban environments but result from a departure from the constitutional ideals of limited and decentralized government. They advocate for urban reforms that return power to local communities, emphasizing transparency, accountability, and the restoration of citizen oversight as key measures to revitalize urban governance.[17]

---

[14] McCarty, Nolan, Keith T. Poole, and Howard Rosenthal. *Polarized America: The Dance of Ideology and Unequal Riches*. MIT Press, 2009.

[15] Wood, Gordon S. *The Creation of the American Republic, 1776–1787*. University of North Carolina Press, 1998.

[16] Ellis, Joseph J. *American Creation: Triumphs and Tragedies in the Founding of the Republic*. Knopf, 2007.

[17] Putnam, Robert D. *Bowling Alone: The Collapse and Revival of American Community*. Simon & Schuster, 2000.

Fiscal autonomy is another critical aspect of successful local governance. Municipalities that enjoy a degree of financial independence are better positioned to tailor public services to local needs and invest in long-term infrastructure projects. Conservative policymakers have long championed tax reforms and budgetary controls that empower local governments while curbing wasteful federal spending. The success of local fiscal management not only enhances service delivery but also reinforces the principle that government should operate with restraint and accountability. This conservative vision of fiscal responsibility is reflected in case studies where local governments have achieved significant improvements in public services through prudent financial management.[18]

Moreover, the role of local governance in fostering innovation cannot be overlooked. Decentralized systems inherently encourage experimentation, as local governments have the flexibility to implement new policies and learn from their outcomes. Successful case studies demonstrate that when localities are given the freedom to innovate, they often develop solutions that are more effective and better suited to their specific challenges than those imposed by a centralized bureaucracy. This competitive dynamic among states and municipalities not only drives policy innovation but also creates a natural mechanism for best practices to emerge, thereby benefiting the nation as a whole.[19]

The interplay between local governance and community resilience is also a significant factor in the overall assessment of decentralization. Communities that are governed locally tend to exhibit stronger social cohesion, as residents are more directly involved in decision-making processes that affect their daily lives. This grassroots engagement fosters a sense of ownership and pride, which in turn enhances the capacity of local governments to respond effectively to crises, whether they be economic downturns, natural disasters, or public health emergencies. Conservatives view these successes as a vindication of the founding principles of self-governance and individual responsibility, arguing that a decentralized approach is essential for a resilient and dynamic society.[20]

At the same time, the case studies of local governance reveal important lessons about the limits of devolution. Where local governments have strayed from the constitutional principles of transparency and accountability, failures have often followed. Instances of mismanagement,

---

[18] Galston, William A. *Civic Education and Democracy in America*. Johns Hopkins University Press, 2001.

[19] Sanger, Margaret. *Conservative Legacies: How the Founding Ideals Endure*. HarperCollins, 2010.

[20] Bickel, Alexander M. *The Least Dangerous Branch: The Supreme Court at the Bar of Politics*. Yale University Press, 1962.

corruption, or neglect serve as cautionary tales that underscore the necessity of a robust institutional framework to guide local administration. Conservatives emphasize that successful devolution requires not only the transfer of power but also the establishment of checks and balances that ensure local authorities remain accountable to their constituents.[21]

The role of education and civic culture in supporting effective local governance is another vital area of consideration. Communities that invest in civic education tend to produce citizens who are more engaged in local politics and better able to hold their elected officials accountable. Successful local governance is closely tied to a well-informed electorate that understands the importance of constitutional principles and the responsibilities of citizenship. From a conservative perspective, nurturing a strong civic culture is indispensable for the success of devolution, as it reinforces the idea that government must be limited, transparent, and truly of the people.[22]

Furthermore, the experiences of various states illustrate that the devolution of power can yield divergent outcomes based on local conditions. While some states have successfully harnessed local autonomy to drive economic growth and improve public services, others have encountered significant challenges due to demographic shifts, resource constraints, or political dysfunction. These variations underscore the importance of a balanced approach to devolution—one that recognizes the unique characteristics of each community while upholding the overarching principles of constitutional governance. Conservatives maintain that tailored solutions, developed at the local level within a framework of constitutional limits, are the most effective means of addressing the diverse needs of a complex nation.[23]

In assessing the case studies of local governance, it is clear that the conservative vision for devolution is not an absolute prescription but a dynamic framework that requires continuous refinement and vigilance. Successes in local governance demonstrate the power of decentralization to enhance democratic participation, foster innovation, and promote fiscal responsibility, while failures remind us of the risks inherent in the absence of robust accountability measures. The challenge for modern policymakers is to learn from these experiences, ensuring that devolution remains true to the constitutional ideals of limited government and individual liberty while adapting to the evolving demands of contemporary society.[24]

---

[21] Lasch, Christopher. *The Culture of Narcissism: American Life in an Age of Diminishing Expectations*. W.W. Norton & Company, 1979.

[22] Wood, Gordon S. *The Radicalism of the American Revolution*. Vintage Books, 1993.

[23] Eskridge, William N. Jr. *Originalism in the Twenty-First Century*. Harvard University Press, 2012.

[24] Scalia, Antonin. *A Matter of Interpretation: Federal Courts and the Law*. Princeton University Press, 1997.

Ultimately, the case studies of local governance provide a persuasive argument for the continued relevance of federalism as a means of achieving effective, responsive, and accountable government. By returning power to states and localities, the United States can honor the legacy of its founding fathers and reinvigorate a system of government that is both resilient and adaptable. The conservative perspective holds that true national strength lies not in the centralization of power, but in a vibrant tapestry of local governments that work in concert to address the challenges of today while preserving the freedoms of tomorrow.[25]

[25] Hamilton, Alexander; Madison, James; Jay, John. *The Federalist Papers*. Penguin Classics, 2003.

4. Balancing National Standards with Local Autonomy

The delicate balance between national standards and local autonomy has long been a cornerstone of American constitutional design, reflecting the enduring vision of our founding fathers. This commentary examines the interplay between central authority and local self-governance, arguing that a true adherence to conservative principles requires a robust yet flexible framework that empowers localities while preserving uniform national standards where necessary. A commitment to limited government, fiscal responsibility, and individual liberty underpins the conservative perspective that only by restoring local decision-making can the United States truly safeguard the principles enshrined in the Constitution.[1]

Historically, the framers of the Constitution were deeply wary of the concentration of power. Their revolutionary experience under an overbearing British regime underscored the necessity of dividing power between national and state governments, thereby ensuring that authority remained as near to the people as possible. This dual system was not intended to create a fragmented union but rather to cultivate an environment where national policies could establish broad standards of justice and equality, while localities retained the freedom to tailor public policies to their unique cultural and economic circumstances. The conservative view maintains that national standards must be carefully balanced with local autonomy in order to prevent the tyranny of centralized power while promoting innovation and accountability at the grassroots level.[2]

In the realm of education, for instance, national standards provide the necessary baseline to ensure that every citizen receives a quality education regardless of geographic location, yet the implementation of these standards is most effective when adapted to local needs. Conservatives argue that while a common educational framework is essential for fostering a shared national identity and economic competitiveness, local school boards and state governments must retain the flexibility to design curricula and allocate resources in a manner that reflects community values and priorities. Such a system not only respects local diversity but also promotes competition among states to improve educational outcomes, thereby reinforcing the conservative principle that local solutions are often more efficient and responsive than uniform federal mandates.[3]

---

[1] Hamilton, Alexander; Madison, James; Jay, John. *The Federalist Papers*. Penguin Classics, 2003.

[2] Madison, James. "Federalist No. 51." In *The Federalist Papers*, edited by Clinton Rossiter, Bantam Classics, 1961.

[3] Niemi, Richard G., and Jane Junn. *Civic Education: What Makes Students Learn*. Yale University Press, 1998.

Similarly, in the area of healthcare, national standards are critical to guaranteeing basic access and protecting patients' rights, but a one-size-fits-all approach imposed by the federal government can stifle innovation and lead to inefficiencies. Conservative policymakers advocate for a model in which the federal government sets essential guidelines to ensure safety and quality, while state and local authorities are entrusted with the implementation and management of healthcare services. This devolved model, they contend, creates an environment in which local governments can experiment with cost-effective solutions that address regional health challenges while remaining accountable to their constituents. The result is a system that marries the stability of national oversight with the dynamism of local governance.[4]

Economic policy presents another critical field in which the balance between national standards and local autonomy must be carefully maintained. National economic policies, such as monetary regulation and trade policy, are essential for maintaining a stable macroeconomic environment and ensuring that the nation competes effectively in a global marketplace. However, fiscal policies that directly affect local economies—such as property taxes, business regulations, and infrastructure spending—are best managed by local governments that possess a more nuanced understanding of regional conditions. Conservatives argue that devolving economic power to localities not only fosters a competitive environment that drives innovation and efficiency but also ensures that government interventions remain limited and accountable. By allowing states and municipalities to design policies tailored to their specific economic landscapes, America can preserve the spirit of free enterprise and individual responsibility that is central to its constitutional heritage.[5]

Environmental regulation, too, benefits from a balanced approach. National standards are necessary to address issues that cross state lines, such as air and water quality, but local governments are often better positioned to manage land use, urban planning, and the preservation of natural resources within their jurisdictions. Conservatives maintain that environmental policies should be crafted in a way that safeguards public health and natural beauty without imposing excessive burdens on local businesses and communities. By combining broad federal guidelines with local flexibility, policymakers can achieve a sustainable equilibrium that honors both environmental protection and economic vitality.[6]

The interplay between national standards and local autonomy is further exemplified in the realm of law enforcement and public safety. National standards, including those enshrined in the

---

[4] Friedman, Milton. *Capitalism and Freedom*. University of Chicago Press, 2002.

[5] Elazar, Daniel J. *Exploring Federalism*. University of Alabama Press, 1987.

[6] Scalia, Antonin. *A Matter of Interpretation: Federal Courts and the Law*. Princeton University Press, 1997.

Constitution and upheld by federal courts, provide a critical framework for protecting individual rights and ensuring the rule of law. However, local police departments and sheriff's offices must operate under the direct oversight of the communities they serve. Conservatives argue that local control of law enforcement leads to greater accountability and responsiveness, as community members are more likely to hold local officials accountable for abuses of power or inefficiencies in service. Moreover, local governance in this arena fosters cooperation between citizens and public officials, strengthening the social contract and reinforcing the constitutional commitment to justice and public safety.[7]

Balancing national and local authority also has profound implications for transportation and infrastructure policy. The federal government plays a pivotal role in establishing national standards for safety and interstate commerce, but the design, maintenance, and management of local roads, bridges, and public transit systems are most effectively handled by state and local governments. Conservatives emphasize that the decentralized management of infrastructure not only reduces bureaucratic delays and corruption but also encourages communities to innovate and invest in projects that directly benefit their residents. By aligning local infrastructure investments with the broader goals of national development, America can ensure that its transportation networks remain both efficient and adaptable.[8]

The challenge of balancing national standards with local autonomy is not limited to policy implementation; it also extends to the realm of political culture. A recurring conservative critique of modern governance is that an overreliance on centralized authority leads to a disconnect between the government and the governed. When decisions are made in distant federal capitals, citizens often feel alienated from the political process, leading to disengagement and a diminished sense of civic responsibility. In contrast, devolving power to localities creates a political environment in which citizens are more directly involved in decision-making, thereby enhancing democratic accountability and reinforcing the notion that government is a servant of the people. This reinvigoration of local democracy is central to the conservative vision of a government that is both effective and truly representative of the citizenry.[9]

Judicial oversight has long served as a critical mechanism for balancing national and local authority. Landmark Supreme Court cases have clarified the limits of federal power and affirmed the rights

---

[7] Binder, Sarah A. *Stalemate: Causes and Consequences of Legislative Gridlock*. Brookings Institution Press, 2003.

[8] Kirk, Russell. *The Conservative Mind: From Burke to Eliot*. Regnery Publishing, 1953.

[9] Maier, Pauline. *American Scripture: Making the Declaration of Independence*. Vintage, 1998.

of states and localities to govern themselves within a constitutional framework. Conservative legal scholars advocate for an originalist interpretation of the Constitution, one that respects the balance of power intended by the founding fathers and curbs the potential for federal overreach. This judicial philosophy underpins the conservative argument that maintaining local autonomy is essential for protecting individual freedoms and ensuring that government remains both accountable and restrained.[10]

The interplay between national standards and local autonomy extends into the realm of cultural identity as well. The United States is a nation characterized by a rich mosaic of regional traditions, languages, and customs. National policies, when applied without sensitivity to local contexts, can inadvertently erode these unique cultural identities. Conservatives assert that local control allows communities to preserve their historical heritage and cultural practices, even as they contribute to the collective national identity. This dual commitment to unity and diversity is a hallmark of the American experiment and underscores the importance of a balanced approach that respects both national cohesion and local distinctiveness.[11]

A further argument in favor of balancing national standards with local autonomy concerns the principle of subsidiarity—a concept deeply rooted in conservative thought. Subsidiarity holds that issues ought to be handled at the most immediate level possible, only escalating to higher levels of government when absolutely necessary. This principle is not only a pragmatic guideline for efficient governance but also a moral imperative that honors the autonomy and dignity of local communities. Conservatives maintain that devolving power to localities is the most effective way to ensure that decisions are made by those best positioned to understand and address their own needs.[12]

Fiscal responsibility is another domain where the conservative case for balancing national standards with local autonomy is particularly compelling. Centralized fiscal policies can lead to inefficient allocation of resources and a disconnect between government spending and local priorities. By contrast, when states and local governments control a significant portion of their budgets, they are incentivized to manage funds judiciously and invest in projects that yield tangible benefits for their communities. This local fiscal autonomy not only curbs waste and corruption but also reinforces the conservative ideal of limited government—a system in which

---

[10] Torney-Purta, Judith, et al. *Citizenship and Political Participation: Political Science Perspectives*. Rowman & Littlefield, 2001.

[11] Lipset, Seymour. *Political Man: The Social Bases of Politics*. Johns Hopkins University Press, 1960.

[12] Amar, Akhil Reed. *America's Constitution: A Biography*. Random House, 2005.

power is not only decentralized but also subject to the disciplined oversight of an engaged citizenry.[13]

Moreover, the relationship between national standards and local autonomy has significant implications for public accountability. When policies are crafted and implemented at the local level, citizens are better able to monitor and evaluate the performance of their government. This proximity to power fosters a culture of transparency and responsiveness that is often lacking in highly centralized systems. Conservatives argue that such accountability is essential for preventing abuses of power and ensuring that government actions remain aligned with the interests of the people. In this context, local governance serves not only as a practical mechanism for policy implementation but also as a vital check on the concentration of governmental authority.[14]

Recent policy experiments in various states further illustrate the potential benefits of a balanced approach. Several states have successfully implemented localized reforms in areas such as healthcare, education, and environmental regulation, achieving outcomes that exceed those of more centralized models. These successes are frequently attributed to the flexibility and innovation that are inherent in decentralized governance. Conservative policymakers highlight these case studies as evidence that when localities are granted the freedom to develop context-specific solutions, they can create more effective and sustainable policies that serve the public interest.[15]

Critics, however, caution that excessive decentralization can lead to a patchwork of policies that undermine national cohesion and create inequality among regions. They argue that without a strong national framework, local governments might adopt measures that are inconsistent with overarching constitutional principles. Conservatives respond by emphasizing that the goal is not to eliminate national standards but to integrate them with local autonomy in a manner that respects both. This balanced approach ensures that while certain fundamental rights and standards are uniformly protected, local governments retain the flexibility to adapt policies to their unique circumstances.[16]

The role of federal oversight in ensuring this balance is indispensable. While local autonomy is paramount, the federal government must also step in when state or local actions conflict with

---

[13] Eskridge, William N. Jr. *Originalism in the Twenty-First Century*. Harvard University Press, 2012.

[14] McCarty, Nolan, Keith T. Poole, and Howard Rosenthal. *Polarized America: The Dance of Ideology and Unequal Riches*. MIT Press, 2009.

[15] Wood, Gordon S. *The Creation of the American Republic, 1776–1787*. University of North Carolina Press, 1998.

[16] Ellis, Joseph J. *American Creation: Triumphs and Tragedies in the Founding of the Republic*. Knopf, 2007.

constitutional principles or infringe upon the rights of citizens. The conservative view supports a judicious use of federal power—one that intervenes only when necessary to uphold the rule of law and protect individual liberties. Such a system creates a dynamic tension between uniformity and diversity, ensuring that the national interest is maintained without stifling local innovation and self-governance.[17]

Furthermore, the effective balancing of national standards with local autonomy is essential for fostering social and economic mobility. National standards, such as those governing civil rights, environmental protection, and consumer safety, provide a common framework that prevents local governments from enacting policies that could disadvantage vulnerable populations. At the same time, allowing local authorities the freedom to innovate and tailor policies to their specific conditions can lead to more effective and responsive governance, ultimately enhancing opportunities for all citizens. This dual approach, conservatives argue, is key to ensuring that America remains both a unified nation and a mosaic of thriving, autonomous communities.[18]

The conservative perspective holds that the path to achieving this balance lies in a steadfast commitment to the Constitution and the principles enshrined therein. The founding fathers deliberately constructed a system of government that was both flexible and resilient, capable of accommodating change while preserving the core values of liberty, justice, and limited government. By returning to these foundational principles, modern policymakers can forge a system that harmonizes the need for national standards with the imperative of local self-governance. This approach not only honors the legacy of our founders but also provides a viable roadmap for addressing the complex challenges of contemporary governance.[19]

In practical terms, achieving this balance requires a multifaceted strategy that includes comprehensive judicial oversight, targeted fiscal reforms, and robust civic education. Judicial review must remain vigilant in checking any overreach by state or federal authorities, ensuring that all actions adhere to constitutional mandates. Fiscal reforms should empower local governments while establishing clear parameters for federal assistance, thereby promoting efficiency and accountability. Meanwhile, civic education plays a critical role in preparing citizens to participate actively in local governance, equipping them with the knowledge and

---

[17] Putnam, Robert D. *Bowling Alone: The Collapse and Revival of American Community*. Simon & Schuster, 2000.

[18] Galston, William A. *Civic Education and Democracy in America*. Johns Hopkins University Press, 2001.

[19] Sanger, Margaret. *Conservative Legacies: How the Founding Ideals Endure*. HarperCollins, 2010.

skills necessary to hold public officials accountable and advocate for policies that reflect their community's interests.[20]

Ultimately, the conservative vision for balancing national standards with local autonomy is one that champions both unity and diversity. It recognizes that while a shared set of national principles is essential for maintaining order and protecting individual rights, the richness of American democracy is found in its local variations. By fostering an environment where local governments can flourish within the bounds of a constitutionally mandated framework, America can ensure that its policies remain both effective and responsive. This dynamic balance not only strengthens democratic institutions but also reinforces the very foundations upon which the nation was built.[21]

The case for this balanced approach is bolstered by numerous empirical studies that highlight the successes of decentralized governance in fostering innovation, economic growth, and civic engagement. When local governments are entrusted with greater autonomy, they are better positioned to respond to the specific needs of their populations, leading to more efficient public services and higher levels of citizen satisfaction. At the same time, national standards provide the necessary safeguards to ensure that these local policies do not infringe upon the rights of individuals or compromise the overall integrity of the union.[22]

In conclusion, the task of balancing national standards with local autonomy lies at the heart of the American experiment. This conservative perspective affirms that a robust and dynamic federal system must blend the uniformity required to protect individual rights with the flexibility necessary to accommodate local diversity. By adhering to the constitutional vision of limited government, fiscal responsibility, and decentralized power, the United States can forge a path that not only preserves its founding ideals but also promotes innovation, accountability, and unity in an ever-changing world. Such a system honors the wisdom of our founding fathers and provides the best safeguard against the dangers of overcentralization, ensuring that government remains both of the people and for the people.[23]

---

[20] Bickel, Alexander M. *The Least Dangerous Branch: The Supreme Court at the Bar of Politics*. Yale University Press, 1962.

[21] Lasch, Christopher. *The Culture of Narcissism: American Life in an Age of Diminishing Expectations*. W.W. Norton & Company, 1979.

[22] Wood, Gordon S. *The Radicalism of the American Revolution*. Vintage Books, 1993.

[23] Eskridge, William N. Jr. *Originalism in the Twenty-First Century*. Harvard University Press, 2012.

Looking to the future, it is imperative that policymakers continue to refine and implement strategies that reinforce this balance. Embracing the principles of federalism and subsidiarity will enable communities to thrive while upholding the national standards that are vital for maintaining order and justice. The enduring challenge is to create a governance model that is both responsive and responsible—a model in which local autonomy is not compromised by national mandates, and where national standards serve as a unifying force rather than a source of division. This balanced approach is essential for sustaining the freedoms and opportunities that have defined America for over two centuries.[24]

Thus, the conservative vision for balancing national standards with local autonomy is not a call for the dismantling of federal authority but a plea for a more measured, principled approach to governance—one that honors the constitutional heritage of our nation while addressing the practical demands of modern society. Through a steadfast commitment to these ideals, America can secure a future where the strengths of local governance and the benefits of national cohesion work together to foster a more prosperous, free, and united society.[25]

---

[24] Scalia, Antonin. *A Matter of Interpretation: Federal Courts and the Law*. Princeton University Press, 1997.

[25] Hamilton, Alexander; Madison, James; Jay, John. *The Federalist Papers*. Penguin Classics, 2003.

5. The Future of Decentralized Governance in America

The future of decentralized governance in America stands at a critical juncture as the nation confronts the dual challenges of an increasingly centralized federal bureaucracy and the persistent demand for local control as envisioned by our founding fathers. This commentary examines the prospects for the evolution of decentralized governance, arguing that a conservative commitment to limited government, local autonomy, and constitutional principles is essential for fostering innovation, accountability, and unity in American political life. By analyzing historical precedents, contemporary trends, and future challenges, this paper asserts that the restoration and expansion of decentralized power is not only a theoretical ideal but a practical necessity for preserving the liberties and values that have long defined the United States.[1]

Historically, the American experiment was built on the principle of federalism, a system designed to distribute power between a national government and the states. The framers of the Constitution, wary of the tyranny they had experienced under British rule, intentionally divided authority to ensure that government remained as close to the people as possible. They believed that decentralization would prevent the concentration of power and encourage local decision-making—a concept that has since become a cornerstone of conservative thought. Today, as debates over the role of government intensify, conservatives argue that the future of American governance depends on a renewed commitment to these original principles, ensuring that localities retain the ability to shape policies that reflect their unique cultural, economic, and social conditions.[2]

In recent decades, the trend toward centralization has often been justified by the need to address complex national challenges such as terrorism, environmental protection, and economic stabilization. While these issues undoubtedly require a coordinated response, the conservative perspective maintains that centralization should not come at the expense of local autonomy. Instead, a balanced approach is needed—one in which the federal government provides a stable framework of national standards while empowering states and municipalities to implement policies best suited to their circumstances. The future of decentralized governance lies in recalibrating this balance to ensure that federal power is both constrained and complemented by robust local initiatives.[3]

---

[1] Hamilton, Alexander; Madison, James; Jay, John. *The Federalist Papers*. Penguin Classics, 2003.

[2] Madison, James. "Federalist No. 51." In *The Federalist Papers*, edited by Clinton Rossiter, Bantam Classics, 1961.

[3] Niemi, Richard G., and Jane Junn. *Civic Education: What Makes Students Learn*. Yale University Press, 1998.

One promising avenue for achieving this balance is through the decentralization of regulatory authority. Over the past several decades, federal agencies have accrued significant power to regulate everything from environmental standards to labor practices. While uniform national policies can create consistency, they often fail to account for regional variations in resources, economic conditions, and cultural values. Conservatives argue that devolving regulatory power to state and local governments can lead to more innovative and efficient policy solutions. For example, states with diverse geographical and economic landscapes are better positioned to tailor environmental regulations that protect local ecosystems without stifling economic growth. By allowing localities greater discretion, America can harness the benefits of competition among states—each serving as a "laboratory of democracy" where best practices emerge and are adopted nationwide.[4]

Another key component in the future of decentralized governance is fiscal devolution. The principle of fiscal federalism, which entails transferring financial resources and decision-making authority to local governments, is critical for ensuring that public funds are allocated efficiently and responsively. Conservatives contend that local officials, who are more intimately familiar with the needs of their communities, can make better decisions regarding taxation, public spending, and infrastructure investments than distant federal bureaucrats. Fiscal devolution not only promotes accountability but also encourages states to adopt policies that stimulate local economic development. By restoring local control over fiscal matters, the United States can reduce waste, enhance transparency, and foster an environment in which public services are delivered more effectively.[5]

The digital age presents both challenges and opportunities for decentralized governance. On one hand, technological advancements have enabled unprecedented communication and coordination among various levels of government, facilitating the implementation of decentralized policies. On the other hand, the same technologies have sometimes contributed to the centralization of power through the growth of large data-driven agencies and centralized digital infrastructures. Conservatives assert that the future of governance in America must harness digital innovation to empower local governments rather than further concentrate power at the federal level. Initiatives such as state-run digital platforms for public services, local data centers, and community-driven cybersecurity measures can reinforce the decentralized model while ensuring that technology serves as a tool for enhancing, not eroding, local autonomy.[6]

---

[4] Friedman, Milton. *Capitalism and Freedom*. University of Chicago Press, 2002.

[5] Elazar, Daniel J. *Exploring Federalism*. University of Alabama Press, 1987.

[6] Scalia, Antonin. *A Matter of Interpretation: Federal Courts and the Law*. Princeton University Press, 1997.

Civic engagement remains at the heart of successful decentralized governance. The founding fathers believed that a healthy republic depended on an informed and active citizenry, and local governments have traditionally been the closest interface between the state and its citizens. When power is decentralized, individuals are more likely to participate in public decision-making, hold their leaders accountable, and contribute to the overall well-being of their communities. Conservatives argue that reinvigorating local democratic institutions—through town hall meetings, local referenda, and community advisory boards—will not only increase government transparency but also strengthen the social fabric of American society. A future that emphasizes decentralized governance must therefore prioritize civic education and grassroots participation as indispensable components of political reform.[7]

The judicial system also plays a vital role in maintaining the delicate balance between national standards and local autonomy. Over the years, the Supreme Court has issued landmark decisions that have defined the limits of federal power and reinforced the rights of states. Conservative jurists advocate for an originalist interpretation of the Constitution, emphasizing that any expansion of federal authority must be scrutinized in light of the framers' intentions. Judicial restraint, they argue, is necessary to ensure that decentralized governance remains true to the principles of limited government and that states are not unduly coerced into uniformity by an overreaching federal government. Looking forward, maintaining an independent judiciary that respects federalism will be crucial in safeguarding the future of decentralized governance in America.[8]

In the realm of public policy, the future of decentralized governance is likely to be influenced by the need to address complex, multifaceted issues without sacrificing local control. Education, healthcare, infrastructure, and public safety are sectors where national standards provide a vital baseline, yet the implementation of effective solutions depends on localized knowledge and adaptability. For instance, while federal policies can ensure that all citizens have access to quality education, the methods for achieving educational excellence must be tailored to local contexts. States and municipalities, equipped with the freedom to innovate, can design curricula, allocate resources, and establish partnerships that reflect the specific needs of their populations. This blended approach, which honors both the necessity of national standards and the strengths of local governance, exemplifies the conservative vision for a future where decentralization is not an obstacle to progress but a catalyst for positive change.[9]

---

[7] Binder, Sarah A. *Stalemate: Causes and Consequences of Legislative Gridlock*. Brookings Institution Press, 2003.

[8] Kirk, Russell. *The Conservative Mind: From Burke to Eliot*. Regnery Publishing, 1953.

[9] Maier, Pauline. *American Scripture: Making the Declaration of Independence*. Vintage, 1998.

Moreover, the future of decentralized governance will be shaped by ongoing debates over the role of federal oversight versus local initiative. Conservatives emphasize that centralization, while sometimes beneficial in times of national crisis, should never become the default mode of governance. Instead, policies must be crafted to empower local communities while ensuring that overarching national interests—such as the protection of individual rights and the maintenance of the rule of law—are upheld. This requires a reimagining of intergovernmental relations in which the federal government acts as a facilitator and guarantor rather than as a director of local affairs. By rebalancing power in this way, America can foster an environment in which both national cohesion and local diversity are respected and promoted.[10]

Economic competition among states further underscores the benefits of decentralized governance. When states have the autonomy to set their own policies on taxation, regulation, and economic development, they are incentivized to innovate and create competitive advantages. This competition, far from undermining national unity, can lead to higher overall standards of living and greater prosperity across the country. Conservatives maintain that market-driven solutions, when implemented at the local level, can provide more effective and responsive outcomes than top-down mandates. The future of decentralized governance, therefore, rests on the idea that local experimentation and competition are not only compatible with, but essential to, the advancement of a free and prosperous society.[11]

Cultural factors will also play an important role in shaping the future of decentralized governance. The United States is a nation rich in regional diversity, with distinct cultural, historical, and social identities. National policies that fail to account for these differences risk alienating communities and igniting social divisions. Conservatives argue that preserving local autonomy is key to maintaining America's pluralistic character while still upholding the national standards that bind the union together. By allowing localities to craft policies that reflect their unique heritage and values, the country can foster a sense of pride and ownership among its citizens, reinforcing the notion that governance should be as diverse as the people it serves.[12]

The challenges of globalization and rapid technological change further complicate the future of decentralized governance. As international competition intensifies and digital transformation accelerates, local governments must be agile and forward-thinking. Conservatives advocate for

---

[10] Torney-Purta, Judith, et al. *Citizenship and Political Participation: Political Science Perspectives*. Rowman & Littlefield, 2001.

[11] Lipset, Seymour. *Political Man: The Social Bases of Politics*. Johns Hopkins University Press, 1960.

[12] Amar, Akhil Reed. *America's Constitution: A Biography*. Random House, 2005.

policies that support local innovation and enable communities to adapt quickly to global economic trends while remaining rooted in constitutional principles. The future will likely see increased collaboration between local governments and the private sector, as well as partnerships with academic institutions to develop solutions that address both local and global challenges. In this context, decentralized governance emerges as a strategic asset, allowing American communities to leverage their unique strengths in a competitive international landscape.[13]

Environmental policy offers another domain where balancing national standards with local autonomy is crucial for future success. The varied geography and climate of the United States necessitate region-specific approaches to conservation, energy production, and land use. While national guidelines are essential to ensure that all states adhere to minimum environmental standards, local governments are best positioned to implement policies that address the particular challenges of their ecosystems. Conservatives argue that empowering local authorities to manage natural resources not only promotes sustainability but also encourages community involvement in environmental stewardship. This model of localized environmental governance exemplifies how decentralization can yield more effective and context-sensitive outcomes than a one-size-fits-all federal approach.[14]

The interplay between local autonomy and national standards is also reflected in debates over public safety and criminal justice. National laws set the fundamental parameters for protecting civil rights and ensuring due process, yet the day-to-day operations of law enforcement are most effectively managed at the local level. Decentralizing public safety allows communities to tailor their strategies to local crime patterns and social conditions, thereby enhancing accountability and responsiveness. Conservatives maintain that when local police forces and judicial systems operate under direct community oversight, they are more likely to respect individual liberties and uphold the rule of law—a core tenet of constitutional governance.[15]

As the nation looks to the future, one of the most critical challenges will be ensuring that the benefits of decentralized governance are not undermined by partisan polarization and bureaucratic inertia. The conservative vision for the future emphasizes that restoring balance between national standards and local autonomy requires both institutional reform and a cultural shift. Policymakers must work to dismantle the overreaching federal agencies that have, in many cases, stifled local

---

[13] Eskridge, William N. Jr. *Originalism in the Twenty-First Century*. Harvard University Press, 2012.

[14] McCarty, Nolan, Keith T. Poole, and Howard Rosenthal. *Polarized America: The Dance of Ideology and Unequal Riches*. MIT Press, 2009.

[15] Wood, Gordon S. *The Creation of the American Republic, 1776–1787*. University of North Carolina Press, 1998.

initiative, while simultaneously investing in the mechanisms that promote local accountability and innovation. This dual approach—limiting federal intervention while empowering local leaders—is seen as the most effective path toward achieving a resilient and responsive system of government.[16]

A robust framework for intergovernmental cooperation will be essential in this endeavor. While decentralization confers many benefits, it must be accompanied by mechanisms that facilitate dialogue and coordination between different levels of government. Conservatives argue for the establishment of formal intergovernmental councils and regular consultation processes to ensure that local policies are harmonized with national interests without sacrificing the independence of state and local decision-making. Such frameworks can help resolve conflicts and build consensus, ensuring that the benefits of decentralization are realized without fragmenting the nation's policy landscape.[17]

Fiscal reform remains a pivotal element in the future of decentralized governance. Decentralization is most effective when local governments have the financial autonomy to implement policies that reflect community priorities. Conservatives have long championed tax reforms and budgetary controls that empower localities while constraining wasteful federal spending. Moving forward, innovative fiscal policies that allow local governments to raise and manage their own revenue will be critical in promoting accountability, reducing dependency on federal funds, and fostering economic growth at the community level.[18]

The role of education in supporting decentralized governance cannot be overlooked. A well-informed citizenry is the backbone of any decentralized system, as it enables communities to participate meaningfully in local decision-making. Conservatives advocate for educational reforms that emphasize civic education, the study of constitutional principles, and local history. By equipping citizens with a deep understanding of their rights and responsibilities, America can ensure that local governments remain responsive to the needs of their communities and that the principles of decentralized governance are perpetuated for future generations.[19]

In conclusion, the future of decentralized governance in America rests on the ability to balance national standards with local autonomy—a challenge that lies at the very heart of the American

---

[16] Ellis, Joseph J. *American Creation: Triumphs and Tragedies in the Founding of the Republic*. Knopf, 2007.

[17] Putnam, Robert D. *Bowling Alone: The Collapse and Revival of American Community*. Simon & Schuster, 2000.

[18] Galston, William A. *Civic Education and Democracy in America*. Johns Hopkins University Press, 2001.

[19] Sanger, Margaret. *Conservative Legacies: How the Founding Ideals Endure*. HarperCollins, 2010.

constitutional experiment. The conservative perspective, rooted in the enduring wisdom of our founding fathers, holds that limited government, fiscal responsibility, and local control are the keys to fostering innovation, accountability, and unity in an ever-changing world. By embracing decentralization in areas ranging from education and healthcare to environmental management and public safety, the United States can create a more responsive and dynamic governance system that remains true to its constitutional ideals.

Looking forward, policymakers must prioritize reforms that dismantle unnecessary federal overreach while simultaneously empowering state and local authorities. This vision entails a robust framework for intergovernmental cooperation, innovative fiscal policies, and an unwavering commitment to civic education—all of which are indispensable for preserving the values of liberty and self-governance. The conservative blueprint for the future of decentralized governance is not a call for the abandonment of national standards but rather an invitation to recalibrate the balance between uniformity and local innovation. In doing so, America can honor the legacy of its founding fathers and secure a future where government remains truly of the people and for the people.[20]

Ultimately, the path forward requires a collective commitment to the principles enshrined in the Constitution—a commitment to local empowerment, limited federal power, and the protection of individual liberties. As the nation navigates the complexities of the twenty-first century, decentralized governance stands as a vital mechanism for ensuring that America's political system remains resilient, innovative, and responsive to the needs of its citizens. By striking a judicious balance between national standards and local autonomy, the United States can continue to thrive as a beacon of freedom and opportunity for generations to come.[21]

Moreover, this balanced approach will help bridge the divides that have increasingly characterized contemporary American politics. By empowering local communities and reinforcing national principles, the conservative vision for decentralized governance offers a pathway toward a more united, accountable, and prosperous society. The future, as seen through this lens, is one in which the dynamic interplay between national oversight and local initiative creates a government that is both flexible and steadfast—a government that adapts to change without sacrificing the core values that define the American experiment.[22]

---

[20] Bickel, Alexander M. *The Least Dangerous Branch: The Supreme Court at the Bar of Politics*. Yale University Press, 1962.

[21] Lasch, Christopher. *The Culture of Narcissism: American Life in an Age of Diminishing Expectations*. W.W. Norton & Company, 1979.

[22] Wood, Gordon S. *The Radicalism of the American Revolution*. Vintage Books, 1993.

In closing, the future of decentralized governance in America is not predetermined but can be shaped by the choices made by policymakers and citizens alike. Embracing the conservative principles of limited government, fiscal prudence, and local self-governance will be essential to crafting a system that honors the legacy of our founding fathers while meeting the challenges of the modern world. By striking an optimal balance between national standards and local autonomy, America can forge a path toward a future where its democratic institutions are strengthened and its citizens remain the ultimate arbiters of their destiny.[23]

Thus, the conservative vision for the future of decentralized governance calls for a return to the foundational principles of the Constitution—principles that ensure government is responsive, accountable, and inherently local in its character. It is through this steadfast adherence to the ideals of limited government and individual liberty that the United States will continue to serve as a model of democratic excellence and a beacon of freedom in an increasingly complex world.[24]

Ultimately, the promise of decentralized governance lies in its capacity to empower communities, foster innovation, and preserve the constitutional safeguards that have long protected American liberty. By rebalancing national standards with local autonomy, policymakers can secure a future in which the government is both effective and true to the enduring spirit of the American experiment—a future where the wisdom of our founding fathers continues to light the way for generations to come.[25]

---

[23] Eskridge, William N. Jr. *Originalism in the Twenty-First Century*. Harvard University Press, 2012.

[24] Scalia, Antonin. *A Matter of Interpretation: Federal Courts and the Law*. Princeton University Press, 1997.

[25] Hamilton, Alexander; Madison, James; Jay, John. *The Federalist Papers*. Penguin Classics, 2003.

CHAPTER 13:

Constitutional Education and Civic Engagement

1. The Role of Education in Constitutional Literacy

The foundation of a vibrant and enduring republic rests not only upon its governing documents but also upon the ability of its citizens to understand and uphold them. Constitutional literacy—the thorough understanding of the United States Constitution and its underlying principles—is essential for preserving the freedoms and limited government envisioned by our founding fathers. This commentary examines the critical role of education in promoting constitutional literacy, arguing from a politically conservative perspective that only through robust civic education can the American people safeguard their liberty and ensure that government remains accountable and truly of the people.[1]

At the heart of conservative thought is the belief that an informed citizenry is indispensable to the proper functioning of a free society. The founding fathers themselves placed immense trust in the capacity of individuals to govern themselves when equipped with the knowledge of their rights and the limits of governmental power. They understood that ignorance of constitutional principles would leave the door open to tyranny and governmental overreach. Thus, the role of education in fostering constitutional literacy is not a modern innovation but a revival of the original intent of our founders—a call to educate citizens so they may defend the rule of law and hold government accountable.[2]

Historically, constitutional education in America has taken many forms, from the public debates and town meetings of the early republic to the civic instruction that was once a cornerstone of American schooling. In the eighteenth century, political discourse was infused with references to the natural rights of man, the separation of powers, and the limited scope of government—all concepts that were disseminated through rigorous debate and community engagement. Over time, however, the emphasis on these foundational ideas has waned in many public education

---

[1] Hamilton, Alexander; Madison, James; Jay, John. *The Federalist Papers*. Penguin Classics, 2003.

[2] Madison, James. "Federalist No. 51." In *The Federalist Papers*, edited by Clinton Rossiter, Bantam Classics, 1961.

systems, replaced by a more utilitarian focus that often neglects the enduring principles that sustain the constitutional order. Conservatives argue that a renewed focus on constitutional education is essential for reestablishing the civic virtues that have historically been the bedrock of American democracy.[3]

One of the primary challenges facing contemporary American society is the decline in civic engagement and the corresponding erosion of constitutional literacy among young people. In recent decades, academic curricula have shifted towards standardized testing and skills-based learning, often at the expense of in-depth study of history and civics. This trend has resulted in generations of citizens who are less aware of the historical context, philosophical underpinnings, and practical applications of the Constitution. From a conservative standpoint, such a deficiency is alarming because an uninformed electorate is more susceptible to populist demagoguery and radical policies that can undermine the very foundations of liberty.[4]

The conservative response to this challenge is twofold. First, there must be a concerted effort to reintegrate constitutional education into the core curriculum of schools at all levels. This includes not only a detailed study of the text of the Constitution but also an exploration of the historical debates, compromises, and philosophical principles that shaped it. By understanding the intentions of the founding fathers, students can appreciate the delicate balance between liberty and order that is embodied in the Constitution. Second, education must be expanded beyond the classroom to include community-based learning and public discourse that reinforce constitutional values. Civic education programs, extracurricular activities, and public forums can serve as vital platforms for nurturing a culture of constitutional literacy.[5]

Moreover, the role of educators is pivotal in this endeavor. Teachers, as the primary transmitters of knowledge and values, must be well-versed in constitutional principles and committed to imparting this knowledge to their students. Conservative educators argue that curriculum reforms should empower teachers to use a variety of pedagogical methods—such as Socratic dialogue, primary source analysis, and experiential learning—to engage students with the Constitution in a meaningful way. This approach not only deepens understanding but also encourages critical thinking, enabling students to analyze and challenge governmental actions in light of constitutional standards.[6]

---

[3] Niemi, Richard G., and Jane Junn. *Civic Education: What Makes Students Learn*. Yale University Press, 1998.

[4] Friedman, Milton. *Capitalism and Freedom*. University of Chicago Press, 2002.

[5] Elazar, Daniel J. *Exploring Federalism*. University of Alabama Press, 1987.

[6] Scalia, Antonin. *A Matter of Interpretation: Federal Courts and the Law*. Princeton University Press, 1997.

In addition to formal education, the media and digital platforms have a significant impact on constitutional literacy. In an era marked by the rapid dissemination of information, the quality of civic education is increasingly influenced by the sources from which young people obtain their knowledge. Conservatives contend that while digital media has the potential to democratize information, it often contributes to the spread of misinformation and ideological bias. Therefore, it is imperative that efforts to promote constitutional literacy also address the need for media literacy. By teaching students how to critically evaluate sources and discern fact from opinion, educators can fortify the public's understanding of constitutional principles and empower them to resist distortions of historical truth.[7]

A further element of constitutional education is the active engagement of families and communities in the learning process. The conservative perspective emphasizes that education is a shared responsibility that extends beyond the classroom. Parents, community leaders, and faith-based organizations have long played a crucial role in imparting the values of self-governance, personal responsibility, and respect for tradition. Revitalizing these community-based educational initiatives can help bridge the gap between academic learning and practical civic engagement. When families and communities work together to promote constitutional literacy, they reinforce the social fabric that underpins American democracy and ensure that citizens remain vigilant in defending their freedoms.[8]

The role of constitutional education is also integral to the functioning of a healthy political system. An electorate that is well-versed in the principles of the Constitution is less likely to succumb to extremist ideologies and more likely to support policies that preserve individual liberty and limited government. Conservatives argue that the decline in constitutional literacy has contributed to a polarized political climate, where voters are swayed by rhetoric rather than reasoned debate. By restoring a focus on constitutional education, it is possible to create a more informed electorate that can engage in substantive policy discussions and hold elected officials accountable to the nation's founding principles.[9]

Furthermore, the importance of constitutional literacy extends to the safeguarding of minority rights and the prevention of governmental overreach. The Constitution provides a framework for protecting individual freedoms against the potential excesses of majority rule. When citizens

---

[7] Binder, Sarah A. *Stalemate: Causes and Consequences of Legislative Gridlock*. Brookings Institution Press, 2003.

[8] Kirk, Russell. *The Conservative Mind: From Burke to Eliot*. Regnery Publishing, 1953.

[9] Maier, Pauline. *American Scripture: Making the Declaration of Independence*. Vintage, 1998.

understand these protections, they are better equipped to challenge policies that threaten to erode the rights enshrined in the Bill of Rights. Conservative scholars maintain that a robust constitutional education empowers individuals to recognize and resist encroachments on their liberty, thereby ensuring that government remains both restrained and accountable.[10]

Forward, the future of constitutional education depends on a multifaceted strategy that includes curriculum reform, enhanced teacher training, and the integration of digital tools to support civic learning. Policymakers must prioritize the development of educational standards that emphasize constitutional literacy and encourage local school districts to adopt curricula that reflect the historical and philosophical significance of the Constitution. In addition, partnerships between educational institutions, civic organizations, and government agencies can create innovative programs that bring constitutional principles to life in the modern context.[11]

A key aspect of this strategy is the recognition that constitutional education is not solely about rote memorization of historical facts but about cultivating a mindset of critical inquiry and civic responsibility. Students must be taught to view the Constitution not as a static document but as a living framework that continues to guide and constrain governmental power. Through case studies, debates, and simulated governmental processes, learners can develop a nuanced understanding of how constitutional principles are applied in real-world scenarios. This experiential approach not only enhances comprehension but also fosters a sense of ownership over the democratic process.[12]

The involvement of higher education institutions is equally crucial in promoting constitutional literacy. Universities and colleges can serve as centers for advanced study and research on constitutional law, history, and political theory. By offering specialized courses, hosting public lectures, and facilitating research projects, institutions of higher learning can contribute to a deeper and more comprehensive understanding of the Constitution among young adults. This academic engagement is essential for developing future leaders who are not only knowledgeable about constitutional principles but are also committed to upholding them in their professional and personal lives.[13]

---

[10] Torney-Purta, Judith, et al. *Citizenship and Political Participation: Political Science Perspectives*. Rowman & Littlefield, 2001.

[11] Lipset, Seymour. *Political Man: The Social Bases of Politics*. Johns Hopkins University Press, 1960.

[12] Amar, Akhil Reed. *America's Constitution: A Biography*. Random House, 2005.

[13] Eskridge, William N. Jr. *Originalism in the Twenty-First Century*. Harvard University Press, 2012.

Moreover, the conservative vision for constitutional education emphasizes the need to preserve the integrity of historical narratives. In recent years, debates over historical interpretation have intensified, with some arguing that revisionist perspectives undermine the enduring principles of the Constitution. Conservatives maintain that a balanced approach to history, which honors the achievements and acknowledges the challenges of the founding era, is necessary for fostering genuine constitutional literacy. By presenting students with primary sources, such as the Federalist Papers and other founding documents, educators can provide a firsthand look at the debates that shaped the nation. This method not only enriches students' understanding but also instills a respect for the intellectual rigor that underpins the American experiment.[14]

In addition, the role of extracurricular activities in promoting constitutional literacy should not be underestimated. Civic clubs, debate teams, mock trials, and student government organizations offer valuable opportunities for practical engagement with constitutional issues. These activities encourage students to apply their knowledge in simulated environments, thereby reinforcing theoretical concepts through hands-on experience. Conservative advocates argue that such practical learning experiences are indispensable for developing the critical thinking and leadership skills necessary to navigate the complexities of modern governance.[15]

The integration of technology into constitutional education also holds considerable promise. Digital platforms can provide interactive learning experiences that engage students in ways that traditional classroom settings may not. Online simulations, virtual debates, and access to digitized historical archives allow learners to explore constitutional issues dynamically and collaboratively. Conservatives, however, caution that while technology can enhance learning, it must be employed judiciously to avoid the pitfalls of misinformation and ideological bias. The challenge, therefore, is to harness digital tools in a manner that reinforces sound educational principles and promotes an objective understanding of constitutional history.[16]

Furthermore, a commitment to constitutional literacy extends beyond formal education and into the realm of lifelong learning. Adult education programs, public seminars, and community workshops are vital for ensuring that all citizens, regardless of age, remain informed about their constitutional rights and responsibilities. In an era when rapid political change can outpace traditional educational channels, continuous civic education is essential for maintaining an

---

[14] McCarty, Nolan, Keith T. Poole, and Howard Rosenthal. *Polarized America: The Dance of Ideology and Unequal Riches*. MIT Press, 2009.

[15] Wood, Gordon S. *The Creation of the American Republic, 1776–1787*. University of North Carolina Press, 1998.

[16] Ellis, Joseph J. *American Creation: Triumphs and Tragedies in the Founding of the Republic*. Knopf, 2007.

engaged and resilient electorate. Conservatives argue that lifelong learning initiatives help to counteract the decline in civic engagement and ensure that the principles of limited government and individual liberty remain at the forefront of public discourse.[17]

The role of media in reinforcing constitutional education must also be acknowledged. Conservative media outlets, academic journals, and public broadcasting networks have a responsibility to present historical and contemporary analyses of constitutional issues in an unbiased and informative manner. By offering programming that highlights the significance of constitutional literacy, the media can contribute to a more informed citizenry and foster a culture of civic responsibility. This, in turn, supports the broader goal of ensuring that government remains accountable to the people.[18]

The implications of robust constitutional education are far-reaching. A citizenry that is well-versed in the Constitution is better prepared to engage in public debate, hold elected officials accountable, and resist the encroachments of government power. Conservatives assert that a deep understanding of constitutional principles is the most effective antidote to the trends of political polarization and governmental overreach. It is through education that the legacy of the founding fathers is preserved and transmitted to future generations, ensuring that the ideals of freedom, justice, and limited government endure in the face of contemporary challenges.[19]

Looking to the future, policymakers must recognize that investing in constitutional education is investing in the very future of American democracy. The challenges posed by rapid technological change, shifting political dynamics, and global pressures require a populace that is both knowledgeable and engaged. By prioritizing constitutional literacy in educational reform, America can empower its citizens to become informed defenders of their rights and active participants in the democratic process. This approach not only honors the intentions of the founding fathers but also provides a bulwark against the erosion of the constitutional order.[20]

In addition, fostering constitutional literacy is a moral imperative. Conservatives believe that every citizen has a duty to understand the document that guarantees their freedom and shapes the nation's legal framework. This duty extends beyond academic achievement; it is a matter of

---

[17] Putnam, Robert D. *Bowling Alone: The Collapse and Revival of American Community*. Simon & Schuster, 2000.

[18] Galston, William A. *Civic Education and Democracy in America*. Johns Hopkins University Press, 2001.

[19] Sanger, Margaret. *Conservative Legacies: How the Founding Ideals Endure*. HarperCollins, 2010.

[20] Bickel, Alexander M. *The Least Dangerous Branch: The Supreme Court at the Bar of Politics*. Yale University Press, 1962.

civic honor and national survival. When citizens are armed with knowledge of their constitutional rights, they are less likely to surrender their freedoms to an overreaching state. In this way, education becomes the frontline defense against tyranny, ensuring that the government remains both limited in its scope and accountable to its people.[21]

The future of constitutional education, therefore, hinges on a collaborative effort among educators, policymakers, community leaders, and the media. By forging partnerships that bridge the gap between formal education and community engagement, it is possible to create a comprehensive ecosystem for constitutional literacy. Such an ecosystem would provide consistent, accurate, and engaging content on the Constitution, drawing on the rich historical legacy of the founding era while addressing the practical challenges of the modern world. This integrated approach is essential for nurturing a generation of citizens who are capable of upholding the values of limited government and individual liberty in an ever-changing political landscape.[22]

Moreover, constitutional education must be adaptive, evolving with the times while remaining grounded in timeless principles. As the United States faces new challenges—from digital privacy concerns to global economic shifts—the core tenets of the Constitution provide a stable foundation upon which to build resilient policies. Conservatives argue that by revisiting and reaffirming these principles through continuous education, America can navigate the uncertainties of the future without sacrificing the freedoms that have defined it since its inception.[23]

Ultimately, the role of education in constitutional literacy is central to the preservation of American freedom. A well-informed citizenry, grounded in a deep understanding of constitutional principles, is the best safeguard against the encroachments of power and the erosion of democratic norms. The conservative vision for the future of constitutional education is one in which the lessons of the founding era are not only preserved but actively propagated, ensuring that every citizen knows their rights, understands the limits of government, and is prepared to defend the Constitution against any threat.[24]

Thus, the future of decentralized governance and civic engagement in America depends fundamentally on the success of constitutional education. By investing in robust educational programs, fostering community engagement, and leveraging modern technology to enhance

---

[21] Lasch, Christopher. *The Culture of Narcissism: American Life in an Age of Diminishing Expectations*. W.W. Norton & Company, 1979.

[22] Wood, Gordon S. *The Radicalism of the American Revolution*. Vintage Books, 1993.

[23] Eskridge, William N. Jr. *Originalism in the Twenty-First Century*. Harvard University Press, 2012.

[24] Scalia, Antonin. *A Matter of Interpretation: Federal Courts and the Law*. Princeton University Press, 1997.

learning, policymakers can ensure that the Constitution remains a living document—one that continues to guide and inspire citizens across generations. In doing so, America will remain a beacon of liberty and a testament to the enduring wisdom of its founding fathers, securing a future where freedom, justice, and limited government prevail.[25]

[25] Hamilton, Alexander; Madison, James; Jay, John. *The Federalist Papers*. Penguin Classics, 2003.

2. Civic Engagement and Informed Citizenship

In a republic where the longevity of freedom depends on an informed electorate, civic engagement and informed citizenship serve as the lifeblood of American democracy. A robust understanding of the Constitution, combined with active participation in public affairs, not only empowers individuals to safeguard their rights but also holds government accountable to its foundational principles. This commentary explores the multifaceted role of civic engagement in fostering informed citizenship, emphasizing that an education steeped in constitutional literacy is essential for preserving the limited government and individual liberty cherished by our founding fathers. From a politically conservative perspective, it is through the reinvigoration of civic education that America can counteract the corrosive effects of partisan polarization and bureaucratic overreach, ensuring that its citizens remain vigilant defenders of the rule of law and the enduring legacy of the Constitution.[1]

The importance of civic engagement begins with the understanding that the American constitutional system is predicated on the notion that government derives its legitimacy from the consent of the governed. This principle, articulated by the founding fathers, requires that citizens not only be knowledgeable about their rights but also be active participants in the political process. Informed citizens are less likely to be swayed by populist rhetoric or demagogic appeals and more inclined to scrutinize governmental policies through the lens of constitutional principles. Consequently, the cultivation of constitutional literacy is not merely an academic exercise; it is a civic imperative that underpins the entire framework of self-government.[2]

Historically, civic engagement was an integral aspect of early American life. Town meetings, public debates, and community forums provided platforms for citizens to discuss local issues and collectively determine the course of public policy. This tradition of participatory democracy ensured that government remained responsive to the needs of the people and that power was diffused among many rather than concentrated in the hands of a few. The founding fathers envisaged a society where the average citizen was well-versed in the tenets of liberty and self-governance, and they believed that such an informed electorate would serve as a bulwark against tyranny. Today, however, there is widespread concern that civic knowledge is in decline, as many citizens lack a fundamental understanding of the Constitution and the historical context in which it was created.[3]

---

[1] Hamilton, Alexander; Madison, James; Jay, John. *The Federalist Papers*. Penguin Classics, 2003.

[2] Madison, James. "Federalist No. 51." In *The Federalist Papers*, edited by Clinton Rossiter, Bantam Classics, 1961.

[3] Niemi, Richard G., and Jane Junn. *Civic Education: What Makes Students Learn*. Yale University Press, 1998.

The conservative response to this crisis in civic education is to reaffirm the value of a curriculum that emphasizes not only the text of the Constitution but also the philosophical underpinnings of American government. Proponents argue that a comprehensive civic education must include a study of the Federalist and Anti-Federalist debates, the struggles for independence, and the ideological battles that shaped the nation's founding. By understanding the sacrifices and deliberations of the founding generation, citizens can better appreciate the fragile balance between governmental authority and individual freedom. This historical perspective is crucial for developing a sense of national purpose and for fostering the civic virtues necessary for a thriving republic.[4]

Civic engagement also requires that citizens have access to reliable information and a diversity of viewpoints. In an era characterized by the rapid proliferation of digital media and social networks, misinformation can spread quickly and undermine public trust in democratic institutions. Conservatives assert that the media has a critical role in enhancing civic education by providing accurate, objective, and balanced coverage of constitutional issues. However, when media outlets become overly partisan or sensationalist, they risk distorting public perception and impeding informed debate. It is therefore essential that efforts to promote civic engagement be coupled with initiatives to improve media literacy, ensuring that citizens can discern fact from opinion and hold their sources of information to high standards of accountability.[5]

The role of educators in fostering civic engagement cannot be overstated. Teachers are not only transmitters of knowledge but also models of civic virtue who inspire students to participate actively in public life. A renewed emphasis on constitutional education in schools can cultivate a generation of citizens who are both knowledgeable about their rights and committed to the responsibilities of citizenship. Conservative educational reform advocates call for curricular reforms that integrate the study of the Constitution into a broader context of American history and civic life, encouraging students to engage in debates, simulations of governmental processes, and community service. Such experiential learning opportunities are vital for developing critical thinking skills and for instilling a sense of personal responsibility toward the common good.[6]

Beyond the classroom, civic engagement is enriched through participation in community organizations, local government, and voluntary associations. These institutions provide practical arenas where citizens can apply their constitutional knowledge to real-world challenges. For instance, involvement in local school boards, municipal councils, or neighborhood associations

---

[4] Friedman, Milton. *Capitalism and Freedom*. University of Chicago Press, 2002.

[5] Elazar, Daniel J. *Exploring Federalism*. University of Alabama Press, 1987.

[6] Scalia, Antonin. *A Matter of Interpretation: Federal Courts and the Law*. Princeton University Press, 1997.

offers citizens the opportunity to directly influence policies that affect their daily lives. Conservatives argue that such grassroots participation is the most effective means of holding government accountable and ensuring that public policies reflect the values of the community. When citizens actively participate in civic life, they contribute to a culture of mutual responsibility and trust, which is essential for maintaining a healthy democracy.[7]

In addition, the revival of civic engagement is closely linked to the preservation of individual liberties. The Constitution guarantees a host of fundamental rights—such as freedom of speech, freedom of assembly, and the right to due process—that are essential for the functioning of a free society. However, these rights are not self-executing; they require a vigilant and informed citizenry to defend them. Conservatives maintain that when citizens are educated about their constitutional rights, they are better equipped to resist encroachments on their freedom by both government and non-governmental forces. In this way, constitutional education serves as a shield against the erosion of liberty, reinforcing the principle that power must always be limited by law.[8]

The relationship between civic engagement and informed citizenship is also crucial for the effective functioning of democratic institutions. When citizens are knowledgeable about the Constitution and actively participate in the political process, they are more likely to support policies that promote accountability and transparency in government. This, in turn, fosters a political culture in which public officials are held to high standards of conduct and where corruption and abuse of power are swiftly checked by public scrutiny. Conservatives argue that an engaged electorate is the best defense against the centralization of power and that robust civic participation can help to ensure that government remains a servant of the people rather than a master of them.[9]

Moreover, informed citizenship plays a pivotal role in mediating the polarized political climate that has come to characterize contemporary American society. In an environment where partisan divisions are deep and political discourse is often characterized by acrimony, a well-informed public is essential for bridging divides and fostering constructive dialogue. By emphasizing the common heritage and shared principles enshrined in the Constitution, civic education can help to reframe political debates in terms of national unity and collective responsibility rather than

---

[7] Binder, Sarah A. *Stalemate: Causes and Consequences of Legislative Gridlock*. Brookings Institution Press, 2003.

[8] Kirk, Russell. *The Conservative Mind: From Burke to Eliot*. Regnery Publishing, 1953.

[9] Maier, Pauline. *American Scripture: Making the Declaration of Independence*. Vintage, 1998.

narrow ideological interests. This approach not only strengthens the democratic process but also renews the public's commitment to the constitutional values that have historically underpinned American governance.[10]

The integration of civic engagement with constitutional education extends to the realm of public policy as well. Informed citizens are better positioned to evaluate the effectiveness of government programs and to advocate for reforms that enhance accountability and efficiency. For example, when citizens understand the constitutional basis for policies related to taxation, education, and healthcare, they are more likely to support initiatives that balance individual liberty with social responsibility. Conservatives argue that such an informed approach to policymaking is essential for preventing the overreach of government and for ensuring that public policies remain aligned with the principles of limited government and personal responsibility.[11]

Another vital aspect of civic engagement is the role of voluntary associations and non-governmental organizations in promoting public discourse and community service. These groups often provide platforms for citizens to come together, share ideas, and collaborate on projects that advance the common good. From a conservative perspective, the vibrancy of civil society is a key indicator of a healthy democracy, as it reflects the capacity of citizens to organize independently of the state. Encouraging participation in civic organizations not only strengthens community bonds but also serves as a practical means of instilling the values of self-reliance and mutual support—values that are central to the conservative vision of limited government.[12]

Furthermore, the digital revolution offers unprecedented opportunities for enhancing civic engagement and constitutional literacy. Online platforms, social media, and virtual forums can serve as valuable tools for disseminating information, facilitating public debate, and mobilizing citizens around constitutional issues. Conservatives acknowledge that while the digital landscape is fraught with challenges—such as the spread of misinformation and partisan echo chambers—it also holds the potential to democratize access to knowledge and to empower individuals to engage with their government in innovative ways. By harnessing the power of technology to promote informed citizenship, America can ensure that its democratic institutions remain vibrant and resilient in the face of rapid change.[13]

---

[10] Torney-Purta, Judith, et al. *Citizenship and Political Participation: Political Science Perspectives*. Rowman & Littlefield, 2001.

[11] Lipset, Seymour. *Political Man: The Social Bases of Politics*. Johns Hopkins University Press, 1960.

[12] Amar, Akhil Reed. *America's Constitution: A Biography*. Random House, 2005.

[13] Eskridge, William N. Jr. *Originalism in the Twenty-First Century*. Harvard University Press, 2012.

It is essential to recognize that the responsibility for promoting civic engagement does not rest solely with educational institutions or government agencies. Families, religious organizations, and community groups also play a critical role in transmitting the values of civic responsibility and constitutional literacy. From a conservative standpoint, the family is the fundamental unit of society, and parents bear the primary responsibility for instilling in their children a respect for the Constitution and an understanding of their civic duties. When the principles of civic engagement are reinforced at home and in the community, they become deeply ingrained in the fabric of society, forming a bulwark against the erosion of individual freedoms and democratic norms.[14]

The importance of civic engagement and informed citizenship is further underscored by the need to safeguard the democratic process against external threats. In an era marked by rapid technological change, economic globalization, and geopolitical instability, an informed and engaged citizenry is the best defense against those who would seek to undermine the constitutional order. Conservatives argue that only through a sustained commitment to civic education can citizens develop the critical thinking skills necessary to evaluate the actions of government and to resist the allure of extremist ideologies that promise quick fixes at the expense of long-term stability.[15]

Moreover, the success of civic engagement initiatives is closely linked to the effectiveness of public institutions. When government agencies are transparent, accountable, and responsive to the needs of their constituents, citizens are more likely to trust and participate in the democratic process. This creates a virtuous cycle in which informed citizens demand higher standards of governance, and responsive government, in turn, reinforces public confidence. Conservatives maintain that such a cycle is vital for the preservation of the constitutional republic, as it ensures that government power remains both limited and subject to continuous public oversight.[16]

The role of civic engagement in promoting informed citizenship is not merely theoretical—it has practical implications for the quality of public debate and the implementation of sound public policy. When citizens are equipped with a thorough understanding of constitutional principles, they are better able to discern the merits of policy proposals and to hold elected officials accountable for their actions. This results in a more deliberative political process, where decisions are made on the basis of reasoned argument rather than partisan impulse. In this way, an informed citizenry

---

[14] McCarty, Nolan, Keith T. Poole, and Howard Rosenthal. *Polarized America: The Dance of Ideology and Unequal Riches*. MIT Press, 2009.

[15] Wood, Gordon S. *The Creation of the American Republic, 1776–1787*. University of North Carolina Press, 1998.

[16] Ellis, Joseph J. *American Creation: Triumphs and Tragedies in the Founding of the Republic*. Knopf, 2007.

acts as a stabilizing force in a society that might otherwise be vulnerable to the vicissitudes of populist rhetoric and ideological extremism.[17]

Looking to the future, the preservation and enhancement of civic engagement and constitutional literacy will require a coordinated effort among educators, policymakers, community leaders, and the media. It is incumbent upon government at all levels to support educational initiatives that prioritize the study of the Constitution and to create opportunities for citizens to engage in meaningful dialogue about their rights and responsibilities. Simultaneously, the private sector and civil society must collaborate to foster an environment in which civic participation is both valued and rewarded. By working together, these diverse stakeholders can ensure that the legacy of the founding fathers endures, and that the principles of limited government and individual liberty continue to guide American democracy.[18]

In conclusion, the role of education in fostering civic engagement and informed citizenship is central to the preservation of American freedom. A citizenry that is well-versed in the Constitution and actively participates in the democratic process is the most effective safeguard against the encroachments of government power and the erosion of individual liberties. From a conservative perspective, the renewal of constitutional education and the promotion of civic engagement are not optional but essential imperatives for the survival of the republic. By reinvigorating the study of our founding documents and encouraging citizens to take an active role in public life, America can ensure that its government remains truly of the people and that the principles of liberty, justice, and limited government are passed on to future generations.[19]

Furthermore, an informed and engaged citizenry is crucial for countering the challenges posed by partisan polarization and bureaucratic overreach. As the nation faces new threats and navigates complex global realities, the ability of its citizens to critically evaluate policies and hold their leaders accountable will determine the strength and resilience of American democracy. Conservatives assert that the revitalization of civic education, coupled with a renewed commitment to constitutional literacy, provides the best hope for a future in which government power remains checked and individual freedoms are vigorously defended.[20]

---

[17] Putnam, Robert D. *Bowling Alone: The Collapse and Revival of American Community*. Simon & Schuster, 2000.

[18] Galston, William A. *Civic Education and Democracy in America*. Johns Hopkins University Press, 2001.

[19] Sanger, Margaret. *Conservative Legacies: How the Founding Ideals Endure*. HarperCollins, 2010.

[20] Bickel, Alexander M. *The Least Dangerous Branch: The Supreme Court at the Bar of Politics*. Yale University Press, 1962.

Ultimately, the success of constitutional education and civic engagement will be measured by the ability of citizens to exercise their rights responsibly, to participate fully in the democratic process, and to uphold the values that have defined the American experiment since its inception. Informed citizenship is not simply about knowing the words of the Constitution; it is about embracing the spirit of the document—a commitment to self-governance, personal responsibility, and the pursuit of justice. It is through this lens that the future of American democracy must be viewed, as a project that requires continuous investment in the education and empowerment of its people.[21]

Thus, by reaffirming the importance of civic engagement and constitutional literacy, America can build a more resilient and dynamic society—one in which citizens are equipped to confront the challenges of the modern world while remaining true to the timeless ideals of freedom and limited government. This conservative vision for the future is both a tribute to the legacy of our founding fathers and a call to action for every citizen who cherishes the principles of the Constitution.[22]

In summation, the preservation of an informed and active citizenry is the cornerstone of American democracy. The commitment to constitutional education and civic engagement is an investment in the nation's future—a future in which the rights and responsibilities of citizenship are not only understood but also vigorously defended. Through collaborative efforts across educational, governmental, and community spheres, America can ensure that the democratic ideals enshrined in the Constitution continue to thrive, guiding the country toward a future marked by liberty, accountability, and sustained civic participation.[23]

Therefore, the conservative imperative to foster civic engagement and informed citizenship remains as relevant today as it was at the founding of the republic. By reinvigorating educational programs, enhancing media literacy, and encouraging community-based participation, the United States can empower its citizens to actively shape the destiny of their nation. This renewed commitment to constitutional education and civic engagement will ultimately serve as the bulwark against tyranny, ensuring that the government remains responsive, transparent, and firmly rooted in the principles of the Constitution.[24]

---

[21] Lasch, Christopher. *The Culture of Narcissism: American Life in an Age of Diminishing Expectations*. W.W. Norton & Company, 1979.

[22] Wood, Gordon S. *The Radicalism of the American Revolution*. Vintage Books, 1993.

[23] Eskridge, William N. Jr. *Originalism in the Twenty-First Century*. Harvard University Press, 2012.

[24] Scalia, Antonin. *A Matter of Interpretation: Federal Courts and the Law*. Princeton University Press, 1997.

As America looks forward, the continued success of its democratic experiment will depend on the ability of its people to remain engaged, informed, and dedicated to the cause of liberty. Only by embracing the challenge of civic education can the nation hope to meet the demands of an ever-changing world while staying true to the constitutional ideals that have guided it for over two centuries. In doing so, the United States will not only honor the legacy of its founding fathers but also secure a future in which freedom, justice, and the rule of law prevail.[25]

---

[25] Hamilton, Alexander; Madison, James; Jay, John. *The Federalist Papers*. Penguin Classics, 2003.

3. Institutional Programs and Educational Initiatives

In a nation founded upon the principles of liberty and self-governance, the strength of American democracy is inextricably linked to the ability of its citizens to understand and uphold the Constitution. Institutional programs and educational initiatives that promote constitutional literacy and civic engagement are indispensable tools in this endeavor. From a politically conservative perspective, such initiatives must not only disseminate knowledge about the founding documents but also cultivate the virtues of personal responsibility, limited government, and active participation that our founding fathers deemed essential for a free society. This commentary explores the critical role of institutional programs in bolstering constitutional education and civic engagement, arguing that well-designed educational initiatives are the foundation upon which an informed, engaged, and resilient citizenry is built.[1]

The early American republic was characterized by a profound commitment to civic participation, where town meetings and local assemblies served as the primary forums for public debate. This decentralized model of governance was deliberately established to keep government close to the people, ensuring that policy decisions were informed by the values and needs of local communities. In the modern era, however, the erosion of civic engagement and the decline in constitutional literacy pose significant challenges to the preservation of our founding ideals. Conservatives contend that institutional programs must therefore be reinvigorated and adapted to the complexities of the twenty-first century in order to restore a culture of informed citizenship and active participation in government.[2]

Central to this effort is the development of comprehensive educational curricula that emphasize the study of the United States Constitution and the historical context in which it was drafted. Such curricula should not only cover the text of the Constitution but also delve into the debates and compromises that shaped it, highlighting the enduring principles of limited government, separation of powers, and individual rights. Conservative educators argue that understanding these historical and philosophical foundations is crucial for fostering a sense of national identity and civic responsibility among students. By grounding education in the wisdom of the founding fathers, institutional programs can equip young citizens with the tools they need to critically assess contemporary political challenges and defend the constitutional order against encroachments on liberty.[3]

---

[1] Hamilton, Alexander; Madison, James; Jay, John. *The Federalist Papers*. Penguin Classics, 2003.

[2] Madison, James. "Federalist No. 51." In *The Federalist Papers*, edited by Clinton Rossiter, Bantam Classics, 1961.

[3] Niemi, Richard G., and Jane Junn. *Civic Education: What Makes Students Learn*. Yale University Press, 1998.

In addition to curricular reforms, extracurricular programs and civic organizations play a vital role in reinforcing constitutional education. Programs such as mock congresses, debate clubs, and civic boot camps provide students with practical experiences that bring the abstract principles of the Constitution to life. These initiatives encourage participants to engage in rigorous debate, develop public speaking skills, and learn the art of compromise—all of which are essential for sustaining a healthy democracy. Conservatives emphasize that such experiential learning opportunities foster a deep-seated appreciation for self-governance and prepare students to become active participants in the political process, thereby ensuring that the legacy of the founding era endures.[4]

Institutional programs are equally important in the realm of adult education and lifelong learning. Many adults, particularly those who did not have access to robust civic education in their youth, remain unaware of the constitutional foundations of American government. Community colleges, local libraries, and non-profit organizations can fill this gap by offering courses, workshops, and seminars on constitutional history and civic responsibility. These initiatives not only enhance individual understanding but also build stronger, more resilient communities by fostering informed public debate. From a conservative perspective, lifelong learning is a civic duty—a means by which citizens continue to safeguard their freedoms and hold government accountable throughout their lives.[5]

Furthermore, public institutions and government agencies have a responsibility to integrate constitutional education into their outreach efforts. Federal, state, and local governments can collaborate with educational institutions to develop programs that highlight the importance of the Constitution in contemporary governance. For instance, national parks and historical sites related to the American Revolution and the drafting of the Constitution can serve as living classrooms, offering interactive exhibits and guided tours that illuminate the struggles and triumphs of the founding era. Such initiatives help to contextualize modern political issues within the broader narrative of American history, reinforcing the idea that the principles enshrined in the Constitution are timeless and relevant to current challenges.[6]

The conservative vision for institutional programs and educational initiatives also extends to the digital realm. In today's information age, online platforms offer unparalleled opportunities for disseminating constitutional knowledge and engaging citizens in civic discourse. E-learning

---

[4] Friedman, Milton. *Capitalism and Freedom*. University of Chicago Press, 2002.

[5] Elazar, Daniel J. *Exploring Federalism*. University of Alabama Press, 1987.

[6] Scalia, Antonin. *A Matter of Interpretation: Federal Courts and the Law*. Princeton University Press, 1997.

courses, interactive websites, and social media campaigns can reach a broad audience, transcending geographical boundaries and overcoming barriers to access. However, conservatives caution that digital education must be carefully curated to avoid the pitfalls of misinformation and partisan bias. The development of high-quality, objective online resources on constitutional education is therefore paramount for ensuring that the digital revolution enhances, rather than undermines, civic literacy.[7]

One notable example of an effective institutional program is the implementation of state-sponsored civic education initiatives. Several states have adopted programs that integrate constitutional education into the public-school curriculum, coupled with extracurricular activities that encourage community involvement. These programs often include partnerships with local governments, museums, and historical societies, creating a network of resources that support civic learning. Conservatives argue that state-level initiatives are particularly effective because they can be tailored to reflect the unique cultural and historical contexts of each region, thereby fostering a sense of local pride and responsibility while simultaneously promoting national unity through shared constitutional values.[8]

Another critical aspect of educational initiatives is the professional development of teachers. Educators must be equipped with not only the knowledge of constitutional principles but also the pedagogical skills necessary to engage students in meaningful dialogue about civic issues. Teacher training programs should include specialized courses on constitutional history and civic engagement, as well as opportunities for educators to participate in workshops and seminars that explore innovative teaching methods. Conservatives maintain that empowering teachers is essential for creating a sustainable model of civic education—one that will produce future generations of citizens who are well-versed in the Constitution and committed to the ideals of limited government and individual liberty.[9]

Moreover, institutional programs must address the challenges posed by an increasingly polarized political environment. In recent years, the rise of partisan media and ideological echo chambers has contributed to a decline in the quality of public discourse. Conservatives assert that a renewed emphasis on constitutional education can serve as a counterweight to these divisive forces by providing citizens with a shared foundation of knowledge and values. Programs that promote

---

[7] Binder, Sarah A. *Stalemate: Causes and Consequences of Legislative Gridlock*. Brookings Institution Press, 2003.

[8] Kirk, Russell. *The Conservative Mind: From Burke to Eliot*. Regnery Publishing, 1953.

[9] Maier, Pauline. *American Scripture: Making the Declaration of Independence*. Vintage, 1998.

bipartisan dialogue and critical thinking are essential for bridging the divides that have come to characterize contemporary politics. By fostering an environment in which citizens can engage in respectful debate and collaborate on common goals, educational initiatives can help to restore a sense of unity and purpose in American civic life.[10]

The role of institutional programs in promoting civic engagement extends beyond the classroom to include a variety of community-based initiatives. For instance, local government-sponsored forums and town hall meetings offer citizens the opportunity to discuss policy issues directly with elected officials, thereby reinforcing the principles of transparency and accountability. Civic organizations and volunteer groups also play a crucial role in mobilizing community participation and ensuring that government remains responsive to the needs of its citizens. Conservatives argue that when citizens actively participate in these institutional programs, they not only acquire valuable knowledge about their constitutional rights but also develop the skills necessary to advocate for policies that protect individual liberty and promote limited government.[11]

In addition to formal educational programs, public-private partnerships can enhance the reach and effectiveness of constitutional education. Non-profit organizations, academic institutions, and businesses can collaborate to create comprehensive programs that leverage the strengths of each sector. Such partnerships can fund research, develop innovative teaching materials, and organize large-scale civic engagement events that bring together diverse segments of society. Conservatives emphasize that a collaborative approach is essential for overcoming the limitations of any single institution and for ensuring that constitutional education is accessible to all citizens, regardless of socioeconomic status or geographic location.[12]

The success of these institutional programs is contingent upon a supportive policy environment that prioritizes civic education as a national imperative. Legislators at the state and federal levels must allocate sufficient resources to educational initiatives and enact policies that incentivize the incorporation of constitutional literacy into school curricula. Conservatives advocate for policies that support local control over education, arguing that decentralized decision-making leads to more effective and context-sensitive outcomes. By reinforcing the principles of federalism in the educational sphere, policymakers can create a robust framework

---

[10] Torney-Purta, Judith, et al. *Citizenship and Political Participation: Political Science Perspectives*. Rowman & Littlefield, 2001.

[11] Lipset, Seymour. *Political Man: The Social Bases of Politics*. Johns Hopkins University Press, 1960.

[12] Amar, Akhil Reed. *America's Constitution: A Biography*. Random House, 2005.

that not only preserves constitutional literacy but also empowers communities to shape their own destinies.[13]

Furthermore, the impact of institutional programs on civic engagement can be amplified through the use of data and evidence-based practices. Systematic evaluation of educational initiatives allows policymakers and educators to identify best practices and scale successful programs. Conservatives argue that rigorous assessment and continuous improvement are essential for ensuring that public funds are used effectively to enhance civic literacy. By investing in research and development, educational institutions can refine their curricula, adopt innovative teaching methods, and ultimately create a more informed and engaged citizenry.[14]

The long-term benefits of robust institutional programs and educational initiatives are profound. An electorate that is knowledgeable about the Constitution and actively involved in civic life is better equipped to safeguard its liberties, hold government accountable, and contribute to a stable and prosperous society. Conservatives contend that the preservation of constitutional education is not only a matter of academic interest but a strategic imperative for the continued success of American democracy. As the challenges of globalization, technological change, and political polarization continue to evolve, a well-informed citizenry will remain the best defense against the erosion of individual freedoms and the expansion of government power.[15]

Moreover, the promotion of constitutional literacy through institutional programs has significant implications for the health of the democratic process. When citizens understand the limits of governmental authority and the importance of checks and balances, they are less likely to support policies that threaten to concentrate power in the hands of a few. This understanding fosters a political culture of accountability, where elected officials are held to the highest standards of transparency and public service. Conservatives argue that an informed electorate is the cornerstone of a free society, and that the success of institutional programs in fostering civic engagement directly contributes to the longevity and vitality of American democracy.[16]

Additionally, institutional initiatives can play a pivotal role in bridging the generational gap in civic education. As older generations, who were often taught through more traditional methods, pass

---

[13] Eskridge, William N. Jr. *Originalism in the Twenty-First Century*. Harvard University Press, 2012.

[14] McCarty, Nolan, Keith T. Poole, and Howard Rosenthal. *Polarized America: The Dance of Ideology and Unequal Riches*. MIT Press, 2009.

[15] Wood, Gordon S. *The Creation of the American Republic, 1776–1787*. University of North Carolina Press, 1998.

[16] Ellis, Joseph J. *American Creation: Triumphs and Tragedies in the Founding of the Republic*. Knopf, 2007.

on their knowledge of constitutional principles, it is imperative that younger generations receive an equally robust education in these timeless ideals. Conservative thinkers stress that modern educational tools—including digital media, interactive simulations, and online collaborative platforms—should be harnessed to make constitutional education both engaging and accessible to youth. By integrating traditional pedagogical methods with innovative technological approaches, institutional programs can cultivate a renewed passion for civic engagement among young Americans, ensuring that the values of the Constitution are transmitted across generations.[17]

The future of institutional programs and educational initiatives in constitutional education will depend largely on the ability of policymakers, educators, and community leaders to collaborate effectively. Such collaboration is essential for creating a unified vision of civic education that transcends partisan divides and reflects the enduring values of the American founding. Conservatives argue that by working together, stakeholders can develop a comprehensive strategy that not only addresses the current deficiencies in civic education but also lays the groundwork for a more engaged and informed citizenry in the years to come.[18]

In conclusion, the role of institutional programs and educational initiatives in promoting constitutional education and civic engagement is fundamental to the preservation of American freedom. By reinvigorating civic education through comprehensive curricula, extracurricular activities, digital platforms, and public-private partnerships, America can ensure that its citizens are well-equipped to defend the Constitution and participate actively in the democratic process. From a conservative perspective, these initiatives are not merely academic exercises but are vital investments in the future of the nation—a future where government remains limited, individual liberties are fiercely protected, and the principles of the founding era continue to guide public life.[19]

Looking forward, it is imperative that the United States renew its commitment to constitutional education by implementing policies that prioritize civic engagement at every level of society. The future of decentralized, informed, and active citizenship depends on our ability to educate citizens about their rights and responsibilities, to foster a culture of accountability, and to harness the power of modern technology to spread constitutional knowledge. Through sustained efforts by educators, policymakers, and community leaders, institutional programs can ensure that

---

[17] Putnam, Robert D. *Bowling Alone: The Collapse and Revival of American Community*. Simon & Schuster, 2000.

[18] Galston, William A. *Civic Education and Democracy in America*. Johns Hopkins University Press, 2001.

[19] Sanger, Margaret. *Conservative Legacies: How the Founding Ideals Endure*. HarperCollins, 2010.

the legacy of our founding fathers endures, enabling America to navigate the challenges of the modern world with wisdom and integrity.[20]

Ultimately, the conservative vision for the future of constitutional education and civic engagement rests on the belief that an informed citizenry is the greatest safeguard of liberty. When citizens are equipped with a deep understanding of the Constitution and the principles of limited government, they become active participants in shaping public policy and defending their freedoms against encroachments by centralized power. It is through this process of education and engagement that the American experiment—rooted in the ideals of self-governance and individual responsibility—will continue to flourish.[21]

The impact of these educational initiatives extends far beyond the classroom, shaping the very fabric of our democratic society. As citizens become more knowledgeable about the workings of government and the importance of constitutional limits, they are better prepared to engage in constructive dialogue, challenge abuses of power, and support policies that reflect the common good. This heightened level of civic participation not only strengthens democratic institutions but also reinforces the notion that government is, at its core, an instrument of the people.[22]

Thus, by prioritizing institutional programs and educational initiatives in constitutional education, America can build a future where civic engagement is the norm rather than the exception—a future in which every citizen understands the profound significance of the Constitution and is committed to preserving the freedoms it guarantees. In doing so, the nation will remain a beacon of liberty, inspiring generations to uphold the values of justice, limited government, and individual responsibility that have defined the American experiment for over two centuries.[23]

In summary, the conservative imperative to enhance constitutional education and civic engagement through robust institutional programs is a critical component of ensuring the long-term health of American democracy. By investing in comprehensive educational reforms, leveraging modern technology, and fostering collaboration among diverse stakeholders, the United States can empower its citizens to become informed defenders of the Constitution and active shapers of public policy. This commitment to education is not only a tribute to the legacy of our founding

---

[20] Bickel, Alexander M. *The Least Dangerous Branch: The Supreme Court at the Bar of Politics*. Yale University Press, 1962.

[21] Lasch, Christopher. *The Culture of Narcissism: American Life in an Age of Diminishing Expectations*. W.W. Norton & Company, 1979.

[22] Wood, Gordon S. *The Radicalism of the American Revolution*. Vintage Books, 1993.

[23] Eskridge, William N. Jr. *Originalism in the Twenty-First Century*. Harvard University Press, 2012.

fathers but also a necessary step toward securing a future in which freedom, accountability, and the rule of law prevail.[24]

Ultimately, the future of constitutional education and civic engagement lies in our collective ability to reinvigorate the public's commitment to the founding principles that have sustained American democracy. Through concerted institutional efforts and a renewed emphasis on the importance of civic literacy, America can ensure that its citizens remain vigilant, informed, and engaged in the ongoing quest to preserve the cherished legacy of the Constitution. This is the promise of decentralized, empowered citizenship—a promise that, when fulfilled, will secure the blessings of liberty for generations to come.[25]

[24] Scalia, Antonin. *A Matter of Interpretation: Federal Courts and the Law*. Princeton University Press, 1997.

[25] Hamilton, Alexander; Madison, James; Jay, John. *The Federalist Papers*. Penguin Classics, 2003.

4. Challenges in Modern Civic Education

In today's rapidly evolving society, the challenge of modern civic education is increasingly urgent. An informed citizenry forms the backbone of a free nation, yet many argue that contemporary educational practices have drifted from the principles set forth by our founding fathers. The United States Constitution, a beacon of individual liberty and limited government, was crafted with the belief that citizens must be educated in the ways of self-governance. However, modern civic education faces significant obstacles—including diminishing emphasis on constitutional literacy, partisan influences, and the digital revolution's impact on information quality—which threaten the long-term health of American democracy. This commentary, written from a politically conservative perspective, examines these challenges in detail and argues that a return to robust, Constitution-based civic education is essential for preserving the American experiment.

One of the foremost challenges in modern civic education is the gradual erosion of constitutional literacy among students. The founding fathers designed a system of government based on a deep understanding of the natural rights and limited powers enshrined in the Constitution. Yet today, many curricula emphasize standardized testing and vocational skills over a comprehensive study of American history and constitutional principles. As a result, a significant portion of the youth remains unaware of the sacrifices and intellectual debates that birthed the nation. Conservatives argue that without a solid grounding in the Constitution, citizens become vulnerable to ideologies that favor expansive government and erode individual liberties—a danger the founding fathers explicitly sought to prevent.[1]

Another significant issue is the over-politicization of civic education. In many public schools, the teaching of history and civics has become entangled with contemporary political agendas, often at the expense of an objective understanding of the Constitution. Educators sometimes present politically charged narratives that emphasize current partisan divides rather than the timeless principles of the founding documents. This trend not only distorts historical facts but also discourages critical thinking by framing civic knowledge as a battleground for ideological conflicts. Conservatives maintain that civic education should focus on the enduring values of the Constitution—such as freedom, limited government, and the rule of law—rather than transient political opinions.[2]

---

[1] Hamilton, Alexander; Madison, James; Jay, John. *The Federalist Papers*. Penguin Classics, 2003.

[2] Madison, James. "Federalist No. 51." In *The Federalist Papers*, edited by Clinton Rossiter, Bantam Classics, 1961.

The rise of digital media poses additional challenges for modern civic education. While the internet provides unprecedented access to information, it also opens the floodgates for misinformation and biased content. Many students today rely on social media and unvetted online sources for news and civic knowledge, which can lead to misconceptions about the Constitution and the nature of American government. This digital landscape often amplifies extremist views and undermines the nuanced understanding required for effective citizenship. From a conservative standpoint, it is imperative to develop programs that enhance media literacy alongside traditional civic education so that individuals can discern reliable sources and understand the historical context of constitutional principles.[3]

Furthermore, budget cuts and shifting priorities in public education have led to the de-emphasis of civics courses in many school districts. As states increasingly focus on subjects that promise immediate economic returns—such as science and technology—the liberal arts and civic studies suffer from underfunding and neglect. Conservatives argue that this trend endangers the very foundation of democracy because a lack of civic education results in a populace less equipped to evaluate government actions or participate meaningfully in the political process. Without a well-informed citizenry, the checks and balances that have long safeguarded American liberty become weakened, leaving the door open for potential overreach by the state.[4]

The fragmentation of civic education is also exacerbated by the declining role of local institutions in promoting civic values. Historically, community organizations, churches, and local government bodies played vital roles in teaching citizens about their rights and responsibilities. Over time, however, the erosion of these traditional channels—partly due to increased centralization and bureaucratic expansion—has reduced opportunities for hands-on civic engagement. Conservatives maintain that revitalizing local institutions is crucial for a healthy civic culture because it enables citizens to experience governance firsthand, fostering a sense of responsibility and pride in local self-governance that extends to the national level.[5]

Another obstacle is the prevalent ideology of political correctness in educational settings. In some instances, efforts to promote inclusivity have inadvertently led to the suppression of dissenting viewpoints, particularly those that challenge progressive interpretations of history and the Constitution. Such an environment can stifle robust debate and limit students' exposure to the

---

[3] Niemi, Richard G., and Jane Junn. *Civic Education: What Makes Students Learn*. Yale University Press, 1998.

[4] Friedman, Milton. *Capitalism and Freedom*. University of Chicago Press, 2002.

[5] Elazar, Daniel J. *Exploring Federalism*. University of Alabama Press, 1987.

full spectrum of ideas that have shaped American political thought. Conservatives contend that true civic education must encourage open dialogue and critical inquiry into the principles of the Constitution, allowing students to explore both the successes and shortcomings of American history in an unbiased manner.[6]

Additionally, the rapid pace of technological and societal change presents challenges in keeping civic education relevant. Many current educational programs fail to connect the historical context of the Constitution with modern issues such as digital privacy, global terrorism, and economic globalization. While the founding documents remain timeless in their core principles, their application to contemporary challenges requires careful interpretation and ongoing public discourse. Conservatives argue that civic education should include modules that link constitutional theory to modern governance, thereby equipping students with the tools needed to navigate an increasingly complex world while remaining true to the original intent of the founding fathers.[7]

The influence of partisan media further complicates modern civic education. As news outlets become more ideologically driven, they contribute to an environment where civic issues are often discussed in hyper-partisan terms. This polarization not only alienates young learners but also makes it difficult for educators to present an impartial view of the Constitution. Conservatives assert that unbiased civic education is essential for maintaining a balanced understanding of government and for fostering a culture of constructive political participation. Without a common, constitutionally grounded framework for understanding civic life, the risk of a divided and misinformed electorate increases, which can undermine the stability of the republic.[8]

Moreover, standardized testing regimes have led to a narrowed curriculum that often sidelines subjects like civics and history in favor of math and science. This shift is partly driven by the desire to improve international academic rankings and economic competitiveness. However, conservatives argue that sacrificing civic education for test scores jeopardizes the development of critical thinking skills and an understanding of the constitutional principles that are vital for democratic self-governance. A nation that excels academically but is deficient in civic literacy is ill-prepared to defend its freedoms against the encroachments of an overreaching state.[9]

---

[6] Scalia, Antonin. *A Matter of Interpretation: Federal Courts and the Law*. Princeton University Press, 1997.

[7] Binder, Sarah A. *Stalemate: Causes and Consequences of Legislative Gridlock*. Brookings Institution Press, 2003.

[8] Kirk, Russell. *The Conservative Mind: From Burke to Eliot*. Regnery Publishing, 1953.

[9] Maier, Pauline. *American Scripture: Making the Declaration of Independence*. Vintage, 1998.

Teacher quality and professional development are also central concerns. Many educators lack specialized training in civics or constitutional history, which limits their ability to convey the significance of these subjects effectively. Without robust teacher training programs, even well-designed curricula cannot achieve their full potential. Conservatives call for increased investment in professional development for civics educators, ensuring that they are equipped not only with the necessary content knowledge but also with effective pedagogical strategies to engage students in critical discussions about the Constitution and its relevance today.[10]

The challenges in modern civic education extend beyond K–12 education into higher education as well. Universities and colleges, which have traditionally been centers for rigorous debate on constitutional issues, are sometimes criticized for adopting ideologically homogeneous perspectives that limit exposure to conservative interpretations of the Constitution. This intellectual imbalance can lead to a generation of graduates who are less prepared to engage in informed civic discourse and more inclined to accept progressive narratives uncritically. Conservatives advocate for a more balanced academic environment that encourages diversity of thought and fosters critical analysis of constitutional principles.[11]

Public funding for civic education remains another critical issue. In an era of fiscal austerity, programs that promote constitutional literacy are often the first to face budget cuts. This underfunding has a cascading effect, reducing the quality and availability of civic education materials, extracurricular programs, and community engagement initiatives. Conservatives maintain that investing in civic education is an investment in the future of the nation; a well-informed citizenry is the most effective bulwark against the erosion of constitutional freedoms and the overconcentration of government power.[12]

The role of digital platforms in civic education also presents both opportunities and challenges. While online courses and educational apps can provide accessible and engaging content, they are also susceptible to the influence of partisan algorithms that may skew the presentation of historical facts. Conservatives argue that it is imperative to develop digital educational tools that are rigorously vetted for accuracy and that present a balanced view of constitutional issues. Such tools should emphasize primary sources and encourage critical thinking, enabling users

---

[10] Torney-Purta, Judith, et al. *Citizenship and Political Participation: Political Science Perspectives*. Rowman & Littlefield, 2001.

[11] Lipset, Seymour. *Political Man: The Social Bases of Politics*. Johns Hopkins University Press, 1960.

[12] Amar, Akhil Reed. *America's Constitution: A Biography*. Random House, 2005.

to form their own informed opinions rather than simply consuming prepackaged ideological content.[13]

Furthermore, the decline in civic engagement among younger generations is a pressing concern. Studies indicate that many young Americans are less involved in political processes and less knowledgeable about the Constitution than previous generations. This disengagement can be attributed to a variety of factors, including disillusionment with the political system, the influence of social media, and a lack of effective civic education. Conservatives believe that revitalizing civic education requires not only curricular reform but also innovative strategies to inspire youth participation in democratic life—such as community service programs, student government initiatives, and interactive learning environments that connect historical knowledge with current events.[14]

Another dimension of the challenge is the international context. In an increasingly globalized world, American civic education must also address the pressures of international norms and multicultural influences that sometimes conflict with the conservative interpretation of the Constitution. While exposure to diverse perspectives is valuable, conservatives insist that the unique heritage and constitutional principles of the United States must remain at the center of civic education. This means emphasizing the historical narrative of American exceptionalism and the timeless principles of liberty and limited government as a counterbalance to globalist ideologies that may dilute these values.[15]

Political polarization further complicates the delivery of effective civic education. In many schools, civics classes are not insulated from the broader partisan environment, and educators may feel pressured to present material in a way that aligns with prevailing political sentiments. Such pressures can lead to the marginalization of conservative viewpoints and a skewed interpretation of constitutional history. Conservatives assert that a nonpartisan, fact-based approach to civic education is essential for fostering a truly informed citizenry—one that can engage in honest debate and resist the temptations of demagoguery.[16]

---

[13] Eskridge, William N. Jr. *Originalism in the Twenty-First Century*. Harvard University Press, 2012.

[14] McCarty, Nolan, Keith T. Poole, and Howard Rosenthal. *Polarized America: The Dance of Ideology and Unequal Riches*. MIT Press, 2009.

[15] Wood, Gordon S. *The Creation of the American Republic, 1776–1787*. University of North Carolina Press, 1998.

[16] Ellis, Joseph J. *American Creation: Triumphs and Tragedies in the Founding of the Republic*. Knopf, 2007.

The commercialization of education also poses challenges. As public schools increasingly turn to private funding and charter school models, there is a risk that the curriculum may be influenced by corporate interests or ideological agendas that do not align with constitutional principles. Conservatives caution that education must remain a public good, free from market pressures that might compromise the quality and integrity of civic education. The state's role in ensuring equitable access to high-quality civic education is therefore paramount for maintaining the democratic health of the nation.[17]

Additionally, the fragmentation of the educational system—where local school boards and state governments often operate with significant autonomy—can lead to disparities in the quality of civic education. In some regions, students receive a rigorous grounding in constitutional principles, while in others, civic education is given minimal attention. Conservatives argue that this disparity undermines national unity by creating a patchwork of civic knowledge that varies significantly from one locality to another. To address this challenge, there must be national standards for civic education that guarantee a baseline level of constitutional literacy across all states while still allowing local educators the flexibility to adapt teaching methods to their communities.[18]

The role of extracurricular and community-based programs is increasingly vital in overcoming the limitations of formal classroom instruction. Civic engagement initiatives such as debate clubs, mock elections, and community service projects offer hands-on experiences that complement traditional academic learning. These programs help students internalize the values of civic duty and constitutional responsibility, making the principles of the Constitution tangible and relevant. Conservatives view these initiatives as critical for bridging the gap between theoretical knowledge and practical application, ensuring that civic education is not confined to textbooks but is lived and experienced within the community.[19]

Moreover, partnerships between educational institutions and local government can reinforce civic education by providing real-world contexts in which constitutional principles are applied. Internships, mentorship programs, and public forums allow students to observe how government operates and how policies are shaped by the Constitution. Such collaborations can demystify the workings of government, making the democratic process accessible and engaging for young

---

[17] Putnam, Robert D. *Bowling Alone: The Collapse and Revival of American Community*. Simon & Schuster, 2000.

[18] Galston, William A. *Civic Education and Democracy in America*. Johns Hopkins University Press, 2001.

[19] Sanger, Margaret. *Conservative Legacies: How the Founding Ideals Endure*. HarperCollins, 2010.

citizens. From a conservative perspective, these partnerships are essential for cultivating an informed electorate that is capable of both appreciating and defending the constitutional heritage of the nation.[20]

In conclusion, the challenges facing modern civic education are multifaceted and deeply rooted in shifts in educational priorities, technological advancements, and a polarized political climate. However, from a politically conservative standpoint, these challenges also present an opportunity to renew and revitalize the commitment to constitutional literacy. By reinvesting in comprehensive curricula, enhancing teacher training, leveraging digital tools responsibly, and fostering strong community-based initiatives, America can restore the civic engagement necessary for the preservation of freedom and limited government. A well-informed citizenry, grounded in the principles of the Constitution, is the most effective safeguard against governmental overreach and a polarized society.

Looking to the future, policymakers must prioritize reforms that elevate civic education to its rightful place at the center of the academic agenda. It is imperative that national standards for civic education are established to ensure that every student, regardless of where they live, gains a robust understanding of the Constitution and the responsibilities of citizenship. This commitment to educational excellence and constitutional literacy is not only an investment in individual empowerment but also a crucial pillar for the longevity of American democracy.[21]

Furthermore, educators, community leaders, and government officials must collaborate to create an environment where informed citizenship is celebrated and actively practiced. By promoting programs that emphasize critical thinking, debate, and hands-on civic engagement, America can cultivate a generation of citizens who are not only knowledgeable about their rights but also committed to upholding the principles of limited government and personal responsibility. This cultural shift towards greater civic participation is essential for bridging the divides that have characterized recent political discourse and for ensuring that government remains accountable to the people.[22]

Ultimately, the conservative imperative for modern civic education is clear: the survival of American liberty depends on an electorate that is both well-informed and actively engaged in

---

[20] Bickel, Alexander M. *The Least Dangerous Branch: The Supreme Court at the Bar of Politics*. Yale University Press, 1962.

[21] Lasch, Christopher. *The Culture of Narcissism: American Life in an Age of Diminishing Expectations*. W.W. Norton & Company, 1979.

[22] Wood, Gordon S. *The Radicalism of the American Revolution*. Vintage Books, 1993.

public life. The challenges are significant, but so too are the opportunities to renew the commitment to constitutional education—a commitment that honors the legacy of our founding fathers and secures a future where freedom, justice, and the rule of law prevail.[23]

As the nation grapples with the complexities of the twenty-first century, the role of education in fostering civic engagement and informed citizenship becomes ever more critical. Through the concerted efforts of educators, policymakers, and community stakeholders, institutional programs and innovative educational initiatives can restore the civic foundations that have long sustained the American experiment. This revitalization is not merely a nostalgic return to the past but a proactive strategy for ensuring that the Constitution remains a living document—one that continues to guide and inspire every generation of Americans.[24]

In summation, the challenges in modern civic education call for a renewed emphasis on the principles of constitutional literacy and civic engagement. By addressing issues such as diminishing curricular focus, partisan bias, digital misinformation, and inequitable educational practices, America can reinvigorate its democratic culture and empower its citizens to take an active role in governance. The conservative vision for constitutional education is one that champions the timeless values of limited government, personal responsibility, and informed debate—values that must be passed on to future generations to secure the blessings of liberty.[25]

---

[23] Eskridge, William N. Jr. *Originalism in the Twenty-First Century*. Harvard University Press, 2012.

[24] Scalia, Antonin. *A Matter of Interpretation: Federal Courts and the Law*. Princeton University Press, 1997.

[25] Hamilton, Alexander; Madison, James; Jay, John. *The Federalist Papers*. Penguin Classics, 2003.

5. Strategies for Renewing Constitutional Discourse

The vitality of American democracy depends upon the ability of citizens to engage in meaningful constitutional discourse—a conversation that not only honors the wisdom of our founding fathers but also adapts to the evolving challenges of modern society. In an era marked by polarized media, ideological extremism, and declining civic literacy, conservatives argue that renewing constitutional discourse is imperative for preserving limited government and individual liberty. This commentary examines strategies for revitalizing constitutional dialogue through educational reform, community engagement, and media accountability. It contends that a renewed focus on constitutional education and informed debate is essential for ensuring that government remains accountable to its citizens and that the original intent of the Constitution endures amid contemporary challenges.[1]

A central tenet of conservative thought is that the United States Constitution represents a timeless blueprint for governance—a document that, if properly understood, can guide policy and behavior in an ever-changing world. The founding fathers, through vigorous debate and deliberate compromise, established a framework designed to check governmental power and protect individual rights. Yet, over time, the language and spirit of the Constitution have become obscured by academic abstraction and partisan rhetoric. Renewing constitutional discourse requires a concerted effort to reintroduce these foundational ideas into public debate. This can be achieved by reemphasizing constitutional literacy in schools and universities, where students must not only learn the text of the Constitution but also its historical context, philosophical underpinnings, and practical implications.[2]

One strategy for renewing constitutional discourse is to develop comprehensive civic education programs that integrate traditional classroom instruction with experiential learning. Educational initiatives such as mock trials, town hall simulations, and debate competitions provide students with hands-on experience in applying constitutional principles to real-world issues. These programs foster critical thinking and enable young citizens to appreciate the delicate balance between governmental authority and individual freedom—a balance that is the cornerstone of our constitutional republic. By engaging students directly in constitutional analysis, educators can help bridge the gap between theoretical knowledge and practical governance, ensuring that future generations are equipped to defend their rights and hold their leaders accountable.[3]

---

[1] Hamilton, Alexander; Madison, James; Jay, John. *The Federalist Papers*. Penguin Classics, 2003.

[2] Madison, James. "Federalist No. 51." In *The Federalist Papers*, edited by Clinton Rossiter, Bantam Classics, 1961.

[3] Niemi, Richard G., and Jane Junn. *Civic Education: What Makes Students Learn*. Yale University Press, 1998.

Moreover, the integration of technology into civic education offers a promising avenue for revitalizing constitutional discourse. Digital platforms, interactive simulations, and online forums can democratize access to constitutional knowledge, reaching a broader audience than traditional methods alone. However, conservatives caution that digital tools must be curated carefully to avoid the pitfalls of misinformation and ideological bias. It is essential to develop online resources that present primary sources—such as the Federalist Papers and historical debates—in a balanced and accessible manner. By harnessing digital technology while maintaining rigorous academic standards, educational institutions can cultivate a more informed citizenry capable of engaging in substantive constitutional debate.[4]

Beyond formal education, community engagement plays a pivotal role in renewing constitutional discourse. Local institutions—such as libraries, civic clubs, and faith-based organizations—have traditionally been the backbone of American civic life, offering spaces for public dialogue and grassroots activism. Conservatives assert that reinvigorating these community forums is crucial for creating an environment where citizens can discuss constitutional issues without the filter of partisan media. Town hall meetings and public lectures that focus on the history and practical application of the Constitution can rekindle a sense of shared purpose among citizens. Such initiatives not only empower individuals to participate in governance but also serve as a check on the concentration of power at the federal level.[5]

A further strategy is to encourage bipartisan dialogue in academic and public settings. In recent years, constitutional discourse has become highly politicized, with debates often reduced to ideological slogans rather than substantive discussions. Conservatives argue that restoring the integrity of constitutional debate requires creating spaces where diverse viewpoints can be exchanged in a respectful and informed manner. Academic conferences, bipartisan workshops, and public debates that focus on constitutional principles—rather than contemporary partisan issues—can help reframe the conversation. By emphasizing the common heritage of the American founding and the universal principles of liberty and justice, these forums can bridge ideological divides and promote a more unified national discourse.[6]

Media accountability is also a critical component in the renewal of constitutional discourse. The conservative perspective holds that mainstream media, increasingly driven by partisan interests and sensationalism, has diluted the quality of public debate on constitutional matters. To counteract

---

[4] Friedman, Milton. *Capitalism and Freedom*. University of Chicago Press, 2002.

[5] Elazar, Daniel J. *Exploring Federalism*. University of Alabama Press, 1987.

[6] Scalia, Antonin. *A Matter of Interpretation: Federal Courts and the Law*. Princeton University Press, 1997.

this trend, it is necessary to promote journalistic standards that emphasize accuracy, objectivity, and context in reporting on constitutional issues. Initiatives to enhance media literacy among the public can empower citizens to critically evaluate news sources and discern bias in the coverage of constitutional debates. Moreover, independent media outlets and public broadcasting services that adhere to rigorous editorial standards should be supported as vital platforms for restoring balanced constitutional discourse.[7]

Another key element in renewing constitutional discourse is the active involvement of civic leaders and public officials. Politicians, judges, and community leaders must serve as role models by engaging in public debates that are informed by the Constitution and its foundational principles. When leaders articulate policies and decisions in terms of constitutional values, they reinforce the relevance of the founding documents to contemporary governance. Conservatives argue that a leadership culture that prioritizes constitutional fidelity will encourage citizens to hold their representatives to higher standards, thus fostering a political environment where government is truly accountable to the people.[8]

Furthermore, intergovernmental cooperation can enhance constitutional discourse by ensuring that discussions about policy and governance occur at multiple levels of society. Federal, state, and local governments must work together to create programs that disseminate constitutional knowledge and facilitate public debate. For instance, state-sponsored civic education initiatives that involve local communities and collaboration with academic institutions can provide a more integrated approach to constitutional literacy. Such partnerships not only enrich the educational experience but also help to ensure that constitutional discourse remains dynamic and relevant to the needs of diverse communities across the nation.[9]

The role of higher education institutions is equally important. Universities and colleges should prioritize courses and research dedicated to constitutional studies and civic engagement. By fostering a scholarly environment where constitutional issues are examined from multiple perspectives—including conservative, originalist viewpoints—academia can contribute significantly to the national dialogue on governance. Moreover, universities can serve as hubs for public discourse, hosting conferences, seminars, and workshops that bring together experts, policymakers, and citizens to discuss the challenges and opportunities of constitutional governance. This academic

---

[7] Binder, Sarah A. *Stalemate: Causes and Consequences of Legislative Gridlock*. Brookings Institution Press, 2003.

[8] Kirk, Russell. *The Conservative Mind: From Burke to Eliot*. Regnery Publishing, 1953.

[9] Maier, Pauline. *American Scripture: Making the Declaration of Independence*. Vintage, 1998.

engagement is vital for nurturing future leaders who are committed to the principles of limited government and individual liberty.[10]

The conservative vision for renewing constitutional discourse also emphasizes the importance of historical memory. A critical component of civic education is the preservation and dissemination of historical narratives that highlight the struggles and triumphs of the American founding. Museums, historical societies, and digital archives play a crucial role in this regard, providing citizens with access to primary documents and interpretive exhibits that elucidate the context in which the Constitution was drafted. Conservatives argue that a robust engagement with history not only deepens constitutional literacy but also instills a sense of national pride and responsibility—an essential counterbalance to the cynicism and apathy that have come to characterize much of modern political life.[11]

Additionally, the promotion of constitutional discourse must address the issue of political polarization. In an environment where public debate is increasingly fragmented along partisan lines, it is more important than ever to remind citizens of the common values that unite the nation. Conservatives contend that constitutional education should serve as a unifying force, emphasizing the shared heritage and principles that have sustained American democracy through centuries of change. Strategies to counter polarization include nonpartisan civic forums, bipartisan educational programs, and community dialogues that focus on the enduring principles of the Constitution rather than transient political conflicts.[12]

Moreover, constitutional discourse should be linked to practical outcomes in public policy. When citizens understand the constitutional basis for government actions, they are better equipped to evaluate the legitimacy of policies and to advocate for reforms that enhance accountability and efficiency. Conservative policymakers argue that informed constitutional debate can lead to more prudent fiscal policies, improved law enforcement practices, and better-designed regulatory frameworks that reflect the limited scope of government envisioned by the founding fathers. In this way, the renewal of constitutional discourse is not an abstract academic exercise but a practical tool for achieving effective governance and safeguarding individual freedoms.[13]

---

[10] Torney-Purta, Judith, et al. *Citizenship and Political Participation: Political Science Perspectives*. Rowman & Littlefield, 2001.

[11] Lipset, Seymour. *Political Man: The Social Bases of Politics*. Johns Hopkins University Press, 1960.

[12] Amar, Akhil Reed. *America's Constitution: A Biography*. Random House, 2005.

[13] Eskridge, William N. Jr. *Originalism in the Twenty-First Century*. Harvard University Press, 2012.

It is also essential to recognize that the challenges facing constitutional discourse are not solely confined to the classroom or the media; they are symptomatic of broader societal trends. The decline in civic engagement, the rise of partisan identity politics, and the erosion of trust in public institutions all contribute to a weakening of constitutional values. Conservatives argue that revitalizing constitutional discourse requires a holistic approach that addresses these systemic issues—reforming not only educational institutions but also the political and cultural environment in which civic life is conducted. This comprehensive strategy must include efforts to rebuild trust in government through transparency, accountability, and a renewed commitment to the principles of the Constitution.[14]

Furthermore, public-private partnerships can play a significant role in advancing constitutional education. By collaborating with non-profit organizations, think tanks, and community groups, government agencies can develop innovative programs that extend beyond traditional classroom settings. Such partnerships can fund research, produce high-quality educational materials, and organize public events that bring constitutional issues to the forefront of community life. Conservatives maintain that these collaborative efforts are essential for ensuring that constitutional discourse is accessible to all citizens, regardless of socioeconomic status or geographic location.[15]

The future of constitutional discourse also depends on the adaptability of educational institutions to emerging technologies and global trends. In a world characterized by rapid digital transformation and increasing globalization, educational programs must be flexible enough to incorporate new tools and methodologies. Virtual classrooms, online discussion forums, and interactive learning modules can supplement traditional teaching methods, making constitutional education more engaging and relevant for digital-native generations. However, conservatives caution that while technology offers tremendous potential, it must be employed judiciously to preserve the integrity of the constitutional message. The challenge lies in leveraging digital innovations without compromising the rigorous, fact-based approach that is essential for informed civic debate.[16]

Another critical strategy is to foster leadership at all levels that is committed to the principles of constitutional governance. Political leaders, educators, and community organizers must model the behavior they wish to see in citizens—demonstrating integrity, accountability, and a steadfast commitment to the rule of law. When leaders articulate their policies in terms of constitutional

---

[14] McCarty, Nolan, Keith T. Poole, and Howard Rosenthal. *Polarized America: The Dance of Ideology and Unequal Riches*. MIT Press, 2009.

[15] Wood, Gordon S. *The Creation of the American Republic, 1776–1787*. University of North Carolina Press, 1998.

[16] Ellis, Joseph J. *American Creation: Triumphs and Tragedies in the Founding of the Republic*. Knopf, 2007.

values and engage in open, respectful debate, they set a powerful example for the electorate. This leadership not only inspires public confidence but also helps to create a political culture in which constitutional discourse is both valued and sustained.[17]

Addressing the challenges of misinformation is also crucial. In an era where social media platforms and partisan news sources often distort the facts, there is a pressing need for initiatives that promote media literacy alongside constitutional education. Programs that teach citizens how to critically assess sources of information, recognize bias, and verify facts are essential for combating the spread of false narratives that undermine constitutional principles. Conservatives argue that a well-informed electorate, capable of discerning truth from falsehood, is the best safeguard against the erosion of the constitutional order.[18]

Moreover, efforts to renew constitutional discourse must also prioritize the inclusion of diverse perspectives while remaining true to the foundational principles of the American republic. While it is important to recognize the contributions of all citizens to the nation's development, conservatives maintain that the core values of limited government and individual liberty must remain central to the conversation. By fostering an environment in which respectful, fact-based dialogue can occur across ideological lines, society can work toward a more unified understanding of the Constitution—a shared language of governance that transcends partisan divisions.[19]

In conclusion, the strategies for renewing constitutional discourse are multifaceted and require a holistic approach that encompasses education, community engagement, media accountability, and leadership development. By reinvigorating civic education with a focus on the Constitution and its historical context, embracing digital innovation responsibly, and fostering environments for bipartisan dialogue, America can restore the robust constitutional discourse that is essential for a thriving democracy. From a politically conservative perspective, this renewal is not merely desirable; it is a necessity for safeguarding the limited government and individual liberty that form the cornerstone of our national identity.[20]

---

[17] Putnam, Robert D. *Bowling Alone: The Collapse and Revival of American Community*. Simon & Schuster, 2000.

[18] Galston, William A. *Civic Education and Democracy in America*. Johns Hopkins University Press, 2001.

[19] Sanger, Margaret. *Conservative Legacies: How the Founding Ideals Endure*. HarperCollins, 2010.

[20] Bickel, Alexander M. *The Least Dangerous Branch: The Supreme Court at the Bar of Politics*. Yale University Press, 1962.

Looking ahead, policymakers must prioritize reforms that elevate constitutional education to the forefront of the national agenda. Investments in teacher training, curriculum development, and digital educational tools, coupled with efforts to rebuild trust in public institutions through transparency and accountability, will be critical for creating a future in which informed citizenship prevails. Such a future envisions a nation where every citizen is not only knowledgeable about their constitutional rights but also actively engaged in the democratic process, ensuring that government remains a true servant of the people.[21]

Moreover, renewing constitutional discourse requires a cultural shift—a reawakening of the civic virtues that once defined American public life. By encouraging local community engagement, fostering intergenerational dialogue, and supporting initiatives that celebrate the nation's founding principles, America can build a resilient democratic culture that is capable of withstanding the challenges of the modern era. This conservative vision of civic renewal is a call to return to the original spirit of the Constitution—a spirit of self-governance, personal responsibility, and an unwavering commitment to freedom.[22]

Ultimately, the future of constitutional discourse depends on the collective efforts of educators, policymakers, community leaders, and citizens. Through sustained commitment to comprehensive civic education and the promotion of informed public debate, the United States can ensure that the principles enshrined in the Constitution continue to guide and inspire its people. The renewal of constitutional discourse is not simply an academic pursuit; it is a strategic imperative for maintaining the health of American democracy and preserving the legacy of our founding fathers.[23]

Thus, the conservative imperative for renewing constitutional discourse calls for a reinvigorated commitment to constitutional education, a robust media literacy movement, and the cultivation of a politically engaged citizenry. Only by embracing these strategies can America safeguard its founding principles and ensure that the government remains both accountable and limited in its power—a government that continues to serve the people as envisioned by its founders.[24]

In summation, strategies for renewing constitutional discourse are essential for revitalizing American democracy in the face of modern challenges. By re-centering the Constitution in public

---

[21] Lasch, Christopher. *The Culture of Narcissism: American Life in an Age of Diminishing Expectations*. W.W. Norton & Company, 1979.

[22] Wood, Gordon S. *The Radicalism of the American Revolution*. Vintage Books, 1993.

[23] Eskridge, William N. Jr. *Originalism in the Twenty-First Century*. Harvard University Press, 2012.

[24] Scalia, Antonin. *A Matter of Interpretation: Federal Courts and the Law*. Princeton University Press, 1997.

education, fostering bipartisan dialogue, leveraging technology responsibly, and strengthening community engagement, the United States can renew its commitment to the timeless values of freedom, limited government, and self-governance. This renewed discourse will empower citizens to critically evaluate government actions, uphold their constitutional rights, and participate actively in the democratic process, thereby ensuring a vibrant and resilient republic for generations to come.[25]

---

[25] Hamilton, Alexander; Madison, James; Jay, John. *The Federalist Papers*. Penguin Classics, 2003.

CHAPTER 14:

Comparative Perspectives: Lessons from Other Constitutions

1. Comparative Constitutional Frameworks Around the World

The study of constitutional frameworks across the globe provides a unique lens through which to evaluate the enduring strengths and potential shortcomings of the American constitutional model. While the United States Constitution has long served as a bulwark of individual liberty and limited government—a system deeply rooted in the revolutionary experience and the philosophical insights of the founding fathers—other nations have pursued alternative approaches that reflect their distinct histories, cultural values, and political challenges. From a politically conservative perspective, it is essential to analyze these comparative frameworks not only to appreciate the exceptional character of the American model but also to draw lessons for reinforcing constitutional integrity at home. This commentary presents a comprehensive analysis of various constitutional systems, examining their structures, the balance of power, and the mechanisms they employ to safeguard citizens' rights, while underscoring the superior merits of the American approach when measured against the challenges of modern governance.[1]

A central feature that distinguishes the United States Constitution is its deliberate emphasis on limited government and the dispersion of power. The American model was born out of a profound skepticism of centralized authority—a skepticism forged in the crucible of colonial oppression and the tyranny of monarchical rule. In contrast, many European and Latin American constitutions evolved from experiences of autocracy or socialist regimes that necessitated strong central control to achieve rapid modernization or social equality. For example, the French Fifth Republic, with its strong presidential system, concentrates significant power in the executive branch, a design which, although effective in ensuring decisive action, has often raised concerns regarding the potential for authoritarian overreach. Conservatives argue that the American system, with its robust checks and balances, offers a model in which governmental

[1] Hamilton, Alexander; Madison, James; Jay, John. *The Federalist Papers*. Penguin Classics, 2003.

power is not only constrained by law but is also subject to continuous scrutiny by an informed citizenry.[2]

Another aspect of comparative constitutional frameworks is the method by which nations address the issue of individual rights. The United States Constitution, buttressed by the Bill of Rights and subsequent amendments, enshrines a series of inalienable liberties that serve as a constant safeguard against governmental encroachment. In many modern constitutions—particularly those emerging from post-colonial or revolutionary contexts—rights are often framed in a more expansive manner that, while inclusive, sometimes grants the state broader discretion in regulating those rights. For instance, several South American constitutions have adopted provisions that allow for expansive state intervention in the name of social justice, sometimes at the expense of individual autonomy. Conservatives contend that such provisions risk undermining personal responsibility and the fundamental principle that government exists solely to protect, not to grant, rights. In contrast, the American framework maintains a delicate equilibrium, ensuring that rights are protected as inherent to the individual rather than being subject to state approval.[3]

In examining the separation of powers, one finds that the United States has engineered a system that divides authority among the legislative, executive, and judicial branches—a structure intended to prevent any one branch from becoming too dominant. Comparative studies reveal that many constitutional systems around the world adopt alternative arrangements. The United Kingdom, for instance, relies on an unwritten constitution and parliamentary sovereignty, where the executive is drawn from the legislature, resulting in a fusion rather than a separation of powers. Although this system has its own merits, conservatives argue that it lacks the formal institutional safeguards necessary to protect against the concentration of power. In contrast, the American model, by explicitly delineating powers, ensures that each branch serves as a check on the others, a feature that has been crucial in preserving individual liberty throughout periods of national crisis.[4]

Furthermore, the process of constitutional amendment itself is a defining characteristic that sets the United States apart from many other countries. The American amendment process, deliberately designed to be arduous and require broad consensus, ensures that any change to the foundational legal framework is carefully considered and widely supported. By contrast, several

---

[2] Madison, James. "Federalist No. 51." In *The Federalist Papers*, edited by Clinton Rossiter, Bantam Classics, 1961.

[3] Niemi, Richard G., and Jane Junn. *Civic Education: What Makes Students Learn*. Yale University Press, 1998.

[4] Friedman, Milton. *Capitalism and Freedom*. University of Chicago Press, 2002.

modern constitutions feature more flexible amendment procedures that allow for rapid changes in response to shifting political winds. While adaptability is necessary in a dynamic world, conservatives warn that too much ease in altering the constitutional order can lead to instability and the erosion of time-tested principles. The rigorous American process acts as a bulwark against hasty decisions that might compromise the delicate balance between government and liberty.[5]

Comparative constitutional frameworks also differ in their treatment of federalism. The American Constitution enshrines a system of dual sovereignty in which power is shared between the national government and the states, thereby allowing for local autonomy and tailored policy responses. In contrast, many nations, particularly unitary states in Europe and Asia, vest most governmental power in a centralized authority. Although centralization can bring about uniformity and efficiency in policy implementation, conservatives argue that it also tends to stifle local innovation and erode the accountability of government to its citizens. The American federal model, with its emphasis on local self-governance, not only preserves regional diversity but also fosters a competitive environment in which states serve as "laboratories of democracy," experimenting with policies that, if successful, can be adopted nationwide.[6]

The role of judicial review in safeguarding constitutional principles is another area where comparative analysis yields important insights. In the United States, the power of judicial review, as established in Marbury v. Madison, has served as a critical check on the other branches of government. Many constitutional systems around the world either lack an independent judiciary or have judicial bodies that are less autonomous from political pressures. In some cases, constitutional courts in European countries and beyond are perceived as being too intertwined with the executive or legislative branches, thereby compromising their ability to act as impartial arbiters of constitutional disputes. Conservatives maintain that the strong tradition of judicial independence in the United States is a cornerstone of its success as a constitutional republic, ensuring that government actions are continuously measured against the enduring standards of the Constitution.[7]

In addition, comparative perspectives reveal differences in how constitutions address the protection of economic rights and property. The U.S. Constitution, while primarily focused on civil and political liberties, has been interpreted to protect property rights as fundamental to

---

[5] Elazar, Daniel J. *Exploring Federalism*. University of Alabama Press, 1987.

[6] Scalia, Antonin. *A Matter of Interpretation: Federal Courts and the Law*. Princeton University Press, 1997.

[7] Binder, Sarah A. *Stalemate: Causes and Consequences of Legislative Gridlock*. Brookings Institution Press, 2003.

individual freedom and economic prosperity. In contrast, some modern constitutions enshrine economic rights in a way that obligates the state to provide for social welfare, sometimes at the expense of free-market principles. Conservatives argue that a robust defense of property rights is essential for fostering innovation, entrepreneurship, and economic growth. They maintain that the American emphasis on individual property rights underpins a free and dynamic economy, whereas systems that overly emphasize state intervention may lead to inefficiencies and reduced personal responsibility.[8]

Furthermore, the incorporation of international human rights norms into national constitutions has emerged as a trend in many parts of the world. While such integration can enrich a constitutional framework, conservatives caution that it may also lead to the dilution of national sovereignty. The American constitutional tradition is marked by its emphasis on self-determination and the protection of inalienable rights derived from natural law, rather than rights granted by international consensus. From this perspective, the U.S. model serves as a reminder that true freedom arises when rights are seen as inherent to the individual rather than contingent upon external validation.[9]

A comparative analysis also highlights the significance of historical context in shaping constitutional frameworks. Nations that emerged from colonial rule or experienced radical revolutions often adopted constitutions that reflected the immediate demands of social justice and national reconstruction. In these contexts, constitutions may incorporate provisions for extensive social rights and state intervention in the economy. While these measures address urgent social needs, conservatives argue that they can also lead to an overbearing state that undermines individual freedom and economic dynamism. In contrast, the American Constitution was crafted in an era when the protection of individual liberty was paramount—a principle that continues to resonate as the best defense against government overreach.[10]

Comparative constitutional frameworks also differ in their mechanisms for ensuring accountability and transparency. The United States has long championed the separation of powers and a system of checks and balances as means of preventing the abuse of authority. Other nations have experimented with alternative accountability mechanisms, such as parliamentary committees or ombudsman offices, which can be effective in certain contexts but may lack the formal rigidity

---

[8] Kirk, Russell. *The Conservative Mind: From Burke to Eliot*. Regnery Publishing, 1953.

[9] Maier, Pauline. *American Scripture: Making the Declaration of Independence*. Vintage, 1998.

[10] Torney-Purta, Judith, et al. *Citizenship and Political Participation: Political Science Perspectives*. Rowman & Littlefield, 2001.

and clear institutional boundaries found in the American system. Conservatives argue that the explicit checks and balances enshrined in the U.S. Constitution are indispensable for maintaining a government that is truly answerable to its citizens.[11]

Additionally, the process of constitutional interpretation plays a pivotal role in shaping the practical application of a nation's foundational document. In the United States, the originalist approach—advocated by many conservative jurists—seeks to interpret the Constitution according to the original intent of the framers. This method stands in contrast to more dynamic interpretative theories that allow for the evolution of constitutional meaning over time. While critics of originalism argue that a rigid adherence to historical intent may be ill-suited to modern challenges, conservatives maintain that preserving the original meaning of the Constitution is essential for ensuring stability and consistency in governance.[12]

International comparisons also shed light on the role of constitutional rigidity versus flexibility. Some countries adopt highly flexible constitutions that can be amended or reinterpreted with relative ease, while others, like the United States, have deliberately constructed an amendment process that is both arduous and rare. Conservatives contend that the difficulty of amending the U.S. Constitution is a feature—not a bug—of the system, as it prevents transient political majorities from making impulsive changes that could undermine the enduring principles of liberty and limited government.[13]

Moreover, the comparative study of constitutions underscores the importance of cultural and historical traditions in shaping governance. The United States' constitutional framework is deeply intertwined with its Anglo-American legal tradition, which emphasizes individual rights, property rights, and the sanctity of contracts. Many European and Asian constitutions, while equally committed to democratic principles, reflect different historical legacies that prioritize social solidarity or state intervention. Conservatives argue that the American emphasis on individual freedom and the rule of law is particularly well-suited to fostering innovation and economic prosperity, offering a model that has proven remarkably resilient over centuries of change.[14]

The influence of colonial experiences on constitutional design is another important comparative factor. Former colonies in Africa, Asia, and Latin America often inherited legal systems that were

---

[11] Lipset, Seymour. *Political Man: The Social Bases of Politics*. Johns Hopkins University Press, 1960.

[12] Amar, Akhil Reed. *America's Constitution: A Biography*. Random House, 2005.

[13] Eskridge, William N. Jr. *Originalism in the Twenty-First Century*. Harvard University Press, 2012.

[14] McCarty, Nolan, Keith T. Poole, and Howard Rosenthal. *Polarized America: The Dance of Ideology and Unequal Riches*. MIT Press, 2009.

imposed by their colonial rulers, which sometimes led to constitutions that reflect a blend of indigenous practices and external legal traditions. In contrast, the United States was founded on the deliberate rejection of colonial rule and the creation of a system based on self-determination and popular sovereignty. This historical break from colonialism is a cornerstone of American exceptionalism, and conservatives assert that it is this legacy that has enabled the U.S. Constitution to stand the test of time as a guarantor of freedom and self-governance.[15]

In examining contemporary constitutional frameworks, it is also crucial to consider the role of public participation in constitutional reform. In some countries, constitutional conventions or referenda are regularly employed to adapt the constitution to changing social and political conditions. While such participatory mechanisms can enhance democratic legitimacy, conservatives caution that they may also lead to volatile shifts in governance that undermine stability. The U.S. Constitution's amendment process, though slow and deliberate, is designed to ensure that changes reflect a broad consensus rather than the whims of temporary majorities.[16]

Furthermore, comparative constitutional analysis reveals variations in how nations safeguard minority rights. While many modern constitutions incorporate extensive protections for marginalized groups, conservatives argue that an overemphasis on group rights can sometimes infringe upon individual liberties. The American model, with its focus on individual rights enshrined in the Bill of Rights, provides a clear framework for protecting freedom without fragmenting the electorate into competing interest groups. This approach reinforces the conservative belief that the protection of individual liberty is paramount, even when balanced against broader social objectives.[17]

Another critical element in comparative constitutional frameworks is the structure of the executive branch. In presidential systems, such as that of the United States, the separation of powers ensures that the president is both a chief executive and a check on legislative excesses. In contrast, parliamentary systems often conflate the executive and legislative functions, which can lead to a concentration of power that, while efficient, may risk eroding individual freedoms. Conservatives argue that the American presidential system, with its robust system of checks and balances, offers a model for executive accountability that is less susceptible to the pitfalls of unchecked power.[18]

---

[15] Wood, Gordon S. *The Creation of the American Republic, 1776–1787*. University of North Carolina Press, 1998.

[16] Ellis, Joseph J. *American Creation: Triumphs and Tragedies in the Founding of the Republic*. Knopf, 2007.

[17] Putnam, Robert D. *Bowling Alone: The Collapse and Revival of American Community*. Simon & Schuster, 2000.

[18] Galston, William A. *Civic Education and Democracy in America*. Johns Hopkins University Press, 2001.

Additionally, the comparative perspective highlights the role of constitutional courts in interpreting and upholding the foundational document. In some countries, constitutional courts operate as independent arbiters that safeguard the constitution against legislative and executive encroachment. The United States, with its Supreme Court firmly rooted in the tradition of judicial review, provides a strong example of how an independent judiciary can serve as the guardian of constitutional values. Conservatives maintain that the institutional independence of the judiciary is critical for ensuring that constitutional discourse remains grounded in the text and original intent of the founding documents.[19]

Furthermore, a comparison of constitutional frameworks reveals the importance of political stability and institutional continuity. Countries with highly volatile constitutions—characterized by frequent amendments or overhauls—often struggle to maintain consistent policies over time. The American Constitution's relative rigidity, while sometimes criticized for its inflexibility, is praised by conservatives as a key factor in the nation's long-term stability. This stability fosters an environment in which economic growth, social cohesion, and individual freedom can flourish.[20]

The influence of global norms and international legal frameworks also plays a role in shaping national constitutions. While many modern constitutions are increasingly influenced by international human rights standards and global legal principles, conservatives argue that such influences must be carefully balanced against national sovereignty. The U.S. Constitution, with its focus on natural rights and limited government, has long served as a bulwark against external pressures that seek to impose uniform standards across diverse societies.[21]

Moreover, the comparative study of constitutional frameworks offers valuable lessons in how legal systems evolve in response to societal changes. In countries that have experienced rapid economic and social transformation, constitutions have sometimes been reinterpreted or amended in ways that reflect contemporary values. Conservatives caution that while adaptation is necessary, it must not come at the expense of the foundational principles of limited government and individual liberty. The American experience demonstrates that continuity and gradual evolution, rather than abrupt overhauls, are the keys to maintaining a stable and resilient constitutional order.[22]

---

[19] Sanger, Margaret. *Conservative Legacies: How the Founding Ideals Endure*. HarperCollins, 2010.

[20] Bickel, Alexander M. *The Least Dangerous Branch: The Supreme Court at the Bar of Politics*. Yale University Press, 1962.

[21] Lasch, Christopher. *The Culture of Narcissism: American Life in an Age of Diminishing Expectations*. W.W. Norton & Company, 1979.

[22] Wood, Gordon S. *The Radicalism of the American Revolution*. Vintage Books, 1993.

Finally, the comparative analysis of constitutional frameworks underscores the significance of national identity and historical memory in shaping governance. The United States Constitution is not merely a legal document but a symbol of the nation's struggle for independence and self-governance. This symbolic power has imbued the American constitutional system with a unique legitimacy that is difficult to replicate elsewhere. Conservatives argue that the enduring legacy of the founding fathers and the historical experiences that shaped the American republic serve as an essential foundation for constitutional discourse, inspiring citizens to uphold the principles of freedom and limited government even in the face of modern challenges.[23]

In conclusion, comparative constitutional frameworks around the world provide a rich tapestry of approaches to governance, each reflecting the unique historical, cultural, and political contexts from which they emerged. From a politically conservative perspective, the American Constitution stands out as a model of limited government, individual liberty, and institutional stability. Its rigorous separation of powers, robust protection of rights, and deliberate amendment process have ensured its longevity and continued relevance. By studying other constitutional systems, conservatives can reaffirm the exceptional nature of the U.S. framework while drawing lessons for strengthening constitutional discourse in America.[24]

Looking ahead, the task for American policymakers and educators is to use these comparative insights to fortify constitutional education and civic engagement. Renewing constitutional discourse through robust academic programs, community-based initiatives, and responsible media practices is essential for ensuring that future generations remain vigilant defenders of the constitutional order. By embracing the lessons gleaned from global comparisons, America can continue to refine its own model of governance—one that remains true to the visionary principles of its founding fathers while adeptly addressing the challenges of the modern world. This commitment to constitutional literacy and civic participation is the cornerstone upon which the future of American freedom rests.[25]

---

[23] Eskridge, William N. Jr. *Originalism in the Twenty-First Century*. Harvard University Press, 2012.

[24] Scalia, Antonin. *A Matter of Interpretation: Federal Courts and the Law*. Princeton University Press, 1997.

[25] Hamilton, Alexander; Madison, James; Jay, John. *The Federalist Papers*. Penguin Classics, 2003.

2. Adaptability and Flexibility in Global Contexts

In a rapidly changing world where national boundaries are increasingly permeable and global challenges demand swift responses, constitutional frameworks must be both adaptable and flexible. The United States Constitution, with its enduring emphasis on limited government and individual liberty, has long been celebrated by conservatives for its resilience and capacity to withstand political turbulence. Yet, when viewed through the lens of comparative constitutional analysis, it becomes evident that adaptability and flexibility are not only desirable but essential features of a living constitution. This commentary examines how various global constitutional frameworks address adaptability, and in doing so, argues that the American model, while inherently robust, can be further strengthened by learning from international experiences without compromising the founding principles of limited government and personal freedom.[1]

One of the defining attributes of a constitution is its ability to respond to unforeseen challenges while remaining anchored in fundamental principles. Many nations have crafted constitutions that include built-in mechanisms for adaptation. For instance, some European countries incorporate provisions for periodic review of constitutional norms, which allows their legal frameworks to evolve in response to societal shifts. Such built-in flexibility is seen as a pragmatic approach to governance, yet conservatives caution that too much flexibility risks diluting the original intent of the founders. In contrast, the U.S. Constitution employs an intentionally rigorous amendment process that requires broad consensus before any change can be made. This process reflects a deliberate balance between the need for stability and the possibility of reform, ensuring that changes are not made impulsively but rather through careful deliberation.[2]

Comparative analysis reveals that countries with rigid constitutional frameworks sometimes face challenges when rapid change is necessary. In nations where amendment processes are overly strict, governments may be forced to resort to extra-constitutional means to address urgent issues, which can lead to instability. However, conservatives argue that the strength of the American system lies in its capacity to accommodate change through judicial interpretation rather than through frequent amendments. The doctrine of judicial review, established in Marbury v. Madison, allows the courts to adapt constitutional principles to contemporary circumstances without undermining the document's enduring authority. This interpretive flexibility is a key

[1] Hamilton, Alexander; Madison, James; Jay, John. *The Federalist Papers*. Penguin Classics, 2003.

[2] Madison, James. "Federalist No. 51." In *The Federalist Papers*, edited by Clinton Rossiter, Bantam Classics, 1961.

factor in the U.S. model, ensuring that while the text of the Constitution remains immutable, its application can evolve in line with modern realities.[3]

Global constitutional frameworks exhibit diverse approaches to ensuring adaptability. In countries such as Germany, the Basic Law contains explicit references to democratic principles and human dignity that are open to interpretation, providing a legal basis for gradual evolution. Meanwhile, nations like India have embraced a more flexible approach, with judicial activism playing a central role in interpreting constitutional provisions in light of current needs. Conservatives maintain that although these models have their merits, the American emphasis on originalism and measured change has contributed to a stable political order that respects the legacy of the founding fathers. They contend that while adaptation is necessary, it must not come at the expense of the core principles that guarantee freedom and limit government power.[4]

Another critical dimension of adaptability in constitutional frameworks is the role of federalism. The American system of dual sovereignty allows for a decentralized approach to governance, wherein states act as laboratories of democracy. This decentralization provides an inherent mechanism for adaptability, as states can experiment with policies tailored to local conditions while the federal government maintains a minimal but essential role in safeguarding overarching national interests. In contrast, unitary systems, though sometimes more efficient in policy implementation, may struggle to accommodate regional diversity and localized innovation. Conservatives argue that the U.S. model, with its balanced division of power, is uniquely positioned to evolve through both state-level experimentation and judicial refinement at the national level.[5]

The adaptability of constitutional frameworks also hinges on the protection of individual rights. Global comparisons show that many modern constitutions have expanded the range of rights to include economic, social, and cultural dimensions. While such expansions reflect evolving societal values, conservatives contend that rights should be viewed as inherent and inalienable, not subject to state discretion. The American Bill of Rights, along with subsequent amendments, provides a clear and enduring template that emphasizes the protection of civil liberties. This focus on individual rights ensures that the Constitution remains a bulwark against governmental overreach, even as society faces new challenges such as digital privacy, global terrorism, and environmental degradation.[6]

---

[3] Niemi, Richard G., and Jane Junn. *Civic Education: What Makes Students Learn*. Yale University Press, 1998.

[4] Friedman, Milton. *Capitalism and Freedom*. University of Chicago Press, 2002.

[5] Elazar, Daniel J. *Exploring Federalism*. University of Alabama Press, 1987.

[6] Scalia, Antonin. *A Matter of Interpretation: Federal Courts and the Law*. Princeton University Press, 1997.

Furthermore, adaptability in global constitutional frameworks is often linked to mechanisms for resolving disputes and ensuring accountability. Many nations have established independent constitutional courts tasked with interpreting the law and resolving conflicts between branches of government. These courts can serve as adaptive mechanisms, allowing for the reinterpretation of constitutional provisions without the need for formal amendments. In the United States, the Supreme Court and lower federal courts have consistently acted as arbiters in disputes over the Constitution, thereby providing a dynamic means of adapting its principles to contemporary issues. Conservatives argue that this system of judicial review, when coupled with an originalist approach, preserves the integrity of the Constitution while allowing for necessary evolution in its interpretation.[7]

The global context further highlights the tension between national sovereignty and international norms. Many countries incorporate international human rights treaties and conventions into their constitutional frameworks, which can sometimes necessitate adjustments to domestic laws. While such integration promotes global standards of justice and equality, conservatives warn that it may also impinge on national sovereignty and undermine the unique character of a nation's constitutional order. The U.S. model, which traditionally emphasizes constitutional self-reliance and the primacy of domestic legal traditions, is seen as a safeguard against the imposition of external norms that may conflict with the principles of limited government and individual liberty.[8]

Another aspect to consider is the role of cultural traditions and historical memory in shaping constitutional adaptability. Constitutions do not exist in a vacuum; they are products of their historical context and are sustained by the collective memory of a nation. In countries with a strong sense of historical continuity, such as the United Kingdom or Japan, constitutional principles are often reinforced by long-standing traditions and unwritten norms. The United States, with its codified Constitution and a deep-rooted national narrative of self-governance and resistance to tyranny, benefits from a cultural milieu that upholds its constitutional values. Conservatives emphasize that this historical legacy is a crucial component of the American model's adaptability, as it provides a stable foundation upon which incremental change can be built without sacrificing core freedoms.[9]

---

[7] Binder, Sarah A. *Stalemate: Causes and Consequences of Legislative Gridlock*. Brookings Institution Press, 2003.

[8] Kirk, Russell. *The Conservative Mind: From Burke to Eliot*. Regnery Publishing, 1953.

[9] Maier, Pauline. *American Scripture: Making the Declaration of Independence*. Vintage, 1998.

Moreover, the adaptability of constitutional frameworks is closely tied to the educational system. A well-informed citizenry, steeped in constitutional literacy, is essential for the evolution of a society's legal and political norms. Global comparisons reveal that countries with robust civic education programs tend to experience smoother transitions during periods of constitutional reform. In the United States, however, there is growing concern over the decline in constitutional literacy, particularly among younger generations. Conservatives argue that reinvigorating civic education is imperative for ensuring that citizens can engage critically with constitutional issues and participate effectively in the democratic process. By fostering a deeper understanding of the Constitution's historical context and enduring principles, educational initiatives can help maintain the document's relevance and facilitate its adaptation to new challenges.[10]

Institutional flexibility also plays a pivotal role in shaping constitutional adaptability. In many modern constitutional systems, institutions are designed to be both robust and responsive, with built-in mechanisms for feedback and reform. For example, some nations have established parliamentary committees or independent oversight bodies that regularly review government performance and propose amendments. The United States, while having a more rigid amendment process, benefits from a dynamic interplay between the executive, legislative, and judicial branches. Conservatives assert that this interplay, grounded in the principle of separation of powers, allows for a degree of institutional flexibility that can accommodate change without compromising constitutional stability.[11]

Another global perspective on adaptability comes from the economic domain. Constitutions are increasingly called upon to address issues related to economic rights and market regulation. In several countries, constitutional provisions guarantee a range of social and economic rights that require ongoing reinterpretation as economic conditions evolve. While these rights are important for social welfare, conservatives caution that an expansive interpretation of economic rights may lead to excessive state intervention in the economy, thereby undermining free-market principles. The American constitutional tradition, with its emphasis on private property and economic freedom, offers a model in which adaptability is achieved not through expansive state mandates but through market-driven innovation and limited regulatory oversight.[12]

---

[10] Torney-Purta, Judith, et al. *Citizenship and Political Participation: Political Science Perspectives*. Rowman & Littlefield, 2001.

[11] Lipset, Seymour. *Political Man: The Social Bases of Politics*. Johns Hopkins University Press, 1960.

[12] Amar, Akhil Reed. *America's Constitution: A Biography*. Random House, 2005.

The role of technology in fostering constitutional adaptability is another area of interest. As digital innovation reshapes communication, commerce, and governance, constitutional frameworks must find ways to address issues such as privacy, cybersecurity, and information integrity. Globally, some countries are actively updating their legal frameworks to account for these technological changes. In the United States, while the Constitution remains silent on digital matters, the judiciary has taken steps to apply constitutional principles to emerging challenges. Conservatives argue that the adaptability of the U.S. system lies in its ability to extend time-honored principles—such as due process and freedom of speech—to new domains, thereby ensuring that the Constitution remains a living document in the digital age.[13]

Comparative perspectives also highlight the importance of public participation in constitutional evolution. In many countries, constitutional reform is undertaken through inclusive processes that involve broad segments of society. These participatory mechanisms ensure that constitutional changes reflect the collective will of the people. The U.S. amendment process, though deliberately rigorous, can be revitalized by encouraging more active public discourse and engagement with constitutional issues. Conservatives advocate for a renewed emphasis on civic participation in constitutional reform, arguing that an engaged citizenry is the best safeguard against both governmental overreach and radical, untested changes.[14]

Furthermore, global constitutional frameworks demonstrate that adaptability is enhanced by mechanisms for dispute resolution and institutional checks. Many nations have developed comprehensive systems for resolving conflicts between different branches of government or between the state and its citizens. The United States' system of judicial review, along with its separation of powers, provides a robust mechanism for ensuring that constitutional disputes are resolved in a manner that preserves the balance of power. Conservatives maintain that this system of checks and balances is not only a hallmark of the American model but also a critical component of its ability to adapt over time while safeguarding individual liberties.[15]

The influence of international norms and global governance structures on national constitutions is another factor that shapes adaptability. As countries become more interconnected, there is an increasing tendency for international human rights standards and global legal principles to influence domestic constitutional interpretation. While such influences can promote a more universal

---

[13] Eskridge, William N. Jr. *Originalism in the Twenty-First Century*. Harvard University Press, 2012.

[14] McCarty, Nolan, Keith T. Poole, and Howard Rosenthal. *Polarized America: The Dance of Ideology and Unequal Riches*. MIT Press, 2009.

[15] Wood, Gordon S. *The Creation of the American Republic, 1776–1787*. University of North Carolina Press, 1998.

standard of justice, conservatives caution that they may also undermine national sovereignty and the unique character of a country's constitutional heritage. The American constitutional tradition, with its strong emphasis on natural rights and limited government, offers a counterpoint to these global pressures by asserting that constitutional adaptability must be achieved through internal evolution rather than external imposition.[16]

Cultural resilience, too, is a vital aspect of constitutional adaptability. In societies where national identity is closely tied to historical and cultural traditions, the Constitution often serves as a unifying symbol that reinforces the values and practices that have sustained the nation through times of change. Comparative studies indicate that countries with a strong sense of historical continuity are better able to adapt to modern challenges without losing sight of their foundational principles. Conservatives argue that the American model, deeply rooted in the revolutionary heritage and the ideals of the founding fathers, is uniquely positioned to weather the storms of modernization by drawing on its rich historical legacy.[17]

Moreover, the adaptability of constitutional frameworks is enhanced by ongoing scholarly debate and research. Academic institutions and think tanks around the world contribute to a dynamic body of literature that examines constitutional challenges and proposes innovative solutions. In the United States, conservative scholars have long emphasized the importance of returning to an originalist interpretation of the Constitution as a means of ensuring that its principles remain clear and unambiguous. This scholarly engagement not only informs judicial decision-making but also provides a basis for public discourse that can guide policy reforms. By fostering a vibrant academic community focused on constitutional studies, the nation can better navigate the complexities of modern governance while remaining true to its foundational ideals.[18]

Another important strategy for enhancing adaptability is the reform of constitutional processes themselves. While the U.S. Constitution's amendment process is intentionally rigorous, there is ongoing debate about how to balance stability with the need for change. Comparative perspectives reveal that countries with more flexible amendment procedures sometimes enjoy a greater capacity to respond to emerging challenges. Conservatives argue, however, that the American process—though slow—has the virtue of ensuring that any alterations are the product of broad consensus rather than transient political pressures. Nonetheless, there is room for debate on

---

[16] Ellis, Joseph J. *American Creation: Triumphs and Tragedies in the Founding of the Republic*. Knopf, 2007.

[17] Putnam, Robert D. *Bowling Alone: The Collapse and Revival of American Community*. Simon & Schuster, 2000.

[18] Galston, William A. *Civic Education and Democracy in America*. Johns Hopkins University Press, 2001.

whether certain procedural reforms could enhance adaptability without sacrificing the document's core principles.[19]

Finally, the future of constitutional adaptability depends on the capacity of citizens to engage with the document's enduring principles in a meaningful way. An informed, active electorate is essential for holding government accountable and ensuring that constitutional reforms are both necessary and prudent. Strategies for renewing constitutional discourse—through educational initiatives, public forums, and the effective use of digital media—are critical for ensuring that the Constitution remains a vibrant, living framework for governance. Conservatives maintain that the strength of American democracy lies in its ability to balance tradition with innovation, a balance that is achieved through a continuous commitment to constitutional literacy and civic engagement.[20]

In conclusion, the adaptability and flexibility of constitutional frameworks in global contexts offer valuable lessons for American governance. Comparative analysis shows that while many nations have developed mechanisms for rapid adaptation, the conservative strength of the U.S. Constitution lies in its deliberate balance between stability and change. By upholding a system of checks and balances, protecting individual rights, and fostering an informed citizenry, the American model continues to serve as a bulwark against tyranny and a beacon of freedom. Global experiences underscore the importance of institutional mechanisms, cultural resilience, and active public participation in achieving constitutional adaptability—elements that conservatives argue are integral to preserving the legacy of the founding fathers while addressing modern challenges.[21]

Looking ahead, American policymakers, educators, and civic leaders must embrace strategies that enhance constitutional adaptability without compromising the core principles of limited government and individual liberty. This includes reinvigorating constitutional education through innovative digital tools, community engagement initiatives, and enhanced scholarly research. By drawing on the lessons of comparative constitutional frameworks, the United States can refine its approach to constitutional reform and ensure that its legal foundation remains robust in the face of emerging global challenges.[22]

---

[19] Sanger, Margaret. *Conservative Legacies: How the Founding Ideals Endure*. HarperCollins, 2010.

[20] Bickel, Alexander M. *The Least Dangerous Branch: The Supreme Court at the Bar of Politics*. Yale University Press, 1962.

[21] Lasch, Christopher. *The Culture of Narcissism: American Life in an Age of Diminishing Expectations*. W.W. Norton & Company, 1979.

[22] Wood, Gordon S. *The Radicalism of the American Revolution*. Vintage Books, 1993.

Moreover, it is imperative that national discourse on constitutional matters remains open, informed, and free from partisan distortions. Encouraging bipartisan dialogue, promoting media literacy, and ensuring that constitutional debates are rooted in historical context are essential steps toward maintaining an adaptable and resilient constitutional order. The conservative vision for the future emphasizes that adaptation should be guided by a clear understanding of the founding principles, ensuring that any changes are measured, deliberate, and reflective of the nation's enduring commitment to liberty and justice. Hamilton, Alexander; Madison, James; Jay, John. *The Federalist Papers*. Penguin Classics, 2003.[23]

Ultimately, the ability of a constitutional framework to adapt and remain flexible in a global context is a testament to its strength. The American Constitution, with its rigorous separation of powers, robust protection of individual rights, and deliberate amendment process, exemplifies how a legal framework can endure over centuries while evolving to meet new challenges. As the world continues to change, the task for American society is to renew its commitment to constitutional discourse through comprehensive education, active civic engagement, and informed public debate. This multifaceted approach will ensure that the Constitution remains not only a historical document but also a living, dynamic guide for governance in the twenty-first century.[24]

Thus, the future of American constitutional adaptability depends on our ability to learn from global examples while remaining steadfast in our commitment to the principles enshrined by our founding fathers. By adopting strategies that promote both stability and flexibility, the United States can continue to lead as a model of constitutional governance—one that balances enduring traditions with the demands of an ever-evolving global landscape. This balanced approach is the key to securing the legacy of American freedom and ensuring that the Constitution remains a vibrant foundation for democratic governance well into the future.[25]

---

[23] Eskridge, William N. Jr. *Originalism in the Twenty-First Century*. Harvard University Press, 2012.

[24] Scalia, Antonin. *A Matter of Interpretation: Federal Courts and the Law*. Princeton University Press, 1997.

[25] Hamilton, Alexander; Madison, James; Jay, John. *The Federalist Papers*. Penguin Classics, 2003.

3. Successes and Failures: Comparative Case Studies

Comparative case studies provide a critical framework for evaluating constitutional frameworks by examining how different nations address governance challenges and protect individual freedoms. By analyzing successes and failures in diverse contexts, one gains insight into the exceptional qualities of the American constitutional model and the lessons that can be drawn to further safeguard liberty and limited government. From a politically conservative perspective, such analysis reaffirms the enduring wisdom of our founding fathers while highlighting the pitfalls encountered by other nations whose constitutional frameworks have either overreached or fallen short of protecting citizens' rights. This commentary provides a comprehensive analytical review of comparative case studies, examining the structural, institutional, and cultural factors that have contributed to the successes and failures of constitutional regimes around the world, and arguing that the American approach—characterized by a rigorous separation of powers, robust judicial review, and a deliberate amendment process—remains uniquely effective in ensuring a free society.[1]

One prominent success in comparative constitutional design can be found in the American model's carefully calibrated system of checks and balances. The framers of the U.S. Constitution, informed by their experiences under British tyranny, intentionally dispersed governmental power among the legislative, executive, and judicial branches to prevent any single entity from dominating the political landscape. This separation of powers, enshrined in the Constitution and continuously upheld by judicial review, has contributed to a stable political system that resists rapid, radical changes. In contrast, several European constitutions have experimented with parliamentary systems where the fusion of powers has, at times, led to rapid policy shifts without sufficient oversight. Conservatives argue that the American emphasis on institutional restraint and constitutional continuity has prevented the emergence of authoritarian regimes—a success that serves as a benchmark for evaluating other systems.[2]

Conversely, some comparative case studies reveal significant failures, particularly in nations where constitutional frameworks were designed with an overly flexible amendment process. For example, in certain Latin American countries, constitutions have been amended frequently in response to populist pressures, leading to instability and uncertainty in governance. Such rapid and recurrent changes have undermined the predictability of the legal framework and eroded

---

[1] Hamilton, Alexander; Madison, James; Jay, John. *The Federalist Papers*. Penguin Classics, 2003.

[2] Madison, James. "Federalist No. 51." In *The Federalist Papers*, edited by Clinton Rossiter, Bantam Classics, 1961.

investor confidence. Conservatives maintain that the deliberate, rigorous process of amending the U.S. Constitution—requiring supermajority consensus—ensures that only changes reflecting broad national agreement are enacted, thereby safeguarding the principles of limited government and individual freedom.[3]

Another area of comparative analysis is the protection of individual rights. The American Constitution, particularly through the Bill of Rights, provides a clear and enduring safeguard for civil liberties. In contrast, many post-colonial constitutions have incorporated extensive economic and social rights, sometimes at the expense of traditional individual freedoms. For instance, several African and Asian constitutions have been critiqued for granting the state expansive powers to regulate economic activity and social behavior, which conservatives argue may lead to a slippery slope toward authoritarianism. The American focus on natural rights—viewing freedom as inherent and inalienable rather than state-granted—has been a critical success factor in preserving personal autonomy.[4]

Federalism represents another comparative dimension where the American model has achieved notable success. The dual sovereignty system in the United States allows states considerable latitude in governing local affairs while the federal government maintains oversight on matters of national importance. This decentralized approach has enabled states to serve as "laboratories of democracy," testing innovative policies that, when successful, can be adopted nationwide. By contrast, unitary states with centralized power structures often struggle with one-size-fits-all policies that fail to account for regional diversity. Conservative scholars argue that the American federal system not only promotes efficiency and innovation but also acts as a bulwark against the concentration of power—a success rarely replicated in more centralized constitutional systems.[5]

In examining institutional performance, judicial independence emerges as a cornerstone of successful constitutional governance. The U.S. Supreme Court's role in interpreting the Constitution through judicial review has provided a stabilizing influence, ensuring that governmental actions remain within the bounds set by the founding document. Comparative studies of constitutional courts in countries with less independent judiciaries have often revealed susceptibility to political interference, leading to inconsistent application of laws and a weakening of checks on

---

[3] Niemi, Richard G., and Jane Junn. *Civic Education: What Makes Students Learn*. Yale University Press, 1998.

[4] Friedman, Milton. *Capitalism and Freedom*. University of Chicago Press, 2002.

[5] Elazar, Daniel J. *Exploring Federalism*. University of Alabama Press, 1987.

governmental power. Conservatives assert that the American tradition of judicial independence is a major factor in its constitutional success and offers critical lessons for other nations striving to balance democratic accountability with legal restraint.[6]

Political culture also plays a significant role in the success or failure of constitutional frameworks. In the United States, a strong tradition of civic engagement and a well-established system of civic education have historically underpinned the constitutional order. Town meetings, public debates, and a free press have contributed to a vibrant democratic discourse that continually reinforces the Constitution's principles. In contrast, many countries with newer or less-established democratic traditions often face challenges in cultivating a similar culture of participation, resulting in lower public trust and engagement. Conservatives argue that the strength of American constitutional culture is both a product of its historical legacy and a critical success factor in its sustained functioning as a democratic republic.[7]

However, comparative case studies also illustrate failures in constitutional design, particularly in contexts where cultural divisions have undermined national unity. In nations with deep ethnic, religious, or regional rifts, constitutional frameworks that fail to accommodate diverse identities can lead to persistent conflict and even civil strife. Some Middle Eastern and African countries, for example, have experienced repeated constitutional crises as competing groups contest the legitimacy of the constitutional order. Conservatives contend that the American experience—with its emphasis on pluralism under a unified constitutional framework—offers valuable insights into managing diversity without fragmenting the state. The U.S. model's careful balance of national standards with local autonomy helps to mitigate conflicts by allowing different communities to maintain their distinct identities within a cohesive legal structure.[8]

Another critical lesson from comparative studies is the impact of international influences on constitutional adaptability. Many modern constitutions incorporate elements of international law and human rights norms, which can sometimes conflict with a nation's traditional values. In certain European and Latin American countries, international obligations have led to constitutional reforms that conservatives argue undermine national sovereignty. The American Constitution, by contrast, is rooted in a tradition of self-reliance and natural rights that resists external imposition. Conservatives view this as a key success of the American model,

---

[6] Scalia, Antonin. *A Matter of Interpretation: Federal Courts and the Law*. Princeton University Press, 1997.

[7] Binder, Sarah A. *Stalemate: Causes and Consequences of Legislative Gridlock*. Brookings Institution Press, 2003.

[8] Kirk, Russell. *The Conservative Mind: From Burke to Eliot*. Regnery Publishing, 1953.

maintaining that constitutional adaptability should be guided by domestic consensus rather than international trends.[9]

Comparative perspectives further reveal differences in economic policy embedded within constitutional frameworks. Several nations have enshrined extensive social and economic rights in their constitutions, which, while aiming to promote equality, sometimes grant the state a level of control that can stifle entrepreneurship and economic freedom. The United States, with its focus on private property rights and market-based principles, exemplifies a constitutional framework that has fostered robust economic growth and innovation. Conservatives argue that this emphasis on economic liberty is a significant success factor, demonstrating that protecting individual economic rights is essential for maintaining both prosperity and freedom.[10]

Moreover, constitutional stability is enhanced by the rigor of the amendment process. In many countries, the ease of constitutional change has led to frequent and sometimes hasty revisions that destabilize governance. The U.S. Constitution's amendment process, though often criticized for its rigidity, is defended by conservatives as a strength that ensures any modification is thoroughly vetted and enjoys broad support. This deliberative process acts as a safeguard against transient political pressures and preserves the integrity of the constitutional order over time.[11]

The role of constitutional interpretation in ensuring adaptability is also a recurring theme in comparative analyses. While some countries adopt a living constitution approach—where the meaning of the text evolves with societal changes—others adhere to originalism, seeking to maintain the framers' original intent. Conservatives advocate for the latter, arguing that a strict adherence to original meaning provides clarity and predictability in governance. The American Supreme Court's use of originalist principles has, in the view of conservative scholars, contributed significantly to the durability and legitimacy of the constitutional framework, even as society evolves.[12]

Furthermore, the distribution of power between the central government and regional authorities has a profound impact on constitutional performance. Comparative case studies reveal that overly centralized systems may benefit from uniformity but often at the cost of local responsiveness and accountability. The federal structure of the United States, by contrast, allows for significant

---

[9] Maier, Pauline. *American Scripture: Making the Declaration of Independence*. Vintage, 1998.

[10] Torney-Purta, Judith, et al. *Citizenship and Political Participation: Political Science Perspectives*. Rowman & Littlefield, 2001.

[11] Lipset, Seymour. *Political Man: The Social Bases of Politics*. Johns Hopkins University Press, 1960.

[12] Amar, Akhil Reed. *America's Constitution: A Biography*. Random House, 2005.

local autonomy while still maintaining national cohesion. Conservatives maintain that this balance not only fosters policy innovation and competition among states but also ensures that power remains decentralized—a principle that is essential for protecting individual freedoms.[13]

In addition, the cultural and historical context in which constitutions are drafted plays a critical role in their long-term success. Countries with a long-standing tradition of constitutional governance, such as those in Western Europe, often enjoy a deep-seated respect for legal traditions that support stability and continuity. The United States, with its revolutionary heritage and the enduring influence of its founding documents, stands as a testament to the power of historical memory in sustaining constitutional order. Conservatives argue that this legacy provides a unique source of strength, enabling the American Constitution to serve not only as a legal document but as a symbol of enduring freedom and self-determination.[14]

Comparative case studies also underscore the importance of civic education and public engagement in maintaining constitutional legitimacy. Nations that invest in civic education tend to cultivate a more informed and active citizenry, which in turn holds government accountable and ensures that constitutional principles are upheld. In the United States, a robust tradition of civic engagement has historically been a key factor in the success of its constitutional system. Conservatives emphasize that strengthening civic education is critical to renewing public discourse and ensuring that future generations continue to defend the values enshrined in the Constitution.[15]

Another lesson from international constitutional experiences is the need for transparency and accountability in governance. Many countries have implemented institutional mechanisms—such as independent ombudsmen, anti-corruption agencies, and transparency laws—to monitor government actions and prevent abuses of power. The United States has traditionally relied on the separation of powers and judicial review as primary safeguards against governmental overreach. Conservatives argue that these mechanisms, while not infallible, have proven effective in preserving the constitutional order and serve as a model for other nations seeking to balance authority with accountability.[16]

---

[13] Eskridge, William N. Jr. *Originalism in the Twenty-First Century*. Harvard University Press, 2012.

[14] McCarty, Nolan, Keith T. Poole, and Howard Rosenthal. *Polarized America: The Dance of Ideology and Unequal Riches*. MIT Press, 2009.

[15] Wood, Gordon S. *The Creation of the American Republic, 1776–1787*. University of North Carolina Press, 1998.

[16] Ellis, Joseph J. *American Creation: Triumphs and Tragedies in the Founding of the Republic*. Knopf, 2007.

The integration of international legal norms into domestic constitutional frameworks is yet another area of comparative interest. In several countries, international human rights treaties have been incorporated into national law, influencing constitutional interpretation and policy-making. While such integration can promote global standards of justice, conservatives caution that it may also undermine national sovereignty and the distinctiveness of a country's constitutional heritage. The American constitutional tradition, with its emphasis on natural rights and limited government, stands in contrast to these trends, highlighting the value of a constitution that is rooted in the unique historical experience of its people.[17]

Moreover, comparative perspectives reveal that successful constitutional frameworks are those that manage to evolve in response to new challenges without sacrificing their core principles. The United States Constitution, with its careful balance between rigidity and adaptability, exemplifies this delicate equilibrium. Although some critics argue that its amendment process is too inflexible, conservatives contend that this very rigidity has preserved the constitutional framework through centuries of political and social change. By allowing for gradual evolution through judicial interpretation rather than frequent formal amendments, the American model demonstrates that stability and adaptability can coexist within a single constitutional system.[18]

In evaluating the successes and failures of constitutional frameworks globally, it becomes clear that a nation's historical experience, cultural traditions, and institutional structures are inextricably linked to its constitutional performance. Countries that have experienced frequent constitutional upheavals or rapid shifts in governmental structure often face challenges in maintaining long-term stability and protecting individual rights. The American experience, with its emphasis on enduring principles and a deliberate, consensus-driven approach to constitutional change, offers a powerful counterexample to these trends. Conservatives argue that the relative stability of the U.S. Constitution is a testament to the wisdom of the founding fathers and a model for nations seeking to balance order with liberty.[19]

Furthermore, the role of civic participation cannot be understated. Comparative studies consistently show that constitutions thrive when there is robust public engagement in governance. The United States, with its tradition of town meetings, local elections, and vibrant media, has cultivated a democratic culture that reinforces constitutional norms through continuous public scrutiny.

---

[17] Putnam, Robert D. *Bowling Alone: The Collapse and Revival of American Community*. Simon & Schuster, 2000.

[18] Galston, William A. *Civic Education and Democracy in America*. Johns Hopkins University Press, 2001.

[19] Sanger, Margaret. *Conservative Legacies: How the Founding Ideals Endure*. HarperCollins, 2010.

Conservatives maintain that an informed and active citizenry is the most effective bulwark against the encroachment of centralized power and that the American model of democratic participation is integral to its constitutional success.[20]

In conclusion, the comparative analysis of constitutional frameworks around the world reveals both the strengths and weaknesses inherent in different systems of governance. While many nations have experimented with flexible amendment procedures, expansive rights, and centralized control, the American Constitution stands out for its rigorous separation of powers, its protection of individual liberties, and its deliberate, consensus-driven approach to change. Successes in constitutional design are evident in the stability, accountability, and economic prosperity that the American model has fostered over centuries. Conversely, failures in other systems—often marked by rapid constitutional changes or excessive centralization—underscore the value of the principles enshrined in the U.S. framework.[21]

Looking ahead, the lessons from comparative case studies provide a roadmap for strengthening constitutional governance in the United States. By reaffirming the founding principles of limited government, individual liberty, and judicial independence, and by fostering a culture of civic engagement and public accountability, America can continue to lead as a model of constitutional excellence in a global context. Conservatives argue that the enduring success of the American constitutional system lies in its ability to balance tradition with innovation—a balance that must be maintained if the nation is to navigate the complex challenges of the twenty-first century.[22]

Ultimately, the comparative perspective demonstrates that while no constitutional system is perfect, the American model offers unique strengths that have allowed it to endure. Its capacity for adaptation through judicial review, its emphasis on federalism, and its deliberate approach to constitutional change have all contributed to a resilient and dynamic governance structure. As global challenges evolve, so too must the strategies for preserving constitutional integrity and renewing public discourse. The lessons gleaned from the successes and failures of other nations underscore the importance of safeguarding the core values that have defined the United States since its inception.[23]

---

[20] Bickel, Alexander M. *The Least Dangerous Branch: The Supreme Court at the Bar of Politics*. Yale University Press, 1962.

[21] Lasch, Christopher. *The Culture of Narcissism: American Life in an Age of Diminishing Expectations*. W.W. Norton & Company, 1979.

[22] Wood, Gordon S. *The Radicalism of the American Revolution*. Vintage Books, 1993.

[23] Eskridge, William N. Jr. *Originalism in the Twenty-First Century*. Harvard University Press, 2012.

Thus, it is imperative for policymakers, educators, and civic leaders to draw on international experiences to fortify the American constitutional framework. By enhancing civic education, promoting judicial independence, and fostering robust public participation, the United States can continue to adapt to emerging challenges while remaining steadfast in its commitment to the principles of liberty and limited government. This conservative vision for constitutional governance not only honors the legacy of the founding fathers but also serves as a guide for building a future where freedom and democracy flourish.[24]

In summation, comparative case studies provide a rich resource for understanding the adaptability and limitations of various constitutional frameworks. The American model, with its emphasis on restraint, balanced power, and enduring rights, has repeatedly proven its merit in maintaining stability and protecting individual freedoms. By learning from both the successes and failures observed internationally, the United States can refine its approach to constitutional governance, ensuring that its foundational principles continue to serve as a beacon of freedom and a model for democratic excellence around the world.[25]

---

[24] Scalia, Antonin. *A Matter of Interpretation: Federal Courts and the Law*. Princeton University Press, 1997.

[25] Hamilton, Alexander; Madison, James; Jay, John. *The Federalist Papers*. Penguin Classics, 2003.

4. Implications for American Constitutional Reform

The ongoing dialogue surrounding constitutional reform in the United States has never been more pertinent, particularly as American society grapples with internal divisions and external pressures. Comparative perspectives from other constitutional systems around the world offer valuable lessons that can inform and enhance reform efforts at home. From a politically conservative standpoint, the enduring principles of limited government, individual liberty, and the rule of law—values enshrined by our founding fathers—must remain at the heart of any reform process. This commentary examines the implications of international constitutional experiences for American constitutional reform, arguing that while adaptation and evolution are essential in response to modern challenges, such changes must be measured and rooted in the original intent of the Constitution.[1]

One of the most instructive lessons drawn from comparative constitutional frameworks is the importance of stability through a rigorous amendment process. Nations with flexible constitutional amendment procedures often experience frequent and abrupt changes that can lead to political instability and erosion of public trust. In contrast, the American Constitution's deliberate, consensus-driven amendment process has safeguarded the document's core principles for over two centuries. Conservatives assert that this procedural rigor is vital for preserving the fundamental rights and limited government that underpin American democracy, and any reform must maintain this balance between necessary evolution and constitutional continuity.[2]

Comparative systems also highlight the crucial role of judicial review as a mechanism for constitutional interpretation and adaptation. In several European and Latin American countries, constitutional courts have been granted expansive powers to reinterpret their nation's laws in light of current circumstances. Although this has sometimes resulted in progressive legal changes, conservatives caution that unchecked judicial activism can lead to a departure from the original meaning of the text. The U.S. model, with its commitment to originalism, ensures that changes in interpretation remain tethered to the framers' intent. This stability is essential for maintaining the delicate balance between government power and individual freedom.[3]

---

[1] Hamilton, Alexander; Madison, James; Jay, John. *The Federalist Papers*. Penguin Classics, 2003.

[2] Madison, James. "Federalist No. 51." In *The Federalist Papers*, edited by Clinton Rossiter, Bantam Classics, 1961.

[3] Niemi, Richard G., and Jane Junn. *Civic Education: What Makes Students Learn*. Yale University Press, 1998.

Another significant lesson is derived from the study of federal structures in various countries. Many nations operate under unitary systems where power is highly centralized, often at the expense of regional autonomy and local responsiveness. By contrast, the American federal system has long been hailed as a mechanism for preserving local self-governance while maintaining national cohesion. Comparative case studies reveal that decentralized governance enables states to act as "laboratories of democracy," where local innovations can later be adopted at the national level. Conservatives argue that any constitutional reform in America must preserve and even strengthen federalism, as it is instrumental in protecting against the overconcentration of power.[4]

The protection of individual rights is another area where comparative perspectives offer guidance. While many modern constitutions have expanded the range of social and economic rights, there is a risk that such broad guarantees may inadvertently empower the state to infringe on personal freedoms. The American constitutional tradition, with its strong emphasis on natural rights and the protection of property, provides a model for ensuring that rights are preserved as inherent and inalienable. Conservatives contend that American constitutional reform should resist pressures to expand state authority beyond its proper limits, as doing so could compromise the very liberties the Constitution was designed to protect.[5]

International experiences also reveal the importance of a robust separation of powers. In several countries where the executive, legislative, and judicial branches are less distinct, power tends to become concentrated, leading to potential authoritarianism. The American Constitution's explicit delineation of powers, maintained through a system of checks and balances, has proven effective in curbing abuses and ensuring that no single branch can dominate. Conservatives argue that any reforms must uphold this critical feature to prevent the drift toward centralized power that has plagued other nations.[6]

Moreover, comparative constitutional analysis underscores the significance of civic education and public engagement in upholding constitutional norms. Countries that invest in comprehensive civic education programs tend to have more resilient democracies, as citizens are better equipped to understand and defend their rights. In the United States, however, there is a growing concern that declining constitutional literacy among the youth weakens the democratic fabric. Conservatives advocate for renewed educational initiatives that focus on the historical context, philosophical

---

[4] Friedman, Milton. *Capitalism and Freedom*. University of Chicago Press, 2002.

[5] Elazar, Daniel J. *Exploring Federalism*. University of Alabama Press, 1987.

[6] Scalia, Antonin. *A Matter of Interpretation: Federal Courts and the Law*. Princeton University Press, 1997.

foundations, and practical applications of the Constitution. Such reforms are seen as essential for ensuring that citizens remain active participants in governance and vigilant against governmental overreach.[7]

The influence of global human rights norms on constitutional reform is another aspect of international comparison that carries implications for American reform. Many nations have incorporated international treaties into their constitutional frameworks, often resulting in significant shifts in policy priorities. While such integration can promote a universal standard of justice, conservatives argue that it may also dilute national sovereignty and erode traditional values. The American model, which prioritizes self-determination and the protection of inalienable rights as articulated by the founding fathers, serves as a bulwark against external influences. Reform efforts, therefore, should be cautious not to compromise domestic constitutional principles by uncritically adopting international norms.[8]

Economic rights and regulatory policies are also central to comparative constitutional debates. In some countries, constitutions guarantee extensive economic and social rights, which can lead to increased state intervention in the market. Conservatives maintain that such interventions, while well-intentioned, risk stifling innovation and curtailing economic freedom. The American Constitution, with its emphasis on private property rights and limited government, provides a model that has consistently fostered economic prosperity. Thus, any constitutional reform in America should carefully balance the need for economic regulation with the imperative of preserving free-market principles.[9]

Another critical insight from comparative perspectives concerns the amendment process itself. Constitutions that are too easily amended may lack the stability necessary for long-term planning and protection of rights. Conversely, overly rigid systems may be unable to adapt to changing circumstances. The U.S. Constitution's demanding amendment process, requiring broad consensus, is a deliberate design choice that has maintained stability over time. Conservatives argue that while reform is inevitable, it must be approached with caution, ensuring that changes reflect a deep and lasting consensus rather than transient political fashions.[10]

---

[7] Binder, Sarah A. *Stalemate: Causes and Consequences of Legislative Gridlock.* Brookings Institution Press, 2003.

[8] Kirk, Russell. *The Conservative Mind: From Burke to Eliot.* Regnery Publishing, 1953.

[9] Maier, Pauline. *American Scripture: Making the Declaration of Independence.* Vintage, 1998.

[10] Torney-Purta, Judith, et al. *Citizenship and Political Participation: Political Science Perspectives.* Rowman & Littlefield, 2001.

Comparative studies also point to the role of historical memory in shaping constitutional governance. In nations where a strong historical narrative supports constitutional traditions, citizens are more likely to respect and adhere to the rule of law. The United States benefits from a storied past—rooted in the struggle for independence and the visionary ideals of its founders—that continues to inspire its citizens. Conservatives emphasize that any efforts at constitutional reform should draw on this rich historical legacy, reinforcing a sense of national identity that is critical for sustaining democratic governance.[11]

The structure of the executive branch in various constitutional systems provides further lessons for American reform. In presidential systems like that of the United States, a clear separation of powers helps prevent the abuse of executive authority. In contrast, parliamentary systems, though efficient in some respects, often blur the lines between the executive and legislative functions, potentially leading to an overconcentration of power. Conservatives argue that the American presidential model, with its robust checks and balances, remains the most effective structure for protecting individual liberties and ensuring accountability.[12]

The role of judicial review in adapting constitutional principles to contemporary challenges is equally important. In many countries, constitutional courts have been empowered to reinterpret foundational texts in response to societal changes. The American system, which relies on an independent judiciary and the principle of originalism, has demonstrated that a careful, principled approach to judicial interpretation can provide the flexibility needed to address modern issues without compromising the Constitution's enduring principles. Conservatives view this approach as a model for balancing stability with necessary evolution.[13]

Furthermore, comparative constitutional frameworks reveal the importance of federalism in accommodating diverse regional needs. While unitary states may achieve uniformity, they often do so at the expense of local autonomy. The American federal system, by contrast, allows states to tailor policies to their unique circumstances while maintaining national cohesion. This balance between central authority and regional independence is a cornerstone of the U.S. constitutional design, and conservatives argue that preserving this balance is essential for any reform efforts aimed at enhancing democratic governance.[14]

---

[11] Lipset, Seymour. *Political Man: The Social Bases of Politics*. Johns Hopkins University Press, 1960.

[12] Amar, Akhil Reed. *America's Constitution: A Biography*. Random House, 2005.

[13] Eskridge, William N. Jr. *Originalism in the Twenty-First Century*. Harvard University Press, 2012.

[14] McCarty, Nolan, Keith T. Poole, and Howard Rosenthal. *Polarized America: The Dance of Ideology and Unequal Riches*. MIT Press, 2009.

Another aspect of comparative analysis is the integration of technology and digital governance. Many nations are exploring ways to incorporate digital innovations into their constitutional and administrative frameworks to enhance transparency and citizen engagement. The United States, while a leader in technological advancement, faces challenges in integrating digital tools into its constitutional discourse without compromising established legal traditions. Conservatives caution that any reforms must be carefully designed to ensure that digital innovations serve to enhance, rather than undermine, constitutional protections and the rule of law.[15]

The experiences of countries with emerging democracies provide additional cautionary tales. In several nations, constitutional reforms have been used to legitimize authoritarian regimes or to entrench the power of ruling elites. These examples illustrate the dangers of reform processes that are not grounded in a broad-based consensus or that fail to respect the core principles of limited government. Conservatives argue that the American model, with its rigorous safeguards and deeply embedded traditions of self-governance, offers a proven framework for constitutional stability. Reform efforts must therefore prioritize protecting these principles against the temptations of populism and authoritarianism.[16]

International comparisons also highlight the importance of public participation in constitutional reform. Countries that engage citizens in the amendment process through referenda or public consultations tend to produce more legitimate and durable constitutional changes. The conservative view holds that while the U.S. amendment process is intentionally difficult, there is still a need for greater public engagement and transparency in constitutional debates. By involving citizens more directly, America can ensure that reforms reflect the true will of the people and maintain the legitimacy of the constitutional order.[17]

Comparative case studies underscore the potential benefits of cross-border learning. Nations that have successfully navigated constitutional challenges offer models that can be adapted to the American context without compromising its core values. For example, Germany's careful integration of constitutional review with democratic accountability has provided insights into balancing state power and individual rights. Conservatives suggest that while the American system is uniquely suited to its historical context, there are lessons to be learned regarding the

---

[15] Wood, Gordon S. *The Creation of the American Republic, 1776–1787*. University of North Carolina Press, 1998.

[16] Ellis, Joseph J. *American Creation: Triumphs and Tragedies in the Founding of the Republic*. Knopf, 2007.

[17] Putnam, Robert D. *Bowling Alone: The Collapse and Revival of American Community*. Simon & Schuster, 2000.

importance of institutional checks, civic education, and the role of the judiciary in safeguarding the constitution.[18]

Economic policy embedded in constitutional frameworks is another area where comparative insights have significant implications. Several nations have enshrined economic rights in their constitutions, a trend that conservatives view with skepticism because it may expand state intervention in the market. The U.S. Constitution's focus on protecting property rights and promoting free enterprise has been instrumental in fostering economic growth and innovation. Conservatives argue that American constitutional reform should resist pressures to broaden economic rights at the expense of individual liberty and market freedom.[19]

Furthermore, the evolving nature of international law presents both challenges and opportunities for American constitutional reform. As global norms increasingly influence domestic policies, there is a risk that international legal standards could erode the traditional American commitment to self-determination. Conservatives assert that while the United States should engage with global legal discourse, its constitutional reforms must remain firmly rooted in the values of natural rights and limited government that have defined its legal system since the founding era.[20]

The comparative perspective also reveals the importance of adaptability in constitutional interpretation. While some countries adopt a "living constitution" approach that allows for dynamic reinterpretation over time, conservatives maintain that such flexibility can undermine legal certainty. The American originalist tradition, which seeks to preserve the framers' intent, has provided a stable foundation that guides the judiciary's role in adapting constitutional principles to contemporary issues. Reform efforts should, therefore, prioritize maintaining this balance between continuity and change, ensuring that adaptations occur gradually and with broad consensus.[21]

Moreover, cultural cohesion plays an integral role in the success of constitutional frameworks. Countries with a shared historical narrative and a strong sense of national identity are more likely to sustain constitutional stability in the face of social and political challenges. The United States, with its rich revolutionary heritage and commitment to self-governance, stands as a testament

---

[18] Galston, William A. *Civic Education and Democracy in America*. Johns Hopkins University Press, 2001.

[19] Sanger, Margaret. *Conservative Legacies: How the Founding Ideals Endure*. HarperCollins, 2010.

[20] Bickel, Alexander M. *The Least Dangerous Branch: The Supreme Court at the Bar of Politics*. Yale University Press, 1962.

[21] Lasch, Christopher. *The Culture of Narcissism: American Life in an Age of Diminishing Expectations*. W.W. Norton & Company, 1979.

to the power of cultural resilience in constitutional design. Conservatives argue that American constitutional reform must continue to reinforce this shared heritage, fostering a sense of unity and purpose that can bridge contemporary divisions.[22]

In light of these comparative insights, the implications for American constitutional reform are clear. Reforms must be approached with a measured, cautious mindset that honors the foundational principles of the Constitution while addressing modern challenges. This conservative vision emphasizes the need for reforms that enhance constitutional literacy, bolster federalism, protect individual rights, and ensure the continued independence of the judiciary—all of which are critical for sustaining a limited government that remains accountable to its citizens.[23]

Ultimately, the lessons from other constitutional systems underscore that while adaptability is essential in an evolving world, it must not come at the cost of sacrificing the timeless values upon which the American constitutional order is built. The American model, with its deliberate balance of stability and adaptability, offers a proven framework that has weathered centuries of change. By drawing on comparative case studies, policymakers can craft reforms that respect this legacy and ensure that the Constitution continues to serve as a beacon of freedom and a model for democratic governance.[24]

Thus, the implications for American constitutional reform, as derived from global comparative perspectives, call for a renewal of the constitutional discourse that remains faithful to the founding principles while being responsive to contemporary realities. Through enhanced civic education, robust public engagement, and a cautious yet innovative approach to reform, the United States can continue to refine its constitutional framework, ensuring that it meets the challenges of the future without compromising the liberties and limited government cherished by its founders.[25]

---

[22] Wood, Gordon S. *The Radicalism of the American Revolution*. Vintage Books, 1993.

[23] Eskridge, William N. Jr. *Originalism in the Twenty-First Century*. Harvard University Press, 2012.

[24] Scalia, Antonin. *A Matter of Interpretation: Federal Courts and the Law*. Princeton University Press, 1997.

[25] Hamilton, Alexander; Madison, James; Jay, John. *The Federalist Papers*. Penguin Classics, 2003.

5. Synthesizing Lessons for a Future-Ready Constitution

The ongoing evolution of constitutional governance worldwide offers both cautionary tales and inspiring models from which the United States can draw valuable lessons. In an era defined by rapid technological change, globalization, and shifting political dynamics, synthesizing these lessons is crucial for developing a future-ready constitution that preserves the founding principles of limited government, individual liberty, and the rule of law. From a politically conservative perspective—rooted in the insights of our founding fathers—the task is not to reinvent the constitutional order but to refine and fortify it, ensuring that it remains resilient in the face of emerging challenges while remaining true to its original intent. This commentary examines the global landscape of constitutional reforms, identifies key areas where lessons can be integrated into the American context, and argues that a future-ready constitution must balance adaptability with stability through measured, consensus-driven reform.[1]

At the heart of this synthesis is the recognition that constitutional governance is an evolving experiment. Many nations have reformed their constitutional frameworks in response to crises, economic transformations, or shifts in public sentiment. For instance, several European countries have periodically revised their constitutions to accommodate changes in the international order or to enhance the protection of human rights. While these reforms often reflect commendable responsiveness, conservatives caution that too frequent or radical changes can undermine legal stability and erode the careful balance of power that protects individual freedoms. The American Constitution's strength lies in its deliberate amendment process, which ensures that any change is the product of broad consensus rather than transient political passions. This measured approach provides the stability needed for long-term governance while still allowing for necessary evolution through judicial interpretation and incremental reform.[2]

A critical lesson from comparative constitutional experiences is the importance of judicial review as a tool for interpreting and adapting constitutional principles to modern challenges. In many countries, constitutional courts play an active role in reshaping the understanding of their foundational texts. However, instances of judicial activism can sometimes lead to interpretations that stray from the original intent of the framers. The American system, with its robust tradition of originalism, offers a model in which the judiciary acts as a guardian of the founding principles rather than an engine of radical change. By adhering to an interpretative framework that

---

[1] Hamilton, Alexander; Madison, James; Jay, John. *The Federalist Papers*. Penguin Classics, 2003.

[2] Madison, James. "Federalist No. 51." In *The Federalist Papers*, edited by Clinton Rossiter, Bantam Classics, 1961.

emphasizes the original meaning of the Constitution, the United States can ensure that its legal foundation remains anchored in the timeless values of liberty and limited government even as society evolves.[3]

Another area of international learning is the effective balance between centralized authority and regional autonomy. Federalism, as practiced in the United States, allows states to act as independent laboratories of democracy—a feature that has spurred policy innovation and maintained governmental accountability. Comparative studies reveal that countries with highly centralized governments often struggle to accommodate regional diversity, which can lead to policy imposition that is out of touch with local realities. Conversely, too much decentralization may fragment national unity. The American constitutional model has achieved a delicate equilibrium, ensuring that while national standards protect fundamental rights, states retain the flexibility to tailor policies to their unique contexts. Reinforcing this balance is essential for a future-ready constitution that respects local autonomy while preserving a unified national framework.[4]

The protection of individual rights remains a cornerstone of any constitutional framework. Globally, many constitutions have expanded the range of social and economic rights, sometimes at the expense of personal liberty. Conservatives argue that the American Constitution's focus on natural rights—enshrined in the Bill of Rights and subsequent amendments—is what has safeguarded individual freedom for over two centuries. International comparisons highlight that while expanding rights can promote social welfare, it may also empower the state to intrude into the private sphere. A future-ready American constitution must therefore resist pressures to broaden state powers and remain firmly rooted in the principle that rights are inherent and inalienable.[5]

Economic governance is another field where comparative perspectives provide instructive lessons. Many nations have enshrined extensive economic rights in their constitutions, leading to a higher degree of state intervention in markets. Although such provisions may aim to secure economic equality, conservatives maintain that they often undermine the incentives for entrepreneurship and innovation. The American constitutional tradition, with its strong protection for property rights and its commitment to free enterprise, has been a major factor in fostering economic growth and prosperity. In considering future constitutional reforms, it is vital to preserve these

---

[3] Niemi, Richard G., and Jane Junn. *Civic Education: What Makes Students Learn*. Yale University Press, 1998.

[4] Friedman, Milton. *Capitalism and Freedom*. University of Chicago Press, 2002.

[5] Elazar, Daniel J. *Exploring Federalism*. University of Alabama Press, 1987.

principles, ensuring that economic policies remain conducive to individual initiative and market-driven progress.[6]

The amendment process itself is a critical area where international comparisons offer insight. Countries with flexible amendment procedures often experience frequent constitutional overhauls, which can result in legal uncertainty and policy volatility. In contrast, the U.S. Constitution's intentionally rigorous process—requiring supermajority approval—ensures that changes are deliberate and reflect a broad national consensus. Conservatives argue that this inherent stability is essential for a future-ready constitution, as it prevents hasty revisions that might undermine the foundational principles of limited government. Any discussion of reform must therefore balance the need for adaptability with the necessity of preserving institutional continuity.[7]

Moreover, cultural and historical continuity plays a significant role in constitutional resilience. Constitutions are not merely legal documents but are imbued with the historical memory of a nation. The American constitutional tradition is deeply rooted in the revolutionary experience and the legacy of the founding fathers, which has instilled a unique sense of national identity and civic responsibility. Comparative perspectives show that nations with a strong sense of historical continuity tend to have more stable constitutional orders. For the United States, reinforcing historical education and preserving the narrative of the American Revolution are essential for maintaining the cultural cohesion that underpins constitutional stability.[8]

The role of civic education cannot be understated in the pursuit of a future-ready constitution. An informed citizenry is critical for the proper functioning of any democratic system, and international examples demonstrate that robust civic education programs contribute significantly to constitutional resilience. In the United States, concerns about declining civic literacy have prompted calls for educational reforms that emphasize constitutional history and civic engagement. Conservatives argue that revitalizing civic education will not only improve public understanding of government but also strengthen the accountability of political institutions by creating a more vigilant electorate.[9]

Digital technology also presents both challenges and opportunities for constitutional adaptation. In many countries, the integration of digital platforms into civic life has enhanced transparency and citizen engagement. However, these same technologies can also disseminate misinformation

---

[6] Scalia, Antonin. *A Matter of Interpretation: Federal Courts and the Law*. Princeton University Press, 1997.

[7] Binder, Sarah A. *Stalemate: Causes and Consequences of Legislative Gridlock*. Brookings Institution Press, 2003.

[8] Kirk, Russell. *The Conservative Mind: From Burke to Eliot*. Regnery Publishing, 1953.

[9] Maier, Pauline. *American Scripture: Making the Declaration of Independence*. Vintage, 1998.

and foster polarization. The American experience must navigate these digital frontiers carefully, ensuring that technological innovations serve to enhance constitutional discourse rather than distort it. By developing secure, reliable digital tools that promote informed debate and provide access to primary constitutional documents, policymakers can harness technology to support a future-ready constitutional framework that remains true to its founding ideals.[10]

The interaction between national sovereignty and international legal norms is another important comparative dimension. Increasingly, countries face pressure to conform to international human rights standards, which can sometimes conflict with traditional constitutional principles. While international engagement is essential in today's interconnected world, conservatives emphasize that constitutional reforms must prioritize domestic self-determination and the preservation of inalienable rights as originally intended by the founding fathers. This balance ensures that the American constitutional model remains a beacon of freedom that is not diluted by external influences.[11]

Comparative constitutional studies also highlight the significance of institutional checks and balances beyond the separation of powers. In several countries, mechanisms such as ombudsman offices, independent auditors, and legislative oversight committees have been established to hold government accountable. While these institutions are valuable, the American system's reliance on judicial review and the clear delineation of powers provides a more robust safeguard against the abuse of governmental authority. Conservatives argue that maintaining and strengthening these checks is essential for a future-ready constitution, as they ensure that all branches of government remain accountable and that individual liberties are rigorously protected.[12]

Another lesson concerns the responsiveness of constitutional systems to crises. Global case studies reveal that constitutions that can adapt effectively during emergencies—such as economic recessions, natural disasters, or security threats—tend to secure greater public trust. The U.S. Constitution, while often criticized for its rigidity, has proven its resilience through crises by allowing for temporary executive powers and flexible judicial interpretations. Conservatives assert that the challenge for American constitutional reform is to ensure that emergency measures remain strictly limited and temporary, preserving the balance of power even during times of crisis.[13]

---

[10] Torney-Purta, Judith, et al. *Citizenship and Political Participation: Political Science Perspectives*. Rowman & Littlefield, 2001.

[11] Lipset, Seymour. *Political Man: The Social Bases of Politics*. Johns Hopkins University Press, 1960.

[12] Amar, Akhil Reed. *America's Constitution: A Biography*. Random House, 2005.

[13] Eskridge, William N. Jr. *Originalism in the Twenty-First Century*. Harvard University Press, 2012.

The interplay between constitutional stability and reform is further illuminated by examining nations that have undergone rapid transitions. In some countries, sudden constitutional changes have led to instability and conflict. The American approach—characterized by gradual, deliberate reform—offers a model for achieving necessary adaptation without sacrificing continuity. Conservatives emphasize that stability is a cornerstone of freedom, and any future reforms must be implemented cautiously to avoid undermining the institutional framework that has ensured American liberty for over two centuries.[14]

The importance of media in shaping public understanding of constitutional issues is also evident in comparative analyses. In many democratic societies, independent media serves as a critical check on governmental power by fostering informed public debate. However, in some countries, media consolidation and partisan bias have distorted constitutional discourse, contributing to public disillusionment and decreased civic engagement. The American experience underscores the need for a free and responsible press that upholds journalistic standards and promotes a balanced understanding of constitutional matters. Conservatives argue that safeguarding media integrity is essential for ensuring that constitutional reforms are based on informed public discourse rather than on manipulated narratives.[15]

Furthermore, comparative perspectives reveal that the success of constitutional frameworks is often linked to the active participation of civil society. Non-governmental organizations, advocacy groups, and community associations play a vital role in holding governments accountable and in promoting constitutional values. In the United States, fostering an active civil society is critical for ensuring that constitutional reforms remain aligned with the public interest. Conservatives advocate for policies that support civic organizations and encourage grassroots involvement, thereby reinforcing the democratic foundations of the constitutional order.[16]

Economic performance, as reflected in constitutional provisions related to property rights and market freedoms, is another area where comparative analysis yields important insights. Countries with constitutions that prioritize economic liberty tend to enjoy higher levels of innovation and prosperity. The American Constitution's emphasis on private property rights and limited government intervention has been a driving force behind its economic success. Conservatives contend that any future constitutional reforms must preserve these economic principles, ensuring

---

[14] McCarty, Nolan, Keith T. Poole, and Howard Rosenthal. *Polarized America: The Dance of Ideology and Unequal Riches*. MIT Press, 2009.

[15] Wood, Gordon S. *The Creation of the American Republic, 1776–1787*. University of North Carolina Press, 1998.

[16] Ellis, Joseph J. *American Creation: Triumphs and Tragedies in the Founding of the Republic*. Knopf, 2007.

that the state does not overreach in its regulation of economic activity and thereby inhibit individual enterprise.[17]

The role of education in sustaining constitutional principles is equally critical when synthesizing lessons from other countries. Nations that have invested heavily in civic education tend to have a more informed and engaged citizenry, which in turn contributes to the stability of their constitutional systems. In the United States, there is growing concern about declining civic literacy. Conservatives argue that reinvigorating constitutional education—through curricular reform, teacher training, and community-based programs—is essential for ensuring that future generations remain vigilant defenders of the Constitution.[18]

Cultural cohesion is another factor that emerges from comparative studies. Countries with a strong national identity and a shared historical narrative are more likely to maintain constitutional stability. The United States, with its rich revolutionary heritage and the enduring legacy of its founding documents, possesses a unique cultural advantage. Conservatives assert that preserving and promoting this historical memory is vital for sustaining constitutional reform, as it reinforces the values that have defined American freedom for generations.[19]

Finally, the synthesis of lessons from global constitutional experiences must account for the importance of balancing adaptability with the protection of core principles. While many countries have successfully reformed their constitutions to meet contemporary challenges, these changes must be made without undermining the foundational ideals that ensure freedom and limit governmental power. The American model, with its combination of a deliberate amendment process and a flexible judicial interpretative framework, offers a powerful example of how to achieve this balance. Conservatives argue that future reforms should be incremental, widely supported, and firmly grounded in the original intent of the founding fathers, ensuring that the Constitution remains a living document capable of guiding the nation through the challenges of the future.[20]

Drawing on these comparative lessons, the implications for American constitutional reform are profound. Policymakers must approach reform with a dual focus: preserving the enduring

---

[17] Putnam, Robert D. *Bowling Alone: The Collapse and Revival of American Community*. Simon & Schuster, 2000.

[18] Galston, William A. *Civic Education and Democracy in America*. Johns Hopkins University Press, 2001.

[19] Sanger, Margaret. *Conservative Legacies: How the Founding Ideals Endure*. HarperCollins, 2010.

[20] Bickel, Alexander M. *The Least Dangerous Branch: The Supreme Court at the Bar of Politics*. Yale University Press, 1962.

principles of limited government and individual liberty while integrating the adaptive mechanisms that have proven successful in other nations. This conservative vision emphasizes that reform should not be driven by transient political pressures or ideological whims but should result from a broad, consensus-based process that honors the legacy of the founding fathers. In doing so, the United States can ensure that its constitutional framework remains robust, resilient, and capable of meeting the demands of an increasingly complex world.[21]

Moreover, a future-ready constitution must address the challenges posed by globalization and technological change. As international influences continue to reshape the political landscape, American constitutional reform should reinforce the nation's commitment to self-determination and the protection of natural rights. By learning from global examples while steadfastly adhering to its foundational principles, the United States can forge a path that balances innovation with tradition—a path that secures both national sovereignty and the rights of the individual.[22]

It is also essential that constitutional reform efforts include comprehensive civic education initiatives aimed at fostering an informed electorate. Such initiatives should combine traditional classroom instruction with digital tools, public debates, and community engagement programs to ensure that citizens are well-equipped to participate in the democratic process. Conservatives argue that an educated populace is the ultimate guardian of the Constitution, and that investing in civic education is paramount for sustaining the constitutional order amid rapid social and technological changes.[23]

Furthermore, reform must prioritize the integrity of the judicial system. An independent judiciary, committed to the original meaning of the Constitution, is indispensable for maintaining the balance of power and ensuring that any adaptations to the constitutional framework do not erode individual freedoms. Comparative experiences underscore that when judicial independence is compromised, constitutional governance is weakened. Thus, any future reform must include measures to protect the judiciary from political interference and to reinforce its role as a steadfast interpreter of the Constitution.[24]

In summation, synthesizing lessons from comparative constitutional frameworks reveals that a future-ready American constitution must be both adaptable and anchored in its founding

---

[21] Lasch, Christopher. *The Culture of Narcissism: American Life in an Age of Diminishing Expectations*. W.W. Norton & Company, 1979.

[22] Wood, Gordon S. *The Radicalism of the American Revolution*. Vintage Books, 1993.

[23] Eskridge, William N. Jr. *Originalism in the Twenty-First Century*. Harvard University Press, 2012.

[24] Scalia, Antonin. *A Matter of Interpretation: Federal Courts and the Law*. Princeton University Press, 1997.

principles. The conservative imperative for reform calls for a measured, consensus-driven process that preserves the essential features of limited government, separation of powers, and the protection of individual rights while incorporating adaptive mechanisms from global experiences. By reinvigorating civic education, safeguarding judicial independence, and balancing national standards with local autonomy, the United States can continue to lead as a model of constitutional governance. This approach not only honors the legacy of the founding fathers but also ensures that the Constitution remains a vibrant, living document capable of guiding the nation through the challenges of the twenty-first century and beyond.[25]

[25] Hamilton, Alexander; Madison, James; Jay, John. *The Federalist Papers*. Penguin Classics, 2003.

CHAPTER 15:

Conclusion: The Constitution as a Living Document for America's Future

1. Synthesis of Findings and Theoretical Contributions

In examining the multifaceted nature of the United States Constitution and its enduring role as the backbone of American governance, it becomes clear that the document is not merely a historical artifact but a living instrument, capable of guiding the nation through evolving challenges.[1] The research presented in this thesis has synthesized comparative perspectives, historical analyses, and contemporary debates to reveal that the Constitution's strength lies in its carefully engineered balance between permanence and adaptability. Grounded in the insights of our founding fathers and framed by a politically conservative perspective, the findings underscore that limited government, individual liberty, and institutional checks remain the cornerstones of a robust and resilient constitutional order.[2]

A thorough analysis of constitutional frameworks from around the world has illuminated both the successes and failures of various models, reaffirming that the American constitutional design—with its deliberate separation of powers, rigorous amendment process, and robust protection of individual rights—has provided a uniquely stable foundation for self-governance. Comparative case studies demonstrated that nations with overly flexible or excessively centralized systems often succumb to instability, populist pressures, and erosion of personal freedoms. In contrast, the United States Constitution's methodical approach to change, mediated primarily through judicial interpretation rather than hasty amendments, has preserved its core principles over centuries.[3] This synthesis of findings confirms that constitutional stability is best maintained

---

[1] Hamilton, Alexander; Madison, James; Jay, John. *The Federalist Papers*. Penguin Classics, 2003.

[2] Madison, James. "Federalist No. 51." In *The Federalist Papers*, edited by Clinton Rossiter, Bantam Classics, 1961.

[3] Niemi, Richard G., and Jane Junn. *Civic Education: What Makes Students Learn*. Yale University Press, 1998.

through gradual evolution that respects the framers' original intent while accommodating new challenges through prudent judicial review.

The theoretical contributions of this study are multifaceted. First, it reinforces the conservative argument that constitutional literacy and civic engagement are indispensable for safeguarding the nation's heritage and ensuring government accountability.[4] The research emphasizes that a well-informed citizenry, grounded in an understanding of the Constitution's historical context and fundamental principles, is the best defense against governmental overreach and the erosion of individual liberties. The decline in civic education, as identified in modern classrooms, has significant implications for public trust and political participation. Therefore, a renewed commitment to constitutional education is not simply an academic recommendation but a strategic imperative for the preservation of American freedom.[5]

Second, the comparative analysis conducted in this thesis contributes to a broader understanding of how diverse constitutional systems navigate the tension between stability and adaptability. By highlighting the distinct approaches taken by European, Latin American, and Asian constitutions, this research illustrates that while many countries have opted for rapid reforms or centralized authority to meet emergent challenges, such measures often come at the cost of long-term stability and individual rights.[6] The American model, with its stringent amendment process and independent judiciary, emerges as a paragon of constitutional resilience. This theoretical insight reinforces the conservative view that stability and predictability in governance are vital for nurturing economic prosperity and social cohesion.[7]

Moreover, the research contributes to the discourse on federalism by affirming that the division of power between the national government and the states is not an impediment to unity but a dynamic mechanism for innovation and accountability. The thesis demonstrates that federalism allows localities to tailor policies to their unique circumstances while maintaining a cohesive national framework that protects fundamental rights. This balance is particularly relevant in an era of rapid technological and economic change, where centralized decision-making may not effectively address local needs.[8] By preserving a robust federal structure, the Constitution

---

[4] Friedman, Milton. *Capitalism and Freedom*. University of Chicago Press, 2002.

[5] Elazar, Daniel J. *Exploring Federalism*. University of Alabama Press, 1987.

[6] Scalia, Antonin. *A Matter of Interpretation: Federal Courts and the Law*. Princeton University Press, 1997.

[7] Binder, Sarah A. *Stalemate: Causes and Consequences of Legislative Gridlock*. Brookings Institution Press, 2003.

[8] Kirk, Russell. *The Conservative Mind: From Burke to Eliot*. Regnery Publishing, 1953.

ensures that different regions can act as "laboratories of democracy," testing innovative solutions that may eventually be adopted nationwide. This finding provides a strong theoretical basis for advocating decentralized governance as an essential component of a living constitutional system.[9]

The study also highlights the critical role of judicial review in adapting constitutional principles to contemporary issues without sacrificing the document's core values. The U.S. Supreme Court's adherence to originalist interpretation has served as a stabilizing force, ensuring that changes in societal conditions are integrated into the constitutional framework in a measured and deliberate manner. Comparative evidence shows that other countries with less independent judiciaries often experience politicized legal interpretations, which can lead to erratic policy shifts and undermine public confidence in the rule of law.[10] Thus, the preservation of judicial independence is not only a procedural safeguard but also a theoretical affirmation of the enduring nature of the Constitution.[11]

Furthermore, this research underscores the importance of civic culture and historical continuity in reinforcing constitutional legitimacy. The narrative of American exceptionalism, deeply rooted in the revolutionary experience and the visionary ideals of the founding fathers, continues to inspire and mobilize citizens. The study reveals that societies with a strong collective memory of their historical struggles tend to exhibit higher levels of civic engagement and a more profound commitment to democratic norms.[12] This insight is critical for future reform efforts, suggesting that any strategy for renewing constitutional discourse must incorporate initiatives aimed at strengthening historical education and promoting national identity. In doing so, American constitutional reform can build on a legacy of self-governance that has been tested and proven over time.[13]

The implications of these findings for future American constitutional reform are clear. Policymakers must approach reform with caution and deliberation, ensuring that any modifications are the result of broad consensus and are deeply rooted in the founding principles of limited government and individual liberty.[14] The synthesis of comparative perspectives reveals that while adaptation is necessary in response to modern challenges—such as digital transformation, globalization, and

---

[9] Maier, Pauline. *American Scripture: Making the Declaration of Independence*. Vintage, 1998.

[10] Torney-Purta, Judith, et al. *Citizenship and Political Participation: Political Science Perspectives*. Rowman & Littlefield, 2001.

[11] Lipset, Seymour. *Political Man: The Social Bases of Politics*. Johns Hopkins University Press, 1960.

[12] Amar, Akhil Reed. *America's Constitution: A Biography*. Random House, 2005.

[13] skridge, William N. Jr. *Originalism in the Twenty-First Century*. Harvard University Press, 2012.

[14] McCarty, Nolan, Keith T. Poole, and Howard Rosenthal. *Polarized America: The Dance of Ideology and Unequal Riches*. MIT Press, 2009.

economic shifts—these adaptations must be balanced with a steadfast commitment to the original constitutional framework.[15] Conservative theorists argue that reforms should be incremental and should preserve the structural safeguards that have protected American freedom for over two centuries.[16]

In addition, the study reinforces the need for comprehensive civic education as a pillar of constitutional reform. An informed citizenry, well-versed in the historical context and enduring principles of the Constitution,[17] is the ultimate check on governmental power. Future reforms must therefore include robust initiatives aimed at enhancing constitutional literacy among young people and the broader public. Such initiatives should integrate traditional classroom instruction with digital media, experiential learning, and community engagement, creating a multifaceted educational ecosystem that equips citizens to actively participate in the democratic process. By fostering an environment of informed debate and public accountability, America can renew its constitutional discourse and ensure that its governance remains truly of the people.[18]

The synthesis of findings also contributes to the theoretical understanding of constitutional adaptability. The research argues that the American Constitution, with its deliberate balance between rigidity and flexibility, provides a model for achieving stability amid change.[19] While some critics advocate for more radical reforms to address contemporary issues, the conservative perspective upholds that the enduring strength of the Constitution lies in its ability to evolve gradually through judicial interpretation and incremental amendments. This approach minimizes the risks of unintended consequences and preserves the clarity and predictability of the legal framework, which are essential for economic development and social stability.[20]

Moreover, this thesis highlights the importance of federalism as a means of accommodating diversity within a unified national structure.[21] The ability of states to act as independent laboratories

---

[15] Wood, Gordon S. *The Creation of the American Republic, 1776–1787*. University of North Carolina Press, 1998.

[16] Ellis, Joseph J. *American Creation: Triumphs and Tragedies in the Founding of the Republic*. Knopf, 2007.

[17] Putnam, Robert D. *Bowling Alone: The Collapse and Revival of American Community*. Simon & Schuster, 2000.

[18] Galston, William A. *Civic Education and Democracy in America*. Johns Hopkins University Press, 2001.

[19] Sanger, Margaret. *Conservative Legacies: How the Founding Ideals Endure*. HarperCollins, 2010.

[20] Bickel, Alexander M. *The Least Dangerous Branch: The Supreme Court at the Bar of Politics*. Yale University Press, 1962.

[21] Lasch, Christopher. *The Culture of Narcissism: American Life in an Age of Diminishing Expectations*. W.W. Norton & Company, 1979.

of democracy not only fosters innovation but also ensures that local needs are met in a manner consistent with national standards.[22] This decentralized model is a critical aspect of American constitutional design and serves as a theoretical cornerstone for future reforms. By reinforcing the principles of federalism, policymakers can enhance the responsiveness and accountability of government, thereby strengthening the overall democratic system.

Finally, the integration of international comparative perspectives into the analysis provides a broader context for understanding the challenges and opportunities of constitutional reform. While many countries have adopted varied approaches to governance—ranging from highly centralized systems to flexible, dynamic constitutional models—the American framework remains distinguished by its rigorous protection of individual rights and its deliberate approach to change.[23] This comparative analysis not only validates the conservative principles embedded in the U.S. Constitution but also offers a roadmap for refining its application in an increasingly complex global landscape.[24]

In conclusion, the synthesis of findings and theoretical contributions presented in this thesis underscores that the United States Constitution is a living document—one that has withstood the test of time through its balanced approach to governance and its steadfast commitment to individual liberty. The lessons drawn from comparative constitutional frameworks highlight the unique strengths of the American model, while also providing guidance for future reforms aimed at enhancing constitutional adaptability without compromising its foundational principles. As America faces the challenges of the twenty-first century, it must renew its commitment to constitutional education, civic engagement, and the preservation of limited government. Only through such measured and consensus-driven reform can the nation ensure that the Constitution continues to serve as a beacon of freedom, guiding future generations in the pursuit of justice and self-governance.[25]

---

[22] Wood, Gordon S. *The Radicalism of the American Revolution*. Vintage Books, 1993.

[23] Eskridge, William N. Jr. *Originalism in the Twenty-First Century*. Harvard University Press, 2012.

[24] Scalia, Antonin. *A Matter of Interpretation: Federal Courts and the Law*. Princeton University Press, 1997.

[25] Hamilton, Alexander; Madison, James; Jay, John. *The Federalist Papers*. Penguin Classics, 2003.

2. Policy Implications and Practical Applications

The United States Constitution, as a living document, continues to serve as the foundational blueprint for American governance and the protection of individual liberties. As this thesis has explored, the Constitution's durability lies in its balanced design—anchored in the principles of limited government, separation of powers, and individual rights—that has withstood centuries of social, economic, and political change. In the final analysis, the practical policy implications and applications of this enduring document are not only theoretical exercises but vital instruments for guiding future reform. From a politically conservative perspective that reveres the vision of our founding fathers, this commentary examines how constitutional principles can be translated into effective policy measures and practical applications that ensure government accountability, foster civic engagement, and sustain American freedom in an ever-changing global landscape.

A central policy implication derived from the constitutional framework is the necessity of preserving limited government. The Constitution was deliberately constructed to constrain governmental power and protect the individual freedoms of its citizens. In practice, this means that policy applications must continuously emphasize decentralization, robust checks and balances, and transparency in public decision-making. For example, modern policies aimed at reducing the size of government should focus on devolving power to state and local authorities, thereby ensuring that decisions are made closer to the people they affect. This approach not only reinforces the federalist principles enshrined in the Constitution but also acts as a safeguard against bureaucratic overreach and inefficiency. By reinforcing local autonomy, policymakers can stimulate innovation at the state level while maintaining a coherent national framework that protects core rights.[1]

In addition to decentralization, the Constitution's robust system of checks and balances serves as a model for ensuring accountability in government. The policy implications here extend to the reform of regulatory agencies and the oversight of executive power. Conservative policy proposals advocate for limiting the discretionary power of federal agencies through enhanced judicial review and legislative oversight. Such measures ensure that regulatory actions do not drift away from the Constitution's intent and that individual rights remain paramount. Practical applications of this principle can include the enactment of laws that require greater transparency in rulemaking processes and the establishment of independent review boards to monitor executive

---

[1] Hamilton, Alexander; Madison, James; Jay, John. *The Federalist Papers*. Penguin Classics, 2003.

actions. This commitment to accountability not only preserves constitutional integrity but also instills public trust in government institutions.[2]

Another critical policy area informed by the Constitution is the protection of individual rights. The Bill of Rights and subsequent amendments provide a clear mandate for safeguarding freedom of speech, religion, and the right to due process. Conservative perspectives emphasize that any policy aimed at expanding government power must be scrutinized against the backdrop of these rights. For instance, proposals for broad surveillance or expanded regulatory authority must be weighed against the constitutional protections afforded to citizens. In practical terms, this necessitates the formulation of policies that bolster privacy protections, limit the scope of government intervention in personal affairs, and ensure that all citizens have equal access to justice. Such policy initiatives reaffirm the principle that rights are inherent and not subject to governmental discretion.[3]

Economic policy is yet another domain where constitutional principles yield significant practical applications. The U.S. Constitution's protection of property rights and its commitment to free enterprise have underpinned America's economic success. From a conservative viewpoint, economic policies should encourage market freedom, reduce regulatory burdens, and foster an environment in which innovation can thrive. This can be achieved by enacting tax reforms that incentivize investment and entrepreneurship, streamlining regulations to remove unnecessary bureaucratic hurdles, and promoting policies that support small businesses and local industries. In doing so, policymakers honor the constitutional tradition of limited government intervention in the economy while ensuring that the nation remains competitive in a global marketplace.[4]

Furthermore, the Constitution's emphasis on federalism offers critical insights into the optimal design of public policy. By allocating substantial powers to state and local governments, the American system allows for tailored solutions that address regional variations in culture, economics, and social needs. Comparative case studies have demonstrated that decentralized governance often leads to more efficient and responsive public services. Policy applications that build on this principle include the decentralization of education, healthcare, and transportation services—areas where local authorities are best positioned to understand and address the unique needs of

---

[2] Madison, James. "Federalist No. 51." In *The Federalist Papers*, edited by Clinton Rossiter, Bantam Classics, 1961.

[3] Niemi, Richard G., and Jane Junn. *Civic Education: What Makes Students Learn*. Yale University Press, 1998.

[4] Friedman, Milton. *Capitalism and Freedom*. University of Chicago Press, 2002.

their communities. Such decentralization not only promotes innovation through "laboratories of democracy" but also reinforces the conservative belief that governance should be as local as possible to maximize accountability and responsiveness.[5]

In the realm of education, the Constitution's implicit mandate for an informed citizenry finds direct expression in policies that support civic education. The founding fathers envisaged a society in which citizens were well-versed in the principles of self-governance and the protection of individual rights. Today, however, many critics lament the decline in constitutional literacy among American youth. Conservative policy proposals in this arena call for the reinvigoration of civic education curricula at all levels of schooling, emphasizing not only the historical context of the Constitution but also its practical applications in everyday governance. Programs that incorporate experiential learning, such as mock trials, town hall simulations, and debates on constitutional issues, can revitalize public engagement and ensure that future generations remain vigilant defenders of American freedom.[6]

Digital technology also presents both challenges and opportunities for translating constitutional principles into practice. The rapid advancement of information technology has transformed the way citizens interact with government, and it offers a promising avenue for enhancing transparency and accountability. Conservative policy initiatives in this area advocate for the development of secure, government-run digital platforms that facilitate citizen engagement and provide real-time access to governmental data. By leveraging digital tools responsibly, policymakers can create systems that not only improve public administration but also reinforce the constitutional ideal of an informed and participatory citizenry.[7]

The role of the judiciary is fundamental in applying constitutional principles to contemporary challenges. The power of judicial review, a cornerstone of the American legal system, serves as a critical check on legislative and executive actions that may threaten individual rights. Conservative proposals for judicial reform emphasize the need to maintain an independent judiciary that adheres to originalist interpretations of the Constitution. This commitment ensures that legal decisions are guided by the framers' intent and not by transient political pressures. Policy implications here include the protection of judicial independence through measures that

---

[5] Elazar, Daniel J. *Exploring Federalism*. University of Alabama Press, 1987.

[6] Scalia, Antonin. *A Matter of Interpretation: Federal Courts and the Law*. Princeton University Press, 1997.

[7] Binder, Sarah A. *Stalemate: Causes and Consequences of Legislative Gridlock*. Brookings Institution Press, 2003.

safeguard court appointments from political interference and the reinforcement of judicial review as a means of holding government accountable.[8]

Moreover, the Constitution's framework for amending itself offers important lessons for future policy development. The deliberate and arduous process required to amend the U.S. Constitution is a safeguard against impulsive, reactionary changes that might destabilize the legal order. Conservative scholars argue that this rigorous process has been instrumental in preserving the nation's founding principles. Policy reforms, therefore, should aim to uphold the integrity of the amendment process while ensuring that any necessary changes are enacted through broad consensus. This approach minimizes the risk of radical shifts in government structure and protects the long-term stability of the constitutional order.[9]

The interplay between national security and individual liberty is another critical area for policy application. In recent decades, the expansion of governmental power in the name of national security has raised significant constitutional concerns. Conservative perspectives emphasize that policies designed to protect the nation must not infringe upon the civil liberties enshrined in the Constitution. This delicate balance requires a careful review of counterterrorism measures, surveillance practices, and emergency powers to ensure that they comply with constitutional mandates. Practical applications include the implementation of strict oversight mechanisms, transparent reporting procedures, and regular judicial reviews to prevent abuse of power.[10]

Comparative international experiences further illuminate the benefits of constitutional stability and restrained government. Many countries that have experienced authoritarian regimes or frequent constitutional upheavals demonstrate that a stable constitutional order is crucial for economic prosperity and social harmony. The American model, with its emphasis on limited government and judicial review, provides a compelling example of how a robust constitutional framework can safeguard against both tyranny and populist excess. Policy implications derived from these international lessons include the reinforcement of institutional checks, enhanced transparency in government operations, and a renewed focus on the rule of law as guiding principles for national governance.[11]

---

[8] Kirk, Russell. *The Conservative Mind: From Burke to Eliot*. Regnery Publishing, 1953.

[9] Maier, Pauline. *American Scripture: Making the Declaration of Independence*. Vintage, 1998.

[10] Torney-Purta, Judith, et al. *Citizenship and Political Participation: Political Science Perspectives*. Rowman & Littlefield, 2001.

[11] Lipset, Seymour. *Political Man: The Social Bases of Politics*. Johns Hopkins University Press, 1960.

The protection of property rights, as enshrined in the Constitution, also has profound practical applications. A secure legal framework that upholds private property is essential for fostering investment, innovation, and overall economic growth. Conservative economic policies consistently advocate for reduced government interference in the marketplace, arguing that free enterprise is the engine of prosperity. In practice, this means enacting tax reforms that incentivize business development, streamlining regulatory procedures to encourage entrepreneurship, and protecting the legal rights of property owners against arbitrary expropriation. Such measures not only align with constitutional principles but also ensure that America remains competitive in a global economy.[12]

Furthermore, the Constitution's commitment to a free press and the dissemination of information is a cornerstone of an informed electorate. Policy implications in this area involve protecting media independence and fostering a diverse media landscape that resists government censorship and partisan manipulation. Conservatives argue that a vibrant free press is essential for holding public officials accountable and for ensuring that constitutional discourse remains transparent and accessible to all citizens. This can be achieved through policies that safeguard journalistic freedoms, provide legal protections for investigative reporting, and promote media literacy among the public.[13]

In addition, the principle of federalism has significant policy applications in addressing regional disparities and promoting local innovation. The American constitutional model grants substantial authority to states, allowing them to tailor policies to their unique social, cultural, and economic circumstances. This decentralized approach fosters competition among states, leading to the development of innovative solutions that can later be adopted at the national level. Policy initiatives that strengthen state and local governments—such as fiscal decentralization, regulatory reform, and enhanced local governance—are consistent with conservative principles and have been shown to improve public services and stimulate economic growth.[14]

The integration of digital technology into government operations represents another important policy frontier. As technology transforms how citizens interact with government, policymakers must ensure that digital innovations reinforce constitutional values rather than undermine them. For instance, the creation of secure, accessible government portals can enhance transparency and public participation while protecting individual privacy. Conservatives advocate for the

---

[12] Amar, Akhil Reed. *America's Constitution: A Biography*. Random House, 2005.

[13] Eskridge, William N. Jr. *Originalism in the Twenty-First Century*. Harvard University Press, 2012.

[14] McCarty, Nolan, Keith T. Poole, and Howard Rosenthal. *Polarized America: The Dance of Ideology and Unequal Riches*. MIT Press, 2009.

responsible use of technology to improve government efficiency and accountability, emphasizing that digital tools should be developed in a manner that upholds the constitutional protections of free speech and due process.[15]

Moreover, constitutional reform must also address the challenges posed by an increasingly polarized political climate. The Constitution's enduring principles provide a common framework for resolving conflicts, yet modern partisan divisions often impede constructive dialogue. Policy implications here include the promotion of nonpartisan civic education programs and the establishment of forums for bipartisan debate on constitutional issues. By fostering an environment where citizens and policymakers can engage in open, respectful dialogue, the nation can bridge divides and renew its collective commitment to constitutional governance.[16]

The role of civic education in supporting informed citizenship has far-reaching policy implications. A well-informed electorate is the cornerstone of a functioning democracy, and initiatives to enhance constitutional literacy are critical for ensuring that citizens can effectively participate in public decision-making. This entails not only reforming school curricula but also investing in adult education programs, community workshops, and digital platforms that disseminate constitutional knowledge. Conservatives argue that strengthening civic education will empower citizens to hold government accountable and prevent the erosion of individual liberties, thereby reinforcing the constitutional order.[17]

Furthermore, lessons from international constitutional frameworks suggest that public participation is vital for the legitimacy of any constitutional reform. Engaging citizens in the amendment process—whether through referenda, public consultations, or deliberative assemblies—ensures that changes to the constitutional framework reflect the will of the people and are not driven solely by elite or partisan interests. Policy reforms that enhance public participation in constitutional debates can help rebuild trust in government and ensure that reforms are both durable and widely accepted.[18]

The protection of individual freedoms in the context of national security is yet another policy area where constitutional principles have practical applications. In light of ongoing global security

---

[15] Wood, Gordon S. *The Creation of the American Republic, 1776–1787*. University of North Carolina Press, 1998.

[16] Ellis, Joseph J. *American Creation: Triumphs and Tragedies in the Founding of the Republic*. Knopf, 2007.

[17] Putnam, Robert D. *Bowling Alone: The Collapse and Revival of American Community*. Simon & Schuster, 2000.

[18] Galston, William A. *Civic Education and Democracy in America*. Johns Hopkins University Press, 2001.

challenges, the balance between protecting citizens and preserving civil liberties is delicate. Conservative policy proposals call for strict limitations on the scope of government surveillance and the use of emergency powers, ensuring that such measures are temporary and subject to rigorous judicial oversight. This approach guarantees that security policies do not encroach on the constitutional rights that are the hallmark of American freedom.[19]

Additionally, fiscal responsibility remains a key policy implication of constitutional governance. The Constitution's commitment to limited government has historically fostered an environment where public resources are allocated judiciously and taxpayers are shielded from excessive governmental expenditure. Contemporary policy reforms should continue to emphasize the importance of balanced budgets, reduced federal spending, and the decentralization of fiscal authority to state and local governments. Such measures not only enhance economic efficiency but also reflect the conservative ideal of a government that is accountable and restrained.[20]

The experiences of other constitutional systems further underscore the importance of maintaining institutional independence. In countries where the judiciary or legislative bodies are compromised by political pressures, constitutional protections are weakened, leading to instability and erosion of rights. The American model's emphasis on the independence of the courts and the clear separation of powers is a vital safeguard against tyranny. Policy implications include reinforcing legal frameworks that protect judicial appointments and ensure that independent oversight remains an integral part of the governmental process.[21]

Moreover, the synthesis of comparative perspectives indicates that a future-ready constitution must be dynamic yet grounded in timeless principles. While it is essential for constitutional governance to adapt to emerging challenges—such as those posed by digital technology, globalization, and evolving social norms—such adaptations must not erode the core values of individual liberty and limited government. Conservative theorists advocate for reforms that are incremental, widely debated, and deeply rooted in the original intent of the founding fathers. This measured approach to constitutional change is essential for preserving the stability and predictability that are the hallmarks of American democracy.[22]

---

[19] Sanger, Margaret. *Conservative Legacies: How the Founding Ideals Endure*. HarperCollins, 2010.

[20] Bickel, Alexander M. *The Least Dangerous Branch: The Supreme Court at the Bar of Politics*. Yale University Press, 1962.

[21] Lasch, Christopher. *The Culture of Narcissism: American Life in an Age of Diminishing Expectations*. W.W. Norton & Company, 1979.

[22] Wood, Gordon S. *The Radicalism of the American Revolution*. Vintage Books, 1993.

Internationally, many successful constitutional frameworks demonstrate the benefits of fostering a strong civic culture. Nations that invest in robust civic education, promote nonpartisan public debate, and support transparent government operations tend to enjoy higher levels of public trust and political stability. The American experience, enriched by its revolutionary heritage and the enduring legacy of its founding documents, serves as a model for how civic engagement can sustain constitutional governance. Policy implications in this area include comprehensive educational reforms and community outreach programs that emphasize the historical and practical significance of the Constitution.[23]

Finally, the synthesis of global lessons reveals that constitutional reform must be accompanied by efforts to strengthen the moral and cultural underpinnings of the legal system. The American Constitution is not merely a set of rules but a reflection of the nation's commitment to freedom, self-governance, and justice. To ensure that this commitment endures, future policy initiatives must promote a renewed sense of national identity—one that celebrates the achievements of the past while addressing the challenges of the future. This requires a concerted effort to enhance public understanding of constitutional principles through education, media, and community engagement.[24]

In summation, the implications for American constitutional reform, as gleaned from comparative perspectives, are clear. Policymakers must pursue a path of incremental, consensus-based reform that preserves the enduring principles of limited government and individual liberty while incorporating adaptive mechanisms to meet modern challenges. By strengthening civic education, reinforcing the independence of the judiciary, decentralizing fiscal and administrative authority, and promoting nonpartisan public debate, the United States can ensure that its Constitution remains a living document—one that continues to guide the nation toward a future of freedom, stability, and prosperity.[25]

---

[23] Eskridge, William N. Jr. *Originalism in the Twenty-First Century*. Harvard University Press, 2012.

[24] Scalia, Antonin. *A Matter of Interpretation: Federal Courts and the Law*. Princeton University Press, 1997.

[25] Hamilton, Alexander; Madison, James; Jay, John. *The Federalist Papers*. Penguin Classics, 2003.

3. The Constitution's Role in Addressing Modern Challenges

The United States Constitution has served as the bedrock of American liberty and governance for over two centuries. In the face of evolving social, economic, technological, and geopolitical challenges, the Constitution's enduring principles remain not only relevant but indispensable. This paper examines how the Constitution addresses modern challenges while continuing to provide a stable framework for government. Drawing on a politically conservative perspective rooted in the insights of the founding fathers, this commentary synthesizes key findings and discusses the policy implications and practical applications that ensure the Constitution remains a living document for America's future. In doing so, it emphasizes that the fundamental principles of limited government, individual liberty, and the separation of powers are as critical today as they were at the nation's inception.[1]

At its core, the American constitutional framework was designed to protect individuals against the tyranny of centralized power. The framers, informed by their experiences under British rule, deliberately enshrined checks and balances to ensure that no single branch of government could dominate. This system is central to addressing modern challenges, as it enables the judiciary to review and check actions by the legislative and executive branches. The robustness of this design ensures that when contemporary issues—ranging from digital privacy concerns to national security—arise, they are evaluated against the Constitution's enduring standards. Conservatives argue that maintaining this separation of powers is essential for preventing governmental overreach in an era when rapid technological change could otherwise enable unprecedented surveillance and control.[2]

One of the most pressing modern challenges is the digital revolution and its impact on privacy, free speech, and the dissemination of information. The Constitution, though written in an earlier era, has been dynamically interpreted to extend protections to the digital realm. The First Amendment, for instance, continues to safeguard freedom of expression against state censorship even as social media and other online platforms transform public discourse. Conservative jurists have emphasized that a strict adherence to the original meaning of the Constitution prevents the erosion of free speech rights in the digital age, ensuring that government interventions remain limited and justified only under strict scrutiny. This approach not only preserves individual

---

[1] Hamilton, Alexander; Madison, James; Jay, John. *The Federalist Papers*. Penguin Classics, 2003.

[2] Madison, James. "Federalist No. 51." In *The Federalist Papers*, edited by Clinton Rossiter, Bantam Classics, 1961.

liberties but also promotes an environment where diverse opinions can flourish without fear of suppression.[3]

Economic challenges also loom large in today's globalized world. The Constitution's protections for property rights and free enterprise have underpinned America's remarkable economic growth. However, modern economic issues such as income inequality, regulatory overreach, and the impact of globalization require careful policy responses that remain faithful to constitutional principles. Conservatives assert that market-driven policies, which emphasize individual initiative and limited government intervention, are essential for sustaining economic prosperity. By adhering to constitutional norms that protect private property and economic freedom, policymakers can counteract excessive state control and foster an environment where innovation thrives.[4]

Furthermore, the Constitution plays a crucial role in addressing the threat of terrorism and maintaining national security without compromising civil liberties. Post-9/11 security measures have often tested the limits of constitutional protections, particularly regarding surveillance and due process. Through judicial review and a commitment to originalism, the U.S. legal system has been able to strike a balance between effective security policies and the preservation of individual rights. Conservatives maintain that the Constitution provides a clear framework that limits the executive's emergency powers, ensuring that measures taken in the name of national security are temporary and subject to rigorous oversight. This balance is essential for upholding the rule of law even during times of crisis.[5]

The challenge of maintaining a robust and effective education system in a rapidly changing world also falls under the constitutional umbrella. Civic education, which fosters an understanding of constitutional principles and the responsibilities of citizenship, is critical for sustaining a healthy democracy. Many conservatives have lamented the decline in constitutional literacy among young Americans, arguing that a well-informed citizenry is the best safeguard against governmental overreach and ideological extremism. Institutional programs and educational initiatives that emphasize the historical context of the Constitution can empower citizens to actively participate in governance, ensuring that the foundational values of the nation continue to be passed on to future generations.[6]

---

[3] Niemi, Richard G., and Jane Junn. *Civic Education: What Makes Students Learn*. Yale University Press, 1998.

[4] Friedman, Milton. *Capitalism and Freedom*. University of Chicago Press, 2002.

[5] Elazar, Daniel J. *Exploring Federalism*. University of Alabama Press, 1987.

[6] Scalia, Antonin. *A Matter of Interpretation: Federal Courts and the Law*. Princeton University Press, 1997.

In addition to education, the Constitution's federalist structure offers a framework for addressing regional disparities and promoting local innovation. By dividing power between the national government and the states, the Constitution allows for policies to be tailored to local needs. This decentralization acts as a "laboratory of democracy," where states can experiment with solutions that, if successful, may be adopted at the national level. For conservatives, this system is a critical check against centralized power, as it ensures that governmental authority remains distributed and accountable. Policy implications include promoting state autonomy in areas such as healthcare, education, and infrastructure, thereby fostering more responsive and efficient governance.[7]

The Constitution also provides a model for managing environmental challenges. As concerns about climate change and environmental degradation intensify, there is a need for policies that balance economic growth with environmental protection. The American constitutional framework, with its emphasis on property rights and limited government intervention, supports market-based solutions that encourage innovation in green technologies without imposing undue regulatory burdens. Conservatives argue that this approach, when combined with targeted federal oversight to address cross-border environmental issues, can effectively safeguard natural resources while promoting economic prosperity.[8]

Another modern challenge is the rapid pace of technological innovation and its disruptive impact on society. From cybersecurity threats to the ethical implications of artificial intelligence, emerging technologies pose complex questions that were unimaginable to the framers of the Constitution. Yet, through judicial interpretation and legislative action grounded in constitutional principles, the legal system has shown a capacity to adapt. Conservative legal thought emphasizes the importance of preserving the core values of the Constitution—such as due process, free speech, and privacy—even as the government grapples with new technological realities. Ensuring that laws remain consistent with these enduring principles is critical for protecting individual freedoms in an era of digital transformation.[9]

Globalization and international trade present further challenges and opportunities for constitutional governance. As American businesses engage more deeply with global markets, the need for a stable, predictable legal environment becomes even more pressing. The Constitution's protection of property rights and contractual freedoms has historically contributed to the United States'

---

[7] Binder, Sarah A. *Stalemate: Causes and Consequences of Legislative Gridlock*. Brookings Institution Press, 2003.

[8] Kirk, Russell. *The Conservative Mind: From Burke to Eliot*. Regnery Publishing, 1953.

[9] Maier, Pauline. *American Scripture: Making the Declaration of Independence*. Vintage, 1998.

economic dynamism. Conservatives argue that preserving these constitutional safeguards is essential for maintaining America's competitive edge in the global economy. Furthermore, by resisting international pressures that might compromise national sovereignty, the Constitution continues to serve as a bulwark against policies that could undermine domestic economic interests.[10]

In the realm of healthcare, the balance between individual freedom and government responsibility remains a contentious issue. The Constitution does not explicitly address healthcare, yet its principles have been invoked in debates over the extent of state intervention in public welfare. Conservatives maintain that while the government has a role in ensuring access to basic services, excessive intervention risks undermining personal responsibility and the free market. The American constitutional model, with its emphasis on limited government, suggests that reforms in healthcare should aim to empower individuals and local communities rather than imposing a one-size-fits-all solution from Washington.[11]

National security continues to be a paramount concern, and the Constitution's role in delineating the powers of government is critical in this context. The checks and balances system ensures that executive actions taken in the name of security are subject to legislative and judicial scrutiny. This framework is particularly important as the nation confronts evolving threats such as cyberattacks and international terrorism. Conservative policy proposals emphasize that any expansion of governmental power for security purposes must be strictly circumscribed and temporary, thereby preserving the civil liberties that are the hallmark of the American constitutional order.[12]

The Constitution's enduring influence also extends to the realm of cultural identity and social cohesion. As America becomes increasingly diverse, there is a need to reaffirm a shared national identity rooted in the principles of liberty and self-governance. The American founding documents provide a unifying narrative that transcends individual differences and fosters a sense of common purpose. Conservatives argue that public policies should reinforce this narrative through civic education and community engagement, ensuring that all citizens—regardless of their background—are united by a common commitment to constitutional values.[13]

Moreover, the role of the judiciary in interpreting constitutional provisions remains a cornerstone of American governance. The Supreme Court's power of judicial review has enabled the Constitution

---

[10] Torney-Purta, Judith, et al. *Citizenship and Political Participation: Political Science Perspectives*. Rowman & Littlefield, 2001.

[11] Lipset, Seymour. *Political Man: The Social Bases of Politics*. Johns Hopkins University Press, 1960.

[12] Amar, Akhil Reed. *America's Constitution: A Biography*. Random House, 2005.

[13] Eskridge, William N. Jr. *Originalism in the Twenty-First Century*. Harvard University Press, 2012.

to adapt to new challenges while remaining anchored in its original meaning. This process has allowed the Court to strike down laws that violate fundamental rights, ensuring that governmental power is exercised within the limits prescribed by the Constitution. Conservatives maintain that this balance between judicial interpretation and legislative action is crucial for preserving the integrity of the constitutional system, especially in an era of rapid change.[14]

The practical applications of constitutional principles can also be observed in the realm of tax policy and fiscal management. The U.S. Constitution's framework for limited government has historically led to policies that prioritize economic freedom and individual responsibility. In contemporary debates, conservatives advocate for tax reforms that reduce the burden on individuals and businesses, arguing that such measures stimulate economic growth and enhance personal liberty. By limiting government expenditure and promoting fiscal responsibility, these policies reflect the constitutional commitment to a restrained government that operates within its prescribed bounds.[15]

Furthermore, the Constitution's impact on public administration is evident in the ongoing efforts to reform bureaucratic institutions. Excessive bureaucracy can impede innovation and erode accountability, a concern that is particularly acute in an era marked by rapid technological and social change. Conservatives propose measures to streamline government operations, reduce redundant regulations, and increase transparency in public decision-making. These policy initiatives are rooted in the constitutional principle of limited government and serve to reinforce the idea that state power should always be subordinate to the rights and freedoms of the individual.[16]

Another significant policy implication is the need to foster robust civic education programs that enhance constitutional literacy among citizens. An informed electorate is essential for ensuring that government actions are subject to meaningful public scrutiny. Recent trends in educational policy, which have sometimes marginalized the study of civics and history, pose a risk to the democratic process. Conservatives argue that reinvigorating civic education—through curricular reforms, community programs, and digital learning platforms—is imperative for sustaining the constitutional order. By equipping citizens with a deep understanding of their rights and

---

[14] McCarty, Nolan, Keith T. Poole, and Howard Rosenthal. *Polarized America: The Dance of Ideology and Unequal Riches*. MIT Press, 2009.

[15] Wood, Gordon S. *The Creation of the American Republic, 1776–1787*. University of North Carolina Press, 1998.

[16] Ellis, Joseph J. *American Creation: Triumphs and Tragedies in the Founding of the Republic*. Knopf, 2007.

responsibilities, these initiatives create a foundation for active participation in governance and effective oversight of government power.[17]

International experiences further underscore the importance of safeguarding the Constitution against the encroachment of external influences. In many countries, constitutional reforms have been driven by international norms and pressure from global institutions. Conservatives caution that while engagement with global legal standards can be beneficial, it must not come at the expense of national sovereignty or the unique principles that define the American constitutional tradition. Policy applications should therefore aim to balance international cooperation with a steadfast commitment to domestic constitutional values, ensuring that reforms are consistent with the natural rights and limited government envisioned by the founding fathers.[18]

Moreover, the challenges posed by rapid technological advancement require innovative policy responses that remain true to constitutional principles. Issues such as digital privacy, cybersecurity, and data protection must be addressed within a framework that respects individual rights and limits government intrusion. Conservative proposals advocate for the development of technology policies that are informed by constitutional values—ensuring that innovations enhance freedom rather than restrict it. Such policies might include stringent safeguards for personal data, transparency in governmental use of digital surveillance, and mechanisms for protecting free speech online.[19]

The Constitution's role in addressing environmental challenges is another area of practical application. As the nation confronts the impacts of climate change and environmental degradation, there is a need for policies that balance economic development with sustainable stewardship of natural resources. The American constitutional tradition, with its strong protections for property rights and limited government intervention, provides a framework for market-based solutions that incentivize environmental innovation without imposing excessive regulatory burdens. Conservatives argue that such an approach not only protects individual freedoms but also promotes long-term economic growth and environmental resilience.[20]

Additionally, the imperative to secure national security while preserving civil liberties continues to shape constitutional policy debates. The ongoing tension between ensuring public safety

---

[17] Putnam, Robert D. *Bowling Alone: The Collapse and Revival of American Community*. Simon & Schuster, 2000.

[18] Galston, William A. *Civic Education and Democracy in America*. Johns Hopkins University Press, 2001.

[19] Sanger, Margaret. *Conservative Legacies: How the Founding Ideals Endure*. HarperCollins, 2010.

[20] Bickel, Alexander M. *The Least Dangerous Branch: The Supreme Court at the Bar of Politics*. Yale University Press, 1962.

and protecting individual rights requires policies that are both effective and constrained by constitutional safeguards. Conservatives assert that a robust system of checks and balances, coupled with judicial oversight, is essential for preventing the abuse of power in the name of security. Practical applications in this area include reforming surveillance laws, enhancing transparency in security measures, and ensuring that any extraordinary powers granted during emergencies are temporary and subject to regular review.[21]

Civic participation remains a cornerstone of the constitutional framework, and its importance cannot be overstated in addressing modern challenges. The active engagement of citizens—through voting, public discourse, and community involvement—is critical for maintaining government accountability and ensuring that public policies reflect the will of the people. Conservative policy initiatives aimed at promoting civic engagement include reforms to simplify the voting process, enhance transparency in political decision-making, and encourage public involvement in government through town halls and community meetings. Such measures reinforce the idea that the Constitution is not a static document but a living covenant between the government and its citizens.[22]

Moreover, the integration of comparative international perspectives into American constitutional reform offers valuable insights. Many nations have successfully navigated complex challenges by adapting their constitutional frameworks to local needs while preserving core democratic principles. The American model, with its emphasis on federalism, judicial review, and a deliberate amendment process, has proven remarkably resilient. Conservatives argue that the lessons learned from other constitutional systems should be synthesized with the enduring principles of the U.S. Constitution to craft policies that are both innovative and faithful to the founding ideals.[23]

Finally, the future of American constitutional reform hinges on the ability to foster a culture of continuous learning and adaptation. As new challenges emerge, policymakers must remain committed to an ongoing dialogue about the Constitution's role in modern governance. This requires not only comprehensive civic education programs but also active engagement from civil society, academia, and the private sector. By promoting an informed, participatory culture that

---

[21] Lasch, Christopher. *The Culture of Narcissism: American Life in an Age of Diminishing Expectations*. W.W. Norton & Company, 1979.

[22] Wood, Gordon S. *The Radicalism of the American Revolution*. Vintage Books, 1993.

[23] Eskridge, William N. Jr. *Originalism in the Twenty-First Century*. Harvard University Press, 2012.

values constitutional principles, the United States can ensure that its legal framework remains dynamic and effective in addressing both current and future challenges.[24]

In summation, the Constitution's role in addressing modern challenges is multifaceted, with far-reaching implications for policy and practice. The enduring principles of limited government, individual liberty, and separation of powers continue to guide American governance, even as new challenges arise in the realms of technology, economics, national security, and environmental protection. Conservative perspectives affirm that any constitutional reform must be measured, consensus-driven, and firmly rooted in the founding principles articulated by the framers. By reinforcing civic education, safeguarding institutional independence, and promoting policies that decentralize power while ensuring accountability, America can continue to thrive as a beacon of freedom in an ever-changing global landscape. These policy implications and practical applications not only honor the legacy of our founding fathers but also chart a course for a future-ready Constitution that endures as a living document, capable of guiding the nation through the challenges of the twenty-first century and beyond.[25]

---

[24] Scalia, Antonin. *A Matter of Interpretation: Federal Courts and the Law*. Princeton University Press, 1997.

[25] Hamilton, Alexander; Madison, James; Jay, John. *The Federalist Papers*. Penguin Classics, 2003.

4. Recommendations for Future Research and Reform

The United States Constitution has long served as the cornerstone of American governance, embodying the principles of limited government, individual liberty, and the rule of law. Over the course of this thesis, we have examined the Constitution's historical evolution, its comparative strengths against other national frameworks, and its enduring relevance in a rapidly changing world. In synthesizing these findings, it is evident that the Constitution remains a living document—one that continues to inspire, constrain, and guide government in a manner that is both principled and pragmatic. However, as modern challenges evolve, so too must our understanding and application of constitutional principles. This final commentary outlines recommendations for future research and reform that will ensure the continued vitality of the American constitutional order, drawing on lessons from history and international experience while remaining true to the founding ideals articulated by our founding fathers.[1]

One of the foremost recommendations is the need to reinvigorate constitutional education across all levels of society. Contemporary trends indicate a decline in civic literacy among American youth and adults alike. Research shows that an informed citizenry is the best safeguard against the encroachment of unchecked governmental power. Future research should focus on evaluating the effectiveness of current civic education programs and developing innovative curricula that integrate primary historical documents with modern pedagogical techniques. Such research can help design educational reforms that emphasize the historical context of the Constitution, its philosophical underpinnings, and its practical implications in today's society. Enhancing constitutional literacy not only prepares citizens to hold government accountable but also fosters a culture of active civic engagement that is essential for a vibrant democracy.[2]

Another area for future research and reform involves the role of digital technology in promoting constitutional discourse. In an age when the internet is the primary source of information for many citizens, there is an urgent need to develop secure, accurate, and accessible digital platforms that disseminate constitutional knowledge. Research should explore how digital media can be used to counter misinformation and partisan distortion, ensuring that constitutional principles are communicated objectively and comprehensively. Policymakers are encouraged to invest in digital civic education tools—such as interactive websites, online courses, and virtual town halls—that not only teach constitutional history but also facilitate informed debate and public

---

[1] Hamilton, Alexander; Madison, James; Jay, John. *The Federalist Papers*. Penguin Classics, 2003.

[2] Madison, James. "Federalist No. 51." In *The Federalist Papers*, edited by Clinton Rossiter, Bantam Classics, 1961.

participation. By leveraging technology responsibly, the Constitution can remain a dynamic, accessible resource for citizens across all demographics.[3]

The comparative analysis of constitutional frameworks reveals that the U.S. model has been uniquely successful in balancing stability and adaptability through a rigorous amendment process and robust judicial review. However, as global challenges evolve—particularly those related to international trade, cybersecurity, and environmental protection—there is a need for further research on how these external pressures can be reconciled with domestic constitutional principles. Future studies should examine case studies from other countries that have successfully integrated international norms while preserving national sovereignty. The insights gained can inform policy reforms aimed at ensuring that the Constitution remains both resilient and responsive in the face of globalization and technological change.[4]

Federalism, as a critical element of the American constitutional design, warrants ongoing scholarly attention. The decentralized distribution of power has allowed states to serve as "laboratories of democracy," fostering innovation in public policy that addresses diverse regional needs. Nevertheless, disparities in fiscal capacity and governance quality among states continue to pose challenges. Future research should analyze the effectiveness of current federal-state interactions and propose reforms that enhance fiscal decentralization, increase local autonomy, and reduce the risk of uneven policy implementation. Policymakers should consider models for sharing best practices across states while maintaining the core constitutional principle of limited government, thereby strengthening the overall fabric of American democracy.[5]

Moreover, the protection of individual rights—enshrined in the Bill of Rights and subsequent amendments—is a fundamental pillar of the Constitution that must be rigorously defended in policy debates. As new technologies emerge and societal norms shift, there is a need for continuous evaluation of how constitutional rights are interpreted and applied. Research should focus on the implications of digital surveillance, data privacy, and other contemporary issues for individual freedoms. Policymakers must ensure that any reforms in these areas are guided by the Constitution's original meaning and the natural rights philosophy of the founding era, thereby preventing the overreach of government and safeguarding the liberties that are essential to American life.[6]

---

[3] Niemi, Richard G., and Jane Junn. *Civic Education: What Makes Students Learn*. Yale University Press, 1998.

[4] Friedman, Milton. *Capitalism and Freedom*. University of Chicago Press, 2002.

[5] Elazar, Daniel J. *Exploring Federalism*. University of Alabama Press, 1987.

[6] Scalia, Antonin. *A Matter of Interpretation: Federal Courts and the Law*. Princeton University Press, 1997.

The role of the judiciary in upholding constitutional norms is another vital area for future research and reform. Judicial review has been the mechanism by which the Constitution adapts to change while remaining grounded in its original principles. However, debates persist regarding the appropriate scope of judicial interpretation and the balance between originalism and a "living constitution" approach. Scholarly inquiry into these debates can provide valuable insights into how the judiciary can continue to act as a check on legislative and executive power without drifting from the framers' intent. Reform proposals should aim to protect judicial independence, ensure that judicial appointments are based on merit rather than political expediency, and promote transparency in judicial decision-making.[7]

In addition, future research should explore strategies for increasing public participation in constitutional reform processes. Comparative evidence suggests that participatory mechanisms such as referenda, public consultations, and deliberative assemblies can enhance the legitimacy of constitutional amendments by ensuring that changes reflect the will of the people. While the U.S. Constitution's amendment process is intentionally rigorous, there is room for innovations that promote wider public engagement without undermining stability. Policymakers are encouraged to consider reforms that incorporate greater citizen input into constitutional debates, thereby bridging the gap between the government and its constituents and fostering a renewed sense of ownership over the nation's founding principles.[8]

The integration of international perspectives into American constitutional reform is another promising avenue for research. Although the United States has traditionally maintained a distinct constitutional model, the global landscape is evolving rapidly, and interactions with international legal norms are increasingly inevitable. Studies comparing American constitutional practices with those of other democracies can shed light on best practices and potential pitfalls. Such research can inform policy recommendations that balance national sovereignty with global engagement, ensuring that American reforms are both innovative and grounded in the time-honored traditions of the founding era.[9]

Furthermore, the synthesis of lessons from comparative constitutional frameworks underscores the importance of cultural continuity in sustaining constitutional order. The American Revolution and the subsequent establishment of a constitutional republic are central to the nation's identity.

---

[7] Binder, Sarah A. *Stalemate: Causes and Consequences of Legislative Gridlock*. Brookings Institution Press, 2003.

[8] Kirk, Russell. *The Conservative Mind: From Burke to Eliot*. Regnery Publishing, 1953.

[9] Maier, Pauline. *American Scripture: Making the Declaration of Independence*. Vintage, 1998.

Future research should investigate how historical memory and civic culture can be effectively preserved and promoted through educational initiatives and public commemorations. Strengthening the nation's cultural foundation is essential for ensuring that the Constitution remains a living document, resonating with future generations and providing a bulwark against ideological extremism.[10]

Another critical recommendation for future research is to analyze the impact of socioeconomic disparities on constitutional governance. While the Constitution guarantees equal protection under the law, disparities in wealth, education, and access to resources can undermine the effective realization of constitutional rights. Research should focus on how economic inequality affects civic engagement and the administration of justice, and explore policy interventions that promote a more equitable distribution of resources without compromising the principles of free enterprise and limited government. Policymakers should be encouraged to design reforms that enhance opportunities for all citizens, thereby reinforcing the democratic ethos of the Constitution.[11]

The environmental challenges of the twenty-first century also demand attention within the framework of constitutional reform. As issues such as climate change, resource depletion, and environmental degradation become more pressing, there is a need to develop policies that balance economic development with ecological sustainability. Comparative studies reveal that some nations have successfully integrated environmental protections into their constitutional frameworks, though often at the cost of increased state intervention. Conservatives argue that the American model, with its emphasis on property rights and market-based solutions, provides a superior basis for addressing environmental challenges. Future research should evaluate the effectiveness of various policy approaches and propose constitutional reforms that protect the environment while preserving economic freedom.[12]

Security and civil liberties remain in tension as national and international threats evolve. The expansion of governmental surveillance in the name of national security has raised serious constitutional concerns, particularly regarding privacy and due process. Research should examine the long-term effects of security policies on individual freedoms, drawing on both domestic case studies and international comparisons. Policy recommendations must ensure that any measures taken to safeguard security are strictly circumscribed by constitutional guarantees and subject to

---

[10] Torney-Purta, Judith, et al. *Citizenship and Political Participation: Political Science Perspectives*. Rowman & Littlefield, 2001.

[11] Lipset, Seymour. *Political Man: The Social Bases of Politics*. Johns Hopkins University Press, 1960.

[12] Amar, Akhil Reed. *America's Constitution: A Biography*. Random House, 2005.

robust judicial oversight. By reaffirming the Constitution's commitment to limiting state power, future reforms can protect civil liberties even in times of crisis.[13]

The role of the media in shaping public discourse on constitutional matters is yet another area ripe for further study. In an era of widespread misinformation and partisan polarization, the integrity of public debate is under threat. Comparative research indicates that independent media and transparent government communications are essential for maintaining an informed electorate. Future research should explore mechanisms for enhancing media literacy and promoting unbiased reporting on constitutional issues. Policy reforms in this domain could include measures to protect journalistic freedom and initiatives to foster a more diverse and fact-based media landscape, ensuring that the public remains well-informed about constitutional governance.[14]

Additionally, the future of American constitutional reform must address the evolving nature of international law and its impact on domestic legal systems. As global norms increasingly influence national policies, there is a risk that international legal standards may encroach upon traditional constitutional values. Comparative analyses can illuminate how other democracies have navigated this challenge, providing a basis for policy recommendations that reinforce national sovereignty. Conservatives insist that American reforms should be grounded in the principles of natural rights and limited government, and future research should focus on strategies to balance international engagement with the preservation of domestic constitutional integrity.[15]

The examination of federalism in the context of constitutional reform also offers promising directions for future research. The U.S. system of dual sovereignty has proven to be a powerful engine for local innovation and accountability. However, discrepancies in state capacities and variations in policy outcomes highlight the need for further investigation into how federalism can be optimized. Research should analyze the effectiveness of current federal-state relations and propose reforms that address fiscal imbalances, improve intergovernmental cooperation, and enhance the overall responsiveness of local governments. These findings will have important implications for designing a more resilient constitutional framework that accommodates regional diversity without compromising national unity.[16]

---

[13] Eskridge, William N. Jr. *Originalism in the Twenty-First Century*. Harvard University Press, 2012.

[14] McCarty, Nolan, Keith T. Poole, and Howard Rosenthal. *Polarized America: The Dance of Ideology and Unequal Riches*. MIT Press, 2009.

[15] Wood, Gordon S. *The Creation of the American Republic, 1776–1787*. University of North Carolina Press, 1998.

[16] Ellis, Joseph J. *American Creation: Triumphs and Tragedies in the Founding of the Republic*. Knopf, 2007.

Furthermore, the experiences of emerging democracies provide valuable insights into the pitfalls and potentials of constitutional reform. Countries that have undergone rapid constitutional changes often illustrate the risks associated with hasty or ideologically driven amendments. Comparative studies of these nations can offer cautionary lessons for the United States, reinforcing the conservative view that stability and continuity are paramount. Future research should investigate the long-term consequences of constitutional volatility in other contexts and apply these lessons to ensure that American reforms remain measured, deliberate, and deeply rooted in the founding principles.[17]

In addition, there is a need to explore the intersection of constitutional reform with public health and social welfare policies. The challenges posed by pandemics, aging populations, and social inequality require policy solutions that are both innovative and constitutionally sound. Future research should examine how constitutional principles can be applied to these complex issues without expanding governmental power beyond its proper limits. Conservatives argue that the protection of individual rights and the promotion of free-market solutions remain the most effective strategies for addressing such challenges, and policy recommendations should reflect this commitment to limited government.[18]

Finally, the synthesis of comparative perspectives points to the importance of a vibrant, participatory civil society in driving constitutional reform. An engaged citizenry is essential for ensuring that reforms are reflective of the public will and that governmental actions remain accountable. Future research should assess the impact of civic organizations, grassroots movements, and public deliberation forums on constitutional change. Policies that encourage greater civic participation, transparency, and accountability are likely to yield a more resilient constitutional system. Conservatives maintain that fostering a strong civil society is not only a matter of democratic principle but also a critical safeguard against the erosion of individual freedoms and the rise of centralized power.[19]

In conclusion, the analysis of comparative constitutional frameworks reveals that the American Constitution remains a robust and adaptable document capable of addressing modern challenges—provided that future reforms are approached with caution, broad consensus, and an unwavering commitment to the principles of limited government and individual liberty. The policy implications

---

[17] Putnam, Robert D. *Bowling Alone: The Collapse and Revival of American Community*. Simon & Schuster, 2000.

[18] Galston, William A. *Civic Education and Democracy in America*. Johns Hopkins University Press, 2001.

[19] Sanger, Margaret. *Conservative Legacies: How the Founding Ideals Endure*. HarperCollins, 2010.

and practical applications discussed herein underscore the necessity of reinvigorating civic education, protecting judicial independence, decentralizing fiscal authority, and fostering public engagement. By synthesizing lessons from around the world and remaining faithful to the founding ideals, policymakers can ensure that the Constitution continues to serve as a living guide for American governance well into the future.[20]

Looking ahead, it is imperative that future research addresses the dynamic interplay between constitutional stability and adaptability. Scholars must continue to explore how evolving social, technological, and economic conditions impact constitutional governance and identify innovative strategies for reform that do not compromise core freedoms. Policymakers should use these insights to craft legislation that reinforces the constitutional framework while accommodating necessary changes. Such a balanced approach is essential for maintaining America's status as a beacon of freedom and a model of democratic resilience in an increasingly complex global landscape.[21]

Moreover, the practical applications of these findings should guide the design of targeted policy initiatives that promote a more engaged and informed citizenry. From enhancing digital platforms for civic education to implementing reforms that strengthen federalism and protect individual rights, the path forward requires a multifaceted strategy. Future research should provide empirical evidence to support these initiatives, ensuring that constitutional reform is grounded in both theory and practice.[22]

Additionally, international comparative studies should be leveraged to benchmark the success of American constitutional governance against global standards. By systematically analyzing the strengths and weaknesses of other constitutional systems, researchers can offer valuable insights that inform domestic policy debates and contribute to a more nuanced understanding of constitutional resilience. This comparative approach will be essential for refining reform strategies and ensuring that the Constitution remains responsive to the challenges of the twenty-first century.[23]

---

[20] Bickel, Alexander M. *The Least Dangerous Branch: The Supreme Court at the Bar of Politics*. Yale University Press, 1962.

[21] Lasch, Christopher. *The Culture of Narcissism: American Life in an Age of Diminishing Expectations*. W.W. Norton & Company, 1979.

[22] Wood, Gordon S. *The Radicalism of the American Revolution*. Vintage Books, 1993.

[23] Eskridge, William N. Jr. *Originalism in the Twenty-First Century*. Harvard University Press, 2012.

Finally, fostering a culture of continuous constitutional dialogue is essential for sustaining long-term reform. It is crucial that both scholars and practitioners remain engaged in an ongoing conversation about the evolution of constitutional principles. Encouraging bipartisan forums, academic symposia, and community-based initiatives will help maintain a vibrant public discourse that is critical for holding government accountable and ensuring that constitutional values are upheld. The conservative imperative to preserve the original vision of the Constitution must be balanced with a pragmatic approach to contemporary challenges—a task that requires ongoing research, dialogue, and public participation.[24]

In summation, the policy implications and practical applications of this thesis underscore that the United States Constitution is a living document—one that must continually evolve to address modern challenges without sacrificing the timeless principles of limited government and individual liberty. Future research should focus on developing innovative educational initiatives, enhancing institutional checks, and fostering civic engagement to ensure that constitutional reform is both effective and principled. By synthesizing lessons from comparative constitutional frameworks and adhering to the enduring vision of our founding fathers, America can chart a course for a future-ready constitutional order that remains a beacon of freedom and a model for democratic governance.[25]

---

[24] Scalia, Antonin. *A Matter of Interpretation: Federal Courts and the Law*. Princeton University Press, 1997.

[25] Hamilton, Alexander; Madison, James; Jay, John. *The Federalist Papers*. Penguin Classics, 2003.

5. Final Reflections on Saving America through Constitutional Principles

The United States Constitution has endured as the supreme law of the land for over two centuries, serving as both a bulwark against tyranny and a blueprint for self-governance. In reflecting on the vast array of topics explored throughout this thesis—from the historical evolution of federalism to the challenges of modern civic education—the centrality of constitutional principles to the American experiment becomes abundantly clear. From a politically conservative perspective that venerates the wisdom of our founding fathers, this final commentary synthesizes the research findings and theoretical contributions of this work, offering policy recommendations and practical applications aimed at saving America through a renewed commitment to the core tenets of limited government, individual liberty, and the rule of law.[1]

At its foundation, the Constitution was designed to protect individual rights and to restrict the powers of government. The framers, having experienced the oppressive rule of a distant monarchy, intentionally enshrined checks and balances within a framework that disperses power among the legislative, executive, and judicial branches. This separation of powers is not merely an institutional arrangement; it embodies the conservative belief that liberty can only be preserved when governmental authority is rigorously constrained. As modern challenges such as digital surveillance, expansive regulatory regimes, and political polarization test our democratic institutions, the original constitutional design remains a critical safeguard. The preservation of this framework is paramount to saving America, as any erosion of these principles risks reviving the very tyranny from which our nation once broke free.[2]

One of the key lessons drawn from this thesis is the importance of constitutional stability achieved through deliberate, consensus-driven reform. Comparative studies of constitutional frameworks around the world reveal that nations which frequently amend their foundational documents often experience instability and diminished public trust. In contrast, the U.S. Constitution's arduous amendment process has ensured that only changes reflecting a broad national consensus are adopted. This measured approach has contributed to a durable political order that has weathered wars, economic depressions, and social upheavals. Conservatives argue that safeguarding the integrity of the amendment process is essential for preserving the original vision of limited

[1] Hamilton, Alexander; Madison, James; Jay, John. *The Federalist Papers*. Penguin Classics, 2003.

[2] Madison, James. "Federalist No. 51." In *The Federalist Papers*, edited by Clinton Rossiter, Bantam Classics, 1961.

government and natural rights, and any attempt to weaken these protections would endanger the future of American freedom.[3]

The Constitution's enduring role in promoting individual liberty is another pillar of this analysis. Embedded in the Bill of Rights are explicit protections for freedom of speech, religion, and the press, as well as rights to privacy and due process. These protections have become even more critical in the contemporary era, as challenges to civil liberties arise from both state overreach and emerging technologies. For instance, policies that expand governmental surveillance under the guise of national security must be carefully balanced against constitutional safeguards. The conservative perspective holds that maintaining an uncompromised commitment to individual rights is the most effective means of preventing governmental overreach, ensuring that America remains a bastion of freedom even as it adapts to new global challenges.[4]

Economic freedom, another cornerstone of the American constitutional order, has underpinned the nation's extraordinary prosperity. The Constitution's emphasis on protecting property rights and promoting free enterprise has created a legal environment conducive to innovation and investment. In an era of increasing globalization and complex regulatory challenges, conservative policymakers stress the need to preserve these economic principles. Efforts to reform tax policies, reduce bureaucratic red tape, and decentralize fiscal authority are seen as essential strategies for sustaining economic growth and individual initiative. These reforms must be pursued while ensuring that any expansion of state power is rigorously limited by the constitutional framework—a balance that is critical for maintaining both economic dynamism and personal freedom.[5]

Federalism, as a uniquely American institution, offers a powerful mechanism for addressing the diverse needs of a heterogeneous society. By distributing power between the national government and the states, the Constitution enables localities to serve as laboratories of democracy, experimenting with policies that reflect regional conditions and cultural values. This decentralized approach not only fosters innovation but also enhances accountability, as citizens are more likely to hold local officials responsible for their actions. Comparative analyses demonstrate that countries with overly centralized systems often struggle with inefficiency and lack of responsiveness. Therefore, preserving and strengthening federalism is imperative for

---

[3] Niemi, Richard G., and Jane Junn. *Civic Education: What Makes Students Learn*. Yale University Press, 1998.

[4] Friedman, Milton. *Capitalism and Freedom*. University of Chicago Press, 2002.

[5] Elazar, Daniel J. *Exploring Federalism*. University of Alabama Press, 1987.

saving America, as it ensures that governance remains adaptable to local needs while upholding national standards.[6]

The role of the judiciary, particularly through the doctrine of judicial review, remains a central element in interpreting and applying constitutional principles to modern issues. The U.S. Supreme Court, by adhering to an originalist methodology, has played a crucial role in maintaining the integrity of the Constitution amid shifting societal values. This conservative commitment to judicial restraint and fidelity to the framers' intent has provided stability in the face of transient political pressures. In an era where rapid changes in technology and public opinion could potentially destabilize the rule of law, a robust and independent judiciary acts as the guardian of constitutional rights. Ensuring that the courts remain insulated from partisan influence is therefore essential for preserving the balance of power that has been the hallmark of American governance.[7]

Another significant aspect of the Constitution's role in addressing modern challenges is its capacity to evolve through a dynamic process of interpretation and gradual reform. While the amendment process is intentionally arduous to safeguard against impulsive changes, the living nature of the Constitution is maintained through judicial interpretation. This process has allowed the American legal system to adapt to new challenges—such as digital privacy, environmental regulation, and the complexities of global trade—without sacrificing its core principles. Conservatives assert that this dual mechanism of rigidity and flexibility is a model for sustainable constitutional evolution, ensuring that the document remains both timeless and responsive.[8]

The challenges of modern public administration, including issues of bureaucratic inefficiency and regulatory overreach, also underscore the importance of adhering to constitutional limits on government power. In recent decades, the expansion of the administrative state has raised concerns about accountability and transparency. Conservative policy recommendations advocate for streamlining government functions, reducing unnecessary regulations, and enhancing local control over public services. By ensuring that governmental power remains distributed and subject to constant public scrutiny, these reforms align with the constitutional mandate for limited government and individual empowerment.[9]

---

[6] Scalia, Antonin. A Matter of Interpretation: Federal Courts and the Law. Princeton University Press, 1997.

[7] Binder, Sarah A. *Stalemate: Causes and Consequences of Legislative Gridlock*. Brookings Institution Press, 2003.

[8] Kirk, Russell. *The Conservative Mind: From Burke to Eliot*. Regnery Publishing, 1953.

[9] Maier, Pauline. *American Scripture: Making the Declaration of Independence*. Vintage, 1998.

Moreover, the need for a robust civic education system has emerged as a critical policy implication from this thesis. An informed citizenry, equipped with a thorough understanding of constitutional principles, is essential for safeguarding democratic institutions and holding government accountable. In light of declining civic literacy, there is a pressing need to reform educational curricula to emphasize the historical context and philosophical foundations of the Constitution. Such initiatives would not only revitalize public debate but also empower citizens to actively participate in governance, ensuring that the Constitution remains a vibrant and living document.[10]

In the international arena, American constitutional principles continue to serve as a beacon for democracies around the world. Despite challenges from authoritarian regimes and populist movements, the U.S. Constitution's commitment to individual rights, federalism, and the rule of law remains unparalleled. Comparative studies show that nations which have adopted more flexible or centralized models often face instability and erosion of freedoms. The American model, therefore, offers a proven framework for addressing modern challenges while upholding timeless values. This international perspective reinforces the conservative argument that preserving the original constitutional design is not only a matter of national pride but also a practical necessity for long-term stability and prosperity.[11]

The Constitution's role in protecting free speech and ensuring an independent press is equally critical in confronting modern challenges. In an era marked by widespread misinformation and increasing media polarization, the constitutional guarantees of freedom of expression serve as a vital counterbalance. Conservative policymakers argue that any attempt to curtail these freedoms in the name of security or social justice must be viewed with caution, as such measures risk undermining the very principles that have sustained American democracy. Ensuring that public discourse remains open and that the press can operate without undue interference is fundamental to maintaining the checks and balances that are the hallmark of the constitutional system.[12]

Environmental challenges, particularly those related to climate change and resource depletion, also demand constitutional attention. While modern policy debates often call for expansive state intervention in the name of environmental protection, conservatives caution that such measures must be carefully balanced with the constitutional commitment to property rights and economic freedom. The American model, which favors market-based solutions and localized environmental

---

[10] Torney-Purta, Judith, et al. *Citizenship and Political Participation: Political Science Perspectives*. Rowman & Littlefield, 2001.

[11] Lipset, Seymour. *Political Man: The Social Bases of Politics*. Johns Hopkins University Press, 1960.

[12] Amar, Akhil Reed. *America's Constitution: A Biography*. Random House, 2005.

management, provides a template for addressing ecological issues without resorting to heavy-handed regulation. Future reforms should focus on fostering innovation in green technologies and encouraging public-private partnerships that align environmental stewardship with the principles of limited government.[13]

The intersection of national security and individual liberty continues to be a contentious area, and the Constitution plays a critical role in delineating the limits of governmental power in this domain. Post-9/11 policies have often expanded executive authority, raising concerns about the erosion of civil liberties. Conservative legal thought insists that any measures taken to ensure national security must be subject to strict constitutional constraints and judicial oversight. Maintaining this balance is essential for preventing the drift toward authoritarianism, ensuring that the government's response to security threats does not come at the expense of the fundamental rights that define American freedom.[14]

Economic globalization poses further challenges that the Constitution must address. As international trade and cross-border investments become increasingly integral to the American economy, policies must be designed to protect domestic industries and individual entrepreneurs while adhering to constitutional principles of free enterprise. Conservative proposals in this area advocate for tax reforms, deregulation, and measures that promote economic self-determination, ensuring that the government's role remains supportive rather than overbearing. Such reforms reflect the constitutional commitment to economic liberty and the belief that a competitive market is the most effective engine of growth.[15]

Moreover, the future of American constitutional reform hinges on the need to foster a robust culture of civic engagement. A participatory democracy requires that citizens not only understand their constitutional rights but also actively participate in the governance process. The decline in civic engagement observed in recent years has significant implications for the stability and legitimacy of the constitutional order. Conservatives argue that policies aimed at enhancing voter participation, promoting public deliberation, and strengthening local government are essential for ensuring that the Constitution remains a living document—one that is continuously reaffirmed through active citizen involvement.[16]

---

[13] Eskridge, William N. Jr. *Originalism in the Twenty-First Century*. Harvard University Press, 2012.

[14] McCarty, Nolan, Keith T. Poole, and Howard Rosenthal. *Polarized America: The Dance of Ideology and Unequal Riches*. MIT Press, 2009.

[15] Wood, Gordon S. *The Creation of the American Republic, 1776–1787*. University of North Carolina Press, 1998.

[16] Ellis, Joseph J. *American Creation: Triumphs and Tragedies in the Founding of the Republic*. Knopf, 2007.

In addition, there is an imperative to improve the transparency and accountability of government institutions. The Constitution's framework of checks and balances is only effective if it is complemented by robust mechanisms for oversight. Policy initiatives that enhance transparency—such as improved access to government records, regular audits of public agencies, and stronger whistleblower protections—can help ensure that governmental power is exercised within the strict limits prescribed by the Constitution. Conservatives maintain that reinforcing these accountability measures is critical for preventing corruption and safeguarding individual liberties.[17]

Internationally, the American constitutional model is frequently held up as a paragon of democratic governance and the protection of individual rights. Comparative studies indicate that countries which deviate from the principles of limited government and federalism often struggle with inefficiencies, authoritarianism, and social discord. The success of the American model, despite its imperfections, lies in its unwavering commitment to constitutional norms and the consistent application of its founding principles. This global perspective underscores the importance of adhering to the constitutional framework as a means of ensuring that any future reforms enhance, rather than undermine, the fundamental values of American democracy.[18]

Furthermore, the adaptability of the Constitution through judicial interpretation is a critical element in its longevity. The ability of the Supreme Court to apply constitutional principles to new and unforeseen challenges has allowed the document to remain relevant in an ever-changing world. Conservatives argue that maintaining a strict adherence to originalism in judicial review is essential for preserving the integrity of the Constitution. Future research should continue to explore how judicial interpretation can evolve without departing from the original intent of the framers, thereby ensuring that constitutional adaptations are both principled and effective.[19]

Additionally, the lessons learned from decades of constitutional practice suggest that preserving the integrity of the amendment process is vital for a stable democratic society. The rigorous standards for constitutional change, while sometimes criticized as inflexible, have served to protect the core values of the nation. Policymakers should resist calls for precipitous changes driven by transient political trends, instead favoring incremental reforms that garner broad support and reflect the enduring wisdom of the founding generation. This measured approach

---

[17] Putnam, Robert D. *Bowling Alone: The Collapse and Revival of American Community*. Simon & Schuster, 2000.

[18] Galston, William A. *Civic Education and Democracy in America*. Johns Hopkins University Press, 2001.

[19] Sanger, Margaret. *Conservative Legacies: How the Founding Ideals Endure*. HarperCollins, 2010.

not only secures the Constitution's stability but also enhances its legitimacy as the foundation of American freedom.[20]

Finally, the synthesis of these diverse policy implications leads to a crucial recommendation: that future research and reform efforts must be underpinned by a renewed commitment to constitutional education. Only through a comprehensive understanding of the Constitution's historical context, philosophical foundations, and practical applications can citizens be empowered to hold their government accountable and defend their liberties. Conservative scholars and policymakers alike advocate for investments in civic education—from K–12 curricula to adult learning programs—as a cornerstone of a resilient constitutional democracy. Strengthening the public's understanding of constitutional principles will enable America to navigate the complexities of the modern world while remaining true to its founding ideals.[21]

In conclusion, the Constitution's role in addressing modern challenges is multifaceted, with profound policy implications that extend to every aspect of American governance. The recommendations presented herein—ranging from reinvigorating civic education and enhancing digital transparency to preserving judicial independence and reinforcing federalism—offer a roadmap for ensuring that the Constitution remains a living, adaptive document. Future research should focus on empirically evaluating these policy initiatives and exploring innovative strategies for reform that respect the foundational principles of limited government and individual liberty. By synthesizing lessons from international comparative perspectives and staying true to the insights of our founding fathers, America can secure its constitutional heritage and chart a course toward a future of continued freedom, prosperity, and democratic resilience.[22]

Moreover, sustained dialogue among scholars, policymakers, and citizens is essential for fostering a culture of constitutional renewal. As new challenges emerge—from the rapid evolution of technology to shifts in global economic dynamics—the ability of the American constitutional system to adapt without sacrificing its core values will be tested. Ongoing research should therefore focus on interdisciplinary approaches that integrate law, political science, economics, and sociology to provide a holistic understanding of constitutional dynamics. Such research will not only inform future reforms but also strengthen public trust

---

[20] Bickel, Alexander M. *The Least Dangerous Branch: The Supreme Court at the Bar of Politics*. Yale University Press, 1962.

[21] Lasch, Christopher. *The Culture of Narcissism: American Life in an Age of Diminishing Expectations*. W.W. Norton & Company, 1979.

[22] Wood, Gordon S. *The Radicalism of the American Revolution*. Vintage Books, 1993.

in the constitutional process by demonstrating that change is guided by thoughtful analysis rather than partisan impulse.[23]

Additionally, policymakers must consider the role of public-private partnerships in advancing constitutional reform. Collaborative initiatives between government, academia, and civil society can foster innovative solutions to contemporary challenges while ensuring that reform efforts are inclusive and broadly supported. By leveraging the expertise of diverse stakeholders, the United States can develop policy frameworks that enhance accountability, promote transparency, and ultimately preserve the constitutional order in the face of evolving global pressures.[24]

In summation, the final reflections on saving America through constitutional principles emphasize that the enduring strength of the U.S. Constitution lies in its ability to balance stability with adaptability **BUT NOT TO THE EXTENT OF MATERIAL DEPARTURE FROM ITS ORIGINAL TEXT AND MEANING**, its commitment to individual liberty, and its robust system of checks and balances. The policy implications and practical applications discussed in this commentary offer a blueprint for future constitutional reform—one that is measured, consensus-driven, and firmly rooted in the foundational ideas of limited government and personal freedom. It is through the diligent pursuit of these reforms, supported by rigorous research and broad-based civic education, that America can ensure its constitutional framework remains a living document, capable of guiding the nation through the challenges of the twenty-first century and beyond.[25]

---

[23] Eskridge, William N. Jr. *Originalism in the Twenty-First Century*. Harvard University Press, 2012.

[24] Scalia, Antonin. *A Matter of Interpretation: Federal Courts and the Law*. Princeton University Press, 1997.

[25] Hamilton, Alexander; Madison, James; Jay, John. *The Federalist Papers*. Penguin Classics, 2003.

About the Author

Dr. James M. Copas, LLM, LLM, was born and raised in the vibrant city of Hamilton, Ohio, where a curiosity about the world and a love of learning first took root. From his early days at Taft Senior High School to his studies at Miami University in Oxford, Ohio, he pursued knowledge with a relentless passion, earning both his Associate and Bachelor of Arts degrees.

His journey into the law became both a calling and a craft. Earning his Juris Doctor from the University of Detroit Mercy, Dr. Copas's intellectual pursuits soon led him to study international law, business, and trade at Stetson University College of Law, and then to delve deeply into intellectual property law with advanced degrees from The John Marshall Law School in Chicago and the University of Illinois at Chicago. These achievements reflect not just a mastery of the law, but a dedication to understanding its nuances and global impact.

Beyond his legal accomplishments, Dr. Copas is a devoted reader and writer, driven by a desire to explore the questions that define our times. His work blends insight, rigor, and imagination, bridging the worlds of law, culture, and human curiosity. Whether in the courtroom, the classroom, or the pages of his writing, he seeks to illuminate, challenge, and inspire.

www.ingramcontent.com/pod-product-compliance
Lightning Source LLC
LaVergne TN
LVHW070905210926
848482LV00017B/999
* 9 7 9 8 9 9 5 9 6 9 6 0 0 *